Daniel Defoe
SELECTIONS

VOLUME II

THE HISTORY OF THE REMARKABLE LIFE
OF JOHN SHEPPARD

❀

EVERYBODY'S BUSINESS IS NOBODY'S BUSINESS

❀

FROM LONDON TO LAND'S END

❀

TWO LETTERS FROM THE "JOURNEY THROUGH
ENGLAND BY A GENTLEMAN."

❀

TOUR THROUGH THE EASTERN COUNTIES OF
ENGLAND, 1722

❀

MEMOIRS OF A CAVALIER

❀

THE COMPLETE ENGLISH TRADESMAN

I

THE HISTORY

Of the remarkable LIFE of

JOHN SHEPPARD,

CONTAINING

A particular Account of his many
ROBBERIES and ESCAPES,

Viz,.

His robbing the Shop of Mr. *Bains* in White-Horse-Yard of 24
Yards of Fustian. Of his breaking and entering the House of the
said Mr. *Bains*, and stealing in Goods and Money to the Value of
20 l. Of his robbing the House of Mr. *Charles* in *May Fair* of
Money, Rings, Plate, &c to the Value of 30 l. Of his robbing the
House of Mrs. *Cook* in *Clare-Market*, along with his pretended
Wife, and his Brother, to the Value of between 50 and 60 l. Of
his breaking the Shop of Mr. *Philips* in *Drury-Lane,* with the
same Persons, and stealing Goods of small Value. Of his entering
the House of Mr. *Carter*, a Mathematical Instrument Maker in
Wytch Street, along with *Anthony Lamb* and *Charles Grace*, and
robbing of Mr. *Barton*, a Master Taylor who lodged therein, of
Goods and Bonds to the Value of near 300 l. Of his breaking and
entering the House of Mr. *Kneebone*, a Woollen-Draper, near the
New Church in the *Strand,* in Company of *Joseph Blake* alias
Blewskin and *William Field,* and stealing Goods to the Value of
near 50 l. Of his robbing of Mr. *Pargiter* on the Highway near
the Turnpike, on the Road *Hampstead,* along with the said
Blewskin. Of his robbing a Lady's Woman in her Mistress's
Coach on the same Road. Of his robbing also a Stage Coach,

with the said *Blewskin*, on the *Hampstead* Road. Likewise of his breaking the Shop of Mr. *Martin* in *Fleet-street*, and stealing 3 silver Watches of 15 l. Value.

ALSO—

A particular Account of his rescuing his pretended Wife from St. *Giles's* Round House. Of the wonderful Escape himself made from the said Round-House. Of the miraculous Escape he and his said pretended Wife made together from *New-Prison*, on the 25th of *May* last. Of his surprizing Escape from the Condemn'd Hold of *Newgate* on the 31st of *August*. Together with the true manner of his being retaken; and of his Behaviour in *Newgate*, till the most astonishing, and never to be forgotten Escape he made from thence, in the Night of the 15th of October. The Whole taken from the most authentick Accounts, as the Informations of divers Justices of the Peace, the several Shop-keepers above-mentioned, the principal Officers of *Newgate* and *New Prison*, and from the Confession of *Sheppard* made to the Rev. Mr. *Wagstaff*, who officiated for the Ordinary at *Newgate*.

TO THE CITIZENS
OF
London and *Westminster.*

GENTLEMEN,

Experience has confirm'd you in that everlasting Maxim, *that there is no other way to protect the* Innocent, *but by Punishing the* Guilty.

Crimes ever were, and ever must be unavoidably frequent in such populous Cities as yours are, being the necessary Consequences, either of the Wants, or the Depravity, of the lowest part of the humane Species.

At this time the most flagrant Offences, as Burning of Dwellings; Burglaries, and Highway Robberies abound; and Frauds common Felonies, and Forgeries are practic'd without Number; thus not only your Properties, but even your very Lives are every way struck at.

The Legislative Power has not been wanting in providing necessary and wholesome Laws against these Evils, the executive part whereof (according to your great Privileges) is lodged in your own Hands: And the Administration hath at all times applyed proper Remedies and Regulations to the Defects which have happen'd in the Magistracy more immediately under their Jurisdiction.

Through the just and salutary Severities of the Magistrates, publick excessive Gaming has been in a manner Surpress'd; and some late Examples of divine Vengeance have overtaken certain of the most notorious lewd Prostitutes of the Town, which together with the laudable endeavours of the great and worthy Societies, has given no small check to that enormous and spreading Vice.

But here's a Criminal bids Defiance to your Laws, and Justice who declar'd and has manifested that the Bars are not made that can either keep him Out, or keep him In, and accordingly hath a second time fled from the very Bosom Of Death.

His History will astonish! and is not compos'd of Fiction, Fable, or Stories plac'd at York, Rome, *or* Jamaica, *but* Facts done at your Doors, Facts *unheard of, altogether new, Incredible, and yet Uncontestable.*

He is gone once more upon his wicked Range in the World. Restless Vengeance is pursuing, and Gentlemen *'tis to be hoped that she will be assisted by your Endeavours to bring to Justice this notorious Offender.*

THE LIFE OF
JOHN SHEPPARD, &c.

This *John Sheppard*, a Youth both in Age and Person, tho' an old Man in Sin; was Born in the Parish of *Stepney* near *London*, in the Year 1702, a Son, Grandson, and great Grandson of a *Carpenter*. His Father died when he was so very Young that he could not recollect that ever he saw him. Thus the burthen of his Maintenance, together with his Brother's and Sister's, lay upon the Shoulders of the Widow Mother, who soon procured an Admittance of her Son *John* into the *Work-House* in *Bishopsgate-street,* where he continued for the space of a Year and half, and in that time received an Education sufficient to qualifie him for the Trade his Mother design'd him, *viz.* a *Carpenter.* Accordingly she was recommended to Mr. *Wood* in *Witch-Street* near *Drury-Lane,* as a Master capable of entertaining and instructing her Son: They agreed and Bound he was for the space of seven Years; the Lad proved an early proficient, had a ready and ingenious Hand, and soon became Master of his Business, and gave entire Satisfaction to his Master Customers, and had the Character of a very sober and orderly Boy. But alas unhappy Youth! before he had compleated six Years of his Apprenticeship, he commenced a fatal Acquaintance with one *Elizabeth Lyon,* otherwise call'd *Edgworth Bess,* from a Town of that Name in *Middlesex* where she was Born, the reputed Wife of a Foot Soldier, and who lived a wicked and debauch'd Life; and our young *Carpenter* became Enamour'd of her, and they must Cohabit together as Man and Wife.

Now was laid the Foundation of his Ruin; *Sheppard* grows weary of the Yoke of Servitude, and began to dispute with his Master; telling him that his way of Jobbing from House to House was not sufficient to furnish him with a due Experience in his Trade; and that if he would not set out to undertake some Buildings, he would step into the World for better Information. Mr. *Wood* a mild, sober, honest Man, indulg'd him; and Mrs. *Wood* with Tears, exhorted him against the Company of this lewd Prostitute: But her Man prompted and harden'd by his HARLOT, D—— n'd *her Blood,* and threw a Stick at his Mistress, and beat her to the Ground. And being with his Master at Work at Mr. *Britt's* the *Sun* Ale-house near *Islington,* upon a very trivial Occasion fell upon his Master, and beat and bruised him in a most barbarous and shameful Manner. Such a sudden and deplorable Change was there in the Behaviour of this promising young Man. Next ensued a neglect of Duty, both to God and his Master, lying out of Nights, perpetual Jarrings, and Animosities; these and such like, were the Consequences of his intimacy with this she *Lyon*; who by the sequel will appear to have been a main loadstone in attracting of him up to this Eminence of Guilt.

Mr. *Wood* having Reason to suspect, that *Sheppard* had robb'd a Neighbour, began to be in great Fear and Terror for himself. And when his Man came not Home in due season at Nights bar'd him out; but he made a mere jest of the Locks and Bolts, and enter'd in, and out at Pleasure; and when Mr. *Wood* and his Wife have had all the Reason in the World to believe him Lock't out, they have found him very quiet in his Bed the next Morning, such was the power of his early Magick.

Edgworth Bess having stol'n a Gold Ring from a Gentleman, whom she had pick'd up in the Streets, was sent to St. *Giles's* Round-house; *Sheppard* went immediately to his Consort, and after a short Discourse with Mr. *Brown* the Beadle, and his Wife, who had the Care of the Place, he fell upon the poor old Couple, took the Keys from them, and let his Lady out at the Door in spight of all the Out-cryes, and Opposition they were capable of making.

About *July* 1723, He was by his Master sent to perform a Repair, at the House of Mr. *Bains*, a Piece-Broker in *White-Horse Yard*; he from thence stole a Roll of Fustain, containing 24 Yards, which was afterwards found in his Trunk. This is supposed to be the first Robbery he ever committed and it was not long e're he Repeated another upon this same Mr. *Bains*, by breaking into his House in the Night-time, and taking out of the *Till* seven Pounds in Money, and Goods to the value of fourteen Pounds more. How he enter'd this House, was a Secret till his being last committed to *Newgate*, when he confessed that he took up the Iron Bars at the Cellar Window, and after he had done his Business, he nailed them down again, so that Mr. *Bains* never believed his House had been broke; and an innocent Woman a Lodger in the House lay all the while under the weight of a suspicion of committing the Robbery.

Sheppard and his Master had now parted, ten Months before the expiration of his Apprenticeship, a woeful parting to the former; he was gone from a good and careful Patronage, and lay expos'd to, and comply'd with the Temptations of the most wicked Wretches this Town could afford as *Joseph Blake*, alias *Blewskins*, *William Field*,

Doleing, James Sykes, alias *Hell* and *Fury*, which last was the first that betray'd, and put him into the Hands of Justice, as will presently appear.

Having deserted his Master's Service, he took Shelter in the House of Mr. *Charles* in *May-Fair*, near *Piccadilly*, and his Landlord having a Necessity for some Repairs in his House, engag'd one Mr. *Panton* a *Carpenter* to Undertake them, and *Sheppard* to assist him as a Journeyman; but on the 23rd of *October*, 1723, e're the Work was compleat, *Sheppard* took Occasion to rob the People of the Effects following, *viz.* seven Pound ten Shillings in Specie, five large silver Spoons, six plain Forks ditto, four Tea-Spoons, six plain Gold Rings, and a Cypher Ring; four Suits of Wearing Apparel, besides Linnen, to a considerable value. This Fact he confess'd to the Reverend Mr. *Wagstaff* before his Escape from the Condemn'd Hold of *Newgate*.

Sheppard had a Brother, nam'd *Thomas*, a *Carpenter* by Profession, tho' a notorious Thief and House-breaker by Practice. This *Thomas* being committed to *Newgate* for breaking the House of Mrs. *Mary Cook* a *Linnen-Draper*, in *Clare-street, Clare-Market*, on the 5th of *February* last, and stealing Goods to the value of between 50, and 60 l. he impeach'd his Brother *John Sheppard*, and *Edgworth Bess* as being concerned with him in the Fact; and these three were also Charg'd with being concern'd together, in breaking the House of Mr. *William Phillips* in *Drury-Lane*, and stealing divers Goods, the Property of Mrs. *Kendrick* a Lodger in the House, on the 14th of the said *February*. All possible endeavours were us'd by Mrs. *Cook* and Mr. *Phillips*, to get *John Sheppard* and *Edgworth Bess* Apprehended, but to no purpose, till the following Accident.

Sheppard was now upon his wicked Range in *London*, committing Robberies every where at Discretion; but one Day meeting with his Acquaintance, *James Sykes*, alias *Hell* and *Fury*, sometimes a Chair-man, and at others a Running Foot-man. This *Sykes* invited him to go to one *Redgate's*, a Victualling-house near the *Seven Dials*, to play at *Skettles*, *Sheppard* comply'd, and *Sykes* secretly sent for Mr. *Price* a Constable in St. *Giles's Parish*, and Charg'd him with his Friend *Sheppard* for the Robbing of Mrs. *Cook*, &c. *Sheppard* was carried before Justice *Parry*, who order'd him to St. *Giles's* Round-house till the next Morning for farther Examination: He was Confin'd in the Upper part of the Place, being two Stories from the Ground, but 'ere two Hours came about, by only the help of a Razor, and the Stretcher of a Chair, he broke open the Top of the Round house, and tying together a Sheet and Blanket, by them descended into the Church-yard and Escap'd, leaving the Parish to Repair the Damage, and Repent of the Affront put upon his Skill and Capacity.

On the 19th of *May* last in the Evening, *Sheppard* with another Robber named *Benson*, were passing thro' *Leicester-fields*, where a Gentleman stood accusing a Woman with an attempt to steal his Watch, a Mobb was gathered about the Disputants, and *Sheppard's* Companion being a *Master*, got in amongst them and pick'd the Gentleman's Pocket in good earnest of the Watch; the Scene was surprizingly chang'd, from an imaginary Robbery to a real one; and in a moment ensued an Out-cry of *stop Thief*, *Sheppard* and *Benson* took to their Heels, and *Sheppard* was seiz'd by a Serjeant of the Guard at *Leicester* House, crying out *stop Thief* with much earnestness. He was convey'd to St. *Ann's Round House* in *Soho*, and kept secure till the next Morning, when *Edgworth Bess* came to visit him, who was seiz'd also; they were carried before Justice *Walters*, when the People in *Drury-Lane* and *Clare-Market* appeared, and charged them with the Robberies aforemention'd: But *Sheppard* pretending to Impeach certain of his Accomplices, the Justice committed them to *New-Prison*, with intent to have them soon removed to *Newgate*, unless there came from them some useful Discoveries. *Sheppard* was now a second time in the hands of Justice, but how long he intended to keep in them, the Reader will soon be able to Judge.

He and his MATE were now in a strong and well guarded Prison, himself loaded with a pair of double *Links* and *Basils*[17] of about fourteen pounds weight, and confined together in the safest Appartment call'd *Newgate Ward*; *Sheppard* conscious of his Crimes, and knowing the *Information* he had made to be but a blind Amusement that would avail him nothing; he began to Meditate an Escape. They had been thus detained for about four Days, and their Friends having the Liberty of seeing them, furnish'd him with Implements proper for his Design, accordingly Mr. *Sheppard* goes to work, and on the 25th of May being *Whit-son Monday* at about two of the Clock in the Morning, he had compleated a practicable breach, and sawed of his Fetters; having with unheard of Diligence and Dexterity, cut off an Iron Bar from the Window, and taken out a Muntin, or Bar of the most solid Oak of about nine Inches in thickness, by boring it thro' in many Places, a work of great Skill and Labour; they had still five and twenty Foot to descend from the Ground; *Sheppard* fasten'd a Sheet and Blanket to the Bars, and causes Madam to take off her Gown and Petticoat, and sent her out first, and she being more Corpulent than himself, it was with great Pain and Difficulty that he got her through the Interval, and observing his Directions, was instantly down, and more frighted than hurt; the *Phylosopher* follow'd, and lighted with Ease and Pleasure; But where are they Escap'd to? Why out of one Prison into another. The Reader is to understand, that the *New Prison* and *Clerkenwell Bridewell* lye Contiguous to one another, and they are got into the Yard of the latter, and have a Wall of twenty-two Foot high to Scale, before their Liberty is perfected; *Sheppard* far from being unprepared to surmount this Difficulty, has his Gimblets and Peircers ready, and makes a Scaleing-Ladder. The Keepers and Prisoners of both Places are a sleep in their Beds; he Mounts his *Bagage*, and in less than ten Minutes carries both her and himself over this wall, and compleats an entire Escape. Altho' his Escape from the Condemn'd Hold of *Newgate*, has made a far greater Noise in the World, than that from this Prison hath. It has been allow'd by all the Jayl-Keepers in *London*, that one so Miraculous was never perform'd before in *England*; the broken Chains and Bars are kept at *New Prison* to Testifie, and preserve the Memory of this extraordinary Villain.

Sheppard not warn'd by this Admonition, returns like a *Dog to his Vomit*, and comes Secretly into his Master *Wood's* Neighbourhood in *Witch-street*, and conceits Measures with one *Anthony Lamb*, an Apprentice to Mr. *Carter* a Mathematical Instrument-maker, for Robbing of Mr. *Barton* a Master Taylor; a Man of Worth and Reputation, who Lodg'd in Mr. *Carter's* House. *Charles Grace*, a graceless Cooper was let into the Secret, and consented, and resolved to Act his Part. The 16th of *June* last was appointed, *Lamb* accordingly lets *Grace* and *Sheppard* into the House at Mid-Night; and they all go up to Mr. *Bartons* Appartment well arm'd with Pistols, and enter'd his Rooms, without being disturb'd. *Grace* was Posted at Mr. *Barton's* Bedside with a loaded Pistol, and positive Orders to shoot him through the Head, if in case he awak'd. *Sheppard* being engag'd in opening the Trunks and Boxes, the mean while. It luckily happen'd for Mr. *Barton*, that he slept Sounder than usual that Night, as having come from a Merry-making with some Friends; tho' poor Man little Dreaming in what dreadful Circumstances. They carried off in Notes, and Bonds, Guineas, Cloaths, Made and Unmade, to the value of between two and three Hundred Pounds; besides a Padesuoy Suit of Cloaths, worth about eighteen or twenty Pounds more; which having been made for a Corpulent Gentleman, *Sheppard* had them reduc'd, and fitted for his own Size and War, as designing to Appear and make a Figure among the *Beau Monde. Grace* and *Sheppard*, having disposed of the Goods at an Ale-house in *Lewkenors Lane* (a Rendezvous of Robbers and Ruffians) took their Flight, and *Grace* had not been since heard of. *Lamb* was apprehended, and carried before Justice *Newton*, and made an ample Confession; and there being nothing but that against him at his Tryal, and withal, a favourable Prosecution, he came off with a Sentence of Transportation only. He as well as *Sheppard* has since confirm'd all the above particulars, and with this Addition, *viz.* That it was Debated among them to have Murder'd all the People in the House, save one Person.

About the latter End of the same Month, *June*, Mr. *Kneebone*, a Woollen-Draper near the New Church in the *Strand*, receiv'd a Caution from the Father of *Anthony Lamb*, who intimated to Mr. *Kneebone* that his House was intended to be broke open and robb'd that very Night. Mr. *Kneebone* prepar'd for the Event, ordering his Servants to sit up, and gave Directions to the Watchman in the Street to observe his House: At about two in the Morning *Sheppard* and his Gang were about the Door, a Maid-Servant went to listen, and heard one of the Wretches, say, *Da—n him, if they could not enter that Night, they would another, and would have 300l. of his,* (meaning) Mr. *Kneebone's* Money. They went off, and nothing more was heard of them till *Sunday* the 12th Day of *July* following, when *Joseph Blake*, alias *Blewskins, John Sheppard*, and *William Field* (as himself Swears) came about 12 o'clock at Night, and cut two large Oaken-Bars over the Cellar-Window, at the back part of the House in *Little-Drury-Lane*, and so entered; Mr. *Kneebone*, and his Family being at Rest, they proceeded to open a Door at the Foot of the Cellar Stairs, with three Bolts, and a large Padlock upon it, and then came up into the Shop and wrench'd off the Hasp, and Padlock that went over the Press, and arriv'd at their desir'd Booty; they continu'd in the House for three Hours, and carry'd off with them One Hundred and eight Yards of Broad Woollen Cloth, five Yards of blue Bays, a light Tye-Wig, and Beaver-Hat, two Silver Spoons, an Handkerchief, and a Penknife. In all to the value of near fifty Pounds.

The *Sunday* following, being the 19th of *July, Sheppard* and *Blewskins* were out upon the *Hampstead* Road, and there stopt a Coach with a Ladies Woman in it, from whom they took but Half-a-Crown; all the Money then about her; the Foot-man behind the Coach came down, and exerted himself; but *Sheppard* sent him in hast up to his Post again, by threat of his Pistol.

The next Night being the 20th of *july*, about Nine, they Robb'd Mr. *Pargiter*, a Chandler of *Hamstead*, near the Halfway-House; *Sheppard* after his being taken at *Finchley* was particularly examin'd about this Robbery. The Reverend Mr. *Wagstaff* having receiv'd a Letter from an unknown Hand, with two Questions, to be propos'd to *Sheppard, viz.* Whether he did Rob *John Pargiter*, on *Monday* the 20th of *July*, about Nine at Night, between the *Turnpike* and *Hamstead*; How much Money he took from him? Whither *Pargiter* was Drunk, or not, and if he had Rings or Watch about him, when robb'd? which, Request was comply'd with, and *Sheppard* affirm'd, that Mr. *Pargiter* was very much in Liquor, having a great Coat on; neither Rings on his Fingers or Watch, and only three Shillings in his Pocket, which they took from him, and that *Blewskins* knock him down twice with the Butt-end of his Pistol to make sure Work, (tho' Excess of drink had done that before) but *Sheppard* did in kindness raise him up as often.

The next Night, *July* 21, they stopt a Stage-Coach, and took from a Passenger in it, Twenty-two Shillings, and were so expeditious in the Matter, that *not two Words were made about the Bargain.*

Now Mr. *Sheppard's* long and wicked Course seemingly draws towards a Period. Mr. *Kneebone* having apply'd to *Jonathan Wild*, and set forth Advertisements in the Papers, complaining of his Robbery. On *Tuesday* the 22d of *July* at Night *Edgworth Bess* was taken in a Brandy-shop, near *Temple-Bar* by *Jonathan Wild*; she being much terrify'd, discover'd where *Sheppard* was: A Warrant was accordingly issued by Justice *Blackerby*, and the next Day he was Apprehended, at the House of *Blewskin's* Mother, in *Rose-Mary-Lane*, by one *Quilt*, a Domestick of Mr. *Wild's* though not without great opposition, for, he clapt a loaded, Pistol to *Quilt's* Breast, and attempted to shoot him, but the Pistol miss'd fire; he was brought back to *New Prison*, confin'd in the Dungeon; and the next Day carried before Justice *Blackerby*. Upon his Examination he Confess'd the three Robberies on the Highway aforemention'd, as also the Robbing of Mr. *Bains*, Mr. *Barton*, and Mr. *Kneebone*, he was committed to Newgate, and at the Sessions of *Oyer* and *Terminer*, and Goal delivery, holden at the *Old-Baily*, on the 12th, 13th and 14th of *August*, he was try'd upon three several indictments, *viz.* First for breaking the House of *William Philips*.

John Sheppard, of the Parish of St. *Martin* in *the Fields*, was indicted for breaking the House of *William Philips*, and stealing divers

Goods, the 14th of *February* last. But there not being sufficient Evidence against the Prisoner, he was acquitted.

He was also indicted a Second Time, of St. *Clement Danes*, for breaking the House of *Mary Cook*, the 5th of *February* last, and stealing divers Goods: But the Evidence against the Prisoner being defficient as to this Indictment also, he was acquitted.

He was also indicted the Third Time, of St. *Mary Savoy*, for breaking the House of *William Kneebone*, in the Night-Time, and stealing, 108 Yards of Woollen Cloth, the 12th of *July* last. The Prosecutor depos'd, That the Prisoner had some Time since been his Servant, and when he went to Bed, the Time mentioned in the Indictment, about 11 a-Clock at Night, he saw all the Doors and Windows fast; but was call'd up about four in the Morning, and found his House broke open, the Bars of a Cellar-Window having been cut, and the Bolts of the Door that comes up Stairs drawn, and the Padlock wrench'd off, and the Shutter in the Shop broken, and his Goods gone; whereupon suspecting the Prisoner, he having committed ill Actions thereabouts before, he acquainted *Jonathan Wild* with it, and he procur'd him to be apprehended. That he went to the Prisoners in New *Prison*, and asking how he could be so ungrateful to rob him, after he had shown him so much Kindness? The Prisoner own'd he had been ungrateful in doing so, informing him of several Circumstances as to the Manner of committing the Fact, but said he had been drawn into it by ill Company. *Jonathan Wild*, depos'd, The Prosecutor came to him, and desir'd him to enquire after his Goods that had been stolen, telling him he suspected the Prisoner to have been concern'd in the Robbery, he having before committed some Robberies in the Neighbourhood. That inquiring after him, and having heard of him before, he was inform'd that he was an Acquaintance of *Joseph Blake*, alias *Blewskins*, and *William Field*. Whereupon he sent for *William Field*, who came to him; upon which he told him, if he would make an ingenuous Confession, he believ'd he could prevail with the Court to make him an Evidence. That he did make a Discovery of the Prisoner, upon which he was apprehended, and also of others since convicted, and gave an Account of some Parcels of the Cloth, which were found accordingly. *William Field* depos'd, That the Prisoner told him, and *Joseph Blake*, that he knew a *Ken* where they might get something of Worth. That they went to take a View of the Prosecutor's House, but disprov'd of the Attempt, as not thinking it easy to be perform'd; But the Prisoner perswaded them that it might easily be done, he knowing the House, he having liv'd with the Prosecutor. That thereupon he cut the Cellar Bar, went into the Cellar, got into the Shop, and brought out three Parcels of Cloth, which they carried away. The Prisoner had also confest the Fact when he was apprehended, and before the Justice. The Fact being plainly prov'd, the Jury found him guilty of the Indictment.

Sentence of Death was pronounc'd upon him accordingly. Several other Prosecutions might have been brought against him, but this was thought sufficient to rid the World of so Capital an Offender: He beg'd earnestly for Transportation, to the most extream Foot of his Majesty's Dominions; and pleaded Youth, and Ignorance as the Motive which had precipitated him into the Guilt; but the Court deaf to his Importunities, as knowing him, and his repeated Crimes to be equally flagrant, gave him no satisfactory Answer: He return'd to his dismal Abode the Condemn'd Hold, where were Nine more unhappy Wretches in as dreadful Circumstances as himself. The Court being at *Windsor*, the Malefactors had a longer Respite than is usual; during that Recess, *James Harman*, *Lumley*, *Davis* and *Sheppard* agreed upon an Escape, concerted Measures, and provided Instruments to make it effectual; but put off the Execution of their Design, on Account the two Gentlemen having their hopes of Life daily renewed by the favourable Answers they receiv'd from some considerable Persons; but those vanishing the day before their Execution, and finding their Sentence irreversible, they two dropt their hopes, together with the Design, they form'd for an Escape, and so in earnest prepar'd to meet Death on the Morrow, (which they accordingly did.). 'Twas on this Day Mr *Davis* gave *Sheppard* the Watch Springs, Files, Saws, &c. to Effect his own Release; and knowing that a Warrant was Hourly expected for his Execution with Two others, on the *Friday* following; he thought it high time to look about him, for he had waited his Tryal, saw his Conviction, and heard his Sentence with some patience; but finding himself irrespitably decreed for Death, he could sit passive no longer, and on the very Day of the Execution of the former; whilst they were having their Fetters taken off, in order for going to the Tree, that Day he began to saw, *Saturday* made a progress; but *Sunday* omitted, by Reason of the Concourse in the *Lodge*. *Edgworth Bess* having been set at Liberty, had frequent Access to him, with others of his Acquaintance. On *Monday* the Death *Warrant* came from *Windsor*, appointing that he, together with *Joseph Ward* and *Anthony Upton* should be Executed on the *Friday* following, being the 4th of *September*. The Keepers acquainted him therewith, and desired him to make good use of that short Time. He thank'd them, said *he would follow their Advice*, and *prepare. Edgworth Bess*, and another Woman had been with him at the Door of the Condemn'd Hold best part of the Afternoon, between five and six he desir'd the other Prisoners, except *Stephen Fowles* to remain above, while he offer'd something in private to his Friends at the Door; they comply'd, and in this interval he got the Spike asunder, which made way for the Skeleton to pass with his Heels foremost, by the Assistance of *Fowles*, whom he most ungenerously betray'd to the Keepers after his being retaken, and the Fellow was as severely punish'd for it.

Having now got clear of his Prison, he took Coach disguis'd in a Night Gown at the corner of the *Old Baily*, along with a Man who waited for him in the Street (and is suppos'd to be *Page* the Butcher) ordering the Coachman to drive to *Black-Fryers Stairs*, where his prostitute gave him the Meeting, and they three took Boat, and went a Shoar at the *Horse-Ferry* at *Westminster*, and at the *White-Hart* they went in, Drank, and stay'd sometime; thence they adjourn'd to a Place in *Holbourn*, where by the help of a Saw he quitted the Chains he had brought with him from *Newgate*; and then like a Freeman took his Ramble through the City and came to *Spittle-Fields*, and there lay with *Edgeworth Bess*.

It may be easy to imagine what an alarm his Escape gave to the Keepers of *Newgate*, three of their People being at the farther End of the *Lodge*, engag'd in a Discourse concerning his wonderful Escape from *New-Prison*, and what Caution ought to be us'd, lest he should give them the slip, at that very Instant as he perfected it.

On *Tuesday* he sent for *William Page* an Apprentice to a Butcher in *Clare-Market*, who came to him, and being Pennyless, he desir'd *Page* to give him what Assistance he could to make his way, and being a Neighbour and Acquaintance, he comply'd with it; but e're he would do any thing, he consulted a near Relation, who as he said, encourag'd him in it; nay, put him upon it, so meeting with this Success in his Application to his Friend, and probable an Assistance in the Pocket, he came to *Sheppard* having bought him a new blue *Butcher's* Frock, and another for himself, and so both took their Rout to *Warnden* in *Northamptonshire*, where they came to a Relation of *Page's*, who receiv'd and Entertain'd them kindly, the People lying from their own Bed to Accommodate them. *Sheppard* pretending to be a *Butcher's* Son in *Clare-Market*, who was going farther in the Country to his Friends, and that *Page* was so kind as to Accompany him; but they as well as their Friend became tir'd of one another; the *Butchers* having but one Shilling left, and the People poor, and Consequently unable to Subsist two such Fellows, after a stay of three or four Days, they return'd, and came for *London*, and reach'd the City on *Tuesday* the 8th of *September*, calling by the way at *Black-Mary's-Hole*, and Drinking with several of their Acquaintance, and then came into *Bishopsgate street*, to one *Cooley's* a *Brandy-shop*, where a *Cobler* being at Work in his Stall, stept out and Swore *ther was* Sheppard, *Sheppard* hearing him, departed immediately. In the Evening they came into *Fleet-street*, at about Eight of the Clock, and observing Mr. *Martins* a Watchmaker's Shop to be open, and a little Boy only to look after it: *Page* goes in and asks the Lad whether Mr. *Taylor* a *Watchmaker* lodg'd in the House? being answer'd in the Negative, he came away, and Reports the Disposition of the Place: *Sheppard* now makes Tryal of his old Master-peice; fixeth a Nail Peircer into the Door post, fastens the Knocker thereto with Packthread, breaks the Glass, and takes out three *Silver Watches* of 15 l. value, the Boy seeing him take them, but could not get out to pursue him, by reason of his Contrivance. One of the Watches he Pledg'd for a Guinea and Half. The same Night they came into *Watch-street*, *Sheppard* going into his *Master's* Yard, and calling for his Fellow 'Prentice, his Mistress heard, knew his Voice, and was dreadfully frightened; he next went to the *Cock* and *Pye Ale-House* in *Drury-Lane*, sent for a Barber his Acquaintance, drank Brandy and eat Oysters in the view of several people. *Page* waiting all the while at the Door, the whole Neighbourhood being alarm'd, yet none durst attempt him, for fear of Pistols, *&c.* He had vow'd Revenge upon a poor Man as kept a Dairy-Cellar, at the End of *White-Horse-Yard*, who having seen him at *Islington* after his Escape, and engag'd not to speak of it, broke his Promise; wherefore *Sheppard* went to his Residence took the Door off the Hinges and threw it down amongst all the Man's Pans, Pipkins, and caus'd a Deluge of Cream and Milk all over the Cellar.

This Night he had a narrow Escape, one Mr. *Ireton* a Sheriffs Officer seeing him and *Page* pass thro' *Drury-Lane*, at about Ten o'clock pursu'd 'em, and laid hold of *Page* instead of *Sheppard*, who got off, thus *Ireton*, missing the main Man, and thinking *Page* of no Consequence, let him go after him.

Edgworth Bess had been apprehended by *Jonathan Wild*, and by Sir *Francis Forbes* one of the Aldermen of *London*, committed to the *Poultry-Compter*, for being aiding and assisting to *Sheppard* in his Escape; the Keepers and others terrify'd and purg'd her as much as was possible to discover where he was, but had it been in her Inclination, it was not in her Power so to do, as it manifestly appear'd soon after.

The People about the *Strand*, *Witch-street* and *Drury-Lane*, whom he had Robb'd, and who had prosecuted him were under great Apprensions and Terror, and in particular Mr. *Kneebone*, on whom he vow'd a bloody Revenge; because he refus'd to sign a Petition in his behalf to the *Recorder* of *London*. This Gentleman was forc'd to keep arm'd People up in his House every Night till he was Re-taken, and had the same fortify'd in the strongest manner. Several other Shop-keepers in this Neighbourhood were also put to great Expence and Trouble to Guard themselves against this dreadful Villian.

The Keepers of *Newgate*, whom the rash World loaded with Infamy, stigmatiz'd and branded with the Title of Persons guilty of Bribery; for Connivance at his Escape, they and what Posse in their Power, either for Love or Money did Contribute their utmost to undeceive a wrong notion'd People. Their Vigilance was remarkably indefatigable, sparing neither Money nor Time, Night nor Day to bring him back to his deserv'd Justice. After many Intelligences, which they endeavour'd for, and receiv'd, they had one which prov'd very Successful. Having learnt for a certainty that their Haunts was about *Finchly Common*, and being very well assur'd of the very House where they lay; on *Thursday* the 10th of *September*, a posse of Men, both of Spirit and Conduct, furnish'd with Arms proper for their Design, went for *Finchley*, some in a Coach and Four, and others on Horseback. They dispers'd themselves upon the *Common* aforesaid, in order to make their View, where they had not been long e're they came in Sight of *SHEPPARD* in Company of *WILLIAM PAGE*, habited like two *Butchers* in new blue Frocks, with white Aprons tuck'd round their Wastes.

Upon *Sheppard's* seeing *Langley* a Turnkey at *Newgate*, he says to his Companion *Page*, *I see a Stag*, upon which their Courage dropt; knowing that now their dealing way of Business was almost at an End; however to make their Flight as secure as they could, they thought it adviseable to take to a Foot-path, to cut off the pursuit of the *Newgate Cavalry*; but this did not prove most successful, *Langley* came up with *Page* (who was hindermost) and Dismounting with Pistol in Hand, commands *Page* to throw up his Hands, which he trembling did, begging for Life, desiring him to *Fisk* him, *viz.* (search him,) which he accordingly did, and found a broad Knife and File; having thus disarm'd him, he takes the *Chubb* along with him in quest of the slippery *Ele*,

Sheppard, who had taken Shelter in an old Stable, belonging to a Farm-House; the pursuit was close, the House invested, and a Girl seeing his Feet as he stood up hid, discover'd him. *Austin* a Turnkey first attach'd his Person. *Langley* seconded him, *Ireton* an Officer help'd to Enclose, and happy was the hindermost who aided in this great Enterprise. He being shock'd with the utmost Fear, told them he submitted, and desir'd they would let him live as long as he could, which they did, and us'd him mildly; upon searching him they found a broad Knife with two of the Watches as he had taken out of Mr. *Martin's* Shop, one under each Armpit; and now having gain'd their Point, and made themselves Masters of what they had often endeavoured for, they came with their *Lost Sheep* to a little House on the *Common* that sold Liquors, with this Inscription on the Sign, *I have brought my* Hogs *to a fair Market*; which our two unfortunate *Butchers* under their then unhappy Circumstances, had too sad Reason to apply to themselves. *Sheppard* had by this time recover'd his Surprize, grew calm and easy, and desir'd them to give him Brandy, they did, and were all good Friends, and Company together.

They adjourn'd with their Booty to another Place, where was waiting a Coach and Four to Convey it to Town, with more Speed and Safety; and Mr. *Sheppard* arriv'd at his old Mansion, at about two in the Afternoon. At his a-lighting, he made a sudden Spring; He declar'd his Intention was to have slipt under the Coach, and had a Race for it; he was put into the Condemn'd-Hold, and Chain'd down to the Floor with double *Basils* about his Feet, *&c.* *Page* was carried before Sir *Francis Forbes* and committed to the same Prison for Accompanying and aiding *Sheppard* in his Escape. The prudence of Mr. *Pitt* caus'd a Separation between him and his Brother the first Night, as a Means to prevent any ensuing Danger, by having two Heads, which (according to our Proverbial Saying) *are better than one*.

The Joy the People of *Newgate* conceiv'd on this Occasion is inexpressible, *Te Deum* was Sung in the *Lodge*, and nothing but Smiles, and Bumpers, were seen there for many Days together. But *Jonathan Wild* unfortunately happen'd to be gone upon a wrong Scent after him to *Sturbridge*, and Lost a Share of the Glory.

His Escape and his being so suddenly Re-taken made such a Noise in the Town, that it was thought all the common People would have gone Mad about him; there being not a *Porter* to be had for Love nor Money, nor getting into an Ale-house, for *Butchers*, *Shoemakers* and *Barbers*, all engag'd in Controversies, and Wagers, about *Sheppard*.

Newgate Night and Day surrounded with the Curious from St. *Giles's* and *Rag-Fair*, and *Tyburn Road* daily lin'd with Women and Children; and the *Gallows* as carefully watch'd by Night, lest he should be hang'd *Incog*. For a Report of that nature, obtain'd much upon the Rabble; In short, it was a Week of the greatest Noise and Idleness among Mechanicks that has been known in *London*, and *Parker* and *Pettis*, two *Lyricks*, subsisted many Days very comfortably upon *Ballads* and *Letters* about *Sheppard*. The vulgar continu'd under great Doubts and Difficulties, in what would be his Case, and whether the *Old Warrant*, or a *New One* must be made for his Execution, or a New Tryal, &c. were the great Questions as arose, and occasion'd various Reasonings and Speculation, till a News Paper, call'd the *Daily Journal* set them all to Rights by the Publication of the Account following, *viz*.

'*J. Sheppard* having been Convicted of Burglary, and Felony, and received Sentence of Death, and afterwards 'Escap'd from *Newgate*; and being since Re-taken'; we are assur'd that it must be prov'd in a *Regular*, and *Judicial* way, that he is the same Person, who was so Convicted and made his Escape, before a Warrant can be obtain'd for his Execution; and that this Affair well be brought before the Court at the *Old Baily* the next Sessions.'

This was enough; People began to grow calm and easy and got *Shav'd*, and their Shoes *finish'd*, and Business returned into its former Channel, the Town resolving to wait the *Sessions* with Patience.

The Reverend Mr. *Wagstaff*, who officiated in the absence of the *Ordinary*, renew'd his former Acquaintance with Mr. *Sheppard*, and examin'd him in a particular manner concerning his Escape from the Condemn'd Hold: He sincerely disown'd, that all, or any, belonging to the Prison were privy thereto; but related it as it has been describ'd. He declar'd that *Edgworth Bess*, who had hitherto pass'd for his *Wife*, was not really so: This was by some thought to be in him Base, and Ungenerous in that, as she had Contributed towards his Escape, and was in Custody on that Account, it might render her more liable to Punishment, than if she had been thought his Wife; but he endeavour'd to acquit himself, by saying, that she was the sole Author of all his Misfortunes; That she betray'd him to *Jonathan Wild*, at the time he was taken in *Rosemary-Lane*; and that when he was contriving his Escape, she disobey'd his orders, as when being requir'd to attend at the Door of the Condemn'd-Hold by Nine, or Ten in the Morning to facilitate his Endeavours, she came not till the Evening, which he said, was an ungrateful Return for the care he had taken in setting her at

Liberty from *New-Prison;* and thus Justify'd himself in what he had done, and said he car'd not what became of her.

He was also Examined about Mr. *Martin's* Watches; and whether *Page* was privy to that Robbery; he carefully guarded himself against uttering any thing that might affect him, peremptorily declar'd him Innocent of that, as well as of being privy to his Escape, and said, that he only out of Kindness, as being an old Companion, was resolv'd to share in his Fortunes after he had Escap'd.

He was again continually meditating a second Escape, as appear'd by his own Hardiness, and the Instruments found upon him, on *Saturday* the 12th, and *Wednesday* the 16th of *September,* the first Time a small File was found conceal'd in his Bible, and the second Time two Files, a Chisel and an Hammer being hid in the Rushes of a Chair; and whenever a Question was mov'd to him, when, or by what Means those Implements came to his Hands; he would passionately fly out, and say, *How can you? you always ask me these, and such like Questions;* and in a particular manner, when he was ask'd, Whether his Companion *Page* was an Accomplice with him, either in the affair of the Watches, or any other? (he reply'd) *That if he knew, he would give no direct Answer,* thinking it to be a Crime in him to detect the Guilty.

It was thought necessary by the Keepers to remove him from the Condemn'd-Hold to a Place, call'd the *Castle,* in the Body of the Goal, and to Chain him down to two large Iron Staples in the Floor; the Concourse of People of tolerable Fashion to see him was exceeding Great, he was always Chearful and Pleasant to a Degree, as turning almost every thing as was said into a Jest and Banter.

Being one *Sunday* at the Chapel, a Gentleman belonging to the *Lord Mayor,* ask'd a Turnkey, Which was *Sheppard,* the Man pointed to him? Says *Sheppard, yes Sir, I am the* Sheppard, *and all the Goalers in the Town are my Flock, and I cannot stir into the Country, but they are all at my Heels* Baughing, *after me, &c.*

He told Mr. *Robins,* the *City Smith, That he had procur'd him a small Job, and that whoever it was that put the Spikes on the Condemn'd-Hold was an honest Man, for a better peice of Metal,* says he, *I never wrought upon in my Life.*

He was loth to believe his frequent Robberies were an Injury to the Public, for he us'd to say, That *if they were ill in one Respect, they were as good in another, and that though he car'd not for Working much himself, yet he was desirous that others should not stand Idle, more especially those of his own Trade, who were always Repairing of his Breaches.*

When serious, and that but seldom, he would Reflect on his past wicked Life. He declar'd to us, that for several Years of his Apprenticeship he had an utter abhorrence to Women of the Town, and us'd to pelt them with Dirt when they have fell in his way; till a *Button-Mould-Maker* his next Neighbour left off that Business, and set up a Victualling-house in *Lewkenhors-Lane*, where himself and other young Apprentices resorted on *Sundays*, and at all other Opportunities. At this House began his Acquaintance with *Edgworth Bess*. His sentiments were strangely alter'd, and from an Aversion to those Prostitutes, he had a more favourable Opinion, and even Conversation with them, till he Contracted an ill Distemper, which as he said, he cur'd himself of by a Medicine of his own preparing.

He inveigh'd bitterly against his Brother *Thomas* for putting him into the Information, for Mrs. *Cook's* Robbery, and pretended that all the Mischiefs that attended him was owing to that Matter. He acknowledg'd that he was concern'd in that Fact, and that his said Brother broke into his Lodgings, and stole from him all his Share and more of the acquir'd Booty.

He often-times averr'd, that *William Field* was no ways concern'd in Mr. *Kneebone's* Robbery; but that being a Brother of the Quill; *Blewskin* and himself told him the particulars, and manner of the Facts, and that all he Swore against him at his Tryal was False, and that he had other Authority for it, than what came out of their (*Sheppard* and *Blewskin*) Mouths, who actually committed the Fact.

And moreover, that *Field* being acquainted with their Warehouse (a Stable) near the *Horse-Ferry* at *Westminster*, which *Sheppard* had hir'd, and usually resposited therein the Goods he stole. He came one Night, and broke open the same, and carried off the best part of the Effects taken out of Mr. *Kneebone's* Shop.

Sheppard said he thought this to be one of the greatest Villanies that could be acted, for another to come and Plunder them of Things for which they had so honourably ventur'd their Lives, and wish'd that *Field*, as well as his Brother *Tom* might meet with forgiveness for it.

He declar'd himself frequently against the Practice of *Whidling*, or *Impeaching*, which he said, had made dreadful Havock among the *Thieves*, and much lamented the depravity of the *Brethren* in that Respect; and said that if all were but such *Tight-Cocks* as himself, the *Reputation* of the *British Thievery* might be carried to a far greater height than it had been done for many Ages, and that there would then be but little Necessity for Jaylors and Hangmen.

These and such like were his constant Discourses, when Company went up with the Turnkeys to the *Castle* to see him, and few or none went away without leaving him Money for his Support; in which he abounded, and did therewith some small Charities to the other Prisoners; however, he was abstemious and sparing enough in his Diet.

Among the many Schemes laid by his Friends, for the preserving himself after his Escape, we were told of a most Remarkable one, propos'd by an ingenious Person, who advis'd, that he might be Expeditiously, and Secretly convey'd to the Palace at *Windsor*, and there to prostrate his Person, and his Case at the Feet of a most Gracious Prince, and his Case being so very singular and new, it might in great probability move the Royal Fountain of unbounded Clemency; but he declin'd this Advice, and follow'd the Judgment and Dictates of *Butchers*, which very speedily brought him very near the Door of the *Slaughterhouse*.

On the 4th of *September*, the Day as *Joseph Ward*, and *Anthony Upton* were Executed, there was publish'd a whimsical Letter, as from *Sheppard*, to *Jack Ketch*, which afforded Diversion to the Town, and Bread to the Author, which is as followeth, *viz.*

SIR,

I Thank you for the Favour you intended me this day: I am a Gentleman, and allow you to be the same, and I hope can forgive Injuries; fond Nature prompted, I obey'd, Oh, propitious Minute! and to show that I am in Charity, I am now drinking your Health, and a *Bon Repo* to poor *Joseph* and *Anthony*. I am gone a few Days for the Air, but design speedily to embark; and this Night I am going upon a Mansion for a Supply; it's a stout Fortification, but what Difficulties can't I encounter, when, dear *Jack*, you find that Bars and Chains are but trifling Obstacles in the way of your Friend and Servant.

JOHN SHEPPARD.

From my Residence in Terra Australi incognito.

P.S. Pray my Service to Mr. *Or——— di——— y* and to Mr. *App— — ee.*

On *Saturday* the 10th of *October*, *Anthony Lamb*, and *Thomas Sheppard*, with 95 other Felons were carried from *Newgate* on Shipboard, for Transportation to the Plantations; the last begg'd to have an opportunity given him of taking his final Leave of his Brother *John*; but this was not to be Granted, and the greatest Favour that could be obtain'd, was that on the *Sunday* before they had an Interview at the *Chapel*, but at such a distance, that they neither saluted, or shook Hands, and the Reason given for it, was that no Implements might be convey'd to *Sheppard* to assist him in making an Escape.

This, Caution seem'd to be absolutely necessary, for it appear'd soon after that *Sheppard* found Means to release himself from the Staples to which he was Chain'd in the Castle, by unlocking a great Padlock with a Nail, which he had pickt up on the Floor, and endeavour'd to pass up the Chimney, but was prevented by the stout Iron Bars fix'd in his way, and wanted nothing but the smallest File to have perfected his Liberty. When the Assistants of the Prison, came as usual with his Victuals, they began to examine his Irons; to their great Surprize they found them loose, and ready to be taken off at Pleasure. Mr. *Pitt* the Head Keeper, and his Deputies were sent for, and *Sheppard* finding this Attempt entirely frustrated, discover'd to them by what means he had got them off; and after they had search'd him, found nothing, and Lock'd and Chain'd him down again; He took up the Nail and unlocked the Padlock before their Faces; they were struck with the greatest Amazement as having never heard, or beheld the like before. He was then Handcuff'd, and more effectually Chain'd.

The next Day, the Reverend Mr. *Purney Ordinary* of the Place came from the Country to visit him, and complain'd of the sad Disposition he found him in, as Meditateing on nothing, but Means to Escape, and declining the great Duty incumbent upon him to prepare for his approaching Change. He began to Relent, and said, that since his last Effort had prov'd not Successful, he would entertain no more Thoughts of that Nature, but entirely Dispose, and Resign himself to the Mercy of Almighty God, of whom he hop'd to find forgiveness of his manifold Offences.

He said, that *Edgworth Bess* and himself kept a little Brandy-shop together in *Lewkenhors-Lane*, and once sav'd about Thirty Pounds; but having such an universal Acquaintance amongst Theives, he had frequent calls to go *Abroad*, and soon quitted that Business, and his Shop.

On *Friday* the 2d, of *October* his old Confederate *Joseph Blake* alias *Blewskin*, was apprehended and taken at a House in St. *Giles's* Parish by *Jonathan Wild*, and by Justice *Blackerby* committed to *Newgate*. *William Field* who was at his liberty, appearing and making Oath, that *Blewskin* together with *John Sheppard* and himself, committed the Burglary and Felony in Mr. *Kneebone's* House, for which *Sheppard* was Condemn'd.

The Sessions commencing at the *Old-Bailey* on *Wednesday* the 14th of *October* following, an Indictment was found against *Blewskin* for the same, and he was brought down from *Newgate* to the *Old-Bailey* to be Arraign'd in order to his Tryal; and being in the Yard within the Gate before the Court: Mr. *Wild* being there Drinking a glass of Wine with him, he said to Mr. *Wild*, *You may put in a word for me, as well as for another Person?* To which Mr. *Wild* reply'd, I cannot do it. *You are certainly a dead Man, and will be tuck'd up very speedily,* or words to that effect: Whereupon *Blewskin* on a sudden seiz'd Mr. *Wild* by the Neck, and with a little Clasp Knife he was provided with he cut his Throat in a very dangerous Manner; and had it not been for a *Muslin* Stock twisted in several Plaits round his Neck, he had in all likelyhood succeeded in his barbarous Design before *Ballard* the Turnkey, who was at Hand, could have time to lay hold of him; the Villain trumph'd afterwards in what he had done, Swearing many bloody Oaths, that if he had murder'd him, he should have died with Satisfaction, and that his Intention was to have cut off his Head, and thrown it into the Sessions House-Yard among the Rabble, and Curs'd both his Hand and the Knife for not Executing it Effectually.

Mr. *Wild* instantly had the Assistance of three able Surgeons, *viz.* Mr. *Dobbins*, Mr. *Marten* and Mr. *Coletheart*, who sew'd up the Wound, and order'd him to his Bed, and he has continu'd ever since, but in a doubtful State of Recovery.

The Felons on the Common Side of *Newgate*, also animated by *Sheppard's* Example, the Night before they were to be Shipt for Transporation, had cut several Iron Bars assunder, and some of them had saw'd off their Fetters, the rest Huzzaing, and making Noises, under pretence of being Joyful that they were to be remov'd on the Morrow, to prevent the Workmen being heard; and in two Hours time more, if their Design had not been discover'd, near One Hundred Villians had been let loose into the World, to have committed new Depredations; nothing was wanted here but *Sheppard's* great Judgment, who was by himself in the strong Room, call'd the *Castle*, meditating his own Deliverance, which he perfected in the manner following.

On *Thursday* the 15th of this Instant *October*, at between One and Two in the Afternoon, *William Austin*, an Assistant to the Keepers, a Man reputed to be a very diligent, and faithful Servant, went to *Sheppard* in the strong Room, call'd the *Castle*, with his Necessaries, as was his Custom every Day. There went along with him Captain *Geary*, the Keeper of *New Prison*, Mr. *Gough*, belonging to the *Gatehouse* in *Westminster*, and two other Gentlemen, who had the Curiosity to see the Prisoner, *Austin* very strictly examined his Fetters, and his Hand-Cuffs, and found them very Safe; he eat his Dinner and talk'd with his usual Gayety to the Company: They took leave of him and wish'd him a good Evening. The Court being sitting at the *Old-Bailey*, the Keepers and most of their Servants were attending there with their Prisoners: And *Sheppard* was told that if he wanted any thing more, then was his Time, because they could not come to him till the next Morning: He thank'd them for their Kindness, and desir'd them to be as *early as possible*.

The same Night, soon after 12 of the Clock Mr. *Bird*, who keeps a Turners-shop adjoyning to *Newgate*, was disturb'd by the Watchman, who found his Street Door open, and call'd up the Family, and they concluding the Accident was owing to the Carelessness of some in the House, shut their Doors, and went to Bed again.

The next Morning *Friday*, at about eight Mr. *Austin* went up as usual to wait on *Sheppard*, and having unlock'd and unbolted the double Doors of the Castle, he beheld almost a Cart-load of Bricks and Rubbish about the Room, and his Prisoner gone: The Man ready to sink, came trembling down again, and was scarce able to Acquaint the People in the *Lodge* with what had happen'd.

The whole Posse of the Prison ran up, and stood like Men depriv'd of their Senses: Their surprize being over, they were in hopes that he might not have yet entirely made his Escape, and got their Keys to open all the strong Rooms adjacent to the *Castle*, in order to Trace him, when to their farther Amazement, they found the Door ready open'd to their Hands; and the strong Locks, Screws and Bolts broken in pieces, and scatter'd about the Jayl. Six great Doors (one whereof having not been open'd for seven Years past) were forc'd, and it appear'd that he had Descended from the Leads of *Newgate* by a Blanket (which he fasten'd to the Wall by an Iron Spike he had taken from the Hatch of the *Chapel*) on the House of Mr. *Bird*, and the Door on the Leads having been left open, it is very reasonable to conclude he past directly to the Street Door down the Stairs; Mr *Bird* and his Wife hearing an odd sort of a Noise on the Stairs as they lay in their Bed, a short time before the Watchman alarm'd the Family.

Infinite Numbers of Citizens came to *Newgate* to behold *Sheppard's* Workmanship, and Mr. *Pitt* and his Officers very readily

Conducted them up Stairs, that the World might be convinc'd there was not the least room to suspect, either a Negligence, or Connivance in the Servants. Every one express'd the greatest Surprize that has been known, and declar'd themselves satisfy'd with the Measures they had taken for the Security of their Prisoner.

One of the Sheriffs came in Person, and went up to the *Castle* to be satisfy'd of the Situation of the Place, &c. Attended by several of the City Officers.

The Court being sat at the *Sessions-House*, the Keepers were sent for and Examin'd, and the Magistrates were in great Consternation, that so horrid a Wretch had escap'd their Justice. It being intended that he should have been brought down to the Court the last Day of the *Sessions*, and order'd for Execution in two or three Days after; if it appear'd that he was the Person Condemn'd for the breaking Mr. *Kneebone's* House, and included in the Warrant for Execution, &c.

Many of the Methods by which this miraculous Escape was effected, remain as yet a Secret, there are some indeed too Evident, the most reasonable Conjecture that has hierto been made, is, that the first Act was his twisting and breaking assunder by the strength of his Hands a small Iron Chain, which together with a great Horse Padlock, (as went from the heavy Fetters about his Legs to the staples) confin'd him to the Floor, and with a Nail open'd the Padlock and set himself at Liberty about the Room: A large flat Iron Bar appears to have been taken out of the Chimney, with the Assistance thereof 'tis plain he broke thro' a Wall of many Foot in Thickness, and made his way from the *Castle* into another strong Room Contiguous, the Door of it not having been open'd since several of the *Preston* Prisoners were Confin'd there about seven Years ago: Three Screws are visibly taken off of the Lock, and the Doors as strong as Art could make them, forc'd open. The Locks and Bolts, either wrench'd or Broke, and the Cases and other Irons made for their Security cut assunder: An Iron Spike broke off from the Hatch in the *Chapel*, which he fix'd in the Wall and fasten'd his Blanket to it, to drop on the Leads of Mr. *Bird's* House, his Stockings were found on the Leads of *Newgate*; 'tis question'd whether sixty Pounds will repair the Damage done to the Jayl.

It will perhaps be inquir'd how all this could be perform'd without his being heard by the Prisoners or the Keepers; 'tis well known that the Place of his Confinement is in the upper part of the Prison, none of the other Felons being Kept any where near him; and 'tis suppos'd that if any had heard him at Work, they would rather have facilitated, than frustrated his Endeavours. In the Course of his Breaches he pass'd by a Door on his Left belonging to the *Common-Side* Felons, who have since Curs'd him heartily for his not giving them an opportunity to kiss his Hand, and lending them a favourable lift when his Hand was in; but that was not a Work proper for Mr. *Sheppard* to do in his then Circumstances.

His Fetters are not to be found any where about the Jayl, from whence 'tis concluded he has either thrown them down some Chimney, or carried them off on his Legs, the latter seems to be Impracticable, and would still render his Escaping in such Manner the more astonishing; and the only Answer that is given to the whole, at *Newgate* is, *That the* Devil *came in Person and assisted him*.

He undoubtedly perform'd most of these Wonders in the darkest part of the Night, and without the least Glimpse of a Candle; a word, he has actually done with his own Hands in a few Hours, what several of the most skilful Artists allow, could not have been acted by a number of Persons furnish'd with proper Implements, and all other Advantages in a full Day.

Never was there anything better Tim'd, the Keepers and all their Assistants being obliged to a strict Attendance on the Sessions at the *Old Bailey*, which held for about a Week; and *Blewskin* having confin'd *Jonathan Wild* to his Chamber, a more favourable opportunity could not have presented for Mr. *Sheppard's* Purposes.

The Jaylors suffer'd much by the Opinion the ignorant Part of the People entertain'd of the Matter, and nothing would satisfie some, but that they not only Conniv'd at, but even assisted him in breaking their own Walls and Fences, and that for this Reason too, *viz.* That he should be at Liberty to instruct and train up others in his Method of House-Breaking; and replenish the Town with a new set of Rogues, to supply the Places of those Transported beyond Sea.

This is indeed a fine way of Judging, the well-known Characters of Mr. *Pitt*, and his Deputies, are sufficient to wipe of such ridiculous Imputations; and 'tis a most lamentable Truth, that they have often-times had in their Charge Villains of the deepest Die; Persons of Quality and great Worth, for whom no Entreaties, no Sums how large soever have been able to interfere between the doleful Prison, and the fatal Tree.

The Officers have done their Duty, they are but Men, and have had to deal with a Creature something more than Man, a *Protoeus*,

Supernatural, Words cannot describe him, his Actions and Workmanship which are too visible, best testifie him.

On *Saturday* the 17th, *Joseph Blake*, alias *Blewskin*, came upon his Tryal at the *Old Bailey*. *Field* gave the same Evidence against him, as he had formerly done against *Sheppard*; and the Prisoner making but a triffling Defence, the Jury found him Guilty of Buglary and Felony. The Criminal when the Verdict was brought in, made his Obeysances to the Court, *and thank'd them for their Kindness*.

It will be necessary that we now return to the Behaviour of Mr. *Sheppard*, some few Days before his last Flight.

Mr. *Figg* the famous Prize Fighter comeing to see him, in *NEWGATE*, there past some pleasant Raillery between them; and after Mr. *Figg* was gone, *Sheppard* declared he had a Mind to send him a formal Challenge to Fight him at all the Weapons in the strong Room; and that let the Consequence be what it would, he should call at Mr. *Figg's* House in his way to Execution, and drink a merry Glass with him by way of Reconciliation.

A young Woman an Acquaintance of his Mother, who wash'd his Linnen and brought him Necessaries, having in an Affray, got her Eyes beaten Black and Blue; says *Sheppard* to her, *How long hast thou been Married?* Replyes the Wench. *I wonder you can ask me such a Question, when you so well know the Contrary*. Nay, says *Sheppard* again, Sarah *don't deny it, for you have gotten your Certificate in your Face*.

Mr. *Ireton* a Bailiff in *Drury-Lane* having pursued *Sheppard* after his Escape from the Condemn'd-Hold with uncommon Diligence; (for the safety of that Neighbourhood which was the chief Scene of his Villainies) *Sheppard* when Re-taken, declared, he would be even with him for it, and if ever he procur'd his Liberty again, *he would give all his Prisoners an* ACT OF GRACE. A Gentleman in a jocose way ask'd him to come and take a Dinner with him, *Sheppard* reply'd, *he accepted of the Invitation, and perhaps might take an opportunity to wait on him*; and there is great Reason to believe he has been as good as his Word.

He would complain of his Nights, as saying, *It was dark with him from Five in the Evening, till Seven in the Morning*; and being not permitted to have either a Bed or Candle, his Circumstances were dismal; and that he never slept but had some confus'd Doses, he said he consider'd all this with the Temper of a Philosopher.

Neither his sad Circumstances, nor the solemn Exhortations of the several Divines who visited him, were able to divert him from this ludicrous way of Expression; he said, *They were all Ginger-bread Fellows*, and came rather out of Curiosity, than Charity; and to form *Papers* and *Ballads* out of his Behaviour.

A *Welch* Clergyman who came pretty often, requested him in a particularly Manner to refrain Drinking; (tho' indeed there was no necessity for that Caution) *Sheppard* says, Doctor, *You set an Example and I'll follow*; this was a smart Satyr and Repartee upon the *Parson*, some Circumstances consider'd.

When he was visited in the *Castle* by the Reverend Mr. *Wagstaff*, he put on the Face only of a Preparation for his End, as appear'd by his frequent Attempts made upon his Escape, and when he has been press'd to Discover those who put him upon Means of Escaping, and furnish'd him with Implements, he would passionately, and with a Motion of striking, say, *ask me no such Questions, one File's worth all the Bibles in the World.*

When ask'd if he had not put off all Thoughts of an Escape and Entertain'd none but those of Death, would Answer by way of Question, not directly, whether they thought it possible, or probable for him to Effect his Release, when Manackled in the manner he was. When mov'd to improve the few Minutes that seem'd to remain of his Life; he did indeed listen to, but not regard the Design and Purport of his Admonition, breaking in with something New of his own, either with respect to his former Accomplices, or Actions, and all too with Pleasure and Gayety of Expression.

When in *Chapel*, he would seemingly make his Responses with Devotion; but would either Laugh, or force Expressions (when as an Auditor of the Sermon) be of Contempt, either of the Preacher, or of his Discourse.

In fine, he behav'd so, in Word, and Action, (since retaken) that demonstrated to the World, that his Escape was the utmost Employ of his Thoughts, whatever Face of Penitence he put on when visited by the Curious.

An Account of SHEPPARD'S Adventures of five Hours immediately after his Escape from *Newgate*, in a Letter to his Friend.

DEAR FRIEND!

Over a Bottle of *Claret* you'll give me leave to *declare it*, that I've fairly put the *Vowels* upon the good Folks at *Newgate, i.o.u.* When I'm able, I may, or may not discharge my *Fees*, 'tis a *Fee-simple*, for a Man in my Condition to acknowledge; and tho' I'm safe out of *Newgate*, I must yet have, or at least, affect, a *New Gate* by Limping, or Turning my Toes in by making a right *Hand* of my *Feet*. Not *to be long*, for I hate *Prolixity* in all Business: *In short*, after *Filing, Defileing, Sawing*, when no Body *Saw. Climbing* (this *Clime in*) it prov'd a good *Turner* of my Affairs, thro' the House of a *Turner*. Being quite past, and safe from *Estreat* on Person or Chattels, and safe in the *Street*, I thought Thanks due to him who cou'd *Deliver hence*; and immediately (for you must know I'm a *Catholick*) to give Thanks for my Deliverance, I stept amongst the *Grey-Fryers* to come an joyn with me, in saying a *Pater-Noster*, or so, at *Amen-Corner*. The *Fryers* being *Fat* began to *Broil*, and soon after *Boild up* into a Passion to be disturb'd at that time of Night. But being got *Loose* and having no Time to *Lose*, I gave them good Words, and so the Business was done. From thence I soon slip'd through *Ludgate*, but was damnably fearful of an *Old Bailey* always lurking thereabout, who might have brought me to the *Fleet* for being too *Nimble*, besides, I was wonderfully apprehensive of receiving some unwelcome *Huggings* from the *W....n* there; therefore with a step and a stride I soon got over *Fleet-ditch*, and (as in Justice I ought) I prais'd the *Bridge* I got over. Being a *Batchelor*, and not being capable to to manage a Bridewell you know. I had no Business near *St. Brides*, so kept the right handside, designing to *Pop* into the *Alley* as usual; but fearing to go thro' there, and *harp* too much on the same *String*, it gave an *Allay* to my Intention, and on I went to *Shoe-lane* end but there meeting with a *Bully Hack* of the Town, he wou'd have shov'd me down, which my Spirit resenting, tho' a *brawny Dog*, I soon *Coller'd* him, fell Souse at him, then with his own Cane I *strapped* till he was force to *Buckle* too, and hold his *Tongue*, in so much he durst not say his *Soul* was his own, and was glad to pack of at *Last*, and turn his *Heels* upon me: I was glad he was gone you may be sure, and *dextrously* made a *Hand* of my *Feet* under the *Leg-Tavern*; but the very Thoughts of *Fetter-Lane* call'd to mind some Passages, which made me avoid the *Passage* at the end of it, (next to the Coffee House you know) so I soon whip'd over the way, yet going along two wooden *Logger-heads* at *St. Dunstan's* made just them a damn'd Noise about their *Quarters*, but the sight of me made perfectly *Hush in a Minute*; now fearing to goe by *Chance-a wry-Lane*, as being upon the *Watch* my self and not to be *debarr'd* at *Temple-Bar*; I stole up *Bell-Yard*, but narrowly escap'd being *Clapper-claw'd* by two Fellows I did not like in the Alley, so was forc'd to goe round with a design to *Sheer-off* into *Sheer-Lane*, but the

Trumpet sounding at that very time, alarm'd me so, I was forc'd to Grope my way back through *Hemlock-Court*, and take my *Passage* by *Ship-Yard* without the Bar again; but there meeting with one of our trusty Friends, (all Ceremonies a-part) he told me under the *Rose* I must expect no *Mercy* in *St. Clement's* Parish, for the *Butchers* there on the *Back* on't would *Face* me, and with their *Cleavers* soon bring me down on my *marrow* Bones; you may believe I soon hastened thence, but by this time being Fainty and night Spent, I put forward, and seeing a *Light* near the *Savoy-Gate*, I was resolv'd not to make *Light* of the Opportunity, but call'd for an hearty Dram of *Luther* and *Calvin*, that is, *Mum* and *Geneva* mix'd; but having Fasted so long before, it soon got into my Noddle, and e'er I had gone twenty steps, it had so intirely *Stranded* my Reason, that by the time I came to *Half-Moon-Street* end, it gave a *New-Exchange* to my Senses, and made me quite *Lunatick*.

However, after a little Rest, I stole down *George-Passage* into *Oaf-Alley* in *York-Buildings*, and thence (tho' a vile Man) into *Villiers-Street*, and so into the *Strand* again, where having gone a little way, *Hefford's-Harp* at the Sign of the *Irish-Harp*, put me a *Jumping and Dancing* to that degree that I could not forbear making a *Somerset* or two before *Northumberland-House*. I thought once of taking the *Windsor* Coach for my self *John Sheppard*, by the Name of *Crook*— — but fearing to be *Hook'd* in before my Journey's End, I stept into *Hedge-Lane*, where two Harlots were up in the *Boughs* (it seems) *Branching* out their Respects to one another, through their Windows, and People beginning to gather thereabout, I ran *Pelmel* to *Piccadilly*, where meeting by meer chance a *Bakers* Cart going to *Turnham-Green*, I being not *Mealy Mouth'd*, nor the Man being *Crusty* I *wheel'd* out of Town.

I did call at *Hammersmith*, having no occasion directly. I shall stay two or three Days in that Neighbourhood, so, if you Direct a letter for Mr. Sligh Bolt, to be left with Mrs. *Tabitha Skymmington* at *Cheesewick*, it's Safety will *Bear Water* by any *Boat*, and come *Current* with the Tyde to

    Dear BOB
Yours from the Top
of *Newgate* to the Bottom

J. *SHEPPARD*.

    P.S. If you see *Blewskin*, tell him I am well, and hope he receiv'd my last—I wou'd write by the *Post* if I durst, but it wou'd be, certainly

Post-pon'd if I did, and it would be *stranger* too, to trust a Line by a *Stranger*, who might *Palm* upon us both and never Deliver it to *Hand.*

I send this by a *Waterman*, (I dare trust) who is very Merry upon me, and says he wou'd not be in my *Jacket. Saturday Octob.* 17, 1724.

We shall conclude with what had been often observ'd by many Persons to *Sheppard, viz.* That it was very Imprudent in him to take Shelter in the City, or the adjacent Parts of it, after his Escape from the Condemn'd Hold; and withal to commit a *Capital Offence,* almost within Sight of *Newgate,* when his Life and all was in such Danger. His Reply was general, *viz.* That it was his Fate: But being ask'd a particular Reason for his not taking a longer Rout than the City, and the Neighbouring parts: pleaded Poverty as his Excuse for Confinement within those Limits; at the same time urging, that had he been Master at that time of five Pounds, *England* should not have been the Place of his Residence, having a good Trade in his Hands to live in any populated Part of the World.

EVERYBODY'S BUSINESS IS NOBODY'S BUSINESS

or,

PRIVATE ABUSES, PUBLIC GRIEVANCES:

EXEMPLIFIED

In the Pride, Insolence, and exorbitant Wages of our Women, Servants, Footmen, &c.

WITH

A Proposal for Amendment of the same; as also for clearing the Streets of those Vermin called Shoe-Cleaners, and substituting in their stead many Thousands of industrious Poor, now ready to starve. With divers other Hints of great Use to the Public.

Humbly submitted the Consideration of our Legislature, and the careful Perusal of all Masters and Mistresses of Families.

BY ANDREW MORETON, Esq.

THE PREFACE

Since this little book appeared in print, it has had no less than three answers, and fresh attacks are daily expected from the powers of Grub-street; but should threescore antagonists more arise, unless they say more to the purpose than the forementioned, they shall not tempt me to reply.

Nor shall I engage in a paper war, but leave my book to answer for itself, having advanced nothing therein but evident truths, and incontestible matters of fact.

The general objection is against my style; I do not set up for an author, but write only to be understood, no matter how plain.

As my intentions are good, so have they had the good fortune to meet with approbation from the sober and substantial part of mankind; as for the vicious and vagabond, their ill-will is my ambition.

It is with uncommon satisfaction I see the magistracy begin to put the laws against vagabonds in force with the utmost vigour, a great many of those vermin, the japanners, having lately been taken up and sent to the several work-houses in and about this city; and indeed high time, for they grow every day more and more pernicious.

My project for putting watchmen under commissioners, will, I hope, be put in practice; for it is scarce safe to go by water unless you know your man.

As for the maid-servants, if I undervalue myself to take notice of them, as they are pleased to say, it is because they overvalue themselves so much they ought to be taken notice of.

This makes the guilty take my subject by the wrong end, but any impartial reader may find, I write not against servants, but bad servants; not against wages, but exorbitant wages, and am entirely of the poet's opinion,

The good should meet with favour and applause,
The wicked be restrain'd by wholesome laws.

The reason why I did not publish this book till the end of the last sessions of parliament was, because I did not care to interfere with more momentous affairs; but leave it to the consideration of that august body during this recess, against the next sessions, when I shall exhibit another complaint against a growing abuse, for which I doubt not but to receive their approbation and the thanks of all honest men.

EVERYBODY'S BUSINESS IS NOBODY'S BUSINESS

This is a proverb so common in everybody's mouth, that I wonder nobody has yet thought it worth while to draw proper inferences from it, and expose those little abuses, which, though they seem trifling, and as it were scarce worth consideration, yet, by insensible degrees, they may become of injurious consequence to the public; like some diseases, whose first symptoms are only trifling disorders, but by continuance and progression, their last periods terminate in the destruction of the whole human fabric.

In contradiction therefore to this general rule, and out of sincere love and well meaning to the public, give me leave to enumerate the abuses insensibly crept in among us, and the inconveniences daily arising from the insolence and intrigues of our servant-wenches, who, by their caballing together, have made their party so considerable, that everybody cries out against them; and yet, to verify the proverb, nobody has thought of, or at least proposed a remedy, although such an undertaking, mean as it seems to be, I hope will one day be thought worthy the consideration of our king, lords, and commons.

Women servants are now so scarce, that from thirty and forty shillings a year, their wages are increased of late to six, seven, nay, eight pounds per annum, and upwards; insomuch that an ordinary tradesman cannot well keep one; but his wife, who might be useful in his shop or business, must do the drudgery of household affairs; and all this because our servant-wenches are so puffed up with pride nowadays, that they never think they go fine enough: it is a hard matter to know the mistress from the maid by their dress; nay, very often the maid shall be much the finer of the two. Our woollen manufacture suffers much by this, for nothing but silks and satins will go down with our kitchen-wenches; to support which intolerable pride, they have insensibly raised their wages to such a height as was never known in any age or nation but this.

Let us trace this from the beginning, and suppose a person has a servant-maid sent him out of the country, at fifty shillings, or three pounds a year. The girl has scarce been a week, nay, a day in her service, but a committee of servant-wenches are appointed to examine her, who advise her to raise her wages, or give warning; to encourage her to which, the herb-woman, or chandler-woman, or some other old intelligencer, provides her a place of four or five pounds a year; this sets madam cock-a-hoop, and she thinks of nothing now but vails and high wages, and so gives warning from place to place, till she has got her wages up to the tip-top.

Her neat's leathern shoes are now transformed into laced ones with high heels; her yarn stockings are turned into fine woollen ones, with silk clocks; and her high wooden pattens are kicked away for leathern clogs; she must have a hoop too, as well as her mistress; and her poor scanty linsey-woolsey petticoat is changed into a good silk one, for four or five yards wide at the least. Not to carry the description farther, in short, plain country Joan is now turned into a fine London madam, can drink tea, take snuff, and carry herself as high as the best.

If she be tolerably handsome, and has any share of cunning, the apprentice or her master's son is enticed away and ruined by her. Thus many good families are impoverished and disgraced by these pert sluts, who, taking the advantage of a young man's simplicity and unruly desires, draw many heedless youths, nay, some of good estates, into their snares; and of this we have but too many instances.

Some more artful shall conceal their condition, and palm themselves off on young fellows for gentlewomen and great fortunes. How many families have been ruined by these ladies? when the father or master of the family, preferring the flirting airs of a young prinked up strumpet, to the artless sincerity of a plain, grave, and good wife, has given his desires aloose, and destroyed soul, body, family, and estate. But they are very favourable if they wheedle nobody into matrimony, but only make a present of a small live creature, no bigger than a bastard, to some of the family, no matter who gets it; when a child is born it must be kept.

Our sessions' papers of late are crowded with instances of servant-maids robbing their places, this can be only attributed to their devilish pride; for their whole inquiry nowadays is, how little they shall do, how much they shall have.

But all this while they make so little reserve, that if they fall sick the parish must keep them, if they are out of place, they must prostitute their bodies, or starve; so that from clopping and changing, they generally proceed to whoring and thieving, and this is the reason why our streets swarm with strumpets.

Thus many of them rove from place to place, from bawdy-house to service, and from service to bawdy-house again, ever unsettled and never easy, nothing being more common than to find these creatures one week in a good family, and the next in a brothel. This amphibious life makes them fit for neither, for if the bawd uses them ill, away they trip to service, and if the mistress gives them a wry word, whip they are at a bawdy-house again, so that in effect they neither make good whores nor good servants.

Those who are not thus slippery in the tail, are light of finger; and of these the most pernicious are those who beggar you inchmeal. If a maid is a downright thief she strips you, it once, and you know your loss; but these retail pilferers waste you insensibly, and though you hardly miss it, yet your substance shall decay to such a degree, that you must have a very good bottom indeed not to feel the ill effects of such moths in your family.

Tea, sugar, wine, &c., or any such trifling commodities, are reckoned no thefts, if they do not directly take your pewter from your shelf, or your linen from your drawers, they are very honest: What harm is there, say they, in cribbing a little matter for a junket, a merry bout or so? Nay, there are those that when they are sent to market for one joint of meat, shall take up two on their master's account, and leave one by the way, for some of these maids are mighty charitable, and can make a shift to maintain a small family with what they can purloin from their masters and mistresses.

If you send them with ready money, they turn factors, and take threepence or fourpence in the shilling brokerage. And here let me take notice of one very heinous abuse, not to say petty felony, which is practised in most of the great families about town, which is, when the tradesman gives the house-keeper or other commanding servant a penny or twopence in the shilling, or so much in the pound, for everything they send in, and which, from thence, is called poundage.

This, in my opinion, is the greatest of villanies, and ought to incur some punishment, yet nothing is more common, and our topping tradesmen, who seem otherwise to stand mightily on their credit, make this but a matter of course and custom. If I do not, says one, another will (for the servant is sure to pick a hole in the person's coat who shall not pay contribution). Thus this wicked practice is carried on and winked at, while receiving of stolen goods, and confederating with felons, which is not a jot worse, is so openly cried out against, and severely punished, witness Jonathan Wild.

And yet if a master or mistress inquire after anything missing, they must be sure to place their words in due form, or madam huffs and flings about at a strange rate, What, would you make a thief of her? Who would live with such mistrustful folks? Thus you are obliged to hold your tongue, and sit down quietly by your loss, for fear of offending your maid, forsooth!

Again, if your maid shall maintain one, two, or more persons from your table, whether they are her poor relations, countryfolk, servants out of place, shoe-cleaners, charwomen, porters, or any other of her menial servants, who do her ladyship's drudgery and go of her errands, you must not complain at your expense, or ask what has become of such a thing, or such a thing; although it might never so reasonably be supposed that it was altogether impossible to have so much expended in your family; but hold your tongue for peace sake, or madam will say, You grudge her victuals; and expose you to the last degree all over the neighbourhood.

Thus have they a salve for every sore, cheat you to your face, and insult you into the bargain; nor can you help yourself without exposing yourself, or putting yourself into a passion.

Another great abuse crept in among us, is the giving of veils to servants; this was intended originally as an encouragement to such as were willing and handy, but by custom and corruption it is now grown to be a thorn in our sides, and, like other good things, abused, does more harm than good; for now they make it a perquisite, a material part of their wages, nor must their master give a supper, but the maid expects the guests should pay for it, nay, sometimes through the nose. Thus have they spirited people up to this unnecessary and burthensome piece of generosity unknown to our forefathers, who only gave gifts to servants at Christmas-tide, which custom is yet kept into the bargain; insomuch that a maid shall have eight pounds per annum in a gentleman's or merchant's family. And if her master is a man of free spirit, who receives much company, she very often doubles her wages by her veils; thus having meat, drink, washing, and lodging for her labour, she throws her whole income upon her back, and by this means looks more like the mistress of the family than the servant-wench.

And now we have mentioned washing, I would ask some good housewifely gentlewoman, if servant-maids wearing printed linens, cottons, and other things of that nature, which require frequent washing, do not, by enhancing the article of soap, add more to housekeeping than the generality of people would imagine? And yet these wretches cry out against great washes, when their own unnecessary dabs are very often the occasion.

But the greatest abuse of all is, that these creatures are become their own lawgivers; nay, I think they are ours too, though nobody would imagine that such a set of slatterns should bamboozle a whole nation; but it is neither better nor worse, they hire themselves to you by their own rule.

That is, a month's wages, or a month's warning; if they don't like you they will go away the next day, help yourself how you can; if you don't like them, you must give them a month's wages to get rid of them.

This custom of warning, as practised by our maid-servants, is now become a great inconvenience to masters and mistresses. You must carry your dish very upright, or miss, forsooth, gives you warning, and you are either left destitute, or to seek for a servant; so that, generally speaking, you are seldom or never fixed, but always at the mercy of every new comer to divulge your family affairs, to inspect your private life, and treasure up the sayings of yourself and friends. A very great confinement, and much complained of in most families.

Thus have these wenches, by their continual plotting and cabals, united themselves into a formidable body, and got the whip hand of their betters; they make their own terms with us; and two servants now, will scarce undertake the work which one might perform with ease; notwithstanding which, they have raised their wages to a most exorbitant pitch; and, I doubt not, if there be not a stop put to their career, but they will bring wages up to 20l. per annum in time, for they are much about half way already.

It is by these means they run away with a great part of our money, which might be better employed in trade, and what is worse, by their insolent behaviour, their pride in dress, and their exorbitant wages, they give birth to the following inconveniences.

First, They set an ill example to our children, our apprentices, our covenant servants, and other dependants, by their saucy and insolent behaviour, their pert, and sometimes abusive answers, their daring defiance of correction, and many other insolences which youth are but too apt to imitate.

Secondly, By their extravagance in dress, they put our wives and daughters upon yet greater excesses, because they will, as indeed they ought, go finer than the maid; thus the maid striving to outdo the mistress, the tradesman's wife to outdo the gentleman's wife, the gentleman's wife emulating the lady, and the ladies one another; it seems as if the whole business of the female sex were nothing but an excess of pride, and extravagance in dress.

Thirdly, The great height to which women-servants have brought their wages, makes a mutiny among the men-servants, and puts them upon raising their wages too; so that in a little time our servants will become our partners; nay, probably, run away with the better part of our profits, and make servants of us *vice versa*. But yet with all these inconveniences, we cannot possibly do without these creatures; let us therefore cease to talk of the abuses arising from them, and begin to think of redressing them. I do not set up for a lawgiver, and therefore shall lay down no certain rules, humbly submitting in all things to the wisdom of our legislature. What I offer shall be under correction; and upon conjecture, my utmost ambition being but to give some hints to remedy this growing evil, and leave the prosecution to abler hands.

And first it would be necessary to settle and limit their wages, from forty and fifty shillings to four and five pounds per annum, that is to say, according to their merits and capacities; for example, a young unexperienced servant should have forty shillings per annum, till she qualifies herself for a larger sum; a servant who can do all household work, or, as the good women term it, can take her work and leave her work, should have four pounds per annum; and those who have lived seven years in one service, should ever after demand five pounds per annum, for I would very fain have some particular encouragements and privileges given to such servants who should continue long in a place; it would incite a desire to please, and cause an emulation very beneficial to the public.

I have heard of an ancient charity in the parish of St. Clement's Danes, where a sum of money, or estate, is left, out of the interest or income of which such maid-servants, who have lived in that parish seven years in one service, receive a reward of ten pounds apiece, if they please to demand it.

This is a noble benefaction, and shows the public spirit of the donor; but everybody's business is nobody's; nor have I heard that such reward has been paid to any servant of late years. A thousand pities a gift of that nature should sink into oblivion, and not be kept up as an example to incite all parishes to do the like.

The Romans had a law called *Jus Trium Liberorum*, by which every man who had been a father of three children, had particular honours and privileges. This incited the youth to quit a dissolute single life and become fathers of families, to the support and glory of the empire.

In imitation of this most excellent law, I would have such servants, who should continue many years in one service, meet with singular esteem and reward.

The apparel of our women-servants should be next regulated, that we may know the mistress from the maid. I remember I was once put very much to the blush, being at a friend's house, and by him required to salute the ladies, I kissed the chamber-jade into the bargain, for she was as well dressed as the best. But I was soon undeceived by a general titter, which gave me the utmost confusion; nor can I believe myself the only person who has made such a mistake.

Things of this nature would be easily avoided, if servant-maids were to wear liveries, as our footmen do; or obliged to go in a dress suitable to their station. What should ail them, but a jacket and petticoat of good yard-wide stuff, or calimanco, might keep them decent and warm.

Our charity children are distinguished by their dress, why then may not our women-servants? why may they not be made frugal per force, and not suffered to put all on their backs, but obliged to save something against a rainy day? I am, therefore, entirely against servants wearing of silks, laces, and other superfluous finery; it sets them above themselves, and makes their mistresses contemptible in their eyes. I am handsomer than my mistress, says a young prinked up baggage, what pity it is I should be her servant, I go as well dressed, or better than she. This makes the girl take the first offer to be made a whore, and there is a good servant spoiled; whereas, were her dress suitable to her condition, it would teach her humility, and put her in mind of her duty.

Besides the fear of spoiling their clothes makes them afraid of household-work; so that in a little time we shall have none but chambermaids and nurserymaids; and of this let me give one instance; my family is composed of myself and sister, a man and a maid; and, being without the last, a young wench came to hire herself. The man was gone out, and my sister above stairs, so I opened the door myself; and this person presented herself to my view, dressed completely, more like a visitor than a servant-maid; she, not knowing me, asked for my sister; pray, madam, said I, be pleased to walk into the parlour, she shall wait on you presently. Accordingly I handed madam in, who took it very cordially. After some apology, I left her alone for a minute or two; while I, stupid wretch! ran up to my sister, and told her there was a gentlewoman below come to visit her. Dear brother, said she, don't leave her alone, go down and entertain her while I dress myself. Accordingly, down I went, and talked of indifferent affairs; meanwhile my sister dressed herself all over again, not being willing to be seen in an undress. At last she came down dressed as clean as her visitor; but how great was my surprise when I found my fine lady a common servant-wench.

My sister understanding what she was, began to inquire what wages she expected? She modestly asked but eight pounds a year. The next question was, what work she could do to deserve such wages? to which she answered, she could clean a house, or dress a common family dinner. But cannot you wash, replied my sister, or get up linen? she answered in the negative, and said, she would undertake neither, nor would she go into a family that did not put out their linen to wash, and hire a charwoman to scour. She desired to see the house, and having carefully surveyed it, said, the work was too hard for her, nor could she undertake it. This put my sister beyond all patience, and me into the greatest admiration. Young woman, said she, you have made a mistake, I want a housemaid, and you are a chambermaid. No, madam, replied she, I am not needlewoman enough for that. And yet you ask eight pounds a year, replied my sister. Yes, madam, said she, nor shall I bate a farthing. Then get you gone for a lazy impudent baggage, said I, you want to be a boarder not a servant; have you a fortune or estate that you dress at that rate? No, sir, said she, but I hope I may wear what I work for without offence. What you work, interrupted my sister, why you do not seem willing to undertake any work; you will not wash nor scour; you cannot dress a dinner for company; you are no needlewoman; and our little house of two rooms on a floor, is too much for you. For God's sake what can you do? Madam, replied she pertly; I know my business; and do not fear a service; there are more places than parish churches; if you wash at home, you should have a laundrymaid; if you give entertainments, you must have a cookmaid; if you have any needlework, you should have a chambermaid; and such a house as this is enough for a housemaid in all conscience.

I was pleased at the wit, and astonished at the impudence of the girl, so dismissed her with thanks for her instructions, assuring her that when I kept four maids she should be housemaid if she pleased.

Were a servant to do my business with cheerfulness, I should not grudge at five or six pounds per annum; nor would I be so unchristian to put more upon any one than they can bear; but to pray and pay too is the devil. It is very hard, that I must keep four servants or none.

In great families, indeed, where many servants are required, those distinctions of chambermaid, housemaid, cookmaid, laundrymaid, nurserymaid, &c., are requisite, to the end that each may take her particular business, and many hands may make the work light; but for a private gentleman, of a small fortune, to be obliged to keep so many idle jades, when one might do the business, is intolerable, and matter of great grievance.

I cannot close this discourse without a gentle admonition and reproof to some of my own sex, I mean those gentlemen who give themselves unnecessary airs, and cannot go to see a friend, but they must kiss and slop the maid; and all this is done with an air of gallantry, and must not be resented. Nay, some gentlemen are so silly, that they shall carry on an underhand affair with their friend's servant-maid, to their own disgrace, and the ruin of many a young creature. Nothing is more base and ungenerous, yet nothing more common, and withal so little taken notice of. D-n me, Jack, says one friend to another, this maid of yours is a pretty girl, you do so and so to her, by G-d. This makes the creature pert, vain, and impudent, and spoils many a good servant.

What gentleman will descend to this low way of intrigue, when he shall consider that he has a footboy or an apprentice for his rival, and that he is seldom or never admitted, but when they have been his tasters; and the fool of fortune, though he comes at the latter end of the feast, yet pays the whole reckoning; and so indeed would I have all such silly cullies served.

If I must have an intrigue, let it be with a woman that shall not shame me. I would never go into the kitchen, when the parlour door was open. We are forbidden at Highgate, to kiss the maid when we may kiss the mistress; why then will gentlemen descend so low, by too much familiarity with these creatures, to bring themselves into contempt?

I have been at places where the maid has been so dizzied with these idle compliments that she has mistook one thing for another, and not regarded her mistress in the least; but put on all the flirting airs imaginable. This behaviour is nowhere so much complained of as in taverns, coffeehouses, and places of public resort, where there are handsome bar-keepers, &c. These creatures being puffed up with the fulsome flattery of a set of flesh-flies, which are continually buzzing about them, carry themselves with the utmost insolence imaginable; insomuch, that you must speak to them with a great deal of deference, or you are sure to be affronted. Being at a coffeehouse the other day, where one of these ladies kept the bar, I had bespoke a dish of rice tea; but madam was so taken up with her sparks, she had quite forgot it. I spake for it again, and with some temper, but was answered after a most taunting manner, not without a toss of the head, a contraction of the nostrils, and other impertinences, too many to enumerate. Seeing myself thus publicly insulted by such an animal, I could not choose but show my resentment. Woman, said I, sternly, I want a dish of rice tea, and not what your vanity and impudence may imagine; therefore treat me as a gentleman and a customer, and serve me with what I call for: keep your impertinent repartees and impudent behaviour for the coxcombs that swarm round your bar, and make you so vain of your blown carcase. And indeed I believe the insolence of this creature will ruin her master at last, by driving away men of sobriety and business, and making the place a den of vagabonds and rakehells.

Gentlemen, therefore, ought to be very circumspect in their behaviour, and not undervalue themselves to servant-wenches, who are but too apt to treat a gentleman ill whenever he puts himself into their power.

Let me now beg pardon for this digression, and return to my subject by proposing some practicable methods for regulating of servants, which, whether they are followed or not, yet, if they afford matter of improvement and speculation, will answer the height of my expectation, and I will be the first who shall approve of whatever improvements are made from this small beginning.

The first abuse I would have reformed is, that servants should be restrained from throwing themselves out of place on every idle vagary. This might be remedied were all contracts between master and servant made before a justice of peace, or other proper officer, and a memorandum thereof taken in writing. Nor should such servant leave his or her place (for men and maids might come under the same regulation) till the time agreed on be expired, unless such servant be misused or denied necessaries, or show some other reasonable cause for their discharge. In that case, the master or mistress should be reprimanded or fined. But if servants misbehave themselves, or leave their places, not being regularly discharged, they ought to be amerced or punished. But all those idle, ridiculous customs, and laws of their own making, as a month's wages, or a month's warning, and suchlike, should be entirely set aside and abolished.

When a servant has served the limited time duly and faithfully, they should be entitled to a certificate, as is practised at present in the wool-combing trade; nor should any person hire a servant without a certificate or other proper security. A servant without a certificate should be deemed a vagrant; and a master or mistress ought to assign very good reasons indeed when they object against giving a servant his or her certificate.

And though, to avoid prolixity, I have not mentioned footmen particularly in the foregoing discourse, yet the complaints alleged against the maids are as well masculine as feminine, and very applicable to our gentlemen's gentlemen; I would, therefore, have them under the very same regulations, and, as they are fellow-servants, would not make fish of one and flesh of the other, since daily experience teaches us, that "never a barrel the better herring."

The next great abuse among us is, that under the notion of cleaning our shoes, above ten thousand wicked, idle, pilfering vagrants are permitted to patrol about our city and suburbs. These are called the black-guard, who black your honour's shoes, and incorporate themselves under the title of the Worshipful Company of Japanners.

Were this all, there were no hurt in it, and the whole might terminate in a jest; but the mischief ends not here, they corrupt our youth, especially our men-servants; oaths and impudence are their only flowers of rhetoric; gaming and thieving are the principal parts of their profession; japanning but the pretence. For example, a gentleman keeps a servant, who among other things is to clean his master's shoes; but our gentlemen's gentlemen are above it nowadays, and your man's man performs the office, for which piece of service you pay double and treble, especially if you keep a table, nay, you are well off if the japanner has no more than his own diet from it.

I have often observed these rascals sneaking from gentlemen's doors with wallets or hats' full of good victuals, which they either carry to their trulls, or sell for a trifle. By this means, our butcher's, our baker's, our poulterer's, and cheesemonger's bills are monstrously exaggerated; not to mention candles just lighted, which sell for fivepence a pound, and many other perquisites best known to themselves and the pilfering villains their confederates.

Add to this, that their continual gaming sets servants upon their wits to supply this extravagance, though at the same time the master's pocket pays for it, and the time which should be spent in a gentleman's service is loitered away among these rakehells, insomuch that half our messages are ineffectual, the time intended being often expired before the message is delivered.

How many frequent robberies are committed by these japanners? And to how many more are they confederates? Silver spoons, spurs, and other small pieces of plate, are every day missing, and very often found upon these sort of gentlemen; yet are they permitted, to the shame of all our good laws, and the scandal of our most excellent government, to lurk about our streets, to debauch our servants and apprentices, and support an infinite number of scandalous, shameless trulls, yet more wicked than themselves, for not a Jack among them but must have his Gill.

By whom such indecencies are daily acted, even in our open streets, as are very offensive to the eyes and ears of all sober persons, and even abominable in a Christian country.

In any riot, or other disturbance, these sparks are always the foremost; for most among them can turn their hands to picking of pockets, to run away with goods from a fire, or other public confusion, to snatch anything from a woman or child, to strip a house when the door is open, or any other branch of a thief's profession.

In short, it is a nursery for thieves and villains; modest women are every day insulted by them and their strumpets; and such children who run about the streets, or those servants who go on errands, do but too frequently bring home some scraps of their beastly profane wit; insomuch, that the conversation of our lower rank of people runs only upon bawdy and blasphemy, notwithstanding our societies for reformation, and our laws in force against profaneness; for this lazy life gets them many proselytes, their numbers daily increasing from runaway apprentices and footboys, insomuch that it is a very hard matter for a gentleman to get him a servant, or for a tradesman to find an apprentice.

Innumerable other mischiefs accrue, and others will spring up from this race of caterpillars, who must be swept from out our streets, or we shall be overrun with all manner of wickedness.

But the subject is so low, it becomes disagreeable even to myself; give me leave, therefore, to propose a way to clear the streets of these vermin, and to substitute as many honest industrious persons in their stead, who are now starving for want of bread, while these execrable villains live, though in rags and nastiness, yet in plenty and luxury.

I, therefore, humbly propose that these vagabonds be put immediately under the command of such taskmasters as the government shall appoint, and that they be employed, punished, or rewarded, according to their capacities and demerits; that is to say, the industrious and docible to wool-combing, and other parts of the woollen manufacture, where hands are wanted, as also to husbandry and other parts of agriculture.

For it is evident that there are scarce hands enow in the country to carry on either of these affairs. Now, these vagabonds might not only by this means be kept out of harm's way, but be rendered serviceable to the nation. Nor is there any need of transporting them beyond seas, for if any are refractory they should be sent to our stannaries and other mines, to our coal works and other places where hard labour is required. And here I must offer one thing never yet thought of, or proposed by any, and that is, the keeping in due repair the navigation of the river Thames, so useful to our trade in general; and yet of late years such vast hills of sand are gathered together in several parts of the river, as are very prejudicial to its navigation, one which is near London Bridge, another near Whitehall, a third near Battersea, and a fourth near Fulham. These are of very great hindrance to the navigation; and indeed the removal of them ought to be a national concern, which I humbly propose may be thus effected.

The rebellious part of these vagabonds, as also other thieves and offenders, should be formed into bodies under the command of proper officers, and under the guard and awe of our soldiery. These should every day at low water carry away these sandhills, and remove every other obstruction to the navigation of this most excellent and useful river.

It may be objected that the ballast men might do this; that as fast as the hills are taken away they would gather together again, or that the watermen might do it. To the first, I answer, that ballast men, instead of taking away from these hills, make holes in other places of the river, which is the reason so many young persons are drowned when swimming or bathing in the river.

Besides, it is a work for many hands, and of long continuance; so that ballast men do more harm than good. The second objection is as silly; as if I should never wash myself, because I shall be dirty again, and I think needs no other answer. And as to the third objection, the watermen are not so public-spirited, they live only from hand to mouth, though not one of them but finds the inconvenience of these hills, every day being obliged to go a great way round about for fear of running aground; insomuch that in a few years the navigation of that part of the river will be entirely obstructed. Nevertheless, every one of these gentlemen-watermen hopes it will last his time, and so they all cry, The devil take the hindmost. But yet I judge it highly necessary that this be made a national concern, like Dagenham breach, and that these hills be removed by some means or other.

And now I have mentioned watermen, give me leave to complain of the insolences and exactions they daily commit on the river Thames, and in particular this one instance, which cries aloud for justice.

A young lady of distinction, in company with her brother, a little youth, took a pair of oars at or near the Temple, on April day last, and ordered the men to carry them to Pepper Alley Stairs. One of the fellows, according to their usual impertinence, asked the lady where she was going? She answered, near St. Olave's church. Upon which he said, she had better go through the bridge. The lady replied she had never gone through the bridge in her life, nor would she venture for a hundred guineas; so commanded him once more to land her at Pepper Alley Stairs. Notwithstanding which, in spite of her fears, threats, and commands; nay, in spite of the persuasion of his fellow, he forced her through London Bridge, which frightened her beyond expression. And to mend the matter, he obliged her to pay double fare, and mobbed her into the bargain.

To resent which abuse, application was made to the hall, the fellow summoned, and the lady ordered to attend, which she did, waiting there all the morning, and was appointed to call again in the afternoon. She came accordingly, they told her the fellow had been there, but was gone, and that she must attend another Friday. She attended again and again, but to the same purpose. Nor have they yet produced the man, but tired out the lady, who has spent above ten shillings in coach-hire, been abused and baffled into the bargain.

It is pity, therefore, there are not commissioners for watermen, as there are for hackney coachmen; or that justices of the peace might not inflict bodily penalties on watermen thus offending. But while watermen are watermen's judges, I shall laugh at those who carry their complaints to the hall.

The usual plea in behalf of abusive watermen is, that they are drunk, ignorant, or poor; but will that satisfy the party aggrieved, or deter the offender from reoffending? Whereas were the offenders sent to the house of correction, and there punished, or sentenced to work at the sandhills aforementioned, for a time suitable to the nature of their crimes, terror of such punishments would make them fearful of offending, to the great quiet of the subject.

Now, it maybe asked, How shall we have our shoes cleaned, or how are these industrious poor to be maintained? To this I answer that the places of these vagabonds may be very well supplied by great numbers of ancient persons, poor widows, and others, who have not enough from their respective parishes to maintain them. These poor people I would have authorised and stationed by the justices of the peace or other magistrates. Each of these should have a particular walk or stand, and no other shoe-cleaner should come into that walk, unless the person misbehave and be removed. Nor should any person clean shoes in the streets, but these authorised shoe-cleaners, who should have some mark of distinction, and be under the immediate government of the justices of the peace.

Thus would many thousands of poor people be provided for, without burthening their parishes. Some of these may earn a shilling or two in the day, and none less than sixpence, or thereabouts. And lest the old japanners should appear again, in the shape of linkboys, and knock down gentlemen in drink, or lead others out of the way into dark remote places, where they either put out their lights, and rob them themselves, or run away and leave them to be pillaged by others, as is daily practised, I would have no person carry a link for hire but some of these industrious poor, and even such, not without some ticket or badge, to let people know whom they trust. Thus would the streets be cleared night and day of these vermin; nor would oaths, skirmishes, blasphemy, obscene talk, or other wicked examples, be so public and frequent. All gaming at orange and gingerbread barrows should be abolished, as also all penny and halfpenny lotteries, thimbles and balls, &c., so frequent in Moorfields, Lincoln's-inn-fields, &c., where idle fellows resort, to play with children and apprentices, and tempt them to steal their parents' or master's money.

There is one admirable custom in the city of London, which I could wish were imitated in the city and liberties of Westminster, and bills of mortality, which is, no porter can carry a burthen or letter in the city, unless he be a ticket porter; whereas, out of the freedom part of London, any person may take a knot and turn porter, till he be entrusted with something of value, and then you never hear of him more.

This is very common, and ought to be amended. I would, therefore, have all porters under some such regulation as coachmen, chairmen, carmen, &c.; a man may then know whom he entrusts, and not run the risk of losing his goods, &c. Nay, I would not have a person carry a basket in the markets, who is not subject to some such regulation; for very many persons oftentimes lose their dinners in sending their meat home by persons they know nothing of.

Thus would all our poor be stationed, and a man or woman able to perform any of these offices, must either comply or be termed an idle vagrant, and sent to a place where they shall be forced to work. By this means industry will be encouraged, idleness punished, and we shall be famed, as well as happy for our tranquillity and decorum.

From London to Land's End.

by
DANIEL DEFOE.

and

Two Letters from the "Journey through England by a Gentleman."

INTRODUCTION.

At the end of this book there are a couple of letters from a volume of the "Travels in England" which were not by Defoe, although resembling Defoe's work so much in form and title, and so near to it in date of publication, that a volume of one book is often found taking the place of a volume of the other. A purchaser of Defoe's "Travels in England" has therefore to take care that he is not buying one of the mixed sets. Each of the two works describes England at the end of the first quarter of the eighteenth century. Our added descriptions of Bath, and of the journey by Chester to Holyhead, were published in 1722; Defoe's "Journey from London to the Land's End" was published in 1724, and both writers help us to compare the past with the present by their accounts of England as it was in the days of George the First, more than a hundred and sixty years ago. The days certainly are gone when, after a good haul of pilchards, seventeen can be bought for a halfpenny, and two gentlemen and their servant can have them broiled at a tavern and dine on them for three farthings, dressing and all. In another of his journeys Defoe gives a seaside tavern bill, in which the charges were ridiculously small for everything except for bread. It was war time, and the bread was the most costly item in the bill.

In the earlier part of this account of the "Journey from London to the Land's End," there is interest in the fresh memories of the rebuilding and planting at Hampton Court by William III. and Queen Mary. The passing away, and in opinion of that day the surpassing, of Wolsey's palace there were none then to regret.

A more characteristic feature in this letter will be found in the details of a project which Defoe says he had himself advocated before the Lord-Treasurer Godolphin, for the settlement of poor refugees from the Palatinate upon land in the New Forest. Our friendly relations with the Palatinate had begun with the marriage of James the First's eldest daughter to the Elector Palatine, who brought on himself much trouble by accepting the crown of Bohemia from the subjects of the Emperor Ferdinand the Second. As a Protestant Prince allied by marriage to England, he drew from England sympathies and ineffectual assistance. Many years afterwards, during the war with France in Queen Anne's time, the allies were unprosperous in 1707, and Marshal Villars was victorious upon the Rhine. The pressure of public feeling on behalf of refugees from the Palatinate did not last long enough for any action to be taken. But if it had seemed well to the Government to accept the project advocated by Defoe, we should have had a clearance of what is now the most beautiful part of the New Forest, near Lyndhurst; and in place of the little area that still preserves all the best features of forest land, we should have had a town of Englishmen descended from the latest of the German settlements upon our soil. Upon the political economy of Defoe's project, and the accuracy of his calculations, and the more or less resemblance of his scheme to the system of free grants of land in unsettled regions beyond the sea, each reader will speculate in his own way.

There are interesting notes on the extent of the sheep farming upon the Downs crossed in this journey. There is high praise of the ladies of Dorsetshire. There are some pleasant notes upon dialect, including the story, often quoted, of the schoolboy whom Defoe saw and heard reading his Bible in class, and while following every word and line with his eye, translating it as he went into his own way of speech. Thus he turned the third verse of the fifth chapter of Solomon's Song, "I have put off my coat; how shall I put it on? I have washed my feet; how shall I defile them?" into "Chav a doffed my cooat; how shall I don't? Chav a washed my veet; how shall I moil 'em?" This is a good example of intelligent reading; for the boy took in the sense of the printed lines, and then made it his own by giving homely utterance to what he understood.

Defoe tells in this letter several tales of the shorefolk about the Great Storm of November, 1703, recollection of which Addison used effectively in the following year in his poem on the Battle of Blenheim. There was the sweeping away of the first Eddystone Lighthouse, with the builder, confident in its strength, who had desired to be in it some night when the wind blew with unusual fury. There was the story also of the man and two boys, in a ship laden with tin, blown out of Helford Haven, and of their hairbreadth escape by counsel of one of the boys who ran the ship through rocks into a narrow creek that he knew in the Isle of Wight. The form of the coast has been changed so much since 1703 by the beat of many storms, that it may be now impossible to know that little cove as the boy knew it. It must have been at the back of the island. Were the storm waves tossing then in Steephill Cove or Luccombe Chine? Does there survive anywhere a tradition of that perilous landing? Probably not. Wreck follows upon wreck, and memory of many tales of death and peril on the rock-bound coast lie between us and the boy who took the helm when he spied the well-known creek as the great storm was sweeping the ship on to destruction. From the next year after that famous storm, Defoe gives a memory of disaster seen by himself at Plymouth in the wreck of a little fleet from Barbadoes. In another part of this letter he tells what he had seen of a fight at sea between three French men-of-war and two English with a convoy of two or three trading vessels.

There will be found also in this letter a good story of a Cornish dog taken from Carew's "Survey of Cornwall," which may pair with that of the London dog who lately took a wounded fellow dog to hospital.

The writer of this letter speaks of the civil war times as a friend of monarchy, but when he tells of the landing of William III. at Torbay, he suggests that the people had good reason for rejoicing, and throughout the journey he takes note of a great inequality he finds in distribution of the right of returning members to Parliament. It is evident that he could propound a project for a Reform Bill, though he is careful so to describe England as to avoid giving offence to Englishmen of any party. The possibility of some change for the better here and there presents itself; Defoe glances and passes on. His theme is England and the English; he shows us, clearly and very simply, what he has seen of the social life and manners of the people, of the features of the land itself, and their relation to its industries; traces of the past, and prospects of the future; shepherds, fishermen, merchants; catching of salmon peel in mill-weirs, and catching of husbands at provincial assemblies; with whatever else he found worth friendly observation.

H. M.

FROM LONDON TO LAND'S END

Sir,

I find so much left to speak of, and so many things to say in every part of England, that my journey cannot be barren of intelligence which way soever I turn; no, though I were to oblige myself to say nothing of anything that had been spoken of before.

I intended once to have gone due west this journey; but then I should have been obliged to crowd my observations so close (to bring Hampton Court, Windsor, Blenheim, Oxford, the Bath and Bristol all into one letter; all those remarkable places lying in a line, as it were, in one point of the compass) as to have made my letter too long, or my observations too light and superficial, as others have done before me.

This letter will divide the weighty task, and consequently make it sit lighter on the memory, be pleasanter to the reader, and make my progress the more regular: I shall therefore take in Hampton Court and Windsor in this journey; the first at my setting out, and the last at my return, and the rest as their situation demands.

As I came down from Kingston, in my last circuit, by the south bank of the Thames, on the Surrey side of the river; so I go up to Hampton Court now on the north bank, and on the Middlesex side, which I mention, because, as the sides of the country bordering on the river lie parallel, so the beauty of the country, the pleasant situations, the glory of innumerable fine buildings (noblemen's and gentlemen's houses, and citizens' retreats), are so equal a match to what I had described on the other side that one knows not which to give the preference to: but as I must speak of them again, when I come to write of the county of Middlesex, which I have now purposely omitted; so I pass them over here, except the palace of Hampton only, which I mentioned in "Middlesex," for the reasons above.

Hampton Court lies on the north bank of the River Thames, about two small miles from Kingston, and on the road from Staines to Kingston Bridge; so that the road straightening the parks a little, they were obliged to part the parks, and leave the Paddock and the great park part on the other side the road—a testimony of that just regard that the kings of England always had, and still have, to the common good, and to the service of the country, that they would not interrupt the course of the road, or cause the poor people to go out of the way of their business to or from the markets and fairs, for any pleasure of their own whatsoever.

The palace of Hampton Court was first founded and built from the ground by that great statesman and favourite of King Henry VIII, Cardinal Wolsey; and if it be a just observation anywhere, as is made from the situation of the old abbeys and monasteries, the clergy were excellent judges of the beauty and pleasantness of the country, and chose always to plant in the best; I say, if it was a just observation in any case, it was in this; for if there be a situation on the whole river between Staines Bridge and Windsor Bridge pleasanter than another, it is this of Hampton; close to the river, yet not offended by the rising of its waters in floods or storms; near to the reflux of the tides, but not quite so near as to be affected with any foulness of the water which the flowing of the tides generally is the occasion of. The gardens extend almost to the bank of the river, yet are never overflowed; nor are there any marshes on either side the river to make the waters stagnate, or the air unwholesome on that account. The river is high enough to be navigable, and low enough to be a little pleasantly rapid; so that the stream looks always cheerful, not slow and sleeping, like a pond. This keeps the waters always clear and clean, the bottom in view, the fish playing and in sight; and, in a word, it has everything that can make an inland (or, as I may call it, a country) river pleasant and agreeable.

I shall sing you no songs here of the river in the first person of a water-nymph, a goddess, and I know not what, according to the humour of the ancient poets; I shall talk nothing of the marriage of old Isis, the male river, with the beautiful Thame, the female river (a whimsey as simple as the subject was empty); but I shall speak of the river as occasion presents, as it really is made glorious by the splendour of its shores, gilded with noble palaces, strong fortifications, large hospitals, and public buildings; with the greatest bridge, and the greatest city in the world, made famous by the opulence of its merchants, the increase and extensiveness of its commerce; by its invincible navies, and by the innumerable fleets of ships sailing upon it to and from all parts of the world.

As I meet with the river upwards in my travels through the inland country I shall speak of it, as it is the channel for conveying an infinite quantity of provisions from remote counties to London, and enriching all the counties again that lie near it by the return of wealth and trade from the city; and in describing these things I expect both to inform and divert my readers, and speak in a more masculine manner, more to the dignity of the subject, and also more to their satisfaction, than I could do any other way.

There is little more to be said of the Thames relating to Hampton Court, than that it adds by its neighbourhood to the pleasure of the situation; for as to passing by water to and from London, though in summer it is exceeding pleasant, yet the passage is a little too long to make it easy to the ladies, especially to be crowded up in the small boats which usually go upon the Thames for pleasure.

The prince and princess, indeed, I remember came once down by water upon the occasion of her Royal Highness's being great with child, and near her time—so near that she was delivered within two or three days after. But this passage being in the royal barges, with strength of oars, and the day exceeding fine, the passage, I say, was made very pleasant, and still the more so for being short. Again, this passage is all the way with the stream, whereas in the common passage upwards great part of the way is against the stream, which is slow and heavy.

But be the going and coming how it will by water, it is an exceeding pleasant passage by land, whether we go by the Surrey side or the Middlesex side of the water, of which I shall say more in its place.

The situation of Hampton Court being thus mentioned, and its founder, it is to be mentioned next that it fell to the Crown in the forfeiture of his Eminence the Cardinal, when the king seized his effects and estate, by which this and Whitehall (another house of his own building also) came to King Henry VIII. Two palaces fit for the kings of England, erected by one cardinal, are standing monuments of the excessive pride as well as the immense wealth of that prelate, who knew no bounds of his insolence and ambition till he was overthrown at once by the displeasure of his master.

Whoever knew Hampton Court before it was begun to be rebuilt, or altered, by the late King William, must acknowledge it was a very complete palace before, and fit for a king; and though it might not, according to the modern method of building or of gardening, pass for a thing exquisitely fine, yet it had this remaining to itself, and perhaps peculiar—namely, that it showed a situation exceedingly capable of improvement, and of being made one of the most delightful palaces in Europe.

This her Majesty Queen Mary was so sensible of, that, while the king had ordered the pulling down the old apartments, and building it up in that most beautiful form which we see them now appear in, her Majesty, impatient of enjoying so agreeable a retreat, fixed upon a building formerly made use of chiefly for landing from the river, and therefore called the Water Galley, and here, as if she had been conscious that she had but a few years to enjoy it, she ordered all the little neat curious things to be done which suited her own conveniences, and made it the pleasantest little thing within doors that could possibly be made, though its situation being such as it could not be allowed to stand after the great building was finished, we now see no remains of it.

The queen had here her gallery of beauties, being the pictures at full-length of the principal ladies attending upon her Majesty, or who were frequently in her retinue; and this was the more beautiful sight because the originals were all in being, and often to be compared with their pictures. Her Majesty had here a fine apartment, with a set of lodgings for her private retreat only, but most exquisitely furnished, particularly a fine chintz bed, then a great curiosity; another of her own work while in Holland, very magnificent, and several others; and here was also her Majesty's fine collection of Delft ware, which indeed was very large and fine; and here was also a vast stock of fine china ware, the like whereof was not then to be seen in England; the long gallery, as above, was filled with this china, and every other place where it could be placed with advantage.

The queen had here also a small bathing-room, made very fine, suited either to hot or cold bathing, as the season should invite; also a dairy, with all its conveniences, in which her Majesty took great delight. All these things were finished with expedition, that here their Majesties might repose while they saw the main building go forward. While this was doing, the gardens were laid out, the plan of them devised by the king himself, and especially the amendments and alterations were made by the king or the queen's particular special command, or by both, for their Majesties agreed so well in their fancy, and had both so good judgment in the just proportions of things, which are the principal beauties of a garden, that it may be said they both ordered everything that was done.

Here the fine parcel of limes which form the semicircle on the south front of the house by the iron gates, looking into the park, were by the dexterous hand of the head gardener removed, after some of them had been almost thirty years planted in other places, though not far off. I know the King of France in the decoration of the gardens of Versailles had oaks removed, which by their dimensions must have been above an hundred years old, and yet were taken up with so much art, and by the strength of such engines, by which such a monstrous quantity of earth was raised with them, that the trees could not feel their remove—that is to say, their growth was not at all hindered. This, I confess, makes the wonder much the less in those trees at Hampton Court gardens; but the performance was not the less difficult or nice, however, in these, and they thrive perfectly well.

While the gardens were thus laid out, the king also directed the laying the pipes for the fountains and *jet-d'eaux*, and particularly the dimensions of them, and what quantity of water they should cast up, and increased the number of them after the first design.

The ground on the side of the other front has received some alterations since the taking down the Water Galley; but not that part immediately next the lodgings. The orange-trees and fine Dutch bays are placed within the arches of the building under the first floor; so that the lower part of the house was all one as a greenhouse for sometime. Here stand advanced, on two pedestals of stone, two marble vases or flower-pots of most exquisite workmanship—the one done by an Englishman, and the other by a German. It is hard to say which is the best performance, though the doing of it was a kind of trial of skill between them; but it gives us room, without any partiality, to say they were both masters of their art.

The *parterre* on that side descends from the terrace-walk by steps, and on the left a terrace goes down to the water-side, from which the garden on the eastward front is overlooked, and gives a most pleasant prospect.

The fine scrolls and *bordure* of these gardens were at first edged with box, but on the queen's disliking the smell those edgings were taken up, but have since been planted again—at least, in many places— nothing making so fair and regular an edging as box, or is so soon brought to its perfection.

On the north side of the house, where the gardens seemed to want screening from the weather or the view of the chapel, and some part of the old building required to be covered from the eye, the vacant ground, which was large, is very happily cast into a wilderness, with a labyrinth and *espaliers* so high that they effectually take off all that part of the old building which would have been offensive to the sight. This labyrinth and wilderness is not only well designed, and completely finished, but is perfectly well kept, and the *espaliers* filled exactly at bottom, to the very ground, and are led up to proportioned heights on the top, so that nothing of that kind can be more beautiful.

The house itself is every way answerable on the outside to the beautiful prospect, and the two fronts are the largest and, beyond comparison, the finest of the kind in England. The great stairs go up from the second court of the palace on the right hand, and lead you to the south prospect.

I hinted in my last that King William brought into England the love of fine paintings as well as that of fine gardens; and you have an example of it in the cartoons, as they are called, being five pieces of such paintings as, if you will believe men of nice judgment and great travelling, are not to be matched in Europe. The stories are known, but especially two of them—viz., that of St. Paul preaching on Mars Hill to the self-wise Athenians, and that of St. Peter passing sentence of death on Ananias—I say, these two strike the mind with the utmost surprise, the passions are so drawn to the life; astonishment, terror, and death in the face of Ananias, zeal and a sacred fire in the eyes of the blessed Apostle, fright and surprise upon the countenances of the beholders in the piece of Ananias; all these describe themselves so naturally that you cannot but seem to discover something of the like passions, even in seeing them.

In the other there is the boldness and courage with which St. Paul undertook to talk to a set of men who, he knew, despised all the world, as thinking themselves able to teach them anything. In the audience there is anticipating pride and conceit in some, a smile or fleer of contempt in others, but a kind of sensible conviction, though crushed in its beginning, on the faces of the rest; and all together appear confounded, but have little to say, and know nothing at all of it; they gravely put him off to hear him another time; all these are seen here in the very dress of the face—that is, the very countenances which they hold while they listen to the new doctrine which the Apostle preached to a people at that time ignorant of it.

The other of the cartoons are exceeding fine but I mention these as the particular two which are most lively, which strike the fancy the soonest at first view. It is reported, but with what truth I know not, that the late French king offered an hundred thousand *louis d'ors* for these pictures; but this, I say, is but a report. The king brought a great many other fine pieces to England, and with them the love of fine paintings so universally spread itself among the nobility and persons of figure all over the kingdom that it is incredible what collections have been made by English gentlemen since that time, and how all Europe has been rummaged, as we may say, for pictures to bring over hither, where for twenty years they yielded the purchasers, such as collected them for sale, immense profit. But the rates are abated since that, and we begin to be glutted with the copies and frauds of the Dutch and Flemish painters who have imposed grossly upon us. But to return to the palace of Hampton Court. Queen Mary lived not to see it completely finished, and her death, with the other difficulties of that reign, put a stop to the works for some time till the king, reviving his good liking of the place, set them to work again, and it was finished as we see it. But I have been assured that had the peace continued, and the king lived to enjoy the continuance of it, his Majesty had resolved to have pulled down all the remains of the old building (such as the chapel and the large court within the first gate), and to have built up the whole palace after the manner of those two fronts already done. In these would have been an entire set of rooms of state for the receiving and, if need had been, lodging and entertaining any foreign prince with his retinue; also offices for all the Secretaries of State, Lords of the Treasury, and of Trade, to have repaired to for the despatch of such business as it might be necessary to have done there upon the king's longer residence there than ordinary; as also apartments for all the great officers of the Household; so that had the house had two great squares added, as was designed, there would have been no room to spare, or that would not have been very well filled. But the king's death put an end to all these things.

Since the death of King William, Hampton Court seemed abandoned of its patron. They have gotten a kind of proverbial saying relating to Hampton Court, viz., that it has been generally chosen by every other prince since it became a house of note. King Charles was the first that delighted in it since Queen Elizabeth's time. As for the reigns before, it was but newly forfeited to the Crown, and was not made a royal house till King Charles I., who was not only a prince that delighted in country retirements, but knew how to make choice of them by the beauty of their situation, the goodness of the air, &c. He took great delight here, and, had he lived to enjoy it in peace, had purposed to make it another thing than it was. But we all know what took him off from that felicity, and all others; and this house was at last made one of his prisons by his rebellious subjects.

His son, King Charles II., may well be said to have an aversion to the place, for the reason just mentioned—namely, the treatment his royal father met with there—and particularly that the rebel and murderer of his father, Cromwell, afterwards possessed this palace, and revelled here in the blood of the royal party, as he had done in that of his sovereign. King Charles II. therefore chose Windsor, and bestowed a vast sum in beautifying the castle there, and which brought it to the perfection we see it in at this day—some few alterations excepted, done in the time of King William.

King William (for King James is not to be named as to his choice of retired palaces, his delight running quite another way)—I say, King William fixed upon Hampton Court, and it was in his reign that Hampton Court put on new clothes, and, being dressed gay and glorious, made the figure we now see it in.

The late queen, taken up for part of her reign in her kind regards to the prince her spouse, was obliged to reside where her care of his health confined her, and in this case kept for the most part at Kensington, where he died; but her Majesty always discovered her delight to be at Windsor, where she chose the little house, as it was called, opposite to the Castle, and took the air in her chaise in the parks and forest as she saw occasion.

Now Hampton Court, by the like alternative, is come into request again; and we find his present Majesty, who is a good judge too of the pleasantness and situation of a place of that kind, has taken Hampton Court into his favour, and has made it much his choice for the summer's retreat of the Court, and where they may best enjoy the diversions of the season. When Hampton Court will find such another favourable juncture as in King William's time, when the remainder of her ashes shall be swept away, and her complete fabric, as designed by King William, shall be finished, I cannot tell; but if ever that shall be, I know no palace in Europe, Versailles excepted, which can come up to her, either for beauty and magnificence, or for extent of building, and the ornaments attending it.

From Hampton Court I directed my course for a journey into the south-west part of England; and to take up my beginning where I concluded my last, I crossed to Chertsey on the Thames, a town I mentioned before; from whence, crossing the Black Desert, as I called it, of Bagshot Heath, I directed my course for Hampshire or Hantshire, and particularly for Basingstoke—that is to say, that a little before, I passed into the great Western Road upon the heath, somewhat west of Bagshot, at a village called Blackwater, and entered Hampshire, near Hartleroe.

Before we reach Basingstoke, we get rid of that unpleasant country which I so often call a desert, and enter into a pleasant fertile country, enclosed and cultivated like the rest of England; and passing a village or two we enter Basingstoke, in the midst of woods and pastures, rich and fertile, and the country accordingly spread with the houses of the nobility and gentry, as in other places. On the right hand, a little before we come to the town, we pass at a small distance the famous fortress, so it was then, of Basing, being a house belonging then to the Marquis of Winchester, the great ancestor of the present family of the Dukes of Bolton.

This house, garrisoned by a resolute band of old soldiers, was a great curb to the rebels of the Parliament party almost through that whole war; till it was, after a vigorous defence, yielded to the conquerors by the inevitable fate of things at that time. The old house is, indeed, demolished but the successor of the family, the first Duke of Bolton, has erected a very noble fabric in the same place, or near it, which, however, is not equal to the magnificence which fame gives to the ancient house, whose strength of building only, besides the outworks, withstood the battery of cannon in several attacks, and repulsed the Roundheads three or four times when they attempted to besiege it. It is incredible what booty the garrison of this place picked up, lying as they did just on the great Western Road, where they intercepted the carriers, plundered the waggons, and suffered nothing to pass—to the great interruption of the trade of the city of London.

Basingstoke is a large populous market-town, has a good market for corn, and lately within a very few years is fallen into a manufacture, viz., of making druggets and shalloons, and such slight goods, which, however, employs a good number of the poor people, and enables them to get their bread, which knew not how to get it before.

From hence the great Western Road goes on to Whitchurch and Andover, two market-towns, and sending members to Parliament; at the last of which the Downs, or open country, begins, which we in general, though falsely, call Salisbury Plain. But my resolution being to take in my view what I had passed by before, I was obliged to go off to the left hand, to Alresford and Winchester.

Alresford was a flourishing market-town, and remarkable for this—that though it had no great trade, and particularly very little, if any, manufactures, yet there was no collection in the town for the poor, nor any poor low enough to take alms of the parish, which is what I do not think can be said of any town in England besides.

But this happy circumstance, which so distinguished Alresford from all her neighbours, was brought to an end in the year ---, when by a sudden and surprising fire the whole town, with both the church and the market-house, was reduced to a heap of rubbish; and, except a few poor huts at the remotest ends of the town, not a house left standing. The town is since that very handsomely rebuilt, and the neighbouring gentlemen contributed largely to the relief of the people, especially by sending in timber towards their building; also their market-house is handsomely built, but the church not yet, though we hear there is a fund raising likewise for that.

Here is a very large pond, or lake of water, kept up to a head by a strong *batter d'eau*, or dam, which the people tell us was made by the Romans; and that it is to this day part of the great Roman highway which leads from Winchester to Alton, and, as it is supposed, went on to London, though we nowhere see any remains of it, except between Winchester and Alton, and chiefly between this town and Alton.

Near this town, a little north-west, the Duke of Bolton has another seat, which, though not large, is a very handsome beautiful palace, and the gardens not only very exact, but very finely situate, the prospect and vistas noble and great, and the whole very well kept.

From hence, at the end of seven miles over the Downs, we come to the very ancient city of Winchester; not only the great church (which is so famous all over Europe, and has been so much talked of), but even the whole city has at a distance the face of venerable, and looks ancient afar off; and yet here are many modern buildings too, and some very handsome; as the college schools, with the bishop's palace, built by Bishop Morley since the late wars—the old palace of the bishop having been ruined by that known church incendiary Sir William Waller and his crew of plunderers, who, if my information is not wrong, as I believe it is not, destroyed more monuments of the dead, and defaced more churches, than all the Roundheads in England beside.

This church, and the schools also are accurately described by several writers, especially by the "Monasticon," where their antiquity and original is fully set forth. The outside of the church is as plain and coarse as if the founders had abhorred ornaments, or that William of Wickham had been a Quaker, or at least a Quietist. There is neither statue, nor a niche for a statue, to be seen on all the outside; no carved work, no spires, towers, pinnacles, balustrades, or anything; but mere walls, buttresses, windows, and coigns necessary to the support and order of the building. It has no steeple, but a short tower covered flat, as if the top of it had fallen down, and it had been covered in haste to keep the rain out till they had time to build it up again.

But the inside of the church has many very good things in it, and worth observation; it was for some ages the burying-place of the English Saxon kings, whose *reliques*, at the repair of the church, were collected by Bishop Fox, and being put together into large wooden chests lined with lead were again interred at the foot of the great wall in the choir, three on one side, and three on the other, with an account whose bones are in each chest. Whether the division of the *reliques* might be depended upon, has been doubted, but is not thought material, so that we do but believe they are all there.

The choir of the church appears very magnificent; the roof is very high, and the Gothic work in the arched part is very fine, though very old; the painting in the windows is admirably good, and easy to be distinguished by those that understand those things: the steps ascending to the choir make a very fine show, having the statues of King James and his son King Charles, in copper, finely cast; the first on the right hand, and the other on the left, as you go up to the choir.

The choir is said to be the longest in England; and as the number of prebendaries, canons, &c., are many, it required such a length. The ornaments of the choir are the effects of the bounty of several bishops. The fine altar (the noblest in England by much) was done by Bishop Morley; the roof and the coat-of-arms of the Saxon and Norman kings were done by Bishop Fox; and the fine throne for the bishop in the choir was given by Bishop Mew in his lifetime; and it was well it was for if he had ordered it by will, there is reason to believe it had never been done—that reverend prelate, notwithstanding he enjoyed so rich a bishopric, scarce leaving money enough behind him to pay for his coffin.

There are a great many persons of rank buried in this church, besides the Saxon kings mentioned above, and besides several of the most eminent bishops of the See. Just under the altar lies a son of William the Conqueror, without any monument; and behind the altar, under a very fine and venerable monument, lies the famous Lord Treasurer Weston, late Earl of Portland, Lord High Treasurer of England under King Charles I. His effigy is in copper armour at full-length, with his head raised on three cushions of the same, and is a very magnificent work. There is also a very fine monument of Cardinal Beaufort in his cardinal's robes and hat.

The monument of Sir John Cloberry is extraordinary, but more because it puts strangers upon inquiring into his story than for anything wonderful in the figure, it being cut in a modern dress (the habit gentlemen wore in those times, which, being now so much out of fashion, appears mean enough). But this gentleman's story is particular, being the person solely entrusted with the secret of the restoration of King Charles II., as the messenger that passed between General Monk on one hand, and Mr. Montague and others entrusted by King Charles II. on the other hand; which he managed so faithfully as to effect that memorable event, to which England owes the felicity of all her happy days since that time; by which faithful service Sir John Cloberry, then a private musketeer only, raised himself to the honour of a knight, with the reward of a good estate from the bounty of the king.

Everybody that goes into this church, and reads what is to be read there, will be told that the body of the church was built by the famous William of Wickham; whose monument, intimating his fame, lies in the middle of that part which was built at his expense.

He was a courtier before a bishop; and, though he had no great share of learning, he was a great promoter of it, and a lover of learned men. His natural genius was much beyond his acquired parts, and his skill in politics beyond his ecclesiastic knowledge. He is said to have put his master, King Edward III., to whom he was Secretary of State, upon the two great projects which made his reign so glorious, viz.:— First, upon setting up his claim to the crown of France, and pushing that claim by force of arms, which brought on the war with France, in which that prince was three times victorious in battle. (2) Upon setting up, or instituting the Order of the Garter; in which he (being before that made Bishop of Winchester) obtained the honour for the Bishops of Winchester of being always prelates of the Order, as an appendix to the bishopric; and he himself was the first prelate of the Order, and the ensigns of that honour are joined with his episcopal ornaments in the robing of his effigy on the monument above.

To the honour of this bishop, there are other foundations of his, as much to his fame as that of this church, of which I shall speak in their order; but particularly the college in this city, which is a noble foundation indeed. The building consists of two large courts, in which are the lodgings for the masters and scholars, and in the centre a very noble chapel; beyond that, in the second court, are the schools, with a large cloister beyond them, and some enclosures laid open for the diversion of the scholars. There also is a great hall, where the scholars dine. The funds for the support of this college are very considerable; the masters live in a very good figure, and their maintenance is sufficient to support it. They have all separate dwellings in the house, and all possible conveniences appointed them.

The scholars have exhibitions at a certain time of continuance here, if they please to study in the new college at Oxford, built by the same noble benefactor, of which I shall speak in its order.

The clergy here live at large, and very handsomely, in the Close belonging to the cathedral; where, besides the bishop's palace mentioned above, are very good houses, and very handsomely built, for the prebendaries, canons, and other dignitaries of this church. The Deanery is a very pleasant dwelling, the gardens very large, and the river running through them; but the floods in winter sometimes incommode the gardens very much.

This school has fully answered the end of the founder, who, though he was no great scholar, resolved to erect a house for the making the ages to come more learned than those that went before; and it has, I say, fully answered the end, for many learned and great men have been raised here, some of whom we shall have occasion to mention as we go on.

Among the many private inscriptions in this church, we found one made by Dr. Over, once an eminent physician in this city, on a mother and child, who, being his patients, died together and were buried in the same grave, and which intimate that one died of a fever, and the other of a dropsy:
"Surrepuit natum Febris, matrem abstulit Hydrops,
Igne Prior Fatis, Altera cepit Aqua."

As the city itself stands in a vale on the bank, and at the conjunction of two small rivers, so the country rising every way, but just as the course of the water keeps the valley open, you must necessarily, as you go out of the gates, go uphill every wry; but when once ascended, you come to the most charming plains and most pleasant country of that kind in England; which continues with very small intersections of rivers and valleys for above fifty miles, as shall appear in the sequel of this journey.

At the west gate of this city was anciently a castle, known to be so by the ruins more than by any extraordinary notice taken of it in history. What they say of it, that the Saxon kings kept their court here, is doubtful, and must be meant of the West Saxons only. And as to the tale of King Arthur's Round Table, which they pretend was kept here for him and his two dozen of knights (which table hangs up still, as a piece of antiquity to the tune of twelve hundred years, and has, as they pretend, the names of the said knights in Saxon characters, and yet such as no man can read), all this story I see so little ground to give the least credit to that I look upon it, and it shall please you, to be no better than a fib.

Where this castle stood, or whatever else it was (for some say there was no castle there), the late King Charles II. marked out a very noble design, which, had he lived, would certainly have made that part of the country the Newmarket of the ages to come; for the country hereabout far excels that of Newmarket Heath for all kinds of sport and diversion fit for a prince, nobody can dispute. And as the design included a noble palace (sufficient, like Windsor, for a summer residence of the whole court), it would certainly have diverted the king from his cursory journeys to Newmarket.

The plan of this house has received several alterations, and as it is never like to be finished, it is scarce worth recording the variety. The building is begun, and the front next the city carried up to the roof and covered, but the remainder is not begun. There was a street of houses designed from the gate of the palace down to the town, but it was never begun to be built; the park marked out was exceeding large, near ten miles in circumference, and ended west upon the open Downs, in view of the town of Stockbridge.

This house was afterwards settled, with a royal revenue also, as an appanage (established by Parliament) upon Prince George of Denmark for his life, in case he had out-lived the queen; but his Royal Highness dying before her Majesty, all hope of seeing this design perfected, or the house finished, is now vanished.

I cannot omit that there are several public edifices in this city and in the neighbourhood, as the hospitals and the building adjoining near the east gate; and towards the north a piece of an old monastery undemolished, and which is still preserved to the religion, being the residence of some private Roman Catholic gentlemen, where they have an oratory, and, as they say, live still according to the rules of St. Benedict. This building is called Hide House; and as they live very usefully, and to the highest degree obliging among their neighbours, they meet with no obstruction or disturbance from anybody.

Winchester is a place of no trade other than is naturally occasioned by the inhabitants of the city and neighbouring villages one with another. Here is no manufacture, no navigation; there was indeed an attempt to make the river navigable from Southampton, and it was once made practicable, but it never answered the expense so as to give encouragement to the undertakers.

Here is a great deal of good company, and abundance of gentry being in the neighbourhood, it adds to the sociableness of the place. The clergy also here are, generally speaking, very rich and very numerous.

As there is such good company, so they are gotten into that new-fashioned way of conversing by assemblies. I shall do no more than mention them here; they are pleasant and agreeable to the young peoples, and sometimes fatal to them, of which, in its place, Winchester has its share of the mirth. May it escape the ill-consequences!

The hospital on the south of this city, at a mile distant on the road to Southampton, is worth notice. It is said to be founded by King William Rufus, but was not endowed or appointed till later times by Cardinal Beaufort. Every traveller that knocks at the door of this house in his way, and asks for it, claims the relief of a piece of white bread and a cup of beer, and this donation is still continued. A quantity of good beer is set apart every day to be given away, and what is left is distributed to other poor, but none of it kept to the next day.

How the revenues of this hospital, which should maintain the master and thirty private gentlemen (whom they call Fellows, but ought to call Brothers), is now reduced to maintain only fourteen, while the master lives in a figure equal to the best gentleman in the country, would be well worth the inquiry of a proper visitor, if such can be named. It is a thing worthy of complaint when public charities, designed for the relief of the poor, are embezzled and depredated by the rich, and turned to the support of luxury and pride.

From Winchester is about twenty-five miles, and over the most charming plains that can anywhere be seen (far, in my opinion, excelling the plains of Mecca), we come to Salisbury. The vast flocks of sheep which one everywhere sees upon these Downs, and the great number of those flocks, is a sight truly worth observation; it is ordinary for these flocks to contain from three thousand to five thousand in a flock, and several private farmers hereabouts have two or three such flocks.

But it is more remarkable still how a great part of these Downs comes, by a new method of husbandry, to be not only made arable (which they never were in former days), but to bear excellent wheat, and great crops, too, though otherwise poor barren land, and never known to our ancestors to be capable of any such thing—nay, they would perhaps have laughed at any one that would have gone about to plough up the wild downs and hills where the sheep were wont to go. But experience has made the present age wiser and more skilful in husbandry; for by only folding the sheep upon the ploughed lands— those lands which otherwise are barren, and where the plough goes within three or four inches of the solid rock of chalk, are made fruitful and bear very good wheat, as well as rye and barley. I shall say more of this when I come to speak of the same practice farther in the country.

This plain country continues in length from Winchester to Salisbury (twenty-five miles), from thence to Dorchester (twenty-two miles), thence to Weymouth (six miles); so that they lie near fifty miles in length and breadth; they reach also in some places thirty-five to forty miles. They who would make any practicable guess at the number of sheep usually fed on these Downs may take it from a calculation made, as I was told, at Dorchester, that there were six hundred thousand sheep fed within six miles of that town, measuring every way round and the town in the centre.

As we passed this plain country, we saw a great many old camps, as well Roman as British, and several remains of the ancient inhabitants of this kingdom, and of their wars, battles, entrenchments, encampments, buildings, and other fortifications, which are indeed very agreeable to a traveller that has read anything of the history of the country. Old Sarum is as remarkable as any of these, where there is a double entrenchment, with a deep graff or ditch to either of them; the area about one hundred yards in diameter, taking in the whole crown of the hill, and thereby rendering the ascent very difficult. Near this there is one farm-house, which is all the remains I could see of any town in or near the place (for the encampment has no resemblance of a town), and yet this is called the borough of Old Sarum, and sends two members to Parliament. Whom those members can justly say they represent would be hard for them to answer.

Some will have it that the old city of *Sorbiodunum* or Salisbury stood here, and was afterwards (for I know not what reasons) removed to the low marshy grounds among the rivers, where it now stands. But as I see no authority for it other than mere tradition, I believe my share of it, and take it *ad referendum.*

Salisbury itself is indeed a large and pleasant city, though I do not think it at all the pleasanter for that which they boast so much of— namely, the water running through the middle of every street—or that it adds anything to the beauty of the place, but just the contrary; it keeps the streets always dirty, full of wet and filth and weeds, even in the middle of summer.

The city is placed upon the confluence of two large rivers, the Avon and the Willy, neither of them considerable rivers, but very large when joined together, and yet larger when they receive a third river (viz., the Naddir), which joins them near Clarendon Park, about three miles below the city; then, with a deep channel and a current less rapid, they run down to Christchurch, which is their port. And where they empty themselves into the sea, from that town upwards towards Salisbury they are made navigable to within two miles, and might be so quite into the city, were it not for the strength of the stream.

As the city of Winchester is a city without trade—that is to say, without any particular manufactures—so this city of Salisbury and all the county of Wilts, of which it is the capital, are full of a great variety of manufactures, and those some of the most considerable in England—namely, the clothing trade and the trade of flannels, druggets, and several other sorts of manufactures, of which in their order.

The city of Salisbury has two remarkable manufactures carried on in it, and which employ the poor of great part of the country round—namely, fine flannels, and long-cloths for the Turkey trade, called Salisbury whites. The people of Salisbury are gay and rich, and have a flourishing trade; and there is a great deal of good manners and good company among them—I mean, among the citizens, besides what is found among the gentlemen; for there are many good families in Salisbury besides the citizens.

This society has a great addition from the Close—that is to say, the circle of ground walled in adjacent to the cathedral, in which the families of the prebendaries and commons, and others of the clergy belonging to the cathedral, have their houses, as is usual in all cities, where there are cathedral churches. These are so considerable here, and the place so large, that it is (as it is called in general) like another city.

The cathedral is famous for the height of its spire, which is without exception the highest and the handsomest in England, being from the ground 410 feet, and yet the walls so exceeding thin that at the upper part of the spire, upon a view made by the late Sir Christopher Wren, the wall was found to be less than five inches thick; upon which a consultation was had whether the spire, or at least the upper part of it, should be taken down, it being supposed to have received some damage by the great storm in the year 1703; but it was resolved in the negative, and Sir Christopher ordered it to be so strengthened with bands of iron plates as has effectually secured it; and I have heard some of the best architects say it is stronger now than when it was first built.

They tell us here long stories of the great art used in laying the first foundation of this church, the ground being marshy and wet, occasioned by the channels of the rivers; that it was laid upon piles, according to some, and upon woolpacks, according to others. But this is not supposed by those who know that the whole country is one rock of chalk, even from the tops of the highest hills to the bottom of the deepest rivers.

They tell us this church was forty years a-building, and cost an immense sum of money; but it must be acknowledged that the inside of the work is not answerable in the decoration of things to the workmanship without. The painting in the choir is mean, and more like the ordinary method of common drawing-room or tavern painting than that of a church; the carving is good, but very little of it; and it is rather a fine church than finely set off.

The ordinary boast of this building (that there were as many gates as months, as many windows as days, as many marble pillars as hours in the year) is now no recommendation at all. However, the mention of it must be preserved:—
"As many days as in one year there be,
So many windows in one church we see;
As many marble pillars there appear
As there are hours throughout the fleeting year;
As many gates as moons one year do view:
Strange tale to tell, yet not more strange than true."

There are, however, some very fine monuments in this church; particularly one belonging to the noble family of Seymours, since Dukes of Somerset (and ancestors of the present flourishing family), which on a most melancholy occasion has been now lately opened again to receive the body of the late Duchess of Somerset, the happy consort for almost forty years of his Grace the present Duke, and only daughter and heiress of the ancient and noble family of Percy, Earls of Northumberland, whose great estate she brought into the family of Somerset, who now enjoy it.

With her was buried at the same time her Grace's daughter the Marchioness of Caermarthen (being married to the Marquis of Caermarthen, son and heir-apparent to the Lord of Leeds), who died

74

for grief at the loss of the duchess her mother, and was buried with her; also her second son, the Duke Percy Somerset, who died a few months before, and had been buried in the Abbey church of Westminster, but was ordered to be removed and laid here with the ancestors of his house. And I hear his Grace designs to have a yet more magnificent monument erected in this cathedral for them, just by the other which is there already.

How the Dukes of Somerset came to quit this church for their burying-place, and be laid in Westminster Abbey, that I know not; but it is certain that the present Duke has chosen to have his family laid here with their ancestors, and to that end has caused the corpse of his son, the Lord Percy, as above, and one of his daughters, who had been buried in the Abbey, to be removed and brought down to this vault, which lies in that they call the Virgin Mary's Chapel, behind the altar. There is, as above, a noble monument for a late Duke and Duchess of Somerset in the place already, with their portraits at full-length, their heads lying upon cushions, the whole perfectly well wrought in fine polished Italian marble, and their sons kneeling by them. Those I suppose to be the father of the great Duke of Somerset, uncle to King Edward IV.; but after this the family lay in Westminster Abbey, where there is also a fine monument for that very duke who was beheaded by Edward VI., and who was the great patron of the Reformation.

Among other monuments of noble men in this cathedral they show you one that is very extraordinary, and to which there hangs a tale. There was in the reign of Philip and Mary a very unhappy murder committed by the then Lord Sturton, or Stourton, a family since extinct, but well known till within a few years in that country.

This Lord Stourton being guilty of the said murder, which also was aggravated with very bad circumstances, could not obtain the usual grace of the Crown (viz., to be beheaded), but Queen Mary positively ordered that, like a common malefactor, he should die at the gallows. After he was hanged, his friends desiring to have him buried at Salisbury, the bishop would not consent that he should be buried in the cathedral unless, as a farther mark of infamy, his friends would submit to this condition—viz., that the silken halter in which he was hanged should be hanged up over his grave in the church as a monument of his crime; which was accordingly done, and there it is to be seen to this day.

The putting this halter up here was not so wonderful to me as it was that the posterity of that lord, who remained in good rank some time after, should never prevail to have that mark of infamy taken off from the memory of their ancestor.

There are several other monuments in this cathedral, as particularly of two noblemen of ancient families in Scotland—one of the name of Hay, and one of the name of Gordon; but they give us nothing of their history, so that we must be content to say there they lie, and that is all.

The cloister, and the chapter-house adjoining to the church, are the finest here of any I have seen in England; the latter is octagon, or eight-square, and is 150 feet in its circumference; the roof bearing all upon one small marble pillar in the centre, which you may shake with your hand; and it is hardly to be imagined it can be any great support to the roof, which makes it the more curious (it is not indeed to be matched, I believe, in Europe).

From hence directing my course to the seaside in pursuit of my first design—viz., of viewing the whole coast of England—I left the great road and went down the east side of the river towards New Forest and Lymington; and here I saw the ancient house and seat of Clarendon, the mansion of the ancient family of Hide, ancestors of the great Earl of Clarendon, and from whence his lordship was honoured with that title, or the house erected into an honour in favour of his family.

But this being a large county, and full of memorable branches of antiquity and modern curiosity, I cannot quit my observations so soon. But being happily fixed, by the favour of a particular friend, at so beautiful a spot of ground as this of Clarendon Park, I made several little excursions from hence to view the northern parts of this county— a county so fruitful of wonders that, though I do not make antiquity my chief search, yet I must not pass it over entirely, where so much of it, and so well worth observation, is to be found, which would look as if I either understood not the value of the study, or expected my readers should be satisfied with a total omission of it.

I have mentioned that this county is generally a vast continued body of high chalky hills, whose tops spread themselves into fruitful and pleasant downs and plains, upon which great flocks of sheep are fed, &c. But the reader is desired to observe these hills and plains are most beautifully intersected and cut through by the course of divers pleasant and profitable rivers; in the course and near the banks of which there always is a chain of fruitful meadows and rich pastures, and those interspersed with innumerable pleasant towns, villages, and houses, and among them many of considerable magnitude. So that, while you view the downs, and think the country wild and uninhabited, yet when you come to descend into these vales you are surprised with the most pleasant and fertile country in England.

There are no less than four of these rivers, which meet all together at or near the city of Salisbury; especially the waters of three of them run through the streets of the city—the Nadder and the Willy and the Avon—and the course of these three lead us through the whole mountainous part of the county. The two first join their waters at Wilton, the shiretown, though a place of no great notice now; and these are the waters which run through the canal and the gardens of Wilton House, the seat of that ornament of nobility and learning, the Earl of Pembroke.

One cannot be said to have seen anything that a man of curiosity would think worth seeing in this county, and not have been at Wilton House; but not the beautiful building, not the ancient trophy of a great family, not the noble situation, not all the pleasures of the gardens, parks, fountains, hare-warren, or of whatever is rare either in art or nature, are equal to that yet more glorious sight of a noble princely palace constantly filled with its noble and proper inhabitants. The lord and proprietor, who is indeed a true patriarchal monarch, reigns here with an authority agreeable to all his subjects (family); and his reign is made agreeable, by his first practising the most exquisite government of himself, and then guiding all under him by the rules of honour and virtue, being also himself perfectly master of all the needful arts of family government—I mean, needful to make that government both easy and pleasant to those who are under it, and who therefore willingly, and by choice, conform to it.

Here an exalted genius is the instructor, a glorious example the guide, and a gentle well-directed hand the governor and law-giver to the whole; and the family, like a well-governed city, appears happy, flourishing, and regular, groaning under no grievance, pleased with what they enjoy, and enjoying everything which they ought to be pleased with.

Nor is the blessing of this noble resident extended to the family only, but even to all the country round, who in their degree feel the effects of the general beneficence, and where the neighbourhood (however poor) receive all the good they can expect, and are sure to have no injury or oppression.

The canal before the house lies parallel with the road, and receives into it the whole river Willy, or at least is able to do so; it may, indeed, be said that the river is made into a canal. When we come into the courtyards before the house there are several pieces of antiquity to entertain the curious, as particularly a noble column of porphyry, with a marble statue of Venus on the top of it. In Italy, and especially at Rome and Naples, we see a great variety of fine columns, and some of them of excellent workmanship and antiquity; and at some of the courts of the princes of Italy the like is seen, as especially at the court of Florence; but in England I do not remember to have seen anything like this, which, as they told me, is two-and-thirty feet high, and of excellent workmanship, and that it came last from Candia, but formerly from Alexandria. What may belong to the history of it any further, I suppose is not known—at least, they could tell me no more of it who showed it me.

On the left of the court was formerly a large grotto and curious water-works; and in a house, or shed, or part of the building, which opened with two folding-doors, like a coach-house, a large equestrian statue of one of the ancestors of the family in complete armour, as also another of a Roman Emperor in brass. But the last time I had the curiosity to see this house, I missed that part; so that I supposed they were removed.

As the present Earl of Pembroke, the lord of this fine palace, is a nobleman of great personal merit many other ways, so he is a man of learning and reading beyond most men of his lordship's high rank in this nation, if not in the world; and as his reading has made him a master of antiquity, and judge of such pieces of antiquity as he has had opportunity to meet with in his own travels and otherwise in the world, so it has given him a love of the study, and made him a collector of valuable things, as well in painting as in sculpture, and other excellences of art, as also of nature; insomuch that Wilton House is now a mere museum or a chamber of rarities, and we meet with several things there which are to be found nowhere else in the world.

As his lordship is a great collector of fine paintings, so I know no nobleman's house in England so prepared, as if built on purpose, to receive them; the largest and the finest pieces that can be imagined extant in the world might have found a place here capable to receive them. I say, they "might have found," as if they could not now, which is in part true; for at present the whole house is so completely filled that I see no room for any new piece to crowd in without displacing some other fine piece that hung there before. As for the value of the piece that might so offer to succeed the displaced, that the great judge of the whole collection, the earl himself, must determine; and as his judgment is perfectly good, the best picture would be sure to possess the place. In a word, here is without doubt the best, if not the greatest, collection of rarities and paintings that are to be seen together in any one nobleman's or gentleman's house in England. The piece of our Saviour washing His disciples' feet, which they show you in one of the first rooms you go into, must be spoken of by everybody that has any knowledge of painting, and is an admirable piece indeed.

You ascend the great staircase at the upper end of the hall, which is very large; at the foot of the staircase you have a Bacchus as large as life, done in fine Peloponnesian marble, carrying a young Bacchus on his arm, the young one eating grapes, and letting you see by his countenance that he is pleased with the taste of them. Nothing can be done finer, or more lively represent the thing intended—namely, the gust of the appetite, which if it be not a passion, it is an affection which is as much seen in the countenance, perhaps more than any other. One ought to stop every two steps of this staircase, as we go up, to contemplate the vast variety of pictures that cover the walls, and of some of the best masters in Europe; and yet this is but an introduction to what is beyond them.

When you are entered the apartments, such variety seizes you every way that you scarce know to which hand to turn yourself. First on one side you see several rooms filled with paintings as before, all so curious, and the variety such, that it is with reluctance that you can turn from them; while looking another way you are called off by a vast collection of busts and pieces of the greatest antiquity of the kind, both Greek and Romans; among these there is one of the Roman emperor Marcus Aurelius in basso-relievo. I never saw anything like what appears here, except in the chamber of rarities at Munich in Bavaria.

Passing these, you come into several large rooms, as if contrived for the reception of the beautiful guests that take them up; one of these is near seventy feet long, and the ceiling twenty-six feet high, with another adjoining of the same height and breadth, but not so long. Those together might be called the Great Gallery of Wilton, and might vie for paintings with the Gallery of Luxembourg, in the Faubourg of Paris.

These two rooms are filled with the family pieces of the house of Herbert, most of them by Lilly or Vandyke; and one in particular outdoes all that I ever met with, either at home or abroad; it is done, as was the mode of painting at that time, after the manner of a family piece of King Charles I., with his queen and children, which before the burning of Whitehall I remember to hang at the east end of the Long Gallery in the palace.

This piece fills the farther end of the great room which I just now mentioned; it contains the Earl of Montgomery, ancestor of the house of Herbert (not then Earls of Pembroke) and his lady, sitting, and as big as life; there are about them their own five sons and one daughter, and their daughter-in-law, who was daughter of the Duke of Buckingham, married to the elder Lord Herbert, their eldest son. It is enough to say of this piece, it is worth the labour of any lover of art to go five hundred miles to see it; and I am informed several gentlemen of quality have come from France almost on purpose. It would be endless to describe the whole set of the family pictures which take up this room, unless we would enter into the roof-tree of the family, and set down a genealogical line of the whole house.

After we have seen this fine range of beauties—for such, indeed, they are—far from being at an end of your surprise, you have three or four rooms still upon the same floor, filled with wonders as before. Nothing can be finer than the pictures themselves, nothing more surprising than the number of them. At length you descend the back stairs, which are in themselves large, though not like the other. However, not a hand's-breadth is left to crowd a picture in of the smallest size; and even the upper rooms, which might be called garrets, are not naked, but have some very good pieces in them.

Upon the whole, the genius of the noble collector may be seen in this glorious collection, than which, take them together, there is not a finer in any private hand in Europe, and in no hand at all in Britain, private or public.

The gardens are on the south of the house, and extend themselves beyond the river, a branch of which runs through one part of them, and still south of the gardens in the great park, which, extending beyond the vale, mounts the hill opening at the last to the great down, which is properly called, by way of distinction, Salisbury Plain, and leads from the city of Salisbury to Shaftesbury. Here also his lordship has a hare-warren, as it is called, though improperly. It has, indeed, been a sanctuary for the hares for many years; but the gentlemen complain that it mars their game, for that as soon as they put up a hare for their sport, if it be anywhere within two or three miles, away she runs for the warren, and there is an end of their pursuit; on the other hand, it makes all the countrymen turn poachers, and destroy the hares by what means they can. But this is a smaller matter, and of no great import one way or other.

From this pleasant and agreeable day's work I returned to Clarendon, and the next day took another short tour to the hills to see that celebrated piece of antiquity, the wonderful Stonehenge, being six miles from Salisbury, north, and upon the side of the River Avon, near the town of Amesbury. It is needless that I should enter here into any part of the dispute about which our learned antiquaries have so puzzled themselves that several books (and one of them in folio) have been published about it; some alleging it to be a heathen or pagan temple and altar, or place of sacrifice, as Mr. Jones; others a monument or trophy of victory; others a monument for the dead, as Mr. Aubrey, and the like. Again, some will have it be British, some Danish, some Saxon, some Roman, and some, before them all, Phoenician.

I shall suppose it, as the majority of all writers do, to be a monument for the dead, and the rather because men's bones have been frequently dug up in the ground near them. The common opinion that no man could ever count them, that a baker carried a basket of bread and laid a loaf upon every stone, and yet never could make out the same number twice, this I take as a mere country fiction, and a ridiculous one too. The reason why they cannot easily be told is that many of them lie half or part buried in the ground; and a piece here and a piece there only appearing above the grass, it cannot be known easily which belong to one stone and which to another, or which are separate stones, and which are joined underground to one another; otherwise, as to those which appear, they are easy to be told, and I have seen them told four times after one another, beginning every time at a different place, and every time they amounted to seventy-two in all; but then this was counting every piece of a stone of bulk which appeared above the surface of the earth, and was not evidently part of and adjoining to another, to be a distinct and separate body or stone by itself.

The form of this monument is not only described but delineated in most authors, and, indeed, it is hard to know the first but by the last. The figure was at first circular, and there were at least four rows or circles within one another. The main stones were placed upright, and they were joined on the top by cross-stones, laid from one to another, and fastened with vast mortises and tenons. Length of time has so decayed them that not only most of the cross-stones which lay on the top are fallen down, but many of the upright also, notwithstanding the weight of them is so prodigious great. How they came thither, or from whence (no stones of that kind being now to be found in that part of England near it) is still the mystery, for they are of such immense bulk that no engines or carriages which we have in use in this age could stir them.

Doubtless they had some method in former days in foreign countries, as well as here, to move heavier weights than we find practicable now. How else did Solomon's workmen build the battlement or additional wall to support the precipice of Mount Moriah, on which the Temple was built, which was all built of stones of Parian marble, each stone being forty cubits long and fourteen cubits broad, and eight cubits high or thick, which, reckoning each cubit at two feet and a half of our measure (as the learned agree to do), was one hundred feet long, thirty-five feet broad, and twenty feet thick?

These stones at Stonehenge, as Mr. Camden describes them, and in which others agree, were very large, though not so large—the upright stones twenty-four feet high, seven feet broad, sixteen feet round, and weigh twelve tons each; and the cross-stones on the top, which he calls coronets, were six or seven tons. But this does not seem equal; for if the cross-stones weighed six or seven tons, the others, as they appear now, were at least five or six times as big, and must weigh in proportion; and therefore I must think their judgment much nearer the case who judge the upright stones at sixteen tons or thereabouts (supposing them to stand a great way into the earth, as it is not doubted but they do), and the coronets or cross-stones at about two tons, which is very large too, and as much as their bulk can be thought to allow.

Upon the whole, we must take them as our ancestors have done—namely, for an erection or building so ancient that no history has handed down to us the original. As we find it, then, uncertain, we must leave it so. It is indeed a reverend piece of antiquity, and it is a great loss that the true history of it is not known. But since it is not, I think the making so many conjectures at the reality, when they know lots can but guess at it, and, above all, the insisting so long and warmly on their private opinions, is but amusing themselves and us with a doubt, which perhaps lies the deeper for their search into it.

The downs and plains in this part of England being so open, and the surface so little subject to alteration, there are more remains of antiquity to be seen upon them than in other places. For example, I think they tell us there are three-and-fifty ancient encampments or fortifications to be seen in this one county—some whereof are exceeding plain to be seen; some of one form, some of another; some of one nation, some of another—British, Danish, Saxon, Roman—as at Ebb Down, Burywood, Oldburgh Hill, Cummerford, Roundway Down, St. Ann's Hill, Bratton Castle, Clay Hill, Stournton Park, Whitecole Hill, Battlebury, Scrathbury, Tanesbury, Frippsbury, Southbury Hill, Amesbury, Great Bodwin, Easterley, Merdon, Aubery, Martenscil Hill, Barbury Castle, and many more.

Also the barrows, as we all agree to call them, are very many in number in this county, and very obvious, having suffered very little decay. These are large hillocks of earth cast up, as the ancients agree, by the soldiers over the bodies of their dead comrades slain in battle; several hundreds of these are to be seen, especially in the north part of this county, about Marlborough and the downs, from thence to St. Ann's Hill, and even every way the downs are full of them.

I have done with matters of antiquity for this county, unless you will admit me to mention the famous Parliament in the reign of Henry II. held at Clarendon, where I am now writing, and another intended to be held there in Richard II.'s time, but prevented by the barons, being then up in arms against the king.

Near this place, at Farlo, was the birthplace of the late Sir Stephen Fox, and where the town, sharing in his good fortune, shows several marks of his bounty, as particularly the building a new church from the foundation, and getting an Act of Parliament passed for making it parochial, it being but a chapel-of-ease before to an adjoining parish. Also Sir Stephen built and endowed an almshouse here for six poor women, with a master and a free school. The master is to be a clergyman, and to officiate in the church—that is to say, is to have the living, which, including the school, is very sufficient.

I am now to pursue my first design, and shall take the west part of Wiltshire in my return, where are several things still to be taken notice of, and some very well worth our stay. In the meantime I went on to Langborough, a fine seat of my Lord Colerain, which is very well kept, though the family, it seems, is not much in this country, having another estate and dwelling at Tottenham High Cross, near London.

From hence in my way to the seaside I came to New Forest, of which I have said something already with relation to the great extent of ground which lies waste, and in which there is so great a quantity of large timber, as I have spoken of already.

This waste and wild part of the country was, as some record, laid open and waste for a forest and for game by that violent tyrant William the Conqueror, and for which purpose he unpeopled the country, pulled down the houses, and, which was worse, the churches of several parishes or towns, and of abundance of villages, turning the poor people out of their habitations and possessions, and laying all open for his deer. The same histories likewise record that two of his own blood and posterity, and particularly his immediate successor William Rufus, lost their lives in this forest—one, viz., the said William Rufus, being shot with an arrow directed at a deer which the king and his company were hunting, and the arrow, glancing on a tree, changed his course, and struck the king full on the breast and killed him. This they relate as a just judgment of God on the cruel devastation made here by the Conqueror. Be it so or not, as Heaven pleases; but that the king was so killed is certain, and they show the tree on which the arrow glanced to this day. In King Charles II.'s time it was ordered to be surrounded with a pale; but as great part of the paling is down with age, whether the tree be really so old or not is to me a great question, the action being near seven hundred years ago.

I cannot omit to mention here a proposal made a few years ago to the late Lord Treasurer Godolphin for re-peopling this forest, which for some reasons I can be more particular in than any man now left alive, because I had the honour to draw up the scheme and argue it before that noble lord and some others who were principally concerned at that time in bringing over—or, rather, providing for when they were come over—the poor inhabitants of the Palatinate, a thing in itself commendable, but, as it was managed, made scandalous to England and miserable to those poor people.

Some persons being ordered by that noble lord above mentioned to consider of measures how the said poor people should be provided for, and whether they could be provided for or no without injury to the public, the answer was grounded upon this maxim—that the number of inhabitants is the wealth and strength of a kingdom, provided those inhabitants were such as by honest industry applied themselves to live by their labour, to whatsoever trades or employments they were brought up. In the next place, it was inquired what employments those poor people were brought up to. It was answered there were husbandmen and artificers of all sorts, upon which the proposal was as follows. New Forest, in Hampshire, was singled out to be the place:—

Here it was proposed to draw a great square line containing four thousand acres of land, marking out two large highways or roads through the centre, crossing both ways, so that there should be a thousand acres in each division, exclusive of the land contained in the said cross-roads.

Then it was proposed to since out twenty men and their families, who should be recommended as honest industrious men, expert in, or at least capable of being instructed in husbandry, curing and cultivating of land, breeding and feeding cattle, and the like. To each of these should be parcelled out, in equal distributions, two hundred acres of this land, so that the whole four thousand acres should be fully distributed to the said twenty families, for which they should have no rent to pay, and be liable to no taxes but such as provided for their own sick or poor, repairing their own roads, and the like. This exemption from rent and taxes to continue for twenty years, and then to pay each £50 a year to the queen—that is to say, to the Crown.

To each of these families, whom I would now call farmers, it was proposed to advance £200 in ready money as a stock to set them to work; to furnish them with cattle, horses, cows, hogs, &c.; and to hire and pay labourers to inclose, clear, and cure the land, which it would be supposed the first year would not be so much to their advantage as afterwards, allowing them timber out of the forest to build themselves houses and barns, sheds and offices, as they should have occasion; also for carts, waggons, ploughs, harrows, and the like necessary things: care to be taken that the men and their families went to work forthwith according to the design.

Thus twenty families would be immediately supplied and provided for, for there would be no doubt but these families, with so much land given them gratis, and so much money to work with, would live very well; but what would this do for the support of the rest, who were supposed to be, to every twenty farmers, forty or fifty families of other people (some of one trade, some of another), with women and children? To this it was answered that these twenty farmers would, by the consequence of their own settlements, provide for and employ such a proportion of others of their own people that, by thus providing for twenty families in a place, the whole number of Palatinates would have been provided for, had they been twenty thousand more in number than they were, and that without being any burden upon or injury to the people of England; on the contrary, they would have been an advantage and an addition of wealth and strength to the nation, and to the country in particular where they should be thus seated. For example:—

As soon as the land was marked out, the farmers put in possession of it, and the money given them, they should be obliged to go to work, in order to their settlement. Suppose it, then, to be in the spring of the year, when such work was most proper. First, all hands would be required to fence and part off the land, and clear it of the timber or bushes, or whatever else was upon it which required to be removed. The first thing, therefore, which the farmer would do would be to single out from the rest of their number every one three servants—that is to say, two men and a maid; less could not answer the preparations they would be obliged to make, and yet work hard themselves also. By the help of these they would, with good management, soon get so much of their land cured, fenced-off, ploughed, and sowed as should yield them a sufficiency of corn and kitchen stuff the very first year, both for horse-meat, hog-meat, food for the family, and some to carry to market, too, by which to bring in money to go farther on, as above.

At the first entrance they were to have the tents allowed them to live in, which they then had from the Tower; but as soon as leisure and conveniences admitted, every farmer was obliged to begin to build him a farm-house, which he would do gradually, some and some, as he could spare time from his other works, and money from his little stock.

In order to furnish himself with carts, waggons, ploughs, harrows, wheel-barrows, hurdles, and all such necessary utensils of husbandry, there would be an absolute necessity of wheelwrights or cartwrights, one at least to each division.

Thus, by the way, there would be employed three servants to each farmer, that makes sixty persons.

Four families of wheelwrights, one to each division—which, suppose five in a family, makes twenty persons. Suppose four head-carpenters, with each three men; and as at first all would be building together, they would to every house building have at least one labourer. Four families of carpenters, five to each family, and three servants, is thirty-two persons; one labourer to each house building is twenty persons more.

Thus here would be necessarily brought together in the very first of the work one hundred and thirty-two persons, besides the head-farmers, who at five also to each family are one hundred more; in all, two hundred and thirty-two.

For the necessary supply of these with provisions, clothes, household stuff, &c. (for all should be done among themselves), first, they must have at least four butchers with their families (twenty persons), four shoemakers with their families and each shoemaker two journeymen (for every trade would increase the number of customers to every trade). This is twenty-eight persons more.

They would then require a hatmaker, a glover, at least two ropemakers, four tailors, three weavers of woollen and three weavers of linen, two basket-makers, two common brewers, ten or twelve shop-keepers to furnish chandlery and grocery wares, and as many for drapery and mercery, over and above what they could work. This makes two-and-forty families more, each at five in a family, which, is two hundred and ten persons; all the labouring part of these must have at least two servants (the brewers more), which I cast up at forty more.

Add to these two ministers, one clerk, one sexton or grave-digger, with their families, two physicians, three apothecaries, two surgeons (less there could not be, only that for the beginning it might be said the physicians should be surgeons, and I take them so); this is forty-five persons, besides servants; so that, in short—to omit many tradesmen more who would be wanted among them—there would necessarily and voluntarily follow to these twenty families of farmers at least six hundred more of their own people.

It is no difficult thing to show that the ready money of £4,000 which the Government was to advance to those twenty farmers would employ and pay, and consequently subsist, all these numerous dependants in the works which must severally be done for them for the first year, after which the farmers would begin to receive their own money back again; for all these tradesmen must come to their own market to buy corn, flesh, milk, butter, cheese, bacon, &c., which after the first year the farmers, having no rent to pay, would have to spare sufficiently, and so take back their own money with advantage. I need not go on to mention how, by consequence provisions increasing and money circulating, this town should increase in a very little time.

It was proposed also that for the encouragement of all the handicraftsmen and labouring poor who, either as servants or as labourers for day-work, assisted the farmers or other tradesmen, they should have every man three acres of ground given them, with leave to build cottages upon the same, the allotments to be upon the waste at the end of the cross-roads where they entered the town.

In the centre of the square was laid out a circle of twelve acres of ground, to be cast into streets for inhabitants to build on as their ability would permit—all that would build to have ground gratis for twenty years, timber out of the forest, and convenient yards, gardens, and orchards allotted to every house.

In the great streets near where they cross each other was to be built a handsome market-house, with a town-hall for parish or corporation business, doing justice and the like; also shambles; and in a handsome part of the ground mentioned to be laid out for streets, as near the centre as might be, was to be ground laid out for the building a church, which every man should either contribute to the building of in money, or give every tenth day of his time to assist in labouring at the building.

I have omitted many tradesmen who would be wanted here, and would find a good livelihood among their country-folks only to get accidental work as day-men or labourers (of which such a town would constantly employ many), as also poor women for assistance in families (such as midwives, nurses, &c.).

Adjacent to the town was to be a certain quantity of common-land for the benefit of the cottages, that the poor might have a few sheep or cows, as their circumstances required; and this to be appointed at the several ends of the town.

There was a calculation made of what increase there would be, both of wealth and people, in twenty years in this town; what a vast consumption of provisions they would cause, more than the four thousand acres of land given them would produce, by which consumption and increase so much advantage would accrue to the public stock, and so many subjects be added to the many thousands of Great Britain, who in the next age would be all true-born Englishmen, and forget both the language and nation from whence they came. And it was in order to this that two ministers were appointed, one of which should officiate in English and the other in High Dutch, and withal to have them obliged by a law to teach all their children both to speak, read, and write the English language.

Upon their increase they would also want barbers and glaziers, painters also, and plumbers; a windmill or two, and the millers and their families; a fulling-mill and a cloth-worker; as also a master clothier or two for making a manufacture among them for their own wear, and for employing the women and children; a dyer or two for dyeing their manufactures; and, which above all is not to be omitted, four families at least of smiths, with every one two servants—considering that, besides all the family work which continually employs a smith, all the shoeing of horses, all the ironwork of ploughs, carts, waggons, harrows, &c., must be wrought by them. There was no allowance made for inns and ale-houses, seeing it would be frequent that those who kept public-houses of any sort would likewise have some other employment to carry on.

This was the scheme for settling the Palatinates, by which means twenty families of farmers, handsomely set up and supported, would lay a foundation, as I have said, for six or seven hundred of the rest of their people; and as the land in New Forest is undoubtedly good, and capable of improvement by such cultivation, so other wastes in England are to be found as fruitful as that; and twenty such villages might have been erected, the poor strangers maintained, and the nation evidently be bettered by it. As to the money to be advanced, which in the case of twenty such settlements, at £1,000 each, would be £80,000, two things were answered to it:—

1. That the annual rent to be received for all those lands after twenty years would abundantly pay the public for the first disburses on the scheme above, that rent being then to amount to £40,000 per annum.

2. More money than would have done this was expended, or rather thrown away, upon them here, to keep them in suspense, and afterwards starve them; sending them a-begging all over the nation, and shipping them off to perish in other countries. Where the mistake lay is none of my business to inquire.

I reserved this account for this place, because I passed in this journey over the very spot where the design was laid out namely, near Lyndhurst, in the road from Rumsey to Lymington, whither I now directed my course.

Lymington is a little but populous seaport standing opposite to the Isle of Wight, in the narrow part of the strait which ships sometimes pass through in fair weather, called the Needles; and right against an ancient town of that island called Yarmouth, and which, in distinction from the great town of Yarmouth in Norfolk, is called South Yarmouth. This town of Lymington is chiefly noted for making fine salt, which is indeed excellent good; and from whence all these south parts of England are supplied, as well by water as by land carriage; and sometimes, though not often, they send salt to London, when, contrary winds having kept the Northern fleets back, the price at

London has been very high; but this is very seldom and uncertain. Lymington sends two members to Parliament, and this and her salt trade is all I can say to her; for though she is very well situated as to the convenience of shipping I do not find they have any foreign commerce, except it be what we call smuggling and roguing; which, I may say, is the reigning commerce of all this part of the English coast, from the mouth of the Thames to the Land's End of Cornwall.

From hence there are but few towns on the sea-coast west, though there are several considerable rivers empty themselves into the sea; nor are there any harbours or seaports of any note except Poole. As for Christchurch, though it stands at the mouth of the Avon (which, as I have said, comes down from Salisbury, and brings with it all the waters of the south and east parts of Wiltshire, and receives also the Stour and Piddle, two Dorsetshire rivers which bring with them all the waters of the north part of Dorsetshire), yet it is a very inconsiderable poor place, scarce worth seeing, and less worth mentioning in this account, only that it sends two members to Parliament, which many poor towns in this part of England do, as well as that.

From hence I stepped up into the country north-west, to see the ancient town of Wimborne, or Wimborneminster; there I found nothing remarkable but the church, which is indeed a very great one, ancient, and yet very well built, with a very firm, strong, square tower, considerably high; but was, without doubt, much finer, when on the top of it stood a most exquisite spire—finer and taller, if fame lies not, than that at Salisbury, and by its situation in a plainer, flatter country visible, no question, much farther; but this most beautiful ornament was blown down by a sudden tempest of wind, as they tell us, in the year 1622.

The church remains a venerable piece of antiquity, and has in it the remains of a place once much more in request than it is now, for here are the monuments of several noble families, and in particular of one king, viz., King Etheldred, who was slain in battle by the Danes. He was a prince famed for piety and religion, and, according to the zeal of these times, was esteemed as a martyr, because, venturing his life against the Danes, who were heathens, he died fighting for his religion and his country. The inscription upon his grave is preserved, and has been carefully repaired, so as to be easily read, and is as follows:—

"In hoc loco quiescit Corpus S. Etheldredi, Regis West Saxonum, Martyris, qui Anno Dom. DCCCLXXII., xxiii Aprilis, per Manos Danorum Paganorum Occubuit."

In English thus:—

"Here rests the Body of Holy Etheldred, King of the West Saxons, and Martyr, who fell by the Hands of the Pagan Danes in the Year of our Lord 872, the 23rd of April."

Here are also the monuments of the great Marchioness of Exeter, mother of Edward Courtney, Earl of Devonshire, and last of the family of Courtneys who enjoyed that honour; as also of John de Beaufort, Duke of Somerset, and his wife, grandmother of King Henry VII., by her daughter Margaret, Countess of Richmond.

This last lady I mention because she was foundress of a very fine free school, which has since been enlarged and had a new benefactress in Queen Elizabeth, who has enlarged the stipend and annexed it to the foundation. The famous Cardinal Pole was Dean of this church before his exaltation.

Having said this of the church, I have said all that is worth naming of the town; except that the inhabitants, who are many and poor, are chiefly maintained by the manufacture of knitting stockings, which employs great part indeed of the county of Dorset, of which this is the first town eastward.

South of this town, over a sandy, wild, and barren country, we came to Poole, a considerable seaport, and indeed the most considerable in all this part of England; for here I found some ships, some merchants, and some trade; especially, here were a good number of ships fitted out every year to the Newfoundland fishing, in which the Poole men were said to have been particularly successful for many years past.

The town sits in the bottom of a great bay or inlet of the sea, which, entering at one narrow mouth, opens to a very great breadth within the entrance, and comes up to the very shore of this town; it runs also west up almost to the town of Wareham, a little below which it receives the rivers Frome and Piddle, the two principal rivers of the county.

This place is famous for the best and biggest oysters in all this part of England, which the people of Poole pretend to be famous for pickling; and they are barrelled up here, and sent not only to London, but to the West Indies, and to Spain and Italy, and other parts. It is observed more pearls are found in the Poole oysters, and larger, than in any other oysters about England.

As the entrance into this large bay is narrow, so it is made narrower by an island, called Branksey, which, lying the very mouth of the passage, divides it into two, and where there is an old castle, called

Branksey Castle, built to defend the entrance, and this strength was very great advantage to the trade of this port in the time of the late war with France.

Wareham is a neat town and full of people, having a share of trade with Poole itself; it shows the ruins of a large town, and, it is apparent, has had eight churches, of which they have three remaining.

South of Wareham, and between the bay I have mentioned and the sea, lies a large tract of land which, being surrounded by the sea except on one side, is called an island, though it is really what should be called a peninsula. This tract of land is better inhabited than the sea-coast of this west end of Dorsetshire generally is, and the manufacture of stockings is carried on there also; it is called the Isle of Purbeck, and has in the middle of it a large market-town, called Corfe, and from the famous castle there the whole town is now called Corfe Castle; it is a corporation, sending members to Parliament.

This part of the country is eminent for vast quarries of stone, which is cut out flat, and used in London in great quantities for paving courtyards, alleys, avenues to houses, kitchens, footways on the sides of the High Streets, and the like; and is very profitable to the place, as also in the number of shipping employed in bringing it to London. There are also several rocks of very good marble, only that the veins in the stone are not black and white, as the Italian, but grey, red, and other colours.

From hence to Weymouth, which is 22 miles, we rode in view of the sea; the country is open, and in some respects pleasant, but not like the northern parts of the county, which are all fine carpet-ground, soft as velvet, and the herbage sweet as garden herbs, which makes their sheep be the best in England, if not in the world, and their wool fine to an extreme.

I cannot omit here a small adventure which was very surprising to me on this journey; passing this plain country, we came to an open piece of ground where a neighbouring gentleman had at a great expense laid out a proper piece of land for a decoy, or duck-coy, as some call it. The works were but newly done, the planting young, the ponds very large and well made; but the proper places for shelter of the fowl not covered, the trees not being grown, and men were still at work improving and enlarging and planting on the adjoining heath or common. Near the decoy-keeper's house were some places where young decoy ducks were hatched, or otherwise kept to fit them for their work. To preserve them from vermin (polecats, kites, and such like), they had set traps, as is usual in such cases, and a gibbet by it, where abundance of such creatures as were taken were hanged up for show.

While the decoy-man was busy showing the new works, he was alarmed with a great cry about this house for "Help! help!" and away he ran like the wind, guessing, as we supposed, that something was catched in the trap.

It was a good big boy, about thirteen or fourteen years old, that cried out, for coming to the place he found a great fowl caught by the leg in the trap, which yet was so strong and so outrageous that the boy going too near him, he flew at him and frighted him, bit him, and beat him with his wings, for he was too strong for the boy; as the master ran from the decoy, so another manservant ran from the house, and finding a strange creature fast in the trap, not knowing what it was, laid at him with a great stick. The creature fought him a good while, but at length he struck him an unlucky blow which quieted him; after this we all came up to see what the matter, and found a monstrous eagle caught by the leg in the trap, and killed by the fellow's cudgel, as above.

When the master came to know what it was, and that his man had killed it, he was ready to kill the fellow for his pains, for it was a noble creature indeed, and would have been worth a great deal to the man to have it shown about the country, or to have sold to any gentleman curious in such things; but the eagle was dead, and there we left it. It is probable this eagle had flown over the sea from France, either there or at the Isle of Wight, where the channel is not so wide; for we do not find that any eagles are known to breed in those parts of Britain.

From hence we turned up to Dorchester, the county town, though not the largest town in the county. Dorchester is indeed a pleasant agreeable town to live in, and where I thought the people seemed less divided into factions and parties than in other places; for though here are divisions, and the people are not all of one mind, either as to religion or politics, yet they did not seem to separate with so much animosity as in other places. Here I saw the Church of England clergyman, and the Dissenting minister or preacher drinking tea together, and conversing with civility and good neighbourhood, like Catholic Christians and men of a Catholic and extensive charity. The town is populous, though not large; the streets broad, but the buildings old and low. However, there is good company, and a good deal of it; and a man that coveted a retreat in this world might as agreeably spend his time and as well in Dorchester as in any town I know in England.

The downs round this town are exceeding pleasant, and come up on, every side, even to the very streets' end; and here it was that they told me that there were six hundred thousand sheep fed on the downs within six miles of the town—that is, six miles every way, which is twelve miles in diameter, and thirty-six miles in circumference. This, I say, I was told—I do not affirm it to be true; but when I viewed the country round, I confess I could not but incline to believe it.

It is observable of these sheep that they are exceeding fruitful, the ewes generally bringing two lambs, and they are for that reason bought by all the farmers through the east part of England, who come to Burford Fair in this country to buy them, and carry them into Kent and Surrey eastward, and into Buckinghamshire and Bedfordshire and Oxfordshire north; even our Banstead Downs in Surrey, so famed for good mutton, is supplied from this place. The grass or herbage of these downs is full of the sweetest and the most aromatic plants, such as nourish the sheep to a strange degree; and the sheep's dung, again, nourishes that herbage to a strange degree; so that the valleys are rendered extremely fruitful by the washing of the water in hasty showers from off these hills.

An eminent instance of this is seen at Amesbury, in Wiltshire, the next county to this; for it is the same thing in proportion over this whole county. I was told that at this town there was a meadow on the bank of the River Avon, which runs thence to Salisbury, which was let for £12 a year per acre for the grass only. This I inquired particularly after at the place, and was assured by the inhabitants, as one man, that the fact was true, and was showed the meadows. The grass which grew on them was such as grew to the length of ten or twelve feet, rising up to a good height and then taking root again, and was of so rich a nature as to answer very well such an extravagant rent.

The reason they gave for this was the extraordinary richness of the soil, made so, as above, by the falling or washing of the rains from the hills adjacent, by which, though no other land thereabouts had such a kind of grass, yet all other meadows and low grounds of the valley were extremely rich in proportion.

There are abundance of good families, and of very ancient lines in the neighbourhood of this town of Dorchester, as the Napiers, the Courtneys, Strangeways, Seymours, Banks, Tregonells, Sydenhams, and many others, some of which have very great estates in the county, and in particular Colonel Strangeways, Napier, and Courtney. The first of these is master of the famous swannery or nursery of swans, the like of which, I believe, is not in Europe. I wonder any man should pretend to travel over this country, and pass by it, too, and then write his account and take no notice of it.

From Dorchester it is six miles to the seaside south, and the ocean in view almost all the way. The first town you come to is Weymouth, or Weymouth and Melcombe, two towns lying at the mouth of a little rivulet which they call the Wey, but scarce claims the name of a river. However, the entrance makes a very good though small harbour, and they are joined by a wooden bridge; so that nothing but the harbour parts them; yet they are separate corporations, and choose each of them two members of Parliament, just as London and Southwark.

Weymouth is a sweet, clean, agreeable town, considering its low situation, and close to the sea; it is well built, and has a great many good substantial merchants in it who drive a considerable trade, and have a good number of ships belonging to the town. They carry on now, in time of peace, a trade with France; but, besides this, they trade also to Portugal, Spain, Newfoundland, and Virginia; and they have a large correspondence also up in the country for the consumption of their returns; especially the wine trade and the Newfoundland trade are considerable here.

Without the harbour is an old castle, called Sandfoot Castle; and over against them, where there is a good road for ships to put in on occasions of bad weather, is Portland Castle, and the road is called Portland Road. While I was here once, there came a merchant-ship into that road called Portland Road under a very hard storm of wind; she was homeward bound from Oporto for London, laden with wines; and as she came in she made signals of distress to the town, firing guns for help, and the like, as is usual in such cases; it was in the dark of the night that the ship came in, and, by the help of her own pilot, found her way into the road, where she came to an anchor, but, as I say, fired guns for help.

The venturous Weymouth men went off, even before it was light, with two boats to see who she was, and what condition she was in; and found she was come to an anchor, and had struck her topmasts; but that she had been in bad weather, had lost an anchor and cable before, and had but one cable to trust to, which did hold her, but was weak; and as the storm continued to blow, they expected every hour to go on shore and split to pieces.

Upon this the Weymouth boats came back with such diligence that in less than three hours they were on board them again with an

95

anchor and cable, which they immediately bent in its place, and let go to assist the other, and thereby secured the ship. It is true that they took a good price of the master for the help they gave him; for they made him draw a bill on his owners at London for £12 for the use of the anchor, cable, and boat, besides some gratuities to the men. But they saved the ship and cargo by it, and in three or four days the weather was calm, and he proceeded on his voyage, returning the anchor and cable again; so that, upon the whole, it was not so extravagant as at first I thought it to be.

The Isle of Portland, on which the castle I mentioned stands, lies right against this Port of Weymouth. Hence it is that our best and whitest freestone comes, with which the Cathedral of St. Paul's, the Monument, and all the public edifices in the City of London are chiefly built; and it is wonderful, and well worth the observation of a traveller, to see the quarries in the rocks from whence they are cut out, what stones, and of what prodigious a size are cut out there.

The island is indeed little more than one continued rock of freestone, and the height of the land is such that from this island they see in clear weather above half over the Channel to France, though the Channel here is very broad. The sea off of this island, and especially to the west of it, is counted the most dangerous part of the British Channel. Due south, there is almost a continued disturbance in the waters, by reason of what they call two tides meeting, which I take to be no more than the sets of the currents from the French coast and from the English shore meeting: this they call Portland Race; and several ships, not aware of these currents, have been embayed to the west of Portland, and been driven on shore on the beach (of which I shall speak presently), and there lost.

To prevent this danger, and guide the mariner in these distresses, they have within these few months set up two lighthouses on the two points of that island; and they had not been many months set up, with the directions given to the public for their bearings, but we found three outward-bound East India ships which were in distress in the night, in a hard extreme gale of wind, were so directed by those lights that they avoided going on shore by it, which, if the lights had not been there, would inevitably happened to their destruction.

This island, though seemingly miserable, and thinly inhabited, yet the inhabitants being almost all stone-cutters, we found there were no very poor people among them, and when they collected money for the re-building St. Paul's, they got more in this island than in the great town of Dorchester, as we were told.

Though Portland stands a league off from the mainland of Britain, yet it is almost joined by a prodigious riff of beach—that is to say, of small stones cast up by the sea—which runs from the island so near the shore of England that they ferry over with a boat and a rope, the water not being above half a stone's-throw over; and the said riff of beach ending, as it were, at that inlet of water, turns away west, and runs parallel with the shore quite to Abbotsbury, which is a town about seven miles beyond Weymouth.

I name this for two reasons: first, to explain again what I said before of ships being embayed and lost here. This is when ships coming from the westward omit to keep a good offing, or are taken short by contrary winds, and cannot weather the high land of Portland, but are driven between Portland and the mainland. If they can come to an anchor, and ride it out, well and good; and if not, they run on shore on that vast beach and are lost without remedy.

On the inside of this beach, and between it and the land, there is, as I have said, an inlet of water which they ferry over, as above, to pass and re-pass to and from Portland: this inlet opens at about two miles west, and grows very broad, and makes a kind of lake within the land of a mile and a half broad, and near three miles in length, the breadth unequal. At the farthest end west of this water is a large duck-coy, and the verge of the water well grown with wood, and proper groves of trees for cover for the fowl: in the open lake, or broad part, is a continual assembly of swans: here they live, feed, and breed, and the number of them is such that, I believe, I did not see so few as 7,000 or 8,000. Here they are protected, and here they breed in abundance. We saw several of them upon the wing, very high in the air, whence we supposed that they flew over the riff of beach, which parts the lake from the sea, to feed on the shores as they thought fit, and so came home again at their leisure.

From this duck-coy west, the lake narrows, and at last almost closes, till the beach joins the shore; and so Portland may be said, not to be an island, but part of the continent. And now we came to Abbotsbury, a town anciently famous for a great monastery, and now eminent for nothing but its ruins.

From hence we went on to Bridport, a pretty large corporation town on the sea-shore, though without a harbour. Here we saw boats all the way on the shore, fishing for mackerel, which they take in the easiest manner imaginable; for they fix one end of the net to a pole set deep into the sand, then, the net being in a boat, they row right out into the water some length, then turn and row parallel with the shore, veering out the net all the while, till they have let go all the net, except the line at the end, and then the boat rows on shore, when the men, hauling the net to the shore at both ends, bring to shore with it such fish as they surrounded in the little way they rowed. This, at that time, proved to be an incredible number, insomuch that the men could hardly draw them on shore. As soon as the boats had brought their fish on shore we observed a guard or watch placed on the shore in several places, who, we found, had their eye, not on the fishermen, but on the country people who came down to the shore to buy their fish; and very sharp we found they were, and some that came with small carts were obliged to go back empty without any fish. When we came to inquire into the particulars of this, we found that these were officers placed on the shore by the justices and magistrates of the towns about, who were ordered to prevent the country farmers buying the mackerel to dung their land with them, which was thought to be dangerous as to infection. In short, such was the plenty of fish that year that the mackerel, the finest and largest I ever saw, were sold at the seaside a hundred for a penny.

From Bridport (a town in which we see nothing remarkable) we came to Lyme, the town particularly made famous by the landing of the Duke of Monmouth and his unfortunate troops in the time of King James II., of which I need say nothing, the history of it being so recent in the memory of so many living.

This is a town of good figure, and has in it several eminent merchants who carry on a considerable trade to France, Spain, Newfoundland, and the Straits; and though they have neither creek or bay, road or river, they have a good harbour, but it is such a one as is not in all Britain besides, if there is such a one in any part of the world.

It is a massy pile of building, consisting of high and thick walls of stone, raised at first with all the methods that skill and art could devise, but maintained now with very little difficulty. The walls are raised in the main sea at a good distance from the shore; it consists of one main and solid wall of stone, large enough for carts and carriages to pass on the top, and to admit houses and warehouses to be built on it, so that it is broad as a street. Opposite to this, but farther into the sea, is another wall of the same workmanship, which crosses the end of the first wall and comes about with a tail parallel to the first wall.

Between the point of the first or main wall is the entrance into the port, and the second or opposite wall, breaking the violence of the sea from the entrance, the ships go into the basin as into a pier or harbour, and ride there as secure as in a millpond or as in a wet dock.

The townspeople have the benefit of this wonderful harbour, and it is carefully kept in repair, as indeed it behoves them to do; but they could give me nothing of the history of it, nor do they, as I could perceive, know anything of the original of it, or who built it. It was lately almost beaten down by a storm, but is repaired again.

This work is called the Cobb. The Custom House officers have a lodge and warehouse upon it, and there were several ships of very good force and rich in value in the basin of it when I was there. It might be strengthened with a fort, and the walls themselves are firm enough to carry what guns they please to plant upon it; but they did not seem to think it needful, and as the shore is convenient for batteries, they have some guns planted in proper places, both for the defence of the Cobb and the town also.

This town is under the government of a mayor and aldermen, and may pass for a place of wealth, considering the bigness of it. Here, we found, the merchants began to trade in the pilchard-fishing, though not to so considerable a degree as they do farther west—the pilchards seldom coming up so high eastward as Portland, and not very often so high as Lyme.

It was in sight of these hills that Queen Elizabeth's fleet, under the command of the Lord Howard of Effingham (then Admiral), began first to engage in a close and resolved fight with the invincible Spanish Armada in 1588, maintaining the fight, the Spaniards making eastward till they came the length of Portland Race, where they gave it over—the Spaniards having received considerable damage, and keeping then closer together. Off of the same place was a desperate engagement in the year 1672 between the English and Dutch, in which the Dutch were worsted and driven over to the coast of France, and then glad to make home to refit and repair.

While we stayed here some time viewing this town and coast, we had opportunity to observe the pleasant way of conversation as it is managed among the gentlemen of this county and their families, which are, without reflection, some of the most polite and well-bred people in the isle of Britain. As their hospitality is very great, and their bounty to the poor remarkable, so their generous friendly way of living with, visiting, and associating one with another is as hard to be described as it is really to be admired; they seem to have a mutual confidence in and friendship with one another, as if they were all relations; nor did I observe the sharping, tricking temper which is too much crept in among the gaming and horse-racing gentry in some parts of England to be so much known among them any otherwise than to be abhorred; and yet they sometimes play, too, and make matches and horse-races, as they see occasion.

The ladies here do not want the help of assemblies to assist in matchmaking, or half-pay officers to run away with their daughters, which the meetings called assemblies in some other parts of England are recommended for. Here is no Bury Fair, where the women are scandalously said to carry themselves to market, and where every night they meet at the play or at the assembly for intrigue; and yet I observed that the women do not seem to stick on hand so much in this country as in those countries where those assemblies are so lately set up—the reason of which, I cannot help saying, if my opinion may bear any weight, is that the Dorsetshire ladies are equal in beauty, and may be superior in reputation. In a word, their reputation seems here to be better kept, guarded by better conduct, and managed with more prudence; and yet the Dorsetshire ladies, I assure you, are not nuns; they do not go veiled about streets, or hide themselves when visited; but a general freedom of conversation—agreeable, mannerly, kind, and good—runs through the whole body of the gentry of both sexes, mixed with the best of behaviour, and yet governed by prudence and modesty such as I nowhere see better in all my observation through the whole isle of Britain. In this little interval also I visited some of the biggest towns in the north-west part of this county, as Blandford—a town on the River Stour in the road between Salisbury and Dorchester—a handsome well-built town, but chiefly famous for making the finest bone-lace in England, and where they showed me some so exquisitely fine as I think I never saw better in Flanders, France, or Italy, and which they said they rated at above £30 sterling a yard; but I suppose there was not much of this to be had. But it is most certain that they make exceeding rich lace in that county, such as no part of England can equal.

From thence I went west to Stourbridge, vulgarly called Strabridge. The town and the country around is employed in the manufacture of stockings, and which was once famous for making the finest, best, and highest-prize knit stocking in England; but that trade now is much decayed by the increase of the knitting-stocking engine or frame, which has destroyed the hand-knitting trade for fine stockings through the whole kingdom, of which I shall speak more in its place.

From hence I came to Sherborne, a large and populous town, with one collegiate or conventual church, and may properly claim to have more inhabitants in it than any town in Dorsetshire, though it is neither the county-town, nor does it send members to Parliament. The church is still a reverend pile, and shows the face of great antiquity. Here begins the Wiltshire medley clothing (though this town be in Dorsetshire), of which I shall speak at large in its place, and therefore I omit any discourse of it here.

Shaftesbury is also on the edge of this county, adjoining to Wiltshire and Dorsetshire, being fourteen miles from Salisbury, over that fine down or carpet ground which they call particularly or properly Salisbury Plain. It has neither house nor town in view all the way; and the road, which often lies very broad and branches off insensibly, might easily cause a traveller to lose his way. But there is a certain never-failing assistance upon all these downs for telling a stranger his way, and that is the number of shepherds feeding or keeping their vast flocks of sheep which are everywhere in the way, and who with a very little pains a traveller may always speak with. Nothing can be like it. The Arcadians' plains, of which we read so much pastoral trumpery in the poets, could be nothing to them.

This Shaftesbury is now a sorry town upon the top of a high hill, which closes the plain or downs, and whence Nature presents you a new scene or prospect—viz., of Somerset and Wiltshire—where it is all enclosed, and grown with woods, forests, and planted hedge-rows; the country rich, fertile, and populous; the towns and houses standing thick and being large and full of inhabitants, and those inhabitants fully employed in the richest and most valuable manufacture in the world—viz., the English clothing, as well the medley or mixed clothing as whites, as well for the home trade as the foreign trade, of which I shall take leave to be very particular in my return through the west and north part of Wiltshire in the latter part of this work.

In my return to my western progress, I passed some little part of Somersetshire, as through Evil or Yeovil, upon the River Ivil, in going to which we go down a long steep hill, which they call Babylon Hill, but from what original I could find none of the country people to inform me.

This Yeovil is a market-town of good resort; and some clothing is carried on in and near it, but not much. Its main manufacture at this time is making of gloves.

It cannot pass my observation here that when we are come this length from London the dialect of the English tongue, or the country way of expressing themselves, is not easily understood—it is so strangely altered. It is true that it is so in many parts of England besides, but in none in so gross a degree as in this part. This way of boorish country speech, as in Ireland it is called the "brogue" upon the tongue, so here it is called "jouring;" and it is certain that though the tongue be all mere natural English, yet those that are but a little acquainted with them cannot understand one-half of what they say. It is not possible to explain this fully by writing, because the difference is not so much in the orthography of words as in the tone and diction— their abridging the speech, "cham" for "I am," "chil" for "I will," "don" for "put on," and "doff" for "put off," and the like. And I cannot omit a short story here on this subject. Coming to a relation's house, who was a school-master at Martock, in Somersetshire, I went into his school to beg the boys a play-day, as is usual in such cases (I should have said, to beg the master a play-day. But that by the way). Coming into the school, I observed one of the lowest scholars was reading his lesson to the usher, which lesson, it seems, was a chapter in the Bible. So I sat down by the master till the boy had read out his chapter. I observed the boy read a little oddly in the tone of the country, which made me the more attentive, because on inquiry I found that the words were the same and the orthography the same as in all our Bibles. I observed also the boy read it out with his eyes still on the book and his head (like a mere boy) moving from side to side as the lines reached cross the columns of the book. His lesson was in the Canticles, v. 3 of chap. v. The words these:—"I have put off my coat. How shall I put it on? I have washed my feet. How shall I defile them?"

The boy read thus, with his eyes, as I say, full on the text:—"Chav a doffed my cooat. How shall I don't? Chav a washed my veet. How shall I moil 'em?"

How the dexterous dunce could form his month to express so readily the words (which stood right printed in the book) in his country jargon, I could not but admire. I shall add to this another piece as diverting, which also happened in my knowledge at this very town of Yeovil, though some years ago.

There lived a good substantial family in the town not far from the "Angel Inn"—a well-known house, which was then, and, I suppose, is still, the chief inn of the town. This family had a dog which, among his other good qualities for which they kept him (for he was a rare house-dog), had this bad one—that he was a most notorious thief, but withal so cunning a dog, and managed himself so warily, that he preserved a mighty good reputation among the neighbourhood. As the family was well beloved in the town, so was the dog. He was known to be a very useful servant to them, especially in the night (when he was fierce as a lion; but in the day the gentlest, lovingest creature that could be), and, as they said, all the neighbours had a good word for this dog.

It happened that the good wife or mistress at the "Angel Inn" had frequently missed several pieces of meat out of the pail, as they say—or powdering-tub, as we call it—and that some were very large pieces. It is also to be observed the dog did not stay to eat what he took upon the spot, in which case some pieces or bones or fragments might be left, and so it might be discovered to be a dog; but he made cleaner work, and when he fastened upon a piece of meat he was sure to carry it quite away to such retreats as he knew he could be safe in, and so feast upon it at leisure.

It happened at last, as with most thieves it does, that the inn-keeper was too cunning for him, and the poor dog was nabbed, taken in the fact, and could make no defence.

Having found the thief and got him in custody, the master of the house, a good-humoured fellow, and loth to disoblige the dog's master by executing the criminal, as the dog law directs, mitigates his sentence, and handled him as follows:—First, taking out his knife, he cut off both his ears; and then, bringing him to the threshold, he chopped off his tail. And having thus effectually dishonoured the poor cur among his neighbours, he tied a string about his neck, and a piece of paper to the string, directed to his master, and with these witty West Country verses on it:—

"To my honoured master, --- Esq.
"Hail master a cham a' com hoam,
So cut as an ape, and tail have I noan,
For stealing of beef and pork out of the pail,
For thease they'v cut my ears, for th' wother my tail;
Nea measter, and us tell thee more nor that
And's come there again, my brains will be flat."

103

I could give many more accounts of the different dialects of the people of this country, in some of which they are really not to be understood; but the particulars have little or no diversion in them. They carry it such a length that we see their "jouring" speech even upon their monuments and grave-stones; as, for example, even in some of the churchyards of the city of Bristol I saw this excellent poetry after some other lines:—

"And when that thou doest hear of thick,
Think of the glass that runneth quick."

But I proceed into Devonshire. From Yeovil we came to Crookorn, thence to Chard, and from thence into the same road I was in before at Honiton.

This is a large and beautiful market-town, very populous and well built, and is so very remarkably paved with small pebbles that on either side the way a little channel is left shouldered up on the sides of it, so that it holds a small stream of fine clear running water, with a little square dipping-place left at every door; so that every family in the town has a clear, clean running river (as it may be called) just at their own door, and this so much finer, so much pleasanter, and agreeable to look on than that at Salisbury (which they boast so much of), that, in my opinion, there is no comparison.

Here we see the first of the great serge manufacture of Devonshire—a trade too great to be described in miniature, as it must be if I undertake it here, and which takes up this whole county, which is the largest and most populous in England, Yorkshire excepted (which ought to be esteemed three counties, and is, indeed, divided as such into the East, West, and North Riding). But Devonshire, one entire county, is so full of great towns, and those towns so full of people, and those people so universally employed in trade and manufactures, that not only it cannot be equalled in England, but perhaps not in Europe.

In my travel through Dorsetshire I ought to have observed that the biggest towns in that county sent no members to Parliament, and that the smallest did—that is to say that Sherborne, Blandford, Wimborneminster, Stourminster, and several other towns choose no members; whereas Weymouth, Melcombe, and Bridport were all burgess towns. But now we come to Devonshire we find almost all the great towns, and some smaller, choosing members also. It is true there are some large populous towns that do not choose, but then there are so many that do, that the county seems to have no injustice, for they send up six-and-twenty members.

However, as I say above, there are several great towns which do not choose Parliament men, of which Bideford is one, Crediton or Kirton another, Ilfracombe a third; but, those excepted, the principal towns in the county do all choose members of Parliament.

Honiton is one of those, and may pass not only for a pleasant good town, as before, but stands in the best and pleasantest part of the whole county, and I cannot but recommend it to any gentlemen that travel this road, that if they please to observe the prospect for half a mile till their coming down the hill and to the entrance into Honiton, the view of the country is the most beautiful landscape in the world—a mere picture—and I do not remember the like in any one place in England. It is observable that the market of this town was kept originally on the Sunday, till it was changed by the direction of King John.

From Honiton the country is exceeding pleasant still, and on the road they have a beautiful prospect almost all the way to Exeter (which is twelve miles). On the left-hand of this road lies that part of the county which they call the South Hams, and which is famous for the best cider in that part of England; also the town of St.-Mary-Ottery, commonly called St. Mary Autree. They tell us the name is derived from the River Ottery, and that from the multitude of otters found always in that river, which however, to me, seems fabulous. Nor does there appear to be any such great number of otters in that water, or in the county about, more than is usual in other counties or in other parts of the county about them. They tell us they send twenty thousand hogsheads of cider hence every year to London, and (which is still worse) that it is most of it bought there by the merchants to mix with their wines—which, if true, is not much to the reputation of the London vintners. But that by-the-bye.

From hence we came to Exeter, a city famous for two things which we seldom find unite in the same town—viz., that it is full of gentry and good company, and yet full of trade and manufactures also. The serge market held here every week is very well worth a stranger's seeing, and next to the Brigg Market at Leeds, in Yorkshire, is the greatest in England. The people assured me that at this market is generally sold from sixty to seventy to eighty, and sometimes a hundred, thousand pounds value in serges in a week. I think it is kept on Mondays.

They have the River Esk here, a very considerable river, and principal in the whole county; and within three miles, or thereabouts, it receives ships of any ordinary burthen, the port there being called

Topsham. But now by the application, and at the expense, of the citizens the channel of the river is so widened, deepened, and cleansed from the shoal, which would otherwise interrupt the navigation, that the ships come now quite up to the city, and there with ease both deliver and take in their lading.

This city drives a very great correspondence with Holland, as also directly to Portugal, Spain, and Italy—shipping off vast quantities of their woollen manufactures especially to Holland, the Dutch giving very large commissions here for the buying of serges perpetuans, and such goods; which are made not only in and about Exeter, but at Crediton, Honiton, Culliton, St.-Mary-Ottery, Newton Bushel, Ashburton, and especially at Tiverton, Cullompton, Bampton, and all the north-east part of the county—which part of the county is, as it may be said, fully employed, the people made rich, and the poor that are properly so called well subsisted and employed by it.

Exeter is a large, rich, beautiful, populous, and was once a very strong city; but as to the last, as the castle, the walls, and all the old works are demolished, so, were they standing, the way of managing sieges and attacks of towns is such now, and so altered from what it was in those days, that Exeter in the utmost strength it could ever boast would not now hold out five days open trenches—nay, would hardly put an army to the trouble of opening trenches against it at all. This city was famous in the late civil unnatural war for its loyalty to the king, and for being a sanctuary to the queen, where her Majesty resided for some time, and here she was delivered of a daughter, being the Princess Henrietta Maria, of whom our histories give a particular account, so I need say no more of it here.

The cathedral church of this city is an ancient beauty, or, as it may be said, it is beautiful for its antiquity; but it has been so fully and often described that it would look like a mere copying from others to mention it. There is a good library kept in it, in which are some manuscripts, and particularly an old missal or mass-book, the leaves of vellum, and famous for its most exquisite writing.

This county, and this part of it in particular, has been famous for the birth of several eminent men as well for learning as for arts and for war, as particularly:—

I. Sir William Petre, who the learned Dr. Wake (now Archbishop of Canterbury, and author of the Additions to Mr. Camden) says was Secretary of State and Privy Councillor to King

Henry VIII., Edward VI., Queen Mary, and Queen Elizabeth, and seven times sent ambassador into foreign countries.

2. Sir Thomas Bodley, famous and of grateful memory to all learned men and lovers of letters for his collecting and establishing the best library in Britain, which is now at Oxford, and is called, after his name, the Bodleian Library to this day.

3. Also Sir Francis Drake, born at Plymouth.

4. Sir Walter Raleigh. Of both those I need say nothing; fame publishes their merit upon every mention of their names.

5. That great patron of learning, Richard Hooker, author of the "Ecclesiastical Polity," and of several other valuable pieces.

6. Of Dr. Arthur Duck, a famed civilian, and well known by his works among the learned advocates of Doctors' Commons.

7. Dr. John Moreman, of Southold, famous for being the first clergyman in England who ventured to teach his parishioners the Lord's Prayer, Creed, and Ten Commandments in the English tongue, and reading them so publicly in the parish church of Mayenhennet in this county, of which he was vicar.

8. Dr. John de Brampton, a man of great learning who flourished in the reign of Henry VI., was famous for being the first that read Aristotle publicly in the University of Cambridge, and for several learned books of his writing, which are now lost.

9. Peter Blundel, a clothier, who built the free school at Tiverton, and endowed it very handsomely; of which in its place.

10. Sir John Glanvill, a noted lawyer, and one of the Judges of the Common Pleas.

11. Sergeant Glanvill, his son; as great a lawyer as his father.

12. Sir John Maynard, an eminent lawyer of later years; one of the Commissioners of the Great Seal under King William III. All these three were born at Tavistock.

13. Sir Peter King, the present Lord Chief Justice of the Common Pleas. And many others.

I shall take the north part of this county in my return from Cornwall; so I must now lean to the south—that is to say, to the South Coast—for in going on indeed we go south-west.

About twenty-two miles from Exeter we go to Totnes, on the River Dart. This is a very good town, of some trade; but has more gentlemen in it than tradesmen of note. They have a very fine stone bridge here over the river, which, being within seven or eight miles of the sea, is very large; and the tide flows ten or twelve feet at the bridge.

Here we had the diversion of seeing them catch fish with the assistance of a dog. The case is this:—On the south side of the river, and on a slip, or narrow cut or channel made on purpose for a mill, there stands a corn-mill; the mill-tail, or floor for the water below the wheels, is wharfed up on either side with stone above high-water mark, and for above twenty or thirty feet in length below it on that part of the river towards the sea; at the end of this wharfing is a grating of wood, the cross-bars of which stand bearing inward, sharp at the end, and pointing inward towards one another, as the wires of a mouse-trap.

When the tide flows up, the fish can with ease go in between the points of these cross-bars, but the mill being shut down they can go no farther upwards; and when the water ebbs again, they are left behind, not being able to pass the points of the grating, as above, outwards; which, like a mouse-trap, keeps them in, so that they are left at the bottom with about a foot or a foot and a half of water. We were carried hither at low water, where we saw about fifty or sixty small salmon, about seventeen to twenty inches long, which the country people call salmon-peal; and to catch these the person who went with us, who was our landlord at a great inn next the bridge, put in a net on a hoop at the end of a pole, the pole going cross the hoop (which we call in this country a shove-net). The net being fixed at one end of the place, they put in a dog (who was taught his trade beforehand) at the other end of the place, and he drives all the fish into the net; so that, only holding the net still in its place, the man took up two or three and thirty salmon-peal at the first time.

Of these we took six for our dinner, for which they asked a shilling (viz., twopence a-piece); and for such fish, not at all bigger, and not so fresh, I have seen six-and-sixpence each given at a London fish-market, whither they are sometimes brought from Chichester by land carriage.

This excessive plenty of so good fish (and other provisions being likewise very cheap in proportion) makes the town of Totnes a very good place to live in; especially for such as have large families and but small estates. And many such are said to come into those parts on purpose for saving money, and to live in proportion to their income.

From hence we went still south about seven miles (all in view of this river) to Dartmouth, a town of note, seated at the mouth of the River Dart, and where it enters into the sea at a very narrow but safe entrance. The opening into Dartmouth Harbour is not broad, but the channel deep enough for the biggest ship in the Royal Navy. The sides of the entrance are high-mounded with rocks, without which, just at the first narrowing of the passage, stands a good strong fort without a platform of guns, which commands the port.

The narrow entrance is not much above half a mile, when it opens and makes a basin or harbour able to receive 500 sail of ships of any size, and where they may ride with the greatest safety, even as in a mill-pond or wet dock. I had the curiosity here, with the assistance of a merchant of the town, to go out to the mouth of the haven in a boat to see the entrance, and castle or fort that commands it; and coming back with the tide of flood, I observed some small fish to skip and play upon the surface of the water, upon which I asked my friend what fish they were. Immediately one of the rowers or seamen starts up in the boat, and, throwing his arms abroad as if he had been bewitched, cries out as loud as he could bawl, "A school! a school!" The word was taken to the shore as hastily as it would have been on land if he had cried "Fire!" And by that time we reached the quays the town was all in a kind of an uproar.

The matter was that a great shoal—or, as they call it, a "school"—of pilchards came swimming with the tide of flood, directly out of the sea into the harbour. My friend whose boat we were in told me this was a surprise which he would have been very glad of if he could but have had a day or two's warning, for he might have taken 200 tons of them. And the like was the case of other merchants in town; for, in short, nobody was ready for them, except a small fishing-boat or two—one of which went out into the middle of the harbour, and at two or three hauls took about forty thousand of them. We sent our servant to the quay to buy some, who for a halfpenny brought us seventeen, and, if he would have taken them, might have had as many more for the same money. With these we went to dinner; the cook at the inn broiled them for us, which is their way of dressing them, with pepper and salt, which cost us about a farthing; so that two of us and a servant dined—and at a tavern, too—for three farthings, dressing and all. And this is the reason of telling the tale. What drink—wine or beer—we had I do not remember; but, whatever it was, that we paid for by itself. But for our food we really dined for three farthings, and very well, too. Our friend treated us the next day with a dish of large lobsters, and I being curious to know the value of such things, and having freedom enough with him to inquire, I found that for 6d. or 8d. they bought as good lobsters there as would have cost in London 3s. to 3s. 6d. each.

In observing the coming in of those pilchards, as above, we found that out at sea, in the offing, beyond the mouth of the harbour, there was a whole army of porpoises, which, as they told us, pursued the pilchards, and, it is probable, drove them into the harbour, as above. The school, it seems, drove up the river a great way, even as high as Totnes Bridge, as we heard afterwards; so that the country people who had boats and nets catched as many as they knew what to do with, and perhaps lived upon pilchards for several days. But as to the merchants and trade, their coming was so sudden that it was no advantage to them.

Round the west side of this basin or harbour, in a kind of a semicircle, lies the town of Dartmouth, a very large and populous town, though but meanly built, and standing on the side of a steep hill; yet the quay is large, and the street before it spacious. Here are some very flourishing merchants, who trade very prosperously, and to the most considerable trading ports of Spain, Portugal, Italy, and the Plantations; but especially they are great traders to Newfoundland, and from thence to Spain and Italy, with fish; and they drive a good trade also in their own fishery of pilchards, which is hereabouts carried on with the greatest number of vessels of any port in the west, except Falmouth.

A little to the southward of this town, and to the east of the port, is Tor Bay, of which I know nothing proper to my observation, more than that it is a very good road for ships, though sometimes (especially with a southerly or south-east wind) ships have been obliged to quit the bay and put out to sea, or run into Dartmouth for shelter.

I suppose I need not mention that they had from the hilly part of this town, and especially from the hills opposite to it, the noble prospect, and at that time particularly delightful, of the Prince of Orange's fleet when he came to that coast, and as they entered into Tor Bay to land—the Prince and his army being in a fleet of about 600 sail of transport ships, besides 50 sail of men-of-war of the line, all which, with a fair wind and fine weather, came to an anchor there at once.

This town, as most of the towns of Devonshire are, is full of Dissenters, and a very large meeting-house they have here. How they act here with respect to the great dispute about the doctrine of the Trinity, which has caused such a breach among those people at Exeter and other parts of the county, I cannot give any account of. This town sends two members to Parliament.

From hence we went to Plympton, a poor and thinly-inhabited town, though blessed with the like privilege of sending members to the

Parliament, of which I have little more to say but that from thence the road lies to Plymouth, distance about six miles.

Plymouth is indeed a town of consideration, and of great importance to the public. The situation of it between two very large inlets of the sea, and in the bottom of a large bay, which is very remarkable for the advantage of navigation. The Sound or Bay is compassed on every side with hills, and the shore generally steep and rocky, though the anchorage is good, and it is pretty safe riding. In the entrance to this bay lies a large and most dangerous rock, which at high-water is covered, but at low-tide lies bare, where many a good ship has been lost, even in the view of safety, and many a ship's crew drowned in the night, before help could be had for them.

Upon this rock (which was called the Eddystone, from its situation) the famous Mr. Winstanley undertook to build a lighthouse for the direction of sailors, and with great art and expedition finished it; which work—considering its height, the magnitude of its building, and the little hold there was by which it was possible to fasten it to the rock—stood to admiration, and bore out many a bitter storm.

Mr. Winstanley often visited, and frequently strengthened, the building by new works, and was so confident of its firmness and stability that he usually said he only desired to be in it when a storm should happen; for many people had told him it would certainly fall if it came to blow a little harder than ordinary.

But he happened at last to be in it once too often—namely, when that dreadful tempest blew, November 27, 1703. This tempest began on the Wednesday before, and blew with such violence, and shook the lighthouse so much, that, as they told me there, Mr. Winstanley would fain have been on shore, and made signals for help; but no boats durst go off to him; and, to finish the tragedy, on the Friday, November 26, when the tempest was so redoubled that it became a terror to the whole nation, the first sight there seaward that the people of Plymouth were presented with in the morning after the storm was the bare Eddystone, the lighthouse being gone; in which Mr. Winstanley and all that were with him perished, and were never seen or heard of since. But that which was a worse loss still was that, a few days after, a merchant's ship called the *Winchelsea*, homeward bound from Virginia, not knowing the Eddystone lighthouse was down, for want of the light that should have been seen, run foul of the rock itself, and was lost with all her lading and most of her men. But there is now another light-house built on the same rock.

What other disasters happened at the same time in the Sound and in the roads about Plymouth is not my business; they are also published in other books, to which I refer.

One thing which I was a witness to on a former journey to this place, I cannot omit. It was the next year after that great storm, and but a little sooner in the year, being in August; I was at Plymouth, and walking on the Hoo (which is a plain on the edge of the sea, looking to the road), I observed the evening so serene, so calm, so bright, and the sea so smooth, that a finer sight, I think, I never saw. There was very little wind, but what was, seemed to be westerly; and about an hour after, it blew a little breeze at south-west, with which wind there came into the Sound that night and the next morning a fleet of fourteen sail of ships from Barbadoes, richly laden for London. Having been long at sea, most of the captains and passengers came on shore to refresh themselves, as is usual after such tedious voyages; and the ships rode all in the Sound on that side next to Catwater. As is customary upon safe arriving to their native country, there was a general joy and rejoicing both on board and on shore.

The next day the wind began to freshen, especially in the afternoon, and the sea to be disturbed, and very hard it blew at night; but all was well for that time. But the night after, it blew a dreadful storm (not much inferior, for the time it lasted, to the storm mentioned above which blew down the lighthouse on the Eddystone). About midnight the noise, indeed, was very dreadful, what with the rearing of the sea and of the wind, intermixed with the firing of guns for help from the ships, the cries of the seamen and people on shore, and (which was worse) the cries of those which were driven on shore by the tempest and dashed in pieces. In a word, all the fleet except three, or thereabouts, were dashed to pieces against the rocks and sunk in the sea, most of the men being drowned. Those three who were saved, received so much damage that their lading was almost all spoiled. One ship in the dark of the night, the men not knowing where they were, run into Catwater, and run on shore there; by which she was, however, saved from shipwreck, and the lives of her crew were saved also.

This was a melancholy morning indeed. Nothing was to be seen but wrecks of the ships and a foaming, furious sea in that very place where they rode all in joy and triumph but the evening before. The captains, passengers, and officers who were, as I have said, gone on shore, between the joy of saving their lives, and the affliction of having lost their ships, their cargoes, and their friends, were objects indeed worth our compassion and observation. And there was a great variety of the passions to be observed in them—now lamenting their losses, their giving thanks for their deliverance. Many of the passengers had lost their all, and were, as they expressed themselves, "utterly undone." They were, I say, now lamenting their losses with violent excesses of grief; then giving thanks for their lives, and that they should be brought on shore, as it were, on purpose to be saved from death; then again in tears for such as were drowned. The various cases were indeed very affecting, and, in many things, very instructing.

As I say, Plymouth lies in the bottom of this Sound, in the centre between the two waters, so there lies against it, in the same position, an island, which they call St. Nicholas, on which there is a castle which commands the entrance into Hamoaze, and indeed that also into Catwater in some degree. In this island the famous General Lambert, one of Cromwell's great agents or officers in the rebellion, was imprisoned for life, and lived many years there.

On the shore over against this island is the citadel of Plymouth, a small but regular fortification, inaccessible by sea, but not exceeding strong by land, except that they say the works are of a stone hard as marble, and would not seen yield to the batteries of an enemy—but that is a language our modern engineers now laugh at.

The town stands above this, upon the same rock, and lies sloping on the side of it, towards the east—the inlet of the sea which is called Catwater, and which is a harbour capable of receiving any number of ships and of any size, washing the eastern shore of the town, where they have a kind of natural mole or haven, with a quay and all other conveniences for bringing in vessels for loading and unloading; nor is the trade carried on here inconsiderable in itself, or the number of merchants small.

The other inlet of the sea, as I term it, is on the other side of the town, and is called Hamoaze, being the mouth of the River Tamar, a considerable river which parts the two counties of Devon and Cornwall. Here (the war with France making it necessary that the ships of war should have a retreat nearer hand than at Portsmouth) the late King William ordered a wet dock—with yards, dry docks, launches, and conveniences of all kinds for building and repairing of ships—to be built; and with these followed necessarily the building of store-houses and warehouses for the rigging, sails, naval and military stores, &c., of such ships as may be appointed to be laid up there, as now several are; with very handsome houses for the commissioners, clerks, and officers of all kinds usual in the king's yards, to dwell in. It is, in short, now become as complete an arsenal or yard for building and fitting men-of-war as any the Government are masters of, and perhaps much more convenient than some of them, though not so large.

The building of these things, with the addition of rope-walks and mast-yards, &c., as it brought abundance of trades-people and workmen to the place, so they began by little and little to build houses on the lands adjacent, till at length there appeared a very handsome street, spacious and large, and as well inhabited; and so many houses are since added that it is become a considerable town, and must of consequence in time draw abundance of people from Plymouth itself.

However, the town of Plymouth is, and will always be, a very considerable town, while that excellent harbour makes it such a general port for the receiving all the fleets of merchants' ships from the southward (as from Spain, Italy, the West Indies, &c.), who generally make it the first port to put in at for refreshment, or safety from either weather or enemies.

The town is populous and wealthy, having, as above, several considerable merchants and abundance of wealthy shopkeepers, whose trade depends upon supplying the sea-faring people that upon so many occasions put into that port. As for gentlemen—I mean, those that are such by family and birth and way of living—it cannot be expected to find many such in a town merely depending on trade, shipping, and sea-faring business; yet I found here some men of value (persons of liberal education, general knowledge, and excellent behaviour), whose society obliges me to say that a gentleman might find very agreeable company in Plymouth.

From Plymouth we pass the Tamar over a ferry to Saltash—a little, poor, shattered town, the first we set foot on in the county of Cornwall. The Tamar here is very wide, and the ferry-boats bad; so that I thought myself well escaped when I got safe on shore in Cornwall.

Saltash seems to be the ruins of a larger place; and we saw many houses, as it were, falling down, and I doubt not but the mice and rats have abandoned many more, as they say they will when they are likely to fall. Yet this town is governed by a mayor and aldermen, has many privileges, sends members to Parliament, takes toll of all vessels that pass the river, and have the sole oyster-fishing in the whole river, which is considerable. Mr. Carew, author of the "Survey of Cornwall," tells us a strange story of a dog in this town, of whom it was observed that if they gave him any large bone or piece of meat, he immediately went out of doors with it, and after having disappeared for some time would return again; upon which, after some time, they watched him, when, to their great surprise, they found that the poor charitable creature carried what he so got to an old decrepit mastiff, which lay in a nest that he had made among the brakes a little way out of the town, and was blind, so that he could not help himself; and there this creature fed him. He adds also that on Sundays or holidays, when he found they made good cheer in the house where he lived, he would go out and bring this old blind dog to the door, and feed him there till he had enough, and then go with him back to his habitation in the country again, and see him safe in. If this story is true, it is very remarkable indeed; and I thought it worth telling, because the author was a person who, they say, might be credited.

This town has a kind of jurisdiction upon the River Tamar down to the mouth of the port, so that they claim anchorage of all small ships that enter the river; their coroner sits upon all dead bodies that are found drowned in the river and the like, but they make not much profit of them. There is a good market here, and that is the best thing to be said of the town; it is also very much increased since the number of the inhabitants are increased at the new town, as I mentioned as near the dock at the mouth of Hamoaze, for those people choose rather to go to Saltash to market by water than to walk to Plymouth by land for their provisions. Because, first, as they go in the town boat, the same boat brings home what they buy, so that it is much less trouble; second, because provisions are bought much cheaper at Saltash than at Plymouth. This, I say, is like to be a very great advantage to the town of Saltash, and may in time put a new face of wealth upon the place.

They talk of some merchants beginning to trade here, and they have some ships that use the Newfoundland fishery; but I could not hear of anything considerable they do in it. There is no other considerable town up the Tamar till we come to Launceston, the county town, which I shall take in my return; so I turned west, keeping the south shore of the county to the Land's End.

From Saltash I went to Liskeard, about seven miles. This is a considerable town, well built; has people of fashion in it, and a very great market; it also sends two members to Parliament, and is one of the five towns called Stannary Towns—that is to say, where the blocks of tin are brought to the coinage; of which, by itself, this coinage of tin is an article very much to the advantage of the towns where it is settled, though the money paid goes another way.

This town of Liskeard was once eminent, had a good castle, and a large house, where the ancient Dukes of Cornwall kept their court in those days; also it enjoyed several privileges, especially by the favour of the Black Prince, who as Prince of Wales and Duke of Cornwall resided here. And in return they say this town and the country round it raised a great body of stout young fellows, who entered into his service and followed his fortunes in his wars in France, as also in Spain. But these buildings are so decayed that there are now scarce any of the ruins of the castle or of the prince's court remaining.

The only public edifices they have now to show are the guild or town hall, on which there is a turret with a fine clock; a very good free school, well provided; a very fine conduit in the market-place; an ancient large church; and, which is something rare for the county of Cornwall, a large, new-built meeting-house for the Dissenters, which I name because they assured me there was but three more, and those very inconsiderable, in all the county of Cornwall; whereas in Devonshire, which is the next county, there are reckoned about seventy, some of which are exceeding large and fine.

This town is also remarkable for a very great trade in all manufactures of leather, such as boots, shoes, gloves, purses, breaches, &c.; and some spinning of late years is set up here, encouraged by the woollen manufacturers of Devonshire.

Between these two towns of Saltash and Liskeard is St. Germans, now a village, decayed, and without any market, but the largest parish in the whole county—in the bounds of which is contained, as they report, seventeen villages, and the town of Saltash among them; for Saltash has no parish church, it seems, of itself, but as a chapel-of-ease to St. Germans. In the neighbourhood of these towns are many pleasant seats of the Cornish gentry, who are indeed very numerous, though their estates may not be so large as is usual in England; yet neither are they despicable in that part; and in particular this may be said of them—that as they generally live cheap, and are more at home than in other counties, so they live more like gentlemen, and keep more within bounds of their estates than the English generally do, take them all together.

Add to this that they are the most sociable, generous, and to one another the kindest, neighbours that are to be found; and as they generally live, as we may say, together (for they are almost always at one another's houses), so they generally intermarry among themselves, the gentlemen seldom going out of the county for a wife, or the ladies for a husband; from whence they say that proverb upon them was raised, viz., "That all the Cornish gentlemen are cousins."

On the hills north of Liskeard, and in the way between Liskeard and Launceston, there are many tin-mines. And, as they told us, some of the richest veins of that metal are found there that are in the whole county—the metal, when cast at the blowing houses into blocks, being, as above, carried to Liskeard to be coined.

From Liskeard, in our course west, we are necessarily carried to the sea-coast, because of the River Fowey or Fowath, which empties itself into the sea at a very large mouth. And hereby this river rising in the middle of the breadth of the county and running south, and the River Camel rising not far from it and running north, with a like large channel, the land from Bodmin to the western part of the county is almost made an island and in a manner cut off from the eastern part—the peninsula, or neck of land between, being not above twelve miles over.

On this south side we came to Foy or Fowey, an ancient town, and formerly very large—nay, not large only, but powerful and potent; for the Foyens, as they were then called, were able to fit out large fleets, not only for merchants' ships, but even of men-of-war; and with these not only fought with, but several times vanquished and routed, the squadron of the Cinque Ports men, who in those days were thought very powerful.

Mr. Camden observes that the town of Foy quarters some part of the arms of every one of those Cinque Ports with their own, intimating that they had at several times trampled over them all. Certain it is they did often beat them, and took their ships, and brought them as good prizes into their haven of Foy; and carried it so high that they fitted out their fleets against the French, and took several of their men-of-war when they were at war with England, and enriched their town by the spoil of their enemies.

Edward IV. favoured them much; and because the French threatened them to come up their river with a powerful navy to burn their town, he caused two forts to be built at the public charge for security of the town and river, which forts—at least, some show of them—remain there still. But the same King Edward was some time after so disgusted at the townsmen for officiously falling upon the French, after a truce was made and proclaimed, that he effectually disarmed them, took away their whole fleet, ships, tackle, apparel, and furniture; and since that time we do not read of any of their naval exploits, nor that they ever recovered or attempted to recover their strength at sea. However, Foy at this time is a very fair town; it lies extended on the east side of the river for above a mile, the buildings fair. And there are a great many flourishing merchants in it, who have a great share in the fishing trade, especially for pilchards, of which they take a great quantity hereabouts. In this town is also a coinage for the tin, of which a great quantity is dug up in the country north and west of the town.

The River Fowey, which is very broad and deep here, was formerly navigable by ships of good burthen as high as Lostwithiel—an ancient and once a flourishing but now a decayed town; and as to trade and navigation, quite destitute; which is occasioned by the river being filled up with sands, which, some say, the tides drive up in stormy weather from the sea; others say it is by sands washed from the lead-mines in the hills; the last of which, by the way, I take to be a mistake, the sand from the hills being not of quantity sufficient to fill up the channel of a navigable river, and, if it had, might easily have been stopped by the townspeople from falling into the river. But that the sea has choked up the river with sand is not only probable, but true; and there are other rivers which suffer in the like manner in this same country.

This town of Lostwithiel retains, however, several advantages which support its figure—as, first, that it is one of the Coinage Towns, as I call them; or Stannary Towns, as others call them; (2) the common gaol for the whole Stannary is here, as are also the County Courts for the whole county of Cornwall.

There is a mock cavalcade kept up at this town, which is very remarkable. The particulars, as they are related by Mr. Carew in his "Survey of Cornwall," take as follows:—

"Upon Little Easter Sunday the freeholders of this town and manor, by themselves or their deputies, did there assemble; amongst whom one (as it fell to his lot by turn), bravely apparelled, gallantly mounted, with a crown on his head, a sceptre in his hand, and a sword borne before him, and dutifully attended by all the rest (also on horseback), rode through the principal street to the church. The curate in his best beseen solemnly received him at the churchyard stile, and conducted him to hear divine service. After which he repaired, with the same pomp, to a house provided for that purpose, made a feast to his attendants, kept the table's-end himself, and was served with kneeling assay and all other rights due to the estate of a prince; with which dinner the ceremony ended, and every man returned home again. The pedigree of this usage is derived from so many descents of ages that the cause and author outreach the remembrance. Howbeit, these circumstances afford a conjecture that it should betoken royalties appertaining to the honour of Cornwall."

Behind Foy and nearer to the coast, at the mouth of a small river which some call Lowe, though without any authority, there stand two towns opposite to one another bearing the name of the River Looe— that is to say, distinguished by the addition of East Looe and West Looe. These are both good trading towns, and especially fishing towns; and, which is very particular, are (like Weymouth and Melcombe, in Dorsetshire) separated only by the creek or river, and yet each of them sends members to Parliament. These towns are joined together by a very beautiful and stately stone bridge having fifteen arches.

East Looe was the ancienter corporation of the two, and for some ages ago the greater and more considerable town; but now they tell us West Looe is the richest, and has the most ships belonging to it. Were they put together, they would make a very handsome seaport town. They have a great fishing trade here, as well for supply of the country as for merchandise, and the towns are not despisable. But as to sending four members to the British Parliament (which is as many as the City of London chooses), that, I confess, seems a little scandalous; but to whom, is none of my business to inquire.

Passing from hence, and ferrying over Foy River or the River Foweth (call it as you please), we come into a large country without many towns in it of note, but very well furnished with gentlemen's seats, and a little higher up with tin-works.

The sea making several deep bays here, they who travel by land are obliged to go higher into the country to pass above the water, especially at Trewardreth Bay, which lies very broad, above ten miles within the country, which passing at Trewardreth (a town of no great note, though the bay takes its name from it), the next inlet of the sea is the famous firth or inlet called Falmouth Haven. It is certainly, next to Milford Haven in South Wales, the fairest and best road for shipping that is in the whole isle of Britain, whether be considered the depth of water for above twenty miles within land; the safety of riding, sheltered from all kind of winds or storms; the good anchorage; and the many creeks, all navigable, where ships may run in and be safe; so that the like is nowhere to be found.

There are six or seven very considerable places upon this haven and the rivers from it—viz., Grampound, Tregony, Truro, Penryn, Falmouth, St. Maws, and Pendennis. The three first of these send members to Parliament. The town of Falmouth, as big as all the three, and richer than ten of them, sends none; which imports no more than this—that Falmouth itself is not of so great antiquity as to its rising as those other towns are; and yet the whole haven takes its name from Falmouth, too, unless, as some think, the town took its name from the haven, which, however, they give no authority to suggest.

St. Maws and Pendennis are two fortifications placed at the points or entrance of this haven, opposite to one another, though not with a communication or view; they are very strong—the first principally by sea, having a good platform of guns pointing athwart the Channel, and planted on a level with the water. But Pendennis Castle is strong by land as well as by water, is regularly fortified, has good out-works, and generally a strong garrison. St. Maws, otherwise called St. Mary's, has a town annexed to the castle, and is a borough sending members to the Parliament. Pendennis is a mere fortress, though there are some habitations in it, too, and some at a small distance near the seaside, but not of any great consideration.

The town of Falmouth is by much the richest and best trading town in this county, though not so ancient as its neighbour town of Truro; and indeed is in some things obliged to acknowledge the seigniority—namely, that in the corporation of Truro the person whom they choose to be their Mayor of Truro is also Mayor of Falmouth of course. How the jurisdiction is managed is an account too long for this place. The Truro-men also receive several duties collected in Falmouth, particularly wharfage for the merchandises landed or shipped off; but let these advantages be what they will, the town of Falmouth has gotten the trade—at least, the best part of it—from the other, which is chiefly owing to the situation. For that Falmouth lying upon the sea, but within the entrance, ships of the greatest burthen come up to the very quays, and the whole Royal Navy might ride safely in the road; whereas the town of Truro lying far within, and at the mouth of two fresh rivers, is not navigable for vessels of above 150 tons or thereabouts.

Some have suggested that the original of Falmouth was the having so large a quay, and so good a depth of water at it. The merchants of Truro formerly used it for the place of lading and unlading their ships, as the merchants of Exeter did at Topsham; and this is the more probable in that, as above, the wharfage of those landing-places is still the property of the corporation of Truro.

But let this be as it will, the trade is now in a manner wholly gone to Falmouth, the trade at Truro being now chiefly (if not only) for the shipping off of block tin and copper ore, the latter being lately found in large quantities in some of the mountains between Truro and St. Michael's, and which is much improved since the several mills are erected at Bristol and other parts for the manufactures of battery ware, as it is called (brass), or which is made out of English copper, most of it duct in these parts—the ore itself ago being found very rich and good.

Falmouth is well built, has abundance of shipping belonging to it, is full of rich merchants, and has a flourishing and increasing trade. I say "increasing," because by the late setting up the English packets between this port and Lisbon, there is a new commerce between Portugal and this town carried on to a very great value.

It is true, part of this trade was founded in a clandestine commerce carried on by the said packets at Lisbon, where, being the king's ships, and claiming the privilege of not being searched or visited by the Custom House officers, they found means to carry off great quantities of British manufactures, which they sold on board to the Portuguese merchants, and they conveyed them on shore, as it is supposed, without paying custom.

But the Government there getting intelligence of it, and complaint being made in England also, where it was found to be very prejudicial to the fair merchant, that trade has been effectually stopped. But the Falmouth merchants, having by this means gotten a taste of the Portuguese trade, have maintained it ever since in ships of their own. These packets bring over such vast quantities of gold in specie, either in *moidores* (which is the Portugal coin) or in bars of gold, that I am very credibly informed the carrier from Falmouth brought by land from thence to London at one time, in the month of January, 1722, or near it, eighty thousand *moidores* in gold, which came from Lisbon in the packet-boats for account of the merchants at London, and that it was attended with a guard of twelve horsemen well armed, for which the said carrier had half per cent. for his hazard.

This is a specimen of the Portugal trade, and how considerable it is in itself, as well as how advantageous to England; but as that is not to the present case, I proceed. The Custom House for all the towns in this port, and the head collector, is established at this town, where the duties (including the other ports) is very considerable. Here is also a very great fishing for pilchards; and the merchants for Falmouth have the chief stroke in that gainful trade.

Truro is, however, a very considerable town, too. It stands up the water north and by east from Falmouth, in the utmost extended branch of the Avon, in the middle between the conflux of two rivers, which, though not of any long course, have a very good appearance for a port, and make it large wharf between them in the front of the town. And the water here makes a good port for small ships, though it be at the influx, but not for ships of burthen. This is the particular town where the Lord-Warden of the Stannaries always holds his famous Parliament of miners, and for stamping of tin. The town is well built, but shows that it has been much fuller, both of houses and inhabitants, than it is now; nor will it probably ever rise while the town of Falmouth stands where it does, and while the trade is settled in it as it is. There are at least three churches in it, but no Dissenters' meeting-house that I could hear of.

Tregony is upon the same water north-east from Falmouth—distance about fifteen miles from it—but is a town of very little trade; nor, indeed, have any of the towns, so far within the shore, notwithstanding the benefit of the water, any considerable trade but what is carried on under the merchants of Falmouth or Truro. The chief thing that is to be said of this town is that it sends members to Parliament, as does also Grampound, a market-town; and Burro', about four miles farther up the water. This place, indeed, has a claim to antiquity, and is an appendix to the Duchy of Cornwall, of which it holds at a fee farm rent and pays to the Prince of Wales as duke £10 11s. 1d. per annum. It has no parish church, but only a chapel-of-ease to an adjacent parish.

Penryn is up the same branch of the Avon as Falmouth, but stands four miles higher towards the west; yet ships come to it of as great a size as can come to Truro itself. It is a very pleasant, agreeable town, and for that reason has many merchants in it, who would perhaps otherwise live at Falmouth. The chief commerce of these towns, as to their sea-affairs, is the pilchards and Newfoundland fishing, which is very profitable to them all. It had formerly a conventual church, with a chantry and a religious house (a cell to Kirton); but they are all demolished, and scarce the ruins of them distinguishable enough to know one part from another.

Quitting Falmouth Haven from Penryn West, we came to Helston, about seven miles, and stands upon the little River Cober, which, however, admits the sea so into its bosom as to make a tolerable good harbour for ships a little below the town. It is the fifth town allowed for the coining tin, and several of the ships called tin-ships are laden here.

This town is large and populous, and has four spacious streets, a handsome church, and a good trade. This town also sends members to Parliament. Beyond this is a market-town, though of no resort for trade, called Market Jew. It lies, indeed, on the seaside, but has no harbour or safe road for shipping.

At Helford is a small but good harbour between Falmouth and this port, where many times the tin-ships go in to load for London; also here are a good number of fishing vessels for the pilchard trade, and abundance of skilful fishermen. It was from this town that in the great storm which happened November 27, 1703, a ship laden with tin was blown out to sea and driven to the Isle of Wight in seven hours, having on board only one man and two boys. The story is as follows:—

"The beginning of the storm there lay a ship laden with tin in Helford Haven, about two leagues and a half west of Falmouth. The tin was taken on board at a place called Guague Wharf, five or six miles up the river, and the vessel was come down to Helford in order to pursue her voyage to London.

"About eight o'clock in the evening the commander, whose name was Anthony Jenkins, went on board with his mate to see that everything was safe, and to give orders, but went both on shore again, leaving only a man and two boys on board, not apprehending any danger, they being in safe harbour. However, he ordered them that if it should blow hard they should carry out the small bower anchor, and so to moor the ship by two anchors, and then giving what other orders he thought to be needful, he went ashore, as above.

"About nine o'clock, the wind beginning to blow harder, they carried out the anchor, according to the master's order; but the wind increasing about ten, the ship began to drive, so they carried out their best bower, which, having a good new cable, brought the ship up. The storm still increasing, they let go the kedge anchor; so that they then rode by four anchors ahead, which were all they had.

"But between eleven and twelve o'clock the wind came about west and by south, and blew in so violent and terrible a manner that, though they rode under the lee of a high shore, yet the ship was driven from all her anchors, and about midnight drove quite out of the harbour (the opening of the harbour lying due east and west) into the open sea, the men having neither anchor or cable or boat to help themselves.

"In this dreadful condition (they driving, I say, out of the harbour) their first and chief care was to go clear of the rocks which lie on either side the harbour's mouth, and which they performed pretty well. Then, seeing no remedy, they consulted what to do next. They could carry no sail at first—no, not a knot; nor do anything but run away afore it. The only thing they had to think on was to keep her out at sea as far as they could, for fear of a point of land called the Dead Man's Head, which lies to the eastward of Falmouth Haven; and then, if they could escape the land, thought to run in for Plymouth next morning, so, if possible, to save their lives.

"In this frighted condition they drove away at a prodigious rate, having sometimes the bonnet of their foresail a little out, but the yard lowered almost to the deck—sometimes the ship almost under water, and sometimes above, keeping still in the offing, for fear of the land, till they might see daylight. But when the day broke they found they were to think no more of Plymouth, for they were far enough beyond it; and the first land they made was Peverel Point, being the southernmost land of the Isle of Purbeck, in Dorsetshire, and a little to the westward of the Isle of Wight; so that now they were in a terrible consternation, and driving still at a prodigious rate. By seven o'clock they found themselves broadside of the Isle of Wight.

"Here they consulted again what to do to save their lives. One of the boys was for running her into the Downs; but the man objected that, having no anchor or cable nor boat to go on shore with, and the storm blowing off shore in the Downs, they should be inevitably blown off and lost upon the unfortunate Goodwin—which, it seems, the man had been on once before and narrowly escaped.

"Now came the last consultation for their lives. The other of the boys said he had been in a certain creek in the Isle of Wight, where, between the rocks, he knew there was room to run the ship in, and at least to save their lives, and that he saw the place just that moment; so he desired the man to let him have the helm, and he would do his best and venture it. The man gave him the helm, and he stood directly in among the rocks, the people standing on the shore thinking they were mad, and that they would in a few minutes be dashed in a thousand pieces.

"But when they came nearer, and the people found they steered as if they knew the place, they made signals to them to direct them as well as they could, and the young bold fellow run her into a small cove, where she stuck fast, as it were, between the rocks on both sides, there being but just room enough for the breadth of the ship. The ship indeed, giving two or three knocks, staved and sunk, but the man and the two youths jumped ashore and were safe; and the lading, being tin, was afterwards secured.

"N.B.—The merchants very well rewarded the three sailors, especially the lad that ran her into that place."

Penzance is the farthest town of any note west, being 254 miles from London, and within about ten miles of the promontory called the Land's End; so that this promontory is from London 264 miles, or thereabouts. This town of Penzance is a place of good business, well built and populous, has a good trade, and a great many ships belonging to it, notwithstanding it is so remote. Here are also a great many good families of gentlemen, though in this utmost angle of the nation; and, which is yet more strange, the veins of lead, tin, and copper ore are said to be seen even to the utmost extent of land at low-water mark, and in the very sea—so rich, so valuable, a treasure is contained in these parts of Great Britain, though they are supposed to be so poor, because so very remote from London, which is the centre of our wealth.

Between this town and St. Burien, a town midway between it and the Land's End, stands a circle of great stones, not unlike those at Stonehenge, in Wiltshire, with one bigger than the rest in the middle. They stand about twelve feet asunder, but have no inscription; neither does tradition offer to leave any part of their history upon record, as whether it was a trophy or a monument of burial, or an altar for worship, or what else; so that all that can be learned of them is that here they are. The parish where they stand is called Boscawone, from whence the ancient and honourable family of Boscawen derive their names.

Near Penzance, but open to the sea, is that gulf they call Mount's Bay; named so from a high hill standing in the water, which they call St. Michael's Mount: the seamen call it only the Cornish Mount. It has been fortified, though the situation of it makes it so difficult of access that, like the Bass in Scotland, there needs no fortification; like the Bass, too, it was once made a prison for prisoners of State, but now it is wholly neglected. There is a very good road here for shipping, which makes the town of Penzance be a place of good resort.

A little up in the county towards the north-west is Godolchan, which though a hill, rather than a town, gives name to the noble and ancient family of Godolphin; and nearer on the northern coast is Royalton, which since the late Sydney Godolphin, Esq., a younger brother of the family, was created Earl of Godolphin, gave title of Lord to his eldest son, who was called Lord Royalton during the life of his father. This place also is infinitely rich in tin-mines.

I am now at my journey's end. As to the islands of Scilly, which lie beyond the Land's End, I shall say something of them presently. I must now return *sur mes pas*, as the French call it; though not literally so, for I shall not come back the same way I went. But as I have coasted the south shore to the Land's End, I shall come back by the north coast, and my observations in my return will furnish very well materials for another letter.

APPENDIX TO LAND'S END.

I have ended this account at the utmost extent of the island of Great Britain west, without visiting those excrescences of the island, as I think I may call them—viz., the rocks of Scilly; of which what is most famous is their infamy or reproach; namely, how many good ships are almost continually dashed in pieces there, and how many brave lives lost, in spite of the mariners' best skill, or the lighthouses' and other sea-marks' best notice.

These islands lie so in the middle between the two vast openings of the north and south narrow seas (or, as the sailors call them, the Bristol Channel, and The Channel—so called by way of eminence) that it cannot, or perhaps never will, be avoided but that several ships in the dark of the night and in stress of weather, may, by being out in their reckonings, or other unavoidable accidents, mistake; and if they do, they are sure, as the sailors call it, to run "bump ashore" upon Scilly, where they find no quarter among the breakers, but are beat to pieces without any possibility of escape.

One can hardly mention the Bishop and his Clerks, as they are called, or the rocks of Scilly, without letting fall a tear to the memory of Sir Cloudesley Shovel and all the gallant spirits that were with him, at one blow and without a moment's warning dashed into a state of immortality—the admiral, with three men-of-war, and all their men (running upon these rocks right afore the wind, and in a dark night) being lost there, and not a man saved. But all our annals and histories are full of this, so I need say no more.

They tell us of eleven sail of merchant-ships homeward bound, and richly laden from the southward, who had the like fate in the same place a great many years ago; and that some of them coming from Spain, and having a great quantity of bullion or pieces of eight on board, the money frequently drives on shore still, and that in good quantities, especially after stormy weather.

This may be the reason why, as we observed during our short stay here, several mornings after it had blown something hard in the night, the sands were covered with country people running to and fro to see if the sea had cast up anything of value. This the seamen call "going a-shoring;" and it seems they do often find good purchase. Sometimes also dead bodies are cast up here, the consequence of shipwrecks among those fatal rocks and islands; as also broken pieces of ships, casks, chests, and almost everything that will float or roll on shore by the surges of the sea.

Nor is it seldom that the voracious country people scuffle and fight about the right to what they find, and that in a desperate manner; so that this part of Cornwall may truly be said to be inhabited by a fierce and ravenous people. For they are so greedy, and eager for the prey, that they are charged with strange, bloody, and cruel dealings, even sometimes with one another; but especially with poor distressed seamen when they come on shore by force of a tempest, and seek help for their lives, and where they find the rooks themselves not more merciless than the people who range about them for their prey.

Here, also, as a farther testimony of the immense riches which have been lost at several times upon this coast, we found several engineers and projectors—some with one sort of diving engine, and some with another; some claiming such a wreck, and some such-and-such others; where they alleged they were assured there were great quantities of money; and strange unprecedented ways were used by them to come at it: some, I say, with one kind of engine, and some another; and though we thought several of them very strange impracticable methods, yet I was assured by the country people that they had done wonders with them under water, and that some of them had taken up things of great weight and in a great depth of water. Others had split open the wrecks they had found in a manner one would have thought not possible to be done so far under water, and had taken out things from the very holds of the ships. But we could not learn that they had come at any pieces of eight, which was the thing they seemed most to aim at and depend upon; at least, they had not found any great quantity, as they said they expected.

However, we left them as busy as we found them, and far from being discouraged; and if half the golden mountains, or silver mountains either, which they promise themselves should appear, they will be very well paid for their labour.

From the tops of the hills on this extremity of the land you may see out into that they call the Chops of the Channel, which, as it is the greatest inlet of commerce, and the most frequented by merchant-ships of any place in the world, so one seldom looks out to seaward but something new presents—that is to say, of ships passing or repassing, either on the great or lesser Channel.

Upon a former accidental journey into this part of the country, during the war with France, it was with a mixture of pleasure and horror that we saw from the hills at the Lizard, which is the southern-most point of this land, an obstinate fight between three French men-of-war and two English, with a privateer and three merchant-ships in their company. The English had the misfortune, not only to be fewer ships of war in number, but of less force; so that while the two biggest French ships engaged the English, the third in the meantime took the two merchant-ships and went off with them. As to the picaroon or privateer, she was able to do little in the matter, not daring to come so near the men-of-war as to take a broadside, which her thin sides would not have been able to bear, but would have sent her to the bottom at once; so that the English men-of-war had no assistance from her, nor could she prevent the taking the two merchant-ships. Yet we observed that the English captains managed their fight so well, and their seamen behaved so briskly, that in about three hours both the Frenchmen stood off, and, being sufficiently banged, let us see that they had no more stomach to fight; after which the English—having damage enough, too, no doubt—stood away to the eastward, as we supposed, to refit.

This point of the Lizard, which runs out to the southward, and the other promontory mentioned above, make the two angles—or horns, as they are called—from whence it is supposed this county received its first name of Cornwall, or, as Mr. Camden says, *Cornubia* in the Latin, and in the British "Kernaw," as running out in two vastly extended horns. And indeed it seems as if Nature had formed this situation for the direction of mariners, as foreknowing of what importance it should be, and how in future ages these seas should be thus thronged with merchant-ships, the protection of whose wealth, and the safety of the people navigating them, was so much her early care that she stretched out the land so very many ways, and extended the points and promontories so far and in so many different places into the sea, that the land might be more easily discovered at a due distance, which way soever the ships should come.

Nor is the Lizard Point less useful (though not so far west) than the other, which is more properly called the Land's End; but if we may credit our mariners, it is more frequently first discovered from the sea. For as our mariners, knowing by the soundings when they are in the mouth of the Channel, do then most naturally stand to the southward, to avoid mistaking the Channel, and to shun the Severn Sea or Bristol Channel, but still more to avoid running upon Scilly and the rocks about it, as is observed before—I say, as they carefully keep to the southward till they think they are fair with the Channel, and then stand to the northward again, or north-east, to make the land, this is the reason why the Lizard is, generally speaking, the first land they make, and not the Land's End.

Then having made the Lizard, they either (first) run in for Falmouth, which is the next port, if they are taken short with easterly winds, or are in want of provisions and refreshment, or have anything out of order, so that they care not to keep the sea; or (secondly) stand away for the Ram Head and Plymouth Sound; or (thirdly) keep an offing to run up the Channel.

So that the Lizard is the general guide, and of more use in these cases than the other point, and is therefore the land which the ships choose to make first; for then also they are sure that they are past Scilly and all the dangers of that part of the island.

Nature has fortified this part of the island of Britain in a strange manner, and so, as is worth a traveller's observation, as if she knew the force and violence of the mighty ocean which beats upon it; and which, indeed, if the land was not made firm in proportion, could not withstand, but would have been washed away long ago.

First, there are the islands of Scilly and the rocks about them; these are placed like out-works to resist the first assaults of this enemy, and so break the force of it, as the piles (or starlings, as they are called) are placed before the solid stonework of London Bridge to fence off the force either of the water or ice, or anything else that might be dangerous to the work.

Then there are a vast number of sunk rocks (so the seamen call them), besides such as are visible and above water, which gradually lessen the quantity of water that would otherwise lie with an infinite weight and force upon the land. It is observed that these rocks lie under water for a great way off into the sea on every side the said two horns or points of land, so breaking the force of the water, and, as above, lessening the weight of it.

But besides this the whole *terra firma*, or body of the land which makes this part of the isle of Britain, seems to be one solid rock, as if it was formed by Nature to resist the otherwise irresistible power of the ocean. And, indeed, if one was to observe with what fury the sea comes on sometimes against the shore here, especially at the Lizard Point, where there are but few, if any, out-works, as I call them, to resist it; how high the waves come rolling forward, storming on the neck of one another (particularly when the wind blows off sea), one would wonder that even the strongest rocks themselves should be able to resist and repel them. But, as I said, the country seems to be, as it were, one great body of stone, and prepared so on purpose.

And yet, as if all this was not enough, Nature has provided another strong fence, and that is, that these vast rocks are, as it were, cemented together by the solid and weighty ore of tin and copper, especially the last, which is plentifully found upon the very outmost edge of the land, and with which the stones may be said to be soldered together, lest the force of the sea should separate and disjoint them, and so break in upon these fortifications of the island to destroy its chief security.

This is certain—that there is a more than ordinary quantity of tin, copper, and lead also placed by the Great Director of Nature in these very remote angles (and, as I have said above, the ore is found upon the very surface of the rocks a good way into the sea); and that it does not only lie, as it were, upon or between the stones among the earth (which in that case might be washed from it by the sea), but that it is even blended or mixed in with the stones themselves, that the stones must be split into pieces to come at it. By this mixture the rocks are made infinitely weighty and solid, and thereby still the more qualified to repel the force of the sea.

Upon this remote part of the island we saw great numbers of that famous kind of crows which is known by the name of the Cornish cough or chough (so the country people call them). They are the same kind which are found in Switzerland among the Alps, and which Pliny pretended were peculiar to those mountains, and calls the *pyrrhocorax*. The body is black; the legs, feet, and bill of a deep yellow, almost to a red. I could not find that it was affected for any good quality it had, nor is the flesh good to eat, for it feeds much on fish and carrion; it is counted little better than a kite, for it is of ravenous quality, and is very mischievous. It will steal and carry away anything it finds about the house that is not too heavy, though not fit for its food—as knives, forks, spoons, and linen cloths, or whatever it can fly away with; sometimes they say it has stolen bits of firebrands, or lighted candles, and lodged them in the stacks of corn and the thatch of barns and houses, and set them on fire; but this I only had by oral tradition.

I might take up many sheets in describing the valuable curiosities of this little Chersonese or Neck Land, called the Land's End, in which there lies an immense treasure and many things worth notice (I mean, besides those to be found upon the surface), but I am too near the end of this letter. If I have opportunity I shall take notice of some part of what I omit here in my return by the northern shore of the county.

TWO LETTERS FROM THE "JOURNEY THROUGH ENGLAND BY A GENTLEMAN."

BATH IN 1722.

Bath.

Sir,

The Bath lies very low, is but a small city, but very compact, and one can hardly imagine it could accommodate near the company that frequents it at least three parts of the year. I have been told of 8,000 families there at a time—some for the benefit of drinking its hot waters, others for bathing, and others for diversion and pleasure (of which, I must say, it affords more than any public place of that kind in Europe).

I told you in my former letters that Epsom and Tunbridge do not allow visiting (the companies there meet only on the walks); but here visits are received and returned, assemblies and balls are given, and parties at play in most houses every night, to which one Mr. Nash hath for many years contributed very much. This gentleman is by custom a sort of master of ceremonies of the place; he is not of any birth nor estate, but by a good address and assurance ingratiates himself into the good graces of the ladies and the best company in the place, and is director of all their parties of pleasure. He wears good clothes, is always affluent of money, plays very much, and whatever he may get in private, yet in public he always seems to lose. The town have been for many years so sensible of the service he does them that they ring the bells generally at his arrival in town, and, it is thought, pay him a yearly contribution for his support.

In the morning early the company of both sexes meet at the Pump (in a great hall enrailed), to drink the waters and saunter about till prayer-time, or divert themselves by looking on those that are bathing in the bath. Most of the company go to church in the morning in dishabille, and then go home to dress for the walks before dinner. The walks are behind the church, spacious and well shaded, planted round with shops filled with everything that contributes to pleasure, and at the end a noble room for gaming, from whence there are hanging-stairs to a pretty garden for everybody that pays for the time they stay, to walk in.

I have often wondered that the physicians of these places prescribe gaming to their patients, in order to keep their minds free from business and thought, that their waters on an undisturbed mind may have the greater effect, when indeed one cross-throw at play must sour a man's blood more than ten glasses of water will sweeten, especially for such great sums as they throw for every day at Bath.

The King and Queen's Baths, which have a communication with one another, are the baths which people of common rank go into promiscuously; and indeed everybody, except the first quality. The way of going into them is very comical: a chair with a couple of chairmen come to your bedside (lie in what storey you will), and there strip you, and give you their dress without your shift, and wrapping you up in blankets carry you to the bath.

When you enter the bath, the water seems very warm; and the heat much increases as you go into the Queen's Bath, where the great spring rises. On a column erected over the spring is an inscription of the first finder-out of these springs, in the following words: that "Bladud, the son of Lud, found them three hundred years before Christ." The smoke and slime of the waters, the promiscuous multitude of the people in the bath, with nothing but their heads and hands above water, with the height of the walls that environ the bath, gave me a lively idea of several pictures I had seen, of Angelo's in Italy of Purgatory, with heads and hands uplifted in the midst of smoke, just as they are here. After bathing, you are carried home in your chair, in the same manner you came.

The Cross Bath, which is used by the people of the first quality, was beautified and inclosed for the convenience of the late King James's queen, who after the priests and physicians had been at work to procure a male successor to the throne of Great Britain, the Sacrament exposed in all the Roman Catholic countries, and for that end a sanctified smock sent from the Virgin Mary at Loretto, the queen was ordered to go to Bath and prepare herself, and the king to make a progress through the western counties and join her there. On his arrival at Bath, the next day after his conjunction with the queen, the Earl of Melfort (then Secretary of State for Scotland) erected a fine prophetic monument in the middle of the Bath, as an everlasting monument of that conjunction. I call it "prophetic," because nine months after a Prince of Wales was born. This monument is still entire and handsome, only some of the inscriptions on the pillar were erased in King William's time. The angels attending the Holy Ghost as He descends, the

Eucharist, the Pillar, and all the ornaments are of fine marble, and must have cost that earl a great deal of money. He was second son to Drummond, Earl of Perth, in North Britain; and was Deputy Governor of the Castle of Edinburgh when the Duke and Duchess of York came to Scotland, in King Charles the Second's time. He was a handsome gentleman, with a good address, and went into all the measures of that court, and at all their balls generally danced with the duchess; who, on their accession to the throne, sent for him up to London, made him Secretary of State for Scotland, created him Earl of Melfort, and Knight of the Order of St. Andrew. His elder brother was also made Chancellor and Governor of Scotland. And on King James's abdication, as the two brothers followed the king's fortunes, the Earl of Perth was made governor to the young prince; and Melfort was created a duke, had the Garter, and was a great man in France to his dying day.

There is another bath for lepers.

The cathedral church is small but well lighted. There are abundance of little monuments in it of people who come there for their health, but meet with their death.

These waters have a wonderful influence on barren ladies, who often prove with child even in their husbands' absence; who must not come near them till their bodies are prepared.

Everything looks gay and serene here; it is plentiful and cheap. Only the taverns do not much improve, for it is a place of universal sobriety. To be drunk at Bath is as scandalous as mad. Common women are not to be met with here so much as at Tunbridge and Epsom. Whether it is the distance from London, or that the gentlemen fly at the highest game, I cannot tell; besides, everything that passes here is known on the walks, and the characters of persons.

In three hours one arrives from Bath at Bristol, a large, opulent, and fine city; but, notwithstanding its nearness, by the different manners of the people seems to be another country. Instead of that politeness and gaiety which you see at Bath, here is nothing but hurry—carts driving along with merchandises, and people running about with cloudy looks and busy faces. When I came to the Exchange I was surprised to see it planted round with stone pillars, with broad boss-plates on them like sun-dials, and coats-of-arms with inscriptions on every plate.

They told me that these pillars were erected by eminent merchants for the benefit of writing and despatching their affairs on them, as on tables; and at 'Change time the merchants take each their stands by their pillars, that masters of ships and owners may know where to find them.

Coffee-houses and taverns lie round the 'Change, just as at London; and the Bristol milk, which is Spanish sherry (nowhere so good as here), is plentifully drunk.

The city of Bristol is situated much like Verona, in Italy. A river runs through almost the middle of it, on which there is a fine stone bridge. The quay may be made the finest, largest, and longest in the world by pulling down an old house or two. Behind the quay is a very noble square, as large as that of Soho in London, in which is kept the Custom House; and most of the eminent merchants who keep their coaches reside here. The cathedral is on the other side of the river, on the top of the hill, and is the meanest I have seen in England. But the square or green adjoining to it has several fine houses, and makes by its situation, in my opinion, much the pleasantest part of the town. There are some churches in the city finer than the cathedral, and your merchants have their little country-seats in the adjacent eminences; of which that of Mr. Southwell hath a very commanding prospect, both of the city, the River Severn, and the shipping that lies below.

There are hot springs near Bristol that are also very much frequented, and are reckoned to be better than the Bath for some distempers.

A traveller when he comes to the Bath must never fail of seeing Badminton, belonging to the Dukes of Beaufort; nor Longleat, belonging to my Lord Weymouth. They are both within a few miles of the Bath. King William, when he took Badminton in his way from Ireland, told the duke that he was not surprised at his not coming to court, having so sumptuous a palace to keep a court of his own in. And indeed the apartments are inferior to few royal palaces. The parks are large, and enclosed with a stone wall; and that duke, whom I described to you in my letter from Windsor, lived up to the grandeur of a sovereign prince. His grandson, who was also Knight of the Garter, made a great figure in the reign of Queen Anne. The family, which is a natural branch of the house of Lancaster, have always distinguished themselves of the Tory side. The present duke is under age.

Longleat, though an old seat, is very beautiful and large; and the gardens and avenue, being full-grown, are very beautiful and well kept. It cost the late Lord Weymouth a good revenue in hospitality to such strangers as came from Bath to see it.

The biggest and most regular house in England was built near Bristol by the late Lord Stawell; but it being judged by his heirs to be too big for the estate, they are pulling it down and selling the materials.

As the weather grows good, I shall proceed through South Wales to Chester, from whence you shall soon hear from me, who am without reserve, sir, your most humble, &c.

FROM CHESTER TO HOLYHEAD.

Chester.

Sir,

I crossed the Severn at the ferry of Ash, about ten miles above Bristol, and got to Monmouth to dinner through a rugged, indifferent country. It is a pitiful old town, and hath nothing remarkable in it; and from thence through a fat fertile country I got to the city of Hereford at night.

Hereford is the dirtiest old city I have seen in England, yet pretty large; the streets are irregular and the houses old, and its cathedral a reverend old pile, but not beautiful; the niches of the walls of the church are adorned with the figures of its bishops as big as the life, in a cumbent posture, with the year of their interments newly painted over. Some of them are in the twelve hundredth year of Christ. Here they drink nothing but cider, which is very cheap and very good; and the very hedges in the country are planted with apple-trees. About three miles from Hereford in my road to Ludlow I saw a fine old seat called Hampton Court, belonging to my Lord Coningsby. The plantations on rising grounds round it give an august splendour to the house, which consists of an oval court with suitable offices, not unlike an house belonging to the Duke of Somerset near London; and from thence in a few hours I arrived at Ludlow, the capital of South Wales, and where the Princes of Wales formerly, and since them the Presidents of Wales, kept their courts.

Ludlow is one of the neatest, clean, pretty towns in England. The street by which you enter the town is spacious, with handsome houses sash-windowed on each side, which leads you by an ascent to the castle on the left of the top of the hill, and the church on the right, from whence there runs also another handsome street. The castle hath a very

137

commanding prospect of the adjacent country; the offices in the outer court are falling down, and a great part of the court is turned into a bowling-green; but the royal apartments in the castle, with some old velvet furniture and a sword of state, are still left. There is also a neat little chapel; but the vanity of the Welsh gentry when they were made councillors has spoiled it by adorning it with their names and arms, of which it is full.

A small expense would still make this castle a habitable and beautiful place, lying high, and overlooking a fine country; there is also a fine prospect from the churchyard, and the church is very neat. I saw abundance of pretty ladies here, and well dressed, who came from the adjacent counties, for the convenience and cheapness of boarding. Provisions of all sorts are extremely plentiful and cheap here, and very good company.

I stayed some days here, to make an excursion into South Wales and know a little of the manners of the country, as I design to do at Chester for North Wales. The gentry are very numerous, exceedingly civil to strangers, if you don't come to purchase and make your abode amongst them. They live much like Gascoynes—affecting their own language, valuing themselves much on the antiquity of their families, and are proud of making entertainments.

The Duke of Powis, of the name of Herbert, hath a noble seat near this town, but I was not at it; the family followed King James's fortunes to France, and I suppose the seat lies neglected. From Ludlow in a short day's riding through a champaign country I arrived at the town of Shrewsbury.

Shrewsbury stands upon an eminence, encircled by the Severn like a horse-shoe; the streets are large, and the houses well built. My Lord Newport, son to the Earl of Bradford, hath a handsome palace, with hanging gardens down to the river; as also Mr. Kinnaston, and some other gentlemen. There is a good town-house, and the most coffee-houses round it that ever I saw in any town; but when you come into them, they are but ale-houses (only they think that the name of coffee-house gives a better air). King Charles would have made them a city, but they chose rather to remain a corporation, as they are, for which they were called the "proud Salopians." There is a great deal of good company in this town, for the convenience of cheapness; and there are assemblies and balls for the young ladies once a week. The Earl of Bradford and several others have handsome seats near it; from hence I came to Wrexham, in Wales, a beautiful market-town; the church is the beautifullest country church in England, and surpasses some cathedrals. I counted fifty-two statues as big as the life in the steeple or tower, which is built after the manner of your Dutch steeples, and as high as any there. I was there on a market-day, and was particularly pleased to see the Welsh ladies come to market in their laced hats, their own hair hanging round their shoulders, and blue and scarlet cloaks like our Amazons—some of them with a greyhound in a string in their hands.

Whitchurch, near it, hath a fine church, built by the Earl of Bridgwater; and so to Chester, an ancient and large city, with a commanding castle. The city consists of four large streets, which make an exact cross, with the town-house and Exchange in the middle; but you don't walk the streets here, but in galleries up one pair of stairs, which keeps you from the rain in winter, and sun in summer; and the houses and shops, with gardens, go all off these galleries, which they call rows. The city is walled round, and the wall so firmly paved that it gives you an agreeable prospect of the country and river, as you walk upon it. The churches are very neat, and the cathedral an august old pile; there is an ancient monument of an Emperor of Germany, with assemblies every week. While I continued at Chester, I made an excursion into North Wales, and went into Denbigh, the capital of that country, where are the remains of a very great and old castle, as is also at Flint, the capital of Flintshire. These castles were the frontier garrisons of Wales before it came under the subjection of England. The country is mountainous, and full of iron and lead works; and here they begin to differ from the English both in language and dress.

From Flint, along the seaside, in three hours I arrived at the famous cold bath called St. Winifred's Well; and the town from thence called Holywell is a pretty large well-built village, in the middle of a grove, in a bottom between, two hills. The well is in the foot of one of the hills, and spouts out about the bigness of a barrel at once, with such force that it turns three or four mills before it falls into the sea. The well where you bathe is floored with stone surrounded with pillars, on which stands a neat little chapel dedicated to St. Winifred, but now turned into a Protestant school. However, to supply the loss of this chapel, the Roman Catholics have chapels erected almost in every inn for the devotion of the pilgrims that flock hither from all the Popish parts of England. The water, you may imagine, is very cold, coming from the bowels of an iron mountain, and never having met with the influence of the sun till it runs from the well.

The legend of St. Winifred is too long and ridiculous for a letter; I leave you to Dr. Fleetwood (when Bishop of St. Asaph) for its description. I will only tell you, in two words, that this St. Winifred was a beautiful damsel that lived on the top of the hill; that a prince of the country fell deeply in love with her; that coming one day when her parents were abroad, and she resisting his passion, turned into rage, and as she was flying from him cut off her head, which rolled down the hill with her body, and at the place where it stopped gushed out this well of water. But there was also a good hermit that lived at the bottom of the hill, who immediately claps her head to her body, and by the force of the water and his prayers she recovered, and lived to perform many miracles for many years after. They give you her printed litanies at the well. And I observed the Roman Catholics in their prayers, not with eyes lifted up to heaven, but intent upon the water, as if it were the real blood of St. Winifred that was to wash them clean from all their sins.

In every inn you meet with a priest, habited like country gentlemen, and very good companions. At the "Cross Keys," where I lodged, there was one that had been marked out to me, to whom I was particularly civil at supper; but finding by my conversation I was none of them, he drank and swore like a dragoon, on purpose, as I imagine, to disguise himself. From Holywell in two hours I came to a handsome seat of Sir John Conway's at Redland, and next day to Conway.

I do not know any place in Europe that would make a finer landscape in a picture than Conway at a mile's distance. It lies on the side of a hill, on the banks of an arm of the sea about the breadth of the Thames at London, and within two little miles of the sea, over which we ferry to go to the town.

The town is walled round, with thirty watch-towers at proper distances on the walls; and the castle with its towers, being very white, makes an august show at a distance, being surrounded with little hills on both sides of the bay or river, covered with wood. But when you cross the ferry and come into the town, there is nothing but poverty and misery. The castle is a heap of rubbish uncovered, and these towers on the walls only standing vestiges of what Wales was when they had a prince of their own.

They speak all Welsh here, and if a stranger should lose his way in this county of Carnarvon, it is ten to one if he meets with any one that has English enough to set him right. The people are also naturally very surly, and even if they understand English, if you ask them a question their answer is, "Dame Salsenach," or "I cannot speak Saxon or

English." Their Bibles and prayer-books are all printed in Welsh in our character; so that an Englishman can read their language, although he doth not understand a word of it. It hath a great resemblance of the Bas-Bretons, but they retain the letter and character as well as language, as the Scots and Highlanders do.

They retain several Popish customs in North Wales, for on Sunday (after morning service) the whole parish go to football till the afternoon service begins, and then they go to the ale-house and play at all manner of games (which ale-house is often kept by the parson, for their livings are very small).

They have also offerings at funerals, which is one of the greatest perquisites the parson hath. When the body is deposited in the church during the service for the dead, every person invited to the burial lays a piece of money upon the altar to defray the dead person's charges to the other world, which, after the ceremony is over, the parson puts in his pocket. From Conway, through the mountainous country of Carnarvon, I passed the famous mountain of Penmaen-Mawr, so dreadfully related by passengers travelling to Ireland. It is a road cut out of the side of the rock, seven feet wide; the sea lies perpendicularly down, about forty fathoms on one side, and the mountain is about the same height above it on the other side. It looks dismal, but not at all dangerous, for there is now a wall breast-high along the precipice. However, there is an ale-house at the bottom of the hill on the other side, with this inscription, "Now your fright is over, take a dram." From hence I proceeded to a little town called Bangor, where there is a cathedral such as may be expected in Wales; and from thence to Carnarvon, the capital of the county. Here are the vestiges of a large old castle, where one of the Henrys, King of England, was born, as was another at Monmouth, in South Wales. For the Welsh were so hard to be reconciled to their union with England at first, it was thought policy to send our queens to lie-in there, to make our princes Welshmen born, and that way ingratiate the inhabitants to their subjection to a prince born in their own country. And for that reason our kings to this day wear a leek (the badge of Wales) on St. David's Day, the patron of this country; as they do the Order of the Thistle on St. Andrew's Day, the patron of Scotland.

Carnarvon is a pretty little town, situated in the bottom of a bay, and might be a place of good trade, if the country afforded a consumption.

The sea flows quite round from Bangor to Carnarvon Bay, which separates Anglesea from the rest of Wales, and makes it an island. Beaumaris, the capital of the island, hath been a flourishing town; there are still two very good streets, and the remains of a very large castle. The Lord Bulkeley hath a noble ancient seat planted with trees on the side of the hill above the town, from whence one hath a fine prospect of the bay and adjacent country; the church is very handsome, and there are some fine ancient monuments of that family and some Knights Templars in it. The family of Bulkeley keep in their family a large silver goblet, with which they entertain their friends, with an inscription round relating to the royal family when in distress, which is often remembered by the neighbouring gentry, whose affections run very much that way all over Wales.

I went from hence to Glengauny, the ancient residence of Owen Tudor, but now belongs to the Bulkeleys, and to be sold. It is a good old house, and I believe never was larger. There is a vulgar error in this country that Owen Tudor was married to a Queen of England, and that the house of York took that surname from him; whereas the Queen of England that was married to him was a daughter of the King of France and dowager of England, and had no relation to the Crown; he had indeed two daughters by her, that were married into English noble families—to one of which Henry VII. was related. But Owen Tudor was neither of the blood of the Princes of Wales himself, nor gave descent to that of the English. He was a private gentleman, of about £3,000 a year, who came to seek his fortune at the English court, and the queen fell in love with him.

I was invited to a cock-match some miles from Glengauny, where were above forty gentlemen, most of them of the names of Owen, Parry, and Griffith; they fought near twenty battles, and every battle a cock was killed. Their cocks are doubtless the finest in the world; and the gentlemen, after they were a little heated with liquor, were as warm as their cocks. A great deal of bustle and noise grew by degrees after dinner was over; but their scolding was all in Welsh, and civilities in English. We had a very great dinner; and the house (called The College) where we dined was built very comically; it is four storeys high, built on the side of a hill, and the stable is in the garret. There is a broad stone staircase on the outside of the house, by which you enter into the several apartments. The kitchen is at the bottom of the hill, a bedchamber above that, the parlour (where we dined) is the third storey, and on the top of the hill is the stable.

From hence I stepped over to Holyhead, where the packet-boats arrive from Ireland. It is a straggling, confused heap of thatched houses built on rocks; yet within doors there are in several of them very good accommodation for passengers, both in lodging and diet.

The packet-boats from Dublin arrive thrice a week, and are larger than those to Holland and France, fitted with all conveniences for passengers; and indeed St. George's Channel requires large ships in winter, the wind being generally very boisterous in these narrow seas.

On my return to Chester I passed over the mountain called Penmaen Ross, where I saw plainly a part of Ireland, Scotland, England, and the Isle of Man all at once.

Tour through the Eastern Counties of England, 1722

I began my travels where I purpose to end them, viz., at the City of London, and therefore my account of the city itself will come last, that is to say, at the latter end of my southern progress; and as in the course of this journey I shall have many occasions to call it a circuit, if not a circle, so I chose to give it the title of circuits in the plural, because I do not pretend to have travelled it all in one journey, but in many, and some of them many times over; the better to inform myself of everything I could find worth taking notice of.

I hope it will appear that I am not the less, but the more capable of giving a full account of things, by how much the more deliberation I have taken in the view of them, and by how much the oftener I have had opportunity to see them.

I set out the 3rd of April, 1722, going first eastward, and took what I think I may very honestly call a circuit in the very letter of it; for I went down by the coast of the Thames through the Marshes or Hundreds on the south side of the county of Essex, till I came to Malden, Colchester, and Harwich, thence continuing on the coast of Suffolk to Yarmouth; thence round by the edge of the sea, on the north and west side of Norfolk, to Lynn, Wisbech, and the Wash; thence back again, on the north side of Suffolk and Essex, to the west, ending it in Middlesex, near the place where I began it, reserving the middle or centre of the several counties to some little excursions, which I made by themselves.

Passing Bow Bridge, where the county of Essex begins, the first observation I made was, that all the villages which may be called the neighbourhood of the city of London on this, as well as on the other sides thereof, which I shall speak to in their order; I say, all those villages are increased in buildings to a strange degree, within the compass of about twenty or thirty years past at the most.

The village of Stratford, the first in this county from London, is not only increased, but, I believe, more than doubled in that time; every vacancy filled up with new houses, and two little towns or hamlets, as they may be called, on the forest side of the town entirely new, namely Maryland Point and the Gravel Pits, one facing the road to Woodford and Epping, and the other facing the road to Ilford; and as for the hither part, it is almost joined to Bow, in spite of rivers, canals, marshy grounds, &c. Nor is this increase of building the case only in this and all the other villages round London; but the increase of the value and rent of the houses formerly standing has, in that compass of years above-mentioned, advanced to a very great degree, and I may venture to say at least the fifth part; some think a third part, above what they were before.

This is indeed most visible, speaking of Stratford in Essex; but it is the same thing in proportion in other villages adjacent, especially on the forest side; as at Low Leyton, Leytonstone, Walthamstow, Woodford, Wanstead, and the towns of West Ham, Plaistow, Upton, etc. In all which places, or near them (as the inhabitants say), above a thousand new foundations have been erected, besides old houses repaired, all since the Revolution; and this is not to be forgotten too, that this increase is, generally speaking, of handsome, large houses, from £20 a year to £60, very few under £20 a year; being chiefly for the habitations of the richest citizens, such as either are able to keep two houses, one in the country and one in the city; or for such citizens as being rich, and having left off trade, live altogether in these neighbouring villages, for the pleasure and health of the latter part of their days.

The truth of this may at least appear, in that they tell me there are no less than two hundred coaches kept by the inhabitants within the circumference of these few villages named above, besides such as are kept by accidental lodgers.

This increase of the inhabitants, and the cause of it, I shall enlarge upon when I come to speak of the like in the counties of Middlesex, Surrey, &c, where it is the same, only in a much greater degree. But this I must take notice of here, that this increase causes those villages to be much pleasanter and more sociable than formerly, for now people go to them, not for retirement into the country, but for good company; of which, that I may speak to the ladies as well as other authors do, there are in these villages, nay, in all, three or four excepted, excellent conversation, and a great deal of it, and that without the mixture of assemblies, gaming-houses, and public foundations of vice and debauchery; and particularly I find none of those incentives kept up on this side the country.

Mr. Camden, and his learned continuator, Bishop Gibson, have ransacked this country for its antiquities, and have left little unsearched;

and as it is not my present design to say much of what has been said already, I shall touch very lightly where two such excellent antiquaries have gone before me; except it be to add what may have been since discovered, which as to these parts is only this: That there seems to be lately found out in the bottom of the Marshes (generally called Hackney Marsh, and beginning near about the place now called the Wick, between Old Ford and the said Wick), the remains of a great stone causeway, which, as it is supposed, was the highway, or great road from London into Essex, and the same which goes now over the great bridge between Bow and Stratford.

That the great road lay this way, and that the great causeway landed again just over the river, where now the Temple Mills stand, and passed by Sir Thomas Hickes's house at Ruckolls, all this is not doubted; and that it was one of those famous highways made by the Romans there is undoubted proof, by the several marks of Roman work, and by Roman coins and other antiquities found there, some of which are said to be deposited in the hands of the Rev. Mr. Strype, vicar of the parish of Low Leyton.

From hence the great road passed up to Leytonstone, a place by some known now as much by the sign of the "Green Man," formerly a lodge upon the edge of the forest; and crossing by Wanstead House, formerly the dwelling of Sir Josiah Child, now of his son the Lord Castlemain (of which hereafter), went over the same river which we now pass at Ilford; and passing that part of the great forest which we now call Hainault Forest, came into that which is now the great road, a little on this side the Whalebone, a place on the road so called because the rib-bone of a great whale, which was taken in the River Thames the same year that Oliver Cromwell died, 1658, was fixed there for a monument of that monstrous creature, it being at first about eight-and-twenty feet long.

According to my first intention of effectually viewing the sea-coast of these three counties, I went from Stratford to Barking, a large market-town, but chiefly inhabited by fishermen, whose smacks ride in the Thames, at the mouth of their river, from whence their fish is sent up to London to the market at Billingsgate by small boats, of which I shall speak by itself in my description of London.

One thing I cannot omit in the mention of these Barking fisher-smacks, viz., that one of those fishermen, a very substantial and experienced man, convinced me that all the pretences to bringing fish alive to London market from the North Seas, and other remote places on the coast of Great Britain, by the new-built sloops called fish-pools, have not been able to do anything but what their fishing-smacks are able on the same occasion to perform. These fishing-smacks are very useful vessels to the public upon many occasions; as particularly, in time of war they are used as press-smacks, running to all the northern and western coasts to pick up seamen to man the navy, when any expedition is at hand that requires a sudden equipment; at other times, being excellent sailors, they are tenders to particular men of war; and on an expedition they have been made use of as machines for the blowing up of fortified ports and havens; as at Calais, St. Malo, and other places.

This parish of Barking is very large, and by the improvement of lands taken in out of the Thames, and out of the river which runs by the town, the tithes, as the townsmen assured me, are worth above £600 per annum, including, small tithes. *Note.*—This parish has two or three chapels of ease, viz., one at Ilford, and one on the side of Hainault Forest, called New Chapel.

Sir Thomas Fanshaw, of an ancient Roman Catholic family, has a very good estate in this parish. A little beyond the town, on the road to Dagenham, stood a great house, ancient, and now almost fallen down, where tradition says the Gunpowder Treason Plot was at first contrived, and that all the first consultations about it were held there.

This side of the county is rather rich in land than in inhabitants, occasioned chiefly by the unhealthiness of the air; for these low marsh grounds, which, with all the south side of the county, have been saved out of the River Thames, and out of the sea, where the river is wide enough to be called so, begin here, or rather begin at West Ham, by Stratford, and continue to extend themselves, from hence eastward, growing wider and wider till we come beyond Tilbury, when the flat country lies six, seven, or eight miles broad, and is justly said to be both unhealthy and unpleasant.

However, the lands are rich, and, as is observable, it is very good farming in the marshes, because the landlords let good pennyworths, for it being a place where everybody cannot live, those that venture it will have encouragement and indeed it is but reasonable they should.

Several little observations I made in this part of the county of Essex.

I. We saw, passing from Barking to Dagenham, the famous breach, made by an inundation of the Thames, which was so great as that it laid near 5,000 acres of land under water, but which after near ten years lying under water, and being several times blown up, has been at last effectually stopped by the application of Captain Perry, the gentleman who, for several years, had been employed in the Czar of Muscovy's works, at Veronitza, on the River Don. This breach appeared now effectually made up, and they assured us that the new work, where the breach was, is by much esteemed the strongest of all the sea walls in that level.

2. It was observable that great part of the lands in these levels, especially those on this side East Tilbury, are held by the farmers, cow-keepers, and grazing butchers who live in and near London, and that they are generally stocked (all the winter half year) with large fat sheep, viz., Lincolnshire and Leicestershire wethers, which they buy in Smithfield in September and October, when the Lincolnshire and Leicestershire graziers sell off their stock, and are kept here till Christmas, or Candlemas, or thereabouts; and though they are not made at all fatter here than they were when bought in, yet the farmer or butcher finds very good advantage in it, by the difference of the price of mutton between Michaelmas, when it is cheapest, and Candlemas, when it is dearest; this is what the butchers value themselves upon, when they tell us at the market that it is right marsh-mutton.

3. In the bottom of these Marshes, and close to the edge of the river, stands the strong fortress of Tilbury, called Tilbury Fort, which may justly be looked upon as the key of the River Thames, and consequently the key of the City of London. It is a regular fortification. The design of it was a pentagon, but the water bastion, as it would have been called, was never built. The plan was laid out by Sir Martin Beckman, chief engineer to King Charles II., who also designed the works at Sheerness. The esplanade of the fort is very large, and the bastions the largest of any in England, the foundation is laid so deep, and piles under that, driven down two an end of one another, so far, till they were assured they were below the channel of the river, and that the piles, which were shed with iron, entered into the solid chalk rock adjoining to, or reaching from, the chalk hills on the other side. These bastions settled considerably at first, as did also part of the curtain, the great quantity of earth that was brought to fill them up, necessarily, requiring to be made solid by time; but they are now firm as the rocks of chalk which they came from, and the filling up one of these bastions, as I have been told by good hands, cost the Government £6,000, being filled with chalk rubbish fetched from the chalk pits at Northfleet, just above Gravesend.

The work to the land side is complete; the bastions are faced with brick. There is a double ditch, or moat, the innermost part of which is 180 feet broad; there is a good counterscarp, and a covered way marked out with ravelins and tenailles, but they are not raised a second time after their first settling.

On the land side there are also two small redoubts of brick, but of very little strength, for the chief strength of this fort on the land side consists in this, that they are able to lay the whole level under water, and so to make it impossible for an enemy to make any approaches to the fort that way.

On the side next the river there is a very strong curtain, with a noble gate called the Water Gate in the middle, and the ditch is palisadoed. At the place where the water bastion was designed to be built, and which by the plan should run wholly out into the river, so to flank the two curtains of each side; I say, in the place where it should have been, stands a high tower, which they tell us was built in Queen Elizabeth's time, and was called the Block House; the side next the water is vacant.

Before this curtain, above and below the said vacancy, is a platform in the place of a counterscarp, on which are planted 106 pieces of cannon, generally all of them carrying from twenty-four to forty-six pound ball; a battery so terrible as well imports the consequence of that place; besides which, there are smaller pieces planted between, and the bastions and curtain also are planted with guns; so that they must be bold fellows who will venture in the biggest ships the world has heard of to pass such a battery, if the men appointed to serve the guns do their duty like stout fellows, as becomes them.

The present government of this important place is under the prudent administration of the Right Honourable the Lord Newbrugh.

From hence there is nothing for many miles together remarkable but a continued level of unhealthy marshes, called the Three Hundreds, till we come before Leigh, and to the mouth of the River Chelmer, and Blackwater. These rivers united make a large firth, or inlet of the sea, which by Mr. Camden is called *Idumanum Fluvium*; but by our fishermen and seamen, who use it as a port, it is called Malden Water.

In this inlet of the sea is Osey, or Osyth Island, commonly called Oosy Island, so well known by our London men of pleasure for the infinite number of wild fowl, that is to say, duck, mallard, teal, and widgeon, of which there are such vast flights, that they tell us the island, namely the creek, seems covered with them at certain times of the year, and they go from London on purpose for the pleasure of shooting; and, indeed, often come home very well laden with game. But it must be remembered too that those gentlemen who are such lovers of the sport, and go so far for it, often return with an Essex ague on their backs, which they find a heavier load than the fowls they have shot.

It is on this shore, and near this creek, that the greatest quantity of fresh fish is caught which supplies not this country only, but London markets also. On the shore, beginning a little below Candy Island, or rather below Leigh Road, there lies a great shoal or sand called the Black Tail, which runs out near three leagues into the sea due east; at the end of it stands a pole or mast, set up by the Trinity House men of London, whose business is to lay buoys and set up sea marks for the direction of the sailors; this is called Shoe Beacon, from the point of land where this sand begins, which is called Shoeburyness, and that from the town of Shoebury, which stands by it. From this sand, and on the edge of Shoebury, before it, or south west of it, all along, to the mouth of Colchester water, the shore is full of shoals and sands, with some deep channels between; all which are so full of fish, that not only the Barking fishing-smacks come hither to fish, but the whole shore is full of small fisher-boats in very great numbers, belonging to the villages and towns on the coast, who come in every tide with what they take; and selling the smaller fish in the country, send the best and largest away upon horses, which go night and day to London market.

N.B.—I am the more particular in my remarks on this place, because in the course of my travels the reader will meet with the like in almost every place of note through the whole island, where it will be seen how this whole kingdom, as well the people as the land, and even the sea, in every part of it, are employed to furnish something, and I may add, the best of everything, to supply the City of London with provisions; I mean by provisions, corn, flesh, fish, butter, cheese, salt, fuel, timber, etc., and clothes also; with everything necessary for building, and furniture for their own use or for trade; of all which in their order.

On this shore also are taken the best and nicest, though not the largest, oysters in England; the spot from whence they have their common appellation is a little bank called Woelfleet, scarce to be called an island, in the mouth of the River Crouch, now called Crooksea Water; but the chief place where the said oysters are now had is from Wyvenhoe and the shores adjacent, whither they are brought by the fishermen, who take them at the mouth of that they call Colchester water and about the sand they call the Spits, and carry them up to Wyvenhoe, where they are laid in beds or pits on the shore to feed, as they call it; and then being barrelled up and carried to Colchester, which is but three miles off, they are sent to London by land, and are from thence called Colchester oysters.

The chief sort of other fish which they carry from this part of the shore to London are soles, which they take sometimes exceeding large, and yield a very good price at London market. Also sometimes middling turbot, with whiting, codling and large flounders; the small fish, as above, they sell in the country.

In the several creeks and openings, as above, on this shore there are also other islands, but of no particular note, except Mersey, which lies in the middle of the two openings between Malden Water and Colchester Water; being of the most difficult access, so that it is thought a thousand men well provided might keep possession of it against a great force, whether by land or sea. On this account, and because if possessed by an enemy it would shut up all the navigation and fishery on that side, the Government formerly built a fort on the south-east point of it; and generally in case of Dutch war, there is a strong body of troops kept there to defend it.

At this place may be said to end what we call the Hundreds of Essex—that is to say, the three Hundreds or divisions which include the marshy country, viz., Barnstable Hundred, Rochford Hundred, and Dengy Hundred.

I have one remark more before I leave this damp part of the world, and which I cannot omit on the women's account, namely, that I took notice of a strange decay of the sex here; insomuch that all along this country it was very frequent to meet with men that had had from five or six to fourteen or fifteen wives; nay, and some more. And I was informed that in the marshes on the other side of the river over against Candy Island there was a farmer who was then living with the five-and-twentieth wife, and that his son, who was but about thirty-five years old, had already had about fourteen. Indeed, this part of the story I only had by report, though from good hands too; but the other is well known and easy to be inquired into about Fobbing, Curringham, Thundersly, Benfleet, Prittlewell, Wakering, Great Stambridge, Cricksea, Burnham, Dengy, and other towns of the like situation. The reason, as a merry fellow told me, who said he had had about a dozen and a half of wives (though I found afterwards he fibbed a little) was this: That they being bred in the marshes themselves and seasoned to the place, did pretty well with it; but that they always went up into the hilly country, or, to speak their own language, into the uplands for a wife. That when they took the young lasses out of the wholesome and fresh air they were healthy, fresh, and clear, and well; but when they came out of their native air into the marshes among the fogs and damps, there they presently changed their complexion, got an ague or two, and seldom held it above half a year, or a year at most; "And then," said he, "we go to the uplands again and fetch another;" so that marrying of wives was reckoned a kind of good farm to them. It is true the fellow told this in a kind of drollery and mirth; but the fact, for all that, is certainly true; and that they have abundance of wives by that very means. Nor is it less true that the inhabitants in these places do not hold it out, as in other countries, and as first you seldom meet with very ancient people among the poor, as in other places we do, so, take it one with another, not one-half of the inhabitants are natives of the place; but such as from other countries or in other parts of this country settle here for the advantage of good farms; for which I appeal to any impartial inquiry, having myself examined into it critically in several places.

From the marshes and low grounds being not able to travel without many windings and indentures by reason of the creeks and waters, I came up to the town of Malden, a noted market town situate at the conflux or joining of two principal rivers in this county, the Chelm or Chelmer, and the Blackwater, and where they enter into the sea. The channel, as I have noted, is called by the sailors Malden Water, and is navigable up to the town, where by that means is a great trade for carrying corn by water to London; the county of Essex being (especially on all that side) a great corn county.

When I have said this I think I have done Malden justice, and said all of it that there is to be said, unless I should run into the old story of its antiquity, and tell you it was a Roman colony in the time of Vespasian, and that it was called Camolodunum. How the Britons, under Queen Boadicea, in revenge for the Romans' ill-usage of her—for indeed they used her majesty ill—they stripped her naked and whipped her publicly through their streets for some affront she had given them. I say how for this she raised the Britons round the country, overpowered, and cut in pieces the Tenth Legion, killed above eighty thousand Romans, and destroyed the colony; but was afterwards overthrown in a great battle, and sixty thousand Britons slain. I say, unless I should enter into this story, I have nothing more to say of Malden, and, as for that story, it is so fully related by Mr. Camden in his history of the Romans in Britain at the beginning of his "Britannia," that I need only refer the reader to it, and go on with my journey.

Being obliged to come thus far into the uplands, as above, I made it my road to pass through Witham, a pleasant, well-situated market town, in which, and in its neighbourhood, there are as many gentlemen of good fortunes and families as I believe can be met with in so narrow a compass in any of the three counties of which I make this circuit.

In the town of Witham dwells the Lord Pasely, oldest son of the Earl of Abercorn of Ireland (a branch of the noble family of Hamilton, in Scotland). His lordship has a small, but a neat, well-built new house, and is finishing his gardens in such a manner as few in that part of England will exceed them.

Nearer Chelmsford, hard by Boreham, lives the Lord Viscount Barrington, who, though not born to the title, or estate, or name which he now possesses, had the honour to be twice made heir to the estates of gentlemen not at all related to him, at least, one of them, as is very much to his honour, mentioned in his patent of creation. His name was Shute, his father a linendraper in London, and served sheriff of the said city in very troublesome times. He changed the name of Shute for that of Barrington by an Act of Parliament obtained for that purpose, and had the dignity of a baron of the kingdom conferred on him by the favour of King George. His lordship is a Dissenter, and seems to love retirement. He was a member of Parliament for the town of Berwick-upon-Tweed.

On the other side of Witham, at Fauburn, an ancient mansion house, built by the Romans, lives Mr. Bullock, whose father married the daughter of that eminent citizen, Sir Josiah Child, of Wanstead, by whom she had three sons; the eldest enjoys the estate, which is considerable.

It is observable, that in this part of the country there are several very considerable estates, purchased and now enjoyed by citizens of London, merchants, and tradesmen, as Mr. Western, an iron merchant, near Kelendon; Mr. Cresnor, a wholesale grocer, who was, a little before he died, named for sheriff at Earl's Coln; Mr. Olemus, a merchant at Braintree; Mr. Westcomb, near Malden; Sir Thomas Webster at Copthall, near Waltham; and several others.

I mention this to observe how the present increase of wealth in the City of London spreads itself into the country, and plants families and fortunes, who in another age will equal the families of the ancient gentry, who perhaps were brought out. I shall take notice of this in a general head, and when I have run through all the counties, collect a list of the families of citizens and tradesmen thus established in the several counties, especially round London.

The product of all this part of the country is corn, as that of the marshy feeding grounds mentioned above is grass, where their chief business is breeding of calves, which I need not say are the best and fattest, and the largest veal in England, if not in the world; and, as an instance, I ate part of a veal or calf, fed by the late Sir Josiah Child at Wanstead, the loin of which weighed above thirty pounds, and the flesh exceeding white and fat.

From hence I went on to Colchester. The story of Kill-Dane, which is told of the town of Kelvedon, three miles from Witham, namely, that this is the place where the massacre of the Danes was begun by the women, and that therefore it was called Kill-Dane; I say of it, as we generally say of improbable news, it wants confirmation. The true name of the town is Kelvedon, and has been so for many hundred years. Neither does Mr. Camden, or any other writer I meet with worth naming, insist on this piece of empty tradition. The town is commonly called Keldon.

Colchester is an ancient corporation. The town is large, very populous, the streets fair and beautiful, and though it may not said to be finely built, yet there are abundance of very good and well-built houses in it. It still mourns in the ruins of a civil war; during which, or rather after the heat of the war was over, it suffered a severe siege, which, the garrison making a resolute defence, was turned into a blockade, in which the garrison and inhabitants also suffered the utmost extremity of hunger, and were at last obliged to surrender at discretion, when their two chief officers, Sir Charles Lucas and Sir George Lisle, were shot to death under the castle wall. The inhabitants had a tradition that no grass would grow upon the spot where the blood of those two gallant gentlemen was spilt, and they showed the place bare of grass for many years; but whether for this reason I will not affirm. The story is now dropped, and the grass, I suppose, grows there, as in other places.

However, the battered walls, the breaches in the turrets, and the ruined churches, still remain, except that the church of St. Mary (where they had the royal fort) is rebuilt; but the steeple, which was two-thirds battered down, because the besieged had a large culverin upon it that did much execution, remains still in that condition.

There is another church which bears the marks of those times, namely, on the south side of the town, in the way to the Hythe, of which more hereafter.

The lines of contravallation, with the forts built by the besiegers, and which surrounded the whole town, remain very visible in many places; but the chief of them are demolished.

The River Colne, which passes through this town, compasses it on the north and east sides, and served in those times for a complete defence on those sides. They have three bridges over it, one called North Bridge, at the north gate, by which the road leads into Suffolk; one called East Bridge, at the foot of the High Street, over which lies the road to Harwich, and one at the Hythe, as above.

The river is navigable within three miles of the town for ships of large burthen; a little lower it may receive even a royal navy; and up to that part called the Hythe, close to the houses, it is navigable for hoys and small barques. This Hythe is a long street, passing from west to east, on the south side of the town. At the west end of it, there is a small intermission of the buildings, but not much; and towards the river it is very populous (it may be called the Wapping of Colchester). There is one church in that part of the town, a large quay by the river, and a good custom-house.

The town may be said chiefly to subsist by the trade of making bays, which is known over most of the trading parts of Europe by the name of Colchester Bays, though indeed all the towns round carry on the same trade—namely, Kelvedon, Witham, Coggeshall, Braintree, Bocking, &c., and the whole county, large as it is, may be said to be employed, and in part maintained, by the spinning of wool for the bay trade of Colchester and its adjacent towns. The account of the siege, A.D. 1648, with a diary of the most remarkable passages, are as follows, which I had from so good a hand as that I have no reason to question its being a true relation.

A Diary:
Or, An Account Of The Siege And Blockade Of Colchester, A.D. 1648.

On the 4th of June, we were alarmed in the town of Colchester that the Lord Goring, the Lord Capel, and a body of two thousand of the loyal party, who had been in arms in Kent, having left a great body of an army in possession of Rochester Bridge, where they resolved to fight the Lord Fairfax and the Parliament army, had given the said General Fairfax the slip, and having passed the Thames at Greenwich, were come to Stratford, and were advancing this way; upon which news, Sir Charles Lucas, Sir George Lisle, Colonel Cook, and several gentlemen of the loyal army, and all that had commissions from the king, with a gallant appearance of gentlemen volunteers, drew together from all parts of the country to join with them.

The 8th, we were further informed that they were advanced to Chelmsford, to New Hall House, and to Witham; and the 9th some of the horse arrived in the town, taking possession of the gates, and having engineers with them, told us that General Goring had resolved to make this town his headquarters, and would cause it to be well fortified. They also caused the drums to beat for volunteers; and a good number of the poor bay-weavers, and such-like people, wanting employment, enlisted; so that they completed Sir Charles Lucas's regiment, which was but thin, to near eight hundred men.

On the 10th we had news that the Lord Fairfax, having beaten the Royalists at Maidstone, and retaken Rochester, had passed the Thames at Gravesend, though with great difficulty, and with some loss, and was come to Horndon-on-the-Hill, in order to gain Colchester before the Royalists; but that hearing Sir Charles Lucas had prevented him, had ordered his rendezvous at Billerecay, and intended to possess the pass at Malden on the 11th, where Sir Thomas Honnywood, with the county-trained bands, was to be the same day.

The same evening the Lord Goring, with all his forces, making about five thousand six hundred men, horse and foot, came to Colchester, and encamping without the suburbs, under command of the cannon of St. Mary's fort, made disposition to fight the Parliament forces if they came up.

The 12th, the Lord Goring came into Colchester, viewed the fort in St. Mary's churchyard, ordered more cannon to be planted upon it, posted two regiments in the suburbs without the head gate, let the town know he would take them into his Majesty's protection, and that he would fight the enemy in that situation. The same evening the Lord Fairfax, with a strong party of one thousand horse, came to Lexden, at two small miles' distance, expecting the rest of his army there the same night.

The Lord Goring brought in prisoners the same day, Sir William Masham, and several other gentlemen of the county, who were secured under a strong guard; which the Parliament hearing, ordered twenty prisoners of the royal party to be singled out, declaring, that they should be used in the same manner as the Lord Goring used Sir William Masham, and the gentlemen prisoners with him.

On the 13th, early in the morning, our spies brought intelligence that the Lord Fairfax, all his forces being come up to him, was making dispositions for a march, resolving to attack the Royalists in their camp; upon which, the Lord Goring drew all his forces together, resolving to fight. The engineers had offered the night before to entrench his camp, and to draw a line round it in one night's time, but his lordship declined it, and now there was no time for it; whereupon the general, Lord Goring, drew up his army in order of battle on both sides the road, the horse in the open fields on the wings; the foot were drawn up, one regiment in the road, one regiment on each side, and two regiments for reserve in the suburb, just at the entrance of the town, with a regiment of volunteers advanced as a forlorn hope, and a regiment of horse at the head-gate, ready to support the reserve, as occasion should require.

About nine in the morning we heard the enemy's drums beat a march, and in half an hour more their first troops appeared on the higher grounds towards Lexden. Immediately the cannon from St. Mary's fired upon them, and put some troops of horse into confusion, doing great execution, which, they not being able to shun it, made them quicken their pace, fall on, when our cannon were obliged to cease firing, lest we should hurt our own troops as well as the enemy. Soon after, their foot appeared, and our cannon saluted them in like manner, and killed them a great many men.

Their first line of foot was led up by Colonel Barkstead, and consisted of three regiments of foot, making about 1,700 men, and these charged our regiment in the lane, commanded by Sir George Lisle and Sir William Campion. They fell on with great fury, and were received with as much gallantry, and three times repulsed; nor could they break in here, though the Lord Fairfax sent fresh men to support them, till the Royalists' horse, oppressed with numbers on the left, were obliged to retire, and at last to come full gallop into the street, and so on into the town. Nay, still the foot stood firm, and the volunteers, being all gentlemen, kept their ground with the greatest resolution; but the left wing being routed, as above, Sir William Campion was obliged to make a front to the left, and lining the hedge with his musketeers, made a stand with a body of pikes against the enemy's horse, and prevented them entering the lane. Here that gallant gentleman was killed with a carabine shot; and after a very gallant resistance, the horse on the right being also overpowered, the word was given to retreat, which, however, was done in such good order, the regiments of reserve standing drawn up at the end of the street, ready to receive the enemy's horse upon the points of their pikes, that the royal troops came on in the openings between the regiments, and entered the town with very little loss, and in very good order.

By this, however, those regiments of reserve were brought at last to sustain the efforts of the enemy's whole army, till being overpowered by numbers they were put into disorder, and forced to get into the town in the best manner they could; by which means near two hundred men were killed or made prisoners.

Encouraged by this success the enemy pushed on, supposing they should enter the town pell-mell with the rest; nor did the Royalists hinder them, but let good part of Barkstead's own regiment enter the head-gate; but then sallying from St. Mary's with a choice body of foot on their left, and the horse rallying in the High Street, and charging them again in the front, they were driven back quite into the street of the suburb, and most of those that had so rashly entered were cut in pieces.

Thus they were repulsed at the south entrance into the town; and though they attempted to storm three times after that with great resolution, yet they were as often beaten back, and that with great havoc of their men; and the cannon from the fort all the while did execution upon those who stood drawn up to support them; so that at last, seeing no good to be done, they retreated, having small joy of their pretended victory.

They lost in this action Colonel Needham, who commanded a regiment called the Tower Guards, and who fought very desperately;

Captain Cox, an old experienced horse officer, and several other officers of note, with a great many private men, though, as they had the field, they concealed their number, giving out that they lost but a hundred, when we were assured they lost near a thousand men besides the wounded.

They took some of our men prisoners, occasioned by the regiment of Colonel Farr, and two more sustaining the shock of their whole army, to secure the retreat of the main body, as above.

The 14th, the Lord Fairfax finding he was not able to carry the town by storm, without the formality of a siege, took his headquarters at Lexden, and sent to London and to Suffolk for more forces; also he ordered the trained bands to be raised and posted on the roads to prevent succours. Notwithstanding which, divers gentlemen, with some assistance of men and arms, found means to get into the town.

The very same night they began to break ground, and particularly to raise a fort between Colchester and Lexden, to cover the general's quarter from the sallies from the town; for the Royalists having a good body of horse, gave them no rest, but scoured the fields every day, and falling all that were found straggling from their posts, and by this means killed a great many.

The 17th, Sir Charles Lucas having been out with 1,200 horse, and detaching parties toward the seaside, and towards Harwich, they brought in a very great quantity of provisions, and abundance of sheep and black cattle sufficient for the supply of the town for a considerable time; and had not the Suffolk forces advanced over Cataway Bridge to prevent it, a larger supply had been brought in that way; for now it appeared plainly that the Lord Fairfax finding the garrison strong and resolute, and that he was not in a condition to reduce them by force, at least without the loss of much blood, had resolved to turn his siege into a blockade, and reduce them by hunger; their troops being also wanted to oppose several other parties, who had, in several parts of the kingdom, taken arms for the king's cause.

This same day General Fairfax sent in a trumpet to propose exchanging prisoners, which the Lord Goring rejected, expecting a reinforcement of troops, which were actually coming to him, and were to be at Linton in Cambridgeshire as the next day.

The same day two ships brought in a quantity of corn and provisions and fifty-six men from the shore of Kent with several gentlemen, who all landed and came up to the town, and the greatest part of the corn was with the utmost application unloaded the same night into some hoys, which brought it up to the Hythe, being apprehensive of the Parliament's ships which lay at Harwich, who having intelligence of the said ships, came the next day into the mouth of the river, and took the said two ships and what corn was left in them. The besieged sent out a party to help the ships, but having no boats they could not assist them.

18th. Sir Charles Lucas sent an answer about exchange of prisoners, accepting the conditions offered, but the Parliament's general returned that he would not treat with Sir Charles, for that he (Sir Charles) being his prisoner upon his parole of honour, and having appeared in arms contrary to the rules of war, had forfeited his honour and faith, and was not capable of command or trust in martial affairs. To this Sir Charles sent back an answer, and his excuse for his breach of his parole, but it was not accepted, nor would the Lord Fairfax enter upon any treaty with him.

Upon this second message Sir William Masham and the Parliament Committee and other gentlemen, who were prisoners in the town, sent a message in writing under their hands to the Lord Fairfax, entreating him to enter into a treaty for peace; but the Lord Fairfax returned, he could take no notice of their request, as supposing it forced from them under restraint; but that if the Lord Goring desired peace, he might write to the Parliament, and he would cause his messenger to have a safe conduct to carry his letter. There was a paper sent enclosed in this paper, signed Capel, Norwich, Charles Lucas, but to that the general would return no answer, because it was signed by Sir Charles for the reasons above.

All this while the Lord Goring, finding the enemy strengthening themselves, gave order for fortifying the town, and drawing lines in several places to secure the entrance, as particularly without the east bridge, and without the north gate and bridge, and to plant more cannon upon the works; to which end some great guns were brought in from some ships at Wivenhoe.

The same day, our men sallied out in three places, and attacked the besiegers, first at their port, called Essex, then at their new works, on the south of the town; a third party sallying at the east bridge, brought in some booty from the Suffolk troops, having killed several of their stragglers on the Harwich road. They also took a lieutenant of horse prisoner, and brought him into the town.

19th. This day we had the unwelcome news that our friends at Linton were defeated by the enemy, and Major Muschamp, a loyal gentleman, killed.

The same night, our men gave the enemy alarm at their new Essex fort, and thereby drew them out as if they would fight, till they brought them within reach of the cannon of St. Mary's, and then our men retiring, the great guns let fly among them, and made them run. Our men shouted after them. Several of them were killed on this occasion, one shot having killed three horsemen in our fight.

20th. We now found the enemy, in order to a perfect blockade, resolved to draw a line of circumvallation round the town; having received a train of forty pieces of heavy cannon from the Tower of London.

This day the Parliament sent a messenger to their prisoners to know how they fared, and how they were used; who returned word, that they fared indifferent well, and were very civilly used, but that provisions were scarce, and therefore dear.

This day a party of horse, with 300 foot, sallied out, and marched as far as the fort on the Isle of Mersey, which they made a show of attacking, to keep in the garrison. Meanwhile the rest took a good number of cattle from the country, which they brought safe into the town, with five waggons laden with corn. This was the last they could bring in that way, the lines being soon finished on that side.

This day the Lord Fairfax sent in a trumpet to the Earl of Norwich and the Lord Goring, offering honourable conditions to them all, allowing all the gentlemen their lives and arms, exemption from plunder, and passes, if they desired to go beyond sea, and all the private men pardon, and leave to go peaceably to their own dwellings. But the Lord Goring and the rest of the gentlemen rejected it, and laughed at them, upon which the Lord Fairfax made proclamation, that his men should give the private soldiers in Colchester free leave to pass through their camp, and go where they pleased without molestation, only leaving their arms, but that the gentlemen should have no quarter. This was a great loss to the Royalists, for now the men foreseeing the great hardships they were like to suffer, began to slip away, and the Lord Goring was obliged to forbid any to desert on pain of present death, and to keep parties of horse continually patrolling to prevent them; notwithstanding which many got away.

21st. The town desired the Lord Goring to give them leave to send a message to Lord Fairfax, to desire they might have liberty to carry on their trade and sell their bays and says, which Lord Goring granted; but the enemy's general returned, that they should have considered that before they let the Royalists into the town; that to desire a free trade from a town besieged was never heard of, or at least, was such a motion, as was never yet granted; that, however, he would give the bay-makers leave to bring their bays and says, and other goods, once a week, or oftener, if they desire it, to Lexden Heath, where they should have a free market, and might sell them or carry them back again, if not sold, as they found occasion.

22nd. The besieged sallied out in the night with a strong party, and disturbed the enemy in their works, and partly ruined one of their forts, called Ewer's Fort, where the besiegers were laying a bridge over the River Colne. Also they sallied again at east bridge, and faced the Suffolk troops, who were now declared enemies. These brought in six-and-fifty good bullocks, and some cows, and they took and killed several of the enemy.

23rd. The besiegers began to fire with their cannon from Essex Fort, and from Barkstead's Fort, which was built upon the Malden road; and finding that the besieged had a party in Sir Harbottle Grimston's house, called, "The Fryery," they fired at it with their cannon, and battered it almost down, and then the soldiers set it on fire.

This day upon the townsmen's treaty for the freedom of the bay trade, the Lord Fairfax sent a second offer of conditions to the besieged, being the same as before, only excepting Lord Goring, Lord Capel, Sir George Lisle, and Sir Charles Lucas.

This day we had news in the town that the Suffolk forces were advanced to assist the besiegers, and that they began a fort called Fort Suffolk, on the north side of the town, to shut up the Suffolk road towards Stratford. This day the besieged sallied out at north bridge, attacked the out-guards of the Suffolk men on Mile End Heath, and drove them into their fort in the woods.

This day the Lord Fairfax sent a trumpet, complaining of chewed and poisoned bullets being shot from the town, and threatening to give no quarter if that practice was allowed; but Lord Goring returned answer, with a protestation, that no such thing was done by his order or consent.

24th. They fired hard from their cannon against St. Mary's steeple, on which was planted a large culverin, which annoyed them even in the general's headquarters at Lexden. One of the best gunners the garrison had was killed with a cannon bullet. This night the besieged sallied towards Audly, on the Suffolk road, and brought in some cattle.

25th. Lord Capel sent a trumpet to the Parliament-General, but the rogue ran away, and came not back, nor sent any answer; whether they received his message or not, was not known.

26th. This day having finished their new bridge, a party of their troops passed that bridge, and took post on the hill over against Mile End Church, where they built a fort, called Fothergall's Fort, and another on the east side of the road, called Rainsbro's Fort, so that the town was entirely shut in, on that side, and the Royalists had no place free but over east bridge, which was afterwards cut off by the enemy's bringing their line from the Hythe within the river to the stone causeway leading to the east bridge.

July 1st. From the 26th to the 1st, the besiegers continued finishing their works, and by the 2nd the whole town was shut in; at which the besiegers gave a general salvo from their cannon at all their forts; but the besieged gave them a return, for they sallied out in the night, attacked Barkstead's fort, scarce finished, with such fury, that they twice entered the work sword in hand, killed most part of the defendants, and spoiled part of the forts cast up; but fresh forces coming up, they retired with little loss, bringing eight prisoners, and having slain, as they reported, above 100.

On the second, Lord Fairfax offered exchange for Sir William Masham in particular, and afterwards for other prisoners, but the Lord Goring refused.

5th. The besieged sallied with two regiments, supported by some horse, at midnight; they were commanded by Sir George Lisle. They fell on with such fury, that the enemy were put into confusion, their works at east bridge ruined, and two pieces of cannon taken, Lieutenant Colonel Sambrook, and several other officers, were killed, and our men retired into the town, bringing the captain, two lieutenants, and about fifty men with them prisoners into the town; but having no horse, we could not bring off the cannon, but they spiked them, and made them unfit for service.

From this time to the 11th, the besieged sallied almost every night, being encouraged by their successes, and they constantly cut off some of the enemy, but not without loss also on their own side.

About this time we received by a spy the bad news of defeating the king's friends almost in all parts of England, and particularly several parties which had good wishes to our gentlemen, and intended to relieve them.

Our batteries from St. Mary's Fort and steeple, and from the north bridge, greatly annoyed them, and killed most of their gunners and firemen. One of the messengers who brought news to Lord Fairfax of the defeat of one of the parties, in Kent, and the taking of Weymer Castle, slipped into the town, and brought a letter to the Lord Goring, and listed in the regiment of the Lord Capel's horse.

14th. The besiegers attacked and took the Hythe Church, with a small work the besieged had there, but the defenders retired in time; some were taken prisoners in the church, but not in the fort; Sir Charles Lucas's horse was attacked by a great body of the besiegers; the besieged defended themselves with good resolution for some time, but a hand-grenade thrown in by the assailants, having fired the magazine, the house was blown up, and most of the gallant defenders buried in the ruins. This was a great blow to the Royalists, for it was a very strong pass, and always well guarded.

15th. The Lord Fairfax sent offers of honourable conditions to the soldiers of the garrison if they would surrender, or quit the service; upon which the Lords Goring and Capel, and Sir Charles Lucas, returned an answer signed by their hands, that it was not honourable or agreeable to the usage of war to offer conditions separately to the soldiers, exclusive of their officers, and therefore civilly desired his lordship to send no more such messages or proposals, or if he did, that he would not take it ill if they hanged up the messenger.

This evening all the gentlemen volunteers, with all the horse of the garrison, with Sir Charles Lucas, Sir George Lisle, and Sir Bernard Gascoigne at the head of them, resolved to break through the enemy, and forcing a pass to advance into Suffolk by Nayland Bridge. To this purpose they passed the river near Middle Mill; but their guides having misled them the enemy took the alarm; upon which their guides, and some pioneers which they had with them to open the hedges and level the banks, for their passing to Boxted, all ran away, so the horse were obliged to retreat, the enemy pretending to pursue, but thinking they had retreated by the north bridge, they missed them; upon which being enraged, they fired the suburbs without the bridge, and burned them quite down.

18th. Some of the horse attempted to escape the same way, and had the whole body been there as before, they had effected it; but there being but two troops, they were obliged to retire. Now the town began to be greatly distressed, provisions failing, and the townspeople, which were numerous, being very uneasy, and no way of breaking through being found practicable, the gentlemen would have joined in any attempt wherein they might die gallantly with their swords in their hands, but nothing presented; they often sallied and cut off many of the enemy, but their numbers were continually supplied, and the besieged diminished; their horse also sunk and became unfit for service, having very little hay, and no corn, and at length they were forced to kill them for food; so that they began to be in a very miserable condition, and the soldiers deserted every day in great numbers, not being able to bear the want of food, as being almost starved with hunger.

22nd. The Lord Fairfax offered again an exchange of prisoners, but the Lord Goring rejected it, because they refused conditions to the chief gentlemen of the garrison.

During this time, two troops of the Royal Horse sallied out in the night, resolving to break out or die: the first rode up full gallop to the enemy's horse guards on the side of Malden road, and exchanged their pistols with the advanced troops, and wheeling made as if they would retire to the town; but finding they were not immediately pursued, they wheeled about to the right, and passing another guard at a distance, without being perfectly discovered, they went clean off, and passing towards Tiptree Heath, and having good guides, they made their escape towards Cambridgeshire, in which length of way they found means to disperse without being attacked, and went every man his own way as fate directed; nor did we hear that many of them were taken: they were led, as we are informed, by Sir Bernard Gascoigne.

Upon these attempts of the horse to break out, the enemy built a small fort in the meadow right against the ford in the river at the Middle Mill, and once set that mill on fire, but it was extinguished without much damage; however, the fort prevented any more attempts that way.

22nd. The Parliament-General sent in a trumpet, to propose again the exchange of prisoners, offering the Lord Capel's son for one, and Mr. Ashburnham for Sir William Masham; but the Lord Capel, Lord Goring, and the rest of the loyal gentlemen rejected it; and Lord Capel, in particular, sent the Lord Fairfax word it was inhuman to surprise his son, who was not in arms, and offer him to insult a father's affection, but that he might murder his son if he pleased, he would leave his blood to be revenged as Heaven should give opportunity; and the

Lord Goring sent word, that as they had reduced the king's servants to eat horseflesh, the prisoners should feed as they fed.

The enemy sent again to complain of the Royalists shooting poisoned bullets, and sent two affidavits of it made by two deserters, swearing it was done by the Lord Norwich's direction; the generals in the town returned under all their hands that they never gave any such command or direction; that they disowned the practice; and that the fellows who swore it were perjured before in running from their colours and the service of their king, and ought not to be credited again; but they added, that for shooting rough-cast slugs they must excuse them, as things stood with them at that time.

About this time, a porter in a soldier's habit got through the enemy's leaguer, and passing their out-guards in the dark, got into the town, and brought letters from London, assuring the Royalists that there were so many strong parties up in arms for the king, and in so many places, that they would be very suddenly relieved. This they caused to be read to the soldiers to encourage them; and particularly it related to the rising of the Earl of Holland, and the Duke of Buckingham, who with 500 horse were gotten together in arms about Kingston in Surrey; but we had notice in a few days after that they were defeated, and the Earl of Holland taken, who was afterwards beheaded.

26th. The enemy now began to batter the walls, and especially on the west side, from St. Mary's towards the north gate; and we were assured they intended a storm; on which the engineers were directed to make trenches behind the walls where the breaches should be made, that in case of a storm they might meet with a warm reception. Upon this, they gave over the design of storming. The Lord Goring finding that the enemy had set the suburbs on fire right against the Hythe, ordered the remaining houses, which were empty of inhabitants, from whence their musketeer fired against the town, to be burned also.

31st. A body of foot sallied out at midnight, to discover what the enemy were doing at a place where they thought a new fort raising; they fell in among the workmen, and put them to flight, cut in pieces several of the guard, and brought in the officer who commanded them prisoner.

August 2nd. The town was now in a miserable condition: the soldiers searched and rifled the houses of the inhabitants for victuals; they had lived on horseflesh several weeks, and most of that also was as lean as carrion, which not being well salted bred wens; and this want of diet made the soldiers sickly, and many died of fluxes, yet they boldly rejected all offers of surrender, unless with safety to their offices. However, several hundreds got out, and either passed the enemy's guards, or surrendered to them and took passes.

7th. The townspeople became very uneasy to the soldiers, and the mayor of the town, with the aldermen, waited upon the general, desiring leave to send to the Lord Fairfax for leave to all the inhabitants to come out of the town, that they might not perish, to which the Lord Goring consented, but the Lord Fairfax refused them.

12th. The rabble got together in a vast crowd about the Lord Goring's quarters, clamouring for a surrender, and they did this every evening, bringing women and children, who lay howling and crying on the ground for bread; the soldiers beat off the men, but the women and children would not stir, bidding the soldiers kill them, saying they had rather be shot than be starved.

16th. The general, moved by the cries and distress of the poor inhabitants, sent out a trumpet to the Parliament-General, demanding leave to send to the Prince, who was with a fleet of nineteen men of war in the mouth of the Thames, offering to surrender, if they were not relieved in twenty days. The Lord Fairfax refused it, and sent them word he would be in the town in person, and visit them in less than twenty days, intimating that they were preparing for a storm. Some tart messages and answers were exchanged on this occasion. The Lord Goring sent word they were willing, in compassion to the poor townspeople, and to save that effusion of blood, to surrender upon honourable terms, but that as for the storming them, which was threatened, they might come on when they thought fit, for that they (the Royalists) were ready for them. This held to the 19th.

20th. The Lord Fairfax returned what he said was his last answer, and should be the last offer of mercy. The conditions offered were, that upon a peaceable surrender, all soldiers and officers under the degree of a captain in commission should have their lives, be exempted from plunder, and have passes to go to their respective dwellings. All the captains and superior officers, with all the lords and gentlemen, as well in commission as volunteers, to surrender prisoners at discretion, only that they should not be plundered by the soldiers.

21st. The generals rejected those offers; and when the people came about them again for bread, set open one of the gates, and bid them go out to the enemy, which a great many did willingly; upon which the Lord Goring ordered all the rest that came about his door to be turned out after them. But when the people came to the Lord

Fairfax's camp the out-guards were ordered to fire at them and drive them all back again to the gate, which the Lord Goring seeing, he ordered them to be received in again. And now, although the generals and soldiers also were resolute to die with their swords in their hands rather than yield, and had maturely resolved to abide a storm, yet the Mayor and Aldermen having petitioned them as well as the inhabitants, being wearied with the importunities of the distressed people, and pitying the deplorable condition they were reduced to, they agreed to enter upon a treaty, and accordingly sent out some officers to the Lord Fairfax, the Parliament-General, to treat, and with them was sent two gentlemen of the prisoners upon their parole to return.

Upon the return of the said messengers with the Lord Fairfax's terms, the Lord Goring, &c., sent out a letter declaring they would die with their swords in their hands rather than yield without quarter for life, and sent a paper of articles on which they were willing to surrender. But in the very interim of this treaty news came that the Scots army, under Duke Hamilton, which was entered into Lancashire, and was joined by the Royalists in that country, making 21,000 men, were entirely defeated. After this the Lord Fairfax would not grant any abatement of articles—viz., to have all above lieutenants surrender at mercy.

Upon this the Lord Goring and the General refused to submit again, and proposed a general sally, and to break through or die, but found upon preparing for it that the soldiers, who had their lives offered them, declined it, fearing the gentlemen would escape, and they should be left to the mercy of the Parliament soldiers; and that upon this they began to mutiny and talk of surrendering the town and their officers too. Things being brought to this pass, the Lords and General laid aside that design, and found themselves obliged to submit; and so the town was surrendered the 28th of August, 1648, upon conditions as follows:-

The Lords and gentlemen all prisoners at mercy.

The common soldiers had passes to go home to their several dwellings, but without arms, and an oath not to serve against the Parliament.

The town to be preserved from pillage, paying £14,000 ready money.

The same day a council of war being called about the prisoners of war, it was resolved that the Lords should be left to the disposal of the Parliament. That Sir Charles Lucas, Sir George Lisle, and Sir Marmaduke Gascoigne should be shot to death, and the other officers prisoners to remain in custody till further order.

The two first of the three gentlemen were shot to death, and the third respited. Thus ended the siege of Colchester.

N.B.—Notwithstanding the number killed in the siege, and dead of the flux, and other distempers occasioned by bad diet, which were very many, and notwithstanding the number which deserted and escaped in the time of their hardships, yet there remained at the time of the surrender:

Earl of Norwich (Goring).
Lord Capell.
Lord Loughbro'.
11 Knights.
9 Colonels.
8 Lieut.-Colonels.
9 Majors.
30 Captains.
72 Lieutenants.
69 Ensigns.
183 Serjeants and Corporals.
3,067 Private Soldiers.
65 Servants to the Lords and General Officers and Gentlemen.
3,526 in all.

The town of Colchester has been supposed to contain about 40,000 people, including the out-villages which are within its liberty, of which there are a great many—the liberty of the town being of a great extent. One sad testimony of the town being so populous is that they buried upwards of 5,259 people in the plague year, 1665. But the town was severely visited indeed, even more in proportion than any of its neighbours, or than the City of London.

The government of the town is by a mayor, high steward, a recorder or his deputy, eleven aldermen, a chamberlain, a town clerk, assistants, and eighteen common councilmen. Their high steward (this year, 1722) is Sir Isaac Rebow, a gentleman of a good family and known character, who has generally for above thirty years been one of their representatives in Parliament. He has a very good house at the entrance in at the south, or head gate of the town, where he has had the honour several times to lodge and entertain the late King William of glorious memory in his returning from Holland by way of Harwich to London. Their recorder is Earl Cowper, who has been twice Lord High Chancellor of England. But his lordship not residing in those parts has put in for his deputy,—Price, Esq., barrister-at-law, and who dwells in the town. There are in Colchester eight churches besides those which are damaged, and five meeting-houses, whereof two for Quakers, besides a Dutch church and a French church.

Public Edifices are -

I. Bay Hall, an ancient society kept up for ascertaining the manufacture of bays, which are, or ought to be, all brought to this hall to be viewed and sealed according to their goodness by the masters; and to this practice has been owing the great reputation of the Colchester bays in foreign markets, where to open the side of a bale and show the seal has been enough to give the buyer a character of the value of the goods without any further search; and so far as they abate the integrity and exactness of their method, which I am told of late is much omitted; I say, so far, that reputation will certainly abate in the markets they go to, which are principally in Portugal and Italy. This corporation is governed by a particular set of men who are called governors of the Dutch Bay Hall. And in the same building is the Dutch church.

2. The guildhall of the town, called by them the moot hall, to which is annexed the town gaol.

3. The workhouse, being lately enlarged, and to which belongs a corporation or a body of the inhabitants, consisting of sixty persons incorporated by Act of Parliament Anno 1698 for taking care of the poor. They are incorporated by the name and title of the governor, deputy governor, assistants, and guardians of the poor of the town of Colchester. They are in number eight-and-forty, to whom are added the mayor and aldermen for the time being, who are always guardians by the same charter. These make the number of sixty, as above. There is also a grammar free-school, with a good allowance to the master, who is chosen by the town.

4. The castle of Colchester is now become only a monument showing the antiquity of the place, it being built as the walls of the town also are, with Roman bricks, and the Roman coins dug up here, and ploughed up in the fields adjoining, confirm it. The inhabitants

boast much that Helena, the mother of Constantine the Great, first Christian Emperor of the Romans, was born there, and it may be so for aught we know. I only observe what Mr. Camden says of the Castle of Colchester, viz.: In the middle of this city stands a castle ready to fall with age.

Though this castle has stood one hundred and twenty years from the time Mr. Camden wrote that account, and it is not fallen yet, nor will another hundred and twenty years, I believe, make it look one jot the older. And it was observable that in the late siege of this town, a common shot, which the besiegers made at this old castle, were so far from making it fall, that they made little or no impression upon it; for which reason, it seems, and because the garrison made no great use of it against the besiegers, they fired no more at it.

There are two charity schools set up here, and carried on by a generous subscription, with very good success.

The title of Colchester is in the family of Earl Rivers, and the eldest son of that family is called Lord Colchester, though as I understand, the title is not settled by the creation to the eldest son till he enjoys the title of earl with it, but that the other is by the courtesy of England; however, this I take *ad referendum*.

From Colchester I took another step down to the coast; the land running out a great way into the sea, south and south-east makes that promontory of land called the Naze, and well known to seamen using the northern trade. Here one sees a sea open as an ocean without any opposite shore, though it be no more than the mouth of the Thames. This point called the Naze, and the north-east point of Kent, near Margate, called the North Foreland, making what they call the mouth of the river and the port of London, though it be here above sixty miles over.

At Walton-under-the-Naze they find on the shore copperas-stone in great quantities; and there are several large works called copperas houses, where they make it with great expense.

On this promontory is a new mark erected by the Trinity House men, and at the public expense, being a round brick tower, near eighty feet high. The sea gains so much upon the land here by the continual winds at south-west, that within the memory of some of the inhabitants there they have lost above thirty acres of land in one place.

From hence we go back into the county about four miles, because of the creeks which lie between; and then turning east again come to Harwich, on the utmost eastern point of this large country.

Harwich is a town so well known and so perfectly described by many writers, I need say little of it. It is strong by situation, and may be made more so by art. But it is many years since the Government of England have had any occasion to fortify towns to the landward; it is enough that the harbour or road, which is one of the best and securest in England, is covered at the entrance by a strong fort and a battery of guns to the seaward, just as at Tilbury, and which sufficiently defend the mouth of the river. And there is a particular felicity in this fortification, viz., that though the entrance or opening of the river into the sea is very wide, especially at high-water, at least two miles, if not three over; yet the Channel, which is deep, and in which the ships must keep and come to the harbour, is narrow, and lies only on the side of the fort, so that all the ships which come in or go out must come close under the guns of the fort—that is to say, under the command of their shot.

The fort is on the Suffolk side of the bay or entrance, but stands so far into the sea upon the point of a sand or shoal, which runs out toward the Essex side, as it were, laps over the mouth of that haven like a blind to it; and our surveyors of the country affirm it to be in the county of Essex. The making this place, which was formerly no other than a sand in the sea, solid enough for the foundation of so good a fortification, has not been done but by many years' labour, often repairs, and an infinite expense of money, but it is now so firm that nothing of storms and high tides, or such things as make the sea dangerous to these kind of works, can affect it.

The harbour is of a vast extent; for, as two rivers empty themselves here, viz., Stour from Manningtree and the Orwell from Ipswich, the channels of both are large and deep; and safe for all weathers; so where they join they make a large bay or road able to receive the biggest ships, and the greatest number that ever the world saw together; I mean ships of war. In the old Dutch war great use has been made of this harbour; and I have known that there has been one hundred sail of men-of-war and their attendants and between three and four hundred sail of collier ships all in this harbour at a time, and yet none of them crowding or riding in danger of one another.

Harwich is known for being the port where the packet boats, between England and Holland, go out and come in. The inhabitants are far from being famed for good usage to strangers, but, on the contrary, are blamed for being extravagant in their reckonings in the public-houses, which has not a little encouraged the setting up of sloops, which they now call passage boats, to Holland, to go directly from the River Thames; this, though it may be something the longer passage, yet as they are said to be more obliging to passengers and more reasonable in the expense, and, as some say, also, the vessels are better sea boats, has been the reason why so many passengers do not go or come by the way of Harwich as formerly were wont to do; insomuch that the stage coaches between this place and London, which ordinarily went twice or three times a week, are now entirely laid down, and the passengers are left to hire coaches on purpose, take post-horses, or hire horses to Colchester, as they find most convenient.

The account of a petrifying quality in the earth here, though some will have it to be in the water of a spring hard by, is very strange. They boast that their town is walled and their streets paved with clay, and yet that one is as strong and the other as clean as those that are built or paved with stone. The fact is indeed true, for there is a sort of clay in the cliff, between the town and the Beacon Hill adjoining, which, when it falls down into the sea, where it is beaten with the waves and the weather, turns gradually into stone. But the chief reason assigned is from the water of a certain spring or well, which, rising in the said cliff, runs down into the sea among those pieces of clay, and petrifies them as it runs; and the force of the sea often stirring, and perhaps turning, the lumps of clay, when storms of wind may give force enough to the water, causes them to harden everywhere alike; otherwise those which were not quite sunk in the water of the spring would be petrified but in part. These stones are gathered up to pave the streets and build the houses, and are indeed very hard. It is also remarkable that some of them taken up before they are thoroughly petrified will, upon breaking them, appear to be hard as a stone without and soft as clay in the middle; whereas others that have lain a due time shall be thorough stone to the centre, and as exceeding hard within as without. The same spring is said to turn wood into iron. But this I take to be no more or less than the quality, which, as I mentioned of the shore at the Naze, is found to be in much of the stone all along this shore, viz., of the copperas kind; and it is certain that the copperas stone (so called) is found in all that cliff, and even where the water of this spring has run; and I presume that those who call the hardened pieces of wood, which they take out of this well by the name of iron, never tried the quality of it with the fire or hammer; if they had, perhaps they would have given some other account of it.

173

On the promontory of land which they call Beacon Hill and which lies beyond or behind the town towards the sea, there is a lighthouse to give the ships directions in their sailing by as well as their coming into the harbour in the night. I shall take notice of these again all together when I come to speak of the Society of Trinity House, as they are called, by whom they are all directed upon this coast.

This town was erected into a marquisate in honour of the truly glorious family of Schomberg, the eldest son of Duke Schomberg, who landed with King William, being styled Marquis of Harwich; but that family (in England, at least) being extinct the title dies also.

Harwich is a town of hurry and business, not much of gaiety and pleasure; yet the inhabitants seem warm in their nests, and some of them are very wealthy. There are not many (if any) gentlemen or families of note either in the town or very near it. They send two members to Parliament; the present are Sir Peter Parker and Humphrey Parsons, Esq.

And now being at the extremity of the county of Essex, of which I have given you some view as to that side next the sea only, I shall break off this part of my letter by telling you that I will take the towns which lie more towards the centre of the county, in my return by the north and west part only, that I may give you a few hints of some towns which were near me in my route this way, and of which being so well known there is but little to say.

On the road from London to Colchester, before I came into it at Witham, lie four good market towns at equal distance from one another, namely, Romford, noted for two markets, viz., one for calves and hogs, the other for corn and other provisions, most, if not all, bought up for London market. At the farther end of the town, in the middle of a stately park, stood Guldy Hall, vulgarly Giddy Hall, an ancient seat of one Coke, sometime Lord Mayor of London, but forfeited on some occasion to the Crown. It is since pulled down to the ground, and there now stands a noble stately fabric or mansion house, built upon the spot by Sir John Eyles, a wealthy merchant of London, and chosen Sub-Governor of the South Sea Company immediately after the ruin of the former Sub-Governor and Directors, whose overthrow makes the history of these times famous.

Brentwood and Ingatestone, and even Chelmsford itself, have very little to be said of them, but that they are large thoroughfare towns, full of good inns, and chiefly maintained by the excessive multitude of

174

carriers and passengers which are constantly passing this way to London with droves of cattle, provisions, and manufactures for London.

The last of these towns is indeed the county town, where the county gaol is kept, and where the assizes are very often held; it stands on the conflux of two rivers—the Chelmer, whence the town is called, and the Cann.

At Lees, or Lee's Priory, as some call it, is to be seen an ancient house in the middle of a beautiful park, formerly the seat of the late Duke of Manchester, but since the death of the duke it is sold to the Duchess Dowager of Buckinghamshire, the present Duke of Manchester retiring to his ancient family seat at Kimbolton in Huntingdonshire, it being a much finer residence. His grace is lately married to a daughter of the Duke of Montagu by a branch of the house of Marlborough.

Four market towns fill up the rest of this part of the country— Dunmow, Braintree, Thaxted, and Coggeshall—all noted for the manufacture of bays, as above, and for very little else, except I shall make the ladies laugh at the famous old story of the Flitch of Bacon at Dunmow, which is this:

One Robert Fitzwalter, a powerful baron in this county in the time of Henry III., on some merry occasion, which is not preserved in the rest of the story, instituted a custom in the priory here: That whatever married man did not repent of his being married, or quarrel or differ and dispute with his wife within a year and a day after his marriage, and would swear to the truth of it, kneeling upon two hard pointed stones in the churchyard, which stones he caused to be set up in the Priory churchyard for that purpose, the prior and convent, and as many of the town as would, to be present, such person should have a flitch of bacon.

I do not remember to have read that any one ever came to demand it; nor do the people of the place pretend to say, of their own knowledge, that they remember any that did so. A long time ago several did demand it, as they say, but they know not who; neither is there any record of it, nor do they tell us, if it were now to be demanded, who is obliged to deliver the flitch of bacon, the priory being dissolved and gone.

The forest of Epping and Hainault spreads a great part of this country still. I shall speak again of the former in my return from this circuit. Formerly, it is thought, these two forests took up all the west and south part of the county; but particularly we are assured, that it reached to the River Chelmer, and into Dengy Hundred, and from

175

thence again west to Epping and Waltham, where it continues to be a forest still.

Probably this forest of Epping has been a wild or forest ever since this island was inhabited, and may show us, in some parts of it, where enclosures and tillage has not broken in upon it, what the face of this island was before the Romans' time; that is to say, before their landing in Britain.

The constitution of this forest is best seen, I mean as to the antiquity of it, by the merry grant of it from Edward the Confessor before the Norman Conquest to Randolph Peperking, one of his favourites, who was after called Peverell, and whose name remains still in several villages in this county; as particularly that of Hatfield Peverell, in the road from Chelmsford to Witham, which is supposed to be originally a park, which they called a field in those days; and Hartfield may be as much as to say a park for doer; for the stags were in those days called harts, so that this was neither more nor less than Randolph Peperking's Hartfield—that is to say, Ralph Peverell's deer-park.

N.B.—This Ralph Randolph, or Ralph Peverell (call him as you please), had, it seems, a most beautiful lady to his wife, who was daughter of Ingelrick, one of Edward the Confessor's noblemen. He had two sons by her—William Peverell, a famed soldier, and lord or governor of Dover Castle, which he surrendered to William the Conqueror, after the battle in Sussex, and Pain Peverell, his youngest, who was lord of Cambridge. When the eldest son delivered up the castle, the lady, his mother, above named, who was the celebrated beauty of the age, was it seems there, and the Conqueror fell in love with her, and whether by force or by consent, took her away, and she became his mistress, or what else you please to call it. By her he had a son, who was called William, after the Conqueror's Christian name, but retained the name of Peverell, and was afterwards created by the Conqueror lord of Nottingham.

This lady afterwards, as is supposed, by way of penance for her yielding to the Conqueror, founded a nunnery at the village of Hatfield Peverell, mentioned above, and there she lies buried in the chapel of it, which is now the parish church, where her memory is preserved by a tombstone under one of the windows.

Thus we have several towns, where any ancient parks have been placed, called by the name of Hatfield on that very account. As Hatfield Broad Oak in this county, Bishop's Hatfield in Hertfordshire, and several others.

But I return to King Edward's merry way, as I call it, of granting this forest to this Ralph Peperking, which I find in the ancient records, in the very words it was passed in, as follows. Take my explanations with it for the sake of those that are not used to the ancient English:

The Grant in Old English.
IChe EDWARD Koning,
Have given of my Forrest the kepen of the Hundred of *Chelmer* and *Dancing.*
To RANDOLPH PEPERKING,
And to his kindling.
With Heorte and Hind, Doe and Bocke,
Hare and Fox, Cat and Brock,
Wild Fowle with his Flock;
Patrich, Pheasant Hen, and Pheasant Cock,
With green and wild Stub and Stock,
To kepen and to yemen with all her might.
Both by Day, and eke by Night;
And Hounds for to hold,
Good and Swift and Bold:
Four Greyhound and six Raches,
For Hare and Fox, and Wild Cattes,
And therefore Iche made him my Book.
Witness the Bishop of *Wolston.*
And Booke ylrede many on,
And *Sweyne* of *Essex,* our Brother,
And taken him many other
And our steward *Howlein,*
That *By sought* me for him.

The Explanation in Modern English

I Edward the king,
Have made ranger of my forest of Chelmsford hundred and Deering hundred,
Ralph Peverell, for him and his heirs for ever;
With both the red and fallow deer.
Hare and fox, otter and badger;
Wild fowl of all sorts,
Partridges and pheasants,

177

Timber and underwood roots and tops;
With power to preserve the forest,
And watch it against deer-stealers and others:
With a right to keep hounds of all sorts,
Four greyhounds and six terriers,
Harriers and foxhounds, and other hounds.
And to this end I have registered this my grant in the crown rolls or books;
To which the bishop has set his hand as a witness for any one to read.
Also signed by the king's brother (or, as some think, the Chancellor Sweyn, then Earl or Count of Essex).
He might call such other witnesses to sign as he thought fit.
Also the king's high steward was a witness, at whose request this grant was obtained of the king.

There are many gentlemen's seats on this side the country, and a great assembly set up at New Hall, near this town, much resorted to by the neighbouring gentry. I shall next proceed to the county of Suffolk, as my first design directed me to do.

From Harwich, therefore, having a mind to view the harbour, I sent my horses round by Manningtree, where there is a timber bridge over the Stour, called Cataway Bridge, and took a boat up the River Orwell for Ipswich. A traveller will hardly understand me, especially a seaman, when I speak of the River Stour and the River Orwell at Harwich, for they know them by no other names than those of Manningtree water and Ipswich water; so while I am on salt water, I must speak as those who use the sea may understand me, and when I am up in the country among the inland towns again, I shall call them out of their names no more.

It is twelve miles from Harwich up the water to Ipswich. Before I come to the town, I must say something of it, because speaking of the river requires it. In former times, that is to say, since the writer of this remembers the place very well, and particularly just before the late Dutch wars, Ipswich was a town of very good business; particularly it was the greatest town in England for large colliers or coal-ships employed between Newcastle and London. Also they built the biggest ships and the best, for the said fetching of coals of any that were employed in that trade. They built, also, there so prodigious strong, that it was an ordinary thing for an Ipswich collier, if no disaster happened to him, to reign (as seamen call it) forty or fifty years, and more.

In the town of Ipswich the masters of these ships generally dwelt, and there were, as they then told me, above a hundred sail of them, belonging to the town at one time, the least of which carried fifteen score, as they compute it, that is, 300 chaldron of coals; this was about the year 1668 (when I first knew the place). This made the town be at that time so populous, for those masters, as they had good ships at sea, so they had large families who lived plentifully, and in very good houses in the town, and several streets were chiefly inhabited by such.

The loss or decay of this trade accounts for the present pretended decay of the town of Ipswich, of which I shall speak more presently. The ships wore out, the masters died off, the trade took a new turn; Dutch flyboats taken in the war, and made free ships by Act of Parliament, thrust themselves into the coal-trade for the interest of the captors, such as the Yarmouth and London merchants, and others; and the Ipswich men dropped gradually out of it, being discouraged by those Dutch flyboats. These Dutch vessels, which cost nothing but the caption, were bought cheap, carried great burthens, and the Ipswich building fell off for want of price, and so the trade decayed, and the town with it. I believe this will be owned for the true beginning of their decay, if I must allow it to be called a decay.

But to return to my passage up the river. In the winter-time those great collier ships, above-mentioned, are always laid up, as they call it; that is to say, the coal trade abates at London, the citizens are generally furnished, their stores taken in, and the demand is over; so that the great ships, the northern seas and coast being also dangerous, the nights long, and the voyage hazardous, go to sea no more, but lie by, the ships are unrigged, the sails, etc., carried ashore, the top-masts struck, and they ride moored in the river, under the advantages and security of sound ground, and a high woody shore, where they lie as safe as in a wet dock; and it was a very agreeable sight to see, perhaps two hundred sail of ships, of all sizes, lie in that posture every winter. All this while, which was usually from Michaelmas to Lady Day, the masters lived calm and secure with their families in Ipswich; and enjoying plentifully, what in the summer they got laboriously at sea, and this made the town of Ipswich very populous in the winter; for as the masters, so most of the men, especially their mates, boatswains, carpenters, etc., were of the same place, and lived in their proportions, just as the masters did; so that in the winter there might be perhaps a thousand men in the town more than in the summer, and perhaps a greater number.

To justify what I advance here, that this town was formerly very full of people, I ask leave to refer to the account of Mr. Camden, and what it was in his time. His words are these:- "Ipswich has a commodious harbour, has been fortified with a ditch and rampart, has a great trade, and is very populous, being adorned with fourteen churches, and large private buildings." This confirms what I have mentioned of the former state of this town; but the present state is my proper work; I therefore return to my voyage up the river.

The sight of these ships thus laid up in the river, as I have said, was very agreeable to me in my passage from Harwich, about five and thirty years before the present journey; and it was in its proportion equally melancholy to hear that there were now scarce forty sail of good colliers that belonged to the whole town.

In a creek in this river, called Lavington Creek, we saw at low water such shoals, or hills rather, of mussels, that great boats might have loaded with them, and no miss have been made of them. Near this creek, Sir Samuel Barnadiston had a very fine seat, as, also, a decoy for wild ducks, and a very noble estate; but it is divided into many branches since the death of the ancient possessor. But I proceed to the town, which is the first in the county of Suffolk of any note this way.

Ipswich is seated, at the distance of twelve miles from Harwich, upon the edge of the river, which, taking a short turn to the west, the town forms, there, a kind of semicircle, or half moon, upon the bank of the river. It is very remarkable, that though ships of 500 ton may, upon a spring tide, come up very near this town, and many ships of that burthen have been built there, yet the river is not navigable any farther than the town itself, or but very little; no, not for the smallest beats; nor does the tide, which rises sometimes thirteen or fourteen feet, and gives them twenty-four feet water very near the town, flow much farther up the river than the town, or not so much as to make it worth speaking of.

He took little notice of the town, or at least of that part of Ipswich, who published in his wild observations on it that ships of 200 ton are built there. I affirm, that I have seen a ship of 400 ton launched at the building-yard, close to the town; and I appeal to the Ipswich colliers (those few that remain) belonging to this town, if several of them carrying seventeen score of coals, which must be upward of 400 ton, have not formerly been built here; but superficial observers must be superficial writers, if they write at all; and to this day, at John's Ness, within a mile and a half of the town itself, ships of any burthen may be built and launched even at neap tides.

I am much mistaken, too, if since the Revolution some very good ships have not been built at this town, and particularly the *Melford* or *Milford* galley, a ship of forty guns; as the *Greyhound* frigate, a man-of-war of thirty-six to forty guns, was at John's Ness. But what is this towards lessening the town of Ipswich, any more than it would be to say, they do not build men-of-war, or East India ships, or ships of five hundred ton burden at St. Catherines, or at Battle Bridge in the Thames? when we know that a mile or two lower, viz., at Radcliffe, Limehouse, or Deptford, they build ships of a thousand ton, and might build first-rate men-of-war too, if there was occasion; and the like might be done in this river of Ipswich, within about two or three miles of the town; so that it would not be at all an out-of-the-way speaking to say, such a ship was built at Ipswich, any more than it is to say, as they do, that the *Royal Prince*, the great ship lately built for the South Sea Company, was London built, because she was built at Limehouse.

And why then is not Ipswich capable of building and receiving the greatest ships in the navy, seeing they may be built and brought up again laden, within a mile and half of the town?

But the neighbourhood of London, which sucks the vitals of trade in this island to itself, is the chief reason of any decay of business in this place; and I shall, in the course of these observations, hint at it, where many good seaports and large towns, though farther off than Ipswich, and as well fitted for commerce, are yet swallowed up by the immense indraft of trade to the City of London; and more decayed beyond all comparison than Ipswich is supposed to be: as Southampton, Weymouth, Dartmouth, and several others which I shall speak to in their order; and if it be otherwise at this time, with some other towns, which are lately increased in trade and navigation, wealth, and people, while their neighbours decay, it is because they have some particular trade, or accident to trade, which is a kind of nostrum to them, inseparable to the place, and which fixes there by the nature of the thing; as the herring-fishery to Yarmouth; the coal trade to Newcastle; the Leeds clothing trade; the export of butter and lead, and the great corn trade for Holland, is to Hull; the Virginia and West India trade at Liverpool; the Irish trade at Bristol, and the like. Thus the war has brought a flux of business and people, and consequently of wealth, to several places, as well as to Portsmouth, Chatham, Plymouth, Falmouth, and others; and were any wars like those, to continue twenty years with the Dutch, or any nation whose fleets lay that way, as the Dutch do, it would be the like perhaps at Ipswich in a few years, and at other places on the same coast.

But at this present time an occasion offers to speak in favour of this port; namely, the Greenland fishery, lately proposed to be carried on by the South Sea Company. On which account I may freely advance this, without any compliment to the town of Ipswich, no place in Britain is equally qualified like Ipswich; whether we respect the cheapness of building and fitting out their ships and shallops; also furnishing, victualling, and providing them with all kinds of stores; convenience for laying up the ships after the voyage, room for erecting their magazines, warehouses, rope walks, cooperages, etc., on the easiest terms; and especially for the noisome cookery, which attends the boiling their blubber, which may be on this river (as it ought to be) remote from any places of resort. Then their nearness to the market for the oil when it is made, and which, above all, ought to be the chief thing considered in that trade, the easiness of their putting out to sea when they begin their voyage, in which the same wind that carries them from the mouth of the haven, is fair to the very seas of Greenland.

I could say much more to this point if it were needful, and in few words could easily prove, that Ipswich must have the preference of all the port towns of Britain, for being the best centre of the Greenland trade, if ever that trade fall into the management of such a people as perfectly understand, and have a due honest regard to its being managed with the best husbandry, and to the prosperity of the undertaking in general. But whether we shall ever arrive at so happy a time as to recover so useful a trade to our country, which our ancestors had the honour to be the first undertakers of, and which has been lost only through the indolence of others, and the increasing vigilance of our neighbours, that is not my business here to dispute.

What I have said is only to let the world see what improvement this town and port is capable of; I cannot think but that Providence, which made nothing in vain, cannot have reserved so useful, so convenient a port to lie vacant in the world, but that the time will some time or other come (especially considering the improving temper of the present age) when some peculiar beneficial business may be found out, to make the port of Ipswich as useful to the world, and the town as flourishing, as Nature has made it proper and capable to be.

As for the town, it is true, it is but thinly inhabited, in comparison of the extent of it; but to say there are hardly any people to be seen there, is far from being true in fact; and whoever thinks fit to look into the churches and meeting-houses on a Sunday, or other public days, will find there are very great numbers of people there. Or if he thinks fit to view the market, and see how the large shambles, called Cardinal Wolsey's Butchery, are furnished with meat, and the rest of the market stocked with other provisions, must acknowledge that it is not for a few people that all those things are provided. A person very curious, and on whose veracity I think I may depend, going through the market in this town, told me, that he reckoned upwards of six hundred country people on horseback and on foot, with baskets and other carriage, who had all of them brought something or other to town to sell, besides the butchers, and what came in carts and waggons.

It happened to be my lot to be once at this town at the time when a very fine new ship, which was built there for some merchants of London, was to be launched; and if I may give my guess at the numbers of people which appeared on the shore, in the houses, and on the river, I believe I am much within compass if I say there were 20,000 people to see it; but this is only a guess, or they might come a great way to see the sight, or the town may be declined farther since that. But a view of the town is one of the surest rules for a gross estimate.

It is true here is no settled manufacture. The French refugees when they first came over to England began a little to take to this place, and some merchants attempted to set up a linen manufacture in their favour; but it has not met with so much success as was expected, and at present I find very little of it. The poor people are, however, employed, as they are all over these counties, in spinning wool for other towns where manufactures are settled.

The country round Ipswich, as are all the counties so near the coast, is applied chiefly to corn, of which a very great quantity is continually shipped off for London; and sometimes they load corn here for Holland, especially if the market abroad is encouraging. They have twelve parish churches in this town, with three or four meetings; but there are not so many Quakers here as at Colchester, and no Anabaptists or Antipoedo Baptists, that I could hear of—at least, there is no meeting-house of that denomination. There is one meeting-house for the Presbyterians, one for the Independents and one for the Quakers; the first is as large and as fine a building of that kind as most on this side of England, and the inside the best finished of any I have seen, London not excepted; that for the Independents is a handsome new-built building, but not so gay or so large as the other.

183

There is a great deal of very good company in this town, and though there are not so many of the gentry here as at Bury, yet there are more here than in any other town in the county; and I observed particularly that the company you meet with here are generally persons well informed of the world, and who have something very solid and entertaining in their society. This may happen, perhaps, by their frequent conversing with those who have been abroad, and by their having a remnant of gentlemen and masters of ships among them who have seen more of the world than the people of an inland town are likely to have seen. I take this town to be one of the most agreeable places in England for families who have lived well, but may have suffered in our late calamities of stocks and bubbles, to retreat to, where they may live within their own compass; and several things indeed recommend it to such:-

1. Good houses at very easy rents.

2. An airy, clean, and well-governed town.

3. Very agreeable and improving company almost of every kind.

4. A wonderful plenty of all manner of provisions, whether flesh or fish, and very good of the kind.

5. Those provisions very cheap, so that a family may live cheaper here than in any town in England of its bigness within such a small distance from London.

6. Easy passage to London, either by land or water, the coach going through to London in a day.

The Lord Viscount Hereford has a very fine seat and park in this town; the house indeed is old built, but very commodious; it is called Christ Church, having been, as it is said, a priory or religious house in former times. The green and park is a great addition to the pleasantness of this town, the inhabitants being allowed to divert themselves there with walking, bowling, etc.

The large spire steeple, which formerly stood upon that they call the tower church, was blown down by a great storm of wind many years ago, and in its a fall did much damage to the church.

The government of this town is by two bailiffs, as at Yarmouth. Mr. Camden says they are chosen out of twelve burgesses called portmen, and two justices out of twenty-four more. There has been lately a very great struggle between the two parties for the choice of these two magistrates, which had this amicable conclusion—namely, that they chose one of either side; so that neither party having the victory, it is to be hoped it may be a means to allay the heats and unneighbourly feuds which such things breed in towns so large as this is. They send two members to Parliament, whereof those at this time are Sir William Thompson, Recorder of London, and Colonel Negus, Deputy Master of the Horse to the king.

There are some things very curious to be seen here, however some superficial writers have been ignorant of them. Dr. Beeston, an eminent physician, began a few years ago a physic garden adjoining to his house in this town; and as he is particularly curious, and, as I was told, exquisitely skilled in botanic knowledge, so he has been not only very diligent, but successful too, in making a collection of rare and exotic plants, such as are scarce to be equalled in England.

One Mr. White, a surgeon, resides also in this town. But before I speak of this gentleman, I must observe that I say nothing from personal knowledge; though if I did, I have too good an opinion of his sense to believe he would be pleased with being flattered or complimented in print. But I must be true to matter of fact. This gentleman has begun a collection or chamber of rarities, and with good success too. I acknowledge I had not the opportunity of seeing them; but I was told there are some things very curious in it, as particularly a sea-horse carefully preserved, and perfect in all its parts; two Roman urns full of ashes of human bodies, and supposed to be above 1,700 years old; besides a great many valuable medals and ancient coins. My friend who gave me this account, and of whom I think I may say he speaks without bias, mentions this gentleman, Mr. White, with some warmth as a very valuable person in his particular employ of a surgeon. I only repeat his words. "Mr. White," says he, "to whom the whole town and country are greatly indebted and obliged to pray for his life, is our most skilful surgeon." These, I say, are his own words, and I add nothing to them but this, that it is happy for a town to have such a surgeon, as it is for a surgeon to have such a character.

The country round Ipswich, as if qualified on purpose to accommodate the town for building of ships, is an inexhaustible store-house of timber, of which, now their trade of building ships is abated, they send very great quantities to the king's building-yards at Chatham, which by water is so little a way that they often run to it from the mouth of the river at Harwich in one tide.

From Ipswich I took a turn into the country to Hadleigh, principally to satisfy my curiosity and see the place where that famous martyr and pattern of charity and religious zeal in Queen Mary's time,

Dr. Rowland Taylor, was put to death. The inhabitants, who have a wonderful veneration for his memory, show the very place where the stake which he was bound to was set up, and they have put a stone upon it which nobody will remove; but it is a more lasting monument to him that he lives in the hearts of the people—I say more lasting than a tomb of marble would be, for the memory of that good man will certainly never be out of the poor people's minds as long as this island shall retain the Protestant religion among them. How long that may be, as things are going, and if the detestable conspiracy of the Papists now on foot should succeed, I will not pretend to say.

A little to the left is Sudbury, which stands upon the River Stour, mentioned above—a river which parts the counties of Suffolk and Essex, and which is within these few years made navigable to this town, though the navigation does not, it seems, answer the charge, at least not to advantage.

I know nothing for which this town is remarkable, except for being very populous and very poor. They have a great manufacture of says and perpetuanas, and multitudes of poor people are employed in working them; but the number of the poor is almost ready to eat up the rich. However, this town sends two members to Parliament, though it is under no form of government particularly to itself other than as a village, the head magistrate whereof is a constable.

Near adjoining to it is a village called Long Melfort, and a very long one it is, from which I suppose it had that addition to its name; it is full of very good houses, and, as they told me, is richer, and has more wealthy masters of the manufacture in it, than in Sudbury itself.

Here and in the neighbourhood are some ancient families of good note; particularly here is a fine dwelling, the ancient seat of the Cordells, whereof Sir William Cordell was Master of the Rolls in the time of Queen Elizabeth; but the family is now extinct, the last heir, Sir John Cordell, being killed by a fall from his horse, died unmarried, leaving three sisters co-heiresses to a very noble estate, most of which, if not all, is now centred on the only surviving sister, and with her in marriage is given to Mr. Firebrass, eldest son of Sir Basil Firebrass, formerly a flourishing merchant in London, but reduced by many disasters. His family now rises by the good fortune of his son, who proves to be a gentleman of very agreeable parts, and well esteemed in the country.

From this part of the country, I returned north-west by Lenham, to visit St. Edmund's Bury, a town of which other writers have talked very largely, and perhaps a little too much. It is a town famed for its pleasant situation and wholesome air, the Montpelier of Suffolk, and perhaps of England. This must be attributed to the skill of the monks of those times, who chose so beautiful a situation for the seat of their retirement; and who built here the greatest and, in its time, the most flourishing monastery in all these parts of England, I mean the monastery of St. Edmund the Martyr. It was, if we believe antiquity, a house of pleasure in more ancient times, or to speak more properly, a court of some of the Saxon or East Angle kings; and, as Mr. Camden says, was even then called a royal village, though it much better merits that name now; it being the town of all this part of England, in proportion to its bigness, most thronged with gentry, people of the best fashion, and the most polite conversation. This beauty and healthiness of its situation was no doubt the occasion which drew the clergy to settle here, for they always chose the best places in the country to build in, either for richness of soil, or for health and pleasure in the situation of their religious houses.

For the like reason, I doubt not, they translated the bones of the martyred king St. Edmund to this place; for it is a vulgar error to say he was murdered here. His martyrdom, it is plain, was at Hoxon or Henilsdon, near Harlston, on the Waveney, in the farthest northern verge of the county; but Segebert, king of the East Angles, had built a religious house in this pleasant rich part of the county; and as the monks began to taste the pleasure of the place, they procured the body of this saint to be removed hither, which soon increased the wealth and revenues of their house, by the zeal of that day, in going on pilgrimage to the shrine of the blessed St. Edmund.

We read, however, that after this the Danes, under King Sweno, over-running this part of the country, destroyed this monastery and burnt it to the ground, with the church and town. But see the turn religion gives to things in the world; his son, King Canutus, at first a Pagan and a tyrant, and the most cruel ravager of all that crew, coming to turn Christian, and being touched in conscience for the soul of his father, in having robbed God and his holy martyr St. Edmund, sacrilegiously destroying the church, and plundering the monastery; I say, touched with remorse, and, as the monks pretend, terrified with a vision of St. Edmund appearing to him, he rebuilt the house, the church, and the town also, and very much added to the wealth of the abbot and his fraternity, offering his crown at the feet of St. Edmund, giving the house to the monks, town and all; so that they were absolute lords of the town, and governed it by their steward for many ages. He also gave them a great many good lordships, which they enjoyed till the general suppression of abbeys, in the time of Henry VIII.

But I am neither writing the history or searching the antiquity of the abbey, or town; my business is the present state of the place.

The abbey is demolished; its ruins are all that is to be seen of its glory: out of the old building, two very beautiful churches are built, and serve the two parishes, into which the town is divided, and they stand both in one churchyard. Here it was, in the path-way between these two churches, that a tragical and almost unheard-of act of barbarity was committed, which made the place less pleasant for some time than it used to be, when Arundel Coke, Esq., a barrister-at-law, of a very ancient family, attempted, with the assistance of a barbarous assassin, to murder in cold blood, and in the arms of hospitality, Edward Crisp, Esq., his brother-in-law, leading him out from his own house, where he had invited him, his wife and children, to supper; I say, leading him out in the night, on pretence of going to see some friend that was known to them both; but in this churchyard, giving a signal to the assassin he had hired, he attacked him with a hedge-bill, and cut him, as one might say, almost in pieces; and when they did not doubt of his being dead, they left him. His head and face was so mangled, that it may be said to be next to a miracle that he was not quite killed: yet so Providence directed for the exemplary punishment of the assassins, that the gentleman recovered to detect them, who (though he outlived the assault) were both executed as they deserved, and Mr. Crisp is yet alive. They were condemned on the statute for defacing and dismembering, called the Coventry Act.

But this accident does not at all lessen the pleasure and agreeable delightful show of the town of Bury; it is crowded with nobility and gentry, and all sorts of the most agreeable company; and as the company invites, so there is the appearance of pleasure upon the very situation; and they that live at Bury are supposed to live there for the sake of it.

The Lord Jermin, afterwards Lord Dover, and, since his lordship's decease, Sir Robert Davers, enjoyed the most delicious seat of Rushbrook, near this town.

The present members of Parliament for this place are Jermyn Davers and James Reynolds, Esquires.

Mr. Harvey, afterwards created Lord Harvey, by King William, and since that made Earl of Bristol by King George, lived many years in this town, leaving a noble and pleasantly situated house in Lincolnshire, for the more agreeable living on a spot so completely qualified for a life of delight as this of Bury.

The Duke of Grafton, now Lord-Lieutenant of Ireland, has also a stately house at Euston, near this town, which he enjoys in right of his mother, daughter to the Earl of Arlington, one of the chief ministers of State in the reign of King Charles II., and who made the second letter in the word "cabal," a word formed by that famous satirist Andrew Marvell, to represent the five heads of the politics of that time, as the word "smectymnus" was on a former occasion.

I shall believe nothing so scandalous of the ladies of this town and the country round it as a late writer insinuates. That the ladies round the country appear mighty gay and agreeable at the time of the fair in this town I acknowledge; one hardly sees such a show in any part of the world; but to suggest they come hither, as to a market, is so coarse a jest, that the gentlemen that wait on them hither (for they rarely come but in good company) ought to resent and correct him for it.

It is true, Bury Fair, like Bartholomew Fair, is a fair for diversion, more than for trade; and it may be a fair for toys and for trinkets, which the ladies may think fit to lay out some of their money in, as they see occasion. But to judge from thence that the knights' daughters of Norfolk, Cambridgeshire, and Suffolk—that is to say, for it cannot be understood any otherwise, the daughters of all the gentry of the three counties—come hither to be picked up, is a way of speaking I never before heard any author have the assurance to make use of in print.

The assembly he justly commends for the bright appearance of the beauties; but with a sting in the tail of this compliment, where he says they seldom end without some considerable match or intrigue; and yet he owns that during the fair these assemblies are held every night. Now that these fine ladies go intriguing every night, and that too after the comedy is done, which is after the fair and raffling is over for the day, so that it must be very late. This is a terrible character for the ladies of Bury, and intimates, in short, that most of them are loose women, which is a horrid abuse upon the whole country.

Now, though I like not the assemblies at all, and shall in another place give them something of their due, yet having the opportunity to see the fair at Bury, and to see that there were, indeed, abundance of the finest ladies, or as fine as any in Britain, yet I must own the number of the ladies at the comedy, or at the assembly, is no way equal to the number that are seen in the town, much less are they equal to the whole body of the ladies in the three counties; and I must also add, that though it is far from true that all that appear at the assembly are there for matches or intrigues, yet I will venture to say that they are not the worst of the ladies who stay away, neither are they the fewest in number or the meanest in beauty, but just the contrary; and I do not at all doubt, but that the scandalous liberty some take at those assemblies will in time bring them out of credit with the virtuous part of the sex here, as it has done already in Kent and other places, and that those ladies who most value their reputation will be seen less there than they have been; for though the institution of them has been innocent and virtuous, the ill use of them, and the scandalous behaviour of some people at them, will in time arm virtue against them, and they will be laid down as they have been set up without much satisfaction.

But the beauty of this town consists in the number of gentry who dwell in and near it, the polite conversation among them, the affluence and plenty they live in, the sweet air they breathe in, and the pleasant country they have to go abroad in.

Here is no manufacturing in this town, or but very little, except spinning, the chief trade of the place depending upon the gentry who live there, or near it, and who cannot fail to cause trade enough by the expense of their families and equipages among the people of a county town. They have but a very small river, or rather but a very small branch of a small river, at this town, which runs from hence to Milden Hall, on the edge of the fens. However, the town and gentlemen about have been at the charge, or have so encouraged the engineer who was at the charge, that they have made this river navigable to the said Milden Hall, from whence there is a navigable dyke, called Milden Hall Drain, which goes into the River Ouse, and so to Lynn; so that all their coal and wine, iron, lead, and other heavy goods, are brought by water from Lynn, or from London, by the way of Lynn, to the great ease of the tradesmen.

This town is famous for two great events. One was that in the year 1447, in the 25th year of Henry VI., a Parliament was held here.

The other was, that at the meeting of this Parliament, the great Humphrey, Duke of Gloucester, regent of the kingdom during the absence of King Henry V. and the minority of Henry VI., and to his last hour the safeguard of the whole nation, and darling of the people, was basely murdered here; by whose death the gate was opened to that dreadful war between the houses of Lancaster and York, which ended in the confusion of that very race who are supposed to have contrived that murder.

From St. Edmund's Bury I returned by Stowmarket and Needham to Ipswich, that I might keep as near the coast as was proper to my designed circuit or journey; and from Ipswich, to visit the sea again, I went to Woodbridge, and from thence to Orford, on the sea side.

Woodbridge has nothing remarkable, but that it is a considerable market for butter and corn to be exported to London; for now begins that part which is ordinarily called High Suffolk, which, being a rich soil, is for a long tract of ground wholly employed in dairies, and they again famous for the best butter, and perhaps the worst cheese, in England. The butter is barrelled, or often pickled up in small casks, and sold, not in London only, but I have known a firkin of Suffolk butter sent to the West Indies, and brought back to England again, and has been perfectly good and sweet, as at first.

The port for the shipping off their Suffolk butter is chiefly Woodbridge, which for that reason is full of corn factors and butter factors, some of whom are very considerable merchants.

From hence, turning down to the shore, we see Orfordness, a noted point of land for the guide of the colliers and coasters, and a good shelter for them to ride under when a strong north-east wind blows and makes a foul shore on the coast.

South of the Ness is Orford Haven, being the mouth of two little rivers meeting together. It is a very good harbour for small vessels, but not capable of receiving a ship of burden.

Orford was once a good town, but is decayed, and as it stands on the land side of the river the sea daily throws up more land to it, and falls off itself from it, as if it was resolved to disown the place, and that it should be a seaport no longer.

A little farther lies Aldborough, as thriving, though without a port, as the other is decaying, with a good river in the front of it.

There are some gentlemen's seats up farther from the sea, but very few upon the coast.

From Aldborough to Dunwich there are no towns of note; even this town seems to be in danger of being swallowed up, for fame reports that once they had fifty churches in the town; I saw but one left, and that not half full of people.

This town is a testimony of the decay of public things, things of the most durable nature; and as the old poet expresses it,

"By numerous examples we may see,
That towns and cities die as well as we."

The ruins of Carthage, of the great city of Jerusalem, or of ancient Rome, are not at all wonderful to me. The ruins of Nineveh, which are so entirely sunk as that it is doubtful where the city stood; the ruins of Babylon, or the great Persepolis, and many capital cities, which time and the change of monarchies have overthrown, these, I say, are not at all wonderful, because being the capitals of great and flourishing kingdoms, where those kingdoms were overthrown, the capital cities necessarily fell with them; but for a private town, a seaport, and a town of commerce, to decay, as it were, of itself (for we never read of Dunwich being plundered or ruined by any disaster, at least, not of late years); this, I must confess, seems owing to nothing but to the fate of things, by which we see that towns, kings, countries, families, and persons, have all their elevation, their medium, their declination, and even their destruction in the womb of time, and the course of nature. It is true, this town is manifestly decayed by the invasion of the waters, and as other towns seem sufferers by the sea, or the tide withdrawing from their ports, such as Orford, just now named, Winchelsea in Kent, and the like, so this town is, as it were, eaten up by the sea, as above; and the still encroaching ocean seems to threaten it with a fatal immersion in a few years more.

Yet Dunwich, however ruined, retains some share of trade, as particularly for the shipping of butter, cheese, and corn, which is so great a business in this county, that it employs a great many people and ships also; and this port lies right against the particular part of the county for butter, as Framlingham, Halstead, etc. Also a very great quantity of corn is bought up hereabout for the London market; for I shall still touch that point how all the counties in England contribute something towards the subsistence of the great city of London, of which the butter here is a very considerable article; as also coarse cheese, which I mentioned before, used chiefly for the king's ships.

Hereabouts they begin to talk of herrings and the fishery; and we find in the ancient records that this town, which was then equal to a large city, paid, among other tribute to the government, fifty thousand of herrings. Here also, and at Swole, or Southole, the next seaport, they cure sprats in the same manner as they do herrings at Yarmouth; that is to say, speaking in their own language, they make red sprats; or to speak good English, they make sprats red.

It is remarkable that this town is now so much washed away by the sea, that what little trade they have is carried on by Walderswick, a little town near Swole, the vessels coming in there, because the ruins of Dunwich make the shore there unsafe and uneasy to the boats; from whence the northern coasting seamen a rude verse of their own using, and I suppose of their own making, as follows,

"Swoul and Dunwich, and Walderswick,
All go in at one lousie creek."

This "lousie creek," in short, is a little river at Swoul, which our late famous atlas-maker calls a good harbour for ships, and rendezvous of the royal navy; but that by-the-bye; the author, it seems, knew no better.

From Dunwich we came to Southwold, the town above-named: this is a small port town upon the coast, at the mouth of a little river called the Blith. I found no business the people here were employed in but the fishery, as above, for herrings and sprats, which they cure by the help of smoke, as they do at Yarmouth.

There is but one church in this town, but it is a very large one and well built, as most of the churches in this county are, and of impenetrable flint; indeed, there is no occasion for its being so large, for staying there one Sabbath day, I was surprised to see an extraordinary large church, capable of receiving five or six thousand people, and but twenty-seven in it besides the parson and the clerk; but at the same time the meeting-house of the Dissenters was full to the very doors, having, as I guessed, from six to eight hundred people in it.

This town is made famous for a very great engagement at sea, in the year 1672, between the English and Dutch fleets, in the bay opposite to the town, in which, not to be partial to ourselves, the English fleet was worsted; and the brave Montague, Earl of Sandwich, Admiral under the Duke of York, lost his life. The ship *Royal Prince*, carrying one hundred guns, in which he was, and which was under him, commanded by Sir Edward Spragg, was burnt, and several other ships lost, and about six hundred seamen; part of those killed in the fight were, as I was told, brought on shore here and buried in the churchyard of this town, as others also were at Ipswich.

At this town in particular, and so at all the towns on this coast, from Orfordness to Yarmouth, is the ordinary place where our summer friends the swallows first land when they come to visit us; and here they may be said to embark for their return, when they go back into warmer climates; and as I think the following remark, though of so trifling a circumstance, may be both instructing as well as diverting, it may be very proper in this place. The case is this; I was some years before at this place, at the latter end of the year, viz., about the beginning of October, and lodging in a house that looked into the churchyard, I observed in the evening, an unusual multitude of birds sitting on the leads of the church. Curiosity led me to go nearer to see what they were, and I found they were all swallows; that there was such an infinite number that they covered the whole roof of the church, and of several houses near, and perhaps might of more houses which I did not see. This led me to inquire of a grave gentleman whom I saw near me, what the meaning was of such a prodigious multitude of swallows sitting there. "Oh, sir," says he, turning towards the sea, "you may see the reason; the wind is off sea." I did not seem fully informed by that expression, so he goes on, "I perceive, sir," says he, "you are a stranger to it; you must then understand first, that this is the season of the year when the swallows, their food here failing, begin to leave us, and return to the country, wherever it be, from whence I suppose they came; and this being the nearest to the coast of Holland, they come here to embark" (this he said smiling a little); "and now, sir," says he, "the weather being too calm or the wind contrary, they are waiting for a gale, for they are all wind-bound."

This was more evident to me, when in the morning I found the wind had come about to the north-west in the night, and there was not one swallow to be seen of near a million, which I believe was there the night before.

How those creatures know that this part of the Island of Great Britain is the way to their home, or the way that they are to go; that this very point is the nearest cut over, or even that the nearest cut is best for them, that we must leave to the naturalists to determine, who insist upon it that brutes cannot think.

Certain it is that the swallows neither come hither for warm weather nor retire from cold; the thing is of quite another nature. They, like the shoals of fish in the sea, pursue their prey; they are a voracious creature, they feed flying; their food is found in the air, viz., the insects, of which in our summer evenings, in damp and moist places, the air is full. They come hither in the summer because our air is fuller of fogs and damps than in other countries, and for that reason feeds great quantities of insects. If the air be hot and dry the gnats die of themselves, and even the swallows will be found famished for want, and fall down dead out of the air, their food being taken from them. In like manner, when cold weather comes in the insects all die, and then of necessity the swallows quit us, and follow their food wherever they go. This they do in the manner I have mentioned above, for sometimes they are seen to go off in vast flights like a cloud. And sometimes again, when the wind grows fair, they go away a few and a few as they come, not staying at all upon the coast.

Note.—This passing and re-passing of the swallows is observed nowhere so much, that I have heard of, or in but few other places, except on this eastern coast, namely, from above Harwich to the east point of Norfolk, called Winterton Ness, North, which is all right against Holland. We know nothing of them any farther north, the passage of the sea being, as I suppose, too broad from Flamborough Head and the shore of Holderness in Yorkshire, etc.

I find very little remarkable on this side of Suffolk, but what is on the sea-shore as above. The inland country is that which they properly call High Suffolk, and is full of rich feeding grounds and large farms, mostly employed in dairies for making the Suffolk butter and cheese, of which I have spoken already. Among these rich grounds stand some market towns, though not of very considerable note; such as Framlingham, where was once a royal castle, to which Queen Mary retired when the Northumberland faction, in behalf of the Lady Jane, endeavoured to supplant her. And it was this part of Suffolk where the Gospellers, as they were then called, preferred their loyalty to their religion, and complimented the Popish line at expense of their share of the Reformation. But they paid dear for it, and their successors have learned better politics since.

In these parts are also several good market towns, some in this county and some in the other, as Beccles, Bungay, Harlston, etc., all on the edge of the River Waveney, which parts here the counties of Suffolk and Norfolk. And here in a bye-place, and out of common remark, lies the ancient town of Hoxon, famous for being the place where St. Edmund was martyred, for whom so many cells and shrines have been set up and monasteries built, and in honour of whom the famous monastery of St. Edmundsbury, above mentioned, was founded, which most people erroneously think was the place where the said murder was committed.

Besides the towns mentioned above, there are Halesworth, Saxmundham, Debenham, Aye, or Eye, all standing in this eastern side of Suffolk, in which, as I have said, the whole country is employed in dairies or in feeding of cattle.

This part of England is also remarkable for being the first where the feeding and fattening of cattle, both sheep as well as black cattle, with turnips, was first practised in England, which is made a very great part of the improvement of their lands to this day, and from whence the practice is spread over most of the east and south parts of England to the great enriching of the farmers and increase of fat cattle. And though some have objected against the goodness of the flesh thus fed with turnips, and have fancied it would taste of the root, yet upon experience it is found that at market there is no difference, nor can they that buy single out one joint of mutton from another by the taste. So that the complaint which our nice palates at first made begins to cease of itself, and a very great quantity of beef and mutton also is brought every year and every week to London from this side of England, and much more than was formerly known to be fed there.

I cannot omit, however little it may seem, that this county of Suffolk is particularly famous for furnishing the City of London and all the counties round with turkeys, and that it is thought there are more turkeys bred in this county and the part of Norfolk that adjoins to it than in all the rest of England, especially for sale, though this may be reckoned, as I say above, but a trifling thing to take notice of in these remarks; yet, as I have hinted, that I shall observe how London is in general supplied with all its provisions from the whole body of the nation, and how every part of the island is engaged in some degree or other of that supply. On this account I could not omit it, nor will it be found so inconsiderable an article as some may imagine, if this be true, which I received an account of from a person living on the place, viz., that they have counted three hundred droves of turkeys (for they drive them all in droves on foot) pass in one season over Stratford Bridge on the River Stour, which parts Suffolk from Essex, about six miles from Colchester, on the road from Ipswich to London. These droves, as they say, generally contain from three hundred to a thousand each drove; so that one may suppose them to contain five hundred one with another, which is one hundred and fifty thousand in all; and yet this is one of the least passages, the numbers which travel by Newmarket Heath and the open country and the forest, and also the numbers that come by Sudbury and Clare being many more.

For the further supplies of the markets of London with poultry, of which these countries particularly abound, they have within these few years found it practicable to make the geese travel on foot too, as well as the turkeys, and a prodigious number are brought up to London in droves from the farthest parts of Norfolk; even from the fen country about Lynn, Downham, Wisbech, and the Washes; as also from all the east side of Norfolk and Suffolk, of whom it is very frequent now to meet droves with a thousand, sometimes two thousand in a drove. They begin to drive them generally in August, by which time the harvest is almost over, and the geese may feed in the stubbles as they go. Thus they hold on to the end of October, when the roads begin to be too stiff and deep for their broad feet and short legs to march in.

Besides these methods of driving these creatures on foot, they have of late also invented a new method of carriage, being carts formed on purpose, with four stories or stages to put the creatures in one above another, by which invention one cart will carry a very great number; and for the smoother going they drive with two horses abreast, like a coach, so quartering the road for the ease of the gentry that thus ride. Changing horses, they travel night and day, so that they bring the fowls seventy, eighty, or, one hundred miles in two days and one night. The horses in this new-fashioned voiture go two abreast, as above, but no perch below, as in a coach, but they are fastened together by a piece of wood lying crosswise upon their necks, by which they are kept even and together, and the driver sits on the top of the cart like as in the public carriages for the army, etc.

In this manner they hurry away the creatures alive, and infinite numbers are thus carried to London every year. This method is also particular for the carrying young turkeys or turkey poults in their season, which are valuable, and yield a good price at market; as also for live chickens in the dear seasons, of all which a very great number are brought in this manner to London, and more prodigiously out of this country than any other part of England, which is the reason of my speaking of it here.

In this part, which we call High Suffolk, there are not so many families of gentry or nobility placed as in the other side of the country. But it is observed that though their seats are not so frequent here, their estates are; and the pleasure of West Suffolk is much of it supported by the wealth of High Suffolk, for the richness of the lands and application of the people to all kinds of improvement is scarce credible; also the farmers are so very considerable and their farms and dairies so large that it is very frequent for a farmer to have £1,000 stock upon his farm in cows only.

NORFOLK

From High Suffolk I passed the Waveney into Norfolk, near Schole Inn. In my passage I saw at Redgrave (the seat of the family) a most exquisite monument of Sir John Holt, Knight, late Lord Chief Justice of the King's Bench several years, and one of the most eminent lawyers of his time. One of the heirs of the family is now building a fine seat about a mile on the south side of Ipswich, near the road.

The epitaph or inscription on this monument is as follows:-

M. S.
D. Johannis Holt, Equitis Aur.
Totius Anglioe in Banco Regis
per 21 Annos continuos
Capitalis Justitiarii
Gulielmo Regi Annoequr Reginae
Consiliarii perpetui:
Libertatis ac Legum Anglicarum
Assertoris, Vindicis, Custodis,
Vigilis Acris & intrepidi,
Rolandus Frater Uncius & Hoeres
Optime de se Merito
posuit,
Die Martis Vto. 1709. Sublatus est
ex Oculis nostris
Natus 30 Decembris, Anno 1642.

When we come into Norfolk, we see a face of diligence spread over the whole country; the vast manufactures carried on (in chief) by the Norwich weavers employs all the country round in spinning yarn for them; besides many thousand packs of yarn which they receive from other countries, even from as far as Yorkshire and Westmoreland, of which I shall speak in its place.

This side of Norfolk is very populous, and thronged with great and spacious market-towns, more and larger than any other part of England so far from London, except Devonshire, and the West Riding of Yorkshire; for example, between the frontiers of Suffolk and the city of Norwich on this side, which is not above 22 miles in breadth, are the following market-towns, viz.:-

Thetford, Hingham, Harleston,
Diss, West Dereham, E. Dereham,
Harling, Attleborough, Watton,
Bucknam, Windham, Loddon, etc.

Most of these towns are very populous and large; but that which is most remarkable is, that the whole country round them is so interspersed with villages, and those villages so large, and so full of people, that they are equal to market-towns in other countries; in a word, they render this eastern part of Norfolk exceeding full of inhabitants.

An eminent weaver of Norwich gave me a scheme of their trade on this occasion, by which, calculating from the number of looms at that time employed in the city of Norwich only, besides those employed in other towns in the same county, he made it appear very plain, that there were 120,000 people employed in the woollen and silk and wool manufactures of that city only; not that the people all lived in the city, though Norwich is a very large and populous city too: but, I say, they were employed for spinning the yarn used for such goods as were all made in that city. This account is curious enough, and very exact, but it is too long for the compass of this work.

This shows the wonderful extent of the Norwich manufacture, or stuff-weaving trade, by which so many thousands of families are maintained. Their trade, indeed, felt a very sensible decay, and the cries of the poor began to be very loud, when the wearing of painted calicoes was grown to such a height in England, as was seen about two or three years ago; but an Act of Parliament having been obtained, though not without great struggle, in the years 1720 and 1721, for prohibiting the use and wearing of calicoes, the stuff trade revived incredibly; and as I passed this part of the country in the year 1723, the manufacturers assured me that there was not, in all the eastern and middle part of Norfolk, any hand unemployed, if they would work; and that the very children, after four or five years of age, could every one earn their own bread. But I return to speak of the villages and towns in the rest of the county; I shall come to the city of Norwich by itself.

This throng of villages continues through all the east part of the country, which is of the greatest extent, and where the manufacture is chiefly carried on. If any part of it be waste and thin of inhabitants, it is the west part, drawing a line from about Brand, or Brandon, south, to Walsinghan, north. This part of the country indeed is full of open plains, and somewhat sandy and barren, and feeds great flocks of good sheep; but put it all together, the county of Norfolk has the most people in the least tract of land of any county in England, except about London, and Exon, and the West Riding of Yorkshire, as above.

Add to this, that there is no single county in England, except as above, that can boast of three towns so populous, so rich, and so famous for trade and navigation, as in this county. By these three towns, I mean the city of Norwich, the towns of Yarmouth and Lynn. Besides that, it has several other seaports of very good trade, as Wisbech, Wells, Burnham, Clye, etc.

Norwich is the capital of all the county, and the centre of all the trade and manufactures which I have just mentioned; an ancient, large, rich, and populous city. If a stranger was only to ride through or view the city of Norwich for a day, he would have much more reason to think there was a town without inhabitants, than there is really to say so of Ipswich; but on the contrary if he was to view the city, either on a Sabbath-day, or on any public occasion, he would wonder where all the people could dwell, the multitude is so great. But the case is this: the inhabitants being all busy at their manufactures, dwell in their garrets at their looms, and in their combing shops (so they call them), twisting-mills, and other work-houses, almost all the works they are employed in being done within doors. There are in this city thirty-two parishes besides the cathedral, and a great many meeting-houses of Dissenters of all denominations. The public edifices are chiefly the castle, ancient and decayed, and now for many years past made use of for a gaol. The Duke of Norfolk's house was formerly kept well, and the gardens preserved for the pleasure and diversion of the citizens, but since feeling too sensibly the sinking circumstances of that once glorious family, who were the first peers and hereditary earl-marshals of England.

The walls of this city are reckoned three miles in circumference, taking in more ground than the City of London, but much of that ground lying open in pasture-fields and gardens; nor does it seem to be, like some ancient places, a decayed, declining town, and that the walls mark out its ancient dimensions; for we do not see room to suppose that it was ever larger or more populous than it is now. But the walls seem to be placed as if they expected that the city would in time increase sufficiently to fill them up with buildings.

The cathedral of this city is a fine fabric, and the spire steeple very high and beautiful. It is not ancient, the bishop's see having been first at Thetford, from whence it was not translated hither till the twelfth century. Yet the church has so many antiquities in it, that our late great scholar and physician, Sir Thomas Brown, thought it worth his while to write a whole book to collect the monuments and inscriptions in this church, to which I refer the reader.

The River Yare runs through this city, and is navigable thus far without the help of any art (that is to say, without locks or stops), and being increased by other waters, passes afterwards through a long tract of the richest meadows, and the largest, take them all together, that are anywhere in England, lying for thirty miles in length, from this city to Yarmouth, including the return of the said meadows on the bank of the Waveney south, and on the River Thyrn north.

Here is one thing indeed strange in itself, and more so, in that history seems to be quite ignorant of the occasion of it. The River Waveney is a considerable river, and of a deep and full channel, navigable for large barges as high as Beccles; it runs for a course of about fifty miles, between the two counties of Suffolk and Norfolk, as a boundary to both; and pushing on, though with a gentle stream, towards the sea, no one would doubt, but, that when they see the river growing broader and deeper, and going directly towards the sea, even to the edge of the beach—that is to say, within a mile of the main ocean—no stranger, I say, but would expect to see its entrance into the sea at that place, and a noble harbour for ships at the mouth of it; when on a sudden, the land rising high by the seaside, crosses the head of the river, like a dam, checks the whole course of it, and it returns, bending its course west, for two miles, or thereabouts; and then turning north, through another long course of meadows (joining to those just now mentioned) seeks out the River Yare, that it may join its water with hers, and find their way to the sea together

Some of our historians tell a long, fabulous story of this river being once open, and a famous harbour for ships belonging to a town of Lowestoft adjoining; but that the town of Yarmouth envying the prosperity of the said town of Lowestoft, made war upon them; and that after many bloody battles, as well by sea as by land, they came at last to a decisive action at sea with their respective fleets, and the victory fell to the Yarmouth men, the Lowestoft fleet being overthrown and utterly destroyed; and that upon this victory, the Yarmouth men either actually did stop up the mouth of the said river, or obliged the vanquished Lowestoft men to do it themselves, and bound them never to attempt to open it again.

I believe my share of this story, and I recommend no more of it to the reader; adding, that I see no authority for the relation, neither do the relators agree either in the time of it, or in the particulars of the fact; that is to say, in whose reign, or under what government all this happened; in what year, and the like; so I satisfy myself with transcribing the matter of fact, and then leave it as I find it.

In this vast tract of meadows are fed a prodigious number of black cattle which are said to be fed up for the fattest beef, though not the largest in England; and the quantity is so great, as that they not only supply the city of Norwich, the town of Yarmouth, and county adjacent, but send great quantities of them weekly in all the winter season to London.

And this in particular is worthy remark, that the gross of all the Scots cattle which come yearly into England are brought hither, being brought to a small village lying north of the city of Norwich, called St. Faith's, where the Norfolk graziers go and buy them.

These Scots runts, so they call them, coming out of the cold and barren mountains of the Highlands in Scotland, feed so eagerly on the rich pasture in these marshes, that they thrive in an unusual manner, and grow monstrously fat; and the beef is so delicious for taste, that the inhabitants prefer them to the English cattle, which are much larger and fairer to look at; and they may very well do so. Some have told me, and I believe with good judgment, that there are above forty thousand of these Scots cattle fed in this county every year, and most of them in the said marshes between Norwich, Beccles, and Yarmouth.

Yarmouth is an ancient town, much older than Norwich; and at present, though not standing on so much ground, yet better built; much more complete; for number of inhabitants, not much inferior; and for wealth, trade, and advantage of its situation, infinitely superior to Norwich.

It is placed on a peninsula between the River Yare and the sea; the two last lying parallel to one another, and the town in the middle. The river lies on the west side of the town, and being grown very large and deep, by a conflux of all the rivers on this side the county, forms the haven; and the town facing to the west also, and open to the river, makes the finest quay in England, if not in Europe, not inferior even to that of Marseilles itself.

The ships ride here so close, and, as it were, keeping up one another, with their headfasts on shore, that for half a mile together they go across the stream with their bowsprits over the land, their bows, or heads touching the very wharf; so that one may walk from ship to ship as on a floating bridge, all along by the shore-side. The quay reaching from the drawbridge almost to the south gate, is so spacious and wide, that in some places it is near one hundred yards from the houses to the wharf. In this pleasant and agreeable range of houses are some very magnificent buildings, and among the rest, the Custom House and Town Hall, and some merchant's houses, which look like little palaces rather than the dwelling-houses of private men.

The greatest defect of this beautiful town seems to be that, though it is very rich and increasing in wealth and trade, and consequently in people, there is not room to enlarge the town by building, which would be certainly done much more than it is, but that the river on the land side prescribes them, except at the north end without the gate; and even there the land is not very agreeable. But had they had a larger space within the gates there would before now have been many spacious streets of noble fine buildings erected, as we see is done in some other thriving towns in England, as at Liverpool, Manchester, Bristol, Frome, etc.

The quay and the harbour of this town during the fishing fair, as they call it, which is every Michaelmas, one sees the land covered with people, and the river with barques and boats, busy day and night landing and carrying of the herrings, which they catch here in such prodigious quantities, that it is incredible. I happened to be there during their fishing fair, when I told in one tide 110 barques and fishing vessels coming up the river all laden with herrings, and all taken the night before; and this was besides what was brought on shore on the Dean (that is the seaside of the town) by open boats, which they call cobles, and which often bring in two or three last of fish at a time. The barques often bring in ten last a piece.

This fishing fair begins on Michaelmas Day, and lasts all the month of October, by which time the herrings draw off to sea, shoot their spawn, and are no more fit for the merchant's business—at least, not those that are taken thereabouts.

The quantity of herrings that are caught in this season are diversely accounted for. Some have said that the towns of Yarmouth and Lowestoft only have taken 40,000 last in a season. I will not venture to confirm that report; but this I have heard the merchants themselves say, viz., that they have cured—that is to say, hanged and dried in the smoke—40,000 barrels of merchantable red herrings in one season, which is in itself (though far short of the other) yet a very considerable article; and it is to be added that this is besides all the herrings consumed in the country towns of both those populous counties for thirty miles from the sea, whither very great quantities are carried every tide during the whole season.

But this is only one branch of the great trade carried on in this town. Another part of this commerce is in the exporting these herrings after they are cured; and for this their merchants have a great trade to Genoa, Leghorn, Naples, Messina, and Venice; as also to Spain and Portugal, also exporting with their herring very great quantities of worsted stuffs, and stuffs made of silk and worsted, camblets, etc., the manufactures of the neighbouring city of Norwich and of the places adjacent.

Besides this, they carry on a very considerable trade with Holland, whose opposite neighbours they are; and a vast quantity of woollen manufactures they export to the Dutch every year. Also they have a fishing trade to the North Seas for white fish, which from the place are called the North Sea cod.

They have also a considerable trade to Norway and to the Baltic, from whence they bring back deals and fir timber, oaken plank, balks, spars, oars, pitch, tar, hemp, flax, spruce canvas, and sail-cloth, with all manner of naval stores, which they generally have a consumption for in their own port, where they build a very great number of ships every year, besides refitting and repairing the old.

Add to this the coal trade between Newcastle and the river of Thames, in which they are so improved of late years that they have now a greater share of it than any other town in England, and have quite worked the Ipswich men out of it who had formerly the chief share of the colliery in their hands.

For the carrying on all these trades they must have a very great number of ships, either of their own or employed by them: and it may in some measure be judged of by this that in the year 1697, I had an account from the town register that there was then 1,123 sail of ships using the sea and belonged to the town, besides such ships as the merchants of Yarmouth might be concerned in, and be part owners of, belonging to any other ports.

To all this I must add, without compliment to the town or to the people, that the merchants, and even the generality of traders of

Yarmouth, have a very good reputation in trade as well abroad as at home for men of fair and honourable dealing, punctual and just in their performing their engagements and in discharging commissions; and their seamen, as well masters as mariners, are justly esteemed among the ablest and most expert navigators in England.

This town, however populous and large, was ever contained in one parish, and had but one church; but within these two years they have built another very fine church near the south end of the town. The old church is dedicated to St. Nicholas, and was built by that famous Bishop of Norwich, William Herbert, who flourished in the reign of William II., and Henry I., William of Malmesbury, calls him *Vir Pecuniosus*; he might have called him *Vir Pecuniosissimus*, considering the times he lived in, and the works of charity and munificence which he has left as witnesses of his immense riches; for he built the Cathedral Church, the Priory for sixty monks, the Bishop's Palace, and the parish church of St. Leonard, all in Norwich; this great church at Yarmouth, the Church of St. Margaret at Lynn, and of St. Mary at Elmham. He removed the episcopal see from Thetford to Norwich, and instituted the Cluniack Monks at Thetford, and gave them or built them a house. This old church is very large, and has a high spire, which is a useful sea-mark.

Here is one of the finest market-places and the best served with provisions in England, London excepted; and the inhabitants are so multiplied in a few years that they seem to want room in their town rather than people to fill it, as I have observed above.

The streets are all exactly straight from north to south, with lanes or alleys, which they call rows, crossing them in straight lines also from east to west, so that it is the most regular built town in England, and seems to have been built all at once; or that the dimensions of the houses and extent of the streets were laid out by consent.

They have particular privileges in this town and a jurisdiction by which they can try, condemn, and execute in especial cases without waiting for a warrant from above; and this they exerted once very smartly in executing a captain of one of the king's ships of war in the reign of King Charles II. for a murder committed in the street, the circumstance of which did indeed call for justice; but some thought they would not have ventured to exert their powers as they did. However, I never heard that the Government resented it or blamed them for it.

It is also a very well-governed town, and I have nowhere in England observed the Sabbath day so exactly kept, or the breach so continually punished, as in this place, which I name to their honour.

Among all these regularities it is no wonder if we do not find abundance of revelling, or that there is little encouragement to assemblies, plays, and gaming meetings at Yarmouth as in some other places; and yet I do not see that the ladies here come behind any of the neighbouring counties, either in beauty, breeding, or behaviour; to which may be added too, not at all to their disadvantage, that they generally go beyond them in fortunes.

From Yarmouth I resolved to pursue my first design, viz., to view the seaside on this coast, which is particularly famous for being one of the most dangerous and most fatal to the sailors in all England—I may say in all Britain—and the more so because of the great number of ships which are continually going and coming this way in their passage between London and all the northern coasts of Great Britain. Matters of antiquity are not my inquiry, but principally observations on the present state of things, and, if possible, to give such accounts of things worthy of recording as have never been observed before; and this leads me the more directly to mention the commerce and the navigation when I come to towns upon the coast as what few writers have yet meddled with.

The reason of the dangers of this particular coast are found in the situation of the county and in the course of ships sailing this way, which I shall describe as well as I can thus:- The shore from the mouth of the River of Thames to Yarmouth Roads lies in a straight line from SSE. *to* NNW., the land being on the W. or larboard side.

From Wintertonness, which is the utmost northerly point of land in the county of Norfolk, and about four miles beyond Yarmouth, the shore falls off for nearly sixty miles to the west, as far as Lynn and Boston, till the shore of Lincolnshire tends north again for about sixty miles more as far as the Humber, whence the coast of Yorkshire, or Holderness, which is the east riding, shoots out again into the sea, to the Spurn and to Flamborough Head, as far east, almost, as the shore of Norfolk had given back at Winterton, making a very deep gulf or bay between those two points of Winterton and the Spurn Head; so that the ships going north are obliged to stretch away to sea from Wintertonness, and leaving the sight of land in that deep bay which I have mentioned, that reaches to Lynn and the shore of Lincolnshire, they go, I say, N. or still NNW. to meet the shore of Holderness, which I said runs out into the sea again at the Spurn; and the first land they make or desire to make, is called as above, Flamborough Head, so that Wintertonness and Flamborough Head are the two extremes of this course, there is, as I said, the Spurn Head indeed between; but as it lies too far in towards the Humber, they keep out to the north to avoid coming near it.

In like manner the ships which come from the north, leave the shore at Flamborough Head, and stretch away SSE. for Yarmouth Roads; and they first land they make is Wintertonness (as above). Now, the danger of the place is this: if the ships coming from the north are taken with a hard gale of wind from the SE., or from any point between NE. and SE., so that they cannot, as the seamen call it, weather Wintertonness, they are thereby kept within that deep bay; and if the wind blows hard, are often in danger of running on shore upon the rocks about Cromer, on the north coast of Norfolk, or stranding upon the flat shore between Cromer and Wells; all the relief they have, is good ground tackle to ride it out, which is very hard to do there, the sea coming very high upon them; or if they cannot ride it out then, to run into the bottom of the great bay I mentioned, to Lynn or Boston, which is a very difficult and desperate push: so that sometimes in this distress whole fleets have been lost here altogether.

The like is the danger to ships going northward, if after passing by Winterton they are taken short with a north-east wind, and cannot put back into the Roads, which very often happens, then they are driven upon the same coast, and embayed just as the latter. The danger on the north part of this bay is not the same, because if ships going or coming should be taken short on this side Flamborough, there is the river Humber open to them, and several good roads to have recourse to, as Burlington Bay, Grimsby Road, and the Spurn Head, and others, where they ride under shelter.

The dangers of this place being thus considered, it is no wonder, that upon the shore beyond Yarmouth there are no less than four lighthouses kept flaming every night, besides the lights at Castor, north of the town, and at Goulston S., all of which are to direct the sailors to keep a good offing in case of bad weather, and to prevent their running into Cromer Bay, which the seamen call the devil's throat.

As I went by land from Yarmouth northward, along the shore towards Cromer aforesaid, and was not then fully master of the reason of these things, I was surprised to see, in all the way from Winterton, that the farmers and country people had scarce a barn, or a shed, or a stable, nay, not the pales of their yards and gardens, not a hogstye, not a necessary house, but what was built of old planks, beams, wales, and timbers, etc., the wrecks of ships, and ruins of mariners' and merchants' fortunes; and in some places were whole yards filled and piled up very high with the same stuff laid up, as I supposed to sell for the like building purposes, as there should be occasion.

About the year 1692 (I think it was that year) there was a melancholy example of what I have said of this place: a fleet of 200 sail of light colliers (so they call the ships bound northward empty to fetch coals from Newcastle to London) went out of Yarmouth Roads with a fair wind, to pursue their voyage, and were taken short with a storm of wind at NE. after they were past Wintertonness, a few leagues; some of them, whose masters were a little more wary than the rest, or perhaps, who made a better judgment of things, or who were not so far out as the rest, tacked, and put back in time, and got safe into the roads; but the rest pushing on in hopes to keep out to sea, and weather it, were by the violence of the storm driven back, when they were too far embayed to weather Wintertonness as above, and so were forced to run west, everyone shifting for themselves as well as they could; some run away for Lynn Deeps, but few of them (the night being so dark) could find their way in there; some, but very few, rode it out at a distance; the rest, being above 140 sail, were all driven on shore and dashed to pieces, and very few of the people on board were saved: at the very same unhappy juncture, a fleet of laden ships were coming from the north, and being just crossing the same bay, were forcibly driven into it, not able to weather the Ness, and so were involved in the same ruin as the light fleet was; also some coasting vessels laden with corn from Lynn and Wells, and bound for Holland, were with the same unhappy luck just come out to begin their voyage, and some of them lay at anchor; these also met with the same misfortune, so that, in the whole, above 200 sail of ships, and above a thousand people, perished in the disaster of that one miserable night, very few escaping.

Cromer is a market town close to the shore of this dangerous coast. I know nothing it is famous for (besides it being thus the terror of the sailors) except good lobsters, which are taken on that coast in great numbers and carried to Norwich, and in such quantities sometimes too as to be conveyed by sea to London.

Farther within the land, and between this place and Norwich, are several good market towns, and innumerable villages, all diligently applying to the woollen manufacture, and the country is exceedingly fruitful and fertile, as well in corn as in pastures; particularly, which was very pleasant to see, the pheasants were in such great plenty as to be seen in the stubbles like cocks and hens—a testimony though, by the way, that the county had more tradesmen than gentlemen in it; indeed, this part is so entirely given up to industry, that what with the seafaring men on the one side, and the manufactures on the other, we saw no idle hands here, but every man busy on the main affair of life, that is to say, getting money; some of the principal of these towns are:- Alsham, North Walsham, South Walsham, Worsted, Caston, Reepham, Holt, Saxthorp, St. Faith's, Blikling, and many others. Near the last, Sir John Hobart, of an ancient family in this county, has a noble seat, but old built. This is that St. Faith's, where the drovers bring their black cattle to sell to the Norfolk graziers, as is observed above.

From Cromer we ride on the strand or open shore to Weyburn Hope, the shore so flat that in some places the tide ebbs out near two miles. From Weyburn west lies Clye, where there are large salt-works and very good salt made, which is sold all over the county, and sometimes sent to Holland and to the Baltic. From Clye we go to Masham and to Wells, all towns on the coast, in each whereof there is a very considerable trade carried on with Holland for corn, which that part of the county is very full of. I say nothing of the great trade driven here from Holland, back again to England, because I take it to be a trade carried on with much less honesty than advantage, especially while the clandestine trade, or the art of smuggling was so much in practice: what it is now, is not to my present purpose.

Near this town lie The Seven Burnhams, as they are called, that is to say, seven small towns, all called by the same name, and each employed in the same trade of carrying corn to Holland, and bringing back,—etc.

From hence we turn to the south-west to Castle Rising, an old decayed borough town, with perhaps not ten families in it, which yet (to the scandal of our prescription right) sends two members to the British Parliament, being as many as the City of Norwich itself or any town in the kingdom, London excepted, can do.

On our left we see Walsingham, an ancient town, famous for the old ruins of a monastery of note there, and the Shrine of our Lady, as noted as that of St. Thomas-à-Becket at Canterbury, and for little else.

Near this place are the seats of the two allied families of the Lord Viscount Townsend and Robert Walpole, Esq.; the latter at this time one of the Lords Commissioners of the Treasury and Minister of State, and the former one of the principal Secretaries of State to King George, of which again.

From hence we went to Lynn, another rich and populous thriving port-town. It stands on more ground than the town of Yarmouth, and has, I think, parishes, yet I cannot allow that it has more people than Yarmouth, if so many. It is a beautiful, well built, and well situated town, at the mouth of the River Ouse, and has this particular attending it, which gives it a vast advantage in trade; namely, that there is the greatest extent of inland navigation here of any port in England, London excepted. The reason whereof is this, that there are more navigable rivers empty themselves here into the sea, including the washes, which are branches of the same port, than at any one mouth of waters in England, except the Thames and the Humber. By these navigable rivers, the merchants of Lynn supply about six counties wholly, and three counties in part, with their goods, especially wine and coals, viz., by the little Ouse, they send their goods to Brandon and Thetford, by the Lake to Mildenhall, Barton Mills, and St. Edmundsbury; by the River Grant to Cambridge, by the great Ouse itself to Ely, to St. Ives, to St. Neots, to Barford Bridge, and to Bedford; by the River Nyne to Peterborough; by the drains and washes to Wisbeach, to Spalding, Market Deeping, and Stamford; besides the several counties, into which these goods are carried by land-carriage, from the places, where the navigation of those rivers end; which has given rise to this observation on the town of Lynn, that they bring in more coals than any sea-port between London and Newcastle; and import more wines than any port in England, except London and Bristol; their trade to Norway and to the Baltic Sea is also great in proportion, and of late years they have extended their trade farther to the southward.

Here are more gentry, and consequently is more gaiety in this town than in Yarmouth, or even in Norwich itself—the place abounding in very good company.

The situation of this town renders it capable of being made very strong, and in the late wars it was so; a line of fortification being drawn round it at a distance from the walls; the ruins, or rather remains of which works appear very fair to this day; nor would it be a hard matter to restore the bastions, with the ravelins, and counterscarp, upon any sudden emergency, to a good state of defence: and that in a little time, a sufficient number of workmen being employed, especially because they are able to fill all their ditches with water from the sea, in such a manner as that it cannot be drawn off.

There is in the market-place of this town a very fine statue of King William on horseback, erected at the charge of the town. The Ouse is mighty large and deep, close to the very town itself, and ships of good burthen may come up to the quay; but there is no bridge, the stream being too strong and the bottom moorish and unsound; nor, for the same reason, is the anchorage computed the best in the world; but there are good roads farther down.

They pass over here in boats into the fen country, and over the famous washes into Lincolnshire, but the passage is very dangerous and uneasy, and where passengers often miscarry and are lost; but then it is usually on their venturing at improper times, and without the guides, which if they would be persuaded not to do, they would very rarely fail of going or coming safe.

From Lynn I bent my course to Downham, where is an ugly wooden bridge over the Ouse; from whence we passed the fen country to Wisbeach, but saw nothing that way to tempt our curiosity but deep roads, innumerable drains and dykes of water, all navigable, and a rich soil, the land bearing a vast quantity of good hemp, but a base unwholesome air; so we came back to Ely, whose cathedral, standing in a level flat country, is seen far and wide, and of which town, when the minster, so they call it, is described, everything remarkable is said that there is room to say. And of the minster, this is the most remarkable thing that I could hear it, namely, that some of it is so ancient, totters so much with every gust of wind, looks so like a decay, and seems so near it, that whenever it does fall, all that it is likely will be thought strange in it will be that it did not fall a hundred years sooner.

From hence we came over the Ouse, and in a few miles to Newmarket. In our way, near Snaybell, we saw a noble seat of the late Admiral Russell, now Earl of Orford, a name made famous by the glorious victory obtained under his command over the French fleet and the burning their ships at La Hogue—a victory equal in glory to, and infinitely more glorious to the English nation in particular, than that at Blenheim, and, above all, more to the particular advantage of the confederacy, because it so broke the heart of the naval power of France that they have not fully recovered it to this day. But of this victory it must be said it was owing to the haughty, rash, and insolent orders given by the King of France to his admiral, viz., to fight the confederate fleet wherever he found them, without leaving room for him to use due caution if he found them too strong, which pride of France was doubtless a fate upon them, and gave a cheap victory to the confederates, the French coming down rashly, and with the most impolitic bravery, with about five-and-forty sail to attack between seventy and eighty sail, by which means they met their ruin. Whereas, had their own fleet been joined, it might have cost more blood to have mastered them if it had been done at all.

The situation of this house is low, and on the edge of the fen country, but the building is very fine, the avenues noble, and the gardens perfectly finished. The apartments also are rich, and I see nothing wanting but a family and heirs to sustain the glory and inheritance of the illustrious ancestor who raised it—*sed caret pedibus*; these are wanting.

Being come to Newmarket in the month of October, I had the opportunity to see the horse races and a great concourse of the nobility and gentry, as well from London as from all parts of England, but they were all so intent, so eager, so busy upon the sharping part of the sport—their wagers and bets—that to me they seemed just as so many horse-coursers in Smithfield, descending (the greatest of them) from their high dignity and quality to picking one another's pockets, and biting one another as much as possible, and that with such eagerness as that it might be said they acted without respect to faith, honour, or good manners.

There was Mr. Frampton the oldest, and, as some say, the cunningest jockey in England; one day he lost one thousand guineas, the next he won two thousand; and so alternately he made as light of throwing away five hundred or one thousand pounds at a time as other men do of their pocket-money, and as perfectly calm, cheerful, and unconcerned when he had lost one thousand pounds as when he had won it. On the other side there was Sir R Fagg, of Sussex, of whom fame says he has the most in him and the least to show for it (relating to jockeyship) of any man there, yet he often carried the prize. His horses, they said, were all cheats, how honest soever their master was, for he scarce ever produced a horse but he looked like what he was not, and was what nobody could expect him to be. If he was as light as the wind, and could fly like a meteor, he was sure to look as clumsy, and as dirty, and as much like a cart-horse as all the cunning of his master and the grooms could make him, and just in this manner he beat some of the greatest gamesters in the field.

I was so sick of the jockeying part that I left the crowd about the posts and pleased myself with observing the horses: how the creatures yielded to all the arts and managements of their masters; how they took their airings in sport, and played with the daily heats which they ran over the course before the grand day. But how, as knowing the difference equally with their riders, would they exert their utmost strength at the time of the race itself! And that to such an extremity that one or two of them died in the stable when they came to be rubbed after the first heat.

Here I fancied myself in the Circus Maximus at Rome seeing the ancient games and the racings of the chariots and horsemen, and in this warmth of my imagination I pleased and diverted myself more and in a more noble manner than I could possibly do in the crowds of gentlemen at the weighing and starting-posts and at their coming in, or at their meetings at the coffee-houses and gaming-tables after the races were over, where there was little or nothing to be seen but what was the subject of just reproach to them and reproof from every wise man that looked upon them.

N.B.—Pray take it with you, as you go, you see no ladies at Newmarket, except a few of the neighbouring gentlemen's families, who come in their coaches on any particular day to see a race, and so go home again directly.

As I was pleasing myself with what was to be seen here, I went in the intervals of the sport to see the fine seats of the gentlemen in the neighbouring county, for this part of Suffolk, being an open champaign country and a healthy air, is formed for pleasure and all kinds of country diversion, Nature, as it were, inviting the gentlemen to visit her where she was fully prepared to receive them, in conformity to which kind summons they came, for the country is, as it were, covered with fine palaces of the nobility and pleasant seats of the gentlemen.

The Earl of Orford's house I have mentioned already; the next is Euston Hall, the seat of the Duke of Grafton. It lies in the open country towards the side of Norfolk, not far from Thetford, a place capable of all that is pleasant and delightful in Nature, and improved by art to every extreme that Nature is able to produce.

From thence I went to Rushbrook, formerly the seat of the noble family of Jermyns, lately Lord Dover, and now of the house of Davers. Here Nature, for the time I was there, drooped and veiled all the beauties of which she once boasted, the family being in tears and the house shut up, Sir Robert Davers, the head thereof, and knight of the

213

shire for the county of Suffolk, and who had married the eldest daughter of the late Lord Dover, being just dead, and the corpse lying there in its funeral form of ceremony, not yet buried. Yet all looked lovely in their sorrow, and a numerous issue promising and grown up intimated that the family of Davers would still flourish, and that the beauties of Rushbrook, the mansion of the family, were not formed with so much art in vain or to die with the present possessor.

After this we saw Brently, the seat of the Earl of Dysert, and the ancient palace of my Lord Cornwallis, with several others of exquisite situation, and adorned with the beauties both of art and Nature, so that I think any traveller from abroad, who would desire to see how the English gentry live, and what pleasures they enjoy, should come into Suffolk and Cambridgeshire, and take but a light circuit among the country seats of the gentlemen on this side only, and they would be soon convinced that not France, no, not Italy itself, can outdo them in proportion to the climate they lived in.

I had still the county of Cambridge to visit to complete this tour of the eastern part of England, and of that I come now to speak.

We enter Cambridgeshire out of Suffolk, with all the advantage in the world; the county beginning upon those pleasant and agreeable plains called Newmarket Heath, where passing the Devil's Ditch, which has nothing worth notice but its name, and that but fabulous too, from the hills called Gogmagog, we see a rich and pleasant vale westward, covered with corn-fields, gentlemen's seats, villages, and at a distance, to crown all the rest, that ancient and truly famous town and university of Cambridge, capital of the county, and receiving its name from, if not, as some say, giving name to it; for if it be true that the town takes its name of Cambridge from its bridge over the river Cam, then certainly the shire or county, upon the division of England into counties, had its name from the town, and Cambridgeshire signifies no more or less than the county of which Cambridge is the capital town.

As my business is not to lay out the geographical situation of places, I say nothing of the buttings and boundings of this county. It lies on the edge of the great level, called by the people here the Fen Country; and great part, if not all, the Isle of Ely lies in this county and Norfolk. The rest of Cambridgeshire is almost wholly a corn country, and of that corn five parts in six of all they sow is barley, which is generally sold to Ware and Royston, and other great malting towns in Hertfordshire, and is the fund from whence that vast quantity of malt, called Hertfordshire malt, is made, which is esteemed the best in

England. As Essex, Suffolk, and Norfolk are taken up in manufactures, and famed for industry, this county has no manufacture at all; nor are the poor, except the husbandmen, famed for anything so much as idleness and sloth, to their scandal be it spoken. What the reason of it is I know not.

It is scarce possible to talk of anything in Cambridgeshire but Cambridge itself; whether it be that the county has so little worth speaking of in it, or, that the town has so much, that I leave to others; however, as I am making modern observations, not writing history, I shall look into the county, as well as into the colleges, for what I have to say.

As I said, I first had a view of Cambridge from Gogmagog hills; I am to add that there appears on the mountain that goes by this name, an ancient camp or fortification, that lies on the top of the hill, with a double, or rather treble, rampart and ditch, which most of our writers say was neither Roman nor Saxon, but British. I am to add that King James II. caused a spacious stable to be built in the area of this camp for his running homes, and made old Mr. Frampton, whom I mentioned above, master or inspector of them. The stables remain still there, though they are not often made use of. As we descended westward we saw the Fen country on our right, almost all covered with water like a sea, the Michaelmas rains having been very great that year, they had sent down great floods of water from the upland countries, and those fens being, as may be very properly said, the sink of no less than thirteen counties—that is to say, that all the water, or most part of the water, of thirteen counties falls into them; they are often thus overflowed. The rivers which thus empty themselves into these fens, and which thus carry off the water, are the Cam or Grant, the Great Ouse and Little Ouse, the Nene, the Welland, and the river which runs from Bury to Milden Hall. The counties which these rivers drain, as above, are as follows:-

Lincoln, Warwick, Norfolk,
* Cambridge, Oxford, Suffolk,
* Huntingdon, Leicester, Essex,
* Bedford, * Northampton
Buckingham, * Rutland.

Those marked with (*) empty all their waters this way, the rest but in part.

In a word, all the water of the middle part of England which does not run into the Thames or the Trent, comes down into these fens.

In these fens are abundance of those admirable pieces of art called decoys that is to say, places so adapted for the harbour and shelter of wild fowl, and then furnished with a breed of those they call decoy ducks, who are taught to allure and entice their kind to the places they belong to, that it is incredible what quantities of wild fowl of all sorts, duck, mallard, teal, widgeon, &c., they take in those decoys every week during the season; it may, indeed, be guessed at a little by this, that there is a decoy not far from Ely which pays to the landlord, Sir Thomas Hare, £500 a year rent, besides the charge of maintaining a great number of servants for the management; and from which decoy alone, they assured me at St. Ives (a town on the Ouse, where the fowl they took was always brought to be sent to London) that they generally sent up three thousand couple a week.

There are more of these about Peterborough, who send the fowl up twice a week in waggon-loads at a time, whose waggons before the late Act of Parliament to regulate carriers I have seen drawn by ten and twelve horses a-piece, they were laden so heavy.

As these fens appear covered with water, so I observed, too, that they generally at this latter part of the year appear also covered with fogs, so that when the downs and higher grounds of the adjacent country were gilded with the beams of the sun, the Isle of Ely looked as if wrapped up in blankets, and nothing to be seen but now and then the lantern or cupola of Ely Minster.

One could hardly see this from the hills and not pity the many thousands of families that were bound to or confined in those fogs, and had no other breath to draw than what must be mixed with those vapours, and that steam which so universally overspreads the country. But notwithstanding this, the people, especially those that are used to it, live unconcerned, and as healthy as other folks, except now and then an ague, which they make light of, and there are great numbers of very ancient people among them.

I now draw near to Cambridge, to which I fancy I look as if I was afraid to come, having made so many circumlocutions beforehand; but I must yet make another digression before I enter the town (for in my way, and as I came in from Newmarket, about the beginning of September), I cannot omit, that I came necessarily through Stourbridge Fair, which was then in its height.

If it is a diversion worthy a book to treat of trifles, such as the gaiety of Bury Fair, it cannot be very unpleasant, especially to the trading part of the world, to say something of this fair, which is not only the greatest in the whole nation, but in the world; nor, if I may believe those who have seen the mall, is the fair at Leipzig in Saxony, the mart at Frankfort-on-the-Main, or the fairs at Nuremberg, or Augsburg, any way to compare to this fair at Stourbridge.

It is kept in a large corn-field, near Casterton, extending from the side of the river Cam, towards the road, for about half a mile square.

If the husbandmen who rent the land, do not get their corn off before a certain day in August, the fair-keepers may trample it under foot and spoil it to build their booths, or tents, for all the fair is kept in tents and booths. On the other hand, to balance that severity, if the fair-keepers have not done their business of the fair, and removed and cleared the field by another certain day in September, the ploughmen may come in again, with plough and cart, and overthrow all, and trample into the dirt; and as for the filth, dung, straw, etc. necessarily left by the fair-keepers, the quantity of which is very great, it is the farmers' fees, and makes them full amends for the trampling, riding, and carting upon, and hardening the ground.

It is impossible to describe all the parts and circumstances of this fair exactly; the shops are placed in rows like streets, whereof one is called Cheapside; and here, as in several other streets, are all sorts of trades, who sell by retail, and who come principally from London with their goods; scarce any trades are omitted—goldsmiths, toyshops, brasiers, turners, milliners, haberdashers, hatters, mercers, drapers, pewterers, china-warehouses, and in a word all trades that can be named in London; with coffee-houses, taverns, brandy-shops, and eating-houses, innumerable, and all in tents, and booths, as above.

This great street reaches from the road, which as I said goes from Cambridge to Newmarket, turning short out of it to the right towards the river, and holds in a line near half a mile quite down to the river-side: in another street parallel with the road are like rows of booths, but larger, and more intermingled with wholesale dealers; and one side, passing out of this last street to the left hand, is a formal great square, formed by the largest booths, built in that form, and which they call the Duddery; whence the name is derived, and what its signification is, I could never yet learn, though I made all possible search into it. The area of this square is about 80 to 100 yards, where the dealers have room before every booth to take down, and open their packs, and to bring in waggons to load and unload.

This place is separated, and peculiar to the wholesale dealers in the woollen manufacture. Here the booths or tents are of a vast extent, have different apartments, and the quantities of goods they bring are so great, that the insides of them look like another Blackwell Hall, being as vast warehouses piled up with goods to the top. In this Duddery, as I have been informed, there have been sold one hundred thousand pounds worth of woollen manufactures in less than a week's time, besides the prodigious trade carried on here, by wholesale men, from London, and all parts of England, who transact their business wholly in their pocket-books, and meeting their chapmen from all parts, make up their accounts, receive money chiefly in bills, and take orders: These they say exceed by far the sales of goods actually brought to the fair, and delivered in kind; it being frequent for the London wholesale men to carry back orders from their dealers for ten thousand pounds' worth of goods a man, and some much more. This especially respects those people, who deal in heavy goods, as wholesale grocers, salters, brasiers, iron-merchants, wine-merchants, and the like; but does not exclude the dealers in woollen manufactures, and especially in mercery goods of all sorts, the dealers in which generally manage their business in this manner.

Here are clothiers from Halifax, Leeds, Wakefield and Huddersfield in Yorkshire, and from Rochdale, Bury, etc., in Lancashire, with vast quantities of Yorkshire cloths, kerseys, pennistons, cottons, etc., with all sorts of Manchester ware, fustiains, and things made of cotton wool; of which the quantity is so great, that they told me there were near a thousand horse-packs of such goods from that side of the country, and these took up a side and half of the Duddery at least; also a part of a street of booths were taken up with upholsterer's ware, such as tickings, sackings, kidderminster stuffs, blankets, rugs, quilts, etc.

In the Duddery I saw one warehouse, or booth with six apartments in it, all belonging to a dealer in Norwich stuffs only, and who, they said, had there above twenty thousand pounds value in those goods, and no other.

Western goods had their share here also, and several booths were filled as full with serges, duroys, druggets, shalloons, cantaloons, Devonshire kerseys, etc., from Exeter, Taunton, Bristol, and other parts west, and some from London also.

But all this is still outdone at least in show, by two articles, which are the peculiars of this fair, and do not begin till the other part of the fair, that is to say for the woollen manufacture begins to draw to a close. These are the wool and the hops; as for the hops, there is scarce any price fixed for hops in England, till they know how they sell at Stourbridge fair; the quantity that appears in the fair is indeed prodigious, and they, as it were, possess a large part of the field on which the fair is kept to themselves; they are brought directly from Chelmsford in Essex, from Canterbury and Maidstone in Kent, and from Farnham in Surrey, besides what are brought from London, the growth of those and other places.

Enquiring why this fair should be thus, of all other places in England, the centre of that trade; and so great a quantity of so bulky a commodity be carried thither so far; I was answered by one thoroughly acquainted with that matter thus: the hops, said he, for this part of England, grow principally in the two counties of Surrey and Kent, with an exception only to the town of Chelmsford in Essex, and there are very few planted anywhere else.

There are indeed in the west of England some quantities growing: as at Wilton, near Salisbury; at Hereford and Broomsgrove, near Wales, and the like; but the quantity is inconsiderable, and the places remote, so that none of them come to London.

As to the north of England, they formerly used but few hops there, their drink being chiefly pale smooth ale, which required no hops, and consequently they planted no hops in all that part of England, north of the Trent; nor did I ever see one acre of hop-ground planted beyond Trent in my observation; but as for some years past, they not only brew great quantities of beer in the north, but also use hops in the brewing their ale much more than they did before; so they all come south of Trent to buy their hops; and here being quantities brought, it is great part of their back carriage into Yorkshire, and Northamptonshire, Derbyshire, Lancashire, and all these counties; nay, of late, since the Union, even to Scotland itself; for I must not omit here also to mention, that the river Grant, or Cam, which runs close by the north-west side of the fair in its way from Cambridge to Ely, is navigable, and that by this means, all heavy goods are brought even to the fair-field, by water carriage from London and other parts; first to the port of Lynn, and then in barges up the Ouse, from the Ouse into the Cam, and so, as I say, to the very edge of the fair.

In like manner great quantities of heavy goods, and the hops among the rest, are sent from the fair to Lynn by water, and shipped there for the Humber, to Hull, York, etc., and for Newcastle-upon-Tyne, and by Newcastle, even to Scotland itself. Now as there is still no planting of hops in the north, though a great consumption, and the consumption increasing daily, this, says my friend, is one reason why at Stourbridge fair there is so great a demand for the hops. He added, that besides this, there were very few hops, if any worth naming, growing in all the counties even on this side Trent, which were above forty miles from London; those counties depending on Stourbridge fair for their supply, so the counties of Suffolk, Norfolk, Cambridge, Huntingdon, Northampton, Lincoln, Leicester, Rutland, and even to Stafford, Warwick, and Worcestershire, bought most if not all of their hops at Stourbridge fair.

These are the reasons why so great a quantity of hops are seen at this fair, as that it is incredible, considering, too, how remote from this fair the growth of them is as above.

This is likewise a testimony of the prodigious resort of the trading people of all parts of England to this fair; the quantity of hops that have been sold at one of these fairs is diversely reported, and some affirm it to be so great, that I dare not copy after them; but without doubt it is a surprising account, especially in a cheap year.

The next article brought thither is wool, and this of several sorts, but principally fleece wool, out of Lincolnshire, where the longest staple is found; the sheep of those countries being of the largest breed.

The buyers of this wool are chiefly indeed the manufacturers of Norfolk and Suffolk and Essex, and it is a prodigious quantity they buy.

Here I saw what I have not observed in any other county of England, namely, a pocket of wool. This seems to be first called so in mockery, this pocket being so big, that it loads a whole waggon, and reaches beyond the most extreme parts of it hanging over both before and behind, and these ordinarily weigh a ton or twenty-five hundredweight of wool, all in one bag.

The quantity of wool only, which has been sold at this place at one fair, has been said to amount to fifty or sixty thousand pounds in value, some say a great deal more.

By these articles a stranger may make some guess at the immense trade carried on at this place; what prodigious quantities of goods are bought and sold here, and what a confluence of people are seen here from all parts of England.

I might go on here to speak of several other sorts of English manufactures which are brought hither to be sold; as all sorts of wrought-iron and brass-ware from Birmingham; edged tools, knives, etc., from Sheffield; glass wares and stockings from Nottingham and Leicester; and an infinite throng of other things of smaller value every morning.

To attend this fair, and the prodigious conflux of people which come to it, there are sometimes no less than fifty hackney coaches which come from London, and ply night and morning to carry the people to and from Cambridge; for there the gross of the people lodge; nay, which is still more strange, there are wherries brought from London on waggons to ply upon the little river Cam, and to row people up and down from the town, and from the fair as occasion presents.

It is not to be wondered at, if the town of Cambridge cannot receive, or entertain the numbers of people that come to this fair; not Cambridge only, but all the towns round are full; nay, the very barns and stables are turned into inns, and made as fit as they can to lodge the meaner sort of people: as for the people in the fair, they all universally eat, drink, and sleep in their booths and tents; and the said booths are so intermingled with taverns, coffee-houses, drinking-houses, eating-houses, cook-shops, etc., and all in tents too; and so many butchers and higglers from all the neighbouring counties come into the fair every morning with beef, mutton, fowls, butter, bread, cheese, eggs, and such things, and go with them from tent to tent, from door to door, that there is no want of any provisions of any kind, either dressed or undressed.

In a word, the fair is like a well-fortified city, and there is the least disorder and confusion I believe, that can be seen anywhere with so great a concourse of people.

Towards the latter end of the fair, and when the great hurry of wholesale business begins to be over, the gentry come in from all parts of the county round; and though they come for their diversion, yet it is not a little money they lay out, which generally falls to the share of the retailers, such as toy-shops, goldsmiths, braziers, ironmongers, turners, milliners, mercers, etc., and some loose coins they reserve for the puppet shows, drolls, rope-dancers, and such like, of which there is no want, though not considerable like the rest. The last day of the fair is the horse-fair, where the whole is closed with both horse and foot races, to divert the meaner sort of people only, for nothing considerable is offered of that kind. Thus ends the whole fair, and in less than a week more, there is scarce any sign left that there has been such a thing there, except by the heaps of dung and straw and other rubbish which is left behind, trod into the earth, and which is as good as a summer's fallow for dunging the land; and as I have said above, pays the husbandman well for the use of it.

I should have mentioned that here is a court of justice always open, and held every day in a shed built on purpose in the fair; this is for keeping the peace, and deciding controversies in matters deriving from the business of the fair. The magistrates of the town of Cambridge are judges in this court, as being in their jurisdiction, or they holding it by special privilege: here they determine matters in a summary way, as is practised in those we call Pye Powder Courts in other places, or as a Court of Conscience; and they have a final authority without appeal.

I come now to the town and university of Cambridge; I say the town and university, for though they are blended together in the situation, and the colleges, halls, and houses for literature are promiscuously scattered up and down among the other parts, and some even among the meanest of the other buildings, as Magdalene College over the bridge is in particular; yet they are all incorporated together by the name of the university, and are governed apart and distinct from the town which they are so intermixed with.

As their authority is distinct from the town, so are their privileges, customs, and government; they choose representatives, or members of Parliament for themselves, and the town does the like for themselves, also apart.

The town is governed by a mayor and aldermen; the university by a chancellor, and vice-chancellor, etc. Though their dwellings are mixed, and seem a little confused, their authority is not so; in some cases the vice-chancellor may concern himself in the town, as in searching houses for the scholars at improper hours, removing scandalous women, and the like.

But as the colleges are many, and the gentlemen entertained in them are a very great number, the trade of the town very much depends upon them, and the tradesmen may justly be said to get their bread by the colleges; and this is the surest hold the university may be said to have of the townsmen, and by which they secure the dependence of the town upon them, and consequently their submission.

I remember some years ago a brewer, who being very rich and popular in the town, and one of their magistrates, had in several things so much opposed the university, and insulted their vice-chancellor, or other heads of houses, that in short the university having no other way to exert themselves, and show their resentment, they made a bye-law or order among themselves, that for the future they would not trade with him; and that none of the colleges, halls, etc., would take any more beer of him; and what followed? The man indeed braved it out a while, but when he found he could not obtain a revocation of the order, he was fain to leave off his brewhouse, and if I remember right, quitted the town.

Thus I say, interest gives them authority; and there are abundance of reasons why the town should not disoblige the university, as there are some also on the other hand, why the university should not differ to any extremity with the town; nor, such is their prudence, do they let any disputes between them run up to any extremities if they can avoid it. As for society; to any man who is a lover of learning, or of learned men, here is the most agreeable under heaven; nor is there any want of mirth and good company of other kinds; but it is to the honour of the university to say, that the governors so well understand their office, and the governed their duty, that here is very little encouragement given to those seminaries of crime, the assemblies, which are so much boasted of in other places.

Again, as dancing, gaming, intriguing are the three principal articles which recommend those assemblies; and that generally the time for carrying on affairs of this kind is the night, and sometimes all night, a time as unseasonable as scandalous; add to this, that the orders of the university admit no such excesses; I therefore say, as this is the case, it is to the honour of the whole body of the university that no encouragement is given to them here.

As to the antiquity of the university in this town, the originals and founders of the several colleges, their revenues, laws, government, and governors, they are so effectually and so largely treated of by other authors, and are so foreign to the familiar design of these letters, that I refer my readers to Mr. Camden's "Britannia" and the author of the "Antiquities of Cambridge," and other such learned writers, by whom they may be fully informed.

The present Vice-Chancellor is Dr. Snape, formerly Master of Eaton School near Windsor, and famous for his dispute with, and evident advantage over, the late Bishop of Bangor in the time of his government; the dispute between the University and the Master of Trinity College has been brought to a head so as to employ the pens of the learned on both sides, but at last prosecuted in a judicial way so as to deprive Dr. Bentley of all his dignities and offices in the university; but the doctor flying to the royal protection, the university is under a writ of mandamus, to show cause why they do not restore the doctor again, to which it seems they demur, and that demur has not, that we hear, been argued, at least when these sheets were sent to the press. What will be the issue time must show.

From Cambridge the road lies north-west on the edge of the fens to Huntingdon, where it joins the great north road. On this side it is all an agreeable corn country as above, adorned with several seats of gentlemen; but the chief is the noble house, seat, or mansion of Wimple or Wimple Hall, formerly built at a vast expense by the late Earl of Radnor, adorned with all the natural beauties of situation, and to which was added all the most exquisite contrivances which the best heads could invent to make it artificially as well as naturally pleasant.

However, the fate of the Radnor family so directing, it was bought with the whole estate about it by the late Duke of Newcastle, in a partition of whose immense estate it fell to the Right Honourable the Lord Harley, son and heir-apparent of the present Earl of Oxford and Mortimer, in right of the Lady Harriet Cavendish, only daughter of the said Duke of Newcastle, who is married to his lordship, and brought him this estate and many other, sufficient to denominate her the richest heiress in Great Britain.

Here his lordship resides, and has already so recommended himself to this county as to be by a great majority chosen Knight of the Shire for the county of Cambridge.

From Cambridge, my design obliging me, and the direct road in part concurring, I came back through the west part of the county of Essex, and at Saffron Walden I saw the ruins of the once largest and most magnificent pile in all this part of England—viz., Audley End—built by, and decaying with, the noble Dukes and Earls of Suffolk.

A little north of this part of the country rises the River Stour, which for a course of fifty miles or more parts the two counties of Suffolk and Essex, passing through or near Haveril, Clare, Cavendish, Halsted, Sudbury, Bowers, Nayland, Stretford, Dedham, Manningtree, and into the sea at Harwich, assisting by its waters to make one of the best harbours for shipping that is in Great Britain—I mean Orwell Haven or Harwich, of which I have spoken largely already.

As we came on this side we saw at a distance Braintree and Bocking, two towns, large, rich, and populous, and made so originally by the bay trade, of which I have spoken at large at Colchester, and which flourishes still among them.

The manor of Braintree I found descended by purchase to the name of Olmeus, the son of a London merchant of the same name, making good what I had observed before, of the great number of such who have purchased estates in this county.

Near this town is Felsted, a small place, but noted for a free school of an ancient foundation, for many years under the mastership of the late Rev. Mr. Lydiat, and brought by him to the meridian of its reputation. It is now supplied, and that very worthily, by the Rev. Mr. Hutchins.

Near to this is the Priory of Lees, a delicious seat of the late Dukes of Manchester, but sold by the present Duke to the Duchess Dowager of Bucks, his Grace the Duke of Manchester removing to his yet finer seat of Kimbolton in Northamptonshire, the ancient mansion of the family. From hence keeping the London Road I came to Chelmsford, mentioned before, and Ingerstone, five miles west, which I mention again, because in the parish church of this town are to be seen the ancient monuments of the noble family of Petre, whose seat and large estate lie in the neighbourhood, and whose whole family, by a constant series of beneficent actions to the poor, and bounty upon all charitable occasions, have gained an affectionate esteem through all that part of the country such as no prejudice of religion could wear out, or perhaps ever may; and I must confess, I think, need not, for good and great actions command our respect, let the opinions of the persons be otherwise what they will.

From hence we crossed the country to the great forest, called Epping Forest, reaching almost to London. The country on that side of Essex is called the Roodings, I suppose, because there are no less than ten towns almost together, called by the name of Roding, and is famous for good land, good malt, and dirty roads; the latter indeed in the winter are scarce passable for horse or man. In the midst of this we see Chipping Onger, Hatfield Broad Oak, Epping, and many forest towns, famed as I have said for husbandry and good malt, but of no other note. On the south side of the county is Waltham Abbey; the ruins of the abbey remain, and though antiquity is not my proper business, I could not but observe that King Harold, slain in the great battle in Sussex against William the Conqueror, lies buried here; his body being begged by his mother, the Conqueror allowed it to be carried hither; but no monument was, as I can find, built for him, only a flat gravestone, on which was engraven *Harold Infelix.*

From hence I came over the forest again—that is to say, over the lower or western part of it, where it is spangled with fine villages, and these villages filled with fine seats, most of them built by the citizens of London, as I observed before, but the lustre of them seems to be entirely swallowed up in the magnificent palace of the Lord Castlemain, whose father, Sir Josiah Child, as it were, prepared it in his life for the design of his son, though altogether unforeseen, by adding to the advantage of its situation innumerable rows of trees, planted in curious order for avenues and vistas to the house, all leading up to the place where the old house stood, as to a centre.

In the place adjoining, his lordship, while he was yet Sir Richard Child only, and some years before he began the foundation of his new house, laid out the most delicious, as well as most spacious, pieces of ground for gardens that is to be seen in all this part of England. The greenhouse is an excellent building, fit to entertain a prince; it is furnished with stoves and artificial places for heat from an apartment in which is a bagnio and other conveniences, which render it both useful and pleasant. And these gardens have been so the just admiration of the world, that it has been the general diversion of the citizens to go out to see them, till the crowds grew too great, and his lordship was obliged to restrain his servants from showing them, except on one or two days in a week only.

The house is built since these gardens have been finished. The building is all of Portland stone in the front, which makes it look extremely glorious and magnificent at a distance, it being the particular property of that stone (except in the streets of London, where it is tainted and tinged with the smoke of the city) to grow whiter and whiter the longer it stands in the open air.

As the front of the house opens to a long row of trees, reaching to the great road at Leightonstone, so the back face, or front (if that be proper), respects the gardens, and, with an easy descent, lands you upon the terrace, from whence is a most beautiful prospect to the river, which is all formed into canals and openings to answer the views from above and beyond the river; the walks and wildernesses go on to such a distance, and in such a manner up the hill, as they before went down, that the sight is lost in the woods adjoining, and it looks all like one planted garden as far as the eye can see.

I shall cover as much as possible the melancholy part of a story which touches too sensibly many, if not most, of the great and flourishing families in England. Pity and matter of grief is it to think that families, by estate able to appear in such a glorious posture as this, should ever be vulnerable by so mean a disaster as that of stock-jobbing. But the general infatuation of the day is a plea for it, so that men are not now blamed on that account. South Sea was a general possession, and if my Lord Castlemain was wounded by that arrow shot in the dark it was a misfortune. But it is so much a happiness that it was not a mortal wound, as it was to some men who once seemed as much out of the reach of it. And that blow, be it what it will, is not remembered for joy of the escape, for we see this noble family, by prudence and management, rise out of all that cloud, if it may be allowed such a name, and shining in the same full lustre as before.

This cannot be said of some other families in this county, whose fine parks and new-built palaces are fallen under forfeitures and alienations by the misfortunes of the times and by the ruin of their masters' fortunes in that South Sea deluge.

But I desire to throw a veil over these things as they come in my way; it is enough that we write upon them, as was written upon King Harold's tomb at Waltham Abbey, *Infelix*, and let all the rest sleep among things that are the fittest to be forgotten.

From my Lord Castlemain's, house and the rest of the fine dwellings on that side of the forest, for there are several very good houses at Wanstead, only that they seem all swallowed up in the lustre of his lordship's palace, I say, from thence, I went south, towards the great road over that part of the forest called the Flats, where we see a very beautiful but retired and rural seat of Mr. Lethulier's, eldest son of the late Sir John Lethulier, of Lusum, in Kent, of whose family I shall speak when I come on that side.

By this turn I came necessarily on to Stratford, where I set out. And thus having finished my first circuit, I conclude my first letter, and am,

Sir, your most humble and obedient servant.

APPENDIX

Whoever travels, as I do, over England, and writes the account of his observations, will, as I noted before, always leave something, altering or undertaking by such a growing improving nation as this, or something to discover in a nation where so much is hid, sufficient to employ the pens of those that come after him, or to add by way of appendix to what he has already observed.

This is my case with respect to the particulars which follow: (I) Since these sheets were in the press, a noble palace of Mr. Walpole's, at present First Commissioner of the Treasury, Privy-counsellor, etc., to King George, is, as it were, risen out of the ruins of the ancient seat of the family of Walpole, at Houghton, about eight miles distant from Lynn, and on the north coast of Norfolk, near the sea.

As the house is not yet finished, and when I passed by it was but newly designed, it cannot be expected that I should be able to give a particular description of what it will be. I can do little more than mention that it appears already to be exceedingly magnificent, and suitable to the genius of the great founder.

But a friend of mine, who lives in that county, has sent me the following lines, which, as he says, are to be placed upon the building, whether on the frieze of the cornice, or over the portico, or on what part of the building, of that I am not as yet certain. The inscription is as follows, viz.:-

"H. M. F.
"Fundamen ut essem Domûs
In Agro Natali Extruendae,
Robertus ille Walpole
Quem nulla nesciet Posteritas:
     Faxit Dues.
     "Postquam Maturus Annis Dominus.
Diu Laetatus fuerit absolutâ
Incolumem tueantur Incolames.
Ad Summam omnium Diem
Et nati natorum et qui nascentur ab illis.
     Hic me Posuit."

A second thing proper to be added here, by way of appendix, relates to what I have mentioned of the Port of London, being bounded by the Naze on the Essex shore, and the North Foreland on the Kentish shore, which some people, guided by the present usage of the Custom House, may pretend is not so, to answer such objectors. The true state of that case stands thus:

"(I) The clause taken from the Act of Parliament establishing the extent of the Port of London, and published in some of the books of rates, is this:

"'To prevent all future differences and disputes touching the extent and limits of the Port of London, the said port is declared to extend, and be accounted from the promontory or point called the North Foreland in the Isle of Thanet, and from thence northward in a right line to the point called the Naze, beyond the Gunfleet upon the coast of Essex, and so continued westward throughout the river Thames, and the several channels, streams, and rivers falling into it, to London Bridge, saving the usual and known rights, liberties, and privileges of the ports of Sandwich and Ipswich, and either of them, and the known members thereof, and of the customers, comptrollers, searchers, and their deputies, of and within the said ports of Sandwich and Ipswich and the several creeks, harbours, and havens to them, or either of them, respectively belonging, within the counties of Kent and Essex.'

"II. Notwithstanding what is above written, the Port of London, as in use since the said order, is understood to reach no farther than Gravesend in Kent and Tilbury Point in Essex, and the ports of Rochester, Milton, and Faversham belong to the port of Sandwich.

"In like manner the ports of Harwich, Colchester, Wivenhoe, Malden, Leigh, etc., are said to be members of the port of Ipswich."

This observation may suffice for what is needful to be said upon the same subject when I may come to speak of the port of Sandwich and its members and their privileges with respect to Rochester, Milton, Faversham, etc., in my circuit through the county of Kent.

MEMOIRS OF A CAVALIER

or

A Military Journal of the Wars in
Germany, and the Wars in England.
From the Year 1632 to the Year 1648.

By Daniel Defoe

INTRODUCTION.

Daniel Defoe is, perhaps, best known to us as the author of *Robinson Crusoe*, a book which has been the delight of generations of boys and girls ever since the beginning of the eighteenth century. For it was then that Defoe lived and wrote, being one of the new school of prose writers which grew up at that time and which gave England new forms of literature almost unknown to an earlier age. Defoe was a vigorous pamphleteer, writing first on the Whig side and later for the Tories in the reigns of William III and Anne. He did much to foster the growth of the newspaper, a form of literature which henceforth became popular. He also did much towards the development of the modern novel, though he did not write novels in our sense of the word. His books were more simple than is the modern novel. What he really wrote were long stories told, as is *Robinson Crusoe*, in the first person and with so much detail that it is hard to believe that they are works of imagination and not true stories. "The little art he is truly master of, is of forging a story and imposing it upon the world as truth." So wrote one of his contemporaries. Charles Lamb, in criticizing Defoe, notices this minuteness of detail and remarks that he is, therefore, an author suited only for "servants" (meaning that this method can appeal only to comparatively uneducated minds). Really as every boy and girl knows, a good story ought to have this quality of seeming true, and the fact that Defoe can so deceive us makes his work the more excellent reading.

The *Memoirs of a Cavalier* resembles *Robinson Crusoe* in so far as it is a tale told by a man of his own experiences and adventures. It has just the same air of truth and for a long time after its first publication in 1720 people were divided in opinion as to whether it was a book of real memoirs or not. A critical examination has shown that it is Defoe's own work and not, as he declares, the contents of a manuscript which he found "by great accident, among other valuable papers" belonging to one of King William's secretaries of state. Although his gifts of imagination enabled him to throw himself into the position of the Cavalier he lapses occasionally into his own characteristic prose and the style is often that of the eighteenth rather than the seventeenth century, more eloquent than quaint. Again, he is not careful to hide inconsistencies between his preface and the text. Thus, he says in his preface that he discovered the manuscript in 1651; yet we find in the *Memoirs* a reference to the Restoration, which shows that it must have been written after 1660 at least. There is abundant proof that the book is really a work of fiction and that the Cavalier is an imaginary character; but, in one sense, it is a true history, inasmuch as the author has studied the events and spirit of the time in which his scene is laid and, though he makes many mistakes of detail, he gives us a very true picture of one of the most interesting periods in English and European history. The *Memoirs* thus represent the English historical novel in its beginnings, a much simpler thing than it was to become in the hands of Scott and later writers.

The period in which the scene is laid is that of the English Civil War, in which the Cavalier fought on the side of King Charles I against the Puritans. But his adventures in this war belong to the second part of the book. In the first part, he tells of his birth and parentage, the foreign travel which was the fashionable completion of the education of a gentleman in the seventeenth century, and his adventures as a volunteer officer in the Swedish army, where he gained the experience which was to serve him well in the Civil War at home. Many a real Cavalier must have had just such a career as Defoe's hero describes as his own. After a short time at Oxford, "long enough for a gentleman," he embarked on a period of travel, going to Italy by way of France. The Cavalier, however, devotes but little space to description, vivid enough as far as it goes, of his adventures in these two countries for a space of over two years. Italy, especially, attracted the attention of gentlemen and scholars in those days, but the Cavalier was more bent on soldiering than sightseeing and he hurries on to tell of his adventures in Germany, where he first really took part in warfare, becoming a volunteer officer in the army of Gustavus Adolphus, the hero King of Sweden, and where he met with those adventures the story of which forms the bulk of the first part of the *Memoirs*.

To appreciate the tale, it will be necessary to have a clear idea of the state of affairs in Europe at the time. The war which was convulsing Germany, and in which almost every other European power interfered at some time, was the Thirty Years' War (1618—1648), a struggle having a special character of its own as the last of the religious wars which had torn Europe asunder for a century and the first of a long series of wars in which the new and purely political principle of the Balance of Power can be seen at work. The struggle was, nominally, between Protestant and Catholic Germany for, during the Reformation period, Germany, which consisted of numerous states under the headship of the Emperor, had split into two great camps. The Northern states had become Protestant under their Protestant princes. The Southern states had remained, for the most part, Catholic or had been won back to Catholicism in the religious reaction known as the Counter-Reformation. As the Catholic movement spread, under a Catholic Emperor like Ferdinand of Styria, who was elected in 1619, it was inevitable that the privileges granted to Protestants should be curtailed. They determined to resist and, as the Emperor had the support of Spain, the Protestant Union found it necessary to call in help from outside. Thus it was that the other European powers came to interfere in German affairs. Some helped the Protestants from motives of religion, more still from considerations of policy, and the long struggle of thirty years may be divided into marked periods in which one power after another, Denmark, Sweden, France, allied themselves with the Protestants against the Emperor. The *Memoirs* are concerned with the first two years of the Swedish period of the war (1630—1634), during which Gustavus Adolphus almost won victory for the Protestants who were, however, to lose the advantage of his brilliant generalship through his death at the battle of Lützen in 1632. Through the death of "this conquering king," the Swedes lost the fruits of their victory and the battle of Lützen marks the end of what may be termed the heroic period of the war. Gustavus Adolphus stands out among the men of his day for the loftiness of his character as well as for the genius of his generalship. It is, therefore, fitting enough that Defoe should make his Cavalier withdraw from the Swedish service after the death of the "glorious king" whom he "could never mention without some remark of his extraordinary merit." For two years longer, he wanders through Germany still watching the course of the war and then returns to England, soon to take part in another war at home, namely the Civil War, in which the English people were divided into two great parties according as they supported King Charles I or the members of the Long Parliament who opposed him. According to the *Memoirs*, the Cavalier "went into arms" without troubling himself "to examine sides." Defoe probably considered this attitude as typical of many of the Cavalier party, and, of course, loyalty to the king's person was one of their strongest motives. The Cavalier does not enter largely into the causes of the war. What he gives us is a picture of army life in that troubled period. It will be well, however, to bear in mind the chief facts in the history of the times.

From the beginning of his reign, Charles had had trouble with his parliaments, which had already become very restless under James I.

Charles's parliaments disapproved of his foreign policy and their unwillingness to grant subsidies led him to fall back on questionable methods of raising money, especially during the eleven years (1629—1640) in which he ruled without a parliament. Charles had no great scheme of tyranny, but avoided parliaments because of their criticism of his policy. At first the opposition had been purely political, but the parliament of 1629 had attacked also Charles's religious policy. He favoured the schemes of Laud (archbishop of Canterbury 1633—1649) and the Arminian school among the clergy, who wished to revive many of the old Catholic practices and some of the beliefs which had been swept away by the Reformation. Many people in England objected not only to these but even to the wearing of the surplice, the simplest of the old vestments, on the use of which Laud tried to insist. This party came to be known as Puritans and they formed the chief strength of the opposition to the King in the Long Parliament which met in 1640. For their attack on the Church led many who had at first opposed the King's arbitrary methods to go over to his side. Thus, the moderate men as well as the loyalists formed a king's party and the opposition was almost confined to men who hated the Church as much as the King. The Puritans who loved simplicity of dress and severity of manners and despised the flowing locks and worldly vanities which the Cavaliers loved were, by these, nicknamed Roundheads on account of their short hair. Defoe, in the *Memoirs*, gives us less of this side of the history of the times than might have been expected. The war actually began in August, 1642, and what Defoe gives us is military history, correct in essentials and full of detail, which is, however, far from accurate. For instance, in his account of the battle of Marston Moor, he makes prince Rupert command the left wing, whereas he really commanded the right wing, the left being led by Lord Goring who, according to Defoe's account, commanded the main battle. He conveys to us, however, the true spirit of the war, emphasizing the ability and the mistakes on both sides, showing how the king's miscalculations or Rupert's rashness deprived the Royalist party of the advantages of the superior generalship and fighting power which were theirs in the first part of the war and how gradually the Roundheads got the better of the Cavaliers. The detailed narrative comes to an end with the delivery of the King to the Parliament by the Scots, to whom he had given himself up in his extremity. A few lines tell of his trial and execution and the *Memoirs* end with some pages of "remarks and observations" on the war and a list of coincidences which had been noted in its course. The latter, savouring somewhat of superstition, appear natural in what purports to be a seventeenth century text, but the summing up of conclusions about the war is rather such as might be made by a more or less impartial observer at a later date than by one who had taken an active part in the struggle. In reading the *Memoirs* this mixture of what belongs to the seventeenth century with the reflections of Defoe, in many ways a typical eighteenth century figure, must be borne in mind. The inaccuracies are pointed out in the notes, but these need not prevent us from entering with zest into the spirit of the story.

E. O'NEILL.

4 *March* 1908.

PREFACE TO THE FIRST EDITION.

As an evidence that 'tis very probable these Memorials were written many years ago, the persons now concerned in the publication assure the reader that they have had them in their possession finished, as they now appear, above twenty years; that they were so long ago found by great accident, among other valuable papers, in the closet of an eminent public minister, of no less figure than one of King William's secretaries of state.

As it is not proper to trace them any farther, so neither is there any need to trace them at all, to give reputation to the story related, seeing the actions here mentioned have a sufficient sanction from all the histories of the times to which they relate, with this addition, that the admirable manner of relating them and the wonderful variety of incidents with which they are beautified in the course of a private gentleman's story, add such delight in the reading, and give such a lustre, as well to the accounts themselves as to the person who was the actor, that no story, we believe, extant in the world ever came abroad with such advantage.

It must naturally give some concern in the reading that the name of a person of so much gallantry and honour, and so many ways valuable to the world, should be lost to the readers. We assure them no small labour has been thrown away upon the inquiry, and all we have been able to arrive to of discovery in this affair is, that a memorandum was found with this manuscript, in these words, but not signed by any name, only the two letters of a name, which gives us no light into the matter, which memoir was as follows:—

Memorandum.

"I found this manuscript among my father's writings, and I understand that he got them as plunder, at, or after, the fight at Worcester, where he served as major of ——'s regiment of horse on the side of the Parliament. I.K."

As this has been of no use but to terminate the inquiry after the person, so, however, it seems most naturally to give an authority to the original of the work, viz., that it was born of a soldier; and indeed it is through every part related with so soldierly a style, and in the very language of the field, that it seems impossible anything but the very person who was present in every action here related, could be the relater of them.

The accounts of battles, the sieges, and the several actions of which this work is so full, are all recorded in the histories of those times; such as the great battle of Leipsic, the sacking of Magdeburg, the siege of Nuremburg, the passing the river Lech in Bavaria; such also as the battle of Kineton, or Edgehill, the battles of Newbury, Marston Moor, and Naseby, and the like: they are all, we say, recorded in other histories, and written by those who lived in those times, and perhaps had good authority for what they wrote. But do those relations give any of the beautiful ideas of things formed in this account? Have they one half of the circumstances and incidents of the actions themselves that this man's eyes were witness to, and which his memory has thus preserved? He that has read the best accounts of those battles will be surprised to see the particulars of the story so preserved, so nicely and so agreeably described, and will confess what we allege, that the story is inimitably told; and even the great actions of the glorious King GUSTAVUS ADOLPHUS receive a lustre from this man's relations which the world was never made sensible of before, and which the present age has much wanted of late, in order to give their affections a turn in favour of his late glorious successor.

In the story of our own country's unnatural wars, he carries on the same spirit. How effectually does he record the virtues and glorious actions of King Charles the First, at the same time that he frequently enters upon the mistakes of his Majesty's conduct, and of his friends, which gave his enemies all those fatal advantages against him, which ended in the overthrow of his armies, the loss of his crown and life, and the ruin of the constitution!

In all his accounts he does justice to his enemies, and honours the merit of those whose cause he fought against; and many accounts recorded in his story, are not to be found even in the best histories of those times.

What applause does he give to gallantry of Sir Thomas Fairfax, to his modesty, to his conduct, under which he himself was subdued, and to the justice he did the king's troops when they laid down their arms!

His description of the Scots troops in the beginning of the war, and the behaviour of the party under the Earl of Holland, who went over against them, are admirable; and his censure of their conduct, who pushed the king upon the quarrel, and then would not let him fight, is no more than what many of the king's friends (though less knowing as soldiers) have often complained of.

In a word, this work is a confutation of many errors in all the writers upon the subject of our wars in England, and even in that extraordinary history written by the Earl of Clarendon; but the editors were so just that when, near twenty years ago, a person who had written a whole volume in folio, by way of answer to and confutation of Clarendon's "History of the Rebellion," would have borrowed the clauses in this account, which clash with that history, and confront it,—we say the editors were so just as to refuse them.

There can be nothing objected against the general credit of this work, seeing its truth is established upon universal history; and almost all the facts, especially those of moment, are confirmed for their general part by all the writers of those times. If they are here embellished with particulars, which are nowhere else to be found, that is the beauty we boast of; and that it is that much recommend this work to all the men of sense and judgment that read it.

The only objection we find possible to make against this work is, that it is not carried on farther, or, as we may say finished, with the finishing the war of the time; and this we complain of also. But then we complain of it as a misfortune to the world, not as a fault in the author; for how do we know but that this author might carry it on, and have another part finished which might not fall into the same hands, or may still remain with some of his family, and which they cannot indeed publish, to make it seem anything perfect, for want of the other parts which we have, and which we have now made public? Nor is it very improbable but that if any such farther part is in being, the publishing these two parts may occasion the proprietors of the third to let the world see it, and that by such a discovery the name of the person may also come to be known, which would, no doubt, be a great satisfaction to the reader as well as us.

This, however, must be said, that if the same author should have written another part of this work, and carried it on to the end of those times, yet as the residue of those melancholy days, to the Restoration, were filled with the intrigues of government, the political management of illegal power, and the dissensions and factions of a people who were then even in themselves but a faction, and that there was very little action in the field, it is more than probable that our author, who was a man of arms, had little share in those things, and might not care to trouble himself with looking at them.

But besides all this, it might happen that he might go abroad again at that time, as most of the gentlemen of quality, and who had an abhorrence for the power that then governed here, did. Nor are we certain that he might live to the end of that time, so we can give no account whether he had any share in the subsequent actions of that time.

'Tis enough that we have the authorities above to recommend this part to us that is now published. The relation, we are persuaded, will recommend itself, and nothing more can be needful, because nothing more can invite than the story itself, which, when the reader enters into, he will find it very hard to get out of till he has gone through it.

MEMOIRS OF A CAVALIER.

PART I

It may suffice the reader, without being very inquisitive after my name, that I was born in the county of Salop, in the year 1608, under the government of what star I was never astrologer enough to examine; but the consequences of my life may allow me to suppose some extraordinary influence affected my birth.

My father was a gentleman of a very plentiful fortune, having an estate of above £5000 per annum, of a family nearly allied to several of the principal nobility, and lived about six miles from the town; and my mother being at —— on some particular occasion, was surprised there at a friend's house, and brought me very safe into the world.

I was my father's second son, and therefore was not altogether so much slighted as younger sons of good families generally are. But my father saw something in my genius also which particularly pleased him, and so made him take extraordinary care of my education.

I was taught, therefore, by the best masters that could be had, everything that was needful to accomplish a young gentleman for the world; and at seventeen years old my tutor told my father an academic education was very proper for a person of quality, and he thought me very fit for it: so my father entered me of —— College in Oxford, where I continued three years.

A collegiate life did not suit me at all, though I loved books well enough. It was never designed that I should be either a lawyer, physician, or divine; and I wrote to my father that I thought I had stayed there long enough for a gentleman, and with his leave I desired to give him a visit.

During my stay at Oxford, though I passed through the proper exercises of the house, yet my chief reading was upon history and geography, as that which pleased my mind best, and supplied me with ideas most suitable to my genius; by one I understood what great actions had been done in the world, and by the other I understood where they had been done.

My father readily complied with my desire of coming home; for besides that he thought, as I did, that three years' time at the university was enough, he also most passionately loved me, and began to think of my settling near him.

At my arrival I found myself extraordinarily caressed by my father, and he seemed to take a particular delight in my conversation. My mother, who lived in perfect union with him both in desires and affection, received me very passionately. Apartments were provided for me by myself, and horses and servants allowed me in particular.

My father never went a-hunting, an exercise he was exceeding fond of, but he would have me with him; and it pleased him when he found me like the sport. I lived thus, in all the pleasures 'twas possible for me to enjoy, for about a year more, when going out one morning with my father to hunt a stag, and having had a very hard chase, and gotten a great way off from home, we had leisure enough to ride gently back; and as we returned my father took occasion to enter into a serious discourse with me concerning the manner of my settling in the world.

He told me, with a great deal of passion, that he loved me above all the rest of his children, and that therefore he intended to do very well for me; and that my eldest brother being already married and settled, he had designed the same for me, and proposed a very advantageous match for me, with a young lady of very extraordinary fortune and merit, and offered to make a settlement of £2000 per annum on me, which he said he would purchase for me without diminishing his paternal estate.

There was too much tenderness in this discourse not to affect me exceedingly. I told him I would perfectly resign myself unto his disposal. But as my father had, together with his love for me, a very nice judgment in his discourse, he fixed his eyes very attentively on me, and though my answer was without the least reserve, yet he thought he saw some uneasiness in me at the proposal, and from thence concluded that my compliance was rather an act of discretion than inclination; and that, however I seemed so absolutely given up to what he had proposed, yet my answer was really an effect of my obedience rather than my choice.

So he returned very quick upon me: "Look you, son, though I give you my own thoughts in the matter, yet I would have you be very plain with me; for if your own choice does not agree with mine, I will be your adviser, but will never impose upon you, and therefore let me know your mind freely." "I don't reckon myself capable, sir," said I, with a great deal of respect, "to make so good a choice for myself as you can for me; and though my opinion differed from yours, its being your opinion would reform mine, and my judgment would as readily comply as my duty." "I gather at least from thence," said my father, "that your designs lay another way before, however they may comply with mine; and therefore I would know what it was you would have asked of me if I had not offered this to you; and you must not deny me your obedience in this, if you expect I should believe your readiness in the other."

"Sir," said I, "'twas impossible I should lay out for myself just what you have proposed; but if my inclinations were never so contrary, though at your command you shall know them, yet I declare them to be wholly subjected to your order. I confess my thoughts did not tend towards marriage or a settlement; for, though I had no reason to question your care of me, yet I thought a gentleman ought always to see something of the world before he confined himself to any part of it. And if I had been to ask your consent to anything, it should have been to give me leave to travel for a short time, in order to qualify myself to appear at home like a son to so good a father."

"In what capacity would you travel?" replied my father. "You must go abroad either as a private gentleman, as a scholar, or as a soldier." "If it were in the latter capacity, sir," said I, returning pretty quick, "I hope I should not misbehave myself; but I am not so determined as not to be ruled by your judgment." "Truly," replied my father, "I see no war abroad at this time worth while for a man to appear in, whether we talk of the cause or the encouragement; and indeed, son, I am afraid you need not go far for adventures of that nature, for times seem to look as if this part of Europe would find us work enough." My father spake then relating to the quarrel likely to happen between the King of England and the Spaniard,' [I] for I believe he had no notions of a civil war in his head.

In short, my father, perceiving my inclinations very forward to go abroad, gave me leave to travel, upon condition I would promise to return in two years at farthest, or sooner, if he sent for me.

While I was at Oxford I happened into the society of a young gentleman, of a good family, but of a low fortune, being a younger brother, and who had indeed instilled into me the first desires of going abroad, and who, I knew, passionately longed to travel, but had not sufficient allowance to defray his expenses as a gentleman. We had contracted a very close friendship, and our humours being very agreeable to one another, we daily enjoyed the conversation of letters. He was of a generous free temper, without the least affectation or deceit, a handsome proper person, a strong body, very good mien, and brave to the last degree. His name was Fielding and we called him

Captain, though it be a very unusual title in a college; but fate had some hand in the title, for he had certainly the lines of a soldier drawn in his countenance. I imparted to him the resolutions I had taken, and how I had my father's consent to go abroad, and would know his mind whether he would go with me. He sent me word he would go with all his heart.

My father, when he saw him, for I sent for him immediately to come to me, mightily approved my choice; so we got our equipage ready, and came away for London.

'Twas on the 22nd of April 1630, when we embarked at Dover, landed in a few hours at Calais, and immediately took post for Paris. I shall not trouble the reader with a journal of my travels, nor with the description of places, which every geographer can do better than I; but these Memoirs being only a relation of what happened either to ourselves, or in our own knowledge, I shall confine myself to that part of it.

We had indeed some diverting passages in our journey to Paris, as first, the horse my comrade was upon fell so very lame with a slip that he could not go, and hardly stand, and the fellow that rid with us express, pretended to ride away to a town five miles off to get a fresh horse, and so left us on the road with one horse between two of us. We followed as well as we could, but being strangers, missed the way, and wandered a great way out the road. Whether the man performed in reasonable time or not we could not be sure, but if it had not been for an old priest, we had never found him. We met this man, by a very good accident, near a little village whereof he was curate. We spoke Latin enough just to make him understand us, and he did not speak it much better himself; but he carried us into the village to his house, gave us wine and bread, and entertained us with wonderful courtesy. After this he sent into the village, hired a peasant, and a horse for my captain, and sent him to guide us into the road. At parting he made a great many compliments to us in French, which we could just understand; but the sum was, to excuse him for a question he had a mind to ask us. After leave to ask what he pleased, it was if we wanted any money for our journey, and pulled out two pistoles, which he offered either to give or lend us.

I mention this exceeding courtesy of the curate because, though civility is very much in use in France, and especially to strangers, yet 'tis a very unusual thing to have them part with their money.

244

We let the priest know, first, that we did not want money, and next that we were very sensible of the obligation he had put upon us; and I told him in particular, if I lived to see him again, I would acknowledge it.

This accident of our horse was, as we afterwards found, of some use to us. We had left our two servants behind us at Calais to bring our baggage after us, by reason of some dispute between the captain of the packet and the custom-house officer, which could not be adjusted, and we were willing to be at Paris. The fellows followed as fast as they could, and, as near as we could learn, in the time we lost our way, were robbed, and our portmanteaus opened. They took what they pleased; but as there was no money there, but linen and necessaries, the loss was not great.

Our guide carried us to Amiens, where we found the express and our two servants, who the express meeting on the road with a spare horse, had brought back with him thither.

We took this for a good omen of our successful journey, having escaped a danger which might have been greater to us than it was to our servants; for the highwaymen in France do not always give a traveller the civility of bidding him stand and deliver his money, but frequently fire on him first, and then take his money.

We stayed one day at Amiens, to adjust this little disorder, and walked about the town, and into the great church, but saw nothing very remarkable there; but going across a broad street near the great church, we saw a crowd of people gazing at a mountebank doctor, who made a long harangue to them with a thousand antic postures, and gave out bills this way, and boxes of physic that way, and had a great trade, when on a sudden the people raised a cry, "*Larron, Larron!*" (in English, "Thief, thief"), on the other side the street, and all the auditors ran away, from Mr Doctor to see what the matter was. Among the rest we went to see, and the case was plain and short enough. Two English gentlemen and a Scotchman, travellers as we were, were standing gazing at this prating doctor, and one of them catched a fellow picking his pocket. The fellow had got some of his money, for he dropped two or three pieces just by him, and had got hold of his watch, but being surprised let it slip again. But the reason of telling this story is for the management of it. This thief had his seconds so ready, that as soon as the Englishman had seized him they fell in, pretended to be mighty zealous for the stranger, takes the fellow by the throat, and makes a great bustle; the gentleman not doubting but the man was secured let go his own hold of him, and left him to them. The hubbub was great, and 'twas these fellows cried, "*Larron, larron!*" but with a dexterity peculiar to themselves had let the right fellow go, and pretended to be all upon one of their own gang. At last they bring the man to the gentleman to ask him what the fellow had done, who, when he saw the person they seized on, presently told them that was not the man. Then they seemed to be in more consternation than before, and spread themselves all over the street, crying, "*Larron, larron!*" pretending to search for the fellow; and so one one way, one another, they were all gone, the noise went over, the gentlemen stood looking one at another, and the bawling doctor began to have the crowd about him again. This was the first French trick I had the opportunity of seeing, but I was told they have a great many more as dexterous as this.

We soon got acquaintance with these gentlemen, who were going to Paris, as well as we; so the next day we made up our company with them, and were a pretty troop of five gentlemen and four servants.

As we had really no design to stay long at Paris, so indeed, excepting the city itself, there was not much to be seen there. Cardinal Richelieu, who was not only a supreme minister in the Church, but Prime Minister in the State, was now made also General of the King's Forces, with a title never known in France before nor since, viz., Lieutenant-General "au place du Roi," in the king's stead, or, as some have since translated it, representing the person of the king.

Under this character he pretended to execute all the royal powers in the army without appeal to the king, or without waiting for orders; and having parted from Paris the winter before had now actually begun the war against the Duke of Savoy, in the process of which he restored the Duke of Mantua, and having taken Pignerol from the duke, put it into such a state of defence as the duke could never force it out of his hands, and reduced the duke, rather by manage and conduct than by force, to make peace without it; so as annexing it to the crown of France it has ever since been a thorn in his foot that has always made the peace of Savoy lame and precarious, and France has since made Pignerol one of the strongest fortresses in the world.

As the cardinal, with all the military part of the court, was in the field, so the king, to be near him, was gone with the queen and all the court, just before I reached Paris, to reside at Lyons. All these considered, there was nothing to do at Paris; the court looked like a citizen's house when the family was all gone into the country, and I thought the whole city looked very melancholy, compared to all the fine things I had heard of it.

The queen-mother and her party were chagrined at the cardinal, who, though he owed his grandeur to her immediate favour, was now grown too great any longer to be at the command of her Majesty, or indeed in her interest; and therefore the queen was under dissatisfaction and her party looked very much down.

The Protestants were everywhere disconsolate, for the losses they had received at Rochelle, Nimes, and Montpelier had reduced them to an absolute dependence on the king's will, without all possible hopes of ever recovering themselves, or being so much as in a condition to take arms for their religion, and therefore the wisest of them plainly foresaw their own entire reduction, as it since came to pass. And I remember very well that a Protestant gentleman told me once, as we were passing from Orleans to Lyons, that the English had ruined them; and therefore, says he, "I think the next occasion the king takes to use us ill, as I know 'twill not be long before he does, we must all fly over to England, where you are bound to maintain us for having helped to turn us out of our own country." I asked him what he meant by saying the English had done it? He returned short upon me: "I do not mean," says he, "by not relieving Rochelle, but by helping to ruin Rochelle, when you and the Dutch lent ships to beat our fleet, which all the ships in France could not have done without you."

I was too young in the world to be very sensible of this before, and therefore was something startled at the charge; but when I came to discourse with this gentleman, I soon saw the truth of what he said was undeniable, and have since reflected on it with regret, that the naval power of the Protestants, which was then superior to the royal, would certainly have been the recovery of all their fortunes, had it not been unhappily broke by their brethren of England and Holland, the former lending seven men-of-war, and the latter twenty, for the destruction of the Rochellers' fleet; and by these very ships the Rochellers' fleet were actually beaten and destroyed, and they never afterwards recovered their force at sea, and by consequence sunk under the siege, which the English afterwards in vain attempted to prevent.

These things made the Protestants look very dull, and expected the ruin of all their party, which had certainly happened had the cardinal lived a few years longer.

We stayed in Paris, about three weeks, as well to see the court and what rarities the place afforded, as by an occasion which had like to have put a short period to our ramble.

Walking one morning before the gate of the Louvre, with a design to see the Swiss drawn up, which they always did, and exercised just before they relieved the guards, a page came up to me, and speaking English to me, "Sir," says he, "the captain must needs have your immediate assistance." I, that had not the knowledge of any person in Paris but my own companion, whom I called captain, had no room to question, but it was he that sent for me; and crying out hastily to him, "Where?" followed the fellow as fast as 'twas possible. He led me through several passages which I knew not, and at last through a tennis-court and into a large room, where three men, like gentlemen, were engaged very briskly two against one. The room was very dark, so that I could not easily know them asunder, but being fully possessed with an opinion before of my captain's danger, I ran into the room with my sword in my hand. I had not particularly engaged any of them, nor so much as made a pass at any, when I received a very dangerous thrust in my thigh, rather occasioned by my too hasty running in, than a real design of the person; but enraged at the hurt, without examining who it was hurt me, I threw myself upon him, and run my sword quite through his body.

The novelty of the adventure, and the unexpected fall of the man by a stranger come in nobody knew how, had becalmed the other two, that they really stood gazing at me. By this time I had discovered that my captain was not there, and that 'twas some strange accident brought me thither. I could speak but little French, and supposed they could speak no English, so I stepped to the door to see for the page that brought me thither, but seeing nobody there and the passage clear, I made off as fast as I could, without speaking a word; nor did the other two gentlemen offer to stop me.

But I was in a strange confusion when, coming into those entries and passages which the page led me through, I could by no means find my way out. At last seeing a door open that looked through a house into the street, I went in, and out at the other door; but then I was at as great a loss to know where I was, and which was the way to my lodgings. The wound in my thigh bled apace, and I could feel the blood in my breeches. In this interval came by a chair; I called, and went into it, and bid them, as well as I could, go to the Louvre; for though I knew not the name of the street where I lodged, I knew I could find the way to it when I was at the Bastille. The chairmen went on their own way, and being stopped by a company of the guards as they went, set me down till the soldiers were marched by; when looking out I found I was just at my own lodging, and the captain was standing at the door looking for me. I beckoned him to me, and, whispering, told him I was very much hurt, but bid him pay the chairmen, and ask no questions but come to me.

I made the best of my way upstairs, but had lost so much blood, that I had hardly spirits enough to keep me from swooning till he came in. He was equally concerned with me to see me in such a bloody condition, and presently called up our landlord, and he as quickly called in his neighbours, that I had a room full of people about me in a quarter of an hour. But this had like to have been of worse consequence to me than the other, for by this time there was great inquiring after the person who killed a man at the tennis-court. My landlord was then sensible of his mistake, and came to me and told me the danger I was in, and very honestly offered to convey me to a friend's of his, where I should be very secure; I thanked him, and suffered myself to be carried at midnight whither he pleased. He visited me very often, till I was well enough to walk about, which was not in less than ten days, and then we thought fit to be gone, so we took post for Orleans. But when I came upon the road I found myself in a new error, for my wound opened again with riding, and I was in a worse condition than before, being forced to take up at a little village on the road, called ———, about ——— miles from Orleans, where there was no surgeon to be had, but a sorry country barber, who nevertheless dressed me as well as he could, and in about a week more I was able to walk to Orleans at three times. Here I stayed till I was quite well, and took coach for Lyons and so through Savoy into Italy.

I spent nearly two years' time after this bad beginning in travelling through Italy, and to the several courts of Rome, Naples, Venice, and Vienna.

When I came to Lyons the king was gone from thence to Grenoble to meet the cardinal, but the queens were both at Lyons.

The French affairs seemed at this time to have but an indifferent aspect. There was no life in anything but where the cardinal was: he pushed on everything with extraordinary conduct, and generally with success; he had taken Susa and Pignerol from the Duke of Savoy, and was preparing to push the duke even out of all his dominions.

But in the meantime everywhere else things looked ill; the troops were ill-paid, the magazines empty, the people mutinous, and a general disorder seized the minds of the court; and the cardinal, who was the soul of everything, desired this interview at Grenoble, in order to put things into some better method.

This politic minister always ordered matters so, that if there was success in anything the glory was his, but if things miscarried it was all laid upon the king. This conduct was so much the more nice, as it is the direct contrary to the custom in like cases, where kings assume the glory of all the success in an action, and when a thing miscarries make themselves easy by sacrificing their ministers and favourites to the complaints and resentments of the people; but this accurate refined statesman got over this point.

While we were at Lyons, and as I remember, the third day after our coming thither, we had like to have been involved in a state broil, without knowing where we were. It was of a Sunday in the evening, the people of Lyons, who had been sorely oppressed in taxes, and the war in Italy pinching their trade, began to be very tumultuous. We found the day before the mob got together in great crowds, and talked oddly; the king was everywhere reviled, and spoken disrespectfully of, and the magistrates of the city either winked at, or durst not attempt to meddle, lest they should provoke the people.

But on Sunday night, about midnight, we were waked by a prodigious noise in the street. I jumped out of bed, and running to the window, I saw the street as full of mob as it could hold, some armed with muskets and halberds, marched in very good order; others in disorderly crowds, all shouting and crying out, "Du paix le roi," and the like. One that led a great party of this rabble carried a loaf of bread upon the top of a pike, and other lesser loaves, signifying the smallness of their bread, occasioned by dearness.

By morning this crowd was gathered to a great height; they ran roving over the whole city, shut up all the shops, and forced all the people to join with them from thence. They went up to the castle, and renewing the clamour, a strange consternation seized all the princes.

They broke open the doors of the officers, collectors of the new taxes, and plundered their houses, and had not the persons themselves fled in time they had been very ill-treated.

The queen-mother, as she was very much displeased to see such consequences of the government, in whose management she had no share, so I suppose she had the less concern upon her. However, she came into the court of the castle and showed herself to the people, gave money amongst them, and spoke gently to them; and by a way peculiar to herself, and which obliged all she talked with, she pacified the mob gradually, sent them home with promises of redress and the like; and so appeased this tumult in two days by her prudence, which the guards in the castle had small mind to meddle with, and if they had, would in all probability have made the better side the worse.

There had been several seditions of the like nature in sundry other parts of France, and the very army began to murmur, though not to mutiny, for want of provisions.

This sedition at Lyons was not quite over when we left the place, for, finding the city all in a broil, we considered we had no business there, and what the consequence of a popular tumult might be we did not see, so we prepared to be gone. We had not rid above three miles out of the city but we were brought as prisoners of war, by a party of mutineers, who had been abroad upon the scout, and were charged with being messengers sent to the cardinal for forces to reduce the citizens. With these pretences they brought us back in triumph, and the queen-mother, being by this time grown something familiar to them, they carried us before her.

When they inquired of us who we were, we called ourselves Scots; for as the English were very much out of favour in France at this time, the peace having been made not many months, and not supposed to be very durable, because particularly displeasing to the people of England, so the Scots were on the other extreme with the French. Nothing was so much caressed as the Scots, and a man had no more to do in France, if he would be well received there, than to say he was a Scotchman.

When we came before the queen-mother she seemed to receive us with some stiffness at first, and caused her guards to take us into custody; but as she was a lady of most exquisite politics, she did this to amuse the mob, and we were immediately after dismissed; and the queen herself made a handsome excuse to us for the rudeness we had suffered, alleging the troubles of the times; and the next morning we had three dragoons of the guards to convoy us out of the jurisdiction of Lyons.

I confess this little adventure gave me an aversion to popular tumults all my life after, and if nothing else had been in the cause, would have biassed me to espouse the king's party in England when our popular heats carried all before it at home.

But I must say, that when I called to mind since, the address, the management, the compliance in show, and in general the whole conduct of the queen-mother with the mutinous people of Lyons, and compared it with the conduct of my unhappy master the King of England, I could not but see that the queen understood much better than King Charles the management of politics and the clamours of the people.

Had this princess been at the helm in England, she would have prevented all the calamities of the Civil War here, and yet not have parted with what that good prince yielded in order to peace neither. She would have yielded gradually, and then gained upon them gradually; she would have managed them to the point she had designed them, as she did all parties in France; and none could effectually subject her but the very man she had raised to be her principal support—I mean the cardinal.

We went from hence to Grenoble, and arrived there the same day that the king and the cardinal with the whole court went out to view a body of 6000 Swiss foot, which the cardinal had wheedled the cantons to grant to the king to help to ruin their neighbour the Duke of Savoy.

The troops were exceeding fine, well-accoutred, brave, clean-limbed, stout fellows indeed. Here I saw the cardinal; there was an air of church gravity in his habit, but all the vigour of a general, and the sprightliness of a vast genius in his face. He affected a little stiffness in his behaviour, but managed all his affairs with such clearness, such steadiness, and such application, that it was no wonder he had such success in every undertaking.

Here I saw the king, whose figure was mean, his countenance hollow, and always seemed dejected, and every way discovering that weakness in his countenance that appeared in his actions.

If he was ever sprightly and vigorous it was when the cardinal was with him, for he depended so much on everything he did, he that was at the utmost dilemma when he was absent, always timorous, jealous, and irresolute.

After the review the cardinal was absent some days, having been to wait on the queen-mother at Lyons, where, as it was discoursed, they were at least seemingly reconciled.

I observed while the cardinal was gone there was no court, the king was seldom to be seen, very small attendance given, and no bustle at the castle; but as soon as the cardinal returned, the great councils were assembled, the coaches of the ambassadors went every day to the castle, and a face of business appeared upon the whole court.

Here the measures of the Duke of Savoy's ruin were concerted, and in order to it the king and the cardinal put themselves at the head of the army, with which they immediately reduced all Savoy, took Chamberri and the whole duchy except Montmelian.

The army that did this was not above 22,000 men, including the Swiss, and but indifferent troops neither, especially the French foot, who, compared to the infantry I have since seen in the German and Swedish armies, were not fit to be called soldiers. On the other hand, considering the Savoyards and Italian troops, they were good troops; but the cardinal's conduct made amends for all these deficiencies.

From hence I went to Pignerol, which was then little more than a single fortification on the hill near the town called St Bride's, but the situation of that was very strong. I mention this because of the prodigious works since added to it, by which it has since obtained the name of "the right hand of France." They had begun a new line below the hill, and some works were marked out on the side of the town next the fort; but the cardinal afterwards drew the plan of the works with his own hand, by which it was made one of the strongest fortresses in Europe.

While I was at Pignerol, the governor of Milan, for the Spaniards, came with an army and sat down before Casale. The grand quarrel, and for which the war in this part of Italy was begun, was this: The Spaniards and Germans pretended to the duchy of Mantua; the Duke of Nevers, a Frenchman, had not only a title to it, but had got possession of it; but being ill-supported by the French, was beaten out by the Imperialists, and after a long siege the Germans took Mantua itself, and drove the poor duke quite out of the country.

The taking of Mantua elevated the spirits of the Duke of Savoy, and the Germans and Spaniards being now at more leisure, with a complete army came to his assistance, and formed the siege of Montferrat.

For as the Spaniards pushed the Duke of Mantua, so the French by way of diversion lay hard upon the Duke of Savoy. They had seized Montferrat, and held it for the Duke of Mantua, and had a strong French garrison under Thoiras, a brave and experienced commander; and thus affairs stood when we came into the French army.

I had no business there as a soldier, but having passed as a Scotch gentleman with the mob at Lyons, and after with her Majesty the queen-mother, when we obtained the guard of her dragoons, we had also her Majesty's pass, with which we came and went where we pleased.

253

And the cardinal, who was then not on very good terms with the queen, but willing to keep smooth water there, when two or three times our passes came to be examined, showed a more than ordinary respect to us on that very account, our passes being from the queen.

Casale being besieged, as I have observed, began to be in danger, for the cardinal, who 'twas thought had formed a design to ruin Savoy, was more intent upon that than upon the succour of the Duke of Mantua; but necessity calling upon him to deliver so great a captain as Thoiras, and not to let such a place as Casale fall into the hands of the enemy, the king, or cardinal rather, ordered the Duke of Montmorency, and the Maréchal D'Effiat, with 10,000 foot and 2000 horse, to march and join the Maréchals De La Force and Schomberg, who lay already with an army on the frontiers of Genoa, but too weak to attempt the raising the siege of Casale.

As all men thought there would be a battle between the French and the Spaniards, I could not prevail with myself to lose the opportunity, and therefore by the help of the passes above mentioned, I came to the French army under the Duke of Montmorency. We marched through the enemy's country with great boldness and no small hazard, for the Duke of Savoy appeared frequently with great bodies of horse on the rear of the army, and frequently skirmished with our troops, in one of which I had the folly—I can call it no better, for I had no business there—to go out and see the sport, as the French gentlemen called it. I was but a raw soldier, and did not like the sport at all, for this party was surrounded by the Duke of Savoy, and almost all killed, for as to quarter they neither asked nor gave. I ran away very fairly, one of the first, and my companion with me, and by the goodness of our horses got out of the fray, and being not much known in the army, we came into the camp an hour or two after, as if we had been only riding abroad for the air.

This little rout made the general very cautious, for the Savoyards were stronger in horse by three or four thousand, and the army always marched in a body, and kept their parties in or very near hand.

I escaped another rub in this French army about five days after, which had like to have made me pay dear for my curiosity.

The Duke de Montmorency and the Maréchal Schomberg joined their army about four or five days after, and immediately, according to the cardinal's instructions, put themselves on the march for the relief of Casale.

The army had marched over a great plain, with some marshy grounds on the right and the Po on the left, and as the country was so well discovered that 'twas thought impossible any mischief should happen, the generals observed the less caution. At the end of this plain was a long wood and a lane or narrow defile through the middle of it.

Through this pass the army was to march, and the van began to file through it about four o'clock. By three hours' time all the army was got through, or into the pass, and the artillery was just entered when the Duke of Savoy with 4000 horse and 1500 dragoons with every horseman a footman behind him, whether he had swam the Po or passed it above at a bridge, and made a long march after, was not examined, but he came boldly up the plain and charged our rear with a great deal of fury.

Our artillery was in the lane, and as it was impossible to turn them about and make way for the army, so the rear was obliged to support themselves and maintain the fight for above an hour and a half.

In this time we lost abundance of men, and if it had not been for two accidents all that line had been cut off. One was, that the wood was so near that those regiments which were disordered presently sheltered themselves in the wood; the other was, that by this time the Maréchal Schomberg, with the horse of the van, began to get back through the lane, and to make good the ground from whence the other had been beaten, till at last by this means it came to almost a pitched battle.

There were two regiments of French dragoons who did excellent service in this action, and maintained their ground till they were almost all killed.

Had the Duke of Savoy contented himself with the defeat of five regiments on the right, which he quite broke and drove into the wood, and with the slaughter and havoc which he had made among the rest, he had come off with honour, and might have called it a victory; but endeavouring to break the whole party and carry off some cannon, the obstinate resistance of these few dragoons lost him his advantages, and held him in play till so many fresh troops got through the pass again as made us too strong for him, and had not night parted them he had been entirely defeated.

At last, finding our troops increase and spread themselves on his flank, he retired and gave over. We had no great stomach to pursue him neither, though some horse were ordered to follow a little way.

The duke lost about a thousand men, and we almost twice as many, and but for those dragoons had lost the whole rear-guard and half our cannon. I was in a very sorry case in this action too. I was with the rear in the regiment of horse of Perigoort, with a captain of which regiment I had contracted some acquaintance. I would have rid off at first, as the captain desired me, but there was no doing it, for the cannon was in the lane, and the horse and dragoons of the van eagerly pressing back through the lane must have run me down or carried me with them. As for the wood, it was a good shelter to save one's life, but was so thick there was no passing it on horseback.

Our regiment was one of the first that was broke, and being all in confusion, with the Duke of Savoy's men at our heels, away we ran into the wood. Never was there so much disorder among a parcel of runaways as when we came to this wood; it was so exceeding bushy and thick at the bottom there was no entering it, and a volley of small shot from a regiment of Savoy's dragoons poured in upon us at our breaking into the wood made terrible work among our horses.

For my part I was got into the wood, but was forced to quit my horse, and by that means, with a great deal of difficulty, got a little farther in, where there was a little open place, and being quite spent with labouring among the bushes I sat down resolving to take my fate there, let it be what it would, for I was not able to go any farther. I had twenty or thirty more in the same condition come to me in less than half-an-hour, and here we waited very securely the success of the battle, which was as before.

It was no small relief to those with me to hear the Savoyards were beaten, for otherwise they had all been lost; as for me, I confess, I was glad as it was because of the danger, but otherwise I cared not much which had the better, for I designed no service among them.

One kindness it did me, that I began to consider what I had to do here, and as I could give but a very slender account of myself for what it was I run all these risks, so I resolved they should fight it among themselves, for I would come among them no more.

The captain with whom, as I noted above, I had contracted some acquaintance in this regiment, was killed in this action, and the French had really a great blow here, though they took care to conceal it all they could; and I cannot, without smiling, read some of the histories and memoirs of this action, which they are not ashamed to call a victory.

We marched on to Saluzzo, and the next day the Duke of Savoy presented himself in battalia on the other side of a small river, giving us a fair challenge to pass and engage him. We always said in our camp that the orders were to fight the Duke of Savoy wherever we met him;

but though he braved us in our view we did not care to engage him, but we brought Saluzzo to surrender upon articles, which the duke could not relieve without attacking our camp, which he did not care to do.

The next morning we had news of the surrender of Mantua to the Imperial army. We heard of it first from the Duke of Savoy's cannon, which he fired by way of rejoicing, and which seemed to make him amends for the loss of Saluzzo.

As this was a mortification to the French, so it quite damped the success of the campaign, for the Duke de Montmorency imagining that the Imperial general would send immediate assistance to the Marquis Spinola, who besieged Casale, they called frequent councils of war what course to take, and at last resolved to halt in Piedmont. A few days after their resolutions were changed again by the news of the death of the Duke of Savoy, Charles Emanuel, who died, as some say, agitated with the extremes of joy and grief.

This put our generals upon considering again whether they should march to the relief of Casale, but the chimera of the Germans put them by, and so they took up quarters in Piedmont. They took several small places from the Duke of Savoy, making advantage of the consternation the duke's subjects were in on the death of their prince, and spread themselves from the seaside to the banks of the Po. But here an enemy did that for them which the Savoyards could not, for the plague got into their quarters and destroyed abundance of people, both of the army and of the country.

I thought then it was time for me to be gone, for I had no manner of courage for that risk; and I think verily I was more afraid of being taken sick in a strange country than ever I was of being killed in battle. Upon this resolution I procured a pass to go for Genoa, and accordingly began my journey, but was arrested at Villa Franca by a slow lingering fever, which held me about five days, and then turned to a burning malignancy, and at last to the plague. My friend, the captain, never left me night nor day; and though for four days more I knew nobody, nor was capable of so much as thinking of myself, yet it pleased God that the distemper gathered in my neck, swelled and broke. During the swelling I was raging mad with the violence of pain, which being so near my head swelled that also in proportion, that my eyes were swelled up, and for the twenty-four hours my tongue and mouth; then, as my servant told me, all the physicians gave me over, as past all remedy, but by the good providence of God the swelling broke.

The prodigious collection of matter which this swelling discharged gave me immediate relief, and I became sensible in less than an hour's time; and in two hours or thereabouts fell into a little slumber which recovered my spirits and sensibly revived me. Here I lay by it till the middle of September. My captain fell sick after me, but recovered quickly. His man had the plague, and died in two days; my man held it out well.

About the middle of September we heard of a truce concluded between all parties, and being unwilling to winter at Villa Franca, I got passes, and though we were both but weak, we began to travel in litters for Milan.

And here I experienced the truth of an old English proverb, that standers-by see more than the gamesters.

The French, Savoyards, and Spaniards made this peace or truce all for separate and several grounds, and every one were mistaken.

The French yielded to it because they had given over the relief of Casale, and were very much afraid it would fall into the hands of the Marquis Spinola. The Savoyards yielded to it because they were afraid the French would winter in Piedmont; the Spaniards yielded to it because the Duke of Savoy being dead, and the Count de Colalto, the Imperial general, giving no assistance, and his army weakened by sickness and the fatigues of the siege, he foresaw he should never take the town, and wanted but to come off with honour.

The French were mistaken, because really Spinola was so weak that had they marched on into Montferrat the Spaniards must have raised the siege; the Duke of Savoy was mistaken, because the plague had so weakened the French that they durst not have stayed to winter in Piedmont; and Spinola was mistaken, for though he was very slow, if he had stayed before the town one fortnight longer, Thoiras the governor must have surrendered, being brought to the last extremity.

Of all these mistakes the French had the advantage, for Casale, was relieved, the army had time to be recruited, and the French had the best of it by an early campaign.

I passed through Montferrat in my way to Milan just as the truce was declared, and saw the miserable remains of the Spanish army, who by sickness, fatigue, hard duty, the sallies of the garrison and such like consequences, were reduced to less than 2000 men, and of them above 1000 lay wounded and sick in the camp.

Here were several regiments which I saw drawn out to their arms that could not make up above seventy or eighty men, officers and all, and those half starved with hunger, almost naked, and in a lamentable condition. From thence I went into the town, and there things were still in a worse condition, the houses beaten down, the walls and works ruined, the garrison, by continual duty, reduced from 4500 men to less than 800, without clothes, money, or provisions, the brave governor weak with continual fatigue, and the whole face of things in a miserable case.

The French generals had just sent them 30,000 crowns for present supply, which heartened them a little, but had not the truce been made as it was, they must have surrendered upon what terms the Spaniards had pleased to make them.

Never were two armies in such fear of one another with so little cause; the Spaniards afraid of the French whom the plague had devoured, and the French afraid of the Spaniards whom the siege had almost ruined.

The grief of this mistake, together with the sense of his master, the Spaniards, leaving him without supplies to complete the siege of Casale, so affected the Marquis Spinola, that he died for grief, and in him fell the last of that rare breed of Low Country soldiers, who gave the world so great and just a character of the Spanish infantry, as the best soldiers of the world; a character which we see them so very much degenerated from since, that they hardly deserve the name of soldiers.

I tarried at Milan the rest of the winter, both for the recovery of my health, and also for supplies from England.

Here it was I first heard the name of Gustavus Adolphus, the king of Sweden, who now began his war with the emperor; and while the king of France was at Lyons, the league with Sweden was made, in which the French contributed 1,200,000 crowns in money, and 600,000 per annum to the attempt of Gustavus Adolphus. About this time he landed in Pomerania, took the towns of Stettin and Stralsund, and from thence proceeded in that prodigious manner of which I shall have occasion to be very particular in the prosecution of these Memoirs.

I had indeed no thoughts of seeing that king or his armies. I had been so roughly handled already, that I had given over the thoughts of appearing among the fighting people, and resolved in the spring to pursue my journey to Venice, and so for the rest of Italy. Yet I cannot deny that as every Gazette gave us some accounts of the conquests and victories of this glorious prince, it prepossessed my thoughts with secret wishes of seeing him, but these were so young and unsettled, that I drew no resolutions from them for a long while after.

About the middle of January I left Milan and came to Genoa, from thence by sea to Leghorn, then to Naples, Rome, and Venice, but saw nothing in Italy that gave me any diversion.

As for what is modern, I saw nothing but lewdness, private murders, stabbing men at the corner of a street, or in the dark, hiring of bravos, and the like. These were to me the modern excellencies of Italy; and I had no gust to antiquities.

'Twas pleasant indeed when I was at Rome to say here stood the Capitol, there the Colossus of Nero, here was the Amphitheatre of Titus, there the Aqueduct of———, here the Forum, there the Catacombs, here the Temple of Venus, there of Jupiter, here the Pantheon, and the like; but I never designed to write a book. As much as was useful I kept in my head, and for the rest, I left it to others.

I observed the people degenerated from the ancient glorious inhabitants, who were generous, brave, and the most valiant of all nations, to a vicious baseness of soul, barbarous, treacherous, jealous and revengeful, lewd and cowardly, intolerably proud and haughty, bigoted to blind, incoherent devotion, and the grossest of idolatry.

Indeed, I think the unsuitableness of the people made the place unpleasant to me, for there is so little in a country to recommend it when the people disgrace it, that no beauties of the creation can make up for the want of those excellencies which suitable society procure the defect of. This made Italy a very unpleasant country to me; the people were the foil to the place, all manner of hateful vices reigning in their general way of living.

I confess I was not very religious myself, and being come abroad into the world young enough, might easily have been drawn into evils that had recommended themselves with any tolerable agreeableness to nature and common manners; but when wickedness presented itself full-grown in its grossest freedoms and liberties, it quite took away all the gust to vice that the devil had furnished me with.

The prodigious stupid bigotry of the people also was irksome to me; I thought there was something in it very sordid. The entire empire the priests have over both the souls and bodies of the people, gave me a specimen of that meanness of spirit, which is nowhere else to be seen but in Italy, especially in the city of Rome.

At Venice I perceived it quite different, the civil authority having a visible superiority over the ecclesiastic, and the Church being more subject there to the State than in any other part of Italy.

For these reasons I took no pleasure in filling my memoirs of Italy with remarks of places or things. All the antiquities and valuable remains of the Roman nation are done better than I can pretend to by such people who made it more their business; as for me, I went to see, and not to write, and as little thought then of these Memoirs as I ill furnished myself to write them.

I left Italy in April, and taking the tour of Bavaria, though very much out of the way, I passed through Munich, Passau, Lintz, and at last to Vienna.

I came to Vienna the 10th of April 1631, intending to have gone from thence down the Danube into Hungary, and by means of a pass, which I had obtained from the English ambassador at Constantinople, I designed to have seen all the great towns on the Danube, which were then in the hands of the Turks, and which I had read much of in the history of the war between the Turks and the Germans; but I was diverted from my design by the following occasion.

There had been a long bloody war in the empire of Germany for twelve years, between the emperor, the Duke of Bavaria, the King of Spain, and the Popish princes and electors on the one side, and the Protestant princes on the other; and both sides having been exhausted by the war, and even the Catholics themselves beginning to dislike the growing power of the house of Austria, 'twas thought all parties were willing to make peace. Nay, things were brought to that pass that some of the Popish princes and electors began to talk of making alliances with the King of Sweden.

Here it is necessary to observe, that the two Dukes of Mecklenburg having been dispossessed of most of their dominions by the tyranny of the Emperor Ferdinand, and being in danger of losing the rest, earnestly solicited the King of Sweden to come to their assistance; and that prince, as he was related to the house of Mecklenburg, and especially as he was willing to lay hold of any opportunity to break with the emperor, against whom he had laid up an implacable prejudice, was very ready and forward to come to their assistance.

The reasons of his quarrel with the emperor were grounded upon the Imperialists concerning themselves in the war of Poland, where the emperor had sent 8000 foot and 2000 horse to join the Polish army against the king, and had thereby given some check to his arms in that war.

In pursuance, therefore, of his resolution to quarrel with the emperor, but more particularly at the instances of the princes above-named, his Swedish Majesty had landed the year before at Stralsund with about 12,000 men, and having joined with some forces which he had left in Polish Prussia, all which did not make 30,000 men, he began a war with the emperor, the greatest in event, filled with the most famous battles, sieges, and extraordinary actions, including its wonderful success and happy conclusion, of any war ever maintained in the world.

The King of Sweden had already taken Stettin, Stralsund, Rostock, Wismar, and all the strong places on the Baltic, and began to spread himself in Germany. He had made a league with the French, as I observed in my story of Saxony; he had now made a treaty with the Duke of Brandenburg, and, in short, began to be terrible to the empire.

In this conjuncture the emperor called the General Diet of the empire to be held at Ratisbon, where, as was pretended, all sides were to treat of peace and to join forces to beat the Swedes out of the empire. Here the emperor, by a most exquisite management, brought the affairs of the Diet to a conclusion, exceedingly to his own advantage, and to the farther oppression of the Protestants; and, in particular, in that the war against the King of Sweden was to be carried on in such manner as that the whole burden and charge would lie on the Protestants themselves, and they be made the instruments to oppose their best friends. Other matters also ended equally to their disadvantage, as the methods resolved on to recover the Church lands, and to prevent the education of the Protestant clergy; and what remained was referred to another General Diet to be held at Frankfort-au-Main in August 1631.

I won't pretend to say the other Protestant princes of Germany had never made any overtures to the King of Sweden to come to their assistance, but 'tis plain they had entered into no league with him; that appears from the difficulties which retarded the fixing of the treaties afterward, both with the Dukes of Brandenburg and Saxony, which unhappily occasioned the ruin of Magdeburg.

But 'tis plain the Swede was resolved on a war with the emperor. His Swedish majesty might, and indeed could not but foresee that if he once showed himself with a sufficient force on the frontiers of the empire, all the Protestant princes would be obliged by their interest or by his arms to fall in with him, and this the consequence made appear to be a just conclusion, for the Electors of Brandenburg and Saxony were both forced to join with him.

First, they were willing to join with him—at least they could not find in their hearts to join with the emperor, of whose power they had such just apprehensions. They wished the Swedes success, and would have been very glad to have had the work done at another man's charge, but, like true Germans, they were more willing to be saved than to save themselves, and therefore hung back and stood upon terms.

Secondly, they were at last forced to it. The first was forced to join by the King of Sweden himself, who being come so far was not to be dallied with, and had not the Duke of Brandenburg complied as he did, he had been ruined by the Swede. The Saxon was driven into the arms of the Swede by force, for Count Tilly, ravaging his country, made him comply with any terms to be saved from destruction.

Thus matters stood at the end of the Diet at Ratisbon. The King of Sweden began to see himself leagued against at the Diet both by Protestant and Papist; and, as I have often heard his Majesty say since, he had resolved to try to force them off from the emperor, and to treat them as enemies equally with the rest if they did not.

But the Protestants convinced him soon after, that though they were tricked into the outward appearance of a league against him at Ratisbon, they had no such intentions; and by their ambassadors to him let him know that they only wanted his powerful assistance to defend their councils, when they would soon convince him that they had a due sense of the emperor's designs, and would do their utmost for their liberty. And these I take to be the first invitations the King of Sweden had to undertake the Protestant cause as such, and which entitled him to say he fought for the liberty and religion of the German nation.

I have had some particular opportunities to hear these things form the mouths of some of the very princes themselves, and therefore am the forwarder to relate them; and I place them here because, previous to the part I acted on this bloody scene, 'tis necessary to let the reader into some part of that story, and to show him in what manner and on what occasions this terrible war began.

The Protestants, alarmed at the usage they had met with at the former Diet, had secretly proposed among themselves to form a general union or confederacy, for preventing that ruin which they saw, unless some speedy remedies were applied, would be inevitable. The Elector of Saxony, the head of the Protestants, a vigorous and politic prince, was the first that moved it; and the Landgrave of Hesse, a zealous and gallant prince, being consulted with, it rested a great while between those two, no method being found practicable to bring it to pass, the emperor being so powerful in all parts, that they foresaw the petty princes would not dare to negotiate an affair of such a nature, being surrounded with the Imperial forces, who by their two generals, Wallenstein and Tilly, kept them in continual subjection and terror.

This dilemma had like to have stifled the thoughts of the union as a thing impracticable, when one Seigensius, a Lutheran minister, a person of great abilities, and one whom the Elector of Saxony made great use of in matters of policy as well as religion, contrived for them this excellent expedient.

I had the honour to be acquainted with this gentleman while I was at Leipsic. It pleased him exceedingly to have been the contriver of so fine a structure as the Conclusions of Leipsic, and he was glad to be entertained on that subject. I had the relation from his own mouth, when, but very modestly, he told me he thought 'twas an inspiration darted on a sudden into his thoughts, when the Duke of Saxony calling him into his closet one morning, with a face full of concern, shaking his head, and looking very earnestly, "What will become of us, doctor?" said the duke; "we shall all be undone at Frankfort-au-Main." "Why so, please your highness?" says the doctor. "Why, they will fight with the King of Sweden with our armies and our money," says the duke, "and devour our friends and ourselves by the help of our friends and ourselves." "But what is become of the confederacy, then," said the doctor, "which your highness had so happily framed in your thoughts, and which the Landgrave of Hesse was so pleased with?" "Become of it?" says the duke, "'tis a good thought enough, but 'tis impossible to bring it to pass among so many members of the Protestant princes as are to be consulted with, for we neither have time to treat, nor will half of them dare to negotiate the matter, the Imperialists being quartered in their very bowels." "But may not some expedient be found out," says the doctor, "to bring them all together to treat of it in a general meeting?" "'Tis well proposed," says the duke, "but in what town or city shall they assemble where the very deputies shall not be besieged by Tilly or Wallenstein in fourteen days' time, and sacrificed to the cruelty and fury of the Emperor Ferdinand?" "Will your highness be the easier in it," replies the doctor, "if a way may be found out to call such an assembly upon other causes, at which the emperor may have no umbrage, and perhaps give his assent? You know the Diet at Frankfort is at hand; 'tis necessary the Protestants should have an assembly of their own to prepare matters for the General Diet, and it may be no difficult matter to obtain it." The duke, surprised with joy at the motion, embraced the doctor with an extraordinary transport. "Thou hast done it, doctor," said he, and immediately caused him to draw a form of a letter to the emperor, which he did with the utmost dexterity of style, in which he was a great master, representing to his Imperial Majesty that, in order to put an end to the troubles of Germany, his Majesty would be pleased to permit the Protestant princes of the empire to hold a Diet to themselves, to consider of such matters as they were to treat of at the General Diet, in order to conform themselves to the will and pleasure of his Imperial Majesty, to drive out foreigners, and settle a lasting peace in the empire. He also insinuated something of their resolutions unanimously to give their suffrages in favour of the King of Hungary at the election of a king of the Romans, a thing which he knew the emperor had in his thought, and would push at with all his might at the Diet. This letter was sent, and the bait so neatly concealed, that the Electors of Bavaria and Mentz, the King of Hungary, and several of the Popish princes, not foreseeing that the ruin of them all lay in the bottom of it, foolishly advised the emperor to consent to it.

In consenting to this the emperor signed his own destruction, for here began the conjunction of the German Protestants with the Swede, which was the fatalest blow to Ferdinand, and which he could never recover.

Accordingly the Diet was held at Leipsic, February 8, 1630, where the Protestants agreed on several heads for their mutual defence, which were the grounds of the following war. These were the famous Conclusions of Leipsic, which so alarmed the emperor and the whole empire, that to crush it in the beginning, the emperor commanded Count Tilly immediately to fall upon the Landgrave of Hesse and the Duke of Saxony as the principal heads of the union; but it was too late.

The Conclusions were digested into ten heads:—

1. That since their sins had brought God's judgments upon the whole Protestant Church, they should command public prayers to be made to Almighty God for the diverting the calamities that attended them.

2. That a treaty of peace might be set on foot, in order to come to a right understanding with the Catholic princes.

3. That a time for such a treaty being obtained, they should appoint an assembly of delegates to meet preparatory to the treaty.

4. That all their complaints should be humbly represented to his Imperial Majesty and the Catholic Electors, in order to a peaceable accommodation.

5. That they claim the protection of the emperor, according to the laws of the empire, and the present emperor's solemn oath and promise.

6. That they would appoint deputies who should meet at certain times to consult of their common interest, and who should be always empowered to conclude of what should be thought needful for their safety.

7. That they will raise a competent force to maintain and defend their liberties, rights, and religion.

8. That it is agreeable to the Constitution of the empire, concluded in the Diet at Augsburg, to do so.

9. That the arming for their necessary defence shall by no means hinder their obedience to his Imperial Majesty, but that they will still continue their loyalty to him.

10. They agree to proportion their forces, which in all amounted to 70,000 men.

The emperor, exceedingly startled at the Conclusions, issued out a severe proclamation or ban against them, which imported much the same thing as a declaration of war, and commanded Tilly to begin, and immediately to fall on the Duke of Saxony with all the fury imaginable, as I have already observed.

Here began the flame to break out; for upon the emperor's ban, the Protestants send away to the King of Sweden for succour.

His Swedish Majesty had already conquered Mecklenburg, and part of Pomerania, and was advancing with his victorious troops, increased by the addition of some regiments raised in those parts, in order to carry on the war against the emperor, having designed to follow up the Oder into Silesia, and so to push the war home to the emperor's hereditary countries of Austria and Bohemia, when the first messengers came to him in this case; but this changed his measures, and brought him to the frontiers of Brandenburg resolved to answer the desires of the Protestants. But here the Duke of Brandenburg began to halt, making some difficulties and demanding terms, which drove the king to use some extremities with him, and stopped the Swedes for a while, who had otherwise been on the banks of the Elbe as soon as Tilly, the Imperial general, had entered Saxony, which if they had done, the miserable destruction of Magdeburg had been prevented, as I observed before. The king had been invited into the union, and when he first came back from the banks of the Oder he had accepted it, and was preparing to back it with all his power.

The Duke of Saxony had already a good army which he had with infinite diligence recruited, and mustered them under the cannon of Leipsic. The King of Sweden having, by his ambassador at Leipsic, entered into the union of the Protestants, was advancing victoriously to their aid, just as Count Tilly had entered the Duke of Saxony's dominions. The fame of the Swedish conquests, and of the hero who commanded them, shook my resolution of travelling into Turkey, being resolved to see the conjunction of the Protestant armies, and before the fire was broke out too far to take the advantage of seeing both sides.

While I remained at Vienna, uncertain which way I should proceed, I remember I observed they talked of the King of Sweden as a prince of no consideration, one that they might let go on and tire himself in Mecklenburg and thereabout, till they could find leisure to deal with him, and then might be crushed as they pleased; but 'tis never safe to despise an enemy, so this was not an enemy to be despised, as they afterwards found.

As to the Conclusions of Leipsic, indeed, at first they gave the Imperial court some uneasiness, but when they found the Imperial armies, began to fright the members out of the union, and that the several branches had no considerable forces on foot, it was the general discourse at Vienna, that the union at Leipsic only gave the emperor an opportunity to crush absolutely the Dukes of Saxony, Brandenburg, and the Landgrave of Hesse, and they looked upon it as a thing certain.

I never saw any real concern in their faces at Vienna till news came to court that the King of Sweden had entered into the union; but as this made them very uneasy, they began to move the powerfulest methods possible to divert this storm; and upon this news Tilly was hastened to fall into Saxony before this union could proceed to a conjunction of forces. This was certainly a very good resolution, and no measure could have been more exactly concerted, had not the diligence of the Saxons prevented it.

The gathering of this storm, which from a cloud began to spread over the empire, and from the little duchy of Mecklenburg began to threaten all Germany, absolutely determined me, as I noted before, as to travelling, and laying aside the thoughts of Hungary, I resolved, if possible, to see the King of Sweden's army.

I parted from Vienna the middle of May, and took post for Great Glogau in Silesia, as if I had purposed to pass into Poland, but designing indeed to go down the Oder to Custrim in the marquisate of Brandenburg, and so to Berlin. But when I came to the frontiers of

Silesia, though I had passes, I could go no farther, the guards on all the frontiers were so strict, so I was obliged to come back into Bohemia, and went to Prague. From hence I found I could easily pass through the Imperial provinces to the lower Saxony, and accordingly took passes for Hamburg, designing, however, to use them no farther than I found occasion.

By virtue of these passes I got into the Imperial army, under Count Tilly, then at the siege of Magdeburg, May the 2nd.

I confess I did not foresee the fate of this city, neither, I believe, did Count Tilly himself expect to glut his fury with so entire a desolation, much less did the people expect it. I did believe they must capitulate, and I perceived by discourse in the army that Tilly would give them but very indifferent conditions; but it fell out otherwise. The treaty of surrender was, as it were, begun, nay, some say concluded, when some of the out-guards of the Imperialists finding the citizens had abandoned the guards of the works, and looked to themselves with less diligence than usual, they broke in, carried an half-moon, sword in hand, with little resistance; and though it was a surprise on both sides, the citizens neither fearing, nor the army expecting the occasion, the garrison, with as much resolution as could be expected under such a fright, flew to the walls, twice beat the Imperialists off, but fresh men coming up, and the administrator of Magdeburg himself being wounded and taken, the enemy broke in, took the city by storm, and entered with such terrible fury, that, without respect to age or condition, they put all the garrison and inhabitants, man, woman, and child, to the sword, plundered the city, and when they had done this set it on fire.

This calamity sure was the dreadfulest sight that ever I saw; the rage of the Imperial soldiers was most intolerable, and not to be expressed. Of 25,000, some said 30,000 people, there was not a soul to be seen alive, till the flames drove those that were hid in vaults and secret places to seek death in the streets rather than perish in the fire. Of these miserable creatures some were killed too by the furious soldiers, but at last they saved the lives of such as came out of their cellars and holes, and so about two thousand poor desperate creatures were left. The exact number of those that perished in this city could never be known, because those the soldiers had first butchered the flames afterwards devoured.

I was on the outer side of the Elbe when this dreadful piece of butchery was done. The city of Magdeburg had a sconce or fort over against it called the toll-house, which joined to the city by a very fine bridge of boats. This fort was taken by the Imperialists a few days before, and having a mind to see it, and the rather because from thence I could have a very good view of the city, I was going over Tilley's bridge of boats to view this fort. About ten o'clock in the morning I perceived they were storming by the firing, and immediately all ran to the works; I little thought of the taking the city, but imagined it might be some outwork attacked, for we all expected the city would surrender that day, or next, and they might have capitulated upon very good terms.

Being upon the works of the fort, on a sudden I heard the dreadfulest cry raised in the city that can be imagined; 'tis not possible to express the manner of it, and I could see the women and children running about the streets in a most lamentable condition.

The city wall did not run along the side where the river was with so great a height, but we could plainly see the market-place and the several streets which run down to the river. In about an hour's time after this first cry all was in confusion; there was little shooting, the execution was all cutting of throats and mere house murders. The resolute garrison, with the brave Baron Falkenberg, fought it out to the last, and were cut in pieces, and by this time the Imperial soldiers having broke open the gates and entered on all sides, the slaughter was very dreadful. We could see the poor people in crowds driven down the streets, flying from the fury of the soldiers, who followed butchering them as fast as they could, and refused mercy to anybody, till driving them to the river's edge, the desperate wretches would throw themselves into the river, where thousands of them perished, especially women and children. Several men that could swim got over to our side, where the soldiers not heated with fight gave them quarter, and took them up, and I cannot but do this justice to the German officers in the fort: they had five small flat boats, and they gave leave to the soldiers to go off in them, and get what booty they could, but charged them not to kill anybody, but take them all prisoners.

Nor was their humanity ill rewarded, for the soldiers, wisely avoiding those places where their fellows were employed in butchering the miserable people, rowed to other places, where crowds of people stood crying out for help, and expecting to be every minute either drowned or murdered; of these at sundry times they fetched over near six hundred, but took care to take in none but such as offered them good pay.

Never was money or jewels of greater service than now, for those that had anything of that sort to offer were soonest helped.

There was a burgher of the town who, seeing a boat coming near him, but out of his call, by the help of a speaking trumpet, told the soldiers in it he would give them 20,000 dollars to fetch him off. They rowed close to the shore, and got him with his wife and six children into the boat, but such throngs of people got about the boat that had like to have sunk her, so that the soldiers were fain to drive a great many out again by main force, and while they were doing this some of the enemies coming down the street desperately drove them all into the water.

The boat, however, brought the burgher and his wife and children safe, and though they had not all that wealth about them, yet in jewels and money he gave them so much as made all the fellows very rich.

I cannot pretend to describe the cruelty of this day: the town by five in the afternoon was all in a flame; the wealth consumed was inestimable, and a loss to the very conqueror. I think there was little or nothing left but the great church and about a hundred houses.

This was a sad welcome into the army for me, and gave me a horror and aversion to the emperor's people, as well as to his cause. I quitted the camp the third day after this execution, while the fire was hardly out in the city; and from thence getting safe-conduct to pass into the Palatinate, I turned out of the road at a small village on the Elbe, called Emerfield, and by ways and towns I can give but small account of, having a boor for our guide, whom we could hardly understand, I arrived at Leipsic on the 17th of May.

We found the elector intense upon the strengthening of his army, but the people in the greatest terror imaginable, every day expecting Tilly with the German army, who by his cruelty at Magdeburg was become so dreadful to the Protestants that they expected no mercy wherever he came.

The emperor's power was made so formidable to all the Protestants, particularly since the Diet at Ratisbon left them in a worse case than it found them, that they had not only formed the Conclusions of Leipsic, which all men looked on as the effect of desperation rather than any probable means of their deliverance, but had privately implored the protection and assistance of foreign powers, and particularly the King of Sweden, from whom they had promises of a speedy and powerful assistance. And truly if the Swede had not with a very strong hand rescued them, all their Conclusions at Leipsic had served but to hasten their ruin. I remember very well when I was in the Imperial army they discoursed with such contempt of the forces of the Protestant, that not only the Imperialists but the Protestants themselves gave them up as lost. The emperor had not less than 200,000 men in several armies on foot, who most of them were on the back of the Protestants in every corner. If Tilly did but write a threatening letter to any city or prince of the union, they presently submitted, renounced the Conclusions of Leipsic, and received Imperial garrisons, as the cities of Ulm and Memmingen, the duchy of Wirtemberg, and several others, and almost all Suaben.

Only the Duke of Saxony and the Landgrave of Hesse upheld the drooping courage of the Protestants, and refused all terms of peace, slighted all the threatenings of the Imperial generals, and the Duke of Brandenburg was brought in afterward almost by force.

The Duke of Saxony mustered his forces under the walls of Leipsic, and I having returned to Leipsic, two days before, saw them pass the review. The duke, gallantly mounted, rode through the ranks, attended by his field-marshal Arnheim, and seemed mighty well pleased with them, and indeed the troops made a very fine appearance; but I that had seen Tilly's army and his old weather-beaten soldiers, whose discipline and exercises were so exact, and their courage so often tried, could not look on the Saxon army without some concern for them when I considered who they had to deal with. Tilly's men were rugged surly fellows, their faces had an air of hardy courage, mangled with wounds and scars, their armour showed the bruises of musket bullets, and the rust of the winter storms. I observed of them their clothes were always dirty, but their arms were clean and bright; they were used to camp in the open fields, and sleep in the frosts and rain, their horses were strong and hardy like themselves, and well taught their exercises; the soldiers knew their business so exactly that general orders were enough; every private man was fit to command, and their wheelings, marchings, counter-marchings and exercise were done with such order and readiness, that the distinct words of command were hardly of any use among them; they were flushed with victory, and hardly knew what it was to fly.

There had passed some messages between Tilly and the duke, and he gave always such ambiguous answers as he thought might serve to gain time; but Tilly was not to be put off with words, and drawing his army towards Saxony, sends four propositions to him to sign, and demands an immediate reply. The propositions were positive.

1. To cause his troops to enter into the emperor's service, and to march in person with them against the King of Sweden.

2. To give the Imperial army quarters in his country, and supply them with necessary provisions.

3. To relinquish the union of Leipsic, and disown the ten Conclusions.

4. To make restitution of the goods and lands of the Church.

The duke being pressed by Tilly's trumpeter for an immediate answer sat all night, and part of the next day, in council with his privy councillors, debating what reply to give him, which at last was concluded, in short, that he would live and die in defence of the Protestant religion, and the Conclusions of Leipsic, and bade Tilly defiance.

The die being thus cast, he immediately decamped with his whole army for Torgau, fearing that Tilly should get there before him, and so prevent his conjunction with the Swede. The duke had not yet concluded any positive treaty with the King of Swedeland, and the Duke of Brandenburg having made some difficulty of joining, they both stood on some niceties till they had like to have ruined themselves all at once.

Brandenburg had given up the town of Spandau to the king by a former treaty to secure a retreat for his army, and the king was advanced as far as Frankfort-upon-the-Oder, when on a sudden some small difficulties arising, Brandenburg seems cold in the matter, and with a sort of indifference demands to have his town of Spandau restored to him again. Gustavus Adolphus, who began presently to imagine the duke had made his peace with the emperor, and so would either be his enemy or pretend a neutrality, generously delivered him his town of Spandau, but immediately turns about, and with his whole army besieges him in his capital city of Berlin. This brought the duke to know his error, and by the interpositions of the ladies, the Queen of Sweden being the duke's sister, the matter was accommodated, and the duke joined his forces with the king.

But the duke of Saxony had like to have been undone by this delay, for the Imperialists, under Count de Furstenberg, were entered his country, and had possessed themselves of Halle, and Tilly was on his march to join him, as he afterwards did, and ravaging the whole country laid siege to Leipsic itself. The duke driven to this extremity rather flies to the Swede than treats with him, and on the 2nd of September the duke's army joined with the King of Sweden.

I had not come to Leipsic but to see the Duke of Saxony's army, and that being marched, as I have said, for Torgau, I had no business there, but if I had, the approach of Tilly and the Imperial army was enough to hasten me away, for I had no occasion to be besieged there; so on the 27th of August I left the town, as several of the principal inhabitants had done before, and more would have done had not the governor published a proclamation against it, and besides they knew not whither to fly, for all places were alike exposed. The poor people were under dreadful apprehensions of a siege, and of the merciless usage of the Imperial soldiers, the example of Magdeburg being fresh before them, the duke and his army gone from them, and the town, though well furnished, but indifferently fortified.

In this condition I left them, buying up stores of provisions, working hard to scour their moats, set up palisadoes, repair their fortifications, and preparing all things for a siege; and following the Saxon army to Torgau, I continued in the camp till a few days before they joined the King of Sweden.

I had much ado to persuade my companion from entering into the service of the Duke of Saxony, one of whose colonels, with whom we had contracted a particular acquaintance, offering him a commission to be cornet in one of the old regiments of horse; but the difference I had observed between this new army and Tilly's old troops had made such an impression on me, that I confess I had yet no manner of inclination for the service, and therefore persuaded him to wait a while till we had seen a little further into affairs, and particularly till we had seen the Swedish army which we had heard so much of.

The difficulties which the Elector-Duke of Saxony made of joining with the king were made up by a treaty concluded with the king on the 2nd of September at Coswig, a small town on the Elbe, whither the king's army was arrived the night before; for General Tilly being now entered into the duke's country, had plundered and ruined all the lower part of it, and was now actually besieging the capital city of Leipsic. These necessities made almost any conditions easy to him; the greatest difficulty was that the King of Sweden demanded the absolute command of the army, which the duke submitted to with less goodwill than he had reason to do, the king's experience and conduct considered.

I had not patience to attend the conclusions of their particular treaties, but as soon as ever the passage was clear I quitted the Saxon camp and went to see the Swedish army. I fell in with the out-guards of the Swedes at a little town called Beltsig, on the river Wersa, just as they were relieving the guards and going to march, and having a pass from the English ambassador was very well received by the officer who changed the guards, and with him I went back into the army. By nine in the morning the army was in full march, the king himself at the head of them on a grey pad, and riding from one brigade to another, ordered the march of every line himself.

When I saw the Swedish troops, their exact discipline, their order, the modesty and familiarity of their officers, and the regular living of the soldiers, their camp seemed a well-ordered city; the meanest country woman with her market ware was as safe from violence as in the streets of Vienna. There were no women in the camp but such as being known to the provosts to be the wives of the soldiers, who were necessary for washing linen, taking care of the soldiers' clothes, and dressing their victuals.

The soldiers were well clad, not gay, furnished with excellent arms, and exceedingly careful of them; and though they did not seem so terrible as I thought Tilly's men did when I first saw them, yet the figure they made, together with what we had heard of them, made them seem to me invincible: the discipline and order of their marchings, camping, and exercise was excellent and singular, and, which was to be seen in no armies but the king's, his own skill, judgment, and vigilance having added much to the general conduct of armies then in use.

As I met the Swedes on their march I had no opportunity to acquaint myself with anybody till after the conjunction of the Saxon army, and then it being but four days to the great battle of Leipsic, our acquaintance was but small, saving what fell out accidentally by conversation.

I met with several gentlemen in the king's army who spoke English very well; besides that there were three regiments of Scots in the army, the colonels whereof I found were extraordinarily esteemed by the king, as the Lord Reay, Colonel Lumsdell, and Sir John Hepburn. The latter of these, after I had by an accident become acquainted with, I found had been for many years acquainted with my father, and on that account I received a great deal of civility from him, which afterwards grew into a kind of intimate friendship. He was a complete soldier indeed, and for that reason so well beloved by that gallant king, that he hardly knew how to go about any great action without him.

It was impossible for me now to restrain my young comrade from entering into the Swedish service, and indeed everything was so inviting that I could not blame him. A captain in Sir John Hepburn's regiment had picked acquaintance with him, and he having as much gallantry in his face as real courage in his heart, the captain had persuaded him to take service, and promised to use his interest to get him a company in the Scotch brigade. I had made him promise me not to part from me in my travels without my consent, which was the only obstacle to his desires of entering into the Swedish pay; and being one evening in the captain's tent with him and discoursing very freely together, the captain asked him very short but friendly, and looking earnestly at me, "Is this the gentleman, Mr Fielding, that has done so much prejudice to the King of Sweden's service?" I was doubly surprised at the expression, and at the colonel, Sir John Hepburn, coming at that very moment into the tent. The colonel hearing something of the question, but knowing nothing of the reason of it, any more than as I seemed a little to concern myself at it, yet after the ceremony due to his character was over, would needs know what I had done to hinder his Majesty's service. "So much truly," says the captain, "that if his Majesty knew it he would think himself very little beholden to him." "I am sorry, sir," said I, "that I should offend in anything, who am but a stranger; but if you would please to inform me, I would endeavour to alter anything in my behaviour that is prejudicial to any one, much less to his Majesty's service." "I shall take you at your word, sir," says the captain; "the King of Sweden, sir, has a particular request to you." "I should be glad to know two things, sir," said I; "first, how that can be possible, since I am not yet known to any man in the army, much less to his Majesty? and secondly, what the request can be?" "Why, sir, his Majesty desires you would not hinder this gentleman from entering into his service, who it seems desires nothing more, if he may have your consent to it." "I have too much honour for his Majesty," returned I, "to deny anything which he pleases to command me; but methinks 'tis some hardship you should make that the king's order, which 'tis very probable he knows nothing of." Sir John Hepburn took the case up something gravely, and drinking a glass of Leipsic beer to the captain, said, "Come, captain, don't press these gentlemen; the king desires no man's service but what is purely volunteer." So we entered into other discourse, and the colonel perceiving by my talk that I had seen Tilly's army, was mighty curious in his questions, and seeming very well satisfied with the account I gave him.

The next day the army having passed the Elbe at Wittenberg, and joined the Saxon army near Torgau, his Majesty caused both armies to draw up in battalia, giving every brigade the same post in the lines as he purposed to fight in. I must do the memory of that glorious general this honour, that I never saw an army drawn up with so much variety, order, and exact regularity since, though I have seen many armies drawn up by some of the greatest captains of the age. The order by which his men were directed to flank and relieve one another, the methods of receiving one body of men if disordered into another, and rallying one squadron without disordering another was so admirable; the horse everywhere flanked lined and defended by the foot, and the foot by the horse, and both by the cannon, was such that if those orders were but as punctually obeyed, 'twere impossible to put an army so modelled into any confusion.

The view being over, and the troops returned to their camps, the captain with whom we drank the day before meeting me told me I must come and sup with him in his tent, where he would ask my pardon for the affront he gave me before. I told him he needed not put himself to the trouble, I was not affronted at all; that I would do myself the honour to wait on him, provided he would give me his word not to speak any more of it as an affront.

We had not been a quarter of an hour in his tent but Sir John Hepburn came in again, and addressing to me, told me he was glad to find me there; that he came to the captain's tent to inquire how to send to me; and that I must do him the honour to go with him to wait on the king, who had a mind to hear the account I could give him of the Imperial army from my own mouth. I must confess I was at some loss in my mind how to make my address to his Majesty, but I had heard so much of the conversable temper of the king, and his particular sweetness of humour with the meanest soldier, that I made no more difficulty, but having paid my respects to Colonel Hepburn, thanked him for the honour he had done me, and offered to rise and wait upon him. "Nay," says the Colonel, "we will eat first, for I find Gourdon," which was the captain's name, "has got something for supper, and the king's order is at seven o'clock." So we went to supper, and Sir John, becoming very friendly, must know my name; which, when I had told him, and of what place and family, he rose from his seat, and embracing me, told me he knew my father very well, and had been intimately acquainted with him, and told me several passages wherein my father had particularly obliged him. After this we went to supper, and the king's health being drank round, the colonel moved the sooner because he had a mind to talk with me.

When we were going to the king he inquired of me where I had been, and what occasion brought me to the army. I told him the short history of my travels, and that I came hither from Vienna on purpose to see the King of Sweden and his army. He asked me if there was any service he could do me, by which he meant, whether I desired an employment. I pretended not to take him so, but told him the protection his acquaintance would afford me was more than I could have asked, since I might thereby have opportunity to satisfy my curiosity, which was the chief end of my coming abroad. He perceiving by this that I had no mind to be a soldier, told me very kindly I should command him in anything; that his tent and equipage, horses and servants should always have orders to be at my service; but that as a piece of friendship, he would advise me to retire to some place distant from the army, for that the army would march to-morrow, and the king was resolved to fight General Tilly, and he would not have me hazard myself; that if I thought fit to take his advice, he would have me take that interval to see the court at Berlin, whither he would send one of his servants to wait on me.

His discourse was too kind not to extort the tenderest acknowledgment from me that I was capable of. I told him his care of me was so obliging, that I knew not what return to make him, but if he pleased to leave me to my choice I desired no greater favour than to trail a pike under his command in the ensuing battle. "I can never answer it to your father," says he, "to suffer you to expose yourself so far." I told him my father would certainly acknowledge his friendship in the proposal made me; but I believed he knew him better than to think he would be well pleased with me if I should accept of it; that I was sure my father would have rode post five hundred miles to have been at such a battle under such a general, and it should never be told him that his son had rode fifty miles to be out of it. He seemed to be something concerned at the resolution I had taken, and replied very quickly upon me, that he approved very well of my courage; "but," says he, "no man gets any credit by running upon needless adventures, nor loses any by shunning hazards which he has no order for. 'Tis enough," says he, "for a gentleman to behave well when he is commanded upon any service; I have had fighting enough," says he, "upon these points of honour, and I never got anything but reproof for it from the king himself."

"Well, sir," said I, "however if a man expects to rise by his valour, he must show it somewhere; and if I were to have any command in an army, I would first try whether I could deserve it. I have never yet seen any service, and must have my induction some time or other. I shall never have a better schoolmaster than yourself, nor a better school than such an army." "Well," says Sir John, "but you may have the same school and the same teaching after this battle is over; for I must tell you beforehand, this will be a bloody touch. Tilly has a great army of old lads that are used to boxing, fellows with iron faces, and 'tis a little too much to engage so hotly the first entrance into the wars. You may see our discipline this winter, and make your campaign with us next summer, when you need not fear but we shall have fighting enough, and you will be better acquainted with things. We do never put our common soldiers upon pitched battles the first campaign, but place our new men in garrisons and try them in parties first." "Sir," said I, with a little more freedom, "I believe I shall not make a trade of the war, and therefore need not serve an apprenticeship to it; 'tis a hard battle where none escapes. If I come off, I hope I shall not disgrace you, and if not, 'twill be some satisfaction to my father to hear his son died fighting under the command of Sir John Hepburn, in the army of the King of Sweden, and I desire no better epitaph upon my tomb."

"Well," says Sir John, and by this time we were just come to the king's quarters, and the guards calling to us interrupted his reply; so we went into the courtyard where the king was lodged, which was in an indifferent house of one of the burghers of Dieben, and Sir John stepping up, met the king coming down some steps into a large room which looked over the town wall into a field where part of the artillery was drawn up. Sir John Hepburn sent his man presently to me to come up, which I did; and Sir John without any ceremony carries me directly up to the king, who was leaning on his elbow in the window. The king turning about, "This is the English gentleman," says Sir John, "who I told your Majesty had been in the Imperial army." "How then did he get hither," says the king, "without being taken by the scouts?" At which question, Sir John saying nothing, "By a pass, and please your Majesty, from the English ambassador's secretary at Vienna," said I, making a profound reverence. "Have you then been at Vienna?" says the king. "Yes, and please your Majesty," said I; upon which the king, folding up a letter he had in his hand, seemed much more earnest to talk about Vienna than about Tilly. "And, pray, what news had you at Vienna?" "Nothing, sir," said I, "but daily accounts one in the neck of another of their own misfortunes, and your Majesty's conquests, which makes a very melancholy court there." "But, pray," said the king, "what is the common opinion there about these affairs?" "The common people are terrified to the last degree," said I, "and when your Majesty took Frankfort-upon-Oder, if your army had marched but twenty miles into Silesia, half the people would have run out of Vienna, and I left them fortifying the city." "They need not," replied the king, smiling; "I have no design to trouble them, it is the Protestant countries I must be for."

Upon this the Duke of Saxony entered the room, and finding the king engaged, offered to retire; but the king, beckoning with his hand, called to him in French; "Cousin," says the king, "this gentleman has been travelling and comes from Vienna," and so made me repeat what I had said before; at which the king went on with me, and Sir John Hepburn informing his Majesty that I spoke High Dutch, he changed his language, and asked me in Dutch where it was that I saw General Tilly's army. I told his Majesty at the siege of Magdeburg. "At Magdeburg!" said the king, shaking his head; "Tilly must answer to me some day for that city, and if not to me, to a greater King than I. Can you guess what army he had with him?" said the king. "He had two armies with him," said I, "but one I suppose will do your Majesty no harm." "Two armies!" said the king. "Yes, sir, he has one army of about 26,000 men," said I, "and another of about 15,000 women and their attendants," at which the king laughed heartily. "Ay, ay," says the king, "those 15,000 do us as much harm as the 26,000, for they eat up the country, and devour the poor Protestants more than the men. Well," says the king, "do they talk of fighting us?" "They talk big enough, sir," said I, "but your Majesty has not been so often fought with as beaten in their discourse." "I know not for the men," says the king, "but the old man is as likely to do it as talk of it, and I hope to try them in a day or two."

The king inquired after that several matters of me about the Low Countries, the Prince of Orange, and of the court and affairs in England; and Sir John Hepburn informing his Majesty that I was the son of an English gentleman of his acquaintance, the king had the goodness to ask him what care he had taken of me against the day of battle. Upon which Sir John repeated to him the discourse we had together by the way; the king seeming particularly pleased with it, began to take me to task himself. "You English gentlemen," says he, "are too forward in the wars, which makes you leave them too soon again." "Your Majesty," replied I, "makes war in so pleasant a manner as makes all the world fond of fighting under your conduct." "Not so pleasant neither," says the king, "here's a man can tell you that sometimes it is not very pleasant." "I know not much of the warrior, sir," said I, "nor of the world, but if always to conquer be the pleasure of the war, your Majesty's soldiers have all that can be desired." "Well," says the king, "but however, considering all things, I think you would do well to take the advice Sir John Hepburn has given you." "Your Majesty may command me to anything, but where your Majesty and so many gallant gentlemen hazard their lives, mine is not worth mentioning; and I should not dare to tell my father at my return into England that I was in your Majesty's army, and made so mean a figure that your Majesty would not permit me to fight under that royal standard." "Nay," replied the king, "I lay no commands upon you, but you are young." "I can never die, sir," said I, "with more honour than in your Majesty's service." I spake this with so much freedom, and his Majesty was so pleased with it, that he asked me how I would choose to serve, on horseback or on foot. I told his Majesty I should be glad to receive any of his Majesty's commands, but if I had not that honour I had purposed to trail a pike under Sir John Hepburn, who had done me so much honour as to introduce me into his Majesty's presence. "Do so, then," replied the king, and turning to Sir John Hepburn, said, "and pray, do you take care of him." At which, overcome with the goodness of his discourse, I could not answer a word, but made him a profound reverence and retired.

The next day but one, being the 7th of September, before day the army marched from Dieben to a large field about a mile from Leipsic, where we found Tilly's army in full battalia in admirable order, which made a show both glorious and terrible. Tilly, like a fair gamester, had taken up but one side of the plain, and left the other free, and all the avenues open for the king's army; nor did he stir to the charge till the king's army was completely drawn up and advanced toward him. He had in his army 44,000 old soldiers, every way answerable to what I have said of them before; and I shall only add, a better army, I believe, never was so soundly beaten.

The king was not much inferior in force, being joined with the Saxons, who were reckoned 22,000 men, and who drew up on the left, making a main battle and two wings, as the king did on the right.

The king placed himself at the right wing of his own horse, Gustavus Horn had the main battle of the Swedes, the Duke of Saxony had the main battle of his own troops, and General Arnheim the right wing of his horse. The second line of the Swedes consisted of the two Scotch brigades, and three Swedish, with the Finland horse in the wings.

In the beginning of the fight, Tilly's right wing charged with such irresistible fury upon the left of the king's army where the Saxons were posted, that nothing could withstand them. The Saxons fled amain, and some of them carried the news over the country that all was lost, and the king's army overthrown; and indeed it passed for an oversight with some that the king did not place some of his old troops among the Saxons, who were new-raised men. The Saxons lost here near 2000 men, and hardly ever showed their faces again all the battle, except some few of their horse.

I was posted with my comrade, the captain, at the head of three Scottish regiments of foot, commanded by Sir John Hepburn, with express directions from the colonel to keep by him. Our post was in the second line, as a reserve to the King of Sweden's main battle, and, which was strange, the main battle, which consisted of four great brigades of foot, were never charged during the whole fight; and yet we, who had the reserve, were obliged to endure the whole weight of the Imperial army. The occasion was, the right wing of the Imperialists having defeated the Saxons, and being eager in the chase, Tilly, who was an old soldier, and ready to prevent all mistakes, forbids any pursuit. "Let them go," says he, "but let us beat the Swedes, or we do nothing." Upon this the victorious troops fell in upon the flank of the king's army, which, the Saxons being fled, lay open to them. Gustavus Horn commanded the left wing of the Swedes, and having first defeated some regiments which charged him, falls in upon the rear of the Imperial right wing, and separates them from the van, who were advanced a great way forward in pursuit of the Saxons, and having routed the said rear or reserve, falls on upon Tilly's main battle, and defeated part of them; the other part was gone in chase of the Saxons, and now also returned, fell in upon the rear of the left wing of the Swedes, charging them in the flank, for they drew up upon the very ground which the Saxons had quitted. This changed the whole front, and made the Swedes face about to the left, and made a great front on their flank to make this good. Our brigades, who were placed as a reserve for the main battle, were, by special order from the king, wheeled about to the left, and placed for the right of this new front to charge the Imperialists; they were about 12,000 of their best foot, besides horse, and flushed with the execution of the Saxons, fell on like furies. The king by this time had almost defeated the Imperialists' left wing; their horse, with more haste than good speed, had charged faster than their foot could follow, and having broke into the king's first line, he let them go, where, while the second line bears the shock, and bravely resisted them, the king follows them on the crupper with thirteen troops of horse, and some musketeers, by which being hemmed in, they were all cut down in a moment as it were, and the army never disordered with them. This fatal blow to the left wing gave the king more leisure to defeat the foot which followed, and to send some assistance to Gustavus Horn in his left wing, who had his hands full with the main battle of the Imperialists.

But those troops who, as I said, had routed the Saxons, being called off from the pursuit, had charged our flank, and were now grown very strong, renewed the battle in a terrible manner. Here it was I saw our men go to wreck. Colonel Hall, a brave soldier, commanded the rear of the Swede's left wing; he fought like a lion, but was slain, and most of his regiment cut off, though not unrevenged, for they entirely ruined Furstenberg's regiment of foot. Colonel Cullembach, with his regiment of horse, was extremely overlaid also, and the colonel and many brave officers killed, and in short all that wing was shattered, and in an ill condition.

In this juncture came the king, and having seen what havoc the enemy made of Cullembach's troops, he comes riding along the front of our three brigades, and himself led us on to the charge; the colonel of his guards, the Baron Dyvel, was shot dead just as the king had given him some orders. When the Scots advanced, seconded by some regiments of horse which the king also sent to the charge, the bloodiest fight began that ever men beheld, for the Scottish brigades, giving fire three ranks at a time over one another's heads, poured in their shot so thick, that the enemy were cut down like grass before a scythe; and following into the thickest of their foot with the clubs of their muskets made a most dreadful slaughter, and yet was there no flying. Tilly's men might be killed and knocked down, but no man turned his back, nor would give an inch of ground, but as they were wheeled, or marched, or retreated by their officers.

There was a regiment of cuirassiers which stood whole to the last, and fought like lions; they went ranging over the field when all their army was broken, and nobody cared for charging them; they were commanded by Baron Kronenburg, and at last went off from the battle whole. These were armed in black armour from head to foot, and they carried off their general. About six o'clock the field was cleared of the enemy, except at one place on the king's side, where some of them rallied, and though they knew all was lost would take no quarter, but fought it out to the last man, being found dead the next day in rank and file as they were drawn up.

I had the good fortune to receive no hurt in this battle, excepting a small scratch on the side of my neck by the push of a pike; but my friend received a very dangerous wound when the battle was as good as over. He had engaged with a German colonel, whose name we could never learn, and having killed his man, and pressed very close upon him, so that he had shot his horse, the horse in the fall kept the colonel down, lying on one of his legs; upon which he demanded quarter, which Captain Fielding granting, helped him to quit his horse, and having disarmed him, was bringing him into the line, when the regiment of cuirassiers, which I mentioned, commanded by Baron Kronenburg, came roving over the field, and with a flying charge saluted our front with a salvo of carabine shot, which wounded us a great many men, and among the rest the captain received a shot in his thigh, which laid him on the ground, and being separated from the line, his prisoner got away with them.

This was the first service I was in, and indeed I never saw any fight since maintained with such gallantry, such desperate valour, together with such dexterity of management, both sides being composed of soldiers fully tried, bred to the wars, expert in everything, exact in their order, and incapable of fear, which made the battle be much more bloody than usual. Sir John Hepburn, at my request, took particular care of my comrade, and sent his own surgeon to look after him; and afterwards, when the city of Leipsic was retaken, provided him lodgings there, and came very often to see him; and indeed I was in great care for him too, the surgeons being very doubtful of him a great while; for having lain in the field all night among the dead, his wound, for want of dressing, and with the extremity of cold, was in a very ill condition, and the pain of it had thrown him into a fever. 'Twas quite dusk before the fight ended, especially where the last rallied troops fought so long, and therefore we durst not break our order to seek out our friends, so that 'twas near seven o'clock the next morning before we found the captain, who, though very weak by the loss of blood, had raised himself up, and placed his back against the buttock of a dead horse. I was the first that knew him, and running to him, embraced him with a great deal of joy; he was not able to speak, but made signs to let me see he knew me, so we brought him into the camp, and Sir John Hepburn, as I noted before, sent his own surgeons to look after him.

The darkness of the night prevented any pursuit, and was the only refuge the enemy had left: for had there been three hours more daylight ten thousand more lives had been lost, for the Swedes (and Saxons especially) enraged by the obstinacy of the enemy, were so thoroughly heated that they would have given quarter but to few. The retreat was not sounded till seven o'clock, when the king drew up the whole army upon the field of battle, and gave strict command that none should stir from their order; so the army lay under their arms all night, which was another reason why the wounded soldiers suffered very much by the cold; for the king, who had a bold enemy to deal with, was not ignorant what a small body of desperate men rallied together might have done in the darkness of the night, and therefore he lay in his coach all night at the head of the line, though it froze very hard.

As soon as the day began to peep the trumpets sounded to horse, and all the dragoons and light-horse in the army were commanded to the pursuit. The cuirassiers and some commanded musketeers advanced some miles, if need were, to make good their retreat, and all the foot stood to their arms for a reverse; but in half-an-hour word was brought to the king that the enemy were quite dispersed, upon which detachments were made out of every regiment to search among the dead for any of our friends that were wounded; and the king himself gave a strict order, that if any were found wounded and alive among the enemy none should kill them, but take care to bring them into the camp—a piece of humanity which saved the lives of near a thousand of the enemies.

This piece of service being over, the enemy's camp was seized upon, and the soldiers were permitted to plunder it; all the cannon, arms, and ammunition was secured for the king's use, the rest was given up to the soldiers, who found so much plunder that they had no reason to quarrel for shares.

For my share, I was so busy with my wounded captain that I got nothing but a sword, which I found just by him when I first saw him; but my man brought me a very good horse with a furniture on him, and one pistol of extraordinary workmanship.

I bade him get upon his back and make the best of the day for himself, which he did, and I saw him no more till three days after, when he found me out at Leipsic, so richly dressed that I hardly knew him; and after making his excuse for his long absence, gave me a very pleasant account where he had been. He told me that, according to my order, being mounted on the horse he had brought me, he first rid into the field among the dead to get some clothes suitable to the equipage of his horse, and having seized on a laced coat, a helmet, a sword, and an extraordinary good cane, was resolved to see what was become of the enemy; and following the track of the dragoons, which he could easily do by the bodies on the road, he fell in with a small party of twenty-five dragoons, under no command but a corporal, making to a village where some of the enemies' horse had been quartered. The dragoons, taking him for an officer by his horse, desired him to command them, told him the enemy was very rich, and they doubted not a good booty. He was a bold, brisk fellow, and told them, with all his heart, but said he had but one pistol, the other being broken with firing; so they lent him a pair of pistols, and a small piece they had taken, and he led them on. There had been a regiment of horse and some troops of Crabats in the village, but they were fled on the first notice of the pursuit, excepting three troops, and these, on sight of this small party, supposing them to be only the first of a greater number, fled in the greatest confusion imaginable. They took the village, and about fifty horses, with all the plunder of the enemy, and with the heat of the service he had spoiled my horse, he said, for which he had brought me two more; for he, passing for the commander of the party, had all the advantage the custom of war gives an officer in like cases.

I was very well pleased with the relation the fellow gave me, and, laughing at him, "Well, captain," said I, "and what plunder have ye got?" "Enough to make me a captain, sir," says he, "if you please, and a troop ready raised too; for the party of dragoons are posted in the village by my command, till they have farther orders." In short, he pulled out sixty or seventy pieces of gold, five or six watches, thirteen or fourteen rings, whereof two were diamond rings, one of which was worth fifty dollars, silver as much as his pockets would hold; besides that he had brought three horses, two of which were laden with baggage, and a boor he had hired to stay with them at Leipsic till he had found me out. "But I am afraid, captain," says I, "you have plundered the village instead of plundering the enemy." "No indeed, not we," says he, "but the Crabats had done it for us and we light of them just as they were carrying it off." "Well," said I, "but what will you do with your men, for when you come to give them orders they will know you well enough?" "No, no," says he, "I took care of that, for just now I gave a soldier five dollars to carry them news that the army was marched to Merseburg, and that they should follow thither to the regiment."

Having secured his money in my lodgings, he asked me if I pleased to see his horses, and to have one for myself? I told him I would go and see them in the afternoon; but the fellow being impatient goes and fetches them. There were three horses, one whereof was a very good one, and by the furniture was an officer's horse of the Crabats, and that my man would have me accept, for the other he had spoiled, as he said. I was but indifferently horsed before, so I accepted of the horse, and went down with him to see the rest of his plunder there. He had got three or four pair of pistols, two or three bundles of officers' linen, and lace, a field-bed, and a tent, and several other things of value; but at last, coming to a small fardel, "And this," says he, "I took whole from a Crabat running away with it under his arm," so he brought it up into my chamber. He had not looked into it, he said, but he understood 'twas some plunder the soldiers had made, and finding it heavy took it by consent. We opened it and found it was a bundle of some linen, thirteen or fourteen pieces of plate, and in a small cup, three rings, a fine necklace of pearl and the value of 100 rix-dollars in money.

The fellow was amazed at his own good fortune, and hardly knew what to do with himself; I bid him go take care of his other things, and of his horses, and come again. So he went and discharged the boor that waited and packed up all his plunder, and came up to me in his old clothes again. "How now, captain," says I, "what, have you altered your equipage already?" "I am no more ashamed, sir, of your livery," answered he, "than of your service, and nevertheless your servant for what I have got by it." "Well," says I to him, "but what will you do now with all your money?" "I wish my poor father had some of it," says he, "and for the rest I got it for you, sir, and desire you would take it." He spoke it with so much honesty and freedom that I could not but take it very kindly; but, however, I told him I would not take a farthing from him as his master, but I would have him play the good husband with it, now he had such good fortune to get it. He told me he would take my directions in everything. "Why, then," said I, "I'll tell you what I would advise you to do, turn it all into ready money, and convey it by return home into England, and follow yourself the first opportunity, and with good management you may put yourself in a good posture of living with it." The fellow, with a sort of dejection in his looks, asked me if he had disobliged me in anything? "Why?" says I. "That I was willing to turn him out of his service." "No, George" (that was his name), says I, "but you may live on this money without being a servant." "I'd throw it all into the Elbe," says he, "over Torgau bridge, rather than leave your service; and besides," says he, "can't I save my money without going from you? I got it in your service, and I'll never spend it out of your service, unless you put me away. I hope my money won't make me the worse servant; if I thought it would, I'd soon have little enough." "Nay, George," says I, "I shall not oblige you to it, for I am not willing to lose you neither: come, then," says I, "let us put it all together, and see what it will come to." So he laid it all together on the table, and by our computation he had gotten as much plunder as was worth about 1400 rix-dollars, besides three horses with their furniture, a tent, a bed, and some wearing linen. Then he takes the necklace of pearl, a very good watch, a diamond ring, and 100 pieces of gold, and lays them by themselves, and having, according to our best calculation, valued the things, he put up all the rest, and as I was going to ask him what they were left out for, he takes them up in his hand, and coming round the table, told me, that if I did not think him unworthy of my service and favour, he begged I would give him leave to make that present to me; that it was my first thought his going out, that he had got it all in my service, and he should think I had no kindness for him if I should refuse it.

I was resolved in my mind not to take it from him, and yet I could find no means to resist his importunity. At last I told him, I would accept of part of his present, and that I esteemed his respect in that as much as the whole, and that I would not have him importune me farther; so I took the ring and watch, with the horse and furniture as before, and made him turn all the rest into money at Leipsic, and not suffering him to wear his livery, made him put himself into a tolerable equipage, and taking a young Leipsicer into my service, he attended me as a gentleman from that time forward.

The king's army never entered Leipsic, but proceeded to Merseberg, and from thence to Halle, and so marched on into Franconia, while the Duke of Saxony employed his forces in recovering Leipsic and driving the Imperialists out of his country. I continued at Leipsic twelve days, being not willing to leave my comrade till he was recovered; but Sir John Hepburn so often importuned me to come into the army, and sent me word that the king had very often inquired for me, that at last I consented to go without him; so having made our appointment where to meet, and how to correspond by letters, I went to wait on Sir John Hepburn, who then lay with the king's army at the city of Erfurt in Saxony. As I was riding between Leipsic and Halle, I observed my horse went very awkwardly and uneasy, and sweat very much, though the weather was cold, and we had rid but very softly; I fancied therefore that the saddle might hurt the horse, and calls my new captain up. "George," says I, "I believe this saddle hurts the horse." So we alighted, and looking under the saddle found the back of the horse extremely galled; so I bid him take off the saddle, which he did, and giving the horse to my young Leipsicer to lead, we sat down to see if we could mend it, for there was no town near us. Says George, pointing with his finger, "If you please to cut open the pannel there, I'll get something to stuff into it which will bear it from the horse's back." So while he looked for something to thrust in, I cut a hole in the pannel of the saddle, and, following it with my finger, I felt something hard, which seemed to move up and down. Again, as I thrust it with my finger, "Here's something that should not be here," says I, not yet imagining what afterwards fell out, and calling, "Run back," bade him put up his finger. "Whatever 'tis," says he, "'tis this hurts the horse, for it bears just on his back when the saddle is set on." So we strove to take hold on it, but could not reach it; at last we took the upper part of the saddle quite from the pannel, and there lay a small silk purse wrapped in a piece of leather, and full of gold ducats. "Thou art born to be rich, George," says I to him, "here's more money." We opened the purse and found in it four hundred and thirty-eight small pieces of gold.

There I had a new skirmish with him whose the money should be. I told him 'twas his, he told me no; I had accepted of the horse and furniture, and all that was about him was mine, and solemnly vowed he would not have a penny of it. I saw no remedy, but put up the money for the present, mended our saddle, and went on. We lay that night at Halle, and having had such a booty in the saddle, I made him search the saddles of the other two horses, in one of which we found three French crowns, but nothing in the other.

We arrived at Erfurt the 28th of September, but the army was removed, and entered into Franconia, and at the siege of Koningshoven we came up with them. The first thing I did was to pay my civilities to Sir John Hepburn, who received me very kindly, but told me withal that I had not done well to be so long from him, and the king had particularly inquired for me, had commanded him to bring me to him at my return. I told him the reason of my stay at Leipsic, and how I had left that place and my comrade, before he was cured of his wounds, to wait on him according to his letters. He told me the king had spoken some things very obliging about me, and he believed would offer me some command in the army, if I thought well to accept of it. I told him

I had promised my father not to take service in an army without his leave, and yet if his Majesty should offer it, I neither knew how to resist it, nor had I an inclination to anything more than the service, and such a leader, though I had much rather have served as a volunteer at my own charge (which, as he knew, was the custom of our English gentlemen) than in any command. He replied, "Do as you think fit; but some gentlemen would give 20,000 crowns to stand so fair for advancement as you do."

The town of Koningshoven capitulated that day, and Sir John was ordered to treat with the citizens, so I had no further discourse with him then; and the town being taken, the army immediately advanced down the river Maine, for the king had his eye upon Frankfort and Mentz, two great cities, both which he soon became master of, chiefly by the prodigious expedition of his march; for within a month after the battle, he was in the lower parts of the empire, and had passed from the Elbe to the Rhine, an incredible conquest, had taken all the strong cities, the bishoprics of Bamberg, of Wurtzburg, and almost all the circle of Franconia, with part of Schawberland—a conquest large enough to be seven years a-making by the common course of arms.

Business going on thus, the king had not leisure to think of small matters, and I being not thoroughly resolved in my mind, did not press Sir John to introduce me. I had wrote to my father with an account of my reception in the army, the civilities of Sir John Hepburn, the particulars of the battle, and had indeed pressed him to give me leave to serve the King of Sweden, to which particular I waited for an answer, but the following occasion determined me before an answer could possibly reach me.

The king was before the strong castle of Marienburg, which commands the city of Wurtzburg. He had taken the city, but the garrison and richer part of the burghers were retired into the castle, and trusting to the strength of the place, which was thought impregnable, they bade the Swedes do their worst; 'twas well provided with all things, and a strong garrison in it, so that the army indeed expected 'twould be a long piece of work. The castle stood on a high rock, and on the steep of the rock was a bastion which defended the only passage up the hill into the castle; the Scots were chose out to make this attack, and the king was an eye-witness of their gallantry. In the action Sir John was not commanded out, but Sir James Ramsey led them on; but I observed that most of the Scotch officers in the other regiments prepared to serve as volunteers for the honour of their countrymen, and Sir John

Hepburn led them on. I was resolved to see this piece of service, and therefore joined myself to the volunteers. We were armed with partisans, and each man two pistols at our belt. It was a piece of service that seemed perfectly desperate, the advantage of the hill, the precipice we were to mount, the height of the bastion, the resolute courage and number of the garrison, who from a complete covert made a terrible fire upon us, all joined to make the action hopeless. But the fury of the Scots musketeers was not to be abated by any difficulties; they mounted the hill, scaled the works like madmen, running upon the enemies' pikes, and after two hours' desperate fight in the midst of fire and smoke, took it by storm, and put all the garrison to the sword. The volunteers did their part, and had their share of the loss too, for thirteen or fourteen were killed out of thirty-seven, besides the wounded, among whom I received a hurt more troublesome than dangerous by a thrust of a halberd into my arm, which proved a very painful wound, and I was a great while before it was thoroughly recovered.

The king received us as we drew off at the foot of the hill, calling the soldiers his brave Scots, and commending the officers by name. The next morning the castle was also taken by storm, and the greatest booty that ever was found in any one conquest in the whole war; the soldiers got here so much money that they knew not what to do with it, and the plunder they got here and at the battle of Leipsic made them so unruly, that had not the king been the best master of discipline in the world, they had never been kept in any reasonable bounds.

The king had taken notice of our small party of volunteers, and though I thought he had not seen me, yet he sent the next morning for Sir John Hepburn, and asked him if I were not come to the army? "Yes," says Sir John, "he has been here two or three days." And as he was forming an excuse for not having brought me to wait on his Majesty, says the king, interrupting him, "I wonder you would let him thrust himself into a hot piece of service as storming the Port Graft. Pray let him know I saw him, and have a very good account of his behaviour." Sir John returned with this account to me, and pressed me to pay my duty to his Majesty the next morning; and accordingly, though I had but an ill night with the pain of my wound, I was with him at the levee in the castle.

I cannot but give some short account of the glory of the morning; the castle had been cleared of the dead bodies of the enemies, and what was not pillaged by the soldiers was placed under a guard. There was first a magazine of very good arms for about 18,000 or 20,000 foot, and 4000 horse, a very good train of artillery of about eighteen pieces of battery, thirty-two brass field-pieces, and four mortars. The bishop's treasure, and other public monies not plundered by the soldiers, was telling out by the officers, and amounted to 400,000 florins in money; and the burghers of the town in solemn procession, bareheaded, brought the king three tons of gold as a composition to exempt the city from plunder. Here was also a stable of gallant horses which the king had the curiosity to go and see.

When the ceremony of the burghers was over, the king came down into the castle court, walked on the parade (where the great train of artillery was placed on their carriages) and round the walls, and gave order for repairing the bastion that was stormed by the Scots; and as at the entrance of the parade Sir John Hepburn and I made our reverence to the king, "Ho, cavalier!" said the king to me, "I am glad to see you," and so passed forward. I made my bow very low, but his Majesty said no more at that time.

When the view was over the king went up into the lodgings, and Sir John and I walked in an antechamber for about a quarter of an hour, when one of the gentlemen of the bedchamber came out to Sir John, and told him the king asked for him; he stayed but a little with the king, and come out to me and told me the king had ordered him to bring me to him.

His Majesty, with a countenance full of honour and goodness, interrupted my compliment, and asked me how I did; at which answering only with a bow, says the king, "I am sorry to see you are hurt; I would have laid my commands on you not to have shown yourself in so sharp a piece of service, if I had known you had been in the camp." "Your Majesty does me too much honour," said I, "in your care of a life that has yet done nothing to deserve your favour." His Majesty was pleased to say something very kind to me relating to my behaviour in the battle of Leipsic, which I have not vanity enough to write; at the conclusion whereof, when I replied very humbly that I was not sensible that any service I had done, or could do, could possibly merit so much goodness, he told me he had ordered me a small testimony of his esteem, and withal gave me his hand to kiss. I was now conquered, and with a sort of surprise told his Majesty I found myself so much engaged by his goodness, as well as my own inclination, that if his Majesty would please to accept of my devoir, I was resolved to serve in his army, or wherever he pleased to command me. "Serve me," says the king, "why, so you do, but I must not have you be a musketeer; a poor soldier at a dollar a week will do that." "Pray, Sir John," says the king, "give him what commission he desires." "No commission, sir," says I, "would please me better than leave to fight near your Majesty's person, and to serve you at my own charge till I am qualified by more experience to receive your commands." "Why, then, it shall be so," said the king, "and I charge you, Hepburn," says he, "when anything offers that is either fit for him, or he desires, that you tell me of it;" and giving me his hand again to kiss, I withdrew.

I was followed before I had passed the castle gate by one of the king's pages, who brought me a warrant, directed to Sir John Hepburn, to go to the master of the horse for an immediate delivery of things ordered by the king himself for my account, where being come, the equerry produced me a very good coach with four horses, harness, and equipage, and two very fine saddle-horses, out of the stable of the bishop's horses afore-mentioned; with these there was a list for three servants, and a warrant to the steward of the king's baggage to defray me, my horses, and servants at the king's charge till farther order. I was very much at a loss how to manage myself in this so strange freedom of so great a prince, and consulting with Sir John Hepburn, I was proposing to him whether it was not proper to go immediately back to pay my duty to his Majesty, and acknowledge his bounty in the best terms I could; but while we were resolving to do so, the guards stood to their arms, and we saw the king go out at the gate in his coach to pass into the city, so we were diverted from it for that time. I acknowledge the bounty of the king was very surprising, but I must say it was not so very strange to me when I afterwards saw the course of his management. Bounty in him was his natural talent, but he never distributed his favours but where he thought himself both loved and faithfully served, and when he was so, even the single actions of his private soldiers he would take particular notice of himself, and publicly own, acknowledge, and reward them, of which I am obliged to give some instances.

A private musketeer at the storming the castle of Wurtzburg, when all the detachment was beaten off, stood in the face of the enemy and fired his piece, and though he had a thousand shot made at him, stood unconcerned, and charged his piece again, and let fly at the enemy, continuing to do so three times, at the same time beckoning with his hand to his fellows to come on again, which they did, animated by his example, and carried the place for the king.

When the town was taken the king ordered the regiment to be drawn out, and calling for that soldier, thanked him before them all for taking the town for him, gave him a thousand dollars in money, and a commission with his own hand for a foot company, or leave to go home, which he would. The soldier took the commission on his knees, kissed it, and put it into his bosom, and told the king, he would never leave his service as long as he lived.

This bounty of the king's, timed and suited by his judgment, was the reason that he was very well served, entirely beloved, and most punctually obeyed by his soldiers, who were sure to be cherished and encouraged if they did well, having the king generally an eye-witness of their behaviour.

My indiscretion rather than valour had engaged me so far at the battle of Leipsic, that being in the van of Sir John Hepburn's brigade, almost three whole companies of us were separated from our line, and surrounded by the enemies' pikes. I cannot but say also that we were disengaged rather by a desperate charge Sir John made with the whole regiment to fetch us off, than by our own valour, though we were not wanting to ourselves neither, but this part of the action being talked of very much to the advantage of the young English volunteer, and possibly more than I deserved, was the occasion of all the distinction the king used me with ever after.

I had by this time letters from my father, in which, though with some reluctance, he left me at liberty to enter into arms if I thought fit, always obliging me to be directed, and, as he said, commanded by Sir John Hepburn. At the same time he wrote to Sir John Hepburn, commending his son's fortunes, as he called it, to his care, which letters Sir John showed the king unknown to me.

I took care always to acquaint my father of every circumstance, and forgot not to mention his Majesty's extraordinary favour, which so affected my father, that he obtained a very honourable mention of it in a letter from King Charles to the King of Sweden, written by his own hand.

I had waited on his Majesty, with Sir John Hepburn, to give him thanks for his magnificent present, and was received with his usual goodness, and after that I was every day among the gentlemen of his ordinary attendance. And if his Majesty went out on a party, as he would often do, or to view the country, I always attended him among the volunteers, of whom a great many always followed him; and he would often call me out, talk with me, send me upon messages to towns, to princes, free cities, and the like, upon extraordinary occasions.

The first piece of service he put me upon had like to have embroiled me with one of his favourite colonels. The king was marching through the Bergstraet, a low country on the edge of the Rhine, and, as all men thought, was going to besiege Heidelberg, but on a sudden orders a party of his guards, with five companies of Scots, to be drawn out; while they were drawing out this detachment the king calls me to him, "Ho, cavalier," says he, that was his usual word, "you shall command this party;" and thereupon gives me orders to march back all night, and in the morning, by break of day, to take post under the walls of the fort of Oppenheim, and immediately to entrench myself as well as I could. Grave Neels, the colonel of his guards, thought himself injured by this command, but the king took the matter upon himself, and Grave Neels told me very familiarly afterwards, "We have such a master," says he, "that no man can be affronted by. I thought myself wronged," says he, "when you commanded my men over my head; and for my life," says he, "I knew not which way to be angry."

I executed my commission so punctually that by break of day I was set down within musket-shot of the fort, under covert of a little mount, on which stood a windmill, and had indifferently fortified myself, and at the same time had posted some of my men on two other passes, but at farther distance from the fort, so that the fort was effectually blocked up on the land side. In the afternoon the enemy sallied on my first entrenchment, but being covered from their cannon, and defended by a ditch which I had drawn across the road, they were so well received by my musketeers that they retired with the loss of six or seven men.

The next day Sir John Hepburn was sent with two brigades of foot to carry on the work, and so my commission ended. The king expressed himself very well pleased with what I had done, and when he was so was never sparing of telling of it, for he used to say that public commendations were a great encouragement to valour.

While Sir John Hepburn lay before the fort and was preparing to storm it, the king's design was to get over the Rhine, but the Spaniards which were in Oppenheim had sunk all the boats they could find. At last the king, being informed where some lay that were sunk, caused them to be weighed with all the expedition possible, and in the night of the 7th of December, in three boats, passed over his regiment of guards, about three miles above the town, and, as the king thought, secure from danger; but they were no sooner landed, and not drawn into order, but they were charged by a body of Spanish horse, and had not the darkness given them opportunity to draw up in the enclosures in several little parties, they had been in great danger of being disordered; but by this means they lined the hedges and lanes so with musketeers, that the remainder had time to draw up in battalia, and saluted the horse with their muskets, so that they drew farther off.

The king was very impatient, hearing his men engaged, having no boats nor possible means to get over to help them. At last, about eleven o'clock at night, the boats came back, and the king thrust another regiment into them, and though his officers dissuaded him, would go over himself with them on foot, and did so. This was three months that very day when the battle of Leipsic was fought, and winter time too, that the progress of his arms had spread from the Elbe, where it parts Saxony and Brandenburg, to the Lower Palatine and the Rhine.

I went over in the boat with the king. I never saw him in so much concern in my life, for he was in pain for his men; but before we got on shore the Spaniards retired. However, the king landed, ordered his men, and prepared to entrench, but he had not time, for by that time the boats were put off again, the Spaniards, not knowing more troops were landed, and being reinforced from Oppenheim, came on again, and charged with great fury; but all things were now in order, and they were readily received and beaten back again. They came on again the third time, and with repeated charges attacked us; but at last finding us too strong for them they gave it over. By this time another regiment of foot was come over, and as soon as day appeared the king with the three regiments marched to the town, which surrendered at the first summons, and the next day the fort yielded to Sir John Hepburn.

The castle at Oppenheim held out still with a garrison of 800 Spaniards, and the king, leaving 200 Scots of Sir James Ramsey's men in the town, drew out to attack the castle. Sir James Ramsey being left wounded at Wurtzburg, the king gave me the command of those 200 men, which were a regiment, that is to say, all that were left of a gallant regiment of 2000 Scots, which the king brought out of Sweden with him, under that brave colonel. There was about thirty officers, who, having no soldiers, were yet in pay, and served as reformadoes with the regiment, and were over and above the 200 men.

The king designed to storm the castle on the lower side by the way that leads to Mentz, and Sir John Hepburn landed from the other side and marched up to storm on the Rhine port.

My reformado Scots, having observed that the town port of the castle was not so well guarded as the rest, all the eyes of the garrison being bent towards the king and Sir John Hepburn, came running to me, and told me they believed they could enter the castle, sword in hand, if I would give them leave. I told them I durst not give them orders, my commission being only to keep and defend the town; but they being very importunate, I told them they were volunteers, and might do what they pleased, that I would lend them fifty men, and draw up the rest to second them, or bring them off, as I saw occasion, so as I might not hazard the town. This was as much as they desired; they sallied immediately, and in a trice the volunteers scaled the port, cut in pieces the guard, and burst open the gate, at which the fifty entered. Finding the gate won, I advanced immediately with 100 musketeers more, having locked up all the gates of the town but the castle port, and leaving fifty still for a reserve just at that gate; the townsmen, too, seeing the castle, as it were, taken, ran to arms, and followed me with above 200 men. The Spaniards were knocked down by the Scots before they knew what the matter was, and the king and Sir John Hepburn, advancing to storm, were surprised when, instead of resistance, they saw the Spaniards throwing themselves over the walls to avoid the fury of the Scots. Few of the garrison got away, but were either killed or taken, and having cleared the castle, I set open the port on the king's side, and sent his Majesty word the castle was his own. The king came on, and entered on foot. I received him at the head of the Scots reformadoes; who all saluted him with their pikes. The king gave them his hat, and turning about, "Brave Scots, brave Scots," says he smiling, "you were too quick for me;" then beckoning to me, made me tell him how and in what manner we had managed the storm, which he was exceeding well pleased with, but especially at the caution I had used to bring them off if they had miscarried, and secured the town.

From hence the army marched to Mentz, which in four days' time capitulated, with the fort and citadel, and the city paid his Majesty 300,000 dollars to be exempted from the fury of the soldiers. Here the king himself drew the plan of those invincible fortifications which to this day makes it one of the strongest cities in Germany.
Friburg, Koningstien, Neustadt, Kaiserslautern, and almost all the Lower Palatinate, surrendered at the very terror of the King of Sweden's approach, and never suffered the danger of a siege.

The king held a most magnificent court at Mentz, attended by the Landgrave of Hesse, with an incredible number of princes and lords of the empire, with ambassadors and residents of foreign princes; and here his Majesty stayed till March, when the queen, with a great retinue of

Swedish nobility, came from Erfurt to see him. The king, attended by a gallant train of German nobility, went to Frankfort, and from thence on to Hoest, to meet the queen, where her Majesty arrived February 8.

During the king's stay in these parts, his armies were not idle, his troops, on one side under the Rhinegrave, a brave and ever-fortunate commander, and under the Landgrave of Hesse, on the other, ranged the country from Lorraine to Luxemburg, and past the Moselle on the west, and the Weser on the north. Nothing could stand before them: the Spanish army which came to the relief of the Catholic Electors was everywhere defeated and beaten quite out of the country, and the Lorraine army quite ruined. 'Twas a most pleasant court sure as ever was seen, where every day expresses arrived of armies defeated, towns surrendered, contributions agreed upon, parties routed, prisoners taken, and princes sending ambassadors to sue for truces and neutralities, to make submissions and compositions, and to pay arrears and contributions.

Here arrived, February 10, the King of Bohemia from England, and with him my Lord Craven, with a body of Dutch horse, and a very fine train of English volunteers, who immediately, without any stay, marched on to Hoest to wait upon his Majesty of Sweden, who received him with a great deal of civility, and was treated at a noble collation by the king and queen at Frankfort. Never had the unfortunate king so fair a prospect of being restored to his inheritance of the Palatinate as at that time, and had King James, his father-in-law, had a soul answerable to the occasion, it had been effected before, but it was a strange thing to see him equipped from the English court with one lord and about forty or fifty English gentlemen in his attendance, whereas had the King of England now, as 'tis well known he might have done, furnished him with 10,000 or 12,000 English foot, nothing could have hindered him taking a full possession of his country; and yet even without that help did the King of Sweden clear almost his whole country of Imperialists, and after his death reinstal his son in the Electorate; but no thanks to us.

The Lord Craven did me the honour to inquire for me by name, and his Majesty of Sweden did me yet more by presenting me to the King of Bohemia, and my Lord Craven gave me a letter from my father. And speaking something of my father having served under the Prince of Orange in the famous battle of Nieuport, the king, smiling, returned, "And pray tell him from me his son has served as well in the warm battle of Leipsic."

My father being very much pleased with the honour I had received from so great a king, had ordered me to acquaint his Majesty that, if he pleased to accept of their service, he would raise him a regiment of English horse at his own charge to be under my command, and to be sent over into Holland; and my Lord Craven had orders from the King of England to signify his consent to the said levy. I acquainted my old friend Sir John Hepburn with the contents of the letter in order to have his advice, who being pleased with the proposal, would have me go to the king immediately with the letter, but present service put it off for some days.

The taking of Creutznach was the next service of any moment. The king drew out in person to the siege of this town. The town soon came to parley, but the castle seemed a work of difficulty, for its situation was so strong and so surrounded with works behind and above one and another, that most people thought the king would receive a check from it; but it was not easy to resist the resolution of the King of Sweden.

He never battered it but with two small pieces, but having viewed the works himself, ordered a mine under the first ravelin, which being sprung with success, he commands a storm. I think there was not more commanded men than volunteers, both English, Scots, French, and Germans. My old comrade was by this time recovered of his wound at Leipsic, and made one. The first body of volunteers, of about forty, were led on by my Lord Craven, and I led the second, among whom were most of the reformado Scots officers who took the castle of Oppenheim. The first party was not able to make anything of it; the garrison fought with so much fury that many of the volunteer gentlemen being wounded, and some killed, the rest were beaten off with loss. The king was in some passion at his men, and rated them for running away, as he called it, though they really retreated in good order, and commanded the assault to be renewed. 'Twas our turn to fall on next. Our Scots officers, not being used to be beaten, advanced immediately, and my Lord Craven with his volunteers pierced in with us, fighting gallantly in the breach with a pike in his hand; and, to give him the honour due to his bravery, he was with the first on the top of the rampart, and gave his hand to my comrade, and lifted him up after him. We helped one another up, till at last almost all the volunteers had gained the height of the ravelin, and maintained it with a great deal of resolution, expecting when the commanded men had gained the same height to advance upon the enemy; when one of the enemy's captains called to my Lord Craven, and told him if they might have honourable terms they would capitulate, which my lord telling him he would engage for, the garrison fired no more, and the captain, leaping down from the next rampart, came with my Lord Craven into the camp, where the conditions were agreed on, and the castle surrendered.

After the taking of this town, the king, hearing of Tilly's approach, and how he had beaten Gustavus Horn, the king's field-marshal, out of Bamberg, began to draw his forces together, and leaving the care of his conquests in these parts to his chancellor Oxenstiern, prepares to advance towards Bavaria.

I had taken an opportunity to wait upon his Majesty with Sir John Hepburn and being about to introduce the discourse of my father's letter, the king told me he had received a compliment on my account in a letter from King Charles. I told him his Majesty had by his exceeding generosity bound me and all my friends to pay their acknowledgments to him, and that I supposed my father had obtained such a mention of it from the King of England, as gratitude moved him to that his Majesty's favour had been shown in me to a family both willing and ready to serve him, that I had received some commands from my father, which, if his Majesty pleased to do me the honour to accept of, might put me in a condition to acknowledge his Majesty's goodness in a manner more proportioned to the sense I had of his favour; and with that I produced my father's letter, and read that clause in it which related to the regiment of horse, which was as follows:—

"I read with a great deal of satisfaction the account you give of the great and extraordinary conquests of the King of Sweden, and with more his Majesty's singular favour to you; I hope you will be careful to value and deserve so much honour. I am glad you rather chose to serve as a volunteer at your own charge, than to take any command, which, for want of experience, you might misbehave in.

"I have obtained of the king that he will particularly thank his Majesty of Sweden for the honour he has done you, and if his Majesty gives you so much freedom, I could be glad you should in the humblest manner thank his Majesty in the name of an old broken soldier.

"If you think yourself officer enough to command them, and his Majesty pleased to accept them, I would have you offer to raise his Majesty a regiment of horse, which, I think, I may near complete in our neighbourhood with some of your old acquaintance, who are very willing to see the world. If his Majesty gives you the word, they shall receive his commands in the Maes, the king having promised me to give them arms, and transport them for that service into Holland; and I hope they may do his Majesty such service as may be for your honour and the advantage of his Majesty's interest and glory."

"YOUR LOVING FATHER."

"'Tis an offer like a gentleman and like a soldier," says the king," and I'll accept of it on two conditions: first," says the king, "that I will pay your father the advance money for the raising the regiment; and next, that they shall be landed in the Weser or the Elbe; for which, if the King of England will not, I will pay the passage; for if they land in Holland, it may prove very difficult to get them to us when the army shall be marched out of this part of the country."

I returned this answer to my father, and sent my man George into England to order that regiment, and made him quartermaster. I sent blank commissions for the officers, signed by the king, to be filled up as my father should think fit; and when I had the king's order for the commissions, the secretary told me I must go back to the king with them. Accordingly I went back to the king, who, opening the packet, laid all the commissions but one upon a table before him, and bade me take them, and keeping that one still in his hand, "Now," says he, "you are one of my soldiers," and therewith gave me his commission, as colonel of horse in present pay. I took the commission kneeling, and humbly thanked his Majesty. "But," says the king, "there is one article-of-war I expect of you more than of others." "Your Majesty can expect nothing of me which I shall not willingly comply with," said I, "as soon as I have the honour to understand what it is." "Why, it is," says the king, "that you shall never fight but when you have orders, for I shall not be willing to lose my colonel before I have the regiment." "I shall be ready at all times, sir," returned I, "to obey your Majesty's orders."

I sent my man express with the king's answer and the commission to my father, who had the regiment completed in less than two months' time, and six of the officers, with a list of the rest, came away to me, whom I presented to his Majesty when he lay before Nuremberg, where they kissed his hand.

One of the captains offered to bring the whole regiment travelling as private men into the army in six weeks' time, and either to transport their equipage, or buy it in Germany, but 'twas thought impracticable. However, I had so many come in that manner that I had a complete troop always about me, and obtained the king's order to muster them as a troop.

On the 8th of March the king decamped, and, marching up the river Maine, bent his course directly for Bavaria, taking several small places by the way, and expecting to engage with Tilly, who he thought would dispute his entrance into Bavaria, kept his army together; but Tilly, finding himself too weak to encounter him, turned away, and leaving Bavaria open to the king, marched into the Upper Palatinate. The king finding the country clear of the Imperialists comes to Nuremberg, made his entrance into that city the 21st of March, and being nobly treated by the citizens, he continued his march into Bavaria, and on the 26th sat down before Donauwerth. The town was taken the next day by storm, so swift were the conquests of this invincible captain. Sir John Hepburn, with the Scots and the English volunteers at the head of them, entered the town first, and cut all the garrison to pieces, except such as escaped over the bridge.

I had no share in the business of Donauwerth, being now among the horse, but I was posted on the roads with five troops of horse, where we picked up a great many stragglers of the garrison, whom we made prisoners of war.

'Tis observable that this town of Donauwerth is a very strong place and well fortified, and yet such expedition did the king make, and such resolution did he use in his first attacks, that he carried the town without putting himself to the trouble of formal approaches. 'Twas generally his way when he came before any town with a design to besiege it; he never would encamp at a distance and begin his trenches a great way off, but bring his men immediately within half musket-shot of the place; there getting under the best cover he could, he would immediately begin his batteries and trenches before their faces; and if there was any place possibly to be attacked, he would fall to storming immediately. By this resolute way of coming on he carried many a town in the first heat of his men, which would have held out many days against a more regular siege.

This march of the king broke all Tilly's measures, for now he was obliged to face about, and leaving the Upper Palatinate, to come to the assistance of the Duke of Bavaria; for the king being 20,000 strong, besides 10,000 foot and 4000 horse and dragoons which joined him from the Duringer Wald, was resolved to ruin the duke, who lay now open to him, and was the most powerful and inveterate enemy of the Protestants in the empire.

Tilly was now joined with the Duke of Bavaria, and might together make about 22,000 men, and in order to keep the Swedes out of the country of Bavaria, had planted themselves along the banks of the river Lech, which runs on the edge of the duke's territories; and having fortified the other side of the river, and planted his cannon for several miles at all the convenient places on the river, resolved to dispute the king's passage.

I shall be the longer in relating this account of the Lech, being esteemed in those days as great an action as any battle or siege of that age, and particularly famous for the disaster of the gallant old General Tilly; and for that I can be more particular in it than other accounts, having been an eye-witness to every part of it.

The king being truly informed of the disposition of the Bavarian army, was once of the mind to have left the banks of the Lech, have repassed the Danube, and so setting down before Ingolstadt, the duke's capital city, by the taking that strong town to have made his entrance into Bavaria, and the conquest of such a fortress, one entire action; but the strength of the place and the difficulty of maintaining his leaguer in an enemy's country while Tilly was so strong in the field, diverted him from that design; he therefore concluded that Tilly was first to be beaten out of the country, and then the siege of Ingolstadt would be the easier.

Whereupon the king resolved to go and view the situation of the enemy. His Majesty went out the 2nd of April with a strong party of horse, which I had the honour to command. We marched as near as we could to the banks of the river, not to be too much exposed to the enemy's cannon, and having gained a little height, where the whole course of the river might be seen, the king halted, and commanded to draw up. The king alighted, and calling me to him, examined every reach and turning of the river by his glass, but finding the river run a long and almost a straight course he could find no place which he liked; but at last turning himself north, and looking down the stream, he found the river, stretching a long reach, doubles short upon itself, making a round and very narrow point. "There's a point will do our business," says the king, "and if the ground be good I'll pass there, let Tilly do his worst."

He immediately ordered a small party of horse to view the ground, and to bring him word particularly how high the bank was on each side and at the point. "And he shall have fifty dollars," says the king, "that will bring me word how deep the water is." I asked his Majesty leave to let me go, which he would by no means allow of; but as the party was drawing out, a sergeant of dragoons told the king, if he pleased to let him go disguised as a boor, he would bring him an account of everything he desired. The king liked the notion well enough, and the fellow being very well acquainted with the country, puts on a ploughman's habit, and went away immediately with a long pole upon his shoulder. The horse lay all this while in the woods, and the king stood undiscerned by the enemy on the little hill aforesaid. The dragoon with his long pole comes down boldly to the bank of the river, and calling to the sentinels which Tilly had placed on the other bank, talked with them, asked them if they could not help him over the river, and pretended he wanted to come to them. At last being come to the point where, as I said, the river makes a short turn, he stands parleying with them a great while, and sometimes, pretending to wade over, he puts his long pole into the water, then finding it pretty shallow he pulls off his hose and goes in, still thrusting his pole in before him, till being gotten up to his middle, he could reach beyond him, where it was too deep, and so shaking his head, comes back again. The soldiers on the other side, laughing at him, asked him if he could swim? He said, "No," "Why, you fool you," says one of the sentinels, "the channel of the river is twenty feet deep." "How do you know that?" says the dragoon. "Why, our engineer," says he, "measured it yesterday." This was what he wanted, but not yet fully satisfied, "Ay, but," says he, "maybe it may not be very broad, and if one of you would wade in to meet me till I could reach you with my pole, I'd give him half a ducat to pull me over." The innocent way of his discourse so deluded the soldiers, that one of them immediately strips and goes in up to the shoulders, and our dragoon goes in on this side to meet him; but the stream took t' other soldier away, and he being a good swimmer, came swimming over to this side. The dragoon was then in a great deal of pain for fear of being discovered, and was once going to kill the fellow, and make off; but at last resolved to carry on the humour, and having entertained the fellow with a tale of a tub, about the Swedes stealing his oats, the fellow being a-cold wanted to be gone, and he as willing to be rid of him, pretended to be very sorry he could not get over the river, and so makes off.

By this, however, he learned both the depth and breadth of the channel, the bottom and nature of both shores, and everything the king wanted to know. We could see him from the hill by our glasses very plain, and could see the soldier naked with him. Says the king, "He will certainly be discovered and knocked on the head from the other side: he is a fool," says the king, "he does not kill the fellow and run off." But when the dragoon told his tale, the king was extremely well satisfied with him, gave him a hundred dollars, and made him a quartermaster to a troop of cuirassiers.

The king having farther examined the dragoon, he gave him a very distinct account of the shore and the ground on this side, which he found to be higher than the enemy's by ten or twelve foot, and a hard gravel.

Hereupon the king resolves to pass there, and in order to it gives, himself, particular directions for such a bridge as I believe never army passed a river on before nor since.

His bridge was only loose planks laid upon large tressels in the same homely manner as I have seen bricklayers raise a low scaffold to build a brick wall; the tressels were made higher than one another to answer to the river as it became deeper or shallower, and was all framed and fitted before any appearance was made of attempting to pass.

When all was ready the king brings his army down to the bank of the river, and plants his cannon as the enemy had done, some here and some there, to amuse them.

At night, April 4th, the king commanded about 2000 men to march to the point, and to throw up a trench on either side, and quite round it with a battery of six pieces of cannon at each end, besides three small mounts, one at the point and one of each side, which had each of them two pieces upon them. This work was begun so briskly and so well carried on, the king firing all the night from the other parts of the river, that by daylight all the batteries at the new work were mounted, the trench lined with 2000 musketeers, and all the utensils of the bridge lay ready to be put together.

Now the Imperialists discovered the design, but it was too late to hinder it; the musketeers in the great trench, and the five new batteries, made such continual fire that the other bank, which, as before, lay twelve feet below them, was too hot for the Imperialists; whereupon Tilly, to be provided for the king at his coming over, falls to work in a wood right against the point, and raises a great battery for twenty pieces of cannon, with a breastwork or line, as near the river as he could, to cover his men, thinking that when the king had built his bridge he might easily beat it down with his cannon.

But the king had doubly prevented him, first by laying his bridge so low that none of Tilly's shot could hurt it; for the bridge lay not above half a foot above the water's edge, by which means the king, who in that showed himself an excellent engineer, had secured it from any batteries to be made within the land, and the angle of the bank secured it from the remoter batteries on the other side, and the continual fire of the cannon and small shot beat the Imperialists from their station just against it, they having no works to cover them.

And in the second place, to secure his passage he sent over about 200 men, and after that 200 more, who had orders to cast up a large ravelin on the other bank, just where he designed to land his bridge. This was done with such expedition too, that it was finished before night, and in condition to receive all the shot of Tilly's great battery, and effectually covered his bridge. While this was doing the king on his side lays over his bridge. Both sides wrought hard all day and night, as if the spade, not the sword, had been to decide the controversy, and that he had got the victory whose trenches and batteries were first ready. In the meanwhile the cannon and musket bullets flew like hail, and made the service so hot that both sides had enough to do to make their men stand to their work. The king, in the hottest of it, animated his men by his presence, and Tilly, to give him his due, did the same; for the execution was so great, and so many officers killed, General Altringer wounded, and two sergeant-majors killed, that at last Tilly himself was obliged to expose himself, and to come up to the very face of our line to encourage his men, and give his necessary orders.

And here about one o'clock, much about the time that the king's brigade and works were finished, and just as they said he had ordered to fall on upon our ravelin with 3000 foot, was the brave old Tilly slain with a musket ball in the thigh. He was carried off to Ingolstadt, and lived some days after, but died of that wound the same day as the king had his horse shot under him at the siege of that town.

We made no question of passing the river here, having brought everything so forward, and with such extraordinary success; but we should have found it a very hot piece of work if Tilly had lived one day more, and, if I may give my opinion of it, having seen Tilly's battery and breastwork, in the face of which we must have passed the river, I must say that, whenever we had marched, if Tilly had fallen in with his horse and foot, placed in that trench, the whole army would have passed as much danger as in the face of a strong town in the storming a counterscarp. The king himself, when he saw with what judgment Tilly had prepared his works, and what danger he must have run, would often say that day's success was every way equal to the victory of Leipsic.

Tilly being hurt and carried off, as if the soul of the army had been lost, they began to draw off. The Duke of Bavaria took horse and rid away as if he had fled out of battle for his life.

The other generals, with a little more caution, as well as courage, drew off by degrees, sending their cannon and baggage away first, and leaving some to continue firing on the bank of the river, to conceal their retreat. The river preventing any intelligence, we knew nothing of the disaster befallen them; and the king, who looked for blows, having finished his bridge and ravelin, ordered to run a line with palisadoes to take in more ground on the bank of the river, to cover the first troops he should send over. This being finished the same night, the king sends over a party of his guards to relieve the men who were in the ravelin, and commanded 600 musketeers to man the new line out of the Scots brigade.

Early in the morning a small party of Scots, commanded by one Captain Forbes, of my Lord Reay's regiment, were sent out to learn something of the enemy, the king observing they had not fired all night; and while this party were abroad, the army stood in battalia; and my old friend Sir John Hepburn, whom of all men the king most depended upon for any desperate service, was ordered to pass the bridge with his brigade, and to draw up without the line, with command to advance as he found the horse, who were to second him, come over.

Sir John being passed without the trench, meets Captain Forbes with some prisoners, and the good news of the enemy's retreat. He sends him directly to the king, who was by this time at the head of his army, in full battalia, ready to follow his vanguard, expecting a hot day's work of it. Sir John sends messenger after messenger to the king, entreating him to give him orders to advance; but the king would not suffer him, for he was ever upon his guard, and would not venture a surprise; so the army continued on this side the Lech all day and the next night. In the morning the king sent for me, and ordered me to draw out 300 horse, and a colonel with 600 horse, and a colonel with 800 dragoons, and ordered us to enter the wood by three ways, but so as to be able to relieve one another; and then ordered Sir John Hepburn with his brigade to advance to the edge of the wood to secure our retreat, and at the same time commanded another brigade of foot to pass the bridge, if need were, to second Sir John Hepburn, so warily did this prudent general proceed.

We advanced with our horse into the Bavarian camp, which we found forsaken. The plunder of it was inconsiderable, for the exceeding caution the king had used gave them time to carry off all their baggage. We followed them three or four miles, and returned to our camp.

I confess I was most diverted that day with viewing the works which Tilly had cast up, and must own again that had he not been taken off we had met with as desperate a piece of work as ever was attempted. The next day the rest of the cavalry came up to us, commanded by Gustavus Horn, and the king and the whole army followed. We advanced through the heart of Bavaria, took Rain at the first summons, and several other small towns, and sat down before Augsburg.

Augsburg, though a Protestant city, had a Popish Bavarian garrison in it of above 5000 men, commanded by a Fugger, a great family in Bavaria. The governor had posted several little parties as out-scouts at the distance of two miles and a half or three miles from the town. The king, at his coming up to this town, sends me with my little troop and three companies of dragoons to beat in these out-scouts. The first party I lighted on was not above sixteen men, who had made a small barricado across the road, and stood resolutely upon their guard. I commanded the dragoons to alight and open the barricado, which, while they resolutely performed, the sixteen men gave them two volleys of their muskets, and through the enclosures made their retreat to a turnpike about a quarter of a mile farther. We passed their first traverse, and coming up to the turnpike, I found it defended by 200 musketeers. I prepared to attack them, sending word to the king how strong the enemy was, and desired some foot to be sent me. My dragoons fell on, and though the enemy made a very hot fire, had beat them from this post before 200 foot, which the king had sent me, had come up. Being joined with the foot, I followed the enemy, who retreated fighting, till they came under the cannon of a strong redoubt, where they drew up, and I could see another body of foot of about 300 join them out of the works; upon which I halted, and considering I was in view of the town, and a great way from the army, I faced about and began to march off. As we marched I found the enemy followed, but kept at a distance, as if they only designed to observe me. I had not marched far, but I heard a volley of small shot, answered by two or three more, which I presently apprehended to be at the turnpike, where I had left a small guard of twenty-six men with a lieutenant. Immediately I detached 100 dragoons to relieve my men and secure my retreat, following myself as fast as the foot could march. The lieutenant sent me back word the post was taken by the enemy, and my men cut off. Upon this I doubled my pace, and when I came up I found it as the lieutenant said; for the post was taken and manned with 300 musketeers and three troops of horse. By this time, also, I found the party in my rear made up towards me, so that I was like to be charged in a narrow place both in front and rear.

I saw there was no remedy but with all my force to fall upon that party before me, and so to break through before those from the town could come up with me; wherefore, commanding my dragoons to alight, I ordered them to fall on upon the foot. Their horse were drawn up in an enclosed field on one side of the road, a great ditch securing the other side, so that they thought if I charged the foot in front they would fall upon my flank, while those behind would charge my rear; and, indeed, had the other come in time, they had cut me off. My dragoons made three fair charges on their foot, but were received with so much resolution and so brisk a fire, that they were beaten off, and sixteen men killed. Seeing them so rudely handled, and the horse ready to fall in, I relieved them with 100 musketeers, and they renewed the attack; at the same time, with my troop of horse, flanked on both wings with fifty musketeers, I faced their horse, but did not offer to charge them. The case grew now desperate, and the enemy behind were just at my heels with near 600 men. The captain who commanded the musketeers who flanked my horse came up to me; says he, "If we do not force this pass all will be lost; if you will draw out your troop and twenty of my foot, and fall in, I'll engage to keep off the horse with the rest." "With all my heart," says I.

Immediately I wheeled off my troop, and a small party of the musketeers followed me, and fell in with the dragoons and foot, who, seeing the danger too as well as I, fought like madmen. The foot at the turnpike were not able to hinder our breaking through, so we made our way out, killing about 150 of them, and put the rest into confusion.

But now was I in as great a difficulty as before how to fetch off my brave captain of foot, for they charged home upon him. He defended himself with extraordinary gallantry, having the benefit of a piece of a hedge to cover him, but he lost half his men, and was just upon the point of being defeated when the king, informed by a soldier that escaped from the turnpike, one of twenty-six, had sent a party of 600 dragoons to bring me off; these came upon the spur, and joined with me just as I had broke through the turnpike. The enemy's foot rallied behind their horse, and by this time their other party was come in; but seeing our relief they drew off together.

I lost above 100 men in these skirmishes, and killed them about 180. We secured the turnpike, and placed a company of foot there with 100 dragoons, and came back well beaten to the army. The king, to prevent such uncertain skirmishes, advanced the next day in view of the town, and, according to his custom, sits down with his whole army within cannon-shot of their walls.

The King won this great city by force of words, for by two or three messages and letters to and from the citizens, the town was gained, the garrison not daring to defend them against their wills. His Majesty made his public entrance into the city on the 14th of April, and receiving the compliments of the citizens, advanced immediately to Ingolstadt, which is accounted, and really is, the strongest town in all these parts.

The town had a very strong garrison in it, and the Duke of Bavaria lay entrenched with his army under the walls of it, on the other side of the river. The king, who never loved long sieges, having viewed the town, and brought his army within musket-shot of it, called a council of war, where it was the king's opinion, in short, that the town would lose him more than 'twas worth, and therefore he resolved to raise his siege.

Here the king going to view the town had his horse shot with a cannon-bullet from the works, which tumbled the king and his horse over one another, that everybody thought he had been killed; but he received no hurt at all. That very minute, as near as could be learnt, General Tilly died in the town of the shot he received on the bank of the Lech, as aforesaid.

I was not in the camp when the king was hurt, for the king had sent almost all the horse and dragoons, under Gustavus Horn, to face the Duke of Bavaria's camp, and after that to plunder the country; which truly was a work the soldiers were very glad of, for it was very seldom they had that liberty given them, and they made very good use of it when it was, for the country of Bavaria was rich and plentiful, having seen no enemy before during the whole war.

The army having left the siege of Ingolstadt, proceeds to take in the rest of Bavaria. Sir John Hepburn, with three brigades of foot, and Gustavus Horn, with 3000 horse and dragoons, went to the Landshut, and took it the same day. The garrison was all horse, and gave us several camisadoes at our approach, in one of which I lost two of my troops, but when we had beat them into close quarters they presently capitulated. The general got a great sum of money of the town, besides a great many presents to the officers. And from thence the king went on to Munich, the Duke of Bavaria's court. Some of the general officers would fain have had the plundering of the duke's palace, but the king was too generous. The city paid him 400,000 dollars; and the duke's magazine was there seized, in which was 140 pieces of cannon, and small arms for above 20,000 men. The great chamber of the duke's rarities was preserved, by the king's special order, with a great deal of care. I expected to have stayed here some time, and to have taken a very exact account of this curious laboratory; but being commanded away, I had no time, and the fate of the war never gave me opportunity to see it again.

The Imperialists, under the command of Commissary Osta, had besieged Biberach, an Imperial city not very well fortified; and the inhabitants being under the Swedes' protection, defended themselves as well as they could, but were in great danger, and sent several expresses to the king for help.

The king immediately detaches a strong body of horse and foot to relieve Biberach, and would be the commander himself. I marched among the horse, but the Imperialists saved us the labour; for the news of the king's coming frighted away Osta, that he left Biberach, and hardly looked behind him till he got up to the Bodensee, on the confines of Switzerland.

At our return from this expedition the king had the first news of Wallenstein's approach, who, on the death of Count Tilly, being declared generalissimo of the emperor's forces, had played the tyrant in Bohemia, and was now advancing with 60,000 men, as they reported, to relieve the Duke of Bavaria.

The king, therefore, in order to be in a posture to receive this great general, resolves to quit Bavaria, and to expect him on the frontiers of Franconia. And because he knew the Nurembergers for their kindness to him would be the first sacrifice, he resolved to defend that city against him whatever it cost.

Nevertheless he did not leave Bavaria without a defence; but, on the one hand, he left Sir John Baner with 10,000 men about Augsburg, and the Duke of Saxe-Weimar with another like army about Ulm and Meningen, with orders so to direct their march as that they might join him upon any occasion in a few days.

We encamped about Nuremberg the middle of June. The army, after so many detachments, was not above 19,000 men. The Imperial army, joined with the Bavarian, were not so numerous as was reported, but were really 60,000 men. The king, not strong enough to fight, yet, as he used to say, was strong enough not to be forced to fight, formed his camp so under the cannon of Nuremberg that there was no besieging the town but they must besiege him too; and he fortified his camp in so formidable a manner that Wallenstein never durst attack him. On the 30th of June Wallenstein's troops appeared, and on the 5th of July encamped close by the king, and posted themselves not on the Bavarian side, but between the king and his own friends of Schwaben and Frankenland, in order to intercept his provisions, and, as they thought, to starve him out of his camp.

Here they lay to see, as it were, who could subsist longest. The king was strong in horse, for we had full 8000 horse and dragoons in the army, and this gave us great advantage in the several skirmishes we had with the enemy. The enemy had possession of the whole country, and had taken effectual care to furnish their army with provisions; they placed their guards in such excellent order, to secure their convoys, that their waggons went from stage to stage as quiet as in a time of peace, and were relieved every five miles by parties constantly posted on the road. And thus the Imperial general sat down by us, not doubting but he should force the king either to fight his way through on very disadvantageous terms, or to rise for want of provisions, and leave the city of Nuremberg a prey to his army; for he had vowed the destruction of the city, and to make it a second Magdeburg.

But the king, who was not to be easily deceived, had countermined all Wallenstein's designs. He had passed his honour to the Nurembergers that he would not leave them, and they had undertaken to victual his army, and secure him from want, which they did so effectually, that he had no occasion to expose his troops to any hazard or fatigues for convoys or forage on any account whatever.

The city of Nuremberg is a very rich and populous city, and the king being very sensible of their danger, had given his word for their defence. And when they, being terrified at the threats of the Imperialists, sent their deputies to beseech the king to take care of them, he sent them word he would, and be besieged with them. They, on the other hand, laid in such stores of all sorts of provision, both for men and horse, that had Wallenstein lain before it six months longer, there would have been no scarcity. Every private house was a magazine, the camp was plentifully supplied with all manner of provisions, and the market always full, and as cheap as in times of peace. The magistrates were so careful, and preserved so excellent an order in the disposal of all sorts of provision, that no engrossing of corn could be practised, for the prices were every day directed at the town-house; and if any man offered to demand more money for corn than the stated price, he could not sell, because at the town store-house you might buy cheaper. Here are two instances of good and bad conduct: the city of Magdeburg had been entreated by the king to settle funds, and raise money for their provision and security, and to have a sufficient garrison to defend them, but they made difficulties, either to raise men for themselves, or to admit the king's troops to assist them, for fear of the charge of maintaining them; and this was the cause of the city's ruin.

The city of Nuremberg opened their arms to receive the assistance proffered by the Swedes, and their purses to defend their town and common cause; and this was the saving them absolutely from destruction. The rich burghers and magistrates kept open houses, where the officers of the army were always welcome; and the council of the city took such care of the poor that there was no complaining nor disorders in the whole city. There is no doubt but it cost the city a great deal of money; but I never saw a public charge borne with so much cheerfulness, nor managed with so much prudence and conduct in my life. The city fed above 50,000 mouths every day, including their own poor, besides themselves; and yet when the king had lain thus three months, and finding his armies longer in coming up than he expected, asked the burgrave how their magazines held out, he answered, they desired his Majesty not to hasten things for them, for they could maintain themselves and him twelve months longer if there was occasion. This plenty kept both the army and city in good health, as well as in good heart; whereas nothing was to be had of us but blows, for we fetched nothing from without our works, nor had no business without the line but to interrupt the enemy.

The manner of the king's encampment deserves a particular chapter. He was a complete surveyor and a master in fortification, not to be outdone by anybody. He had posted his army in the suburbs of the town, and drawn lines round the whole circumference, so that he begirt the whole city with his army. His works were large, the ditch deep, flanked with innumerable bastions, ravelins, horn-works, forts, redoubts, batteries, and palisadoes, the incessant work of 8000 men for about fourteen days; besides that, the king was adding something or other to it every day, and the very posture of his camp was enough to tell a bigger army than Wallenstein's that he was not to be assaulted in his trenches.

The king's design appeared chiefly to be the preservation of the city; but that was not all. He had three armies acting abroad in three several places. Gustavus Horn was on the Moselle, the chancellor Oxenstiern about Mentz, Cologne, and the Rhine, Duke William and

Duke Bernhard, together with General Baner, in Bavaria. And though he designed they should all join him, and had wrote to them all to that purpose, yet he did not hasten them, knowing that while he kept the main army at bay about Nuremberg, they would, without opposition, reduce those several countries they were acting in to his power. This occasioned his lying longer in the camp at Nuremberg than he would have done, and this occasioned his giving the Imperialists so many alarms by his strong parties of horse, of which he was well provided, that they might not be able to make any considerable detachments for the relief of their friends. And here he showed his mastership in the war, for by this means his conquests went on as effectually as if he had been abroad himself.

In the meantime it was not to be expected two such armies should lie long so near without some action. The Imperial army, being masters of the field, laid the country for twenty miles round Nuremberg in a manner desolate. What the inhabitants could carry away had been before secured in such strong towns as had garrisons to protect them, and what was left the hungry Crabats devoured or set on fire; but sometimes they were met with by our men, who often paid them home for it. There had passed several small rencounters between our parties and theirs; and as it falls out in such cases, sometimes one side, sometimes the other, got the better. But I have observed there never was any party sent out by the king's special appointment but always came home with victory.

The first considerable attempt, as I remember, was made on a convoy of ammunition. The party sent out was commanded by a Saxon colonel, and consisted of 1000 horse and 500 dragoons, who burnt above 600 waggons loaded with ammunition and stores for the army, besides taking about 2000 muskets, which they brought back to the army.

The latter end of July the king received advice that the Imperialists had formed a magazine for provision at a town called Freynstat, twenty miles from Nuremberg. Hither all the booty and contributions raised in the Upper Palatinate, and parts adjacent, was brought and laid up as in a place of security, a garrison of 600 men being placed to defend it; and when a quantity of provisions was got together, convoys were appointed to fetch it off.

The king was resolved, if possible, to take or destroy this magazine; and sending for Colonel Dubalt, a Swede, and a man of extraordinary conduct, he tells him his design, and withal that he must be the man to put it in execution, and ordered him to take what forces he thought convenient. The colonel, who knew the town very well, and the country about it, told his Majesty he would attempt it with all his heart; but he was afraid 'twould require some foot to make the attack. "But we can't stay for that," says the king; "you must then take some dragoons with you;" and immediately the king called for me. I was just coming up the stairs as the king's page was come out to inquire for me, so I went immediately in to the king. "Here is a piece of hot work for you," says the king, "Dubalt will tell it you; go together and contrive it."

We immediately withdrew, and the colonel told me the design, and what the king and he had discoursed; that, in his opinion, foot would be wanted: but the king had declared there was no time for the foot to march, and had proposed dragoons. I told him, I thought dragoons might do as well; so we agreed to take 1600 horse and 400 dragoons. The king, impatient in his design, came into the room to us to know what we had resolved on, approved our measures, gave us orders immediately; and, turning to me, "You shall command the dragoons," says the king, "but Dubalt must be general in this case, for he knows the country." "Your Majesty," said I, "shall be always served by me in any figure you please." The king wished us good speed, and hurried us away the same afternoon, in order to come to the place in time. We marched slowly on because of the carriages we had with us, and came to Freynstat about one o'clock in the night perfectly undiscovered. The guards were so negligent, that we came to the very port before they had notice of us, and a sergeant with twelve dragoons thrust in upon the out-sentinels, and killed them without noise.

Immediately ladders were placed to the half-moon which defended the gate, which the dragoons mounted and carried in a trice, about twenty-eight men being cut in pieces within. As soon as the ravelin was taken, they burst open the gate, at which I entered at the head of 200 dragoons, and seized the drawbridge. By this time the town was in alarm, and the drums beat to arms, but it was too late, for by the help of a petard we broke open the gate, and entered the town. The garrison made an obstinate fight for about half-an-hour, but our men being all in, and three troops of horse dismounted coming to our assistance with their carabines, the town was entirely mastered by three of the clock, and guards set to prevent anybody running to give notice to the enemy. There were about 200 of the garrison killed, and the rest taken prisoners. The town being thus secured, the gates were opened, and Colonel Dubalt came in with the horse.

The guards being set, we entered the magazine, where we found an incredible quantity of all sorts of provision. There was 150 tons of bread, 8000 sacks of meal, 4000 sacks of oats, and of other provisions in proportion. We caused as much of it as could be loaded to be brought away in such waggons and carriages as we found, and set the rest on fire, town and all. We stayed by it till we saw it past a possibility of being saved, and then drew off with 800 waggons, which we found in the place, most of which we loaded with bread, meal, and oats. While we were doing this we sent a party of dragoons into the fields, who met us again as we came out, with above 1000 head of black cattle, besides sheep.

Our next care was to bring this booty home without meeting with the enemy, to secure which, the colonel immediately despatched an express to the king, to let him know of our success, and to desire a detachment might be made to secure our retreat, being charged with so much plunder.

And it was no more than need; for though we had used all the diligence possible to prevent any notice, yet somebody, more forward than ordinary, had escaped away, and carried news of it to the Imperial army. The general, upon this bad news, detaches Major-General Sparr with a body of 6000 men to cut off our retreat. The king, who had notice of this detachment, marches out in person with 3000 men to wait upon General Sparr. All this was the account of one day. The king met General Sparr at the moment when his troops were divided, fell upon them, routed one part of them, and the rest in a few hours after, killed them 1000 men, and took the general prisoner.

In the interval of this action we came safe to the camp with our booty, which was very considerable, and would have supplied our whole army for a month. Thus we feasted at the enemy's cost, and beat them into the bargain.

The king gave all the live cattle to the Nurembergers, who, though they had really no want of provisions, yet fresh meat was not so plentiful as such provisions which were stored up in vessels and laid by.

After this skirmish we had the country more at command than before, and daily fetched in fresh provisions and forage in the fields.

The two armies had now lain a long time in sight of one another, and daily skirmishes had considerably weakened them; and the king, beginning to be impatient, hastened the advancement of his friends to join him, in which also they were not backward; but having drawn together their forces from several parts, and all joined the chancellor Oxenstiern, news came, the 15th of August, that they were in full march to join us; and being come to a small town called Brock, the king went out of the camp with about 1000 horse to view them. I went along with the horse, and the 21st of August saw the review of all the armies together, which were 30,000 men, in extraordinary equipage, old soldiers, and commanded by officers of the greatest conduct and experience in the world. There was the rich chancellor of Sweden, who commanded as general; Gustavus Horn and John Baner, both Swedes and old generals; Duke William and Duke Bernhard of Weimar; the Landgrave of Hesse-Cassel, the Palatine of Birkenfelt, and abundance of princes and lords of the empire.

The armies being joined, the king, who was now a match for Wallenstein, quits his camp and draws up in battalia before the Imperial trenches: but the scene was changed. Wallenstein was no more able to fight now than the king was before; but, keeping within his trenches, stood upon his guard. The king coming up close to his works, plants batteries, and cannonaded him in his very camp. The Imperialists, finding the king press upon them, retreat into a woody country about three leagues, and, taking possession of an old ruined castle, posted their army behind it.

This old castle they fortified, and placed a very strong guard there. The king, having viewed the place, though it was a very strong post, resolved to attack it with the whole right wing. The attack was made with a great deal of order and resolution, the king leading the first party on with sword in hand, and the fight was maintained on both sides with the utmost gallantry and obstinacy all the day and the next night too, for the cannon and musket never gave over till the morning; but the Imperialists having the advantage of the hill, of their works and batteries, and being continually relieved, and the Swedes naked, without cannon or works, the post was maintained, and the king, finding it would cost him too much blood, drew off in the morning.

This was the famous fight at Altemberg, where the Imperialists boasted to have shown the world the King of Sweden was not invincible. They call it the victory at Altemberg; 'tis true the king failed in his attempt of carrying their works, but there was so little of a victory in it, that the Imperial general thought fit not to venture a second brush, but to draw off their army as soon as they could to a safer quarter.

I had no share in this attack, very few of the horse being in the action, but my comrade, who was always among the Scots volunteers, was wounded and taken prisoner by the enemy. They used him very civilly, and the king and Wallenstein straining courtesies with one another, the king released Major-General Sparr without ransom, and the Imperial general sent home Colonel Tortenson, a Swede, and sixteen volunteer gentlemen, who were taken in the heat of the action, among whom my captain was one.

The king lay fourteen days facing the Imperial army, and using all the stratagems possible to bring them to a battle, but to no purpose, during which time we had parties continually out, and very often skirmishes with the enemy.

I had a command of one of these parties in an adventure, wherein I got no booty, nor much honour. The King had received advice of a convoy of provisions which was to come to the enemy's camp from the Upper Palatinate, and having a great mind to surprise them, he commanded us to waylay them with 1200 horse, and 800 dragoons. I had exact directions given me of the way they were to come, and posting my horse in a village a little out of the road, I lay with my dragoons in a wood, by which they were to pass by break of day. The enemy appeared with their convoy, and being very wary, their out-scouts discovered us in the wood, and fired upon the sentinel I had posted in a tree at the entrance of the wood. Finding myself discovered, I would have retreated to the village where my horse were posted, but in a moment the wood was skirted with the enemy's horse, and 1000 commanded musketeers advanced to beat me out. In this pickle I sent away three messengers one after another for the horse, who were within two miles of me, to advance to my relief; but all my messengers fell into the enemy's hands. Four hundred of my dragoons on foot, whom I had placed at a little distance before me, stood to their work, and beat off two charges of the enemy's foot with some loss on both sides. Meantime 200 of my men faced about, and rushing out of the wood, broke through a party of the enemy's horse, who stood to watch our coming out. I confess I was exceedingly surprised at it, thinking those fellows had done it to make their escape, or else were gone over to the enemy; and my men were so discouraged at it, that they began to look about which way to run to save themselves, and were just upon the point of disbanding to shift for themselves, when one of the captains called to me aloud to beat a parley and treat. I made no answer, but, as if I had not heard him, immediately gave the word for all the captains

317

to come together. The consultation was but short, for the musketeers were advancing to a third charge, with numbers which we were not likely to deal with. In short, we resolved to beat a parley, and demand quarter, for that was all we could expect, when on a sudden the body of horse I had posted in the village, being directed by the noise, had advanced to relieve me, if they saw occasion, and had met the 200 dragoons, who guided them directly to the spot where they had broke through, and altogether fell upon the horse of the enemy, who were posted on that side, and, mastering them before they could be relieved, cut them all to pieces and brought me off. Under the shelter of this party, we made good our retreat to the village, but we lost above 300 men, and were glad to make off from the village too, for the enemy were very much too strong for us.

Returning thence towards the camp, we fell foul with 200 Crabats, who had been upon the plundering account. We made ourselves some amends upon them for our former loss, for we showed them no mercy; but our misfortunes were not ended, for we had but just despatched those Crabats when we fell in with 3000 Imperial horse, who, on the expectation of the aforesaid convoy, were sent out to secure them. All I could do could not persuade my men to stand their ground against this party; so that finding they would run away in confusion, I agreed to make off, and facing to the right, we went over a large common a full trot, till at last fear, which always increases in a flight, brought us to a plain flight, the enemy at our heels. I must confess I was never so mortified in my life; 'twas to no purpose to turn head, no man would stand by us; we run for life, and a great many we left by the way who were either wounded by the enemy's shot, or else could not keep race with us.

At last, having got over the common, which was near two miles, we came to a lane; one of our captains, a Saxon by country, and a gentleman of a good fortune, alighted at the entrance of the lane, and with a bold heart faced about, shot his own horse, and called his men to stand by him and defend the lane. Some of his men halted, and we rallied about 600 men, which we posted as well as we could, to defend the pass; but the enemy charged us with great fury. The Saxon gentleman, after defending himself with exceeding gallantry, and refusing quarter, was killed upon the spot. A German dragoon, as I thought him, gave me a rude blow with the stock of his piece on the side of my head, and was just going to repeat it, when one of my men shot him dead. I was so stunned with the blow, that I knew nothing;

but recovering, I found myself in the hands of two of the enemy's officers, who offered me quarter, which I accepted; and indeed, to give them their due, they used me very civilly. Thus this whole party was defeated, and not above 500 men got safe to the army; nor had half the number escaped, had not the Saxon captain made so bold a stand at the head of the lane.

Several other parties of the king's army revenged our quarrel, and paid them home for it; but I had a particular loss in this defeat, that I never saw the king after; for though his Majesty sent a trumpet to reclaim us as prisoners the very next day, yet I was not delivered, some scruple happening about exchanging, till after the battle of Lützen, where that gallant prince lost his life.

The Imperial army rose from their camp about eight or ten days after the king had removed, and I was carried prisoner in the army till they sat down to the siege of Coburg Castle, and then was left with other prisoners of war, in the custody of Colonel Spezuter, in a small castle near the camp called Neustadt. Here we continued indifferent well treated, but could learn nothing of what action the armies were upon, till the Duke of Friedland, having been beaten off from the castle of Coburg, marched into Saxony, and the prisoners were sent for into the camp, as was said, in order to be exchanged.

I came into the Imperial leaguer at the siege of Leipsic, and within three days after my coming, the city was surrendered, and I got liberty to lodge at my old quarters in the town upon my parole.

The King of Sweden was at the heels of the Imperialists, for finding Wallenstein resolved to ruin the Elector of Saxony, the king had re-collected as much of his divided army as he could, and came upon him just as he was going to besiege Torgau.

As it is not my design to write a history of any more of these wars than I was actually concerned in, so I shall only note that, upon the king's approach, Wallenstein halted, and likewise called all his troops together, for he apprehended the king would fall on him, and we that were prisoners fancied the Imperial soldiers went unwillingly out, for the very name of the King of Sweden was become terrible to them. In short, they drew all the soldiers of the garrison they could spare out of Leipsic; sent for Pappenheim again, who was gone but three days before with 6000 men on a private expedition. On the 16th of November, the armies met on the plains of Lützen; a long and bloody battle was fought, the Imperialists were entirely routed and beaten, 12,000 slain upon the spot, their cannon, baggage, and 2000 prisoners taken, but the

King of Sweden lost his life, being killed at the head of his troops in the beginning of the fight.

It is impossible to describe the consternation the death of this conquering king struck into all the princes of Germany; the grief for him exceeded all manner of human sorrow. All people looked upon themselves as ruined and swallowed up; the inhabitants of two-thirds of all Germany put themselves into mourning for him; when the ministers mentioned him in their sermons or prayers, whole congregations would burst out into tears. The Elector of Saxony was utterly inconsolable, and would for several days walk about his palace like a distracted man, crying the saviour of Germany was lost, the refuge of abused princes was gone, the soul of the war was dead; and from that hour was so hopeless of out-living the war, that he sought to make peace with the emperor.

Three days after this mournful victory, the Saxons recovered the town of Leipsic by stratagem. The Duke of Saxony's forces lay at Torgau, and perceiving the confusion the Imperialists were in at the news of the overthrow of their army, they resolved to attempt the recovery of the town. They sent about twenty scattering troopers, who, pretending themselves to be Imperialists fled from the battle, were let in one by one, and still as they came in, they stayed at the court of guard in the port, entertaining the soldiers with discourse about the fight, and how they escaped, and the like, till the whole number being got in, at a watchword they fell on the guard, and cut them all in pieces; and immediately opening the gate to three troops of Saxon horse, the town was taken in a moment.

It was a welcome surprise to me, for I was at liberty of course; and the war being now on another foot, as I thought, and the king dead, I resolved to quit the service.

I had sent my man, as I have already noted, into England, in order to bring over the troops my father had raised for the King of Sweden. He executed his commission so well, that he landed with five troops at Embden in very good condition; and orders were sent them by the king, to join the Duke of Lunenberg's army, which they did at the siege of Boxtude, in the Lower Saxony. Here by long and very sharp service they were most of them cut off, and though they were several times recruited, yet I understood there were not three full troops left.

The Duke of Saxe-Weimar, a gentleman of great courage, had the command of the army after the king's death, and managed it with so much prudence, that all things were in as much order as could be expected, after so great a loss; for the Imperialists were everywhere beaten, and Wallenstein never made any advantage of the king's death.

I waited on him at Heilbronn, whither he was gone to meet the great chancellor of Sweden, where I paid him my respects, and desired he would bestow the remainder of my regiment on my comrade the captain, which he did with all the civility and readiness imaginable. So I took my leave of him, and prepared to come for England.

I shall only note this, that at this Diet, the Protestant princes of the empire renewed their league with one another, and with the crown of Sweden, and came to several regulations and conclusions for the carrying on the war, which they afterwards prosecuted, under the direction of the said chancellor of Sweden. But it was not the work of a small difficulty nor of a short time. And having been persuaded to continue almost two years afterwards at Frankfort, Heilbronn, and there-about, by the particular friendship of that noble wise man, and extraordinary statesman, Axeli Oxenstiern, chancellor of Sweden, I had opportunity to be concerned in, and present at, several treaties of extraordinary consequence, sufficient for a history, if that were my design.

Particularly I had the happiness to be present at, and have some concern in, the treaty for the restoring the posterity of the truly noble Palsgrave, King of Bohemia. King James of England had indeed too much neglected the whole family; and I may say with authority enough, from my own knowledge of affairs, had nothing been done for them but what was from England, that family had remained desolate and forsaken to this day.

But that glorious king, whom I can never mention without some remark of his extraordinary merit, had left particular instructions with his chancellor to rescue the Palatinate to its rightful lord, as a proof of his design to restore the liberty of Germany, and reinstate the oppressed princes who were subjected to the tyranny of the house of Austria.

Pursuant to this resolution, the chancellor proceeded very much like a man of honour; and though the King of Bohemia was dead a little before, yet he carefully managed the treaty, answered the objections of several princes, who, in the general ruin of the family, had reaped private advantages, settled the capitulations for the quota of contributions very much for their advantage, and fully reinstalled the Prince Charles in the possession of all his dominions in the Lower Palatinate, which afterwards was confirmed to him and his posterity by the peace of Westphalia, where all these bloody wars were finished in a peace, which has since been the foundation of the Protestants' liberty, and the best security of the whole empire.

I spent two years rather in wandering up and down than travelling; for though I had no mind to serve, yet I could not find in my heart to leave Germany; and I had obtained some so very close intimacies with the general officers that I was often in the army, and sometimes they did me the honour to bring me into their councils of war.

Particularly, at that eminent council before the battle of Nördlingen, I was invited to the council of war, both by Duke Bernhard of Weimar and by Gustavus Horn. They were generals of equal worth, and their courage and experience had been so well, and so often tried, that more than ordinary regard was always given to what they said. Duke Bernhard was indeed the younger man, and Gustavus had served longer under our great schoolmaster the king; but it was hard to judge which was the better general, since both had experience enough, and shown undeniable proofs both of their bravery and conduct.

I am obliged, in the course of my relation, so often to mention the great respect I often received from these great men, that it makes me sometimes jealous, lest the reader may think I affect it as a vanity. The truth is, that I am ready to confess, the honours I received, upon all occasions, from persons of such worth, and who had such an eminent share in the greatest action of that age, very much pleased me, and particularly, as they gave me occasions to see everything that was doing on the whole stage of the war. For being under no command, but at liberty to rove about, I could come to no Swedish garrison or party, but, sending my name to the commanding officer, I could have the word sent me; and if I came into the army, I was often treated as I was now at this famous battle of Nördlingen.

But I cannot but say, that I always looked upon this particular respect to be the effect of more than ordinary regard the great king of Sweden always showed me, rather than any merit of my own; and the veneration they all had for his memory, made them continue to show me all the marks of a suitable esteem.

But to return to the council of war, the great and, indeed, the only question before us was, Shall we give battle to the Imperialists, or not? Gustavus Horn was against it, and gave, as I thought, the most invincible arguments against a battle that reason could imagine.

First, they were weaker than the enemy by above 5000 men.

Secondly, the Cardinal-Infant of Spain, who was in the Imperial army with 8000 men, was but there *en passant*, being going from Italy to Flanders, to take upon him the government of the Low Countries; and if he saw no prospect of immediate action, would be gone in a few days.

Thirdly, they had two reinforcements, one of 5000 men, under the command of Colonel Cratz, and one of 7000 men, under the Rhinegrave, who were just at hand—the last within three days' march of them: and,

Lastly, they had already saved their honour; in that they had put 600 foot into the town of Nördlingen, in the face of the enemy's army, and consequently the town might hold out some days the longer.

Fate, rather than reason, certainly blinded the rest of the generals against such arguments as these. Duke Bernhard and almost all the generals were for fighting, alleging the affront it would be to the Swedish reputation to see their friends in the town lost before their faces.

Gustavus Horn stood stiff to his cautious advice, and was against it, and I thought the Baron D'Offkirk treated him a little indecently; for, being very warm in the matter, he told them, that if Gustavus Adolphus had been governed by such cowardly counsel, he had never been conqueror of half Germany in two years. "No," replied old General Horn, very smartly, "but he had been now alive to have testified for me, that I was never taken by him for a coward: and yet," says he, "the king was never for a victory with a hazard, when he could have it without."

I was asked my opinion, which I would have declined, being in no commission; but they pressed me to speak. I told them I was for staying at least till the Rhinegrave came up, who, at least, might, if expresses were sent to hasten him, be up with us in twenty four hours. But Offkirk could not hold his passion, and had not he been overruled he would have almost quarrelled with Marshal Horn. Upon which the old general, not to foment him, with a great deal of mildness stood up, and spoke thus—

"Come, Offkirk," says he, "I'll submit my opinion to you, and the majority of our fellow-soldiers. We will fight, but, upon my word, we shall have our hands full."

The resolution thus taken, they attacked the Imperial army. I must confess the counsels of this day seemed as confused as the resolutions of the night.

Duke Bernhard was to lead the van of the left wing, and to post himself upon a hill which was on the enemy's right without their entrenchments, so that, having secured that post, they might level their cannon upon the foot, who stood behind the lines, and relieved the town at pleasure. He marched accordingly by break of day, and falling with great fury upon eight regiments of foot, which were posted at the foot of the hill, he presently routed them, and made himself master of the post. Flushed with this success, he never regards his own concerted measures of stopping there and possessing what he had got, but pushes on and falls in with the main body of the enemy's army.

While this was doing, Gustavus Horn attacks another post on the hill, where the Spaniards had posted and lodged themselves behind some works they had cast up on the side of the hill. Here they defended themselves with extreme obstinacy for five hours, and at last obliged the Swedes to give it over with loss. This extraordinary gallantry of the Spaniards was the saving of the Imperial army; for Duke Bernhard having all this while resisted the frequent charges of the Imperialists, and borne the weight of two-thirds of their army, was not able to stand any longer, but sending one messenger on the neck of another to Gustavus Horn for more foot, he, finding he could not carry his point, had given it over, and was in full march to second the duke. But now it was too late, for the King of Hungary seeing the duke's men, as it were, wavering, and having notice of Horn's wheeling about to second him, falls in with all his force upon his flank, and with his Hungarian hussars, made such a furious charge, that the Swedes could stand no longer.

The rout of the left wing was so much the more unhappy, as it happened just upon Gustavus Horn's coming up; for, being pushed on with the enemies at their heels, they were driven upon their own friends, who, having no ground to open and give them way, were trodden down by their own runaway brethren. This brought all into the utmost confusion. The Imperialists cried "Victoria!" and fell into the middle of the infantry with a terrible slaughter.

I have always observed, 'tis fatal to upbraid an old experienced officer with want of courage. If Gustavus Horn had not been whetted with the reproaches of the Baron D'Offkirk, and some of the other general officers, I believe it had saved the lives of a thousand men; for when all was thus lost, several officers advised him to make a retreat with such regiments as he had yet unbroken; but nothing could persuade him to stir a foot. But turning his flank into a front, he saluted the enemy, as they passed by him in pursuit of the rest, with such terrible volleys of small shot, as cost them the lives of abundance of their men.

The Imperialists, eager in the pursuit, left him unbroken, till the Spanish brigade came up and charged him. These he bravely repulsed with a great slaughter, and after them a body of dragoons; till being laid at on every side, and most of his men killed, the brave old general, with all the rest who were left, were made prisoners.

The Swedes had a terrible loss here, for almost all their infantry were killed or taken prisoners. Gustavus Horn refused quarter several times; and still those that attacked him were cut down by his men, who fought like furies, and by the example of their general, behaved themselves like lions. But at last, these poor remains of a body of the bravest men in the world were forced to submit. I have heard him say, he had much rather have died than been taken, but that he yielded in compassion to so many brave men as were about him; for none of them would take quarter till he gave his consent.

I had the worst share in this battle that ever I had in any action of my life; and that was to be posted among as brave a body of horse as any in Germany, and yet not be able to succour our own men; but our foot were cut in pieces (as it were) before our faces, and the situation of the ground was such as we could not fall in. All that we were able to do, was to carry off about 2000 of the foot, who, running away in the rout of the left wing, rallied among our squadrons, and got away with us. Thus we stood till we saw all was lost, and then made the best retreat we could to save ourselves, several regiments having never charged, nor fired a shot; for the foot had so embarrassed themselves among the lines and works of the enemy, and in the vineyards and mountains, that the horse were rendered absolutely unserviceable.

The Rhinegrave had made such expedition to join us, that he reached within three miles of the place of action that night, and he was a great safeguard for us in rallying our dispersed men, who else had fallen into the enemy's hands, and in checking the pursuit of the enemy.

And indeed, had but any considerable body of the foot made an orderly retreat, it had been very probable they had given the enemy a brush that would have turned the scale of victory; for our horse being whole, and in a manner untouched, the enemy found such a check in the pursuit, that 1600 of their forwardest men following too eagerly, fell in with the Rhinegrave's advanced troops the next day, and were cut in pieces without mercy.

This gave us some satisfaction for the loss, but it was but small compared to the ruin of that day. We lost near 8000 men upon the spot, and above 3000 prisoners, all our cannon and baggage, and 120 colours. I thought I never made so indifferent a figure in my life, and so we thought all; to come away, lose our infantry, our general, and our honour, and never fight for it. Duke Bernhard was utterly disconsolate for old Gustavus Horn, for he concluded him killed; he tore the hair from his head like a madman, and telling the Rhinegrave the story of the council of war, would reproach himself with not taking his advice, often repeating it in his passion. "Tis I," said he, "have been the death of the bravest general in Germany;" would call himself fool and boy, and such names, for not listening to the reasons of an old experienced soldier. But when he heard he was alive in the enemy's hands he was the easier, and applied himself to the recruiting his troops, and the like business of the war; and it was not long before he paid the Imperialists with interest.

I returned to Frankfort-au-Main after this action, which happened the 17th of August 1634; but the progress of the Imperialists was so great that there was no staying at Frankfort. The chancellor Oxenstiern removed to Magdeburg, Duke Bernhard and the Landgrave marched into Alsatia, and the Imperialists carried all before them for all the rest of the campaign. They took Philipsburg by surprise; they took Augsburg by famine, Spire and Treves by sieges, taking the Elector prisoner. But this success did one piece of service to the Swedes, that it brought the French into the war on their side, for the Elector of Treves was their confederate. The French gave the conduct of the war to Duke Bernhard. This, though the Duke of Saxony fell off, and fought against them, turned the scale so much in their favour, that they recovered their losses, and proved a terror to all Germany. The farther accounts of the war I refer to the histories of those times, which I have since read with a great deal of delight.

I confess when I saw the progress of the Imperial army, after the battle of Nördlingen, and the Duke of Saxony turning his arms against them, I thought their affairs declining; and, giving them over for lost, I left Frankfort, and came down the Rhine to Cologne, and from thence into Holland.

I came to the Hague the 8th of March 1635, having spent three years and a half in Germany, and the greatest part of it in the Swedish army.

I spent some time in Holland viewing the wonderful power of art, which I observed in the fortifications of their towns, where the very bastions stand on bottomless morasses, and yet are as firm as any in the world. There I had the opportunity of seeing the Dutch army, and their famous general, Prince Maurice. 'Tis true, the men behaved themselves well enough in action, when they were put to it, but the prince's way of beating his enemies without fighting, was so unlike the gallantry of my royal instructor, that it had no manner of relish with me. Our way in Germany was always to seek out the enemy and fight him; and, give the Imperialists their due, they were seldom hard to be found, but were as free of their flesh as we were. Whereas Prince Maurice would lie in a camp till he starved half his men, if by lying there he could but starve two-thirds of his enemies; so that indeed the war in Holland had more of fatigues and hardships in it, and ours had more of fighting and blows. Hasty marches, long and unwholesome encampments, winter parties, counter-marching, dodging and entrenching, were the exercises of his men, and oftentimes killed him more men with hunger, cold and diseases, than he could do with fighting. Not that it required less courage, but rather more, for a soldier had at any time rather die in the field *a la coup de mousquet*, than be starved with hunger, or frozen to death in the trenches.

Nor do I think I lessen the reputation of that great general; for 'tis most certain he ruined the Spaniard more by spinning the war thus out in length, than he could possibly have done by a swift conquest. For had he, Gustavus-like, with a torrent of victory dislodged the Spaniard of all the twelve provinces in five years, whereas he was forty years a-beating them out of seven, he had left them rich and strong at home, and able to keep them in constant apprehensions of a return of his power. Whereas, by the long continuance of the war, he so broke the very heart of the Spanish monarchy, so absolutely and irrecoverably impoverished them, that they have ever since languished of the disease, till they are fallen from the most powerful, to be the most despicable nation in the world.

The prodigious charge the King of Spain was at in losing the seven provinces, broke the very spirit of the nation; and that so much, that all the wealth of their Peruvian mountains have not been able to retrieve it; King Philip having often declared that war, besides his Armada for invading England, had cost him 370,000,000 of ducats, and 4,000,000 of the best soldiers in Europe; whereof, by an unreasonable Spanish obstinacy, above 60,000 lost their lives before

Ostend, a town not worth a sixth part either of the blood or money it cost in a siege of three years; and which at last he had never taken, but that Prince Maurice thought it not worth the charge of defending it any longer.

However, I say, their way of fighting in Holland did not relish with me at all. The prince lay a long time before a little fort called Schenkenschanz, which the Spaniard took by surprise, and I thought he might have taken it much sooner. Perhaps it might be my mistake, but I fancied my hero, the King of Sweden, would have carried it sword in hand, in half the time.

However it was, I did not like it; so in the latter end of the year I came to the Hague, and took shipping for England, where I arrived, to the great satisfaction of my father and all my friends.

My father was then in London, and carried me to kiss the king's hand. His Majesty was pleased to receive me very well, and to say a great many very obliging things to my father upon my account.

I spent my time very retired from court, for I was almost wholly in the country; and it being so much different from my genius, which hankered after a warmer sport than hunting among our Welsh mountains, I could not but be peeping in all the foreign accounts from Germany, to see who and who was together. There I could never hear of a battle, and the Germans being beaten, but I began to wish myself there. But when an account came of the progress of John Baner, the Swedish general in Saxony, and of the constant victories he had there over the Saxons, I could no longer contain myself, but told my father this life was very disagreeable to me; that I lost my time here, and might to much more advantage go into Germany, where I was sure I might make my fortune upon my own terms; that, as young as I was, I might have been a general officer by this time, if I had not laid down my commission; that General Baner, or the Marshal Horn, had either of them so much respect for me, that I was sure I might have anything of them; and that if he pleased to give me leave, I would go for Germany again. My father was very unwilling to let me go, but seeing me uneasy, told me that, if I was resolved, he would oblige me to stay no longer in England than the next spring, and I should have his consent.

The winter following began to look very unpleasant upon us in England, and my father used often to sigh at it; and would tell me sometimes he was afraid we should have no need to send Englishmen to fight in Germany.

The cloud that seemed to threaten most was from Scotland. My father, who had made himself master of the arguments on both sides, used to be often saying he feared there was some about the king who exasperated him too much against the Scots, and drove things too high. For my part, I confess I did not much trouble my head with the cause; but all my fear was they would not fall out, and we should have no fighting. I have often reflected since, that I ought to have known better, that had seen how the most flourishing provinces of Germany were reduced to the most miserable condition that ever any country in the world was, by the ravagings of soldiers, and the calamities of war.

How much soever I was to blame, yet so it was, I had a secret joy at the news of the king's raising an army, and nothing could have withheld me from appearing in it; but my eagerness was anticipated by an express the king sent to my father, to know if his son was in England; and my father having ordered me to carry the answer myself, I waited upon his Majesty with the messenger. The king received me with his usual kindness, and asked me if I was willing to serve him against the Scots?

I answered, I was ready to serve him against any that his Majesty thought fit to account his enemies, and should count it an honour to receive his commands. Hereupon his Majesty offered me a commission. I told him, I supposed there would not be much time for raising of men; that if his Majesty pleased I would be at the rendezvous with as many gentlemen as I could get together, to serve his Majesty as volunteers.

The truth is, I found all the regiments of horse the king designed to raise were but two as regiments; the rest of the horse were such as the nobility raised in their several countries, and commanded them themselves; and, as I had commanded a regiment of horse abroad, it looked a little odd to serve with a single troop at home; and the king took the thing presently. "Indeed 'twill be a volunteer war," said the king, "for the Northern gentry have sent me an account of above 4000 horse they have already." I bowed, and told his Majesty I was glad to hear his subjects were forward to serve him. So taking his Majesty's orders to be at York by the end of March, I returned to my father.

My father was very glad I had not taken a commission, for I know not from what kind of emulation between the western and northern gentry. The gentlemen of our side were not very forward in the service; their loyalty to the king in the succeeding times made it appear it was not for any disaffection to his Majesty's interest or person, or to the cause; but this, however, made it difficult for me when I came home to get any gentlemen of quality to serve with me, so that I presented myself to his Majesty only as a volunteer, with eight gentlemen and about thirty-six countrymen well mounted and armed.

And as it proved, these were enough, for this expedition ended in an accommodation with the Scots; and they not advancing so much as to their own borders, we never came to any action. But the armies lay in the counties of Northumberland and Durham, ate up the country, and spent the king a vast sum of money; and so this war ended, a pacification was made, and both sides returned.

The truth is, I never saw such a despicable appearance of men in arms to begin a war in my life; whether it was that I had seen so many braver armies abroad that prejudiced me against them, or that it really was so; for to me they seemed little better than a rabble met together to devour, rather than fight for their king and country. There was indeed a great appearance of gentlemen, and those of extraordinary quality; but their garb, their equipages, and their mien, did not look like war; their troops were filled with footmen and servants, and wretchedly armed, God wot. I believe I might say, without vanity, one regiment of Finland horse would have made sport at beating them all. There were such crowds of parsons (for this was a Church war in particular) that the camp and court was full of them; and the king was so eternally besieged with clergymen of one sort or another, that it gave offence to the chief of the nobility.

As was the appearance, so was the service. The army marched to the borders, and the headquarter was at Berwick-upon-Tweed; but the Scots never appeared, no, not so much as their scouts; whereupon the king called a council of war, and there it was resolved to send the Earl of Holland with a party of horse into Scotland, to learn some news of the enemy. And truly the first news he brought us was, that finding their army encamped about Coldingham, fifteen miles from Berwick, as soon as he appeared, the Scots drew out a party to charge him, upon which most of his men halted—I don't say run away, but 'twas next door to it—for they could not be persuaded to fire their pistols, and wheel of like soldiers, but retreated in such a disorderly and shameful manner, that had the enemy but had either the courage or conduct to have followed them, it must have certainly ended in the ruin of the whole party.[1]

---

[1] Upon the breach of the match between the King of England and the Infanta of Spain; and particularly upon the old quarrel of the King of Bohemia and the Palatinate.

THE SECOND PART

I confess, when I went into arms at the beginning of this war, I never troubled myself to examine sides: I was glad to hear the drums beat for soldiers, as if I had been a mere Swiss, that had not cared which side went up or down, so I had my pay. I went as eagerly and blindly about my business, as the meanest wretch that 'listed in the army; nor had I the least compassionate thought for the miseries of my native country, till after the fight at Edgehill. I had known as much, and perhaps more than most in the army, what it was to have an enemy ranging in the bowels of a kingdom; I had seen the most flourishing provinces of Germany reduced to perfect deserts, and the voracious Crabats, with inhuman barbarity, quenching the fires of the plundered villages with the blood of the inhabitants. Whether this had hardened me against the natural tenderness which I afterwards found return upon me, or not, I cannot tell; but I reflected upon myself afterwards with a great deal of trouble, for the unconcernedness of my temper at the approaching ruin of my native country.

I was in the first army at York, as I have already noted, and, I must confess, had the least diversion there that ever I found in an army in my life. For when I was in Germany with the King of Sweden, we used to see the king with the general officers every morning on horseback viewing his men, his artillery, his horses, and always something going forward. Here we saw nothing but courtiers and clergymen, bishops and parsons, as busy as if the direction of the war had been in them. The king was seldom seen among us, and never without some of them always about him.

Those few of us that had seen the wars, and would have made a short end of this for him, began to be very uneasy; and particularly a certain nobleman took the freedom to tell the king that the clergy would certainly ruin the expedition. The case was this: he would have had the king have immediately marched into Scotland, and put the matter to the trial of a battle; and he urged it every day. And the king finding his reasons very good, would often be of his opinion; but next morning he would be of another mind.

This gentleman was a man of conduct enough, and of unquestioned courage, and afterwards lost his life for the king. He saw we had an army of young stout fellows numerous enough; and though they had not yet seen much service, he was for bringing them to action, that the Scots might not have time to strengthen themselves, nor they have time by idleness and sotting, the bane of soldiers, to make themselves unfit for anything.

I was one morning in company with this gentleman; and as he was a warm man, and eager in his discourse, "A pox of these priests," says he, "'tis for them the king has raised this army, and put his friends to a vast charge; and now we are come, they won't let us fight."

But I was afterwards convinced the clergy saw further into the matter than we did. They saw the Scots had a better army than we had—bold and ready, commanded by brave officers—and they foresaw that if we fought we should be beaten, and if beaten, they were undone. And 'twas very true, we had all been ruined if we had engaged.

It is true when we came to the pacification which followed, I confess I was of the same mind the gentleman had been of; for we had better have fought and been beaten than have made so dishonourable a treaty without striking a stroke. This pacification seems to me to have laid the scheme of all the blood and confusion which followed in the Civil War. For whatever the king and his friends might pretend to do by talking big, the Scots saw he was to be bullied into anything, and that when it came to the push the courtiers never cared to bring it to blows.

I have little or nothing to say as to action in this mock expedition. The king was persuaded at last to march to Berwick; and, as I have said already, a party of horse went out to learn news of the Scots, and as soon as they saw them, ran away from them bravely.

This made the Scots so insolent that, whereas before they lay encamped behind a river, and never showed themselves, in a sort of modest deference to their king, which was the pretence of not being aggressors or invaders, only arming in their own defence, now, having been invaded by the English troops entering Scotland, they had what they wanted. And to show it was not fear that retained them before, but policy, now they came up in parties to our very gates, braving and facing us every day.

I had, with more curiosity than discretion, put myself as a volunteer at the head of one of our parties of horse, under my Lord Holland, when they went out to discover the enemy; they went, they said, to see what the Scots were a-doing.

We had not marched far, but our scouts brought word they had discovered some horse, but could not come up to them, because a river parted them. At the heels of these came another party of our men upon the spur to us, and said the enemy was behind, which might be true for aught we knew; but it was so far behind that nobody could see them, and yet the country was plain and open for above a mile before us. Hereupon we made a halt, and, indeed, I was afraid it would have been an odd sort of a halt, for our men began to look one upon another, as they do in like cases, when they are going to break; and when the scouts came galloping in the men were in such disorder, that had but one man broke away, I am satisfied they had all run for it.

I found my Lord Holland did not perceive it; but after the first surprise was a little over I told my lord what I had observed, and that unless some course was immediately taken they would all run at the first sight of the enemy. I found he was much concerned at it, and began to consult what course to take to prevent it. I confess 'tis a hard question how to make men stand and face an enemy, when fear has possessed their minds with an inclination to run away. But I'll give that honour to the memory of that noble gentleman, who, though his experience in matters of war was small, having never been in much service, yet his courage made amends for it; for I daresay he would not have turned his horse from an army of enemies, nor have saved his life at the price of running away for it.

My lord soon saw, as well as I, the fright the men were in, after I had given him a hint of it; and to encourage them, rode through their ranks and spoke cheerfully to them, and used what arguments he thought proper to settle their minds. I remembered a saying which I heard old Marshal Gustavus Horn speak in Germany, "If you find your men falter, or in doubt, never suffer them to halt, but keep them advancing; for while they are going forward, it keeps up their courage."

As soon as I could get opportunity to speak to him, I gave him this as my opinion. "That's very well," says my lord, "but I am studying," says he, "to post them so as that they can't run if they would; and if they stand but once to face the enemy, I don't fear them afterwards."

While we were discoursing thus, word was brought that several parties of the enemies were seen on the farther side of the river, upon which my lord gave the word to march; and as we were marching on, my lord calls out a lieutenant who had been an old soldier, with only five troopers whom he had most confidence in, and having given him his lesson, he sends him away. In a quarter of an hour one of the five troopers comes back galloping and hallooing, and tells us his lieutenant had, with his small party, beaten a party of twenty of the enemy's horse over the river, and had secured the pass, and desired my lord would march up to him immediately.

'Tis a strange thing that men's spirits should be subjected to such sudden changes, and capable of so much alteration from shadows of things. They were for running before they saw the enemy, now they are in haste to be led on, and but that in raw men we are obliged to bear with anything, the disorder in both was intolerable.

The story was a premeditated sham, and not a word of truth in it, invented to raise their spirits, and cheat them out of their cowardly phlegmatic apprehensions, and my lord had his end in it; for they were all on fire to fall on. And I am persuaded, had they been led immediately into a battle begun to their hands, they would have laid about them like furies; for there is nothing like victory to flush a young soldier. Thus, while the humour was high, and the fermentation lasted, away we marched, and, passing one of their great commons, which they call moors, we came to the river, as he called it, where our lieutenant was posted with his four men; 'twas a little brook fordable with ease, and, leaving a guard at the pass, we advanced to the top of a small ascent, from whence we had a fair view of the Scots army, as they lay behind another river larger than the former.

Our men were posted well enough, behind a small enclosure, with a narrow lane in their front. And my lord had caused his dragoons to be placed in the front to line the hedges; and in this posture he stood viewing the enemy at a distance. The Scots, who had some intelligence of our coming, drew out three small parties, and sent them by different ways to observe our number; and, forming a fourth party, which I guessed to be about 600 horse, advanced to the top of the plain, and drew up to face us, but never offered to attack us.

One of the small parties, making about 100 men, one third foot, passes upon our flank in view, but out of reach; and, as they marched, shouted at us, which our men, better pleased with that work than with fighting, readily enough answered, and would fain have fired at them for the pleasure of making a noise, for they were too far off to hit them.

I observed that these parties had always some foot with them; and yet if the horse galloped, or pushed on ever so forward, the foot were as forward as they, which was an extraordinary advantage.

Gustavus Adolphus, that king of soldiers, was the first that I have ever observed found the advantage of mixing small bodies of musketeers among his horse; and, had he had such nimble strong fellows as these, he would have prized them above all the rest of his men. These were those they call Highlanders. They would run on foot with their arms and all their accoutrements, and keep very good order too, and yet keep pace with the horse, let them go at what rate they would. When I saw the foot thus interlined among the horse, together with the way of ordering their flying parties, it presently occurred to my mind that here was some of our old Scots come home out of Germany that had the ordering of matters, and if so, I knew we were not a match for them.

Thus we stood facing the enemy till our scouts brought us word the whole Scots army was in motion, and in full march to attack us; and, though it was not true, and the fear of our men doubled every object, yet 'twas thought convenient to make our retreat. The whole matter was that the scouts having informed them what they could of our strength, the 600 were ordered to march towards us, and three regiments of foot were drawn out to support the horse.

I know not whether they would have ventured to attack us, at least before their foot had come up; but whether they would have put it to the hazard or no, we were resolved not to hazard the trial, so we drew down to the pass. And, as retreating looks something like running away, especially when an enemy is at hand, our men had much ado to make their retreat pass for a march, and not a flight; and, by their often looking behind them, anybody might know what they would have done if they had been pressed.

I confess, I was heartily ashamed when the Scots, coming up to the place where we had been posted, stood and shouted at us. I would have persuaded my lord to have charged them, and he would have done it with all his heart, but he saw it was not practicable; so we stood at gaze with them above two hours, by which time their foot were come up to them, and yet they did not offer to attack us. I never was so ashamed of myself in my life; we were all dispirited. The Scots gentlemen would come out single, within shot of our post, which in a time of war is always accounted a challenge to any single gentleman, to come out and exchange a pistol with them, and nobody would stir; at last our old lieutenant rides out to meet a Scotchman that came pickeering on his quarter. This lieutenant was a brave and a strong fellow, had been a soldier in the Low Countries; and though he was not of any quality, only a mere soldier, had his preferment for his conduct. He gallops bravely up to his adversary, and exchanging their pistols, the lieutenant's horse happened to be killed. The Scotchman very generously dismounts, and engages him with his sword, and fairly masters him, and carries him away prisoner; and I think this horse was all the blood was shed in that war.

The lieutenant's name thus conquered was English, and as he was a very stout old soldier, the disgrace of it broke his heart. The Scotchman, indeed, used him very generously; for he treated him in the camp very courteously, gave him another horse, and set him at liberty, gratis. But the man laid it so to heart, that he never would appear in the army, but went home to his own country and died.

I had enough of party-making, and was quite sick with indignation at the cowardice of the men; and my lord was in as great a fret as I, but there was no remedy. We durst not go about to retreat, for we should have been in such confusion that the enemy must have discovered it; so my lord resolved to keep the post, if possible, and send to the king for some foot. Then were our men ready to fight with one another who should be the messenger; and at last when a lieutenant with twenty dragoons was despatched, he told us afterwards he found himself an hundred strong before he was gotten a mile from the place.

In short, as soon as ever the day declined, and the dusk of the evening began to shelter the designs of the men, they dropped away from us one by one; and at last in such numbers, that if we had stayed till the morning, we had not had fifty men left; out of 1200 horse and dragoons.

When I saw how it was, consulting with some of the officers, we all went to my Lord Holland, and pressed him to retreat, before the enemy should discern the flight of our men; so he drew us off, and we came to the camp the next morning, in the shamefullest condition that ever poor men could do. And this was the end of the worst expedition ever I made in my life.

To fight and be beaten is a casualty common to a soldier, and I have since had enough of it; but to run away at the sight of an enemy, and neither strike or be stricken, this is the very shame of the profession, and no man that has done it ought to show his face again in the field, unless disadvantages of place or number make it tolerable, neither of which was our case.

My Lord Holland made another march a few days after, in hopes to retrieve this miscarriage; but I had enough of it, so I kept in my quarters. And though his men did not desert him as before, yet upon the appearance of the enemy they did not think fit to fight, and came off with but little more honour than they did before.

There was no need to go out to seek the enemy after this, for they came, as I have noted, and pitched in sight of us, and their parties came up every day to the very out-works of Berwick, but nobody cared to meddle with them. And in this posture things stood when the pacification was agreed on by both parties, which, like a short truce, only gave both sides breath to prepare for a new war more ridiculously managed than the former. When the treaty was so near a conclusion as that conversation was admitted on both sides, I went over to the Scotch camp to satisfy my curiosity, as many of our English officers did also.

I confess the soldiers made a very uncouth figure, especially the Highlanders. The oddness and barbarity of their garb and arms seemed to have something in it remarkable.

They were generally tall swinging fellows; their swords were extravagantly, and, I think, insignificantly broad, and they carried great wooden targets, large enough to cover the upper part of their bodies. Their dress was as antique as the rest; a cap on their heads, called by them a bonnet, long hanging sleeves behind, and their doublet, breeches, and stockings of a stuff they called plaid, striped across red and yellow, with short cloaks of the same. These fellows looked, when drawn out, like a regiment of merry-andrews, ready for Bartholomew Fair. They are in companies all of a name, and therefore call one another only by their Christian names, as Jemmy, Jocky, that is, John, and Sawny, that is, Alexander, and the like. And they scorn to be commanded but by one of their own clan or family. They are all gentlemen, and proud enough to be kings. The meanest fellow among them is as tenacious of his honour as the best nobleman in the country, and they will fight and cut one another's throats for every trifling affront.

But to their own clans or lairds, they are the willingest and most obedient fellows in nature. Give them their due, were their skill in exercises and discipline proportioned to their courage, they would make the bravest soldiers in the world. They are large bodies, and prodigiously strong; and two qualities they have above other nations, viz., hardy to endure hunger, cold, and hardships, and wonderfully swift of foot. The latter is such an advantage in the field that I know none like it; for if they conquer, no enemy can escape them, and if they run, even the horse can hardly overtake them. These were some of them, who, as I observed before, went out in parties with their horse.

There were three or four thousand of these in the Scots army, armed only with swords and targets; and in their belts some of them had a pistol, but no muskets at that time among them.

But there were also a great many regiments of disciplined men, who, by their carrying their arms, looked as if they understood their business, and by their faces, that they durst see an enemy.

I had not been half-an-hour in their camp after the ceremony of giving our names, and passing their out-guards and main-guard was over, but I was saluted by several of my acquaintance; and in particular, by one who led the Scotch volunteers at the taking the castle of Oppenheim, of which I have given an account. They used me with all the respect they thought due to me, on account of old affairs, gave me the word, and a sergeant waited upon me whenever I pleased to go abroad.

I continued twelve or fourteen days among them, till the pacification was concluded; and they were ordered to march home. They spoke very respectfully of the king, but I found were exasperated to the last degree at Archbishop Laud and the English bishops, for endeavouring to impose the Common Prayer Book upon them; and they always talked with the utmost contempt of our soldiers and army. I always waived the discourse about the clergy, and the occasion of the war, but I could not but be too sensible what they said of our men was true; and by this I perceived they had an universal intelligence from among us, both of what we were doing, and what sort of people we were that were doing it; and they were mighty desirous of coming to blows with us. I had an invitation from their general, but I declined it, lest I should give offence. I found they accepted the pacification as a thing not likely to hold, or that they did not design should hold; and that they were resolved to keep their forces on foot, notwithstanding the agreement. Their whole army was full of brave officers, men of as much experience and conduct as any in the world; and all men who know anything of the war, know good officers presently make a good army.

Things being thus huddled up, the English came back to York, where the army separated, and the Scots went home to increase theirs; for I easily foresaw that peace was the farthest thing from their thoughts.

The next year the flame broke out again. The king draws his forces down into the north, as before, and expresses were sent to all the gentlemen that had commands to be at the place by the 15th of July. As I had accepted of no command in the army, so I had no inclination at all to go, for I foresaw there would be nothing but disgrace attend it. My father, observing such an alteration in my usual forwardness, asked me one day what was the matter, that I who used to be so forward to go into the army, and so eager to run abroad to fight, now showed no inclination to appear when the service of the king and country called me to it? I told him I had as much zeal as ever for the king's service, and for the country too: but he knew a soldier could not abide to be beaten; and being from thence a little more inquisitive, I told him the observations I had made in the Scots army, and the people I had conversed with there. "And, sir," says I, "assure yourself, if the king offers to fight them, he will be beaten; and I don't love to engage when my judgment tells me beforehand I shall be worsted." And as I had foreseen, it came to pass; for the Scots resolving to proceed, never stood upon the ceremony of aggression, as before, but on the 20th of August they entered England with their army.

However, as my father desired, I went to the king's army, which was then at York, but not gotten all together. The king himself was at London, but upon this news takes post for the army, and advancing a part of his forces, he posted the Lord Conway and Sir Jacob Astley, with a brigade of foot and some horse, at Newburn, upon the river Tyne, to keep the Scots from passing that river.

The Scots could have passed the Tyne without fighting; but to let us see that they were able to force their passage, they fall upon his body of men and notwithstanding all the advantages of the place, they beat them from the post, took their baggage and two pieces of cannon, with some prisoners. Sir Jacob Astley made what resistance he could, but the Scots charged with so much fury, and being also overpowered, he was soon put into confusion. Immediately the Scots made themselves masters of Newcastle, and the next day of Durham, and laid those two counties under intolerable contributions.

Now was the king absolutely ruined; for among his own people the discontents before were so plain, that had the clergy had any forecast, they would never have embroiled him with the Scots, till he had fully brought matters to an understanding at home. But the case was thus: the king, by the good husbandry of Bishop Juxon, his treasurer, had a million of ready money in his treasury, and upon that account, having no need of a Parliament, had not called one in twelve years; and perhaps had never called another, if he had not by this unhappy circumstance been reduced to a necessity of it; for now this ready money was spent in two foolish expeditions, and his army appeared in a condition not fit to engage the Scots. The detachment under Sir Jacob Astley, which were of the flower of his men, had been routed at Newburn, and the enemy had possession of two entire counties.

All men blamed Laud for prompting the king to provoke the Scots, a headstrong nation, and zealous for their own way of worship; and Laud himself found too late the consequences of it, both to the whole cause and to himself; for the Scots, whose native temper is not easily to forgive an injury, pursued him by their party in England, and never gave it over till they laid his head on the block.

The ruined country now clamoured in his Majesty's ears with daily petitions, and the gentry of other neighbouring counties cry out for peace and Parliament. The king, embarrassed with these difficulties, and quite empty of money, calls a great council of the nobility at York, and demands their advice, which any one could have told him before would be to call a Parliament.

I cannot, without regret, look back upon the misfortune of the king, who, as he was one of the best princes in his personal conduct that ever reigned in England, had yet some of the greatest unhappinesses in his conduct as a king, that ever prince had, and the whole course of his life demonstrated it.

1. An impolitic honesty. His enemies called it obstinacy; but as I was perfectly acquainted with his temper, I cannot but think it was his judgment, when he thought he was in the right, to adhere to it as a duty though against his interest.

2. Too much compliance when he was complying. No man but himself would have denied what at some times he denied, and have granted what at other times he granted; and this uncertainty of counsel proceeded from two things.

1. The heat of the clergy, to whom he was exceedingly devoted, and for whom, indeed, he ruined himself.

2. The wisdom of his nobility.

Thus when the counsel of his priests prevailed, all was fire and fury; the Scots were rebels, and must be subdued, and the Parliament's demands were to be rejected as exorbitant. But whenever the king's judgment was led by the grave and steady advice of his nobility and counsellors, he was always inclined by them to temperate his measures between the two extremes. And had he gone on in such a temper, he had never met with the misfortunes which afterward attended him, or had so many thousands of his friends lost their lives and fortunes in his service.

I am sure we that knew what it was to fight for him, and that loved him better than any of the clergy could pretend to, have had many a consultation how to bring over our master from so espousing their interest, as to ruin himself for it; but 'twas in vain.

I took this interval when I sat still and only looked on, to make these remarks, because I remember the best friends the king had were at this time of that opinion, that 'twas an unaccountable piece of indiscretion, to commence a quarrel with the Scots, a poor and obstinate people, for a ceremony and book of Church discipline, at a time when the king stood but upon indifferent terms with his people at home.

The consequence was, it put arms into the hands of his subjects to rebel against him; it embroiled him with his Parliament in England, to whom he was fain to stoop in a fatal and unusual manner to get money, all his own being spent, and so to buy off the Scots whom he could not beat off.

I cannot but give one instance of the unaccountable politics of his ministers. If they overruled this unhappy king to it, with design to exhaust and impoverish him, they were the worst of traitors; if not, the grossest of fools. They prompted the king to equip a fleet against the Scots, and to put on board it 5000 land men. Had this been all, the design had been good, that while the king had faced the army upon the borders, these 5000, landing in the Firth of Edinburgh, might have put that whole nation into disorder. But in order to this, they advised the king to lay out his money in fitting out the biggest ships he had, and the "Royal Sovereign," the biggest ship the world had ever seen, which cost him no less than £100,000, was now built, and fitted out for this voyage.

This was the most incongruous and ridiculous advice that could be given, and made us all believe we were betrayed, though we knew not by whom.

To fit out ships of 100 guns to invade Scotland, which had not one man-of-war in the world, nor any open confederacy with any prince or state that had any fleet, 'twas a most ridiculous thing. An hundred sail of Newcastle colliers, to carry the men with their stores and provisions, and ten frigates of 40 guns each, had been as good a fleet as reason and the nature of the thing could have made tolerable.

Thus things were carried on, till the king, beggared by the mismanagement of his counsels, and beaten by the Scots, was driven to the necessity of calling a Parliament in England.

It is not my design to enter into the feuds and brangles of this Parliament. I have noted, by observations of their mistakes, who brought the king to this happy necessity of calling them.

His Majesty had tried Parliaments upon several occasions before, but never found himself so much embroiled with them but he could send them home, and there was an end of it; but as he could not avoid calling these, so they took care to put him out of a condition to dismiss them.

The Scots army was now quartered upon the English. The counties, the gentry, and the assembly of lords at York, petitioned for a Parliament.

The Scots presented their demands to the king, in which it was observed that matters were concerted between them and a party in England; and I confess when I saw that, I began to think the king in an ill case; for as the Scots pretended grievances, we thought, the king redressing those grievances, they could ask no more; and therefore all men advised the king to grant their full demands. And whereas the king had not money to supply the Scots in their march home, I know there were several meetings of gentlemen with a design to advance considerable sums of money to the king to set him free, and in order to reinstate his Majesty, as before. Not that we ever advised the king to rule without a Parliament, but we were very desirous of putting him out of the necessity of calling them, at least just then.

But the eighth article of the Scots' demands expressly required, that an English Parliament might be called to remove all obstructions of commerce, and to settle peace, religion, and liberty; and in another article they tell the king, the 24th of September being the time his Majesty appointed for the meeting of the peers, will make it too long ere the Parliament meet. And in another, that a Parliament was the only way of settling peace, and bring them to his Majesty's obedience.

When we saw this in the army, 'twas time to look about. Everybody perceived that the Scots army would call an English Parliament; and whatever aversion the king had to it, we all saw he would be obliged to comply with it; and now they all began to see their error, who advised the king to this Scotch war.

While these things were transacting, the assembly of the peers meet at York, and by their advice a treaty was begun with the Scots. I had the honour to be sent with the first message which was in writing.

I brought it, attended by a trumpet and a guard of 500 horse, to the Scots quarters. I was stopped at Darlington, and my errand being known, General Leslie sent a Scots major and fifty horses to receive me, but would let neither my trumpet or guard set foot within their quarters. In this manner I was conducted to audience in the chapter-house at Durham, where a committee of Scots lords who attended the army received me very courteously, and gave me their answer in writing also.

'Twas in this answer that they showed, at least to me, their design of embroiling the king with his English subjects; they discoursed very freely with me, and did not order me to withdraw when they debated their private opinions. They drew up several answers but did not like them; at last they gave me one which I did not receive, I thought it was too insolent to be borne with. As near as I can remember it was thus: The commissioners of Scotland attending the service in the army, do refuse any treaty in the city of York.

One of the commissioners who treated me with more distinction than the rest, and discoursed freely with me, gave me an opportunity to speak more freely of this than I expected.

I told them if they would return to his Majesty an answer fit for me to carry, or if they would say they would not treat at all, I would deliver such a message. But I entreated them to consider the answer was to their sovereign, and to whom they made a great profession of duty and respect, and at least they ought to give their reasons why they declined a treaty at York, and to name some other place, or humbly to desire his Majesty to name some other place; but to send word they would not treat at York, I could deliver no such message, for when put into English it would signify they would not treat at all.

I used a great many reasons and arguments with them on this head, and at last with some difficulty obtained of them to give the reason, which was the Earl of Strafford's having the chief command at York, whom they declared their mortal enemy, he having declared them rebels in Ireland.

With this answer I returned. I could make no observations in the short time I was with them, for as I stayed but one night, so I was guarded as a close prisoner all the while. I saw several of their officers whom I knew, but they durst not speak to me, and if they would have ventured, my guard would not have permitted them.

In this manner I was conducted out of their quarters to my own party again, and having delivered my message to the king and told his Majesty the circumstances, I saw the king receive the account of the haughty behaviour of the Scots with some regret; however, it was his

Majesty's time now to bear, and therefore the Scots were complied with, and the treaty appointed at Ripon; where, after much debate, several preliminary articles were agreed on, as a cessation of arms, quarters, and bounds to the armies, subsistence to the Scots army, and the residue of the demands was referred to a treaty at London, &c.

We were all amazed at the treaty, and I cannot but remember we used to wish much rather we had been suffered to fight; for though we had been worsted at first, the power and strength of the king's interest, which was not yet tried, must, in fine, have been too strong for the Scots, whereas now we saw the king was for complying with anything, and all his friends would be ruined.

I confess I had nothing to fear, and so was not much concerned, but our predictions soon came to pass, for no sooner was this Parliament called but abundance of those who had embroiled their king with his people of both kingdoms, like the disciples when their Master was betrayed to the Jews, forsook him and fled; and now Parliament tyranny began to succeed Church tyranny, and we soldiers were glad to see it at first. The bishops trembled, the judges went to gaol, the officers of the customs were laid hold on; and the Parliament began to lay their fingers on the great ones, particularly Archbishop Laud and the Earl of Strafford. We had no great concern for the first, but the last was a man of so much conduct and gallantry, and so beloved by the soldiers and principal gentry of England, that everybody was touched with his misfortune.

The Parliament now grew mad in their turn, and as the prosperity of any party is the time to show their discretion, the Parliament showed they knew as little where to stop as other people. The king was not in a condition to deny anything, and nothing could be demanded but they pushed it. They attainted the Earl of Strafford, and thereby made the king cut off his right hand to save his left, and yet not save it neither. They obtained another bill to empower them to sit during their own pleasure, and after them, triennial Parliaments to meet, whether the king call them or no; and granting this completed his Majesty's ruin.

Had the House only regulated the abuses of the court, punished evil counsellors, and restored Parliaments to their original and just powers, all had been well, and the king, though he had been more than mortified, had yet reaped the benefit of future peace; for now the Scots were sent home, after having eaten up two countries, and received a prodigious sum of money to boot. And the king, though too late, goes in person to Edinburgh, and grants them all they could desire, and more

345

than they asked; but in England, the desires of ours were unbounded, and drove at all extremes.

They drew out the bishops from sitting in the House, made a protestation equivalent to the Scotch Covenant, and this done, print their remonstrance. This so provoked the king, that he resolves upon seizing some of the members, and in an ill hour enters the House in person to take them. Thus one imprudent thing on one hand produced another of the other hand, till the king was obliged to leave them to themselves, for fear of being mobbed into something or other unworthy of himself.

These proceedings began to alarm the gentry and nobility of England; for, however willing we were to have evil counsellors removed, and the government return to a settled and legal course, according to the happy constitution of this nation, and might have been forward enough to have owned the king had been misled, and imposed upon to do things which he had rather had not been done, yet it did not follow, that all the powers and prerogatives of the crown should devolve upon the Parliament, and the king in a manner be deposed, or else sacrificed to the fury of the rabble.

The heats of the House running them thus to all extremes, and at last to take from the king the power of the militia, which indeed was all that was left to make him anything of a king, put the king upon opposing force with force; and thus the flame of civil war began.

However backward I was in engaging in the second year's expedition against the Scots, I was as forward now, for I waited on the king at York, where a gallant company of gentlemen as ever were seen in England, engaged themselves to enter into his service; and here some of us formed ourselves into troops for the guard of his person.

The king having been waited upon by the gentry of Yorkshire, and having told them his resolution of erecting his royal standard, and received from them hearty assurances of support, dismisses them, and marches to Hull, where lay the train of artillery, and all the arms and ammunition belonging to the northern army which had been disbanded. But here the Parliament had been beforehand with his Majesty, so that when he came to Hull, he found the gates shut, and Sir John Hotham, the governor, upon the walls, though with a great deal of seeming humility and protestations of loyalty to his person, yet with a positive denial to admit any of the king's attendants into the town. If his Majesty pleased to enter the town in person with any reasonable number of his household, he would submit, but would not be prevailed on to receive the king as he would be received, with his forces, though those forces were then but very few.

The king was exceedingly provoked at this repulse, and indeed it was a great surprise to us all, for certainly never prince began a war against the whole strength of his kingdom under the circumstances that he was in. He had not a garrison, or a company of soldiers in his pay, not a stand of arms, or a barrel of powder, a musket, cannon or mortar, not a ship of all the fleet, or money in his treasury to procure them; whereas the Parliament had all his navy, and ordnance, stores, magazines, arms, ammunition, and revenue in their keeping. And this I take to be another defect of the king's counsel, and a sad instance of the distraction of his affairs, that when he saw how all things were going to wreck, as it was impossible but he should see it, and 'tis plain he did see it, that he should not long enough before it came to extremities secure the navy, magazines, and stores of war, in the hands of his trusty servants, that would have been sure to have preserved them for his use, at a time when he wanted them.

It cannot be supposed but the gentry of England, who generally preserved their loyalty for their royal master, and at last heartily showed it, were exceedingly discouraged at first when they saw the Parliament had all the means of making war in their own hands, and the king was naked and destitute either of arms or ammunition, or money to procure them. Not but that the king, by extraordinary application, recovered the disorder the want of these things had thrown him into, and supplied himself with all things needful.

But my observation was this, had his Majesty had the magazines, navy, and forts in his own hand, the gentry, who wanted but the prospect of something to encourage them, had come in at first, and the Parliament, being unprovided, would have been presently reduced to reason. But this was it that balked the gentry of Yorkshire, who went home again, giving the king good promises, but never appeared for him, till by raising a good army in Shropshire and Wales, he marched towards London, and they saw there was a prospect of their being supported.

In this condition the king erected his standard at Nottingham, 22nd August 1642, and I confess, I had very melancholy apprehensions of the king's affairs, for the appearance to the royal standard was but small. The affront the king had met with at Hull, had balked and dispirited the northern gentry, and the king's affairs looked with a very dismal aspect. We had expresses from London of the prodigious success of the Parliament levies, how their men came in faster than they could entertain them, and that arms were delivered out to whole companies listed together, and the like. And all this while the king had not got together a thousand foot, and had no arms for them neither. When the king saw this, he immediately despatches five several messengers, whereof one went to the Marquis of Worcester into Wales; one went to the queen, then at Windsor; one to the Duke of Newcastle, then Marquis of Newcastle, into the north; one into Scotland; and one into France, where the queen soon after arrived to raise money, and buy arms, and to get what assistance she could among her own friends. Nor was her Majesty idle, for she sent over several ships laden with arms and ammunition, with a fine train of artillery, and a great many very good officers; and though one of the first fell into the hands of the Parliament, with three hundred barrels of powder and some arms, and one hundred and fifty gentlemen, yet most of the gentlemen found means, one way or other, to get to us, and most of the ships the queen freighted arrived; and at last her Majesty came herself, and brought an extraordinary supply both of men, money, arms, &c., with which she joined the king's forces under the Earl of Newcastle in the north.

Finding his Majesty thus bestirring himself to muster his friends together, I asked him if he thought it might not be for his Majesty's service to let me go among my friends, and his loyal subjects about Shrewsbury? "Yes," says the king, smiling, "I intend you shall, and I design to go with you myself." I did not understand what the king meant then, and did not think it good manners to inquire, but the next day I found all things disposed for a march, and the king on horseback by eight of the clock; when calling me to him, he told me I should go before, and let my father and all my friends know he would be at Shrewsbury the Saturday following. I left my equipages, and taking post with only one servant, was at my father's the next morning by break of day. My father was not surprised at the news of the king's coming at all, for, it seems, he, together with the royal gentry of those parts, had sent particularly to give the king an invitation to move that way, which I was not made privy to, with an account what encouragement they had there in the endeavours made for his interest. In short, the whole country was entirely for the king, and such was the universal joy the people showed when the news of his Majesty's coming down was positively known, that all manner of business was laid aside, and the whole body of the people seemed to be resolved upon the war.

As this gave a new face to the king's affairs, so I must own it filled me with joy; for I was astonished before, when I considered what the king and his friends were like to be exposed to. The news of the proceedings of the Parliament, and their powerful preparations, were now no more terrible; the king came at the time appointed, and having lain at my father's house one night, entered Shrewsbury in the morning. The acclamations of the people, the concourse of the nobility and gentry about his person, and the crowds which now came every day into the standard, were incredible.

The loyalty of the English gentry was not only worth notice, but the power of the gentry is extraordinary visible in this matter. The king, in about six weeks' time, which was the most of his stay at Shrewsbury, was supplied with money, arms, ammunition, and a train of artillery, and listed a body of an army upwards of 20,000 men.

His Majesty seeing the general alacrity of his people, immediately issued out commissions, and formed regiments of horse and foot; and having some experienced officers about him, together with about sixteen who came from France, with a ship loaded with arms and some field-pieces which came very seasonably into the Severn, the men were exercised, regularly disciplined, and quartered, and now we began to look like soldiers. My father had raised a regiment of horse at his own charge, and completed them, and the king gave out arms to them from the supplies which I mentioned came from abroad. Another party of horse, all brave stout fellows, and well mounted, came in from Lancashire, and the Earl of Derby at the head of them. The Welshmen came in by droves; and so great was the concourse of people, that the king began to think of marching, and gave the command, as well as the trust of regulating the army, to the brave Earl of Lindsey, as general of the foot. The Parliament general being the Earl of Essex, two braver men, or two better officers, were not in the kingdom; they had both been old soldiers, and had served together as volunteers in the Low Country wars, under Prince Maurice. They had been comrades and companions abroad, and now came to face one another as enemies in the field.

Such was the expedition used by the king and his friends, in the levies of this first army, that notwithstanding the wonderful expedition the Parliament made, the king was in the field before them; and now the gentry in other parts of the nation bestirred themselves, and seized upon, and garrisoned several considerable places, for the king. In the north, the Earl of Newcastle not only garrisoned the most considerable places, but even the general possession of the north was for the king, excepting Hull, and some few places, which the old Lord Fairfax had taken up for the Parliament. On the other hand, entire Cornwall and most of the western counties were the king's. The Parliament had their chief interest in the south and eastern part of England, as Kent, Surrey, and, Sussex, Essex, Suffolk, Norfolk, Cambridge, Bedford, Huntingdon, Hertford, Buckinghamshire, and the other midland counties. These were called, or some of them at least, the associated counties, and felt little of the war, other than the charges; but the main support of the Parliament was the city of London.

The king made the seat of his court at Oxford, which he caused to be regularly fortified. The Lord Say had been here, and had possession of the city for the enemy, and was debating about fortifying it, but came to no resolution, which was a very great over-sight in them; the situation of the place, and the importance of it, on many accounts, to the city of London, considered; and they would have retrieved this error afterwards, but then 'twas too late; for the king made it the headquarter, and received great supplies and assistance from the wealth of the colleges, and the plenty of the neighbouring country. Abingdon, Wallingford, Basing, and Reading, were all garrisoned and fortified as outworks to defend this as the centre. And thus all England became the theatre of blood, and war was spread into every corner of the country, though as yet there was no stroke struck. I had no command in this army. My father led his own regiment, and, old as he was, would not leave his royal master, and my elder brother stayed at home to support the family. As for me, I rode a volunteer in the royal troop of guards, which may very well deserve the title of a royal troop, for it was composed of young gentlemen, sons of the nobility, and some of the prime gentry of the nation, and I think not a person of so mean a birth or fortune as myself. We reckoned in this troop two and thirty lords, or who came afterwards to be such, and eight and thirty of younger sons of the nobility, five French noblemen, and all the rest gentlemen of very good families and estates.

And that I may give the due to their personal valour, many of this troop lived afterwards to have regiments and troops under their command in the service of the king, many of them lost their lives for him, and most of them their estates. Nor did they behave unworthy of themselves in their first showing their faces to the enemy, as shall be mentioned in its place.

While the king remained at Shrewsbury, his loyal friends bestirred themselves in several parts of the kingdom. Goring had secured Portsmouth, but being young in matters of war, and not in time relieved, though the Marquis of Hertford was marching to relieve him, yet he was obliged to quit the place, and shipped himself for Holland, from whence he returned with relief for the king, and afterwards did very good service upon all occasions, and so effectually cleared himself of the scandal the hasty surrender of Portsmouth had brought upon his courage.

The chief power of the king's forces lay in three places, in Cornwall, in Yorkshire, and at Shrewsbury. In Cornwall, Sir Ralph Hopton, afterwards Lord Hopton, Sir Bevil Grenvile, and Sir Nicholas Slanning secured all the country, and afterwards spread themselves over Devonshire and Somersetshire, took Exeter from the Parliament, fortified Bridgewater and Barnstaple, and beat Sir William Waller at the battle of Roundway Down, as I shall touch at more particularly when I come to recite the part of my own travels that way.

In the north, The Marquis of Newcastle secured all the country, garrisoned York, Scarborough, Carlisle, Newcastle, Pomfret, Leeds, and all the considerable places, and took the field with a very good army, though afterwards he proved more unsuccessful than the rest, having the whole power of a kingdom at his back, the Scots coming in with an army to the assistance of the Parliament, which, indeed, was the general turn of the scale of the war; for had it not been for this Scots army, the king had most certainly reduced the Parliament, at least to good terms of peace, in two years' time.

The king was the third article. His force at Shrewsbury I have noted already. The alacrity of the gentry filled him with hopes, and all his army with vigour, and the 8th of October 1642, his Majesty gave orders to march. The Earl of Essex had spent above a month after his leaving London (for he went thence the 9th of September) in modelling and drawing together his forces; his rendezvous was at St Albans, from whence he marched to Northampton, Coventry, and Warwick, and leaving garrisons in them, he comes on to Worcester. Being thus advanced, he possesses Oxford, as I noted before, Banbury, Bristol, Gloucester, and Worcester, out of all which places, except Gloucester, we drove him back to London in a very little while.

Sir John Byron had raised a very good party of 500 horse, most gentlemen, for the king, and had possessed Oxford; but on the approach of the Lord Say quitted it, being now but an open town, and retreated to Worcester, from whence, on the approach of Essex's army, he retreated to the king. And now all things grew ripe for action, both parties having secured their posts, and settled their schemes of the war, taken their posts and places as their measures and opportunities directed. The field was next in their eye, and the soldiers began to inquire when they should fight, for as yet there had been little or no blood drawn; and 'twas not long before they had enough of it; for, I believe, I may challenge all the historians in Europe to tell me of any war in the world where, in the space of four years, there were so many pitched battles, sieges, fights, and skirmishes, as in this war. We never encamped or entrenched, never fortified the avenues to our posts, or lay fenced with rivers and defiles; here was no leaguers in the field, as at the story of Nuremberg, neither had our soldiers any tents, or what they call heavy baggage. 'Twas the general maxim of this war, "Where is the enemy? let us go and fight them," or, on the other hand, if the enemy was coming, "What was to be done?" "Why, what should be done? Draw out into the fields and fight them." I cannot say 'twas the prudence of the parties, and had the king fought less he had gained more. And I shall remark several times when the eagerness of fighting was the worst counsel, and proved our loss. This benefit, however, happened in general to the country, that it made a quick, though a bloody, end of the war, which otherwise had lasted till it might have ruined the whole nation.

On the 10th of October the king's army was in full march, his Majesty, generalissimo, the Earl of Lindsey, general of the foot, Prince Rupert, general of the horse; and the first action in the field was by Prince Rupert and Sir John Byron. Sir John had brought his body of 500 horse, as I noted already, from Oxford to Worcester; the Lord Say, with a strong party, being in the neighbourhood of Oxford, and expected in the town, Colonel Sandys, a hot man, and who had more courage than judgment, advances with about 1500 horse and dragoons, with design to beat Sir John Byron out of Worcester, and take post there for the Parliament.

The king had notice that the Earl of Essex designed for Worcester, and Prince Rupert was ordered to advance with a body of horse and dragoons to face the enemy, and bring off Sir John Byron. This his Majesty did to amuse the Earl of Essex, that he might expect him that way; whereas the king's design was to get between the Earl of Essex's army and the city of London; and his Majesty's end was doubly answered, for he not only drew Essex on to Worcester, where he spent more time than he needed, but he beat the party into the bargain.

I went volunteer in this party, and rode in my father's regiment; for though we really expected not to see the enemy, yet I was tired with lying still. We came to Worcester just as notice was brought to Sir John Byron, that a party of the enemy was on their march for Worcester, upon which the prince immediately consulting what was to be done, resolves to march the next morning and fight them.

The enemy, who lay at Pershore, about eight miles from Worcester, and, as I believe, had no notice of our march, came on very confidently in the morning, and found us fairly drawn up to receive them. I must confess this was the bluntest, downright way of making war that ever was seen. The enemy, who, in all the little knowledge I had of war, ought to have discovered our numbers, and guessed by our posture what our design was, might easily have informed themselves that we intended to attack them, and so might have secured the advantage of a bridge in their front; but without any regard to these methods of policy, they came on at all hazards. Upon this notice, my father proposed to the prince to halt for them, and suffer ourselves to be attacked, since we found them willing to give us the advantage. The prince approved of the advice, so we halted within view of a bridge, leaving space enough on our front for about half the number of their forces to pass and draw up; and at the bridge was posted about fifty dragoons, with orders to retire as soon as the enemy advanced, as if they had been afraid. On the right of the road was a ditch, and a very high bank behind, where we had placed 300 dragoons, with orders to lie flat on their faces till the enemy had passed the bridge, and to let fly among them as soon as our trumpets sounded a charge. Nobody but Colonel Sandys would have been caught in such a snare, for he might easily have seen that when he was over the bridge there was not room enough for him to fight in. But the Lord of hosts was so much in their mouths, for that was the word for that day, that they took little heed how to conduct the host of the Lord to their own advantage.

As we expected, they appeared, beat our dragoons from the bridge, and passed it. We stood firm in one line with a reserve, and expected a charge, but Colonel Sandys, showing a great deal more judgment than we thought he was master of, extends himself to the left, finding the ground too strait, and began to form his men with a great deal of readiness and skill, for by this time he saw our number was greater than he expected. The prince perceiving it, and foreseeing that the stratagem of the dragoons would be frustrated by this, immediately charges with the horse, and the dragoons at the same time standing upon their feet, poured in their shot upon those that were passing the bridge. This surprise put them into such disorder, that we had but little work with them. For though Colonel Sandys with the troops next him sustained the shock very well, and behaved themselves gallantly enough, yet the confusion beginning in their rear, those that had not yet passed the bridge were kept back by the fire of the dragoons, and the rest were easily cut in pieces. Colonel Sandys was mortally wounded and taken prisoner, and the crowd was so great to get back, that many pushed into the water, and were rather smothered than drowned. Some of them who never came into the fight, were so frighted, that they never looked behind them till they came to Pershore, and, as we were afterwards informed, the lifeguards of the general who had quartered in the town, left it in disorder enough, expecting us at the heels of their men.

If our business had been to keep the Parliament army from coming to Worcester, we had a very good opportunity to have secured the bridge at Pershore; but our design lay another way, as I have said, and the king was for drawing Essex on to the Severn, in hopes to get behind him, which fell out accordingly.

Essex, spurred by this affront in the infancy of their affairs, advances the next day, and came to Pershore time enough to be at the funeral of some of his men; and from thence he advances to Worcester.

We marched back to Worcester extremely pleased with the good success of our first attack, and our men were so flushed with this little victory that it put vigour into the whole army. The enemy lost about 3000 men, and we carried away near 150 prisoners, with 500 horses, some standards and arms, and among the prisoners their colonel; but he died a little after of his wounds.

Upon the approach of the enemy, Worcester was quitted, and the forces marched back to join the king's army, which lay then at Bridgnorth, Ludlow, and thereabout. As the king expected, it fell out; Essex found so much work at Worcester to settle Parliament quarters, and secure Bristol, Gloucester, and Hereford, that it gave the king a full day's march of him. So the king, having the start of him, moves towards London; and Essex, nettled to be both beaten in fight and outdone in conduct, decamps, and follows the king.

The Parliament, and the Londoners too, were in a strange consternation at this mistake of their general; and had the king, whose great misfortune was always to follow precipitant advices,—had the king, I say, pushed on his first design, which he had formed with very good reason, and for which he had been dodging with Essex eight or ten days, viz., of marching directly to London, where he had a very great interest, and where his friends were not yet oppressed and impoverished, as they were afterwards, he had turned the scale of his affairs. And every man expected it; for the members began to shift for themselves, expresses were sent on the heels of one another to the Earl of Essex to hasten after the king, and, if possible, to bring him to a battle. Some of these letters fell into our hands, and we might easily discover that the Parliament were in the last confusion at the thoughts of our coming to London. Besides this, the city was in a worse fright than the House, and the great moving men began to go out of town. In short, they expected us, and we expected to come, but Providence for our ruin had otherwise determined it.

Essex, upon news of the king's march, and upon receipt of the Parliament's letters, makes long marches after us, and on the 23rd of October reaches the village of Kineton, in Warwickshire. The king was almost as far as Banbury, and there calls a council of war. Some of the old officers that foresaw the advantage the king had, the concern the city was in, and the vast addition, both to the reputation of his forces and the increase of his interest, it would be if the king could gain that point, urged the king to march on to London. Prince Rupert and the fresh colonels pressed for fighting, told the king it dispirited their men to march with the enemy at their heels; that the Parliament army was inferior to him by 6000 men, and fatigued with hasty marching; that as their orders were to fight, he had nothing to do but to post himself to advantage, and receive them to their destruction; that the action near Worcester had let them know how easy it was to deal with a rash enemy; and that 'twas a dishonour for him, whose forces were so much superior, to be pursued by his subjects in rebellion. These and the like arguments prevailed with the king to alter his wiser measures and resolve to fight. Nor was this all; when a resolution of fighting was taken, that part of the advice which they who were for fighting gave, as a reason for their opinion, was forgot, and instead of halting and posting ourselves to advantage till the enemy came up, we were ordered to march back and meet them.

Nay, so eager was the prince for fighting, that when, from the top of Edgehill, the enemy's army was descried in the bottom between them and the village of Kineton, and that the enemy had bid us defiance, by discharging three cannons, we accepted the challenge, and answering with two shots from our army, we must needs forsake the advantages of the hills, which they must have mounted under the command of our cannon, and march down to them into the plain. I confess, I thought here was a great deal more gallantry than discretion; for it was plainly taking an advantage out of our own hands, and putting it into the hands of the enemy. An enemy that must fight, may always be fought with to advantage. My old hero, the glorious Gustavus Adolphus, was as forward to fight as any man of true valour mixed with any policy need to be, or ought to be; but he used to say, "An enemy reduced to a necessity of fighting is half beaten."

Tis true, we were all but young in the war; the soldiers hot and forward, and eagerly desired to come to hands with the enemy. But I take the more notice of it here, because the king in this acted against his own measures; for it was the king himself had laid the design of getting the start of Essex, and marching to London. His friends had invited him thither, and expected him, and suffered deeply for the omission; and yet he gave way to these hasty counsels, and suffered his judgment to be overruled by majority of voices; an error, I say, the King of Sweden was never guilty of. For if all the officers at a council of war were of a different opinion, yet unless their reasons mastered his judgment, their votes never altered his measures. But this was the error of our good, but unfortunate master, three times in this war, and particularly in two of the greatest battles of the time, viz., this of Edgehill, and that of Naseby.

The resolution for fighting being published in the army, gave an universal joy to the soldiers, who expressed an extraordinary ardour for fighting. I remember my father talking with me about it, asked me what I thought of the approaching battle. I told him I thought the king had done very well; for at that time I did not consult the extent of the design, and had a mighty mind, like other rash people, to see it brought to a day, which made me answer my father as I did. "But," said I, "sir, I doubt there will be but indifferent doings on both sides, between two armies both made up of fresh men, that have never seen any service." My father minded little what I spoke of that; but when I seemed pleased that the king had resolved to fight, he looked angrily at me, and told me he was sorry I could see no farther into things. "I tell you," says he hastily, "if the king should kill and take prisoners this whole army, general and all, the Parliament will have the victory; for we have lost more by slipping this opportunity of getting into London, than we shall ever get by ten battles." I saw enough of this afterwards to convince me of the weight of what my father said, and so did the king too; but it was then too late. Advantages slipped in war are never recovered.

We were now in a full march to fight the Earl of Essex. It was on Sunday morning the 24th of October 1642, fair weather overhead, but the ground very heavy and dirty. As soon as we came to the top of Edgehill, we discovered their whole army. They were not drawn up, having had two miles to march that morning, but they were very busy forming their lines, and posting the regiments as they came up. Some of their horse were exceedingly fatigued, having marched forty-eight hours together; and had they been suffered to follow us three or four days' march farther, several of their regiments of horse would have been quite ruined, and their foot would have been rendered unserviceable for the present. But we had no patience.

As soon as our whole army was come to the top of the hill, we were drawn up in order of battle. The king's army made a very fine appearance; and indeed they were a body of gallant men as ever appeared in the field, and as well furnished at all points; the horse exceedingly well accoutred, being most of them gentlemen and volunteers, some whole regiments serving without pay; their horses very good and fit for service as could be desired. The whole army were not above 18,000 men, and the enemy not 1000 over or under, though we had been told they were not above 12,000; but they had been reinforced with 4000 men from Northampton. The king was with the general, the Earl of Lindsey, in the main battle; Prince Rupert commanded the right wing, and the Marquis of Hertford, the Lord Willoughby, and several other very good officers the left.

The signal of battle being given with two cannon shots, we marched in order of battalia down the hill, being drawn up in two lines with bodies of reserve; the enemy advanced to meet us much in the same form, with this difference only, that they had placed their cannon on their right, and the king had placed ours in the centre, before, or rather between two great brigades of foot. Their cannon began with us first, and did some mischief among the dragoons of our left wing; but our officers, perceiving the shot took the men and missed the horses, ordered all to alight, and every man leading his horse, to advance in the same order; and this saved our men, for most of the enemy's shot flew over their heads. Our cannon made a terrible execution upon their foot for a quarter of an hour, and put them into great confusion, till the general obliged them to halt, and changed the posture of his front, marching round a small rising ground by which he avoided the fury of our artillery.

By this time the wings were engaged, the king having given the signal of battle, and ordered the right wing to fall on. Prince Rupert, who, as is said, commanded that wing, fell on with such fury, and pushed the left wing of the Parliament army so effectually, that in a moment he filled all with terror and confusion. Commissary-General Ramsey, a Scotsman, a Low Country Soldier, and an experienced officer, commanded their left wing, and though he did all that an expert soldier, and a brave commander could do, yet 'twas to no purpose; his lines were immediately broken, and all overwhelmed in a trice. Two regiments of foot, whether as part of the left wing, or on the left of the main body, I know not, were disordered by their own horse, and rather trampled to death by the horses, than beaten by our men; but they were so entirely broken and disordered, that I do not remember that ever they made one volley upon our men; for their own horse running away, and falling foul on these foot, were so vigorously followed by our men, that the foot never had a moment to rally or look behind them. The point of the left wing of horse were not so soon broken as the rest, and three regiments of them stood firm for some time. The dexterous officers of the other regiments taking the opportunity, rallied a great many of their scattered men behind them, and pieced in some troops with those regiments; but after two or three charges, which a brigade of our second line, following the prince, made upon them, they also were broken with the rest.

I remember that at the great battle of Leipsic, the right wing of the Imperialists having fallen in upon the Saxons with like fury to this, bore down all before them, and beat the Saxons quite out of the field; upon which the soldiers cried, "Victoria, let us follow." "No, no," said the old General Tilly, "let them go, but let us beat the Swedes too, and then all's our own." Had Prince Rupert taken this method, and instead of following the fugitives, who were dispersed so effectually that two regiments would have secured them from rallying—I say, had he fallen in upon the foot, or wheeled to the left, and fallen in upon the rear of the enemy's right wing of horse, or returned to the assistance of the left wing of our horse, we had gained the most absolute and complete victory that could be; nor had 1000 men of the enemy's army got off. But this prince, who was full of fire, and pleased to see the rout of an enemy, pursued them quite to the town of Kineton, where indeed he killed abundance of their men, and some time also was lost in plundering the baggage.

But in the meantime, the glory and advantage of the day was lost to the king, for the right wing of the Parliament horse could not be so broken. Sir William Balfour made a desperate charge upon the point of the king's left, and had it not been for two regiments of dragoons who were planted in the reserve, had routed the whole wing, for he broke through the first line, and staggered the second, who advanced to their assistance, but was so warmly received by those dragoons, who came seasonably in, and gave their first fire on horseback, that his fury was checked, and having lost a great many men, was forced to wheel about to his own men; and had the king had but three regiments of horse at hand to have charged him, he had been routed. The rest of this wing kept their ground, and received the first fury of the enemy with great firmness; after which, advancing in their turn, they were at once masters of the Earl of Essex's cannon. And here we lost another advantage; for if any foot had been at hand to support these horse, they had carried off the cannon, or turned it upon the main battle of the enemy's foot, but the foot were otherwise engaged. The horse on this side fought with great obstinacy and variety of success a great while. Sir Philip Stapleton, who commanded the guards of the Earl of Essex, being engaged with a party of our Shrewsbury cavaliers, as we called them, was once in a fair way to have been cut off by a brigade of our foot, who, being advanced to fall on upon the Parliament's main body, flanked Sir Philip's horse in their way, and facing to the left, so furiously charged him with their pikes, that he was obliged to retire in great disorder, and with the loss of a great many men and horses.

All this while the foot on both sides were desperately engaged, and coming close up to the teeth of one another with the clubbed musket and push of pike, fought with great resolution, and a terrible slaughter on both sides, giving no quarter for a great while; and they continued to do thus, till, as if they were tired, and out of wind, either party seemed willing enough to leave off, and take breath. Those which suffered most were that brigade which had charged Sir William Stapleton's horse, who being bravely engaged in the front with the enemy's foot, were, on the sudden, charged again in front and flank by Sir William Balfour's horse and disordered, after a very desperate defence. Here the king's standard was taken, the standard-bearer, Sir Edward Verney, being killed; but it was rescued again by Captain Smith, and brought to the king the same night, for which the king knighted the captain.

This brigade of foot had fought all the day, and had not been broken at last, if any horse had been at hand to support them. The field began to be now clear; both armies stood, as it were, gazing at one another, only the king, having rallied his foot, seemed inclined to renew the charge, and began to cannonade them, which they could not return, most of their cannon being nailed while they were in our possession, and all the cannoniers killed or fled; and our gunners did execution upon Sir William Balfour's troops for a good while.

My father's regiment being in the right with the prince, I saw little of the fight but the rout of the enemy's left, and we had as full a victory there as we could desire, but spent too much time in it. We killed about 2000 men in that part of the action, and having totally dispersed them, and plundered their baggage, began to think of our fellows when 'twas too late to help them. We returned, however, victorious to the king, just as the battle was over. The king asked the prince what news? He told him he could give his Majesty a good account of the enemy's horse. "Ay, by G—d," says a gentleman that stood by me, "and of their carts too." That word was spoken with such a sense of the misfortune, and made such an impression on the whole army, that it occasioned some ill blood afterwards among us; and but that the king took up the business, it had been of ill consequence, for some person who had heard the gentleman speak it, informed the prince who it was, and the prince resenting it, spoke something about it in the hearing of the party when the king was present. The gentleman, not at all surprised, told his Highness openly he had said the words; and though he owned he had no disrespect for his Highness, yet he could not but say, if it had not been so, the enemy's army had been better beaten. The prince replied something very disobliging; upon which the gentleman came up to the king, and kneeling, humbly besought his Majesty to accept of his commission, and to give him leave to tell the prince, that whenever his Highness pleased, he was ready to give him satisfaction. The prince was exceedingly provoked, and as he was very passionate, began to talk very oddly, and without all government of himself. The gentleman, as bold as he, but much calmer preserved his temper, but maintained his quarrel; and the king was so concerned, that he was very much out of humour with the prince about it. However, his Majesty, upon consideration, soon ended the dispute, by laying his commands on them both to speak no more of it for that day; and refusing the commission from the colonel, for he was no less, sent for them both next morning in private, and made them friends again.

But to return to our story. We came back to the king timely enough to put the Earl of Essex's men out of all humour of renewing the fight, and as I observed before, both parties stood gazing at one another, and our cannon playing upon them obliged Sir William Balfour's horse to wheel off in some disorder, but they returned us none again, which, as we afterwards understood, was, as I said before, for want of both powder and gunners, for the cannoniers and firemen were killed, or had quitted their train in the fight, when our horse had possession of their artillery; and as they had spiked up some of the cannon, so they had carried away fifteen carriages of powder.

Night coming on, ended all discourse of more fighting, and the king drew off and marched towards the hills. I know no other token of victory which the enemy had than their lying in the field of battle all night, which they did for no other reason than that, having lost their baggage and provisions, they had nowhere to go, and which we did not, because we had good quarters at hand.

The number of prisoners and of the slain were not very unequal; the enemy lost more men, we most of quality. Six thousand men on both sides were killed on the spot, whereof, when our rolls were examined, we missed 2500. We lost our brave general the old Earl of Lindsey, who was wounded and taken prisoner, and died of his wounds; Sir Edward Stradling, Colonel Lundsford, prisoners; and Sir Edward Verney and a great many gentlemen of quality slain. On the other hand, we carried off Colonel Essex, Colonel Ramsey, and the Lord St John, who also died of his wounds; we took five ammunition waggons full of powder, and brought off about 500 horse in the defeat of the left wing, with eighteen standards and colours, and lost seventeen.

The slaughter of the left wing was so great, and the flight so effectual, that several of the officers rid clear away, coasting round, and got to London, where they reported that the Parliament army was entirely defeated—all lost, killed, or taken, as if none but them were left alive to carry the news. This filled them with consternation for a while, but when other messengers followed, all was restored to quiet again, and the Parliament cried up their victory and sufficiently mocked God and their general with their public thanks for it. Truly, as the fight was a deliverance to them, they were in the right to give thanks for it; but as to its being a victory, neither side had much to boast of, and they less a great deal than we had.

I got no hurt in this fight, and indeed we of the right wing had but little fighting; I think I had discharged my pistols but once, and my carabine twice, for we had more fatigue than fight; the enemy fled, and we had little to do but to follow and kill those we could overtake. I spoiled a good horse, and got a better from the enemy in his room, and came home weary enough. My father lost his horse, and in the fall was bruised in his thigh by another horse treading on him, which disabled him for some time, and at his request, by his Majesty's consent, I commanded the regiment in his absence.

The enemy received a recruit of 4000 men the next morning; if they had not, I believe they had gone back towards Worcester; but, encouraged by that reinforcement, they called a council of war, and had a long debate whether they could attack us again; but notwithstanding their great victory, they durst not attempt it, though this addition of strength made them superior to us by 3000 men.

The king indeed expected, that when these troops joined them they would advance, and we were preparing to receive them at a village called Aynho, where the headquarters continued three or four days; and had they really esteemed the first day's work a victory, as they called it, they would have done it, but they thought not good to venture, but march away to Warwick, and from thence to Coventry. The king, to urge them to venture upon him, and come to a second battle, sits down before Banbury, and takes both town and castle; and two entire regiments of foot, and one troop of horse, quit the Parliament service, and take up their arms for the king. This was done almost before their faces, which was a better proof of a victory on our side, than any they could pretend to. From Banbury we marched to Oxford; and now all men saw the Parliament had made a great mistake, for they were not always in the right any more than we, to leave Oxford without a garrison. The king caused new regular works to be drawn round it, and seven royal bastions with ravelins and out-works, a double ditch, counterscarp, and covered way; all which, added to the advantage of its situation, made it a formidable place, and from this time it became our place of arms, and the centre of affairs on the king's side.

If the Parliament had the honour of the field, the king reaped the fruits of the victory; for all this part of the country submitted to him. Essex's army made the best of their way to London, and were but in an ill condition when they came there, especially their horse.

The Parliament, sensible of this, and receiving daily accounts of the progress we made, began to cool a little in their temper, abated of their first rage, and voted an address for peace; and sent to the king to let him know they were desirous to prevent the effusion of more blood, and to bring things to an accommodation, or, as they called it, a right understanding.

I was now, by the king's particular favour, summoned to the councils of war, my father continuing absent and ill; and now I began to think of the real grounds, and which was more, of the fatal issue of this war. I say, I now began it; for I cannot say that I ever rightly stated matters in my own mind before, though I had been enough used to blood, and to see the destruction of people, sacking of towns, and plundering the country; yet 'twas in Germany, and among strangers; but I found a strange, secret and unaccountable sadness upon my spirits, to see this acting in my own native country. It grieved me to the heart, even in the rout of our enemies, to see the slaughter of them; and even in the fight, to hear a man cry for quarter in English, moved me to a compassion which I had never been used to; nay, sometimes it looked to me as if some of my own men had been beaten; and when I heard a soldier cry, "O God, I am shot," I looked behind me to see which of my own troop was fallen. Here I saw myself at the cutting of the throats of my friends; and indeed some of my near relations. My old comrades and fellow-soldiers in Germany were some with us, some against us, as their opinions happened to differ in religion. For my part, I confess I had not much religion in me, at that time; but I thought religion rightly practised on both sides would have made us all better friends; and therefore sometimes I began to think, that both the bishops of our side, and the preachers on theirs, made religion rather the pretence than the cause of the war. And from those thoughts I vigorously argued it at the council of war against marching to Brentford, while the address for a treaty of peace from the Parliament was in hand: for I was for taking the Parliament by the handle which they had given us, and entering into a negotiation, with the advantage of its being at their own request.

I thought the king had now in his hands an opportunity to make an honourable peace; for this battle of Edgehill, as much as they boasted of the victory to hearten up their friends, had sorely weakened their army, and discouraged their party too, which in effect was worse as to their army. The horse were particularly in an ill case, and the foot greatly diminished, and the remainder very sickly; but besides this, the Parliament were greatly alarmed at the progress we made afterward; and still fearing the king's surprising them, had sent for the Earl of Essex to London, to defend them; by which the country was, as it were, defeated and abandoned, and left to be plundered; our parties overrun all places at pleasure. All this while I considered, that whatever the soldiers of fortune meant by the war, our desires were to suppress the exorbitant power of a party, to establish our king in his just and legal rights; but not with a design to destroy the constitution of government, and the being of Parliament. And therefore I thought now was the time for peace, and there were a great many worthy gentlemen in the army of my mind; and, had our master had ears to hear us, the war might have had an end here.

This address for peace was received by the king at Maidenhead, whither this army was now advanced, and his Majesty returned answer by Sir Peter Killegrew, that he desired nothing more, and would not be wanting on his part. Upon this the Parliament name commissioners, and his Majesty excepting against Sir John Evelyn, they left him out, and sent others; and desired the king to appoint his residence near London, where the commissioners might wait upon him. Accordingly the king appointed Windsor for the place of treaty, and desired the treaty might be hastened. And thus all things looked with a favourable aspect, when one unlucky action knocked it all on the head, and filled both parties with more implacable animosities than they had before, and all hopes of peace vanished.

During this progress of the king's armies, we were always abroad with the horse ravaging the country, and plundering the Roundheads. Prince Rupert, a most active vigilant party man, and I must own, fitter for such than for a general, was never lying still, and I seldom stayed behind; for our regiment being very well mounted, he would always send for us, if he had any extraordinary design in hand.

One time in particular he had a design upon Aylesbury, the capital of Buckinghamshire; indeed our view at first was rather to beat the enemy out of town and demolish their works, and perhaps raise some contributions on the rich country round it, than to garrison the place, and keep it; for we wanted no more garrisons, being masters of the field.

The prince had 2500 horse with him in this expedition, but no foot; the town had some foot raised in the country by Mr Hampden, and two regiments of country militia, whom we made light of, but we found they stood to their tackle better than well enough. We came very early to the town, and thought they had no notice of us; but some false brother had given them the alarm, and we found them all in arms, the hedges without the town lined with musketeers, on that side in particular where they expected us, and two regiments of foot drawn up in view to support them, with some horse in the rear of all.

The prince, willing, however, to do something, caused some of his horse to alight, and serve as dragoons; and having broken a way into the enclosures, the horse beat the foot from behind the hedges, while the rest who were alighted charged them in the lane which leads to the town. Here they had cast up some works, and fired from their lines very regularly, considering them as militia only, the governor encouraging them by his example; so that finding without some foot there would be no good to be done, we gave it over, and drew off; and so Aylesbury escaped a scouring for that time.

I cannot deny but these flying parties of horse committed great spoil among the country people; and sometimes the prince gave a liberty to some cruelties which were not at all for the king's interest; because it being still upon our own country, and the king's own subjects, whom in all his declarations he protested to be careful of, it seemed to contradict all those protestations and declarations, and served to aggravate and exasperate the common people; and the king's enemies made all the advantages of it that was possible, by crying out of twice as many extravagancies as were committed.

'Tis true, the king, who naturally abhorred such things, could not restrain his men, no, nor his generals, so absolutely as he would have done. The war, on his side, was very much à la volunteer; many gentlemen served him at their own charge, and some paid whole regiments themselves: sometimes also the king's affairs were straiter than ordinary, and his men were not very well paid, and this obliged him to wink at their excursions upon the country, though he did not approve of them. And yet I must own, that in those parts of England where the war was hottest, there never was seen that ruin and depopulation, murders, and barbarities, which I have seen even among Protestant armies abroad, in Germany and other foreign parts of the world. And if the Parliament people had seen those things abroad, as I had, they would not have complained.

The most I have seen was plundering the towns for provisions, drinking up their beer, and turning our horses into their fields, or stacks of corn; and sometimes the soldiers would be a little rude with the wenches; but alas! what was this to Count Tilly's ravages in Saxony? Or what was our taking of Leicester by storm, where they cried out of our barbarities, to the sacking of New Brandenburg, or the taking of Magdeburg? In Leicester, of 7000 or 8000 people in the town, 300 were killed; in Magdeburg, of 25,000 scarce 2700 were left, and the whole town burnt to ashes. I myself have seen seventeen or eighteen villages on fire in a day, and the people driven away from their dwellings, like herds of cattle. I do not instance these greater barbarities to justify lesser actions, which are nevertheless irregular; but I do say, that circumstances considered, this war was managed with as much humanity on both sides as could be expected, especially also considering the animosity of parties.

But to return to the prince: he had not always the same success in these enterprises, for sometimes we came short home. And I cannot omit one pleasant adventure which happened to a party of ours, in one of these excursions into Buckinghamshire. The major of our regiment was soundly beaten by a party, which, as I may say, was led by a woman; and, if I had not rescued him, I know not but he had been taken prisoner by a woman. It seems our men had besieged some fortified house about Oxfordshire, towards Thame, and the house being defended by the lady in her husband's absence, she had yielded the house upon a capitulation; one of the articles of which was, to march out with all her servants, soldiers, and goods, and to be conveyed to Thame. Whether she thought to have gone no farther, or that she reckoned herself safe there, I know not; but my major, with two troops of horse, meets with this lady and her party, about five miles from Thame, as we were coming back from our defeated attack of Aylesbury. We reckoned ourselves in an enemy's country, and had lived a little at large, or at discretion, as 'tis called abroad; and these two troops, with the major, were returning to our detachment from a little village, where, at the farmer's house, they had met with some liquor, and truly some of his men were so drunk they could but just sit upon their horses. The major himself was not much better, and the whole body were but in a sorry condition to fight. Upon the road they meet this party; the lady having no design of fighting, and being, as she thought, under the protection of the articles, sounds a parley, and desired to speak with the officer. The major, as drunk as he was, could tell her, that by the articles she was to be assured no farther than Thame, and being now five miles beyond it, she was a fair enemy, and therefore demanded to render themselves prisoners. The lady seemed surprised, but being sensible she was in the wrong, offered to compound for her goods, and would have given him £300, and I think seven or eight horses. The major would certainly have taken it, if he had not been drunk; but he refused it, and gave threatening words to her, blustering in language which he thought proper to fright a woman, viz., that he would cut them all to pieces, and give no quarter, and the like.

The lady, who had been more used to the smell of powder than he imagined, called some of her servants to her, and, consulting with them what to do, they all unanimously encouraged her to let them fight; told her it was plain that the commander was drunk, and all that were with him were rather worse than he, and hardly able to sit their horses; and that therefore one bold charge would put them all into confusion. In a word, she consented, and, as she was a woman, they desired her to secure herself among the waggons; but she refused, and told them bravely she would take her fate with them. In short, she boldly bade my major defiance, and that he might do his worst, since she had offered him fair, and he had refused it; her mind was altered now, and she would give him nothing, and bade his officer that parleyed longer with her be gone; so the parley ended. After this she gave him fair leave to go back to his men; but before he could tell his tale to them she was at his heels with all her men, and gave him such a home charge as put his men into disorder, and, being too drunk to rally, they were knocked down before they knew what to do with themselves, and in a few minutes more they took to a plain flight. But what was still worse, the men, being some of them very drunk, when they came to run for their lives fell over one another, and tumbled over their horses, and made such work that a troop of women might have beaten them all. In this pickle, with the enemy at his heels, I came in with him, hearing the noise. When I appeared the pursuers retreated, and, seeing what a condition my people were in, and not knowing the strength of the enemy, I contented myself with bringing them off without pursuing the other; nor could I ever hear positively who this female captain was. We lost seventeen or eighteen of our men, and about thirty horses; but when the particulars of the story was told us, our major was so laughed at by the whole army, and laughed at everywhere, that he was ashamed to show himself for a week or a fortnight after.

But to return to the king: his Majesty, as I observed, was at Maidenhead addressed by the Parliament for peace, and Windsor being appointed for the place of treaty, the van of his army lay at Colebrook. In the meantime, whether it were true or only a pretence, but it was reported the Parliament general had sent a body of his troops, with a train of artillery, to Hammersmith, in order to fall upon some part of our army, or to take some advanced post, which was to the prejudice of our men; whereupon the king ordered the army to march, and, by the favour of a thick mist, came within half a mile of Brentford before he was discovered. There were two regiments of foot, and about 600 horse into the town, of the enemy's best troops; these taking the alarm, posted themselves on the bridge at the west end of the town. The king attacked them with a select detachment of his best infantry, and they defended themselves with incredible obstinacy. I must own I never saw raw men, for they could not have been in arms above four months, act like them in my life. In short, there was no forcing these men, for, though two whole brigades of our foot, backed by our horse, made five several attacks upon them they could not break them, and we lost a great many brave men in that action. At last, seeing the obstinacy of these men, a party of horse was ordered to go round from Osterley; and, entering the town on the north side, where, though the horse made some resistance, it was not considerable, the town was presently taken. I led my regiment through an enclosure, and came into the town nearer to the bridge than the rest, by which means I got first into the town; but I had this loss by my expedition, that the foot charged me before the body was come up, and poured in their shot very furiously. My men were but in an ill case, and would not have stood much longer, if the rest of the horse coming up the lane had not found them other employment. When the horse were thus entered, they immediately dispersed the enemy's horse, who fled away towards London, and falling in sword in hand upon the rear of the foot, who were engaged at the bridge, they were all cut in pieces, except about 200, who, scorning to ask quarter, desperately threw themselves into the river of Thames, where they were most of them drowned.

The Parliament and their party made a great outcry at this attempt—that it was base and treacherous while in a treaty of peace; and that the king, having amused them with hearkening to a treaty, designed to have seized upon their train of artillery first, and, after that, to have surprised both the city of London and the Parliament. And I have observed since, that our historians note this action as contrary to the laws of honour and treaties, though as there was no cessation of arms agreed on, nothing is more contrary to the laws of war than to suggest it.

That it was a very unhappy thing to the king and whole nation, as it broke off the hopes of peace, and was the occasion of bringing the Scots army in upon us, I readily acknowledge, but that there was anything dishonourable in it, I cannot allow. For though the Parliament had addressed to the king for peace, and such steps were taken in it as before, yet, as I have said, there was no proposals made on either side for a cessation of arms, and all the world must allow, that in such cases the war goes on in the field, while the peace goes on in the cabinet. And if the war goes on, admit the king had designed to surprise the city or Parliament, or all of them, it had been no more than the custom of war allows, and what they would have done by him if they could. The treaty of Westphalia, or peace of Munster, which ended the bloody wars of Germany, was a precedent for this. That treaty was actually negotiating seven years, and yet the war went on with all the vigour and rancour imaginable, even to the last. Nay, the very time after the conclusion of it, but before the news could be brought to the army, did he that was afterwards King of Sweden, Carolus Gustavus, take the city of Prague by surprise, and therein an inestimable booty. Besides, all the wars of Europe are full of examples of this kind, and therefore I cannot see any reason to blame the king for this action as to the fairness of it. Indeed, as to the policy of it, I can say little; but the case was this. The king had a gallant army, flushed with success, and things hitherto had gone on very prosperously, both with his own army and elsewhere; he had above 35,000 men in his own army, including his garrison left at Banbury, Shrewsbury, Worcester, Oxford, Wallingford, Abingdon, Reading, and places adjacent. On the other hand, the Parliament army came back to London in but a very sorry condition;[1] for what with their loss in their victory, as they called it, at Edgehill, their sickness, and a hasty march to London, they were very much diminished, though at London they soon recruited them again. And this prosperity of the king's affairs might encourage him to strike this blow, thinking to bring the Parliament to the better terms by the apprehensions of the superior strength of the king's forces.

But, however it was, the success did not equally answer the king's expectation. The vigorous defence the troops posted at Brentford made as above, gave the Earl of Essex opportunity, with extraordinary application, to draw his forces out to Turnham Green. And the exceeding alacrity of the enemy was such, that their whole army appeared with them, making together an army of 24,000 men, drawn up in view of our forces by eight o'clock the next morning. The city regiments were placed between the regular troops, and all together offered us battle, but we were not in a condition to accept it. The king indeed was sometimes of the mind to charge them, and once or twice ordered parties to advance to begin to skirmish, but upon better advice altered his mind, and indeed it was the wisest counsel to defer the fighting at that time. The Parliament generals were as unfixed in their resolutions, on the other side, as the king; sometimes they sent out parties, and then called them back again. One strong party of near 3000 men marched off towards Acton, with orders to amuse us on that side, but were countermanded. Indeed, I was of the opinion we might have ventured the battle, for though the Parliament's army were more numerous, yet the city trained bands, which made up 4000 of their foot, were not much esteemed, and the king was a great deal stronger in horse than they. But the main reason that hindered the engagement, was want of ammunition, which the king having duly weighed, he caused the carriages and cannon to draw off first, and then the foot, the horse continuing to force the enemy till all was clear gone; and then we drew off too and marched to Kingston, and the next day to Reading.

Now the king saw his mistake in not continuing his march for London, instead of facing about to fight the enemy at Edgehill. And all the honour we had gained in so many successful enterprises lay buried in this shameful retreat from an army of citizens' wives; for truly that appearance at Turnham Green was gay, but not great. There was as many lookers-on as actors. The crowds of ladies, apprentices, and mob was so great, that when the parties of our army advanced, and as they thought, to charge, the coaches, horsemen, and crowd, that cluttered away to be out of harm's way, looked little better than a rout. And I was persuaded a good home charge from our horse would have sent their whole army after them. But so it was, that this crowd of an army was to triumph over us, and they did it, for all the kingdom was carefully informed how their dreadful looks had frightened us away.

Upon our retreat, the Parliament resent this attack, which they call treacherous, and vote no accommodation; but they considered of it afterwards, and sent six commissioners to the king with propositions. But the change of the scene of action changed the terms of peace, and now they made terms like conquerors, petition him to desert his army, and return to the Parliament, and the like. Had his Majesty, at the head of his army, with the full reputation they had before, and in the ebb of their affairs, rested at Windsor, and commenced a treaty, they had certainly made more reasonable proposals; but now the scabbard seemed to be thrown away on both sides.

The rest of the winter was spent in strengthening parties and places, also in fruitless treaties of peace, messages, remonstrances, and paper war on both sides, and no action remarkable happened anywhere that I remember. Yet the king gained ground everywhere, and his forces in the north increased under the Earl of Newcastle; also my Lord Goring, then only called Colonel Goring, arrived from Holland, bringing three ships laden with arms and ammunition, and notice that the queen was following with more. Goring brought 4000 barrels of gunpowder, and 20,000 small arms; all which came very seasonably, for the king was in great want of them, especially the powder. Upon this recruit the Earl of Newcastle draws down to York, and being above 16,000 strong, made Sir Thomas Fairfax give ground, and retreat to Hull.

Whoever lay still, Prince Rupert was always abroad, and I chose to go out with his Highness as often as I had opportunity, for hitherto he was always successful. About this time the prince being at Oxford, I gave him intelligence of a party of the enemy who lived a little at large, too much for good soldiers, about Cirencester. The prince, glad of the news, resolved to attack them, and though it was a wet season, and the ways exceeding bad, being in February, yet we marched all night in the dark, which occasioned the loss of some horses and men too, in sloughs and holes, which the darkness of the night had suffered them to fall into. We were a very strong party, being about 3000 horse and dragoons, and coming to Cirencester very early in the morning, to our great satisfaction the enemy were perfectly surprised, not having the least notice of our march, which answered our end more ways than one. However, the Earl of Stamford's regiment made some resistance; but the town having no works to defend it, saving a slight breastwork at the entrance of the road, with a turnpike, our dragoons alighted, and forcing their way over the bellies of Stamford's foot, they beat them from their defence, and followed them at their heels into the town. Stamford's regiment was entirely cut in pieces, and several others, to the number of about 800 men, and the town entered without any other resistance. We took 1200 prisoners, 3000 arms, and the county magazine, which at that time was considerable; for there was about 120 barrels of powder, and all things in proportion.

I received the first hurt I got in this war at this action, for having followed the dragoons and brought my regiment within the barricado which they had gained, a musket bullet struck my horse just in the head, and that so effectually that he fell down as dead as a stone all at once. The fall plunged me into a puddle of water and daubed me; and my man having brought me another horse and cleaned me a little, I was just getting up, when another bullet struck me on my left hand, which I had just clapped on the horse's main to lift myself into the saddle. The blow broke one of my fingers, and bruised my hand very much; and it proved a very painful hurt to me. For the present I did not much concern myself about it, but made my man tie it up close in my handkerchief, and led up my men to the market-place, where we had a very smart brush with some musketeers who were posted in the churchyard; but our dragoons soon beat them out there, and the whole town was then our own. We made no stay here, but marched back with all our booty to Oxford, for we knew the enemy were very strong at Gloucester, and that way.

Much about the same time, the Earl of Northampton, with a strong party, set upon Lichfield, and took the town, but could not take the Close; but they beat a body of 4000 men coming to the relief of the town, under Sir John Gell, of Derbyshire, and Sir William Brereton, of Cheshire, and killing 600 of them, dispersed the rest.

Our second campaign now began to open; the king marched from Oxford to relieve Reading, which was besieged by the Parliament forces; but General Fielding, Lieutenant-Governor, Sir Arthur Ashton being wounded, surrendered to Essex before the king could come up; for which he was tried by martial law, and condemned to die, but the king forbore to execute the sentence. This was the first town we had lost in the war, for still the success of the king's affairs was very encouraging. This bad news, however, was overbalanced by an account brought the king at the same time, by an express from York, that the queen had landed in the north, and had brought over a great magazine of arms and ammunition, besides some men. Some time after this her Majesty, marching southward to meet the king, joined the army near Edgehill, where the first battle was fought. She brought the king 3000 foot, 1500 horse and dragoons, six pieces of cannon, 1500 barrels of powder, 12,000 small arms.

During this prosperity of the king's affairs his armies increased mightily in the western counties also. Sir William Waller, indeed, commanded for the Parliament in those parts too, and particularly in Dorsetshire, Hampshire, and Berkshire, where he carried on their cause but too fast; but farther west, Sir Nicholas Slanning, Sir Ralph Hopton, and Sir Bevil Grenvile had extended the king's quarters from Cornwall through Devonshire, and into Somersetshire, where they took Exeter, Barnstaple, and Bideford; and the first of these they fortified very well, making it a place of arms for the west, and afterwards it was the residence of the queen.

At last, the famous Sir William Waller and the king's forces met, and came to a pitched battle, where Sir William lost all his honour again. This was at Roundway Down in Wiltshire. Waller had engaged our Cornish army at Lansdown, and in a very obstinate fight had the better of them, and made them retreat to the Devizes. Sir William Hopton, however, having a good body of foot untouched, sent expresses and messengers one in the neck of another to the king for some horse, and the king being in great concern for that army, who were composed of the flower of the Cornish men, commanded me to march with all possible secrecy, as well as expedition, with 1200 horse and dragoons from Oxford, to join them. We set out in the depth of the night, to avoid, if possible, any intelligence being given of our route, and soon joined with the Cornish army, when it was as soon resolved to give battle to Waller; and, give him his due, he was as forward to fight as we. As it is easy to meet when both sides are willing to be found, Sir William Waller met us upon Roundway Down, where we had a fair field on both sides, and room enough to draw up our horse. In a word, there was little ceremony to the work; the armies joined, and we charged his horse with so much resolution, that they quickly fled, and quitted the field; for we over-matched him in horse, and this was the entire destruction of their army. For the infantry, which outnumbered ours by 1500, were now at our mercy; some faint resistance they made, just enough to give us occasion to break into their ranks with our horse, where we gave time to our foot to defeat others that stood to their work, upon which they began to disband, and run every way they could; but our horse having surrounded them, we made a fearful havoc of them.

We lost not about 200 men in this action; Waller lost about 4000 killed and taken, and as many dispersed that never returned to their colours. Those of foot that escaped got into Bristol, and Waller, with the poor remains of his routed regiments, got to London; so that it is plain some ran east, and some ran west, that is to say, they fled every way they could.

My going with this detachment prevented my being at the siege of Bristol, which Prince Rupert attacked much about the same time, and it surrendered in three days. The Parliament questioned Colonel Nathaniel Fiennes, the governor, and had him tried as a coward by a court-martial, and condemned to die, but suspended the execution also, as the king did the governor of Reading. I have often heard Prince Rupert say, they did Colonel Fiennes wrong in that affair; and that if the colonel would have summoned him, he would have demanded a passport of the Parliament, and have come up and convinced the court that Colonel Fiennes had not misbehaved himself, and that he had not a sufficient garrison to defend a city of that extent; having not above 1200 men in the town, excepting some of Waller's runaways, most of whom were unfit for service, and without arms; and that the citizens in general being disaffected to him, and ready on the first occasion to open the gates to the king's forces, it was impossible for him to have kept the city. "And when I had farther informed them," said the prince, "of the measures I had taken for a general assault the next day, I am confident I should have convinced them that I had taken the city by storm, if he had not surrendered."

The king's affairs were now in a very good posture, and three armies in the north, west, and in the centre, counted in the musters about 70,000 men besides small garrisons and parties abroad. Several of the lords, and more of the commons, began to fall off from the Parliament, and make their peace with the king; and the affairs of the Parliament began to look very ill. The city of London was their inexhaustible support and magazine, both for men, money, and all things necessary; and whenever their army was out of order, the clergy of their party in but one Sunday or two, would preach the young citizens out of their shops, the labourers from their masters, into the army, and recruit them on a sudden. And all this was still owing to the omission I first observed, of not marching to London, when it might have been so easily effected.

We had now another, or a fairer opportunity, than before, but as ill use was made of it. The king, as I have observed, was in a very good posture; he had three large armies roving at large over the kingdom. The Cornish army, victorious and numerous, had beaten Waller, secured and fortified Exeter, which the queen had made her residence, and was there delivered of a daughter, the Princess Henrietta Maria, afterwards Duchess of Orleans, and mother of the Duchess Dowager of Savoy, commonly known in the French style by the title of Madam Royal. They had secured Salisbury, Sherborne Castle, Weymouth, Winchester, and Basing-house, and commanded the whole country, except Bridgewater and Taunton, Plymouth and Lynn; all which places they held blocked up. The king was also entirely master of all Wales, Monmouthshire, Cheshire, Shropshire, Staffordshire, Worcestershire, Oxfordshire, Berkshire, and all the towns from Windsor up the Thames to Cirencester, except Reading and Henley; and of the whole Severn, except Gloucester.

The Earl of Newcastle had garrisons in every strong place in the north, from Berwick-upon-Tweed to Boston in Lincolnshire, and

Newark-upon-Trent, Hull only excepted, whither the Lord Fairfax and his son Sir Thomas were retreated, their troops being routed and broken, Sir Thomas Fairfax his baggage, with his lady and servants taken prisoners, and himself hardly scaping.

And now a great council of war was held in the king's quarters, what enterprise to go upon; and it happened to be the very same day when the Parliament were in a serious debate what should become of them, and whose help they should seek. And indeed they had cause for it; and had our counsels been as ready and well-grounded as theirs, we had put an end to the war in a month's time.

In this council the king proposed the marching to London, to put an end to the Parliament and encourage his friends and loyal subjects in Kent, who were ready to rise for him; and showed us letters from the Earl of Newcastle, wherein he offered to join his Majesty with a detachment of 4000 horse, and 8000 foot, if his Majesty thought fit to march southward, and yet leave forces sufficient to guard the north from any invasion. I confess, when I saw the scheme the king had himself drawn for this attempt, I felt an unusual satisfaction in my mind, from the hopes that he might bring this war to some tolerable end; for I professed myself on all occasions heartily weary with fighting with friends, brothers, neighbours, and acquaintance, and I made no question but this motion of the king's would effectually bring the Parliament to reason.

All men seemed to like the enterprise but the Earl of Worcester, who, on particular views for securing the country behind, as he called it, proposed the taking in the town of Gloucester and Hereford first. He made a long speech of the danger of leaving Massey, an active bold fellow, with a strong party in the heart of all the king's quarters, ready on all occasions to sally out and surprise the neighbouring garrisons, as he had done Sudley Castle and others; and of the ease and freedom to all those western parts to have them fully cleared of the enemy. Interest presently backs this advice, and all those gentlemen whose estates lay that way, or whose friends lived about Worcester, Shrewsbury, Bridgnorth, or the borders, and who, as they said, had heard the frequent wishes of the country to have the city of Gloucester reduced, fell in with this advice, alleging the consequence it was for the commerce of the country to have the navigation of the Severn free, which was only interrupted by this one town from the sea up to Shrewsbury, &c.

I opposed this, and so did several others. Prince Rupert was vehemently against it; and we both offered, with the troops of the country, to keep Gloucester blocked up during the king's march for London, so that Massey should not be able to stir.

This proposal made the Earl of Worcester's party more eager for the siege than before, for they had no mind to a blockade which would leave the country to maintain the troops all the summer; and of all men the prince did not please them, for, he having no extraordinary character for discipline, his company was not much desired even by our friends. Thus, in an ill hour, 'twas resolved to sit down before Gloucester. The king had a gallant army of 28,000 men whereof 11,000 horse, the finest body of gentlemen that ever I saw together in my life; their horses without comparison, and their equipages the finest and the best in the world, and their persons Englishmen, which, I think, is enough to say of them.

According to the resolution taken in the council of war, the army marched westward, and sat down before Gloucester the beginning of August. There we spent a month to the least purpose that ever army did. Our men received frequent affronts from the desperate sallies of an inconsiderable enemy. I cannot forbear reflecting on the misfortunes of this siege. Our men were strangely dispirited in all the assaults they gave upon the place; there was something looked like disaster and mismanagement, and our men went on with an ill will and no resolution. The king despised the place, and thinking to carry it sword in hand, made no regular approaches, and the garrison, being desperate, made therefore the greater slaughter. In this work our horse, who were so numerous and so fine, had no employment. Two thousand horse had been enough for this business, and the enemy had no garrison or party within forty miles of us, so that we had nothing to do but look on with infinite regret upon the losses of our foot.

The enemy made frequent and desperate sallies, in one of which I had my share. I was posted upon a parade, or place of arms, with part of my regiment, and part of Colonel Goring's regiment of horse, in order to support a body of foot, who were ordered to storm the point of a breastwork which the enemy had raised to defend one of the avenues to the town. The foot were beat off with loss, as they always were; and Massey, the governor, not content to have beaten them from his works, sallies out with near 400 men, and falling in upon the foot as they were rallying under the cover of our horse, we put ourselves in the best posture we could to receive them. As Massey did not expect, I suppose, to engage with any horse, he had no pikes with him, which encouraged us to treat him the more rudely; but as to desperate men danger is no danger, when he found he must clear his hands of us, before he could despatch the foot, he faces up to us, fires but one volley of his small shot, and fell to battering us with the stocks of their muskets in such a manner that one would have thought they had been madmen.

We at first despised this way of clubbing us, and charging through them, laid a great many of them upon the ground, and in repeating our charge, trampled more of them under our horses' feet; and wheeling thus continually, beat them off from our foot, who were just upon the point of disbanding. Upon this they charged us again with their fire, and at one volley killed thirty-three or thirty-four men and horses; and had they had pikes with them, I know not what we should have done with them. But at last charging through them again, we divided them; one part of them being hemmed in between us and our own foot, were cut in pieces to a man; the rest as I understood afterwards, retreated into the town, having lost 300 of their men.

In this last charge I received a rude blow from a stout fellow on foot with the butt end of his musket which perfectly stunned me, and fetched me off from my horse; and had not some near me took care of me, I had been trod to death by our own men. But the fellow being immediately killed, and my friends finding me alive, had taken me up, and carried me off some distance, where I came to myself again after some time, but knew little of what I did or said that night. This was the reason why I say I afterwards understood the enemy retreated; for I saw no more what they did then, nor indeed was I well of this blow for all the rest of the summer, but had frequent pains in my head, dizzinesses and swimming, that gave me some fears the blow had injured the skull; but it wore off again, nor did it at all hinder my attending my charge.

This action, I think, was the only one that looked like a defeat given the enemy at this siege. We killed them near 300 men, as I have said, and lost about sixty of our troopers.

All this time, while the king was harassing and weakening the best army he ever saw together during the whole war, the Parliament generals, or rather preachers, were recruiting theirs; for the preachers were better than drummers to raise volunteers, zealously exhorting the London dames to part with their husbands, and the city to send some of their trained bands to join the army for the relief of Gloucester; and now they began to advance towards us.

The king hearing of the advance of Essex's army, who by this time was come to Aylesbury, had summoned what forces he had within call, to join him; and accordingly he received 3000 foot from Somersetshire; and having battered the town for thirty-six hours, and made a fair breach, resolves upon an assault, if possible, to carry the town before the enemy came up. The assault was begun about seven in the evening, and the men boldly mounted the breach; but after a very obstinate and bloody dispute, were beaten out again by the besieged with great loss.

Being thus often repulsed, and the Earl of Essex's army approaching, the king calls a council of war, and proposed to fight Essex's army. The officers of the horse were for fighting; and without doubt we were superior to him both in number and goodness of our horse, but the foot were not in an equal condition; and the colonels of foot representing to the king the weakness of their regiments, and how their men had been balked and disheartened at this cursed siege, the graver counsel prevailed, and it was resolved to raise the siege, and retreat towards Bristol, till the army was recruited. Pursuant to this resolution, the 5th of September, the king, having before sent away his heavy cannon and baggage, raised the siege, and marched to Berkeley Castle. The Earl of Essex came the next day to Birdlip Hills; and understanding by messengers from Colonel Massey, that the siege was raised, sends a recruit of 2500 men into the city, and followed us himself with a great body of horse.

This body of horse showed themselves to us once in a large field fit to have entertained them in; and our scouts having assured us they were not above 4000, and had no foot with them, the king ordered a detachment of about the same number to face them. I desired his Majesty to let us have two regiments of dragoons with us, which was then 800 men in a regiment, lest there might be some dragoons among the enemy; which the king granted, and accordingly we marched, and drew up in view of them. They stood their ground, having, as they supposed, some advantage of the manner they were posted in, and expected we would charge them. The king, who did us the honour to command this party, finding they would not stir, calls me to him, and ordered me with the dragoons, and my own regiment, to take a circuit round by a village to a certain lane, where in their retreat they must have passed, and which opened to a small common on the flank; with orders, if they engaged, to advance and charge them in the flank. I marched immediately; but though the country about there was almost all enclosures, yet their scouts were so vigilant, that they discovered me, and gave notice to the body; upon which their whole party moved to the left, as if they intended to charge me, before the king with his body of horse could come. But the king was too vigilant to be circumvented so; and therefore his Majesty perceiving this, sends away three regiments of horse to second me, and a messenger before them, to order me to halt, and expect the enemy, for that he would follow with the whole body.

But before this order reached me, I had halted for some time; for finding myself discovered, and not judging it safe to be entirely cut off from the main body, I stopped at the village, and causing my dragoons to alight, and line a thick hedge on my left, I drew up my horse just at the entrance into the village opening to a common. The enemy came up on the trot to charge me, but were saluted with a terrible fire from the dragoons out of the hedge, which killed them near 100 men. This being a perfect surprise to them, they halted, and just at that moment they received orders from their main body to retreat; the king at the same time appearing upon some heights in their rear, which obliged them to think of retreating, or coming to a general battle, which was none of their design.

I had no occasion to follow them, not being in a condition to attack the whole body; but the dragoons coming out into the common, gave them another volley at a distance, which reached them effectually, for it killed about twenty of them, and wounded more; but they drew off, and never fired a shot at us, fearing to be enclosed between two parties, and so marched away to their general's quarters, leaving ten or twelve more of their fellows killed, and about 180 horses. Our men, after the country fashion, gave them a shout at parting, to let them see we knew they were afraid of us.

However, this relieving of Gloucester raised the spirits as well as the reputation of the Parliament forces, and was a great defeat to us; and from this time things began to look with a melancholy aspect, for the prosperous condition of the king's affairs began to decline. The opportunities he had let slip were never to be recovered, and the Parliament, in their former extremity, having voted an invitation to the Scots to march to their assistance, we had now new enemies to encounter; and, indeed, there began the ruin of his Majesty's affairs, for the Earl of Newcastle, not able to defend himself against the Scots on his rear, the Earl of Manchester in his front, and Sir Thomas Fairfax on his flank, was everywhere routed and defeated, and his forces obliged to quit the field to the enemy.

About this time it was that we first began to hear of one Oliver Cromwell, who, like a little cloud, rose out of the east, and spread first into the north, till it shed down a flood that overwhelmed the three kingdoms.

He first was a private captain of horse, but now commanded a regiment whom he armed *cap-à-pie à la cuirassier*; and, joining with the Earl of Manchester, the first action we heard of him that made him anything famous was about Grantham, where, with only his own regiment, he defeated twenty-four troops of horse and dragoons of the king's forces; then, at Gainsborough, with two regiments, his own of horse and one of dragoons, where he defeated near 3000 of the Earl of Newcastle's men, killed Lieutenant-General Cavendish, brother to the Earl of Devonshire, who commanded them, and relieved Gainsborough; and though the whole army came in to the rescue, he made good his retreat to Lincoln with little loss; and the next week he defeated Sir John Henderson at Winceby, near Horncastle, with sixteen regiments of horse and dragoons, himself having not half that number; killed the Lord Widdrington, Sir Ingram Hopton, and several gentlemen of quality. Thus this firebrand of war began to blaze, and he soon grew a terror to the north; for victory attended him like a page of honour, and he was scarce ever known to be beaten during the whole war.

Now we began to reflect again on the misfortune of our master's counsels. Had we marched to London, instead of besieging Gloucester, we had finished the war with a stroke. The Parliament's army was in a most despicable condition, and had never been recruited, had we not given them a month's time, which we lingered away at this fatal town of Gloucester. But 'twas too late to reflect; we were a disheartened army, but we were not beaten yet, nor broken. We had a large country to recruit in, and we lost no time but raised men apace. In the meantime his Majesty, after a short stay at Bristol, makes back again towards Oxford with a part of the foot and all the horse.

At Cirencester we had a brush again with Essex; that town owed us a shrewd turn for having handled them coarsely enough before, when Prince Rupert seized the county magazine. I happened to be in the town that night with Sir Nicholas Crisp, whose regiment of horse quartered there with Colonel Spencer and some foot; my own regiment was gone before to Oxford. About ten at night, a party of Essex's men beat up our quarters by surprise, just as we had served them before. They fell in with us, just as people were going to bed, and having beaten the out-guards, were gotten into the middle of the town before our men could get on horseback. Sir Nicholas Crisp, hearing the alarm, gets up, and with some of his clothes on, and some off, comes into my chamber. "We are all undone," says he, "the Roundheads are upon us." We had but little time to consult, but being in one of the principal inns in the town, we presently ordered the gates of the inn to be shut, and sent to all the inns where our men were quartered to do the like, with orders, if they had any back-doors, or ways to get out, to come to us. By this means, however, we got so much time as to get on horseback, and so many of our men came to us by back ways, that we had near 300 horse in the yards and places behind the house. And now we began to think of breaking out by a lane which led from the back side of the inn, but a new accident determined us another, though a worse way.

The enemy being entered, and our men cooped up in the yards of the inns, Colonel Spencer, the other colonel, whose regiment of horse lay also in the town, had got on horseback before us, and engaged with the enemy, but being overpowered, retreated fighting, and sends to Sir Nicholas Crisp for help. Sir Nicholas, moved to see the distress of his friend, turning to me, says he, "What can we do for him?" I told him I thought 'twas time to help him, if possible; upon which, opening the inn gates, we sallied out in very good order, about 300 horse. And several of the troops from other parts of the town joining us, we recovered Colonel Spencer, and charging home, beat back the enemy to their main body. But finding their foot drawn up in the churchyard, and several detachments moving to charge us, we retreated in as good order as we could. They did not think fit to pursue us, but they took all the carriages which were under the convoy of this party, and laden with provisions and ammunition, and above 500 of our horse, the foot shifted away as well as they could. Thus we made off in a shattered condition towards Farringdon, and so to Oxford, and I was very glad my regiment was not there.

We had small rest at Oxford, or indeed anywhere else; for the king was marched from thence, and we followed him. I was something uneasy at my absence from my regiment, and did not know how the king might resent it, which caused me to ride after them with all expedition. But the armies were engaged that very day at Newbury, and I came in too late. I had not behaved myself so as to be suspected of a wilful shunning the action; but a colonel of a regiment ought to avoid absence from his regiment in time of fight, be the excuse never so just, as carefully as he would a surprise in his quarters. The truth is, 'twas an error of my own, and owing to two day's stay I made at the Bath, where

I met with some ladies who were my relations. And this is far from being an excuse; for if the king had been a Gustavus Adolphus, I had certainly received a check for it.

This fight was very obstinate, and could our horse have come to action as freely as the foot, the Parliament army had suffered much more; for we had here a much better body of horse than they, and we never failed beating them where the weight of the work lay upon the horse.

Here the city train-bands, of which there was two regiments, and whom we used to despise, fought very well. They lost one of their colonels, and several officers in the action; and I heard our men say, they behaved themselves as well as any forces the Parliament had.

The Parliament cried victory here too, as they always did; and indeed where the foot were concerned they had some advantage; but our horse defeated them evidently. The king drew up his army in battalia, in person, and faced them all the next day, inviting them to renew the fight; but they had no stomach to come on again.

It was a kind of a hedge fight, for neither army was drawn out in the field; if it had, 'twould never have held from six in the morning to ten at night. But they fought for advantages; sometimes one side had the better, sometimes another. They fought twice through the town, in at one end, and out at the other; and in the hedges and lanes, with exceeding fury. The king lost the most men, his foot having suffered for want of the succour of their horse, who on two several occasions could not come at them. But the Parliament foot suffered also, and two regiments were entirely cut in pieces, and the king kept the field.

Essex, the Parliament general, had the pillage of the dead, and left us to bury them; for while we stood all day to our arms, having given them a fair field to fight us in, their camp rabble stripped the dead bodies, and they not daring to venture a second engagement with us, marched away towards London.

The king lost in this action the Earls of Carnarvon and Sunderland, the Lord Falkland, a French marquis and some very gallant officers, and about 1200 men. The Earl of Carnarvon was brought into an inn in Newbury, where the king came to see him. He had just life enough to speak to his Majesty, and died in his presence. The king was exceedingly concerned for him, and was observed to shed tears at the sight of it. We were indeed all of us troubled for the loss of so brave a gentleman, but the concern our royal master discovered, moved us more than ordinary. Everybody endeavoured to have the king out of the room, but he would not stir from the bedside, till he saw all hopes of life was gone.

The indefatigable industry of the king, his servants and friends, continually to supply and recruit his forces, and to harass and fatigue the enemy, was such, that we should still have given a good account of the war had the Scots stood neuter. But bad news came every day out of the north; as for other places, parties were always in action. Sir William Waller and Sir Ralph Hopton beat one another by turns; and Sir Ralph had extended the king's quarters from Launceston in Cornwall, to Farnham in Surrey, where he gave Sir William Waller a rub, and drove him into the castle. But in the north, the storm grew thick, the Scots advanced to the borders, and entered England in confederacy with the Parliament, against their king; for which the Parliament requited them afterwards as they deserved.

Had it not been for this Scotch army, the Parliament had easily been reduced to terms of peace; but after this they never made any proposals fit for the king to receive. Want of success before had made them differ among themselves. Essex and Waller could never agree; the Earl of Manchester and the Lord Willoughby differed to the highest degree; and the king's affairs went never the worse for it. But this storm in the north ruined us all; for the Scots prevailed in Yorkshire, and being joined with Fairfax, Manchester, and Cromwell, carried all before them; so that the king was obliged to send Prince Rupert, with a body of 4000 horse, to the assistance of the Earl of Newcastle, where that prince finished the destruction of the king's interest, by the rashest and unaccountablest action in the world, of which I shall speak in its place.

Another action of the king's, though in itself no greater a cause of offence than the calling the Scots into the nation, gave great offence in general, and even the king's own friends disliked it; and was carefully improved by his enemies to the disadvantage of the king, and of his cause.

The rebels in Ireland had, ever since the bloody massacre of the Protestants, maintained a war against the English, and the Earl of Ormond was general and governor for the king. The king, finding his affairs pinch him at home, sends orders to the Earl of Ormond to consent to a cessation of arms with the rebels, and to ship over certain of his regiments hither to his Majesty's assistance. 'Tis true, the Irish had deserved to be very ill treated by the English; but while the Parliament pressed the king with a cruel and unnatural war at home, and called in an army out of Scotland to support their quarrel with their king, I could never be convinced, that it was such a dishonourable action for the king to suspend the correction of his Irish rebels till he was in a capacity to do it with safety to himself; or to delay any farther assistance to preserve himself at home; and the troops he recalled being his own, it was no breach of his honour to make use of them, since he now wanted them for his own security against those who fought against him at home.

But the king was persuaded to make one step farther, and that, I confess, was unpleasing to us all; and some of his best and most faithful servants took the freedom to speak plainly to him of it; and that was bringing some regiments of the Irish themselves over. This cast, as we thought, an odium upon our whole nation, being some of those very wretches who had dipped their hands in the innocent blood of the Protestants, and, with unheard-of butcheries, had massacred so many thousands of English in cool blood.

Abundance of gentlemen forsook the king upon this score; and seeing they could not brook the fighting in conjunction with this wicked generation, came into the declaration of the Parliament, and making composition for their estates, lived retired lives all the rest of war, or went abroad.

But as exigences and necessities oblige us to do things which at other times we would not do, and is, as to man, some excuse for such things; so I cannot but think the guilt and dishonour of such an action must lie, very much of it, at least, at their doors, who drove the king to these necessities and distresses, by calling in an army of his own subjects whom he had not injured, but had complied with them in everything, to make war upon him without any provocation.

As to the quarrel between the king and his Parliament, there may something be said on both sides; and the king saw cause himself to disown and dislike some things he had done, which the Parliament objected against, such as levying money without consent of Parliament, infractions on their privileges, and the like. Here, I say, was some room for an argument at least, and concessions on both sides were needful to come to a peace. But for the Scots, all their demands had been answered, all their grievances had been redressed, they had made articles with their sovereign, and he had performed those articles; their capital enemy Episcopacy was abolished; they had not one thing to demand of the king which he had not granted. And therefore they had no more cause to take up arms against their sovereign than they had against the Grand Seignior. But it must for ever lie against them as a brand of infamy, and as a reproach on their whole nation that, purchased by the Parliament's money, they sold their honesty, and rebelled against their king for hire; and it was not many years before, as I have said already, they were fully paid the wages of their unrighteousness, and chastised for their treachery by the very same people whom they thus basely assisted. Then they would have retrieved it, if it had not been too late.

But I could not but accuse this age of injustice and partiality, who while they reproached the king for his cessation of arms with the Irish rebels, and not prosecuting them with the utmost severity, though he was constrained by the necessities of the war to do it, could yet, at the same time, justify the Scots taking up arms in a quarrel they had no concern in, and against their own king, with whom they had articled and capitulated, and who had so punctually complied with all their demands, that they had no claim upon him, no grievances to be redressed, no oppression to cry out of, nor could ask anything of him which he had not granted.

But as no action in the world is so vile, but the actors can cover with some specious pretence, so the Scots now passing into England publish a declaration to justify their assisting the Parliament. To which I shall only say, in my opinion, it was no justification at all; for admit the Parliament's quarrel had been never so just, it could not be just in them to aid them, because 'twas against their own king too, to whom they had sworn allegiance, or at least had crowned him, and thereby had recognised his authority. For if maladministration be, according to Prynne's doctrine, or according to their own Buchanan, a sufficient reason for subjects to take up arms against their prince, the breach of his coronation oath being supposed to dissolve the oath of allegiance, which however I cannot believe; yet this can never be extended to make it lawful, that because a king of England may, by maladministration, discharge the subjects of England from their allegiance, that therefore the subjects of Scotland may take up arms against the King of Scotland, he having not infringed the compact of government as to them, and they having nothing to complain of for themselves. Thus I thought their own arguments were against them, and Heaven seemed to concur with it; for although they did carry the cause for the English rebels, yet the most of them left their bones here in the quarrel.

But what signifies reason to the drum and the trumpet! The Parliament had the supreme argument with those men, viz., the money; and having accordingly advanced a good round sum, upon payment of this (for the Scots would not stir a foot without it) they entered

England on the 15th of January 1643[-4], with an army of 12,000 men, under the command of old Leslie, now Earl of Leven, an old soldier of great experience, having been bred to arms from a youth in the service of the Prince of Orange.

The Scots were no sooner entered England but they were joined by all the friends to the Parliament party in the north; and first, Colonel Grey, brother to the Lord Grey, joined them with a regiment of horse, and several out of Westmoreland and Cumberland, and so they advanced to Newcastle, which they summon to surrender. The Earl of Newcastle, who rather saw than was able to prevent this storm, was in Newcastle, and did his best to defend it; but the Scots, increased by this time to above 20,000, lay close siege to the place, which was but meanly fortified, and having repulsed the garrison upon several sallies, and pressing the place very close, after a siege of twelve days, or thereabouts, they enter the town sword in hand. The Earl of Newcastle got away, and afterwards gathered what forces together he could, but [was] not strong enough to hinder the Scots from advancing to Durham, which he quitted to them, nor to hinder the conjunction of the Scots with the forces of Fairfax, Manchester, and Cromwell. Whereupon the earl, seeing all things thus going to wreck, he sends his horse away, and retreats with his foot into York, making all necessary preparations for a vigorous defence there, in case he should be attacked, which he was pretty sure of, as indeed afterwards happened. York was in a very good posture of defence, the fortifications very regular, and exceeding strong; well furnished with provisions, and had now a garrison of 12,000 men in it. The governor under the Earl of Newcastle was Sir Thomas Glemham, a good soldier, and a gentleman brave enough.

The Scots, as I have said, having taken Durham, Tynemouth Castle, and Sunderland, and being joined by Sir Thomas Fairfax, who had taken Selby, resolve, with their united strength, to besiege York; but when they came to view the city, and saw a plan of the works, and had intelligence of the strength of the garrison, they sent expresses to Manchester and Cromwell for help, who came on, and joined them with 9000, making together about 30,000 men, rather more than less.

Now had the Earl of Newcastle's repeated messengers convinced the king that it was absolutely necessary to send some forces to his assistance, or else all would be lost in the north. Whereupon Prince Rupert was detached, with orders first to go into Lancashire and relieve Lathom House, defended by the brave Countess of Derby, and then, taking all the forces he could collect in Cheshire, Lancashire, and Yorkshire, to march to relieve York.

The prince marched from Oxford with but three regiments of horse and one of dragoons, making in all about 2800 men. The colonels of horse were Colonel Charles Goring, the Lord Byron, and myself; the dragoons were of Colonel Smith. In our march we were joined by a regiment of horse from Banbury, one of dragoons from Bristol, and three regiments of horse from Chester, so that when we came into Lancashire we were about 5000 horse and dragoons. These horse we received from Chester were those who, having been at the siege of Nantwich, were obliged to raise the siege by Sir Thomas Fairfax; and the foot having yielded, the horse made good their retreat to Chester, being about 2000, of whom three regiments now joined us. We received also 2000 foot from West Chester, and 2000 more out of Wales, and with this strength we entered Lancashire. We had not much time to spend, and a great deal of work to do.

Bolton and Liverpool felt the first fury of our prince; at Bolton, indeed, he had some provocation, for here we were like to be beaten off. When first the prince came to the town, he sent a summons to demand the town for the king, but received no answer but from their guns, commanding the messenger to keep off at his peril. They had raised some works about the town, and having by their intelligence learnt that we had no artillery, and were only a flying party (so they called us), they contemned the summons, and showed themselves upon their ramparts, ready for us. The prince was resolved to humble them, if possible, and takes up his quarters close to the town. In the evening he orders me to advance with one regiment of dragoons and my horse, to bring them off, if occasion was, and to post myself as near as possible I could to the lines, yet so as not to be discovered; and at the same time, having concluded what part of the works to fall upon, he draws up his men on two other sides, as if he would storm them there; and, on a signal, I was to begin the real assault on my side with my dragoons.

I had got so near the town with my dragoons, making them creep upon their bellies a great way, that we could hear the soldiers talk on the walls, when the prince, believing one regiment would be too few, sends me word that he had ordered a regiment of foot to help, and that I should not discover myself till they were come up to me. This broke our measures, for the march of this regiment was discovered by the enemy, and they took the alarm. Upon this I sent to the prince, to desire he would put off the storm for that night, and I would answer for it the next day; but the prince was impatient, and sent orders we should fall on as soon as the foot came up to us. The foot marched out of the way, missed us, and fell in with a road that leads to another part of the town; and being not able to find us, make an attack upon the town themselves; but the defendants, being ready for them, received them very warmly, and beat them off with great loss.

I was at a loss now what to do; for hearing the guns, and by the noise knowing it was an assault upon the town, I was very uneasy to have my share in it; but as I had learnt under the King of Sweden punctually to adhere to the execution of orders, and my orders being to lie still till the foot came up with me, I would not stir if I had been sure to have done never so much service; but, however, to satisfy myself, I sent to the prince to let him know that I continued in the same place expecting the foot, and none being yet come, I desired farther orders. The prince was a little amazed at this, and finding there must be some mistake, came galloping away in the dark to the place and drew off the men, which was no hard matter, for they were willing enough to give it over.

As for me, the prince ordered me to come off so privately as not to be discovered, if possible, which I effectually did; and so we were balked for that night. The next day the prince fell on upon another quarter with three regiments of foot, but was beaten off with loss, and the like a third time. At last the prince resolved to carry it, doubled his numbers, and, renewing the attack with fresh men, the foot entered the town over their works, killing in the first heat of the action all that came in their way; some of the foot at the same time letting in the horse, and so the town was entirely won. There was about 600 of the enemy killed, and we lost above 400 in all, which was owing to the foolish mistakes we made. Our men got some plunder here, which the Parliament made a great noise about; but it was their due, and they bought it dear enough.

Liverpool did not cost us so much, nor did we get so much by it, the people having sent their women and children and best goods on board the ships in the road; and as we had no boats to board them with, we could not get at them. Here, as at Bolton, the town and fort was taken by storm, and the garrison were many of them cut in pieces, which, by the way, was their own faults.

Our next step was Lathom House, which the Countess of Derby had gallantly defended above eighteen weeks against the Parliament forces; and this lady not only encouraged her men by her cheerful and noble maintenance of them, but by examples of her own undaunted spirit, exposing herself upon the walls in the midst of the enemy's shot, would be with her men in the greatest dangers; and she well deserved our care of her person, for the enemy were prepared to use her very rudely if she fell into their hands.

Upon our approach the enemy drew off, and the prince not only effectually relieved this vigorous lady, but left her a good quantity of all sorts of ammunition, three great guns, 500 arms, and 200 men, commanded by a major, as her extraordinary guard.

Here the way being now opened, and our success answering our expectation, several bodies of foot came in to us from Westmoreland and from Cumberland; and here it was that the prince found means to surprise the town of Newcastle-upon-Tyne, which was recovered for the king by the management of the mayor of the town, and some loyal gentlemen of the county, and a garrison placed there again for the king.

But our main design being the relief of York, the prince advanced that way apace, his army still increasing; and being joined by the Lord Goring from Richmondshire with 4000 horse, which were the same the Earl of Newcastle had sent away when he threw himself into York with the infantry, we were now 18,000 effective men, whereof 10,000 horse and dragoons; so the prince, full of hopes, and his men in good heart, boldly marched directly for York.

The Scots, as much surprised at the taking of Newcastle as at the coming of their enemy, began to inquire which way they should get home, if they should be beaten; and calling a council of war, they all agreed to raise the siege. The prince, who drew with him a great train of carriages charged with provision and ammunition for the relief of the city, like a wary general, kept at a distance from the enemy, and fetching a great compass about, brings all safe into the city, and enters into York himself with all his army.

No action of this whole war had gained the prince so much honour, or the king's affairs so much advantage, as this, had the prince but had the power to have restrained his courage after this, and checked his fatal eagerness for fighting. Here was a siege raised, the reputation of the enemy justly stirred, a city relieved, and furnished with all things necessary in the face of an army superior in a number by near 10,000 men, and commanded by a triumvirate of Generals Leven, Fairfax, and Manchester. Had the prince but remembered the proceeding of the great Duke of Parma at the relief of Paris, he would have seen the relieving the city was his business; 'twas the enemy's business to fight if possible, 'twas his to avoid it; for, having delivered the city, and put the disgrace of raising the siege upon the enemy, he had nothing further to do but to have waited till he had seen what course the enemy would take, and taken his further measures from their motion.

But the prince, a continual friend to precipitant counsels, would hear no advice. I entreated him not to put it to the hazard; I told him that he ought to consider if he lost the day he lost the kingdom, and took the crown off from the king's head. I put him in mind that it was impossible those three generals should continue long together; and that if they did, they would not agree long in their counsels, which would be as well for us as their separating. 'Twas plain Manchester and Cromwell must return to the associated counties, who would not suffer them to stay, for fear the king should attempt them. That he could subsist well enough, having York city and river at his back; but the Scots would eat up the country, make themselves odious, and dwindle away to nothing, if he would but hold them at bay a little. Other general officers were of the same mind; but all I could say, or they either, to a man deaf to anything but his own courage, signified nothing. He would draw out and fight; there was no persuading him to the contrary, unless a man would run the risk of being upbraided with being a coward, and afraid of the work. The enemy's army lay on a large common, called Marston Moor, doubtful what to do. Some were for fighting the prince, the Scots were against it, being uneasy at having the garrison of Newcastle at their backs; but the prince brought their councils of war to a result, for he let them know they must fight him, whether they would or no; for the prince being, as before, 18,000 men, and the Earl of Newcastle having joined him with 8000 foot out of the city, were marched in quest of the enemy, had entered the moor in view of their army, and began to draw up in order of battle; but the night coming on, the armies only viewed each other at a distance for that time. We lay all night upon our arms, and with the first of the day were in order of battle; the enemy was getting ready, but part of Manchester's men were not in the field, but lay about three miles off, and made a hasty march to come up.

The prince's army was exceedingly well managed; he himself commanded the left wing, the Earl of Newcastle the right wing; and the Lord Goring, as general of the foot, assisted by Major-General Porter and Sir Charles Lucas, led the main battle. I had prevailed with the prince, according to the method of the King of Sweden, to place some small bodies of musketeers in the intervals of his horse, in the left wing, but could not prevail upon the Earl of Newcastle to do it in the right, which he afterwards repented. In this posture we stood facing the enemy, expecting they would advance to us, which at last they did; and the prince began the day by saluting them with his artillery, which, being placed very well, galled them terribly for a quarter of an hour. They could not shift their front, so they advanced the hastier to get within our great guns, and consequently out of their danger, which brought the fight the sooner on.

The enemy's army was thus ordered; Sir Thomas Fairfax had the right wing, in which was the Scots horse, and the horse of his own and his father's army; Cromwell led the left wing, with his own and the Earl of Manchester's horse, and the three generals, Leslie, old Fairfax, and Manchester, led the main battle.

The prince, with our left wing, fell on first, and, with his usual fury, broke like a clap of thunder into the right wing of the Scots horse, led by Sir Thomas Fairfax, and, as nothing could stand in his way, he broke through and through them, and entirely routed them, pursuing them quite out of the field. Sir Thomas Fairfax, with a regiment of lances, and about 500 of his own horse, made good the ground for some time; but our musketeers, which, as I said, were such an unlooked-for sort of an article in a fight among the horse, that those lances, which otherwise were brave fellows, were mowed down with their shot, and all was put into confusion. Sir Thomas Fairfax was wounded in the face, his brother killed, and a great slaughter was made of the Scots, to whom I confess we showed no favour at all.

While this was doing on our left, the Lord Goring with the main battle charged the enemy's foot; and particularly one brigade commanded by Major-General Porter, being mostly pikemen, not regarding the fire of the enemy, charged with that fury in a close body of pikes, that they overturned all that came in their way, and breaking into the middle of the enemy's foot, filled all with terror and confusion, insomuch that the three generals, thinking all had been lost, fled, and quitted the field.

But matters went not so well with that always unfortunate gentleman the Earl of Newcastle and our right wing of horse; for Cromwell charged the Earl of Newcastle with a powerful body of horse. And though the earl, and those about him, did what men could do, and behaved themselves with all possible gallantry, yet there was no withstanding Cromwell's horse, but, like Prince Rupert, they bore down all before them. And now the victory was wrung out of our hands by our own gross miscarriage; for the prince, as 'twas his custom, too eager in the chase of the enemy, was gone and could not be heard of. The foot in the centre, the right wing of the horse being routed by Cromwell, was left, and without the guard of his horse; Cromwell having routed the Earl of Newcastle, and beaten him quite out of the field, and Sir Thomas Fairfax rallying his dispersed troops, they fall all together upon the foot. General Lord Goring, like himself, fought like a lion, but, forsaken of his horse, was hemmed in on all sides, and overthrown; and an hour after this, the prince returning, too late to recover his friends, was obliged with the rest to quit the field to conquerors.

This was a fatal day to the king's affairs, and the risk too much for any man in his wits to run; we lost 4000 men on the spot, 3000 prisoners, among whom was Sir Charles Lucas, Major-General Porter, Major-General Tilyard, and about 170 gentlemen of quality. We lost all our baggage, twenty-five pieces of cannon, 3000 carriages, 150 barrels of powder, 10,000 arms. The prince got into York with the Earl of Newcastle, and a great many gentlemen; and 7000 or 8000 of the men, as well horse as foot.

I had but very coarse treatment in this fight; for returning with the prince from the pursuit of the right wing, and finding all lost, I halted with some other officers, to consider what to do. At first we were for making our retreat in a body, and might have done so well enough, if we had known what had happened, before we saw ourselves in the middle of the enemy; for Sir Thomas Fairfax, who had got together his scattered troops, and joined by some of the left wing, knowing who we were, charged us with great fury. 'Twas not a time to think of anything but getting away, or dying upon the spot; the prince kept on in the front, and Sir Thomas Fairfax by this charge cut off about three regiments of us from our body; but bending his main strength at the prince, left us, as it were, behind him, in the middle of the field of battle. We took this for the only opportunity we could have to get off, and joining together, we made across the place of battle in as good order as we could, with our carabines presented. In this posture we passed by several bodies of the enemy's foot, who stood with their pikes charged to keep us off; but they had no occasion, for we had no design to meddle with them, but to get from them.

Thus we made a swift march, and thought ourselves pretty secure; but our work was not done yet, for on a sudden we saw ourselves under a necessity of fighting our way through a great body of Manchester's horse, who came galloping upon us over the moor. They had, as we suppose, been pursuing some of our broken troops which were fled before, and seeing us, they gave us a home charge. We received them as well as we could, but pushed to get through them, which at last we did with a considerable loss to them. However, we lost so many men, either killed or separated from us (for all could not follow the same way), that of our three regiments we could not be above 400 horse together when we got quite clear, and these were mixed men, some of one troop and regiment, some of another. Not that I believe many of us were killed in the last attack, for we had plainly the better of the enemy, but our design being to get off, some shifted for themselves one way and some another, in the best manner they could, and as their several fortunes guided them. Four hundred more of this body, as I afterwards understood, having broke through the enemy's body another way, kept together, and got into Pontefract Castle, and 300 more made northward and to Skipton, where the prince afterwards fetched them off.

These few of us that were left together, with whom I was, being now pretty clear of pursuit, halted, and began to inquire who and who we were, and what we should do; and on a short debate, I proposed we should make to the first garrison of the king's that we could recover, and that we should keep together, lest the country people should insult us upon the roads. With this resolution we pushed on westward for Lancashire, but our misfortunes were not yet at an end. We travelled very hard, and got to a village upon the river Wharfe, near Wetherby. At Wetherby there was a bridge, but we understood that a party from Leeds had secured the town and the post, in order to stop the flying Cavaliers, and that 'twould be very hard to get through there, though, as we understood afterwards, there were no soldiers there but a guard of the townsmen. In this pickle we consulted what course to take. To stay where we were till morning, we all concluded, would not be safe. Some advised to take the stream with our horses, but the river, which is deep, and the current strong, seemed to bid us have a care what we did of that kind, especially in the night. We resolved therefore to refresh ourselves and our horses, which indeed is more than we did, and go on till we might come to a ford or bridge, where we might get over. Some guides we had, but they either were foolish or false, for after we had rode eight or nine miles, they plunged us into a river at a place they called a ford, but 'twas a very ill one, for most of our horses swam, and seven or eight were lost, but we saved the men. However, we got all over.

We made bold with our first convenience to trespass upon the country for a few horses, where we could find them, to remount our men whose horses were drowned, and continued our march. But being obliged to refresh ourselves at a small village on the edge of Bramham Moor, we found the country alarmed by our taking some horses, and we were no sooner got on horseback in the morning, and entering on the moor, but we understood we were pursued by some troops of horse. There was no remedy but we must pass this moor; and though our horses were exceedingly tired, yet we pressed on upon a round trot, and recovered an enclosed country on the other side, where we halted. And here, necessity putting us upon it, we were obliged to look out for more horses, for several of our men were dismounted, and others' horses disabled by carrying double, those who lost their horses getting up behind them. But we were supplied by our enemies against their will.

The enemy followed us over the moor, and we having a woody enclosed country about us, where we were, I observed by their moving, they had lost sight of us; upon which I proposed concealing ourselves till we might judge of their numbers. We did so, and lying close in a wood, they passed hastily by us, without skirting or searching the wood, which was what on another occasion they would not have done. I found they were not above 150 horse, and considering, that to let them go before us, would be to alarm the country, and stop our design, I thought, since we might be able to deal with them, we should not meet with a better place for it, and told the rest of our officers my mind, which all our party presently (for we had not time for a long debate) agreed to.

Immediately upon this I caused two men to fire their pistols in the wood, at two different places, as far asunder as I could. This I did to give them an alarm, and amuse them; for being in the lane, they would otherwise have got through before we had been ready, and I resolved to engage them there, as soon as 'twas possible. After this alarm, we rushed out of the wood, with about a hundred horse, and charged them on the flank in a broad lane, the wood being on their right. Our passage into the lane being narrow, gave us some difficulty in our getting out; but the surprise of the charge did our work; for the enemy, thinking we had been a mile or two before, had not the least thoughts of this onset, till they heard us in the wood, and then they who were before could not come back. We broke into the lane just in the middle of them, and by that means divided them; and facing to the left, charged the rear. First our dismounted men, which were near fifty, lined the edge of the wood, and fired with their carabines upon those which were before, so warmly, that they put them into a great disorder. Meanwhile fifty more of our horse from the farther part of the wood showed themselves in the lane upon their front. This put them of the foremost party into a great perplexity, and they began to face about, to fall upon us who were engaged in the rear. But their facing about in a lane where there was no room to wheel, as one who understands the manner of wheeling a troop of horse must imagine, put them into a great disorder. Our party in the head of the lane taking the advantage of this mistake of the enemy, charged in upon them, and routed them entirely.

Some found means to break into the enclosures on the other side of the lane, and get away. About thirty were killed, and about twenty-five made prisoners, and forty very good horses were taken; all this while not a man of ours was lost, and not above seven or eight wounded. Those in the rear behaved themselves better, for they stood our charge with a great deal of resolution, and all we could do could not break them; but at last our men who had fired on foot through the hedges at the other party, coming to do the like here, there was no standing it any longer. The rear of them faced about and retreated out of the lane, and drew up in the open field to receive and rally their fellows. We killed about seventeen of them, and followed them to the end of the lane, but had no mind to have any more fighting than needs must, our condition at that time not making it proper, the towns round us being all in the enemy's hands, and the country but indifferently pleased with us; however, we stood facing them till they thought fit to march away. Thus we were supplied with horses enough to remount our men, and pursued our first design of getting into Lancashire. As for our prisoners, we let them off on foot.

But the country being by this time alarmed, and the rout of our army everywhere known, we foresaw abundance of difficulties before us; we were not strong enough to venture into any great towns, and we were too many to be concealed in small ones. Upon this we resolved to halt in a great wood about three miles beyond the place where we had the last skirmish, and sent our scouts to discover the country, and learn what they could, either of the enemy or of our friends.

Anybody may suppose we had but indifferent quarters here, either for ourselves or for our horses; but, however, we made shift to lie here two days and one night. In the interim I took upon me, with two more, to go to Leeds to learn some news; we were disguised like country ploughmen; the clothes we got at a farmer's house, which for that particular occasion we plundered; and I cannot say no blood was shed in a manner too rash, and which I could not have done at another time;

but our case was desperate, and the people too surly, and shot at us out of the window, wounded one man and shot a horse, which we counted as great a loss to us as a man, for our safety depended upon our horses. Here we got clothes of all sorts, enough for both sexes, and thus dressing myself up *au paysan,* with a white cap on my head, and a fork on my shoulder, and one of my comrades in the farmer's wife's russet gown and petticoat, like a woman, the other with an old crutch like a lame man, and all mounted on such horses as we had taken the day before from the country, away we go to Leeds by three several ways, and agreed to meet upon the bridge. My pretended country woman acted her part to the life, though the party was a gentleman of good quality, of the Earl of Worcester's family; and the cripple did as well as he; but I thought myself very awkward in my dress, which made me very shy, especially among the soldiers. We passed their sentinels and guards at Leeds unobserved, and put up our horses at several houses in the town, from whence we went up and down to make our remarks. My cripple was the fittest to go among the soldiers, because there was less danger of being pressed. There he informed himself of the matters of war, particularly that the enemy sat down again to the siege of York; that flying parties were in pursuit of the Cavaliers; and there he heard that 500 horse of the Lord Manchester's men had followed a party of Cavaliers over Bramham Moor, and that entering a lane, the Cavaliers, who were 1000 strong, fell upon them, and killed them all but about fifty. This, though it was a lie, was very pleasant to us to hear, knowing it was our party, because of the other part of the story, which was thus: That the Cavaliers had taken possession of such a wood, where they rallied all the troops of their flying army; that they had plundered the country as they came, taking all the horses they could get; that they had plundered Goodman Thomson's house, which was the farmer I mentioned, and killed man, woman, and child; and that they were about 2000 strong.

My other friend in woman's clothes got among the good wives at an inn, where she set up her horse, and there she heard the same sad and dreadful tidings; and that this party was so strong, none of the neighbouring garrisons durst stir out; but that they had sent expresses to York, for a party of horse to come to their assistance.

I walked up and down the town, but fancied myself so ill disguised, and so easy to be known, that I cared not to talk with anybody. We met at the bridge exactly at our time, and compared our intelligence, found it answered our end of coming, and that we had nothing to do but to get back to our men; but my cripple told me, he would not stir till he bought some victuals: so away he hops with his crutch, and buys four or five great pieces of bacon, as many of hung beef, and two or three loaves; and borrowing a sack at the inn (which I suppose he never restored), he loads his horse, and getting a large leather bottle, he filled that of aqua-vitae instead of small beer; my woman comrade did the like. I was uneasy in my mind, and took no care but to get out of the town; however, we all came off well enough; but 'twas well for me that I had no provisions with me, as you will hear presently.

We came, as I said, into the town by several ways, and so we went out; but about three miles from the town we met again exactly where we had agreed. I being about a quarter of a mile from the rest, I meets three country fellows on horseback; one had a long pole on his shoulder, another a fork, the third no weapon at all, that I saw. I gave them the road very orderly, being habited like one of their brethren; but one of them stopping short at me, and looking earnestly calls out, "Hark thee, friend," says he, in a broad north-country tone, "whar hast thou thilk horse?" I must confess I was in the utmost confusion at the question, neither being able to answer the question, nor to speak in his tone; so I made as if I did not hear him, and went on. "Na, but ye's not gang soa," says the boor, and comes up to me, and takes hold of the horse's bridle to stop me; at which, vexed at heart that I could not tell how to talk to him, I reached him a great knock on the pate with my fork, and fetched him off of his horse, and then began to mend my pace. The other clowns, though it seems they knew not what the fellow wanted, pursued me, and finding they had better heels than I, I saw there was no remedy but to make use of my hands, and faced about.

The first that came up with me was he that had no weapons, so I thought I might parley with him, and speaking as country like as I could, I asked him what he wanted? "Thou'st knaw that soon," says Yorkshire, "and ise but come at thee." "Then keep awa', man," said I, "or ise brain thee." By this time the third man came up, and the parley ended; for he gave me no words, but laid at me with his long pole, and that with such fury, that I began to be doubtful of him. I was loth to shoot the fellow, though I had pistols under my grey frock, as well for that the noise of a pistol might bring more people in, the village being on our rear, and also because I could not imagine what the fellow meant, or would have. But at last, finding he would be too many for me with that long weapon, and a hardy strong fellow, I threw myself off my

397

horse, and running in with him, stabbed my fork into his horse. The horse being wounded, staggered awhile, and then fell down, and the booby had not the sense to get down in time, but fell with him. Upon which, giving him a knock or two with my fork, I secured him. The other, by this time, had furnished himself with a great stick out of a hedge, and before I was disengaged from the last fellow, gave me two such blows, that if the last had not missed my head and hit me on the shoulder, I had ended the fight and my life together. 'Twas time to look about me now, for this was a madman. I defended myself with my fork, but 'twould not do. At last, in short, I was forced to pistol him and get on horseback again, and with all the speed I could make, get away to the wood to our men.

If my two fellow-spies had not been behind, I had never known what was the meaning of this quarrel of the three countrymen, but my cripple had all the particulars. For he being behind us, as I have already observed, when he came up to the first fellow who began the fray, he found him beginning to come to himself. So he gets off, and pretends to help him, and sets him up upon his breech, and being a very merry fellow, talked to him: "Well, and what's the matter now?" says he to him. "Ah, wae's me," says the fellow, "I is killed." "Not quite, mon," says the cripple. "Oh, that's a fau thief," says he, and thus they parleyed. My cripple got him on's feet, and gave him a dram of his aqua-vitae bottle, and made much of him, in order to know what was the occasion of the quarrel. Our disguised woman pitied the fellow too, and together they set him up again upon his horse, and then he told him that that fellow was got upon one of his brother's horses who lived at Wetherby. They said the Cavaliers stole him, but 'twas like such rogues. No mischief could be done in the country, but 'twas the poor Cavaliers must bear the blame, and the like, and thus they jogged on till they came to the place where the other two lay. The first fellow they assisted as they had done t'other, and gave him a dram out of the leather bottle, but the last fellow was past their care, so they came away. For when they understood that 'twas my horse they claimed, they began to be afraid that their own horses might be known too, and then they had been betrayed in a worse pickle than I, and must have been forced to have done some mischief or other to have got away.

I had sent out two troopers to fetch them off, if there was any occasion; but their stay was not long and the two troopers saw them at a distance coming towards us, so they returned.

I had enough of going for a spy, and my companions had enough of staying in the wood for other intelligences agreed with ours, and all concurred in this, that it was time to be going; however, this use we made of it, that while the country thought us so strong we were in the less danger of being attacked, though in the more of being observed; but all this while we heard nothing of our friends till the next day. We heard Prince Rupert, with about 1000 horse, was at Skipton, and from thence marched away to Westmoreland.

We concluded now we had two or three days' time good; for, since messengers were sent to York for a party to suppress us, we must have at least two days' march of them, and therefore all concluded we were to make the best of our way. Early in the morning, therefore, we decamped from those dull quarters; and as we marched through a village we found the people very civil to us, and the women cried out, "God bless them, 'tis pity the Roundheads should make such work with such brave men," and the like. Finding we were among our friends, we resolved to halt a little and refresh ourselves; and, indeed, the people were very kind to us, gave us victuals and drink, and took care of our horses. It happened to be my lot to stop at a house where the good woman took a great deal of pains to provide for us; but I observed the good man walked about with a cap upon his head, and very much out of order. I took no great notice of it, being very sleepy, and having asked my landlady to let me have a bed, I lay down and slept heartily. When I waked I found my landlord on another bed groaning very heavily.

When I came downstairs, I found my cripple talking with my landlady; he was now out of his disguise, but we called him cripple still; and the other, who put on the woman's clothes, we called Goody Thompson. As soon as he saw me, he called me out, "Do you know," says he, "the man of the house you are quartered in?" "No, not I," says I. "No; so I believe, nor they you," says he; "if they did, the good wife would not have made you a posset, and fetched a white loaf for you." "What do you mean?" says I. "Have you seen the man?" says he. "Seen him," says I; "yes, and heard him too; the man's sick, and groans so heavily," says I, "that I could not lie upon the bed any longer for him." "Why, this is the poor man," says he, "that you knocked down with your fork yesterday, and I have had all the story out yonder at the next door." I confess it grieved me to have been forced to treat one so roughly who was one of our friends, but to make some amends, we contrived to give the poor man his brother's horse; and my cripple told him a formal story, that he believed the horse was taken away from the fellow by some of our men, and if he knew him again, if 'twas his friend's horse, he should have him. The man came down upon the news, and I caused six or seven horses, which were taken at the same time, to be shown him; he immediately chose the right; so I gave him the horse, and we pretended a great deal of sorrow for the man's hurt, and that we had not knocked the fellow on the head as well as took away the horse. The man was so overjoyed at the revenge he thought was taken on the fellow, that we heard him groan no more.

We ventured to stay all day at this town and the next night, and got guides to lead us to Blackstone Edge, a ridge of mountains which part this side of Yorkshire from Lancashire. Early in the morning we marched, and kept our scouts very carefully out every way, who brought us no news for this day. We kept on all night, and made our horses do penance for that little rest they had, and the next morning we passed the hills and got into Lancashire, to a town called Littlebrough, and from thence to Rochdale, a little market town. And now we thought ourselves safe as to the pursuit of enemies from the side of York. Our design was to get to Bolton, but all the county was full of the enemy in flying parties, and how to get to Bolton we knew not. At last we resolved to send a messenger to Bolton; but he came back and told us he had with lurking and hiding tried all the ways that he thought possible, but to no purpose, for he could not get into the town. We sent another, and he never returned, and some time after we understood he was taken by the enemy. At last one got into the town, but brought us word they were tired out with constant alarms, had been strictly blocked up, and every day expected a siege, and therefore advised us either to go northward where Prince Rupert and the Lord Goring ranged at liberty, or to get over Warrington Bridge, and so secure our retreat to Chester.

This double direction divided our opinions. I was for getting into Chester, both to recruit myself with horses and with money, both which I wanted, and to get refreshment, which we all wanted; but the major part of our men were for the north. First they said there was their general, and 'twas their duty to the cause, and the king's interest obliged us to go where we could do best service; and there was their friends, and every man might hear some news of his own regiment, for we belonged to several regiments. Besides, all the towns to the left of us were possessed by Sir William Brereton, Warrington, and Northwich, garrisoned by the enemy, and a strong party at Manchester, so that 'twas very likely we should be beaten and dispersed before we could get to Chester. These reasons, and especially the last, determined us for the north, and we had resolved to march the next morning, when other intelligence brought us to more speedy resolutions. We kept our scouts continually abroad to bring us intelligence of the enemy, whom we expected on our backs, and also to keep an eye upon the country; for, as we lived upon them something at large, they were ready enough to do us any ill turn, as it lay in their power.

The first messenger that came to us was from our friends at Bolton, to inform us that they were preparing at Manchester to attack us. One of our parties had been as far as Stockport, on the edge of Cheshire, and was pursued by a party of the enemy, but got off by the help of the night. Thus, all things looked black to the south, we had resolved to march northward in the morning, when one of our scouts from the side of Manchester, assured us Sir Thomas Middleton, with some of the Parliament forces and the country troops, making above 1200 men, were on the march to attack us, and would certainly beat up our quarters that night. Upon this advice we resolved to be gone; and, getting all things in readiness, we began to march about two hours before night. And having gotten a trusty fellow for a guide, a fellow that we found was a friend to our side, he put a project into my head which saved us all for that time; and that was, to give out in the village that we were marched to Yorkshire, resolving to get into Pontefract Castle; and accordingly he leads us out of the town the same way we came in, and, taking a boy with him, he sends the boy back just at night, and bade him say he saw us go up the hills at Blackstone Edge; and it happened very well, for this party were so sure of us, that they had placed 400 men on the road to the northward to intercept our retreat that way, and had left no way for us, as they thought, to get away but back again.

About ten o'clock at night, they assaulted our quarters, but found we were gone; and being informed which way, they followed upon the spur, and travelling all night, being moonlight, they found themselves the next day about fifteen miles east, just out of their way. For we had, by the help of our guide, turned short at the foot of the hills, and through blind, untrodden paths, and with difficulty enough, by noon the next day had reached almost twenty-five miles north, near a town called Clitheroe. Here we halted in the open field, and sent out our people to see how things were in the country. This part of the country, almost unpassable, and walled round with hills, was indifferent quiet, and we got some refreshment for ourselves, but very little horse-meat, and so went on. But we had not marched far before we found ourselves discovered, and the 400 horse sent to lie in wait for us as before, having understood which way we went, followed us hard; and by letters to some of their friends at Preston, we found we were beset again.

Our guide began now to be out of his knowledge, and our scouts brought us word, the enemy's horse was posted before us, and we knew they were in our rear. In this exigence, we resolved to divide our small body, and so amusing them, at least one might get off, if the other miscarried. I took about eighty horse with me, among which were all that I had of our own regiment, amounting to above thirty-two, and took the hills towards Yorkshire. Here we met with such unpassable hills, vast moors, rocks, and stonyways, as lamed all our horses and tired our men; and some times I was ready to think we should never be able to get over them, till our horses failing, and jackboots being but indifferent things to travel in, we might be starved before we should find any road, or towns; for guide we had none, but a boy who knew but little, and would cry when we asked him any questions. I believe neither men nor horses ever passed in some places where we went, and for twenty hours we saw not a town nor a house, excepting sometimes from the top of the mountains, at a vast distance. I am persuaded we might have encamped here, if we had had provisions, till the war had been over, and have met with no disturbance; and I have often wondered since, how we got into such horrible places, as much as how we got out. That which was worse to us than all the rest, was, that we knew not where we were going, nor what part of the country we should come into, when we came out of those desolate crags. At last, after a terrible fatigue, we began to see the western parts of Yorkshire, some few villages, and the country at a distance looked a little like England, for I thought before it looked like old Brennus Hill, which the Grisons call "the grandfather of the Alps." We got some relief in the villages, which indeed some of us had so much need of, that they were hardly able to sit their horses, and others were forced to help them off, they were so faint. I never felt so much of the power of hunger in my life, for having not eaten in thirty hours, I was as ravenous as a hound; and if I had had a piece of horse-flesh, I believe I should not have had patience to have staid dressing it, but have fallen upon it raw, and have eaten it as greedily as a Tartar. However I ate very cautiously, having often seen the danger of men's eating heartily after long fasting.

Our next care was to inquire our way. Halifax, they told us, was on our right. There we durst not think of going. Skipton was before us, and there we knew not how it was, for a body of 3000 horse, sent out by the enemy in pursuit of Prince Rupert, had been there but two days before, and the country people could not tell us whether they were gone, or no. And Manchester's horse, which were sent out after our party, were then at Halifax, in quest of us, and afterwards marched into Cheshire. In this distress we would have hired a guide, but none of the country people would go with us, for the Roundheads would hang them, they said, when they came there. Upon this I called a fellow to me, "Hark ye, friend," says I, "dost thee know the way so as to bring us into Westmoreland, and not keep the great road from York?" "Ay, merry," says he, "I ken the ways weel enou!" "And you would go and guide us," said I, "but that you are afraid the Roundheads will hang you?" "Indeed would I," says the fellow. "Why then," says I, "thou hadst as good be hanged by a Cavalier as a Roundhead, for if thou wilt not go, I'll hang thee just now." "Na, and ye serve me soa," says the fellow, "Ise ene gang with ye, for I care not for hanging; and ye'll get me a good horse, Ise gang and be one of ye, for I'll nere come heame more." This pleased us still better, and we mounted the fellow, for three of our men died that night with the extreme fatigue of the last service.

Next morning, when our new trooper was mounted and clothed we hardly knew him; and this fellow led us by such ways, such wildernesses, and yet with such prudence, keeping the hills to the left, that we might have the villages to refresh ourselves, that without him, we had certainly either perished in those mountains, or fallen into the enemy's hands. We passed the great road from York so critically as to time, that from one of the hills he showed us a party of the enemy's horse who were then marching into Westmoreland. We lay still that day, finding we were not discovered by them; and our guide proved the best scout that we could have had; for he would go out ten miles at a time, and bring us in all the news of the country. Here he brought us word, that York was surrendered upon articles, and that Newcastle, which had been surprised by the king's party, was besieged by another army of Scots advanced to help their brethren.

Along the edges of those vast mountains we passed with the help of our guide, till we came into the forest of Swale; and finding ourselves perfectly concealed here, for no soldier had ever been here all the war, nor perhaps would not, if it had lasted seven years, we thought we wanted a few days' rest, at least for our horses. So we resolved to halt; and while we did so, we made some disguises, and sent out some spies into the country; but as here were no great towns, nor no post road, we got very little intelligence. We rested four days, and then marched again; and indeed having no great stock of money about us, and not very free of that we had, four days was enough for those poor places to be able to maintain us.

We thought ourselves pretty secure now; but our chief care was how to get over those terrible mountains; for having passed the great road that leads from York to Lancaster, the crags, the farther northward we looked, looked still the worse, and our business was all on the other side. Our guide told us, he would bring us out, if we would have patience, which we were obliged to, and kept on this slow march, till he brought us to Stanhope, in the country of Durham; where some of Goring's horse, and two regiments of foot, had their quarters. This was nineteen days from the battle of Marston Moor. The prince, who was then at Kendal in Westmoreland, and who had given me over as lost, when he had news of our arrival, sent an express to me, to meet him at Appleby. I went thither accordingly, and gave him an account of our journey, and there I heard the short history of the other part of our men, whom we parted from in Lancashire. They made the best of their way north; they had two resolute gentlemen who commanded; and being so closely pursued by the enemy, that they found themselves under a necessity of fighting, they halted, and faced about, expecting the charge. The boldness of the action made the officer who led the enemy's horse (which it seems were the county horse only) afraid of them; which they perceiving, taking the advantage of his fears, bravely advance, and charge them; and though they were above 200 horse, they routed them, killed about thirty or forty, got some horses, and some money, and pushed on their march night and day; but coming near Lancaster, they were so waylaid and pursued, that they agreed to separate, and shift every man for himself. Many of them fell into the enemy's hands; some were killed attempting to pass through the river Lune; some went back, six or seven got to Bolton, and about eighteen got safe to Prince Rupert.

The prince was in a better condition hereabouts than I expected; he and my Lord Goring, with the help of Sir Marmaduke Langdale, and the gentlemen of Cumberland, had gotten a body of 4000 horse, and about 6000 foot; they had retaken Newcastle, Tynemouth, Durham, Stockton, and several towns of consequence from the Scots, and might have cut them out work enough still, if that base people, resolved to engage their whole interest to ruin their sovereign, had not sent a second army of 10,000 men, under the Earl of Callander, to help their first. These came and laid siege to Newcastle, but found more vigorous resistance now than they had done before.

There were in the town Sir John Morley, the Lord Crawford, Lord Reay, and Maxwell, Scots; and old soldiers, who were resolved their countrymen should buy the town very dear, if they had it; and had it not been for our disaster at Marston Moor, they had never had it; for Callander, finding he was not able to carry the town, sends to General Leven to come from the siege of York to help him.

Meantime the prince forms a very good army, and the Lord Goring, with 10,000 men, shows himself on the borders of Scotland, to try if that might not cause the Scots to recall their forces; and, I am persuaded, had he entered Scotland, the Parliament of Scotland had recalled the Earl of Callander, for they had but 5000 men left in arms to send against him; but they were loth to venture. However, this effect it had, that it called the Scots northward again, and found them work there for the rest of the summer to reduce the several towns in the bishopric of Durham.

I found with the prince the poor remains of my regiment, which, when joined with those that had been with me, could not all make up three troops, and but two captains, three lieutenants, and one cornet; the rest were dispersed, killed, or taken prisoners. However, with those, which we still called a regiment, I joined the prince, and after having done all we could on that side, the Scots being returned from York, the prince returned through Lancashire to Chester.

The enemy often appeared and alarmed us, and once fell on one of our parties, and killed us about a hundred men; but we were too many for them to pretend to fight us, so we came to Bolton, beat the troops of the enemy near Warrington, where I got a cut with a halberd in my face, and arrived at Chester the beginning of August.

The Parliament, upon their great success in the north, thinking the king's forces quite unbroken, had sent their General Essex into the west, where the king's army was commanded by Prince Maurice, Prince Rupert's elder brother, but not very strong; and the king being, as they supposed, by the absence of Prince Rupert, weakened so much as that he might be checked by Sir William Waller, who, with 4500 foot, and 1500 horse, was at that time about Winchester, having lately beaten Sir Ralph Hopton;—upon all these considerations, the Earl of Essex marches westward.

The forces in the west being too weak to oppose him, everything gave way to him, and all people expected he would besiege Exeter, where the queen was newly lying-in, and sent a trumpet to desire he would forbear the city, while she could be removed, which he did, and passed on westward, took Tiverton, Bideford, Barnstaple, Launceston, relieved Plymouth, drove Sir Richard Grenvile up into Cornwall, and followed him thither, but left Prince Maurice behind him with 4000 men about Barnstaple and Exeter. The king, in the meantime, marches from Oxford into Worcester, with Waller at his heels. At Edgehill his Majesty turns upon Waller, and gave him a brush, to put him in mind of the place. The king goes on to Worcester, sends 300 horse to relieve Durley Castle, besieged by the Earl of Denby, and sending part of his forces to Bristol, returns to Oxford.

His Majesty had now firmly resolved to march into the west, not having yet any account of our misfortunes in the north. Waller and Middleton waylay the king at Cropredy Bridge. The king assaults Middleton at the bridge.

Waller's men were posted with some cannon to guard a pass. Middleton's men put a regiment of the king's foot to the rout, and pursued them. Waller's men, willing to come in for the plunder, a thing their general had often used them to, quit their post at the pass, and their great guns, to have part in the victory. The king coming in seasonably to the relief of his men, routs Middleton, and at the same time sends a party round, who clapped in between Sir William Waller's men and their great guns, and secured the pass and the cannon too. The king took three colonels, besides other officers, and about 300 men prisoners, with eight great guns, nineteen carriages of ammunition, and killed about 200 men.

Waller lost his reputation in this fight, and was exceedingly slighted ever after, even by his own party; but especially by such as were of General Essex's party, between whom and Waller there had been jealousies and misunderstandings for some time.

The king, about 8000 strong, marched on to Bristol, where Sir William Hopton joined him, and from thence he follows Essex into Cornwall. Essex still following Grenvile, the king comes to Exeter, and joining with Prince Maurice, resolves to pursue Essex; and now the Earl of Essex began to see his mistake, being cooped up between two seas, the king's army in his rear, the country his enemy, and Sir Richard Grenvile in his van.

The king, who always took the best measures when he was left to his own counsel, wisely refuses to engage, though superior in number, and much stronger in horse. Essex often drew out to fight, but the king fortifies, takes the passes and bridges, plants cannon, and secures the country to keep off provisions, and continually straitens their quarters, but would not fight.

Now Essex sends away to the Parliament for help, and they write to Waller, and Middleton, and Manchester to follow, and come up with the king in his rear; but some were too far off, and could not, as Manchester and Fairfax; others made no haste, as having no mind to it, as Waller and Middleton, and if they had, it had been too late.

At last the Earl of Essex, finding nothing to be done, and unwilling to fall into the king's hands, takes shipping, and leaves his army to shift for themselves. The horse, under Sir William Balfour, the best horse officer, and, without comparison, the bravest in all the Parliament army, advanced in small parties, as if to skirmish, but following in with the whole body, being 3500 horse, broke through, and got off. Though this was a loss to the king's victory, yet the foot were now in a condition so much the worse. Brave old Skippon proposed to fight through with the foot and die, as he called it, like Englishmen, with sword in hand; but the rest of the officers shook their heads at it, for, being well paid, they had at present no occasion for dying.

Seeing it thus, they agreed to treat, and the king grants them conditions, upon laying down their arms, to march off free. This was too much. Had his Majesty but obliged them upon oath not to serve again for a certain time, he had done his business; but this was not thought of; so they passed free, only disarmed, the soldiers not being allowed so much as their swords.

The king gained by this treaty forty pieces of cannon, all of brass, 300 barrels of gunpowder, 9000 arms, 8000 swords, match and bullet in proportion, 200 waggons, 150 colours and standards, all the bag and baggage of the army, and about 1000 of the men listed in his army. This was a complete victory without bloodshed; and had the king but secured the men from serving but for six months, it had most effectually answered the battle of Marston Moor.

As it was, it infused new life into all his Majesty's forces and friends, and retrieved his affairs very much; but especially it encouraged us in the north, who were more sensible of the blow received at Marston Moor, and of the destruction the Scots were bringing upon us all.

While I was at Chester, we had some small skirmishes with Sir William Brereton. One morning in particular Sir William drew up, and faced us, and one of our colonels of horse observing the enemy to be not, as he thought, above 200, desires leave of Prince Rupert to attack them with the like number, and accordingly he sallied out with 200 horse. I stood drawn up without the city with 800 more, ready to bring him off, if he should be put to the worst, which happened accordingly; for, not having discovered neither the country nor the enemy as he ought, Sir William Brereton drew him into an ambuscade; so that before he came up with Sir William's forces, near enough to charge, he finds about 300 horse in his rear. Though he was surprised at this, yet, being a man of a ready courage, he boldly faces about with 150 of his men, leaving the other fifty to face Sir William. With this small party, he desperately charges the 300 horse in his rear, and putting them into disorder, breaks through them, and, had there been no greater force, he had cut them all in pieces. Flushed with this success, and loth to desert the fifty men he had left behind, he faces about again, and charges through them again, and with these two charges entirely routs them. Sir William Brereton finding himself a little disappointed, advances, and falls upon the fifty men just as the colonel came up to them; they fought him with a great deal of bravery, but the colonel being unfortunately killed in the first charge, the men gave way, and came flying all in confusion, with the enemy at their heels. As soon as I saw this, I advanced, according to my orders, and the enemy, as soon as I appeared, gave over the pursuit. This gentleman, as I remember, was Colonel Marrow; we fetched off his body, and retreated into Chester.

The next morning the prince drew out of the city with about 1200 horse and 2000 foot, and attacked Sir William Brereton in his quarters. The fight was very sharp for the time, and near 700 men, on both sides, were killed; but Sir William would not put it to a general engagement, so the prince drew off, contenting himself to have insulted him in his quarters.

We now had received orders from the king to join him; but I representing to the prince the condition of my regiment, which was now 100 men, and that, being within twenty-five miles of my father's house, I might soon recruit it, my father having got some men together already, I desired leave to lie at Shrewsbury for a month, to make up my men. Accordingly, having obtained his leave, I marched to Wrexham, where in two days' time I got twenty men, and so on to Shrewsbury. I had not been here above ten days, but I received an express to come away with what recruits I had got together, Prince Rupert having positive orders to meet the king by a certain day. I had not mounted 100 men, though

I had listed above 200, when these orders came; but leaving my father to complete them for me, I marched with those I had and came to Oxford.

The king, after the rout of the Parliament forces in the west, was marched back, took Barnstaple, Plympton, Launceston, Tiverton, and several other places, and left Plymouth besieged by Sir Richard Grenvile, met with Sir William Waller at Shaftesbury, and again at Andover, and boxed him at both places, and marched for Newbury. Here the king sent for Prince Rupert to meet him, who with 3000 horse made long marches to join him; but the Parliament having joined their three armies together, Manchester from the north, Waller and Essex (the men being clothed and armed) from the west, had attacked the king and obliged him to fight the day before the prince came up.

The king had so posted himself, as that he could not be obliged to fight but with advantage, the Parliament's forces being superior in number, and therefore, when they attacked him, he galled them with his cannon, and declining to come to a general battle, stood upon the defensive, expecting Prince Rupert with the horse.

The Parliament's forces had some advantage over our foot, and took the Earl of Cleveland prisoner. But the king, whose foot were not above one to two, drew his men under the cannon of Donnington Castle, and having secured his artillery and baggage, made a retreat with his foot in very good order, having not lost in all the fight above 300 men, and the Parliament as many. We lost five pieces of cannon and took two, having repulsed the Earl of Manchester's men on the north side of the town, with considerable loss.

The king having lodged his train of artillery and baggage in Donnington Castle, marched the next day for Oxford. There we joined him with 3000 horse and 2000 foot. Encouraged with this reinforcement, the king appears upon the hills on the north-west of Newbury, and faces the Parliament army. The Parliament having too many generals as well as soldiers, they could not agree whether they should fight or no. This was no great token of the victory they boasted of, for they were now twice our number in the whole, and their foot three for one. The king stood in battalia all day, and finding the Parliament forces had no stomach to engage him, he drew away his cannon and baggage out of Donnington Castle in view of their whole army, and marched away to Oxford.

This was such a false step of the Parliament's generals, that all the people cried shame of them. The Parliament appointed a committee to inquire into it. Cromwell accused Manchester, and he Waller, and so they laid the fault upon one another. Waller would have been glad to have charged it upon Essex, but as it happened he was not in the army, having been taken ill some days before. But as it generally is when a mistake is made, the actors fall out among themselves, so it was here. No doubt it was as false a step as that of Cornwall, to let the king fetch away his baggage and cannon in the face of three armies, and never fire a shot at them.

The king had not above 8000 foot in his army, and they above 25,000. 'Tis true the king had 8000 horse, a fine body, and much superior to theirs; but the foot might, with the greatest ease in the world, have prevented the removing the cannon, and in three days' time have taken the castle, with all that was in it.

Those differences produced their self-denying ordinance, and the putting by most of their old generals, as Essex, Waller, Manchester, and the like; and Sir Thomas Fairfax, a terrible man in the field, though the mildest of men out of it, was voted to have the command of all their forces, and Lambert to take the command of Sir Thomas Fairfax's troops in the north, old Skippon being Major-General.

This winter was spent on the enemy's side in modelling, as they called it, their army, and on our side in recruiting ours, and some petty excursions. Amongst the many addresses I observed one from Sussex or Surrey, complaining of the rudeness of their soldiers, from which I only observed that there were disorders among them as well as among us, only with this difference, that they, for reasons I mentioned before, were under circumstances to prevent it better than the king. But I must do the king's memory that justice, that he used all possible methods, by punishment of soldiers, charging, and sometimes entreating, the gentlemen not to suffer such disorders and such violences in their men; but it was to no purpose for his Majesty to attempt it, while his officers, generals, and great men winked at it; for the licentiousness of the soldier is supposed to be approved by the officer when it is not corrected.

The rudeness of the Parliament soldiers began from the divisions among their officers; for in many places the soldiers grew so out of all discipline and so unsufferably rude, that they, in particular, refused to march when Sir William Waller went to Weymouth. This had turned to good account for us, had these cursed Scots been out of our way, but they were the staff of the party; and now they were daily solicited to

410

march southward, which was a very great affliction to the king and all his friends.

One booty the king got at this time, which was a very seasonable assistance to his affairs, viz., a great merchant ship, richly laden at London, and bound to the East Indies, was, by the seamen, brought into Bristol, and delivered up to the king. Some merchants in Bristol offered the king £40,000 for her, which his Majesty ordered should be accepted, reserving only thirty great guns for his own use.

The treaty at Uxbridge now was begun, and we that had been well beaten in the war heartily wished the king would come to a peace; but we all foresaw the clergy would ruin it all. The Commons were for Presbytery, and would never agree the bishops should be restored. The king was willinger to comply with anything than this, and we foresaw it would be so; from whence we used to say among ourselves, "That the clergy was resolved if there should be no bishop there should be no king."

This treaty at Uxbridge was a perfect war between the men of the gown, ours was between those of the sword; and I cannot but take notice how the lawyers, statesmen, and the clergy of every side bestirred themselves, rather to hinder than promote the peace.

There had been a treaty at Oxford some time before, where the Parliament insisting that the king should pass a bill to abolish Episcopacy, quit the militia, abandon several of his faithful servants to be exempted from pardon, and making several other most extravagant demands, nothing was done, but the treaty broke off, both parties being rather farther exasperated, than inclined to hearken to conditions.

However, soon after the success in the west, his Majesty, to let them see that victory had not puffed him up so as to make him reject the peace, sends a message to the Parliament, to put them in mind of messages of like nature which they had slighted; and to let them know, that notwithstanding he had beaten their forces, he was yet willing to hearken to a reasonable proposal for putting an end to the war.

The Parliament pretended the king, in his message, did not treat with them as a legal Parliament, and so made hesitations; but after long debates and delays they agreed to draw up propositions for peace to be sent to the king. As this message was sent to the Houses about August, I think they made it the middle of November before they brought the propositions for peace; and, when they brought them, they had no power to enter either upon a treaty, or so much as preliminaries for a treaty, only to deliver the letter, and receive an answer.

However, such were the circumstances of affairs at this time, that the king was uneasy to see himself thus treated, and take no notice of it: the king returned an answer to the propositions, and proposed a treaty by commissioners which the Parliament appointed.

Three months more were spent in naming commissioners. There was much time spent in this treaty, but little done; the commissioners debated chiefly the article of religion, and of the militia; in the latter they were very likely to agree, in the former both sides seemed too positive. The king would by no means abandon Episcopacy nor the Parliament Presbytery; for both in their opinion were *jure divino*.

The commissioners finding this point hardest to adjust, went from it to that of the militia; but the time spinning out, the king's commissioners demanded longer time for the treaty; the other sent up for instructions, but the House refused to lengthen out the time.

This was thought an insolence upon the king, and gave all good people a detestation of such haughty behaviour; and thus the hopes of peace vanished, both sides prepared for war with as much eagerness as before.

The Parliament was employed at this time in what they called a-modelling their army; that is to say, that now the Independent party [was] beginning to prevail; and, as they outdid all the others in their resolution of carrying on the war to all extremities, so they were both the more vigorous and more politic party in carrying it on.

Indeed, the war was after this carried on with greater animosity than ever, and the generals pushed forward with a vigour that, as it had something in it unusual, so it told us plainly from this time, whatever they did before, they now pushed at the ruin even of the monarchy itself.

All this while also the war went on, and though the Parliament had no settled army, yet their regiments and troops were always in action; and the sword was at work in every part of the kingdom.

Among an infinite number of party skirmishings and fights this winter, one happened which nearly concerned me, which was the surprise of the town and castle of Shrewsbury. Colonel Mitton, with about 1200 horse and foot, having intelligence with some people in the town, on a Sunday morning early broke into the town and took it, castle and all. The loss for the quality, more than the number, was very great to the king's affairs. They took there fifteen pieces of cannon, Prince Maurice's magazine of arms and ammunition, Prince Rupert's baggage, above fifty persons of quality and officers. There was not above eight or ten men killed on both sides, for the town was surprised, not stormed. I had a particular loss in this action; for all the men and horses my father had got together for the recruiting my regiment were here lost and dispersed, and, which was the worse, my father happening to be then in the town, was taken prisoner, and carried to Beeston Castle in Cheshire.

I was quartered all this winter at Banbury, and went little abroad; nor had we any action till the latter end of February, when I was ordered to march to Leicester with Sir Marmaduke Langdale, in order, as we thought, to raise a body of men in that county and Staffordshire to join the king.

We lay at Daventry one night, and continuing our march to pass the river above Northampton, that town being possessed by the enemy, we understood a party of Northampton forces were abroad, and intended to attack us. Accordingly, in the afternoon our scouts brought us word the enemy were quartered in some villages on the road to Coventry. Our commander, thinking it much better to set upon them in their quarters, than to wait for them in the field, resolves to attack them early in the morning before they were aware of it. We refreshed ourselves in the field for that day, and, getting into a great wood near the enemy, we stayed there all night, till almost break of day, without being discovered.

In the morning very early we heard the enemy's trumpets sound to horse. This roused us to look abroad, and, sending out a scout, he brought us word a part of the enemy was at hand. We were vexed to be so disappointed, but finding their party small enough to be dealt with, Sir Marmaduke ordered me to charge them with 300 horse and 200 dragoons, while he at the same time entered the town. Accordingly I lay still till they came to the very skirt of the wood where I was posted, when I saluted them with a volley from my dragoons out of the wood, and immediately showed myself with my horse on their front ready to charge them. They appeared not to be surprised, and received our charge with great resolution; and, being above 400 men, they pushed me vigorously in their turn, putting my men into some disorder. In this extremity I sent to order my dragoons to charge them in the flank, which they did with great bravery, and the other still maintained the fight with desperate resolution. There was no want of courage in our men on both sides, but our dragoons had the advantage, and at last routed them, and drove them back to the village. Here Sir Marmaduke Langdale had his hands full too, for my firing had alarmed the towns adjacent, that when he came into the town he found them all in arms, and, contrary to his expectation, two regiments of foot, with about 500 horse more. As Sir Marmaduke had no foot, only horse and dragoons, this was a surprise to him; but he caused his dragoons to enter the town and charge the foot, while his horse secured the avenues of the town.

The dragoons bravely attacked the foot, and Sir Marmaduke falling in with his horse, the fight was obstinate and very bloody, when the horse that I had routed came flying into the street of the village, and my men at their heels. Immediately I left the pursuit, and fell in with all my force to the assistance of my friends, and, after an obstinate resistance, we routed the whole party; we killed about 700 men, took 350, 27 officers, 100 arms, all their baggage, and 200 horses, and continued our march to Harborough, where we halted to refresh ourselves.

Between Harborough and Leicester we met with a party of 800 dragoons of the Parliament forces. They, found themselves too few to attack us, and therefore to avoid us they had gotten into a small wood; but perceiving themselves discovered, they came boldly out, and placed themselves at the entrance into a lane, lining both sides of the hedges with their shot. We immediately attacked them, beat them from their hedges, beat them into the wood, and out of the wood again, and forced them at last to a downright run away, on foot, among the enclosures, where we could not follow them, killed about 100 of them, and took 250 prisoners, with all their horses, and came that night to Leicester. When we came to Leicester, and had taken up our quarters, Sir Marmaduke Langdale sent for me to sup with him, and told me that he had a secret commission in his pocket, which his Majesty had commanded him not to open till he came to Leicester; that now he had sent for me to open it together, that we might know what it was we were to do, and to consider how to do it; so pulling out his sealed orders, we found we were to get what force we could together, and a certain number of carriages with ammunition, which the governor of Leicester was to deliver us, and a certain quantity of provision, especially corn and salt, and to relieve Newark. This town had been long besieged. The fortifications of the place, together with its situation, had rendered it the strongest place in England; and, as it was the greatest pass in England, so it was of vast consequence to the king's affairs. There was in it a garrison of brave old rugged boys, fellows that, like Count Tilly's Germans, had iron faces, and they had defended themselves with extraordinary bravery a great while, but were reduced to an exceeding strait for want of provisions.

Accordingly we received the ammunition and provision, and away we went for Newark; about Melton Mowbray, Colonel Rossiter set upon us, with above 3000 men; we were about the same number, having 2500 horse, and 800 dragoons. We had some foot, but they were still at Harborough, and were ordered to come after us.

Rossiter, like a brave officer as he was, charged us with great fury, and rather outdid us in number, while we defended ourselves with all the eagerness we could, and withal gave him to understand we were not so soon to be beaten as he expected. While the fight continued doubtful, especially on our side, our people, who had charge of the carriages and provisions, began to enclose our flanks with them, as if we had been marching, which, though it was done without orders, had two very good effects, and which did us extraordinary service. First, it secured us from being charged in the flank, which Rossiter had twice attempted; and secondly, it secured our carriages from being plundered, which had spoiled our whole expedition. Being thus enclosed, we fought with great security; and though Rossiter made three desperate charges upon us; he could never break us. Our men received him with so much courage, and kept their order so well, that the enemy, finding it impossible to force us, gave it over, and left us to pursue our orders. We did not offer to chase them, but contented enough to have repulsed and beaten them off, and our business being to relieve Newark, we proceeded.

If we are to reckon by the enemy's usual method, we got the victory, because we kept the field, and had the pillage of their dead; but otherwise, neither side had any great cause to boast. We lost about 150 men, and near as many hurt; they left 170 on the spot, and carried off some. How many they had wounded we could not tell; we got seventy or eighty horses, which helped to remount some of our men that had lost theirs in the fight. We had, however, this advantage, that we were to march on immediately after this service, the enemy only to retire to their quarters, which was but hard by. This was an injury to our wounded men, who we were after obliged to leave at Belvoir Castle, and from thence we advanced to Newark.

Our business at Newark was to relieve the place, and this we resolved to do whatever it cost, though, at the same time, we resolved not to fight unless we were forced to it. The town was rather blocked up than besieged; the garrison was strong, but ill-provided; we had sent them word of our coming to them, and our orders to relieve them, and they proposed some measures for our doing it. The chief strength of the enemy lay on the other side of the river; but they having also some notice of our design, had sent over forces to strengthen their leaguer on this side. The garrison had often surprised them by sallies, and indeed had chiefly subsisted for some time by what they brought in on this manner.

Sir Marmaduke Langdale, who was our general for the expedition, was for a general attempt to raise the siege, but I had persuaded him off of that; first, because, if we should be beaten, as might be probable, we then lost the town. Sir Marmaduke briskly replied, "A soldier ought never to suppose he shall be beaten." "But, sir," says I, "you'll get more honour by relieving the town, than by beating them. One will be a credit to your conduct, as the other will be to your courage; and if you think you can beat them, you may do it afterward, and then if you are mistaken, the town is nevertheless secured, and half your victory gained."

He was prevailed with to adhere to this advice, and accordingly we appeared before the town about two hours before night. The horse drew up before the enemy's works; the enemy drew up within their works, and seeing no foot, expected when our dragoons would dismount and attack them. They were in the right to let us attack them, because of the advantage of their batteries and works, if that had been our design; but, as we intended only to amuse them, this caution of theirs effected our design; for, while we thus faced them with our horse, two regiments of foot, which came up to us but the night before, and was all the infantry we had, with the waggons of provisions, and 500 dragoons, taking a compass clean round the town, posted themselves on the lower side of the town by the river. Upon a signal the garrison agreed on before, they sallied out at this very juncture with all the men they could spare, and dividing themselves in two parties, while one party moved to the left to meet our relief, the other party fell on upon part of that body which faced us. We kept in motion, and upon this signal advanced to their works, and our dragoons fired upon them, and the horse, wheeling and counter-marching often, kept them continually expecting to be attacked. By this means the enemy were kept employed, and our foot, with the waggons, appearing on that quarter where they were least expected, easily defeated the advanced guards and forced that post, where, entering the leaguer, the other part of the garrison, who had sallied that way, came up to them, received the waggons, and the dragoons entered with them into the town. That party which we faced on the other side of the works knew nothing of what was done till all was over; the garrison retreated in good order, and we drew off, having finished what we came for without fighting. Thus we plentifully stored the town with all things wanting, and with an addition of 500 dragoons to their garrison; after which we marched away without fighting a stroke.

Our next orders were to relieve Pontefract Castle, another garrison of the king's, which had been besieged ever since a few days after the fight at Marston Moor, by the Lord Fairfax, Sir Thomas Fairfax, and other generals in their turn. By the way we were joined with 800 horse out of Derbyshire, and some foot, so many as made us about 4500 men in all.

Colonel Forbes, a Scotchman, commanded at the siege, in the absence of the Lord Fairfax. The colonel had sent to my lord for more troops, and his lordship was gathering his forces to come up to him, but he was pleased to come too late. We came up with the enemy's leaguer about the break of day, and having been discovered by their scouts, they, with more courage than discretion, drew out to meet us. We saw no reason to avoid them, being stronger in horse than they; and though we had but a few foot, we had 1000 dragoons, which helped us out. We had placed our horse and foot throughout in one line, with two reserves of horse, and between every division of horse a division of foot, only that on the extremes of our wings there were two parties of horse on each point by themselves, and the dragoons in the centre on foot. Their foot charged us home, and stood with push of pike a great while; but their horse charging our horse and musketeers, and being closed on the flanks, with those two extended troops on our wings, they were presently disordered, and fled out of the field. The foot, thus deserted, were charged on every side and broken. They retreated still fighting, and in good order for a while; but the garrison sallying upon them at the same time, and being followed close by our horse, they were scattered, entirely routed, and most of them killed. The Lord Fairfax was come with his horse as far as Ferrybridge, but the fight was over, and all he could do was to rally those that fled, and save some of their carriages, which else had fallen into our hands. We drew up our little army in order of battle the next day, expecting the Lord Fairfax would have charged us; but his lordship was so far from any such thoughts that he placed a party of dragoons, with orders to fortify the pass at Ferrybridge, to prevent our falling upon him in his retreat, which he needed not have done; for, having raised the siege of Pontefract, our business was done, we had nothing to say to him, unless we had been strong enough to stay.

We lost not above thirty men in this action, and the enemy 300, with about 150 prisoners, one piece of cannon, all their ammunition, 1000 arms, and most of their baggage, and Colonel Lambert was once taken prisoner, being wounded, but got off again.

We brought no relief for the garrison, but the opportunity to furnish themselves out of the country, which they did very plentifully. The ammunition taken from the enemy was given to them, which they wanted, and was their due, for they had seized it in the sally they made, before the enemy was quite defeated.

I cannot omit taking notice on all occasions how exceeding serviceable this method was of posting musketeers in the intervals, among the horse, in all this war. I persuaded our generals to it as much as possible, and I never knew a body of horse beaten that did so: yet I had great difficulty to prevail upon our people to believe it, though it was taught me by the greatest general in the world, viz., the King of Sweden. Prince Rupert did it at the battle of Marston Moor; and had the Earl of Newcastle not been obstinate against it in his right wing, as I observed before, the day had not been lost. In discoursing this with Sir Marmaduke Langdale, I had related several examples of the serviceableness of these small bodies of firemen, and with great difficulty brought him to agree, telling him I would be answerable for the success. But after the fight, he told me plainly he saw the advantage of it, and would never fight otherwise again if he had any foot to place. So having relieved these two places, we hastened by long marches through Derbyshire, to join Prince Rupert on the edge of Shropshire and Cheshire. We found Colonel Rossiter had followed us at a distance ever since the business at Melton Mowbray, but never cared to attack us, and we found he did the like still. Our general would fain have been doing with him again, but we found him too shy. Once we laid a trap for him at Dovebridge, between Derby and Burton-upon-Trent, the body being marched two days before. Three hundred dragoons were left to guard the bridge, as if we were afraid he should fall upon us. Upon this we marched, as I said, on to Burton, and the next day, fetching a compass round, came to a village near Titbury Castle, whose name I forgot, where we lay still expecting our dragoons would be attacked.

Accordingly, the colonel, strengthened with some troops of horse from Yorkshire, comes up to the bridge, and finding some dragoons posted, advances to charge them. The dragoons immediately get a-horseback, and run for it, as they were ordered. But the old lad was not to be caught so, for he halts immediately at the bridge, and would not come over till he had sent three or four flying parties abroad to discover the country. One of these parties fell into our hands, and received but coarse entertainment. Finding the plot would not take, we appeared and drew up in view of the bridge, but he would not stir. So we continued our march into Cheshire, where we joined Prince Rupert and Prince Maurice, making together a fine body, being above 8000 horse and dragoons.

This was the best and most successful expedition I was in during this war. 'Twas well concerted, and executed with as much expedition and conduct as could be desired, and the success was answerable to it. And indeed, considering the season of the year (for we set out from Oxford the latter end of February), the ways bad, and the season wet, it was a terrible march of above 200 miles, in continual action, and continually dodged and observed by a vigilant enemy, and at a time when the north was overrun by their armies, and the Scots wanting employment for their forces. Yet in less than twenty-three days we marched 200 miles, fought the enemy in open field four times, relieved one garrison besieged, and raised the siege of another, and joined our friends at last in safety.

The enemy was in great pain for Sir William Brereton and his forces, and expresses rode night and day to the Scots in the north, and to the parties in Lancashire to come to his help. The prince, who used to be rather too forward to fight than otherwise, could not be persuaded to make use of this opportunity, but loitered, if I may be allowed to say so, till the Scots, with a brigade of horse and 2000 foot, had joined him; and then 'twas not thought proper to engage them.

I took this opportunity to go to Shrewsbury to visit my father, who was a prisoner of war there, getting a pass from the enemy's governor. They allowed him the liberty of the town, and sometimes to go to his own house upon his parole, so that his confinement was not very much to his personal injury. But this, together with the charges he had been at in raising the regiment, and above £20,000 in money and plate, which at several times he had lent, or given rather to the king, had reduced our family to very ill circumstances; and now they talked of cutting down his woods.

I had a great deal of discourse with my father on this affair; and, finding him extremely concerned, I offered to go to the king and desire his leave to go to London and treat about his composition, or to render myself a prisoner in his stead, while he went up himself. In this difficulty I treated with the governor of the town, who very civilly offered me his pass to go for London, which I accepted, and, waiting on Prince Rupert, who was then at Worcester, I acquainted him with my design. The prince was unwilling I should go to London; but told me he had some prisoners of the Parliament's friends in Cumberland, and he would get an exchange for my father. I told him if he would give me his word for it I knew I might depend upon it, otherwise there was so many of the king's party in their hands, that his Majesty was tired with solicitations for exchanges, for we never had a prisoner but there was ten offers of exchanges for him. The prince told me I should depend upon him; and he was as good as his word quickly after.

While the prince lay at Worcester he made an incursion into Herefordshire, and having made some of the gentlemen prisoners, brought them to Worcester; and though it was an action which had not been usual, they being persons not in arms, yet the like being my father's case, who was really not in commission, nor in any military service, having resigned his regiment three years before to me, the prince insisted on exchanging them for such as the Parliament had in custody in like circumstances. The gentlemen seeing no remedy, solicited their own case at the Parliament, and got it passed in their behalf; and by this means my father got his liberty, and by the assistance of the Earl of Denbigh got leave to come to London to make a composition as a delinquent for his estate. This they charged at £7000, but by the assistance of the same noble person he got off for £4000. Some members of the committee moved very kindly that my father should oblige me to quit the king's service, but that, as a thing which might be out of his power, was not insisted on.

The modelling the Parliament army took them up all this winter, and we were in great hopes the divisions which appeared amongst them might have weakened their party; but when they voted Sir Thomas Fairfax to be general, I confess I was convinced the king's affairs were lost and desperate. Sir Thomas, abating the zeal of his party, and the mistaken opinion of his cause, was the fittest man amongst them to undertake the charge. He was a complete general, strict in his discipline, wary in conduct, fearless in action, unwearied in the fatigue of the war, and withal, of a modest, noble, generous disposition. We all apprehended danger from him, and heartily wished him of our own side; and the king was so sensible, though he would not discover it, that when an account was brought him of the choice they had made, he replied, "he was sorry for it; he had rather it had been anybody than he."

The first attempts of this new general and new army were at Oxford, which, by the neighbourhood of a numerous garrison in Abingdon, began to be very much straitened for provisions; and the new forces under Cromwell and Skippon, one lieutenant-general, the other major-general to Fairfax, approaching with a design to block it up, the king left the place, supposing his absence would draw them away, as it soon did.

The king resolving to leave Oxford, marches from thence with all his forces, the garrison excepted, with design to have gone to Bristol; but the plague was in Bristol, which altered the measures, and changed the course of the king's designs, so he marched for Worcester about the beginning of June 1645. The foot, with a train of forty pieces of cannon, marching into Worcester, the horse stayed behind some time in Gloucestershire.

The first action our army did, was to raise the siege of Chester; Sir William Brereton had besieged it, or rather blocked it up, and when his Majesty came to Worcester, he sent Prince Rupert with 4000 horse and dragoons, with orders to join some foot out of Wales, to raise the siege; but Sir William thought fit to withdraw, and not stay for them, and the town was freed without fighting. The governor took care in this interval to furnish himself with all things necessary for another siege; and, as for ammunition and other necessaries, he was in no want.

I was sent with a party into Staffordshire, with design to intercept a convoy of stores coming from London, for the use of Sir William Brereton; but they having some notice of the design, stopped, and went out of the road to Burton-upon-Trent, and so I missed them; but that we might not come back quite empty, we attacked Hawkesley House, and took it, where we got good booty, and brought eighty prisoners back to Worcester. From Worcester the king advanced into Shropshire, and took his headquarters at Bridgnorth. This was a very happy march of the king's, and had his Majesty proceeded, he had certainly cleared the north once more of his enemies, for the country was generally for him. At his advancing so far as Bridgnorth, Sir William Brereton fled up into Lancashire; the Scots brigades who were with him retreated into the north, while yet the king was above forty miles from them, and all things lay open for conquest. The new generals, Fairfax and Cromwell, lay about Oxford, preparing as if they would besiege it, and gave the king's army so much leisure, that his Majesty might have been at Newcastle before they could have been half way to him. But Heaven, when the ruin of a person or party is determined, always so infatuates their counsels as to make them instrumental to it themselves.

The king let slip this great opportunity, as some thought, intending to break into the associated counties of Northampton, Cambridge, Norfolk, where he had some interests forming. What the design was, we knew not, but the king turns eastward, and marches into Leicestershire, and having treated the country but very indifferently, as having deserved no better of us, laid siege to Leicester.

This was but a short siege; for the king, resolving not to lose time, fell on with his great guns, and having beaten down their works, our foot entered, after a vigorous resistance, and took the town by storm. There was some blood shed here, the town being carried by assault; but it was their own faults; for after the town was taken, the soldiers and townsmen obstinately fought us in the market-place; insomuch that the horse was called to enter the town to clear the streets. But this was not all; I was commanded to advance with these horse, being three regiments, and to enter the town; the foot, who were engaged in the streets, crying out, "Horse, horse." Immediately I advanced to the gate, for we were drawn up about musket-shot from the works, to have supported our foot in case of a sally. Having seized the gate, I placed a guard of horse there, with orders to let nobody pass in or out, and dividing my troops, rode up by two ways towards the market-place. The garrison defending themselves in the market-place, and in the churchyard with great obstinacy, killed us a great many men; but as soon as our horse appeared they demanded quarter, which our foot refused them in the first heat, as is frequent in all nations, in like cases, till at last they threw down their arms, and yielded at discretion; and then I can testify to the world, that fair quarter was given them. I am the more particular in this relation, having been an eye-witness of the action, because the king was reproached in all the public libels, with which those times abounded, for having put a great many to death, and hanged the committee of the Parliament, and some Scots, in cold blood, which was a notorious forgery; and as I am sure there was no such thing done, so I must acknowledge I never saw any inclination in his Majesty to cruelty, or to act anything which was not practised by the general laws of war, and by men of honour in all nations.

But the matter of fact, in respect to the garrison, was as I have related; and, if they had thrown down their arms sooner, they had had mercy sooner; but it was not for a conquering army, entering a town by storm, to offer conditions of quarter in the streets.

Another circumstance was, that a great many of the inhabitants, both men and women, were killed, which is most true; and the case was thus: the inhabitants, to show their over-forward zeal to defend the town, fought in the breach; nay, the very women, to the honour of the Leicester ladies, if they like it, officiously did their parts; and after the town was taken, and when, if they had had any brains in their zeal, they would have kept their houses, and been quiet, they fired upon our men out of their windows, and from the tops of their houses, and threw tiles upon their heads; and I had several of my men wounded so, and seven or eight killed. This exasperated us to the last degree; and, finding one house better manned than ordinary, and many shot fired at us out of the windows, I caused my men to attack it, resolved to make them an example for the rest; which they did, and breaking open the doors, they killed all they found there, without distinction; and I appeal to the world if they were to blame. If the Parliament committee, or the Scots deputies were here, they ought to have been quiet, since the town was taken; but they began with us, and, I think, brought it upon themselves. This is the whole case, so far as came within my knowledge, for which his Majesty was so much abused.

We took here Colonel Gray and Captain Hacker, and about 300 prisoners, and about 300 more were killed. This was the last day of May 1645.

His Majesty having given over Oxford for lost, continued here some days, viewed the town, ordered the fortifications to be augmented, and prepares to make it the seat of war. But the Parliament, roused at this appearance of the king's army, orders their general to raise the siege of Oxford, where the garrison had, in a sally, ruined some of their works, and killed them 150 men, taking several prisoners, and carrying them with them into the city; and orders him to march towards Leicester, to observe the king.

The king had now a small, but gallant army, all brave tried soldiers, and seemed eager to engage the new-modelled army; and his Majesty, hearing that Sir Thomas Fairfax, having raised the siege of Oxford, advanced towards him, fairly saves him the trouble of a long march, and meets him half way.

The army lay at Daventry, and Fairfax at Towcester, about eight miles off. Here the king sends away 600 horse, with 3000 head of cattle, to relieve his people in Oxford; the cattle he might have spared better than the men. The king having thus victualled Oxford, changes his resolution of fighting Fairfax, to whom Cromwell was now joined with 4000 men, or was within a day's march, and marches northward. This was unhappy counsel, because late given. Had we marched northward at first, we had done it; but thus it was. Now we marched with a triumphing enemy at our heels, and at Naseby their advanced parties attacked our rear. The king, upon this, alters his resolution again, and resolves to fight, and at midnight calls us up at Harborough to come to a council of war. Fate and the king's opinion determined the council of war; and 'twas resolved to fight. Accordingly the van, in which was Prince Rupert's brigade of horse, of which my regiment was a part, counter-marched early in the morning.

By five o'clock in the morning, the whole army, in order of battle, began to descry the enemy from the rising grounds, about a mile from Naseby, and moved towards them. They were drawn up on a little ascent in a large common fallow field, in one line extended from one side of the field to the other, the field something more than a mile over, our army in the same order, in one line, with the reserve.

The king led the main battle of foot, Prince Rupert the right wing of the horse, and Sir Marmaduke Langdale the left. Of the enemy Fairfax and Skippon led the body, Cromwell and Rossiter the right, and Ireton the left, the numbers of both armies so equal, as not to differ 500 men, save that the king had most horse by about 1000, and Fairfax most foot by about 500. The number was in each army about 18,000 men. The armies coming close up, the wings engaged first. The prince with his right wing charged with his wonted fury, and drove all the Parliament's wing of horse, one division excepted, clear out of the field; Ireton, who commanded this wing, give him his due, rallied often, and fought like a lion; but our wing bore down all before them, and pursued them with a terrible execution.

Ireton seeing one division of his horse left, repaired to them, and keeping his ground, fell foul of a brigade of our foot, who coming up to the head of the line, he like a madman charges them with his horse. But they with their pikes tore him to pieces; so that this division was entirely ruined. Ireton himself, thrust through the thigh with a pike, wounded in the face with a halberd, was unhorsed and taken prisoner.

Cromwell, who commanded the Parliament's right wing, charged Sir Marmaduke Langdale with extraordinary fury, but he, an old tried soldier, stood firm, and received the charge with equal gallantry, exchanging all their shot, carabines and pistols and then fell on sword in hand. Rossiter and Whalley had the better on the point of the wing, and routed two divisions of horse, pushed them behind the reserves, where they rallied and charged again, but were at last defeated; the rest of the horse, now charged in the flank, retreated fighting, and were pushed behind the reserves of foot.

While this was doing the foot engaged with equal fierceness, and for two hours there was a terrible fire. The king's foot, backed with gallant officers, and full of rage at the rout of their horse, bore down the enemy's brigade led by Skippon. The old man, wounded, bleeding, retreats to their reserves. All the foot, except the general's brigade, were thus driven into the reserves, where their officers rallied them, and bring them on to a fresh charge; and here the horse, having driven our horse above a quarter of a mile from the foot, face about, and fall in on the rear of the foot.

Had our right wing done thus, the day had been secured; but Prince Rupert, according to his custom, following the flying enemy, never concerned himself with the safety of those behind; and yet he returned sooner than he had done in like cases too. At our return we found all in confusion, our foot broken, all but one brigade, which, though charged in the front, flank, and rear, could not be broken till Sir Thomas Fairfax himself came up to the charge with fresh men, and then they were rather cut in pieces than beaten, for they stood with their pikes charged every way to the last extremity.

In this condition, at the distance of a quarter of a mile, we saw the king rallying his horse, and preparing to renew the fight; and our wing of horse coming up to him, gave him opportunity to draw up a large body of horse, so large that all the enemy's horse facing us stood still and looked on, but did not think fit to charge us till their foot, who had entirely broken our main battle, were put in order again, and brought up to us.

The officers about the king advised his Majesty rather to draw off; for, since our foot were lost, it would be too much odds to expose the horse to the fury of their whole army, and would but be sacrificing his best troops without any hopes of success. The king, though with great regret at the loss of his foot, yet seeing there was no other hope, took this advice, and retreated in good order to Harborough, and from thence to Leicester.

This was the occasion of the enemy having so great a number of prisoners; for the horse being thus gone off, the foot had no means to make their retreat, and were obliged to yield themselves. Commissary-

General Ireton being taken by a captain of foot, makes the captain his prisoner, to save his life, and gives him his liberty for his courtesy before.

Cromwell and Rossiter, with all the enemy's horse, followed us as far as Leicester, and killed all that they could lay hold on straggling from the body, but durst not attempt to charge us in a body. The king, expecting the enemy would come to Leicester, removes to Ashby-de-la-Zouch, where we had some time to recollect ourselves.

This was the most fatal action of the whole war, not so much for the loss of our cannon, ammunition, and baggage, of which the enemy boasted so much, but as it was impossible for the king ever to retrieve it. The foot, the best that ever he was master of, could never be supplied; his army in the west was exposed to certain ruin, the north overrun with the Scots; in short, the case grew desperate, and the king was once upon the point of bidding us all disband, and shift for ourselves.

We lost in this fight not above 2000 slain, and the Parliament near as many, but the prisoners were a great number; the whole body of foot being, as I have said, dispersed, there were 4500 prisoners, besides 400 officers, 2000 horses, 12 pieces of cannon, 40 barrels of powder, all the king's baggage, coaches, most of his servants, and his secretary, with his cabinet of letters, of which the Parliament made great improvement, and basely enough caused his private letters—between his Majesty and the queen, her Majesty's letters to the king, and a great deal of such stuff—to be printed.

After this fatal blow, being retreated, as I have said, to Ashby-de-la-Zouch in Leicestershire, the king ordered us to divide; his Majesty, with a body of horse, about 3000, went to Lichfield, and through Cheshire into North Wales, and Sir Marmaduke Langdale, with about 2500, went to Newark.

The king remained in Wales for several months; and though the length of the war had almost drained that country of men, yet the king raised a great many men there, recruited his horse regiments, and got together six or seven regiments of foot, which seemed to look like the beginning of a new army.

I had frequent discourses with his Majesty in this low ebb of his affairs, and he would often wish he had not exposed his army at Naseby. I took the freedom once to make a proposition to his Majesty, which, if it had taken effect, I verily believe would have given a new turn to his affairs; and that was, at once to slight all his garrisons in the kingdom, and give private orders to all the soldiers in every place, to join in bodies, and meet at two general rendezvous, which I would have appointed to be, one at Bristol, and one at West Chester. I demonstrated how easily all the forces might reach these two places; and both being strong and wealthy places, and both seaports, he would have a free communication by sea with Ireland, and with his friends abroad; and having Wales entirely his own, he might yet have an opportunity to make good terms for himself, or else have another fair field with the enemy.

Upon a fair calculation of his troops in several garrisons and small bodies dispersed about, I convinced the king, by his own accounts, that he might have two complete armies, each of 25,000 foot, 8000 horse, and 2000 dragoons; that the Lord Goring and the Lord Hopton might ship all their forces, and come by sea in two tides, and be with him in a shorter time than the enemy could follow. With two such bodies he might face the enemy, and make a day of it; but now his men were only sacrificed, and eaten up by piecemeal in a party-war, and spent their lives and estates to do him no service. That if the Parliament garrisoned the towns and castles he should quit, they would lessen their army, and not dare to see him in the field: and if they did not, but left them open, then 'twould be no loss to him, but he might possess them as often as he pleased.

This advice I pressed with such arguments, that the king was once going to despatch orders for the doing it; but to be irresolute in counsel is always the companion of a declining fortune; the king was doubtful, and could not resolve till it was too late.

And yet, though the king's forces were very low, his Majesty was resolved to make one adventure more, and it was a strange one; for, with but a handful of men, he made a desperate march, almost 250 miles in the middle of the whole kingdom, compassed about with armies and parties innumerable, traversed the heart of his enemy's country, entered their associated counties, where no army had ever yet come, and in spite of all their victorious troops facing and following him, alarmed even London itself and returned safe to Oxford.

His Majesty continued in Wales from the battle at Naseby till the 5th or 6th of August, and till he had an account from all parts of the progress of his enemies, and the posture of his own affairs.

Here we found, that the enemy being hard pressed in Somersetshire by the Lord Goring, and Lord Hopton's forces, who had taken Bridgewater, and distressed Taunton, which was now at the point of surrender, they had ordered Fairfax and Cromwell, and the whole army, to march westward to relieve the town; which they did, and Goring's troops were worsted, and himself wounded at the fight at Langport.

The Scots, who were always the dead weight upon the king's affairs, having no more work to do in the north, were, at the Parliament's desire, advanced southward, and then ordered away towards South Wales, and were set down to the siege of Hereford. Here this famous Scotch army spent several months in a fruitless siege, ill provided of ammunition, and worse with money; and having sat near three months before the town, and done little but eaten up the country round them, upon the repeated accounts of the progress of the Marquis of Montrose in that kingdom, and pressing instances of their countrymen, they resolved to raise their siege, and go home to relieve their friends.

The king, who was willing to be rid of the Scots, upon good terms, and therefore to hasten them, and lest they should pretend to push on the siege to take the town first, gives it out, that he was resolved with all his forces to go into Scotland, and join Montrose; and so having secured Scotland, to renew the war from thence.

And accordingly his Majesty marches northwards, with a body of 4000 horse; and, had the king really done this, and with that body of horse marched away (for he had the start of all his enemies, by above a fortnight's march), he had then had the fairest opportunity for a general turn of all his affairs, that he ever had in all the latter part of this war. For Montrose, a gallant daring soldier, who from the least shadow of force in the farthest corner of this country, had, rolling like a snowball, spread all over Scotland, was come into the south parts, and had summoned Edinburgh, frighted away their statesmen, beaten their soldiers at Dundee and other places; and letters and messengers in the heels of one another, repeated their cries to their brethren in England, to lay before them the sad condition of the country, and to hasten the army to their relief. The Scots lords of the enemy's party fled to Berwick, and the chancellor of Scotland goes himself to General Leslie, to press him for help.

In this extremity of affairs Scotland lay when we marched out of Wales. The Scots, at the siege of Hereford, hearing the king was gone northward with his horse, conclude he was gone directly for Scotland, and immediately send Leslie with 4000 horse and foot to follow, but did not yet raise the siege. But the king, still irresolute, turns away to the eastward, and comes to Lichfield, where he showed his resentments at Colonel Hastings for his easy surrender of Leicester.

In this march the enemy took heart. We had troops of horse on every side upon us like hounds started at a fresh stag. Leslie, with the Scots, and a strong body followed in our rear, Major-General Poyntz, Sir John Gell, Colonel Rossiter, and others in our way; they pretended to be 10,000 horse, and yet never durst face us. The Scots made one attempt upon a troop which stayed a little behind, and took some prisoners; but when a regiment of our horse faced them they retired. At a village near Lichfield another party of about 1000 horse attacked my regiment. We were on the left of the army, and at a little too far a distance. I happened to be with the king at that time, and my lieutenant-colonel with me, so that the major had charge of the regiment. He made a very handsome defence, but sent messengers for speedy relief. We were on a march, and therefore all ready, and the king orders me a regiment of dragoons and 300 horse, and the body halted to bring us off, not knowing how strong the enemy might be. When I came to the place I found my major hard laid to, but fighting like a lion. The enemy had broke in upon him in two places, and had routed one troop, cutting them off from the body, and had made them all prisoners. Upon this I fell in with the 300 horse, and cleared my major from a party who charged him in the flank; the dragoons immediately lighting, one party of them comes up on my wing, and saluting the enemy with their muskets, put them to a stand, the other party of dragoons wheeling to the left endeavouring to get behind them. The enemy, perceiving they should be overpowered, retreated in as good order as they could, but left us most of our prisoners, and about thirty of their own. We lost about fifteen of our men, and the enemy about forty, chiefly by the fire of our dragoons in their retreat.

In this posture we continued our march; and though the king halted at Lichfield—which was a dangerous article, having so many of the enemy's troops upon his hands, and this time gave them opportunity to get into a body—yet the Scots, with their General Leslie, resolving for the north, the rest of the troops were not able to face us, till, having ravaged the enemy's country through Staffordshire, Warwick, Leicester, and Nottinghamshire, we came to the leaguer before Newark.

The king was once more in the mind to have gone into Scotland, and called a council of war to that purpose; but then it was resolved by all hands that it would be too late to attempt it, for the Scots and

Major-General Poyntz were before us, and several strong bodies of horse in our rear; and there was no venturing now, unless any advantage presented to rout one of those parties which attended us.

Upon these and like considerations we resolved for Newark; on our approach the forces which blocked up that town drew off, being too weak to oppose us, for the king was now above 5000 horse and dragoons, besides 300 horse and dragoons he took with him from Newark.

We halted at Newark to assist the garrison, or give them time rather to furnish themselves from the country with what they wanted, which they were very diligent in doing; for in two days' time they filled a large island which lies under the town, between the two branches of the Trent, with sheep, oxen, cows, and horses, an incredible number; and our affairs being now something desperate, we were not very nice in our usage of the country, for really if it was not with a resolution both to punish the enemy and enrich ourselves, no man can give any rational account why this desperate journey was undertaken. 'Tis certain the Newarkers, in the respite they gained by our coming, got above £50,000 from the country round them in corn, cattle, money, and other plunder.

From hence we broke into Lincolnshire, and the king lay at Belvoir Castle, and from Belvoir Castle to Stamford. The swiftness of our march was a terrible surprise to the enemy; for our van being at a village on the great road called Stilton, the country people fled into the Isle of Ely, and every way, as if all was lost. Indeed our dragoons treated the country very coarsely, and all our men in general made themselves rich. Between Stilton and Huntingdon we had a small bustle with some of the associated troops of horse, but they were soon routed, and fled to Huntingdon, where they gave such an account of us to their fellows that they did not think fit to stay for us, but left their foot to defend themselves as well as they could.

While this was doing in the van a party from Burleigh House, near Stamford, the seat of the Earl of Exeter, pursued four troops of our horse, who, straggling towards Peterborough, and committing some disorders there, were surprised before they could get into a posture of fighting; and encumbered, as I suppose, with their plunder, they were entirely routed, lost most of their horses, and were forced to come away on foot; but finding themselves in this condition, they got in a body into the enclosures, and in that posture turning dragoons, they lined the hedges, and fired upon the enemy with their carabines. This way of fighting, though not very pleasant to troopers, put the enemy's horse to some stand, and encouraged our men to venture into a village, where the enemy had secured forty of their horse; and boldly charging the guard, they beat them off, and recovering those horses, the rest made their retreat good to Wansford Bridge; but we lost near 100 horses, and about twelve of our men taken prisoners.

The next day the king took Huntingdon; the foot which were left in the town, as I observed by their horse, had posted themselves at the foot of the bridge, and fortified the pass, with such things as the haste and shortness of the time would allow; and in this posture they seemed resolute to defend themselves. I confess, had they in time planted a good force here, they might have put a full stop to our little army; for the river is large and deep, the country on the left marshy, full of drains and ditches, and unfit for horse, and we must have either turned back, or took the right hand into Bedfordshire; but here not being above 400 foot, and they forsaken of their horse, the resistance they made was to no other purpose than to give us occasion to knock them on the head, and plunder the town.

However, they defended the bridge, as I have said, and opposed our passage. I was this day in the van, and our forlorn having entered Huntingdon without any great resistance till they came to the bridge, finding it barricaded, they sent me word; I caused the troops to halt, and rode up to the forlorn, to view the countenance of the enemy, and found by the posture they had put themselves in, that they resolved to sell us the passage as dear as they could.

I sent to the king for some dragoons, and gave him account of what I observed of the enemy, and that I judged them to be 1000 men; for I could not particularly see their numbers. Accordingly the king ordered 500 dragoons to attack the bridge, commanded by a major; the enemy had 200 musketeers placed on the bridge, their barricade served them for a breastwork on the front, and the low walls on the bridge served to secure their flanks. Two bodies of their foot were placed on the opposite banks of the river, and a reserve stood in the highway on the rear. The number of their men could not have been better ordered, and they wanted not courage answerable to the conduct of the party. They were commanded by one Bennet, a resolute officer, who stood in the front of his men on the bridge with a pike in his hand.

Before we began to fall on, the king ordered to view the river, to see if it was nowhere passable, or any boat to be had; but the river being not fordable, and the boats all secured on the other side, the attack was resolved on, and the dragoons fell on with extraordinary bravery. The foot defended themselves obstinately, and beat off our dragoons twice, and though Bennet was killed upon the spot, and after him his lieutenant, yet their officers relieving them with fresh men, they would certainly have beat us all off, had not a venturous fellow, one of our dragoons, thrown himself into the river, swam over, and, in the midst of a shower of musket-bullets, cut the rope which tied a great flat-bottom boat, and brought her over. With the help of this boat, I got over 100 troopers first, and then their horses, and then 200 more without their horses; and with this party fell in with one of the small bodies of foot that were posted on that side, and having routed them, and after them the reserve which stood on the road, I made up to the other party. They stood their ground, and having rallied the runaways of both the other parties, charged me with their pikes, and brought me to a retreat; but by this time the king had sent over 300 men more, and they coming up to me, the foot retreated. Those on the bridge finding how 'twas, and having no supplies sent them, as before, fainted, and fled; and the dragoons rushing forward, most of them were killed; about 150 of the enemy were killed, of which all the officers at the bridge, the rest run away.

The town suffered for it, for our men left them little of anything they could carry. Here we halted and raised contributions, took money of the country and of the open towns, to exempt them from plunder. Twice we faced the town of Cambridge, and several of our officers advised his Majesty to storm it. But having no foot, and but 1200 dragoons, wiser heads diverted him from it, and leaving Cambridge on the left, we marched to Woburn, in Bedfordshire, and our parties raised money all over the country quite into Hertfordshire, within five miles of St Alban's.

The swiftness of our march, and uncertainty which way we intended, prevented all possible preparation to oppose us, and we met with no party able to make head against us. From Woburn the king went through Buckingham to Oxford; some of our men straggling in the villages for plunder, were often picked up by the enemy. But in all this long march we did not lose 200 men, got an incredible booty, and brought six waggons laden with money, besides 2000 horses and 3000 head of cattle, into Oxford. From Oxford his Majesty moves again into Gloucestershire, having left about 1500 of his horse at Oxford to scour the country, and raise contributions, which they did as far as Reading.

Sir Thomas Fairfax was returned from taking Bridgewater, and was sat down before Bristol, in which Prince Rupert commanded with a strong garrison, 2500 foot and 1000 horse. We had not force enough to attempt anything there. But the Scots, who lay still before Hereford, were afraid of us, having before parted with all their horse under Lieutenant-General Leslie, and but ill stored with provisions; and if we came on their backs, were in a fair way to be starved, or made to buy their provisions at the price of their blood.

His Majesty was sensible of this, and had we had but ten regiments of foot, would certainly have fought the Scots. But we had no foot, or so few as was not worth while to march them. However, the king marched to Worcester, and the Scots, apprehending they should be blocked up, immediately raised the siege, pretending it was to go help their brethren in Scotland, and away they marched northwards.

We picked up some of their stragglers, but they were so poor, had been so ill paid, and so harassed at the siege, that they had neither money nor clothes; and the poor soldiers fed upon apples and roots, and ate the very green corn as it grew in the fields, which reduced them to a very sorry condition of health, for they died like people infected with the plague.

'Twas now debated whether we should yet march for Scotland, but two things prevented—(1.) The plague was broke out there, and multitudes died of it, which made the king backward, and the men more backward. (2.) The Marquis of Montrose, having routed a whole brigade of Leslie's best horse, and carried all before him, wrote to his Majesty that he did not now want assistance, but was in hopes in a few days to send a body of foot into England to his Majesty's assistance. This over-confidence of his was his ruin; for, on the contrary, had he earnestly pressed the king to have marched, and fallen in with his horse, the king had done it, and been absolutely master of Scotland in a fortnight's time; but Montrose was too confident, and defied them all, till at last they got their forces together, and Leslie with his horse out of England, and worsted him in two or three encounters, and then never left him till they drove him out of Scotland.

While his Majesty stayed at Worcester, several messengers came to him from Cheshire for relief, being exceedingly straitened by the forces of the Parliament; in order to which the king marched, but Shrewsbury being in the enemy's hands, he was obliged to go round by Ludlow, where he was joined by some foot out of Wales. I took this opportunity to ask his Majesty's leave to go by Shrewsbury to my father's, and, taking only two servants, I left the army two days before they marched.

This was the most unsoldier-like action that ever I was guilty of, to go out of the army to pay a visit when a time of action was just at hand; and, though I protest I had not the least intimation, no, not from my own thoughts, that the army would engage, at least before they came to Chester, before which I intended to meet them, yet it looked so ill, so like an excuse or a sham of cowardice, or disaffection to the cause and to my master's interest, or something I know not what, that I could not bear to think of it, nor never had the heart to see the king's face after it.

From Ludlow the king marched to relieve Chester. Poyntz, who commanded the Parliament's forces, follows the king, with design to join with the forces before Chester, under Colonel Jones, before the king could come up. To that end Poyntz passes through Shrewsbury the day that the king marched from Ludlow; yet the king's forces got the start of him, and forced him to engage. Had the king engaged him but three hours sooner, and consequently farther off from Chester, he had ruined him, for Poyntz's men, not able to stand the shock of the king's horse, gave ground, and would in half-an-hour more have been beaten out of the field; but Colonel Jones, with a strong party from the camp, which was within two miles; comes up in the heat of the action, falls on in the king's rear, and turned the scale of the day. The body was, after an obstinate fight, defeated, and a great many gentlemen of quality killed and taken prisoners. The Earl of Lichfield was of the number of the former, and sixty-seven officers of the latter, with 1000 others. The king, with about 500 horse, got into Chester, and from thence into Wales, whither all that could get away made up to him as fast as they could, but in a bad condition.

This was the last stroke they struck; the rest of the war was nothing but taking all his garrisons from him one by one, till they finished the war with the captivating his person, and then, for want of other business, fell to fighting with one another.

I was quite disconsolate at the news of this last action, and the more because I was not there. My regiment wholly dispersed, my lieutenant-colonel, a gentleman of a good family, and a near relation to my mother, was prisoner, my major and three captains killed, and most of the rest prisoners.

The king, hopeless of any considerable party in Wales, Bristol being surrendered, sends for Prince Rupert and Prince Maurice, who came to him. With them, and the Lord Digby, Sir Marmaduke

Langdale, and a great train of gentlemen, his Majesty marches to Newark again, leaves 1000 horse with Sir William Vaughan to attempt the relief of Chester, in doing whereof he was routed the second time by Jones and his men, and entirely dispersed.

The chief strength the king had in these parts was at Newark, and the Parliament were very earnest with the Scots to march southward and to lay siege to Newark; and while the Parliament pressed them to it, and they sat still and delayed it, several heats began, and some ill blood between them, which afterwards broke out into open war. The English reproached the Scots with pretending to help them, and really hindering their affairs. The Scots returned that they came to fight for them, and are left to be starved, and can neither get money nor clothes. At last they came to this, the Scots will come to the siege if the Parliament will send them money, but not before. However, as people sooner agree in doing ill than in doing well, they came to terms, and the Scots came with their whole army to the siege of Newark.

The king, foreseeing the siege, calls his friends about him, tells them he sees his circumstances are such that they can help him but little, nor he protect them, and advises them to separate. The Lord Digby, with Sir Marmaduke Langdale, with a strong body of horse, attempt to get into Scotland to join with Montrose, who was still in the Highlands, though reduced to a low ebb, but these gentlemen are fallen upon on every side and routed, and at last, being totally broken and dispersed, they fly to the Earl of Derby's protection in the Isle of Man.

Prince Rupert, Prince Maurice, Colonel Gerard, and above 400 gentlemen, all officers of horse, lay their commissions down, and seizing upon Wootton House for a retreat, make proposals to the Parliament to leave the kingdom, upon their parole not to return again in arms against the Parliament, which was accepted, though afterwards the prince declined it. I sent my man post to the prince to be included in this treaty, and for leave for all that would accept of like conditions, but they had given in the list of their names, and could not alter it.

This was a sad time. The poor remains of the king's fortunes went everywhere to wreck. Every garrison of the enemy was full of the Cavalier prisoners, and every garrison the king had was beset with enemies, either blocked up or besieged. Goring and the Lord Hopton were the only remainders of the king's forces which kept in a body, and Fairfax was pushing them with all imaginable vigour with his whole army about Exeter and other parts of Devonshire and Cornwall.

435

In this condition the king left Newark in the night, and got to Oxford. The king had in Oxford 8000 men, and the towns of Banbury, Farringdon, Donnington Castle, and such places as might have been brought together in twenty-four hours, 15,000 or 20,000 men, with which, if he had then resolved to have quitted the place, and collected the forces in Worcester, Hereford, Lichfield, Ashby-de-la-Zouch, and all the small castles and garrisons he had thereabouts, he might have had near 40,000 men, might have beaten the Scots from Newark, Colonel Jones from Chester, and all, before Fairfax, who was in the west, could be able to come to their relief. And this his Majesty's friends in North Wales had concerted; and, in order to it, Sir Jacob Ashby gathered what forces he could, in our parts, and attempted to join the king at Oxford, and to have proposed it to him; but Sir Jacob was entirely routed at Stow-on-the-Wold, and taken prisoner, and of 3000 men not above 600 came to Oxford.

All the king's garrisons dropped one by one; Hereford, which had stood out against the whole army of the Scots, was surprised by six men and a lieutenant dressed up for country labourers, and a constable pressed to work, who cut the guards in pieces, and let in a party of the enemy. Chester was reduced by famine, all the attempts the king made to relieve it being frustrated.

Sir Thomas Fairfax routed the Lord Hopton at Torrington, and drove him to such extremities, that he was forced up into the farthest corner of Cornwall. The Lord Hopton had a gallant body of horse with him of nine brigades, but no foot; Fairfax, a great army.

Heartless, and tired out with continual ill news, and ill success, I had frequent meetings with some gentlemen who had escaped from the rout of Sir William Vaughan, and we agreed upon a meeting at Worcester, of all the friends we could get, to see if we could raise a body fit to do any service; or, if not, to consider what was to be done. At this meeting we had almost as many opinions as people; our strength appeared too weak to make any attempt, the game was too far gone in our parts to be retrieved; all we could make up did not amount to above 800 horse.

'Twas unanimously agreed not to go into the Parliament as long as our royal master did not give up the cause; but in all places, and by all possible methods, to do him all the service we could. Some proposed one thing, some another; at last we proposed getting vessels to carry us to the Isle of Man to the Earl of Derby, as Sir Marmaduke Langdale, Lord Digby, and others had done. I did not foresee any service it would be to the king's affairs, but I started a proposal that, marching to Pembroke in a body, we should there seize upon all the vessels we could, and embarking ourselves, horses, and what foot we could get, cross the Severn Sea, and land in Cornwall to the assistance of Prince Charles, who was in the army of the Lord Hopton, and where only there seemed to be any possibility of a chance for the remaining part of our cause.

This proposal was not without its difficulties, as how to get to the seaside, and, when there, what assurance of shipping. The enemy, under Major-General Langhorn, had overrun Wales, and 'twould be next to impossible to effect it.

We could never carry our proposal with the whole assembly; but, however, about 200 of us resolved to attempt it, and [the] meeting being broken up without coming to any conclusion, we had a private meeting among ourselves to effect it.

We despatched private messengers to Swansea and Pembroke, and other places; but they all discouraged us from the attempt that way, and advised us to go higher towards North Wales, where the king's interest had more friends, and the Parliament no forces. Upon this we met, and resolved, and having sent several messengers that way, one of my men provided us two small vessels in a little creek near Harlech Castle, in Merionethshire. We marched away with what expedition we could, and embarked in the two vessels accordingly. It was the worst voyage sure that ever man went; for first we had no manner of accommodation for so many people, hay for our horses we got none, or very little, but good store of oats, which served us for our own bread as well as provender for the horses.

In this condition we put off to sea, and had a fair wind all the first night, but early in the morning a sudden storm drove us within two or three leagues of Ireland. In this pickle, sea-sick, our horses rolling about upon one another, and ourselves stifled for want of room, no cabins nor beds, very cold weather, and very indifferent diet, we wished ourselves ashore again a thousand times; and yet we were not willing to go ashore in Ireland if we could help it; for the rebels having possession of every place, that was just having our throats cut at once. Having rolled about at the mercy of the winds all day, the storm ceasing in the evening, we had fair weather again, but wind enough, which being large, in two days and a night we came upon the coast of Cornwall, and, to our no small comfort, landed the next day at St Ives, in the county of Cornwall.

We rested ourselves here, and sent an express to the Lord Hopton, who was then in Devonshire, of our arrival, and desired him to assign us quarters, and send us his farther orders. His lordship expressed a very great satisfaction at our arrival, and left it to our own conduct to join him as we saw convenient.

We were marching to join him, when news came that Fairfax had given him an entire defeat at Torrington. This was but the old story over again. We had been used to ill news a great while, and 'twas the less surprise to us.

Upon this news we halted at Bodmin, till we should hear farther; and it was not long before we saw a confirmation of the news before our eyes, for the Lord Hopton, with the remainder of his horse, which he had brought off at Torrington in a very shattered condition, retreated to Launceston, the first town in Cornwall, and hearing that Fairfax pursued him, came on to Bodmin. Hither he summoned all the troops which he had left, which, when he had got together, were a fine body indeed of 5000 horse, but few foot but what were at Pendennis, Barnstaple, and other garrisons. These were commanded by the Lord Hopton. The Lord Goring had taken shipping for France to get relief a few days before.

Here a grand council of war was called, and several things were proposed, but as it always is in distress, people are most irresolute, so 'twas here. Some were for breaking through by force, our number being superior to the enemy's horse. To fight them with their foot would be desperation and ridiculous; and to retreat would but be to coop up themselves in a narrow place, where at last they must be forced to fight upon disadvantage, or yield at mercy. Others opposed this as a desperate action, and without probability of success, and all were of different opinions. I confess, when I saw how things were, I saw 'twas a lost game, and I was for the opinion of breaking through, and doing it now, while the country was open and large, and not being forced to it when it must be with more disadvantage. But nothing was resolved on, and so we retreated before the enemy. Some small skirmishes there happened near Bodmin, but none that were very considerable.

'Twas the 1st of March when we quitted Bodmin, and quartered at large at Columb, St Dennis, and Truro, and the enemy took his quarters at Bodmin, posting his horse at the passes from Padstow on the north, to Wadebridge, Lostwithiel, and Fowey, spreading so from sea to sea, that now breaking through was impossible. There was no more room for counsel; for unless we had ships to carry us off, we had nothing to do but when we were fallen upon, to defend ourselves, and sell victory as dear as we could to the enemies.

The Prince of Wales seeing the distress we were in, and loth to fall into the enemy's hands, ships himself on board some vessels at Falmouth, with about 400 lords and gentlemen. And as I had no command here to oblige my attendance, I was once going to make one, but my comrades, whom I had been the principal occasion of bringing hither, began to take it ill, that I would leave them, and so I resolved we would take our fate together.

While thus we had nothing before us but a soldier's death, a fair field, and a strong enemy, and people began to look one upon another, the soldiers asked how their officers looked, and the officers asked how their soldiers looked, and every day we expected to be our last, when unexpectedly the enemy's general sent a trumpet to Truro to my Lord Hopton, with a very handsome gentlemanlike offer:—

That since the general could not be ignorant of his present condition, and that the place he was in could not afford him subsistence or defence; and especially considering that the state of our affairs were such, that if we should escape from thence we could not remove to our advantage, he had thought good to let us know, that if we would deliver up our horses and arms, he would, for avoiding the effusion of Christian blood, or the putting any unsoldierly extremities upon us, allow such honourable and safe conditions, as were rather better than our present circumstances could demand, and such as should discharge him to all the world, as a gentleman, as a soldier, and as a Christian.

After this followed the conditions he would give us, which were as follows, viz.:—That all the soldiery, as well English as foreigners, should have liberty to go beyond the seas, or to their own dwellings, as they pleased; and to such as shall choose to live at home, protection for their liberty, and from all violence and plundering of soldiers, and to give them bag and baggage, and all their goods, except horses and arms.

That for officers in commissions, and gentlemen of quality, he would allow them horses for themselves and one servant, or more, suitable to their quality, and such arms as are suitable to gentlemen of such quality travelling in times of peace; and such officers as would go beyond sea, should take with them their full arms and number of horses as are allowed in the army to such officers.

That all the troopers shall receive on the delivery of their horses, 20s. a man to carry them home; and the general's pass and recommendation to any gentleman who desires to go to the Parliament to settle the composition for their estates.

Lastly, a very honourable mention of the general, and offer of their mediation to the Parliament, to treat him as a man of honour, and one who has been tender of the country, and behaved himself with all the moderation and candour that could be expected from an enemy.

Upon the unexpected receipt of this message, a council of war was called, and the letter read; no man offered to speak a word; the general moved it, but every one was loth to begin.

At last an old colonel starts up, and asked the general what he thought might occasion the writing this letter? The general told him, he could not tell; but he could tell, he was sure, of one thing, that he knew what was not the occasion of it, viz., that is, not any want of force in their army to oblige us to other terms. Then a doubt was started, whether the king and Parliament were not in any treaty, which this agreement might be prejudicial to.

This occasioned a letter to my Lord Fairfax, wherein our general returning the civilities, and neither accepting nor refusing his proposal, put it upon his honour, whether there was not some agreement or concession between his Majesty and the Parliament, in order to a general peace, which this treaty might be prejudicial to, or thereby be prejudicial to us.

The Lord Fairfax ingenuously declared, he had heard the king had made some concessions, and he heartily wished he would make such as would settle the kingdom in peace, that Englishmen might not wound and destroy one another; but that he declared he knew of no treaty commenced, nor anything passed which could give us the least shadow of hope for any advantage in not accepting his conditions; at last telling us, that though he did not insult over our circumstances, yet if we thought fit, upon any such supposition, to refuse his offers, he was not to seek in his measures.

And it appeared so, for he immediately advanced his forlorns, and dispossessed us of two advanced quarters, and thereby straitened us yet more.

We had now nothing to say, but treat, and our general was so sensible of our condition, that he returned the trumpet with a safe-conduct for commissioners at twelve o'clock that night; upon which a cessation of arms was agreed on, we quitting Truro to the Lord Fairfax, and he left St Allen to us to keep our headquarters.

The conditions were soon agreed on; we disbanded nine full brigades of horse, and all the conditions were observed with the most honour and care by the enemy that ever I saw in my life.

Nor can I omit to make very honourable mention of this noble gentleman, though I did not like his cause; but I never saw a man of a more pleasant, calm, courteous, downright, honest behaviour in my life; and for his courage and personal bravery in the field, that we had felt enough of. No man in the world had more fire and fury in him while in action, or more temper and softness out of it. In short, and I cannot do him greater honour, he exceedingly came near the character of my foreign hero, Gustavus Adolphus, and in my account is, of all the soldiers in Europe, the fittest to be reckoned in the second place of honour to him.

I had particular occasion to see much of his temper in all this action, being one of the hostages given by our general for the performance of the conditions, in which circumstance the general did me several times the honour to send to me to dine with him; and was exceedingly pleased to discourse with me about the passages of the wars in Germany, which I had served in, he having been at the same time in the Low Countries in the service of Prince Maurice; but I observed if at any time my civilities extended to commendations of his own actions, and especially to comparing him to Gustavus Adolphus, he would blush like a woman, and be uneasy, declining the discourse, and in this he was still more like him.

Let no man scruple my honourable mention of this noble enemy, since no man can suspect me of favouring the cause he embarked in, which I served as heartily against as any man in the army; but I cannot conceal extraordinary merit for its being placed in an enemy.

This was the end of our making war, for now we were all under parole never to bear arms against the Parliament; and though some of us did not keep our word, yet I think a soldier's parole ought to be the most sacred in such case, that a soldier may be the easier trusted at all times upon his word. For my part, I went home fully contented, since I could do my royal master no better service, that I had come off no worse.

The enemy going now on in a full current of success, and the king reduced to the last extremity, and Fairfax, by long marches, being come back within five miles of Oxford, his Majesty, loth to be cooped up in a town which could on no account hold long out, quits the town in a disguise, leaving Sir Thomas Clemham governor, and being only attended with Mr Ashburnham and one more, rides away to Newark, and there fatally committed himself to the honour and fidelity of the Scots under General Leven.

There had been some little bickering between the Parliament and the Scots commissioners concerning the propositions which the Scots were for a treaty with the king upon, and the Parliament refused it. The Parliament, upon all proposals of peace, had formerly invited the king to come and throw himself upon the honour, fidelity, and affection of his Parliament. And now the king from Oxford offering to come up to London on the protection of the Parliament for the safety of his person, they refused him, and the Scots differed from them in it, and were for a personal treaty.

This, in our opinion, was the reason which prompted the king to throw himself upon the fidelity of the Scots, who really by their infidelity had been the ruin of all his affairs, and now, by their perfidious breach of honour and faith with him, will be virtually and mediately the ruin of his person.

The Scots were, as all the nation besides them was, surprised at the king's coming among them; the Parliament began very high with them, and send an order to General Leven to send the king to Warwick Castle; but he was not so hasty to part with so rich a prize. As soon as the king came to the general, he signs an order to Colonel Bellasis, the governor of Newark, to surrender it, and immediately the Scots decamp homewards, carrying the king in the camp with them, and marching on, a house was ordered to be provided for the king at Newcastle.

And now the Parliament saw their error, in refusing his Majesty a personal treaty, which, if they had accepted (their army was not yet taught the way of huffing their masters), the kingdom might have been settled in peace. Upon this the Parliament send to General Leven to have his Majesty not be sent, which was their first language, but be suffered to come to London to treat with his Parliament; before it was, "Let the king be sent to Warwick Castle"; now 'tis, "To let his Majesty come to London to treat with his people."

But neither one or the other would do with the Scots; but we who knew the Scots best knew that there was one thing would do with them, if the other would not, and that was money; and therefore our hearts ached for the king.

The Scots, as I said, had retreated to Newcastle with the king, and there they quartered their whole army at large upon the country; the Parliament voted they had no farther occasion for the Scots, and desired them to go home about their business. I do not say it was in these words, but in whatsoever good words their messages might be expressed, this and nothing less was the English of it. The Scots reply, by setting forth their losses, damages, and dues, the substance of which was, "Pay us our money and we will be gone, or else we won't stir." The Parliament call for an account of their demands, which the Scots give in, amounting to a million; but, according to their custom, and especially finding that the army under Fairfax inclined gradually that way, fall down to £500,000, and at last to £400,000; but all the while this is transacting a separate treaty is carried on at London with the commissioners of Scotland, and afterwards at Edinburgh, by which it is given them to understand that, whereas upon payment of the money, the Scots army is to march out of England, and to give up all the towns and garrisons which they hold in this kingdom, so they are to take it for granted that 'tis the meaning of the treaty that they shall leave the king in the hands of the English Parliament.

To make this go down the better, the Scotch Parliament, upon his Majesty's desire to go with their army into Scotland, send him for answer, that it cannot be for the safety of his Majesty or of the State to come into Scotland, not having taken the Covenant, and this was carried in their Parliament but by two voices.

The Scots having refused his coming into Scotland, as was concerted between the two Houses, and their army being to march out of England, the delivering up the king became a consequence of the thing—unavoidable, and of necessity.

His Majesty, thus deserted of those into whose hands he had thrown himself, took his leave of the Scots general at Newcastle, telling him only, in few words, this sad truth, that he was bought and sold. The Parliament commissioners received him at Newcastle from the Scots, and brought him to Holmby House, in Northamptonshire; from whence, upon the quarrels and feuds of parties, he was fetched by a party of horse, commanded by one Cornet Joyce, from the army, upon their mutinous rendezvous at Triplow Heath; and, after this, suffering many violences and varieties of circumstances among the army, was carried to Hampton Court, from whence his Majesty very readily made his escape; but not having notice enough to provide effectual means for his more effectual deliverance, was obliged to deliver himself to Colonel Hammond in the Isle of Wight. Here, after some very indifferent usage, the Parliament pursued a farther treaty with him, and all points were agreed but two: the entire abolishing Episcopacy, which the king declared to be against his conscience and his coronation oath; and the sale of the Church lands, which he declared, being most of them gifts to God and the Church, by persons deceased, his Majesty thought could not be alienated without the highest sacrilege, and if taken from the uses to which they were appointed by the wills of the donors, ought to be restored back to the heirs and families of the persons who bequeathed them.

And these two articles so stuck with his Majesty, that he ventured his fortune, and royal family, and his own life for them. However, at last, the king condescended so far in these, that the Parliament voted his Majesty's concessions to be sufficient to settle and establish the peace of the nation.

This vote discovered the bottom of all the counsels which then prevailed; for the army, who knew if peace were once settled, they should be undone, took the alarm at this, and clubbing together in committees and councils, at last brought themselves to a degree of hardness above all that ever this nation saw; for calling into question the proceedings of their masters who employed them, they immediately fall to work upon the Parliament, remove Colonel Hammond, who had the charge of the king, and used him honourably, place a new guard upon him, dismiss the commissioners, and put a stop to the treaty; and, following their blow, march to London, place regiments of foot at the Parliament-house door, and, as the members came up, seize upon all those whom they had down in a list as promoters of the settlement and treaty, and would not suffer them to sit; but the rest who, being of their own stamp, are permitted to go on, carry on the designs of the army, revive their votes of non-addresses to the king, and then, upon the army's petition to bring all delinquents to justice, the mask was thrown off, the word all is declared to be meant the king, as well as every man else they pleased. 'Tis too sad a story, and too much a matter of grief to me, and to all good men, to renew the blackness of those days, when law and justice was under the feet of power; the army ruled the Parliament, the private officers their generals, the common soldiers their officers, and confusion was in every part of the government. In this hurry they sacrificed their king, and shed the blood of the English nobility without mercy.

The history of the times will supply the particulars which I omit, being willing to confine myself to my own accounts and observations. I was now no more an actor, but a melancholy observator of the misfortunes of the times. I had given my parole not to take up arms against the Parliament, and I saw nothing to invite me to engage on their side. I saw a world of confusion in all their counsels, and I always expected that in a chain of distractions, as it generally falls out, the last link would be destruction; and though I pretended to no prophecy, yet the progress of affairs have brought it to pass, and I have seen Providence, who suffered, for the correction of this nation, the sword to govern and devour us, has at last brought destruction by the sword upon the head of most of the party who first drew it.

* * * * *

If together with the brief account of what concern I had in the active part of the war, I leave behind me some of my own remarks and observations, it may be pertinent enough to my design, and not unuseful to posterity.

I. I observed by the sequel of things that it may be some excuse to the first Parliament, who began this war, to say that they manifested their designs were not aimed at the monarchy, nor their quarrel at the person of the king; because, when they had in their power, though against his will, they would have restored both his person and dignity as a king, only loading it with such clogs of the people's power as they at first pretended to, viz., the militia, and power of naming the great officers at court, and the like; which powers, it was never denied, had been stretched too far in the beginning of this king's reign, and several things done illegally, which his Majesty had been sensible of, and was willing to rectify; but they having obtained the power by victory, resolved so to secure themselves, as that, whenever they laid down their arms, the king should not be able to do the like again. And thus far they were not to be so much blamed, and we did not on our own part blame them, when they had obtained the power, for parting with it on good terms.

But when I have thus far advocated for the enemies, I must be very free to state the crimes of this bloody war by the events of it. 'Tis manifest there were among them from the beginning a party who aimed at the very root of the government, and at the very thing which they brought to pass, viz., the deposing and murdering of their sovereign; and, as the devil is always master where mischief is the work, this party prevailed, turned the other out of doors, and overturned all that little honesty that might be in the first beginning of this unhappy strife.

The consequence of this was, the Presbyterians saw their error when it was too late, and then would gladly have joined the royal party to have suppressed this new leaven which had infected the lump; and this is very remarkable, that most of the first champions of this war who bore the brunt of it, when the king was powerful and prosperous, and when there was nothing to be got by it but blows, first or last, were so ill used by this independent, powerful party, who tripped up the heels of all their honesty, that they were either forced by ill treatment to take up arms on our side, or suppressed and reduced by them. In this the justice of Providence seemed very conspicuous, that these having pushed all things by violence against the king, and by arms and force brought him to their will, were at once both robbed of the end, their Church government, and punished for drawing their swords against their masters, by their own servants drawing the sword against them; and God, in His due time, punished the others too. And what was yet farther strange, the punishment of this crime of making war against their king, singled out those very men, both in the army and in the Parliament, who were the greatest champions of the Presbyterian cause in the council and in the field. Some minutes, too, of circumstances I cannot forbear observing, though they are not very material, as to the fatality and revolutions of days and times. A Roman Catholic gentleman of Lancashire, a very religious man in his way, who had kept a calculate of times, and had observed mightily the fatality of times, places, and actions, being at my father's house, was discoursing once upon the just judgment of God in dating His providences, so as to signify to us His displeasure at particular circumstances; and, among an infinite number of collections he had made, these were some which I took particular notice of, and from whence I began to observe the like:—

1. That King Edward VI. died the very same day of the same month in which he caused the altar to be taken down, and the image of the Blessed Virgin in the Cathedral of St Paul's.

2. That Cranmer was burnt at Oxford the same day and month that he gave King Henry VIII. advice to divorce his Queen Catherine.

3. That Queen Elizabeth died the same day and month that she resolved, in her Privy Council, to behead the Queen of Scots.

4. That King James died the same day that he published his book against Bellarmine.

5. That King Charles's long Parliament, which ruined him, began the very same day and month which that Parliament began, that at the request of his predecessor robbed the Roman Church of all her revenues, and suppressed abbeys and monasteries.

How just his calculations were, or how true the matter of fact, I cannot tell, but it put me upon the same in several actions and successes of this war. And I found a great many circumstances, as to time or action, which befell both his Majesty and his parties first;

Then others which befell the Parliament and Presbyterian faction, which raised the war;

Then the Independent tyranny which succeeded and supplanted the first party;

Then the Scots who acted on both sides;

Lastly, the restoration and re-establishment of the loyalty and religion of our ancestors.

1. For King Charles I.; 'tis observable, that the charge against the Earl of Strafford, a thing which his Majesty blamed himself for all the days of his life, and at the moment of his last suffering, was first read in the Lords' House on the 30th of January, the same day of the month six years that the king himself was brought to the block.

2. That the king was carried away prisoner from Newark, by the Scots, May 10, the same day six years that, against his conscience and promise, he passed the bill of attainder against the loyal, noble Earl of Strafford.

3. The same day seven years that the king entered the House of Commons for the five members, which all his friends blamed him for, the same day the Rump voted bringing his Majesty to trial, after they had set by the Lords for not agreeing to it, which was the 3rd of January 1648.

4. The 12th of May 1646, being the surrender of Newark, the Parliament held a day of thanksgiving and rejoicing, for the reduction of the king and his party, and finishing the war, which was the same day five years that the Earl of Strafford was beheaded.

5. The battle at Naseby, which ruined the king's affairs, and where his secretary and his office was taken, was the 14th of June, the same day and month the first commission was given out by his Majesty to raise forces.

6. The queen voted a traitor by the Parliament the 3rd of May, the same day and month she carried the jewels into France.

7. The same day the king defeated Essex in the west, his son, King Charles II., was defeated at Worcester.

8. Archbishop Laud's house at Lambeth assaulted by the mob, the same day of the same month that he advised the king to make war upon the Scots.

9. Impeached the 15th of December 1640, the same day twelvemonth that he ordered the Common Prayer-book of Scotland to be printed, in order to be imposed upon the Scots, from which all our troubles began.

But many more, and more strange, are the critical junctures of affairs in the case of the enemy, or at least more observed by me:—

1. Sir John Hotham, who repulsed his Majesty and refused him admittance into Hull before the war, was seized at Hull by the same Parliament for whom he had done it, the same 10th day of August two years that he drew the first blood in that war.

2. Hampden of Buckinghamshire killed the same day one year that the mob petition from Bucks was presented to the king about him, as one of the five members.

3. Young Captain Hotham executed the 1st of January, the same day that he assisted Sir Thomas Fairfax in the first skirmish with the king's forces at Bramham Moor.

4. The same day and month, being the 6th of August 1641, that the Parliament voted to raise an army against the king, the same day and month, *anno* 1648, the Parliament were assaulted and turned out of doors by that very army, and none left to sit but who the soldiers pleased, which were therefore called the Rump.

5. The Earl of Holland deserted the king, who had made him general of the horse, and went over to the Parliament, and the 9th of March 1641, carried the Commons' reproaching declaration to the king; and afterwards taking up arms for the king against the Parliament, was beheaded by them the 9th of March 1648, just seven years after.

6. The Earl of Holland was sent by the king to come to his assistance and refused, the 11th of July 1641, and that very day seven years after was taken by the Parliament at St Neots.

7. Colonel Massey defended Gloucester against the king, and beat him off the 5th of September 1643; was taken after by Cromwell's men fighting for the king, on the 5th of September 1651, two or three days after the fight at Worcester.

8. Richard Cromwell resigning, because he could not help it, the Parliament voted a free Commonwealth, without a single person or House of Lords. This was the 25th of May 1658; the 25th of May 1660, the king landed at Dover, and restored the government of a single person and House of Lords.

9. Lambert was proclaimed a traitor by the Parliament April the 20th, being the same day he proposed to Oliver Cromwell to take upon him the title of king.

10. Monk being taken prisoner at Nantwich by Sir Thomas Fairfax, revolted to the Parliament the same day nineteen years he declared for the king, and thereby restored the royal authority.

11. The Parliament voted to approve of Sir John Hotham's repulsing the king at Hull, the 28th of April 1642; the 28th of April 1660, the Parliament first debated in the House the restoring the king to the crown.

12. The agitators of the army formed themselves into a cabal, and held their first meeting to seize on the king's person, and take him into their custody from Holmby, the 28th of April 1647; the same day, 1660, the Parliament voted the agitators to be taken into custody, and committed as many of them as could be found.

13. The Parliament voted the queen a traitor for assisting her husband, the king, May the 3rd, 1643; her son, King Charles II., was presented with the votes of Parliament to restore him, and the present of £50,000, the 3rd of May 1660.

14. The same day the Parliament passed the Act for recognition of Oliver Cromwell, October 13th, 1654, Lambert broke up the Parliament and set up the army, 1659, October the 13th.

Some other observations I have made, which, as not so pertinent, I forbear to publish, among which I have noted the fatality of some days to parties, as—

The 2nd of September: The fight at Dunbar; the fight at Worcester; the oath against a single person passed; Oliver's first Parliament called. For the enemy

The 2nd of September: Essex defeated in Cornwall; Oliver died; city works demolished. For the king.

The 29th of May: Prince Charles born; Leicester taken by storm; King
Charles II. restored. Ditto.

Fatality of circumstances in this unhappy war, as—

1. The English Parliament call in the Scots, to invade their king, and are invaded themselves by the same Scots, in defence of the king whose case, and the design of the Parliament, the Scots had mistaken.

2. The Scots, who unjustly assisted the Parliament to conquer their lawful sovereign, contrary to their oath of allegiance, and without any

pretence on the king's part, are afterwards absolutely conquered and subdued by the same Parliament they assisted.

3. The Parliament, who raised an army to depose their king, deposed by the very army they had raised.

4. The army broke three Parliaments, and are at last broke by a free Parliament; and all they had done by the military power, undone at once by the civil.

5. Abundance of the chief men, who by their fiery spirits involved the nation in a civil war, and took up arms against their prince, first or last met with ruin or disgrace from their own party.

(I.) Sir John Hotham and his son, who struck the first stroke, both beheaded or hanged by the Parliament.

(2.) Major-General Massey three times taken prisoner by them, and once wounded at Worcester.

(3.) Major-General Langhorn,

(4.) Colonel Poyer, and

(5.) Colonel Powell, changed sides, and at last taken, could obtain no other favour than to draw lots for their lives; Colonel Poyer drew the dead lot, and was shot to death.

(6.) Earl of Holland: who, when the House voted who should be reprieved, Lord Goring, who had been their worst enemy, or the Earl of Holland, who excepting one offence, had been their constant servant, voted Goring to be spared, and the Earl to die.

(7.) The Earl of Essex, their first general;

(8.) Sir William Waller;

(9.) Lieutenant-General Ludlow;

(10.) The Earl of Manchester;

—all disgusted and voted out of the army, though they had stood the first shock of the war, to make way for the new model of the army, and introduce a party.

* * * * *

In all these confusions I have observed two great errors, one of the king, and one of his friends.

Of the king, that when he was in their custody, and at their mercy, he did not comply with their propositions of peace, before their army, for want of employment, fell into heats and mutinies; that he did not at first grant the Scots their own conditions, which, if he had done, he had gone into Scotland; and then, if the English would have fought the Scots for him, he had a reserve of his loyal friends, who would have had

450

room to have fallen in with the Scots to his assistance, who were after dispersed and destroyed in small parties attempting to serve him.

While his Majesty remained at Newcastle, the queen wrote to him, persuading him to make peace upon any terms; and in politics her Majesty's advice was certainly the best. For, however low he was brought by a peace, it must have been better than the condition he was then in.

The error I mention of the king's friends was this, that after they saw all was lost, they could not be content to sit still, and reserve themselves for better fortunes, and wait the happy time when the divisions of the enemy would bring them to certain ruin; but must hasten their own miseries by frequent fruitless risings, in the face of a victorious enemy, in small parties; and I always found these effects from it:—

I. The enemy, who were always together by the ears, when they were let alone, were united and reconciled when we gave them any interruption; as particularly, in the case of the first assault the army made upon them, when Colonel Pride, with his regiment, garbled the House, as they called it. At that time a fair opportunity offered; but it was omitted till it was too late. That insult upon the House had been attempted the year before, but was hindered by the little insurrection of the royal party, and the sooner they had fallen out, the better.

2. These risings being desperate, with vast disadvantages, and always suppressed, ruined all our friends; the remnants of the Cavaliers were lessened, the stoutest and most daring were cut off, and the king's interest exceedingly weakened, there not being less than 30,000 of his best friends cut off in the several attempts made at Maidstone, Colchester, Lancashire, Pembroke, Pontefract, Kingston, Preston, Warrington, Worcester, and other places. Had these men all reserved their fortunes to a conjunction with the Scots, at either of the invasions they made into this kingdom, and acted with the conduct and courage they were known masters of, perhaps neither of those Scots armies had been defeated.

But the impatience of our friends ruined all; for my part, I had as good a mind to put my hand to the ruin of the enemy as any of them, but I never saw any tolerable appearance of a force able to match the enemy, and I had no mind to be beaten and then hanged. Had we let them alone, they would have fallen into so many parties and factions, and so effectually have torn one another to pieces, that whichsoever party had come to us, we should, with them, have been too hard for all the rest.

This was plain by the course of things afterwards; when the Independent army had ruffled the Presbyterian Parliament, the soldiery of that party made no scruple to join us, and would have restored the king with all their hearts, and many of them did join us at last.

And the consequence, though late, ended so; for they fell out so many times, army and Parliament, Parliament and army, and alternately pulled one another down so often till at last the Presbyterians who began the war, ended it, and, to be rid of their enemies, rather than for any love to the monarchy, restored King Charles the Second, and brought him in on the very day that they themselves had formerly resolved the ruin of his father's government, being the 29th of May, the same day twenty years that the private cabal in London concluded their secret league with the Scots, to embroil his father King Charles the First.[2]

---

[2] General Ludlow, in his Memoirs, p. 52, says their men returned from Warwick to London, not like men who had obtained a victory, but like men that had been beaten

THE COMPLETE ENGLISH TRADESMAN

BY

DANIEL DEFOE

AUTHOR'S PREFACE

The title of this work is an index of the performance. It is a collection of useful instructions for a young tradesman. The world is grown so wise of late, or (if you will) fancy themselves so, are so *opiniatre*, as the French well express it, so self-wise, that I expect some will tell us beforehand they know every thing already, and want none of my instructions; and to such, indeed, these instructions are not written.

Had I not, in a few years' experience, seen many young tradesmen miscarry, for want of those very cautions which are here given, I should have thought this work needless, and I am sure had never gone about to write it; but as the contrary is manifest, I thought, and think still, the world greatly wanted it.

And be it that those unfortunate creatures that have thus blown themselves up in trade, have miscarried for want of knowing, or for want of practising, what is here offered for their direction, whether for want of wit, or by too much wit, the thing is the same, and the direction is equally needful to both.

An old experienced pilot sometimes loses a ship by his assurance and over confidence of his knowledge, as effectually as a young pilot does by his ignorance and want of experience—this very thing, as I have been informed, was the occasion of the fatal disaster in which Sir Cloudesley Shovel, and so many hundred brave fellows, lost their lives in a moment upon the rocks of Scilly.[3]

He that is above informing himself when he is in danger, is above pity when he miscarries—a young tradesman who sets up thus full of himself, and scorning advice from those who have gone before him, like

---

[3] October 22, 1707.—Admiral Shovel, with the confederate fleet from the Mediterranean, as he was coming home, apprehended himself near the rocks of Scilly about noon, and the weather being hazy, he brought to and lay by till evening, when he made a signal for sailing. What induced him to be more cautious in the day than in the night is not known; but the fleet had not been long under sail before his own ship, the *Association*, with the *Eagle* and *Romney*, were dashed to pieces upon the rocks called the *Bishop and his Clerks*, and all their men lost; the *Ferdinand* was also cast away, and but twenty-four of her men saved. Admiral Byng, perceiving the misfortune, altered his course, whereby he preserved himself and the rest of the fleet which sailed after him.—*Salmon's Chronological Historian.* London, 1723.

a horse that rushes into the battle, is only fearless of danger because he does not understand it.

If there is not something extraordinary in the temper and genius of the tradesmen of this age, if there is not something very singular in their customs and methods, their conduct and behaviour in business; also, if there is not something different and more dangerous and fatal in the common road of trading, and tradesmen's management now, than ever was before, what is the reason that there are so many bankrupts and broken tradesmen now among us, more than ever were known before? I make no doubt but there is as much trade now, and as much gotten by trading, as there ever was in this nation, at least in our memory; and if we will allow other people to judge, they will tell us there is much more trade, and trade is much more gainful; what, then, must be the reason that the tradesmen cannot live on their trades, cannot keep open their shops, cannot maintain themselves and families, as well now as they could before? Something extraordinary must be the case.

There must be some failure in the tradesman—it can be nowhere else—either he is less sober and less frugal, less cautious of what he does, whom he trusts, how he lives, and how he behaves, than tradesmen used to be, or he is less industrious, less diligent, and takes less care and pains in his business, or something is the matter; it cannot be but if he had the same gain, and but the same expense which the former ages suffered tradesmen to thrive with, he would certainly thrive as they did. There must be something out of order in the foundation; he must fail in the essential part, or he would not fail in his trade. The same causes would have the same effects in all ages; the same gain, and but the same expense, would just leave him in the same place as it would have left his predecessor in the same shop; and yet we see one grow rich, and the other starve, under the very same circumstances.

The temper of the times explains the case to every body that pleases but to look into it. The expenses of a family are quite different now from what they have been. Tradesmen cannot live as tradesmen in the same class used to live; custom, and the manner of all the tradesmen round them, command a difference; and he that will not do as others do, is esteemed as nobody among them, and the tradesman is doomed to ruin by the fate of the times.

In short, there is a fate upon a tradesman; either he must yield to the snare of the times, or be the jest of the times; the young tradesman cannot resist it; he must live as others do, or lose the credit of living, and be run down as if he were bankrupt. In a word, he must spend more than he can afford to spend, and so be undone; or not spend it, and so be undone.

If he lives as others do, he breaks, because he spends more than he gets; if he does not, he breaks too, because he loses his credit, and that is to lose his trade. What must he do?[4]

The following directions are calculated for this exigency, and to prepare the young tradesman to stem the attacks of those fatal customs, which otherwise, if he yields to them, will inevitably send him the way of all the thoughtless tradesmen that have gone before him.

Here he will be effectually, we hope, encouraged to set out well; to begin wisely and prudently; and to avoid all those rocks which the gay race of tradesmen so frequently suffer shipwreck upon. And here he will have a true plan of his own prosperity drawn out for him, by which, if it be not his own fault, he may square his conduct in an unerring manner, and fear neither bad fortune nor bad friends. I had purposed to give a great many other cautions and directions in this work, but it would have spun it out too far, and have made it tedious. I would indeed have discoursed of some branches of home trade, which necessarily embarks the inland tradesman in some parts of foreign business, and so makes a merchant of the shopkeeper almost whether he will or no. For example, almost all the shopkeepers and inland traders in seaport towns, or even in the water-side part of London itself, are necessarily brought in to be owners of ships, and concerned at least in the vessel, if not in the voyage. Some of their trades, perhaps, relate to, or are employed in, the building, or fitting, or furnishing out ships, as is the case at Shoreham, at Ipswich, Yarmouth, Hull, Whitby, Newcastle, and the like. Others are concerned in the cargoes, as in the herring fishery at Yarmouth and the adjacent ports, the colliery at Newcastle, Sunderland, &c., and the like in many other cases.

In this case, the shopkeeper is sometimes a merchant adventurer, whether he will or not, and some of his business runs into sea-adventures, as in the salt trade at Sheffield, in Northumberland, and Durham, and again at Limington; and again in the coal trade, from Whitehaven in Cumberland to Ireland, and the like.

---

[4] There is much reason for receiving all such complaints as the above with caution. The extravagance of the present, in contrast with the frugality of a past age, has always been a favourite topic of declamation, and appears to have no other foundation than whim. Indeed, it is next to impossible that any great body of men could exist in the circumstances described in the text.

These considerations urged me to direct due cautions to such tradesmen, and such as would be particular to them, especially not to launch out in adventures beyond the compass of their stocks,[5] and withal to manage those things with due wariness. But this work had not room for those things; and as that sort of amphibious tradesmen, for such they are, trading both by water and by land, are not of the kind with those particularly aimed at in these sheets, I thought it was better to leave them quite out than to touch but lightly upon them.

I had also designed one chapter or letter to my inland tradesmen, upon the most important subject of borrowing money upon interest, which is one of the most dangerous things a tradesman is exposed to. It is a pleasant thing to a tradesman to see his credit rise, and men offer him money to trade with, upon so slender a consideration as five per cent. interest, when he gets ten per cent. perhaps twice in the year; but it is a snare of the most dangerous kind in the event, and has been the ruin of so many tradesmen, that, though I had not room for it in the work, I could not let it pass without this notice in the preface.

I. Interest-money eats deep into the tradesman's profits, because it is a payment certain, whether the tradesman gets or loses, and as he may often get double, so sometimes he loses, and then his interest is a double payment; it is a partner with him under this unhappy circumstance, namely, that it goes halves when he gains, but not when he loses.

2. The lender calls for his money when he pleases, and often comes for it when the borrower can ill spare it; and then, having launched out in trade on the supposition of so much in stock, he is left to struggle with the enlarged trade with a contracted stock, and thus he sinks under the weight of it, cannot repay the money, is dishonoured, prosecuted, and at last undone, by the very loan which he took in to help him. Interest of money is a dead weight upon the tradesman, and as the interest always keeps him low, the principal sinks him quite down, when that comes to be paid out again. Payment of interest, to a tradesman, is like Cicero bleeding to death in a warm bath;[6] the pleasing warmth of the bath makes him die in a kind of dream, and not feel himself decay, till at last he is exhausted, falls into convulsions, and expires.

---

[5] Stock is in this book invariably used for what we express by the term *capital*.
[6] Cicero is here given by mistake for Seneca, who thus suffered death by order of the tyrant Nero.

A tradesman held up by money at interest, is sure to sink at last by the weight of it, like a man thrown into the sea with a stone tied about his neck, who though he could swim if he was loose, drowns in spite of all his struggle.

Indeed, this article would require not a letter, but a book by itself; and the tragical stories of tradesmen undone by usury are so many, and the variety so great, that they would make a history by themselves. But it must suffice to treat it here only in general, and give the tradesmen a warning of it, as the Trinity-house pilots warn sailors of a sand, by hanging a buoy upon it, or as the Eddystone light-house upon a sunk rock, which, as the poet says, 'Bids men stand off, and live; come near, and die.'

For a tradesman to borrow money upon interest, I take to be like a man going into a house infected with the plague; it is not only likely that he may be infected and die, but next to a miracle if he escapes.

This part being thus hinted at, I think I may say of the following sheets, that they contain all the directions needful to make the tradesman thrive; and if he pleases to listen to them with a temper of mind willing to be directed, he must have some uncommon ill luck if he miscarries.

INTRODUCTION

Being to direct this discourse to the tradesmen of this nation, it is needful, in order to make the substance of this work and the subject of it agree together, that I should in a few words explain the terms, and tell the reader who it is we understand by the word tradesman, and how he is to be qualified in order to merit the title of *complete*.

This is necessary, because the said term tradesman is understood by several people, and in several places, in a different manner: for example, in the north of Britain, and likewise in Ireland, when you say a tradesman, you are understood to mean a mechanic, such as a smith, a carpenter, a shoemaker, and the like, such as here we call a handicraftsman. In like manner, abroad they call a tradesman such only as carry goods about from town to town, and from market to market, or from house to house, to sell; these in England we call petty chapmen, in the north pethers, and in our ordinary speech pedlars.

But in England, and especially in London, and the south parts of Britain, we take it in another sense, and in general, all sorts of warehouse-keepers, shopkeepers, whether wholesale dealers or retailers of goods, are called tradesmen, or, to explain it by another word, trading men: such are, whether wholesale or retail, our grocers, mercers, linen and woollen drapers, Blackwell-hall factors, tobacconists, haberdashers, whether of hats or small wares, glovers, hosiers, milliners, booksellers, stationers, and all other shopkeepers, who do not actually work upon, make, or manufacture, the goods they sell.

On the other hand, those who make the goods they sell, though they do keep shops to sell them, are not called tradesmen, but handicrafts, such as smiths, shoemakers, founders, joiners, carpenters, carvers, turners, and the like; others, who only make, or cause to be made, goods for other people to sell, are called manufacturers and artists, &c. Thus distinguished, I shall speak of them all as occasion requires, taking this general explication to be sufficient; and I thus mention it to prevent being obliged to frequent and further particular descriptions as I go on.

As there are several degrees of people employed in trade below these, such as workmen, labourers, and servants, so there is a degree of traders above them, which we call merchants; where it is needful to observe, that in other countries, and even in the north of Britain and Ireland, as the handicraftsmen and artists are called tradesmen, so the shopkeepers whom we here call tradesmen, are all called merchants; nay, even the very pedlars are called travelling merchants.[7] But in England the word merchant is understood of none but such as carry on foreign correspondences, importing the goods and growth of other countries, and exporting the growth and manufacture of England to other countries; or, to use a vulgar expression, because I am speaking to and of those who use that expression, such as trade beyond sea. These in England, and these only, are called merchants, by way of honourable distinction; these I am not concerned with in this work, nor is any part of it directed to them.

As the tradesmen are thus distinguished, and their several occupations divided into proper classes, so are the trades. The general commerce of England, as it is the most considerable of any nation in the world, so that part of it which we call the home or inland trade, is equal, if not superior, to that of any other nation, though some of those nations are infinitely greater than England, and more populous also, as France and Germany in particular.

I insist that the trade of England is greater and more considerable than that of any other nation, for these reasons: I. Because England produces more goods as well for home consumption as for foreign exportation, and those goods all made of its own produce or manufactured by its own inhabitants, than any other nation in the world. 2. Because England consumes within itself more goods of foreign growth, imported from the several countries where they are produced or wrought, than any other nation in the world. And—3. Because for the doing this England employs more shipping and more seamen than any other nation, and, some think, than all the other nations, of Europe.

Hence, besides the great number of wealthy merchants who carry on this great foreign *negoce* [*negotium* (Latin) business], and who, by their corresponding with all parts of the world, import the growth of all countries hither—I say, besides these, we have a very great number of considerable dealers, whom we call tradesmen, who are properly called warehouse-keepers, who supply the merchants with all the several kinds of manufactures, and other goods of the produce of England, for exportation; and also others who are called wholesalemen, who buy and take off from the merchants all the foreign goods which they import; these, by their corresponding with a like sort of tradesmen in the

---

[7] This misuse of the term *merchant* continues to exist in Scotland to the present day.

country, convey and hand forward those goods, and our own also, among those country tradesmen, into every corner of the kingdom, however remote, and by them to the retailers, and by the retailer to the last consumer, which is the last article of all trade. These are the tradesmen understood in this work, and for whose service these sheets are made public.

Having thus described the person whom I understand by the English tradesman, it is then needful to inquire into his qualifications, and what it is that renders him a finished or complete man in his business.

I. That he has a general knowledge of not his own particular trade and business only—that part, indeed, well denominates a handicraftsman to be a complete artist; but our complete tradesman ought to understand all the inland trade of England, so as to be able to turn his hand to any thing, or deal in any thing or every thing of the growth and product of his own country, or the manufacture of the people, as his circumstances in trade or other occasions may require; and may, if he sees occasion, lay down one trade and take up another when he pleases, without serving a new apprenticeship to learn it.

2. That he not only has a knowledge of the species or kinds of goods, but of the places and peculiar countries where those goods, whether product or manufacture, are to be found; that is to say, where produced or where made, and how to come at them or deal in them, at the first hand, and to his best advantage.

3. That he understands perfectly well all the methods of correspondence, returning money or goods for goods, to and from every county in England; in what manner to be done, and in what manner most to advantage; what goods are generally bought by barter and exchange, and what by payment of money; what for present money, and what for time; what are sold by commission from the makers, what bought by factors, and by giving commission to buyers in the country, and what bought by orders to the maker, and the like; what markets are the most proper to buy every thing at, and where and when; and what fairs are proper to go to in order to buy or sell, or meet the country dealer at, such as Sturbridge, Bristol, Chester, Exeter; or what marts, such as Beverly, Lynn, Boston, Gainsborough, and the like.

In order to complete the English tradesman in this manner, the first thing to be done is lay down such general maxims of trade as are fit for his instruction, and then to describe the English or British product, being the fund of its inland trade, whether we mean its produce as the growth of the country, or its manufactures, as the labour of her people; then to acquaint the tradesman with the manner of the circulation where those things are found, how and by what methods all those goods are brought to London, and from London again conveyed into the country; where they are principally bought at best hand, and most to the advantage of the buyer, and where the proper markets are to dispose of them again when bought.

These are the degrees by which the complete tradesman is brought up, and by which he is instructed in the principles and methods of his commerce, by which he is made acquainted with business, and is capable of carrying it on with success, after which there is not a man in the universe deserves the title of a complete tradesman, like the English shopkeeper.

CHAPTER I
THE TRADESMAN IN HIS PREPARATIONS WHILE AN APPRENTICE

The first part of a trader's beginning is ordinarily when he is very young, I mean, when he goes as an apprentice, and the notions of trade are scarcely got into his head; for boys go apprentices while they are but boys; to talk to them in their first three or four years signifies nothing; they are rather then to be taught submission to families, and subjection to their masters, and dutiful attendance in their shops or warehouses; and this is not our present business.

But after they have entered the fifth or sixth year, they may then be entertained with discourses of another nature; and as they begin then to look forward beyond the time of their servitude, and think of setting up and being for themselves, I think then is the time to put them upon useful preparations for the work, and to instruct them in such things as may qualify them best to enter upon the world, and act for themselves when they are so entered.

The first thing a youth in the latter part of his time is to do, is to endeavour to gain a good judgment in the wares of all kinds that he is likely to deal in—as, for example, if a draper, the quality of cloths; if a stationer, the quality of papers; if a grocer, the quality of sugars, teas, &c.; and so on with all other trades. During the first years of a young man's time, he of course learns to weigh and measure either liquids or solids, to pack up and make bales, trusses, packages, &c., and to do the coarser and laborious part of business; but all that gives him little knowledge in the species and quality of the goods, much less a nice judgment in their value and sorts, which however is one of the principal things that belong to trade.

It is supposed that, by this time, if his master is a man of considerable business, his man is become the eldest apprentice, and is taken from the counter, and from sweeping the warehouse, into the counting-house, where he, among other things, sees the bills of parcels of goods bought, and thereby knows what every thing costs at first hand, what gain is made of them, and if a miscarriage happens, he knows what loss too; by which he is led of course to look into the goodness of the goods, and see the reason of things: if the goods are not to expectation, and consequently do not answer the price, he sees the reason of that loss, and he looks into the goods, and sees where and how far they are deficient, and in what; this, if he be careful to make his observations, brings him naturally to have a good judgment in the goods.

If a young man neglects this part, and passes over the season for such improvement, he very rarely ever recovers it; for this part has its season, and that more remarkable than in many other cases, and that season lost, never comes again; a judgment in goods taken in early, is never lost, and a judgment taken in late is seldom good.

If the youth slips this occasion, and, not minding what is before him, goes out of his time without obtaining such a skill as this in the goods he is to deal in, he enters into trade without his most useful tools, and must use spectacles before his time.

For want of this knowledge of the goods, he is at a loss in the buying part, and is liable to be cheated and imposed upon in the most notorious manner by the sharp-sighted world, for his want of judgment is a thing that cannot be hid; the merchants or manufacturers of whom he buys, presently discover him; the very boys in the wholesalemen's warehouses, and in merchant's warehouses, will play upon him, sell him one thing for another, show him a worse sort when he calls for a better, and, asking a higher price for it, persuade him it is better; and when they have thus bubbled him, they triumph over his ignorance when he is gone, and expose him to the last degree.

Besides, for want of judgment in the goods he is to buy, he often runs a hazard of being cheated to a very great degree, and perhaps some time or other a tradesman may be ruined by it, or at least ruin his reputation.

When I lived abroad, I had once a commission sent me from a merchant in London, to buy a large parcel of brandy: the goods were something out of my way, having never bought any in that country before. However, it happened that I had frequently bought and imported brandies in England, and had some judgment in them, so much that I ventured to buy without taking a cooper with me, which was not usual in that place. The first parcel of brandy I saw was very good, and I bought freely to the value of about £600, and shipped them for England, where they gave very good satisfaction to my employer. But I could not complete my commission to my mind in that parcel. Some days after, some merchants, who had seen me buy the other, and thought me a novice in the business, and that I took no cooper to taste the brandy, laid a plot for me, which indeed was such a plot as I was not in the least aware of; and had not the little judgment which I had in the commodity prevented, I had been notoriously abused. The case was thus:—They gave me notice by the same person who helped me to the sight of the first brandy, that there was a cellar of extraordinary good brandy at such a place, and invited me to see it. Accordingly I went in an afternoon, and tasted the brandy, being a large parcel, amounting to about £460.

I liked the goods very well; but the merchant, as they called him, that is to say, the knave appointed to cheat the poor stranger, was cunningly out of the way, so that no bargain was to be made that night. But as I had said that I liked the brandy, the same person who brought me an account of them, comes to my lodgings to treat with me about the price. We did not make many words: I bade him the current price which I had bought for some days before, and after a few struggles for five crowns a-tun more, he came to my price, and his next word was to let me know the gage of the cask; and as I had seen the goods already, he thought there was nothing to do but to make a bargain, and order the goods to be delivered.

But young as I was, I was too old for that too; and told him, I could not tell positively how many I should take, but that I would come in the afternoon, and taste them again, and mark out what I wanted. He seemed uneasy at that, and pretended he had two merchants waiting to see them, and he could sell them immediately, and I might do him a prejudice if I made him wait and put them off, who perhaps might buy in the mean time.

I answered him coldly, I would not hinder him selling them by any means if he could have a better chapman, that I could not come sooner, and that I would not be obliged to take the whole parcel, nor would I buy any of them without tasting them again: he argued much to have me buy them, seeing, as he said, I had tasted them before, and liked them very well.

'I did so,' said I, 'but I love to have my palate confirm one day what it approved the day before.' 'Perhaps,' says he, 'you would have some other person's judgment of them, and you are welcome to do so, sir, with all my heart; send any body you please:' but still he urged for a bargain, when the person sent should make his report; and then he had his agents ready, I understood afterwards, to manage the persons I should send.

I answered him frankly, I had no great judgment, but that, such as it was, I ventured to trust to it; I thought I had honest men to deal with, and that I should bring nobody to taste them for me but myself.

This pleased him, and was what he secretly wished; and now, instead of desiring me to come immediately, he told me, that seeing I would not buy without seeing the goods again, and would not go just then, he could not be in the way in the afternoon, and so desired I would defer it till next morning, which I readily agreed to.

In the morning I went, but not so soon as I had appointed; upon which, when I came, he seemed offended, and said I had hindered him—that he could have sold the whole parcel, &c. I told him I could not have hindered him, for that I had told him he should not wait for me, but sell them to the first good customer he found. He told me he had indeed sold two or three casks, but he would not disoblige me so much as to sell the whole parcel before I came. This I mention, because he made it a kind of a bite upon me, that I should not be alarmed at seeing the casks displaced in the cellar.

When I came to taste the brandy, I began to be surprised. I saw the very same casks which I had touched with the marking-iron when I was there before, but I did not like the brandy by any means, but did not yet suspect the least foul play.

I went round the whole cellar, and I could not mark above three casks which I durst venture to buy; the rest apparently showed themselves to be mixed, at least I thought so. I marked out the three casks, and told him my palate had deceived me, that the rest of the brandy was not for my turn.

I saw the man surprised, and turn pale, and at first seemed to be very angry, that I should, as he called it, disparage the goods—that sure I did not understand brandy, and the like—and that I should have brought somebody with me that did understand it. I answered coldly, that if I ventured my money upon my own judgment, the hazard was not to the seller, but to the buyer, and nobody had to do with that; if I did not like his goods, another, whose judgment was better, might like them, and so there was no harm done: in a word, he would not let me have the three casks I had marked, unless I took more, and I would take no more—so we parted, but with no satisfaction on his side; and I afterwards came to hear that he had sat up all the night with his coopers, mixing spirits in every cask, whence he drew off a quantity of the right brandy, and corrupted it, concluding, that as I had no judgment to choose by but my own, I could not discover it; and it came out by his quarrelling with the person who brought me to him, for telling him I did not understand the goods, upon which presumption he ventured to spoil the whole parcel.

I give you this story as a just caution to a young tradesman, and to show how necessary it is that a tradesman should have judgment in the goods he buys, and how easily he may be imposed upon and abused, if he offers to buy upon his own judgment, when really it is defective. I could enlarge this article with many like examples, but I think this may suffice.

The next thing I recommend to an apprentice at the conclusion of his time, is to acquaint himself with his master's chapmen;[8] I mean of both kinds, as well those he sells to, as those he buys of, and, if he is a factor, with his master's employers. But what I aim at now is the chapmen and customers whom his master chiefly sells to. I need not explain myself not to mean by this the chance customers of a retailer's shop, for there can be no acquaintance, or very little, made with them; I mean the country shopkeepers, or others, who buy in parcels, and who buy to sell again, or export as merchants. If the young man comes from his master, and has formed no acquaintance or interest among the customers whom his master dealt with, he has, in short, slipt or lost one of the principal ends and reasons of his being an apprentice, in which he has spent seven years, and perhaps his friends given a considerable sum of money.

For a young man coming out of his time to have his shop or warehouse stocked with goods, and his customers all to seek, will make his beginning infinitely more difficult to him than it would otherwise be; and he not only has new customers to seek, but has their characters to seek also, and knows not who is good and who not, till he buys that knowledge by his experience, and perhaps sometimes pays too dear for it.

It was an odd circumstance of a tradesman in this city a few years ago, who, being out of his time, and going to solicit one of his master's customers to trade with him, the chapman did not so much as know him, or remember that he had ever heard his name, except as he had heard his master call his apprentice Jacob. I know some masters diligently watch to prevent their apprentices speaking to their customers, and to keep them from acquainting themselves with the buyers, that when they come out of their times they may not carry the trade away with them.

To hinder an apprentice from an acquaintance with the dealers of both sorts, is somewhat like Laban's usage of Jacob, namely, keeping

---

[8] Individuals dealt with.

back the beloved Rachel, whom he served his seven years' time for, and putting him off with a blear-eyed Leah in her stead; it is, indeed, a kind of robbing him, taking from him the advantage which he served his time for, and sending him into the world like a man out of a ship set on shore among savages, who, instead of feeding him, are indeed more ready to eat him up and devour him.[9]

An apprentice who has served out his time faithfully and diligently, ought to claim it as a debt to his indentures, that his master should let him into an open acquaintance with his customers; he does not else perform his promise to teach him the art and mystery of his trade; he does not make him master of his business, or enable him as he ought to set up in the world; for, as buying is indeed the first, so selling is the last end of trade, and the faithful apprentice ought to be fully made acquainted with them both.

Next to being acquainted with his master's customers and chapmen, the apprentice, when his time is near expiring, ought to acquaint himself with the books, that is to say, to see and learn his master's method of book-keeping, that he may follow it, if the method is good, and may learn a better method in time, if it is not.

The tradesman should not be at a loss how to keep his books, when he is to begin his trade; that would be to put him to school when he is just come from school; his apprenticeship is, and ought in justice to be, a school to him, where he ought to learn every thing that should qualify him for his business, at least every thing that his master can teach him; and if he finds his master either backward or unwilling to teach him, he should complain in time to his own friends, that they may some how or other supply the defect.

A tradesman's books are his repeating clock, which upon all occasions are to tell him how he goes on, and how things stand with him in the world: there he will know when it is time to go on, or when

***

[9] It would be hard to doubt that Defore was sincere in this pleading of the rights of the apprentice; but its morality is certainly far from clear. The master may have gained customers with difficulty, by the exercise of much ingenuity, patience, and industry, or through some peculiar merit of his own. Indeed, it is always to be presumed that a tradesman's customers are attached to him from some of these causes. Of course, it would be hard if his apprentices, instead of collecting customers for themselves by the same means, seduced away those of his master. The true and direct object of an apprenticeship is to acquire a trade, not to acquire customers.

it is time to give over; and upon his regular keeping, and fully acquainting himself with his books, depends at least the comfort of his trade, if not the very trade itself. If they are not duly posted, and if every thing is not carefully entered in them, the debtor's accounts kept even, the cash constantly balanced, and the credits all stated, the tradesman is like a ship at sea, steered without a helm; he is all in confusion, and knows not what he does, or where he is; he may be a rich man, or a bankrupt—for, in a word, he can give no account of himself to himself, much less to any body else.

His books being so essential to his trade, he that comes out of his time without a perfect knowledge of the method of book-keeping, like a bride undrest, is not fit to be married; he knows not what to do, or what step to take; he may indeed have served his time, but he has not learned his trade, nor is he fit to set up; and be the fault in himself for not learning, or in his master for not teaching him, he ought not to set up till he has gotten some skilful person to put him in a way to do it, and make him fully to understand it.

It is true, there is not a great deal of difficulty in keeping a tradesman's books, especially if he be a retailer only; but yet, even in the meanest trades, they ought to know how to keep books. But the advice is directed to those who are above the retailer, as well as to them; if the book-keeping be small, it is the sooner learned, and the apprentice is the more to blame if he neglects it. Besides, the objection is much more trifling than the advice. The tradesman cannot carry on any considerable trade without books; and he must, during his apprenticeship, prepare himself for business by acquainting himself with every thing needful for his going on with his trade, among which that of book-keeping is absolutely necessary.

The last article, and in itself essential to a young tradesman, is to know how to buy; if his master is kind and generous, he will consider the justice of this part, and let him into the secret of it of his own free will, and that before his time is fully expired; but if that should not happen, as often it does not, let the apprentice know, that it is one of the most needful things to him that can belong to his apprenticeship, and that he ought not to let his time run over his head, without getting as much insight into it as possible; that therefore he ought to lose no opportunity to get into it, even whether his master approves of it or no; for as it is a debt due to him from his master to instruct him in it, it is highly just he should use all proper means to come at it.

Indeed, the affair in this age between masters and their apprentices, stands in a different view from what the same thing was a few years past; the state of our apprenticeship is not a state of servitude now, and hardly of subjection, and their behaviour is accordingly more like gentlemen than tradesmen; more like companions to their masters, than like servants. On the other hand, the masters seem to have made over their authority to their apprentices for a sum of money, the money taken now with apprentices being most exorbitantly great, compared to what it was in former times.

Now, though this does not at all exempt the servant or apprentice from taking care of himself, and to qualify himself for business while he is an apprentice, yet it is evident that it is no furtherance to apprentices; the liberties they take towards the conclusion of their time, are so much employed to worse purposes, that apprentices do not come out of their times better finished for business and trade than they did formerly, but much the worse: and though it is not the proper business and design of this work to enlarge on the injustice done both to master and servant by this change of custom, yet to bring it to my present purpose, it carries this force with it, namely, that the advice to apprentices to endeavour to finish themselves for business during the time of the indenture, is so much the more needful and seasonable.

Nor is this advice for the service of the master, but of the apprentice; for if the apprentice neglects this advice, if he omits to qualify himself for business as above, if he neither will acquaint himself with the customers, nor the books, nor with the buying part, nor gain judgment in the wares he is to deal in, the loss is his own, not his master's—and, indeed, he may be said to have served not himself, but his master—and both his money and his seven years are all thrown away.

CHAPTER II
THE TRADESMAN'S WRITING LETTERS

As plainness, and a free unconstrained way of speaking, is the beauty and excellence of speech, so an easy free concise way of writing is the best style for a tradesman. He that affects a rumbling and bombast style, and fills his letters with long harangues, compliments, and flourishes, should turn poet instead of tradesman, and set up for a wit, not a shopkeeper. Hark how such a young tradesman writes, out of the country, to his wholesale-man in London, upon his first setting up.

'SIR—The destinies having so appointed it, and my dark stars concurring, that I, who by nature was framed for better things, should be put out to a trade, and the gods having been so propitious to me in the time of my servitude, that at length the days are expired, and I am launched forth into the great ocean of business, I thought fit to acquaint you, that last month I received my fortune, which, by my father's will, had been my due two years past, at which time I arrived to man's estate, and became major, whereupon I have taken a house in one of the principal streets of the town of——, where I am entered upon my business, and hereby let you know that I shall have occasion for the goods hereafter mentioned, which you may send to me by the carrier.'

This fine flourish, and which, no doubt, the young fellow dressed up with much application, and thought was very well done, put his correspondent in London into a fit of laughter, and instead of sending him the goods he wrote for, put him either first upon writing down into the country to inquire after his character, and whether he was worth dealing with, or else it obtained to be filed up among such letters as deserved no answer.

The same tradesman in London received by the post another letter, from a young shopkeeper in the country, to the purpose following:—

'Being obliged, Sir, by my late master's decease, to enter immediately upon his business, and consequently open my shop without coming up to London to furnish myself with such goods as at present I want, I have here sent you a small order, as underwritten. I hope you will think yourself obliged to use me well, and particularly that the goods may be good of the sorts, though I cannot be at London to look them out myself. I have enclosed a bill of exchange for £75, on Messrs A.B. and Company, payable to you, or your order, at one-and-twenty days' sight; be pleased to get it accepted, and if the goods amount to more than that sum, I shall, when I have your bill of parcels, send you the remainder. I repeat my desire, that you will send me the goods well sorted, and well chosen, and as cheap as possible, that I may be encouraged to a further correspondence. I am, your humble servant,

C.K.'

This was writing like a man that understood what he was doing; and his correspondent in London would presently say—'This young man writes like a man of business; pray let us take care to use him well, for in all probability he will be a very good chapman.'

The sum of the matter is this: a tradesman's letters should be plain, concise, and to the purpose; no quaint expressions, no book-phrases, no flourishes, and yet they must be full and sufficient to express what he means, so as not to be doubtful, much less unintelligible. I can by no means approve of studied abbreviations, and leaving out the needful copulatives of speech in trading letters; they are to an extreme affected; no beauty to the style, but, on the contrary, a deformity of the grossest nature. They are affected to the last degree, and with this aggravation, that it is an affectation of the grossest nature; for, in a word, it is affecting to be thought a man of more than ordinary sense by writing extraordinary nonsense; and affecting to be a man of business, by giving orders and expressing your meaning in terms which a man of business may not think himself bound by. For example, a tradesman at Hull writes to his correspondent at London the following letter:—

'SIR, yours received, have at present little to reply. Last post you had bills of loading, with invoice of what had loaden for your account in Hamburgh factor bound for said port. What have farther orders for, shall be dispatched with expedition. Markets slacken much on this side; cannot sell the iron for more than 37s. Wish had your orders if shall part with it at that rate. No ships since the 11th. London fleet may be in the roads before the late storm, so hope they are safe: if have not insured, please omit the same till hear farther; the weather proving good, hope the danger is over.

My last transmitted three bills exchange, import £315; please signify if are come to hand, and accepted, and give credit in account current to your humble servant.'

I pretend to say there is nothing in all this letter, though appearing to have the face of a considerable dealer, but what may be taken any way, *pro* or *con*. The Hamburgh factor may be a ship, or a horse—be

473

bound to Hamburgh or London. What shall be dispatched may be one thing, or any thing, or every thing, in a former letter. No ships since the 11th, may be no ships come in, or no ships gone out. The London fleet being in the roads, it may be the London fleet from Hull to London, or from London to Hull, both being often at sea together. The roads may be Yarmouth roads, or Grimsby, or, indeed, any where.

By such a way of writing, no orders can be binding to him that gives them, or to him they are given to. A merchant writes to his factor at Lisbon:—

'Please to send, per first ship, 150 chests best Seville, and 200 pipes best Lisbon white. May value yourself per exchange £1250 sterling, for the account of above orders. Suppose you can send the sloop to Seville for the ordered chests, &c. I am.'

Here is the order to send a cargo, with a *please to send*; so the factor may let it alone if he does not please.[10] The order is 150 chests Seville; it is supposed he means oranges, but it may be 150 chests orange-trees as well, or chests of oil, or any thing. Lisbon white, may be wine or any thing else, though it is supposed to be wine. He may draw £1250, but he may refuse to accept it if he pleases, for any thing such an order as that obliges him.

On the contrary, orders ought to be plain and explicit; and he ought to have assured him, that on his drawing on him, his bills should be honoured—that is, accepted and paid.

I know this affectation of style is accounted very grand, looks modish, and has a kind of majestic greatness in it; but the best merchants in the world are come off from it, and now choose to write plain and intelligibly: much less should country tradesmen, citizens, and shopkeepers, whose business is plainness and mere trade, make use of it.

I have mentioned this in the beginning of this work, because, indeed, it is the beginning of a tradesman's business. When a tradesman takes an apprentice, the first thing he does for him, after he takes him from behind his counter, after he lets him into his counting-house and his books, and after trusting him with his more private business—I say, the first thing is to let him write letters to his dealers, and correspond with his friends; and this he does in his master's name, subscribing his letters thus:—

I am, for my master, A.B. and Company, your
humble servant, C.D.

---

[10] The practice of trade now sanctions courteous expressions of this kind.

And beginning thus:—Sir, I am ordered by my master A.B. to advise you that—

Or thus:—

Sir, By my master's order, I am to signify to you that

Orders for goods ought to be very explicit and particular, that the dealer may not mistake, especially if it be orders from a tradesman to a manufacturer to make goods, or to buy goods, either of such a quality, or to such a pattern; in which, if the goods are made to the colours, and of a marketable goodness, and within the time limited, the person ordering them cannot refuse to receive them, and make himself debtor to the maker. On the contrary, if the goods are not of a marketable goodness, or not to the patterns, or are not sent within the time, the maker ought not to expect they should be received. For example—

The tradesman, or warehouseman, or what else we may call him, writes to his correspondent at Devizes, in Wiltshire, thus:—

'Sir—The goods you sent me last week are not at all for my purpose, being of a sort which I am at present full of: however, if you are willing they should lie here, I will take all opportunities to sell them for your account; otherwise, on your first orders, they shall be delivered to whoever you shall direct: and as you had no orders from me for such sorts of goods, you cannot take this ill. But I have here enclosed sent you five patterns as under, marked 1 to 5; if you think fit to make me fifty pieces of druggets of the same weight and goodness with the fifty pieces, No. A.B., which I had from you last October, and mixed as exactly as you can to the enclosed patterns, ten to each pattern, and can have the same to be delivered here any time in February next, I shall take them at the same price which I gave you for the last; and one month after the delivery you may draw upon me for the money, which shall be paid to your content. Your friend and servant.

P.S. Let me have your return per next post, intimating that you can or cannot answer this order, that I may govern myself accordingly. *To Mr H.G., clothier, Devizes.*'

The clothier, accordingly, gives him an answer the next post, as follows:—

'Sir—I have the favour of yours of the 22d past, with your order for fifty fine druggets, to be made of the like weight and goodness with the two packs, No. A.B., which I made for you and sent last October, as also the five patterns enclosed, marked 1 to 5, for my direction in the mixture. I give you this trouble, according to your order, to let you know I have already put the said fifty pieces in hand; and as I am always willing to serve you to the best of my power, and am thankful for your favours, you may depend upon them within the time, that is to say, some time in February next, and that they shall be of the like fineness and substance with the other, and as near to the patterns as possible. But in regard our poor are very craving, and money at this time very scarce, I beg you will give me leave (twenty or thirty pieces of them being finished and delivered to you at any time before the remainder), to draw fifty pounds on you for present occasion; for which I shall think myself greatly obliged, and shall give you any security you please that the rest shall follow within the time.

As to the pack of goods in your hands, which were sent up without your order, I am content they remain in your hands for sale on my account, and desire you will sell them as soon as you can, for my best advantage. I am,' &c.

Here is a harmony of business, and every thing exact; the order is given plain and express; the clothier answers directly to every point; here can be no defect in the correspondence; the diligent clothier applies immediately to the work, sorts and dyes his wool, mixes his colours to the patterns, puts the wool to the spinners, sends his yarn to the weavers, has the pieces brought home, then has them to the thicking or fulling-mill, dresses them in his own workhouse, and sends them up punctually by the time; perhaps by the middle of the month. Having sent up twenty pieces five weeks before, the warehouse-keeper, to oblige him, pays his bill of £50, and a month after the rest are sent in, he draws for the rest of the money, and his bills are punctually paid. The consequence of this exact writing and answering is this—

The warehouse-keeper having the order from his merchant, is furnished in time, and obliges his customer; then says he to his servant, 'Well, this H.G. of Devizes is a clever workman, understands his business, and may be depended on: I see if I have an order to give that requires any exactness and honest usage, he is my man; he understands orders when they are sent, goes to work immediately, and answers them punctually.'

Again, the clothier at Devizes says to his head man, or perhaps his son, 'This Mr H. is a very good employer, and is worth obliging; his orders are so plain and so direct, that a man cannot mistake, and if the goods are made honestly and to his time, there's one's money; bills are cheerfully accepted, and punctually paid; I'll never disappoint him; whoever goes without goods, he shall not.'

On the contrary, when orders are darkly given, they are doubtfully observed; and when the goods come to town, the merchant dislikes them, the warehouseman shuffles them back upon the clothier, to lie for his account, pretending they are not made to his order; the clothier is discouraged, and for want of his money discredited, and all their correspondence is confusion, and ends in loss both of money and credit.

CHAPTER III
THE TRADING STYLE

In the last chapter I gave my thoughts for the instruction of young tradesmen in writing letters with orders, and answering orders, and especially about the proper style of a tradesman's letters, which I hinted should be plain and easy, free in language, and direct to the purpose intended. Give me leave to go on with the subject a little farther, as I think it is useful in another part of the tradesman's correspondence.

I might have made some apology for urging tradesmen to write a plain and easy style; let me add, that the tradesmen need not be offended at my condemning them, as it were, to a plain and homely style—easy, plain, and familiar language is the beauty of speech in general, and is the excellency of all writing, on whatever subject, or to whatever persons they are we write or speak. The end of speech is that men might understand one another's meaning; certainly that speech, or that way of speaking, which is most easily understood, is the best way of speaking. If any man were to ask me, which would be supposed to be a perfect style, or language, I would answer, that in which a man speaking to five hundred people, of all common and various capacities, idiots or lunatics excepted, should be understood by them all in the same manner with one another, and in the same sense which the speaker intended to be understood—this would certainly be a most perfect style.

All exotic sayings, dark and ambiguous speakings, affected words, and, as I said in the last chapter, abridgement, or words cut off, as they are foolish and improper in business, so, indeed, are they in any other things; hard words, and affectation of style in business, is like bombast in poetry, a kind of rumbling nonsense, and nothing of the kind can be more ridiculous.

The nicety of writing in business consists chiefly in giving every species of goods their trading names, for there are certain peculiarities in the trading language, which are to be observed as the greatest proprieties, and without which the language your letters are written in would be obscure, and the tradesmen you write to would not understand you—for example, if you write to your factor at Lisbon, or at Cadiz, to make you returns in hardware, he understands you, and sends you so many bags of pieces of eight. So, if a merchant comes to me to hire a small ship of me, and tells me it is for the pipin trade, or to buy a vessel, and tells me he intends to make a pipiner of her, the meaning is, that she is to run to Seville for oranges, or to Malaga for lemons. If he says he intends to send her for a lading of fruit, the meaning is, she is to go to Alicant, Denia, or Xevia, on the coast of Spain, for raisins of the sun, or to Malaga for Malaga raisins. Thus, in the home trade in England: if in Kent a man tells me he is to go among the night-riders, his meaning is, he is to go a-carrying wool to the sea-shore—the people that usually run the wool off in boats, are called owlers—those that steal customs, smugglers, and the like. In a word, there is a kind of slang in trade, which a tradesman ought to know, as the beggars and strollers know the gipsy cant, which none can speak but themselves; and this in letters of business is allowable, and, indeed, they cannot understand one another without it.

A brickmaker being hired by a brewer to make some bricks for him at his country-house, wrote to the brewer that he could not go forward unless he had two or three loads *of spanish*, and that otherwise his bricks would cost him six or seven chaldrons of coals extraordinary, and the bricks would not be so good and hard neither by a great deal, when they were burnt.

The brewer sends him an answer, that he should go on as well as he could for three or four days, and then the *spanish* should be sent him: accordingly, the following week, the brewer sends him down two carts loaded with about twelve hogsheads or casks of molasses, which frighted the brickmaker almost out of his senses. The case was this:-The brewers formerly mixed molasses with their ale to sweeten it, and abate the quantity of malt, molasses, being, at that time, much cheaper in proportion, and this they called *spanish*, not being willing that people should know it. Again, the brickmakers all about London, do mix sea-coal ashes, or laystal-stuff, as we call it, with the clay of which they make bricks, and by that shift save eight chaldrons of coals out of eleven, in proportion to what other people use to burn them with, and these ashes they call *spanish*.

Thus the received terms of art, in every particular business, are to be observed, of which I shall speak to you in its turn: I name them here to intimate, that when I am speaking of plain writing in matters of business, it must be understood with an allowance for all these things—and a tradesman must be not only allowed to use them in his style, but cannot write properly without them—it is a particular excellence in a tradesman to be able to know all the terms of art in every separate business, so as to be able to speak or write to any particular handicraft or manufacturer in his own dialect, and it is as necessary as it is for a seaman to understand the names of all the several things belonging to a ship. This, therefore, is not to be understood when I say, that a tradesman should write plain and explicit, for these things belong to, and are part of, the language of trade.

But even these terms of art, or customary expressions, are not to be used with affectation, and with a needless repetition, where they are not called for.

Nor should a tradesman write those out-of-the-way words, though it is in the way of the business he writes about, to any other person, who he knows, or has reason to believe, does not understand them—I say, he ought not to write in those terms to such, because it shows a kind of ostentation, and a triumph over the ignorance of the person they are written to, unless at the very same time you add an explanation of the terms, so as to make them assuredly intelligible at the place, and to the person to whom they are sent.

A tradesman, in such cases, like a parson, should suit his language to his auditory; and it would be as ridiculous for a tradesman to write a letter filled with the peculiarities of this or that particular trade, which trade he knows the person he writes to is ignorant of, and the terms whereof he is unacquainted with, as it would be for a minister to quote the Chrysostome and St Austin, and repeat at large all their sayings in the Greek and the Latin, in a country church, among a parcel of ploughmen and farmers. Thus a sailor, writing a letter to a surgeon, told him he had a swelling on the north-east side of his face—that his windward leg being hurt by a bruise, it so put him out of trim, that he always heeled to starboard when he made fresh way, and so run to leeward, till he was often forced aground; then he desired him to give him some directions how to put himself into a sailing posture again. Of all which the surgeon understood little more than that he had a swelling on his face, and a bruise in his leg.

It would be a very happy thing, if tradesmen had all their *lexicon technicum* at their fingers' ends; I mean (for pray, remember, that I observe my own rule, not to use a hard word without explaining it), that every tradesman would study so the terms of art of other trades, that he might be able to speak to every manufacturer or artist in his own language, and understand them when they talked one to another: this would make trade be a kind of universal language, and the particular marks they are obliged to, would be like the notes of music, an universal character, in which all the tradesmen in England might write to one another in the language and characters of their several trades, and be as intelligible to one another as the minister is to his people, and perhaps much more.

I therefore recommend it to every young tradesman to take all occasions to converse with mechanics of every kind, and to learn the particular language of their business; not the names of their tools only, and the way of working with their instruments as well as hands, but the very cant of their trade, for every trade has its *nostrums*, and its little made words, which they often pride themselves in, and which yet are useful to them on some occasion or other.

There are many advantages to a tradesman in thus having a general knowledge of the terms of art, and the cant, as I call it, of every business; and particularly this, that they could not be imposed upon so easily by other tradesmen, when they came to deal with them.

If you come to deal with a tradesman or handicraft man, and talk his own language to him, he presently supposes you understand his business; that you know what you come about; that you have judgment in his goods, or in his art, and cannot easily be imposed upon; accordingly, he treats you like a man that is not to be cheated, comes close to the point, and does not crowd you with words and rattling talk to set out his wares, and to cover their defects; he finds you know where to look or feel for the defect of things, and how to judge their worth. For example:—

What trade has more hard words and peculiar ways attending it, than that of a jockey, or horse-courser, as we call them! They have all the parts of the horse, and all the diseases attending him, necessary to be mentioned in the market, upon every occasion of buying or bargaining. A jockey will know you at first sight, when you do but go round a horse, or at the first word you say about him, whether you are a dealer, as they call themselves, or a stranger. If you begin well, if you take up the horse's foot right, if you handle him in the proper places, if you bid his servant open his mouth, or go about it yourself like a workman, if you speak of his shapes or goings in the proper words—'Oh!' says the jockey to his fellow, 'he understands a horse, he speaks the language:' then he knows you are not to be cheated, or, at least, not so easily; but if you go awkwardly to work, whisper to your man you bring with you to ask every thing for you, cannot handle the horse yourself, or speak the language of the trade, he falls upon you with his flourishes, and with a flux of horse rhetoric imposes upon you with oaths and asseverations, and, in a word, conquers you with the mere clamour of his trade.

481

Thus, if you go to a garden to buy flowers, plants, trees, and greens, if you know what you go about, know the names of flowers, or simples, or greens; know the particular beauties of them, when they are fit to remove, and when to slip and draw, and when not; what colour is ordinary, and what rare; when a flower is rare, and when ordinary—the gardener presently talks to you as to a man of art, tells you that you are a lover of art, a friend to a florist, shows you his exotics, his green-house, and his stores; what he has set out, and what he has budded or enarched, and the like; but if he finds you have none of the terms of art, know little or nothing of the names of plants, or the nature of planting, he picks your pocket instantly, shows you a fine trimmed fuz-bush for a juniper, sells you common pinks for painted ladies, an ordinary tulip for a rarity, and the like. Thus I saw a gardener sell a gentleman a large yellow auricula, that is to say, a *running away*, for a curious flower, and take a great price. It seems, the gentleman was a lover of a good yellow; and it is known, that when nature in the auricula is exhausted, and has spent her strengh in showing a fine flower, perhaps some years upon the same root, she faints at last, and then turns into a yellow, which yellow shall be bright and pleasant the first year, and look very well to one that knows nothing of it, though another year it turns pale, and at length almost white. This the gardeners call a *run flower*, and this they put upon the gentleman for a rarity, only because he discovered at his coming that he knew nothing of the matter. The same gardener sold another person a root of white painted thyme for the right *Marum Syriacum;* and thus they do every day.

A person goes into a brickmaker's field to view his clamp, and buy a load of bricks; he resolves to see them loaded, because he would have good ones; but not understanding the goods, and seeing the workmen loading them where they were hard and well burnt, but looked white and grey, which, to be sure, were the best of the bricks, and which perhaps they would not have done if he had not been there to look at them, they supposing he understood which were the best; but he, in the abundance of his ignorance, finds fault with them, because they were not a good colour, and did not look red; the brickmaker's men took the hint immediately, and telling the buyer they would give him red bricks to oblige him, turned their hands from the grey hard well-burnt bricks to the soft *sammel*[11] half-burnt bricks, which they were glad to dispose of, and which nobody that had understood them would have taken off their hands.

I mention these lower things, because I would suit my writing to the understanding of the meanest people, and speak of frauds used in the most ordinary trades; but it is the like in almost all the goods a tradesman can deal in. If you go to Warwickshire to buy cheese, you demand the cheese 'of the first make,' because that is the best. If you go to Suffolk to buy butter, you refuse the butter of the first make, because that is not the best, but you bargain for 'the right rowing butter,' which is the butter that is made when the cows are turned into the grounds where the grass has been mowed, and the hay carried off, and grown again: and so in many other cases. These things demonstrate the advantages there are to a tradesman, in his being thoroughly informed of the terms of art, and the peculiarities belonging to every particular business, which, therefore, I call the language of trade.

As a merchant should understand all languages, at least the languages of those countries which he trades to, or corresponds with, and the customs and usages of those countries as to their commerce, so an English tradesman ought to understand all the languages of trade, within the circumference of his own country, at least, and particularly of such as he may, by any of the consequences of his commerce, come to be any way concerned with.

Especially, it is his business to acquaint himself with the terms and trading style, as I call it, of those trades which he buys of, as to those he sells to; supposing he sells to those who sell again, it is their business to understand him, not his to understand them: and if he finds they do not understand him, he will not fail to make their ignorance be his advantage, unless he is honester and more conscientious in his dealings than most of the tradesmen of this age seem to be.

---

[11] *Sammel* is a term of art the brickmakers use for those bricks which are not well burnt, and which generally look of a pale red colour, and as fair as the other, but are soft.

CHAPTER IV
OF THE TRADESMAN ACQUAINTING HIMSELF WITH ALL BUSINESS IN GENERAL

It is the judgment of some experienced tradesmen, that no man ought to go from one business to another, and launch out of the trade or employment he was bred to: *Tractent fabrilia fabri*—'Every man to his own business;' and, they tell us, men never thrive when they do so.

I will not enter into that dispute here. I know some good and encouraging examples of the contrary, and which stand as remarkable instances, or as exceptions to the general rule: but let that be as it will, sometimes providence eminently calls upon men out of one employ into another, out of a shop into a warehouse, out of a warehouse into a shop, out of a single hand into a partnership, and the like; and they trade one time here, another time there, and with very good success too. But I say, be that as it will, a tradesman ought so far to acquaint himself with business, that he should not be at a loss to turn his hand to this or that trade, as occasion presents, whether in or out of the way of his ordinary dealing, as we have often seen done in London and other places, and sometimes with good success.

This acquainting himself with business does not intimate that he should learn every trade, or enter into the mystery of every employment. That cannot well be; but that he should have a true notion of business in general, and a knowledge how and in what manner it is carried on; that he should know where every manufacture is made, and how bought at first hand; that he should know which are the proper markets, and what the particular kinds of goods to exchange at those markets; that he should know the manner how every manufacture is managed, and the method of their sale.

It cannot be expected that he should have judgment in the choice of all kinds of goods, though in a great many he may have judgment too: but there is a general understanding in trade, which every tradesman both may and ought to arrive to; and this perfectly qualifies him to engage in any new undertaking, and to embark with other persons better qualified than himself in any new trade, which he was not in before; in which, though he may not have a particular knowledge and judgment in the goods they are to deal in or to make, yet, having the benefit of the knowledge his new partner is master of, and being himself apt to take in all additional lights, he soon becomes experienced, and the knowledge of all the other parts of business qualifies him to be a sufficient partner. For example—A.B. was bred a dry-salter, and he goes in partner with with C.D., a scarlet-dyer, called a bow-dyer, at Wandsworth.

As a salter, A.B. has had experience enough in the materials for dyeing, as well scarlets as all other colours, and understands very well the buying of cochineal, indigo, galls, shumach, logwood, fustick, madder, and the like; so that he does his part very well. C.D. is an experienced scarlet-dyer; but now, doubling their stock, they fall into a larger work, and they dye bays and stuffs, and other goods, into differing colours, as occasion requires; and this brings them to an equality in the business, and by hiring good experienced servants, they go on very well together.

The like happens often when a tradesman turns his hand from one trade to another; and when he embarks, either in partnership or out of it, in any new business, it is supposed he seldom changes hands in such a manner without some such suitable person to join with, or that he has some experienced head workman to direct him, which, if that workman proves honest, is as well as a partner. On the other hand, his own application and indefatigable industry supply the want of judgment. Thus, I have known several tradesmen turn their hands from one business to another, or from one trade entirely to another, and very often with good success. For example, I have seen a confectioner turn a sugar-baker; another a distiller; an apothecary turn chemist, and not a few turn physicians, and prove very good physicians too; but that is a step beyond what I am speaking of.

But my argument turns upon this—that a tradesman ought to be able to turn his hand to any thing; that is to say, to lay down one trade and take up another, if occasion leads him to it, and if he sees an evident view of profit and advantage in it; and this is only done by his having a general knowledge of trade, so as to have a capacity of judging: and by but just looking upon what is offered or proposed, he sees as much at first view as others do by long inquiry, and with the judgment of many advisers.

When I am thus speaking of the tradesman's being capable of making judgment of things, it occurs, with a force not to be resisted, that I should add, he is hereby fenced against bubbles and projects, and against those fatal people called projectors, who are, indeed, among tradesmen, as birds of prey are among the innocent fowls—devourers and destroyers. A tradesman cannot be too well armed, nor too much cautioned, against those sort of people; they are constantly surrounded with them, and are as much in jeopardy from them, as a man in a crowd is of having his pocket picked—nay, almost as a man is when in a crowd of pickpockets.

Nothing secures the tradesman against those men so well as his being thoroughly knowing in business, having a judgment to weigh all the delusive schemes and the fine promises of the wheedling projector, and to see which are likely to answer, or which not; to examine all his specious pretences, his calculations and figures, and see whether they are as likely to answer the end as he takes upon him to say they will; to make allowances for all his fine flourishes and outsides, and then to judge for himself. A projector is to a tradesman a kind of incendiary; he is in a constant plot to blow him up, or set fire to him; for projects are generally as fatal to a tradesman as fire in a magazine of gunpowder.

The honest tradesman is always in danger, and cannot be too wary; and therefore to fortify his judgment, that he may be able to guard against such people as these, is one of the most necessary things I can do for him.

In order, then, to direct the tradesman how to furnish himself thus with a needful stock of trading knowledge, first, I shall propose to him to converse with tradesmen chiefly: he that will be a tradesman should confine himself within his own sphere: never was the Gazette so full of the advertisements of commissions of bankrupt as since our shopkeepers are so much engaged in parties, formed into clubs to hear news, and read journals and politics; in short, when tradesmen turn statesmen, they should either shut up their shops, or hire somebody else to look after them.

The known story of the upholsterer is very instructive,[12] who, in his abundant concern for the public, ran himself out of his business into a jail; and even when he was in prison, could not sleep for the concern he had for the liberties of his dear country: the man was a good patriot, but a bad shopkeeper; and, indeed, should rather have shut up his shop, and got a commission in the army, and then he had served his country in the way of his calling. But I may speak to this more in its turn.

My present subject is not the negative, what he should not do, but the affirmative, what he should do; I say, he should take all occasions to

---

[12] The story of the political upholsterer forms the subject of several amusing papers by Addison in the *Tatler*.

converse within the circuit of his own sphere, that is, dwell upon the subject of trade in his conversation, and sort with and converse among tradesmen as much as he can; as writing teaches to write—*scribendo discis scribere*—so conversing among tradesmen will make him a tradesman. I need not explain this so critically as to tell you I do not mean he should confine or restrain himself entirely from all manner of conversation but among his own class: I shall speak to that in its place also. A tradesman may on occasion keep company with gentlemen as well as other people; nor is a trading man, if he is a man of sense, unsuitable or unprofitable for a gentleman to converse with, as occasion requires; and you will often find, that not private gentlemen only, but even ministers of state, privy-councillors, members of parliament, and persons of all ranks in the government, find it for their purpose to converse with tradesmen, and are not ashamed to acknowledge, that a tradesman is sometimes qualified to inform them in the most difficult and intricate, as well as the most urgent, affairs of government; and this has been the reason why so many tradesmen have been advanced to honours and dignities above their ordinary rank, as Sir Charles Duncombe, a goldsmith; Sir Henry Furnese, who was originally a retail hosier; Sir Charles Cook, late one of the board of trade, a merchant; Sir Josiah Child, originally a very mean tradesman; the late Mr Lowndes, bred a scrivener; and many others, too many to name.

But these are instances of men called out of their lower sphere for their eminent usefulness, and their known capacities, being first known to be diligent and industrious men in their private and lower spheres; such advancements make good the words of the wise man—'Seest thou a man diligent in his calling, he shall stand before kings; he shall not stand before mean men.[13]

In the mean time, the tradesman's proper business is in his shop or warehouse, and among his own class or rank of people; there he sees how other men go on, and there he learns how to go on himself; there he sees how other men thrive, and learns to thrive himself; there he hears all the trading news—as for state news and politics, it is none of his business; there he learns how to buy, and there he gets oftentimes opportunities to sell; there he hears of all the disasters in trade, who breaks, and why; what brought such and such a man to misfortunes and disasters; and sees the various ways how men go down in the world, as

---

[13] To stand in the presence of a prince is the highest mark of honour in the east, as to sit is with us.

well as the arts and management, by which others from nothing arise to wealth and estates.

Here he sees the Scripture itself thwarted, and his neighbour tradesman, a wholesale haberdasher, in spite of a good understanding, in spite of a good beginning, and in spite of the most indefatigable industry, sink in his circumstances, lose his credit, then his stock, and then break and become bankrupt, while the man takes more pains to be poor than others do to grow rich.

There, on the other hand, he sees G.D., a plodding, weak-headed, but laborious wretch, of a confined genius, and that cannot look a quarter of a mile from his shop-door into the world, and beginning with little or nothing, yet rises apace in the mere road of business, in which he goes on like the miller's horse, who, being tied to the post, is turned round by the very wheel which he turns round himself; and this fellow shall get money insensibly, and grow rich even he knows not how, and no body else knows why.

Here he sees F.M. ruined by too much trade, and there he sees M.F. starved for want of trade; and from all these observations he may learn something useful to himself, and fit to guide his own measures, that he may not fall into the same mischiefs which he sees others sink under, and that he may take the advantage of that prudence which others rise by.

All these things will naturally occur to him, in his conversing among his fellow-tradesmen. A settled little society of trading people, who understand business, and are carrying on trade in the same manner with himself, no matter whether they are of the very same trades or no, and perhaps better not of the same—such a society, I say, shall, if due observations are made from it, teach the tradesman more than his apprenticeship; for there he learned the operation, here he learns the progression; his apprenticeship is his grammar-school, this is his university; behind his master's counter, or in his warehouse, he learned the first rudiments of trade, but here he learns the trading sciences; here he comes to learn the *arcana*, speak the language, understand the meaning of every thing, of which before he only learned the beginning: the apprenticeship inducts him, and leads him as the nurse the child; this finishes him; there he learned the beginning of trade, here he sees it in its full extent; in a word, there he learned to trade, here he is made a complete tradesman.

Let no young tradesman object, that, in the conversation I speak of, there are so many gross things said, and so many ridiculous things

488

argued upon, there being always a great many weak empty heads among the shopkeeping trading world: this may be granted without any impeachment of what I have advanced—for where shall a man converse, and find no fools in the society?—and where shall he hear the weightiest things debated, and not a great many empty weak things offered, out of which nothing can be learned, and from which nothing can be deduced?—for 'out of nothing, nothing can come.'

But, notwithstanding, let me still insist upon it to the tradesman to keep company with tradesmen; let the fool run on in his own way; let the talkative green-apron rattle in his own way; let the manufacturer and his factor squabble and brangle; the grave self-conceited puppy, who was born a boy, and will die before he is a man, chatter and say a great deal of nothing, and talk his neighbours to death—out of every one you will learn something—they are all tradesmen, and there is always something for a young tradesman to learn from them. If, understanding but a little French, you were to converse every day a little among some Frenchmen in your neighbourhood, and suppose those Frenchmen, you thus kept company with, were every one of them fools, mere ignorant, empty, foolish fellows, there might be nothing learnt from their sense, but you would still learn French from them, if it was no more than the tone and accent, and the ordinary words usual in conversation.

Thus, among your silly empty tradesmen, let them be as foolish and empty other ways as you can suggest, though you can learn no philosophy from them, you may learn many things in trade from them, and something from every one; for though it is not absolutely necessary that every tradesman should be a philosopher, yet every tradesman, in his way, knows something that even a philosopher may learn from.

I knew a philosopher that was excellently skilled in the noble science or study of astronomy, who told me he had some years studied for some simile, or proper allusion, to explain to his scholars the phenomena of the sun's motion round its own axis, and could never happen upon one to his mind, till by accident he saw his maid Betty trundling her mop: surprised with the exactness of the motion to describe the thing he wanted, he goes into his study, calls his pupils about him, and tells them that Betty, who herself knew nothing of the matter, could show them the sun revolving about itself in a more lively manner than ever he could. Accordingly, Betty was called, and bidden bring out her mop, when, placing his scholars in a due-position, opposite not to the face of the maid, but to her left side, so that they could see the end of the mop, when it whirled round upon her arm.

They took it immediately—there was the broad-headed nail in the centre, which was as the body of the sun, and the thrums whisking round, flinging the water about every way by innumerable little streams, describing exactly the rays of the sun, darting light from the centre to the whole system.

If ignorant Betty, by the natural consequences of her operation, instructed the astronomer, why may not the meanest shoemaker or pedlar, by the ordinary sagacity of his trading wit, though it may be indeed very ordinary, coarse, and unlooked for, communicate something, give some useful hint, dart some sudden thought into the mind of the observing tradesman, which he shall make his use of, and apply to his own advantage in trade, when, at the same time, he that gives such hint shall himself, like Betty and her mop, know nothing of the matter?

Every tradesman is supposed to manage his business his own way, and, generally speaking, most tradesmen have some ways peculiar and particular to themselves, which they either derived from the masters who taught them, or from the experience of things, or from something in the course of their business, which had not happened to them before.

And those little *nostrums* are oftentime very properly and with advantage communicated from one to another; one tradesman finds out a nearer way of buying than another, another finds a vent for what is bought beyond what his neighbour knows of, and these, in time, come to be learned of them by their ordinary conversation.

I am not for confining the tradesman from keeping better company, as occasion and leisure requires; I allow the tradesman to act the gentleman sometimes, and that even for conversation, at least if his understanding and capacity make him suitable company to them, but still his business is among those of his own rank. The conversation of gentlemen, and what they call keeping good company, may be used as a diversion, or as an excursion, but his stated society must be with his neighbours, and people in trade; men of business are companions for men of business; with gentlemen he may converse pleasantly, but here he converses profitably; tradesmen are always profitable to one another; as they always gain by trading together, so they never lose by conversing together; if they do not get money, they gain knowledge in business, improve their experience, and see farther and farther into the world.

A man of but an ordinary penetration will improve himself by conversing in matters of trade with men of trade; by the experience of the old tradesmen they learn caution and prudence, and by the rashness

490

and the miscarriages of the young, they learn what are the mischiefs that themselves may be exposed to.

Again, in conversing with men of trade, they get trade; men first talk together, then deal together—many a good bargain is made, and many a pound gained, where nothing was expected, by mere casual coming to talk together, without knowing any thing of the matter before they met. The tradesmen's meetings are like the merchants' exchange, where they manage, negociate, and, indeed, beget business with one another.

Let no tradesman mistake me in this part; I am not encouraging them to leave their shops and warehouses, to go to taverns and ale-houses, and spend their time there in unnecessary prattle, which, indeed, is nothing but sotting and drinking; this is not meeting to do business, but to neglect business. Of which I shall speak fully afterwards.

But the tradesmen conversing with one another, which I mean, is the taking suitable occasions to discourse with their fellow tradesmen, meeting them in the way of their business, and improving their spare hours together. To leave their shops, and quit their counters, in the proper seasons for their attendance there, would be a preposterous negligence, would be going out of business to gain business, and would be cheating themselves, instead of improving themselves. The proper hours of business are sacred to the shop and the warehouse. He that goes out of the order of trade, let the pretence of business be what it will, loses his business, not increases it; and will, if continued, lose the credit of his conduct in business also.

CHAPTER V
DILIGENCE AND APPLICATION IN BUSINESS

Solomon was certainly a friend to men of business, as it appears by his frequent good advice to them. In Prov. xviii. 9, he says, 'He that is slothful in business, is brother to him that is a great waster:' and in another place, 'The sluggard shall be clothed in rags,' (Prov. xxiii. I), or to that purpose. On the contrary, the same wise man, by way of encouragement, tells them, 'The diligent hand maketh rich,' (Prov. x. 4), and, 'The diligent shall bear rule, but the slothful shall be under tribute.'

Nothing can give a greater prospect of thriving to a young tradesman, than his own diligence; it fills himself with hope, and gives him credit with all who know him; without application, nothing in this world goes forward as it should do: let the man have the most perfect knowledge of his trade, and the best situation for his shop, yet without application nothing will go on. What is the shop without the master? what the books without the book-keeper? what the credit without the man? Hark how the people talk of such conduct as the slothful negligent trader discovers in his way.

'Such a shop,' says the customer, 'stands well, and there is a good stock of goods in it, but there is nobody to serve but a 'prentice-boy or two, and an idle journeyman: one finds them always at play together, rather than looking out for customers; and when you come to buy, they look as if they did not care whether they showed you any thing or no. One never sees a master in the shop, if we go twenty times, nor anything that bears the face of authority. Then, it is a shop always exposed, it is perfectly haunted with thieves and shop-lifters; they see nobody but raw boys in it, that mind nothing, and the diligent devils never fail to haunt them, so that there are more outcries of 'Stop thief!' at their door, and more constables fetched to that shop, than to all the shops in the row. There was a brave trade at that shop in Mr—'s time: he was a true shopkeeper; like the quack doctor, you never missed him from seven in the morning till twelve, and from two till nine at night, and he throve accordingly—he left a good estate behind him. But I don't know what these people are; they say there are two partners of them, but there had as good be none, for they are never at home, nor in their shop: one wears a long wig and a sword, I hear, and you see him often in the Mall and at court, but very seldom in his shop, or waiting on his customers; and the other, they say, lies a-bed till eleven o'clock every day, just comes into the shop and shows himself, then stalks about to the tavern to take a whet, then to Child's coffee-house to hear the news, comes home to dinner at one, takes a long sleep in his chair after it, and about four o'clock comes into the shop for half an hour, or thereabouts, then to the tavern, where he stays till two in the morning, gets drunk, and is led home by the watch, and so lies till eleven again; and thus he walks round like the hand of a dial. And what will it all come to?—they'll certainly break, that you may be sure of; they can't hold it long.'

'This is the town's way of talking, where they see an example of it in the manner as is described; nor are the inferences unjust, any more than the description is unlike, for such certainly is the end of such management, and no shop thus neglected ever made a tradesman rich.

On the contrary, customers love to see the master's face in the shop, and to go to a shop where they are sure to find him at home. When he does not sell, or cannot take the price offered, yet the customers are not disobliged, and if they do not deal now, they may another time: if they do deal, the master generally gets a better price for his goods than a servant can, besides that he gives better content; and yet the customers always think they buy cheaper of the master too.

I seem to be talking now of the mercer or draper, as if my discourse were wholly bent and directed to them; but it is quite contrary, for it concerns every tradesman—the advice is general, and every tradesman claims a share in it; the nature of trade requires it. It is an old Anglicism, 'Such a man drives a trade;' the allusion is to a carter, that with his voice, his hands, his whip, and his constant attendance, keeps the team always going, helps himself, lifts at the wheel in every slough, doubles his application upon every difficulty, and, in a word, to complete the simile, if he is not always with his horses, either the wagon is set in a hole, or the team stands still, or, which is worst of all, the load is spoiled by the waggon overthrowing.

It is therefore no improper speech to say, such a man drives his trade; for, in short, if trade is not driven, it will not go.

Trade is like a hand-mill, it must always be turned about by the diligent hand of the master; or, if you will, like the pump-house at Amsterdam, where they put offenders in for petty matters, especially beggars; if they will work and keep pumping, they sit well, and dry and safe, and if they work very hard one hour or two, they may rest, perhaps, a quarter of an hour afterwards; but if they oversleep themselves, or grow lazy, the water comes in upon them and wets them, and they have no dry place to stand in, much less to sit down in; and, in short, if they continue obstinately idle, they must sink; so that it is nothing but *pump* or *drown*, and they may choose which they like best.

He that engages in trade, and does not resolve to work at it, is *felo de se*; it is downright murdering himself; that is to say, in his trading capacity, he murders his credit, he murders his stock, and he starves, which is as bad as murdering, his family.

Trade must not be entered into as a thing of light concern; it is called business very properly, for it is a business *for* life, and ought to be followed as one of the great businesses *of* life—I do not say the chief, but one of the great businesses of life it certainly is—trade must, I say, be worked at, not played with; he that trades in jest, will certainly break in earnest; and this is one reason indeed why so many tradesmen come to so hasty a conclusion of their affairs.

There was another old English saying to this purpose, which shows how much our old fathers were sensible of the duty of a shopkeeper: speaking of the tradesman as just opening his shop, and beginning a dialogue with it; the result of which is, that the shop replies to the tradesman thus: 'Keep me, and I will keep thee.' It is the same with driving the trade; if the shopkeeper will not keep, that is, diligently attend to his shop, the shop will not keep, that is, maintain him: and in the other sense it is harsher to him, if he will not drive his trade, the trade will drive him; that is, drive him out of the shop, drive him away.

All these old sayings have this monitory substance in them; namely, they all concur to fill a young tradesman with true notions of what he is going about; and that the undertaking of a trade is not a sport or game, in which he is to meet with diversions only, and entertainment, and not to be in the least troubled or disturbed: trade is a daily employment, and must be followed as such, with the full attention of the mind, and full attendance of the person; nothing but what are to be called the necessary duties of life are to intervene; and even these are to be limited so as not to be prejudicial to business.

And now I am speaking of the necessary things which may intervene, and which may divide the time with our business or trade, I shall state the manner in a few words, that the tradesman may neither give too much, nor take away too much, to or from any respective part of what may be called his proper employment, but keep as due a balance of his time as he should of his books or cash.

The life of man is, or should be, a measure of allotted time; as his time is measured out to him, so the measure is limited, must end, and the end of it is appointed.

The purposes for which time is given, and life bestowed, are very momentous; no time is given uselessly, and for nothing; time is no more to be unemployed, than it is to be ill employed. Three things are chiefly before us in the appointment of our time: 1. Necessaries of nature. 2. Duties of religion, or things relating to a future life. 3. Duties of the present life, namely, business and calling.

I. Necessities of nature, such as eating and drinking; rest, or sleep; and in case of disease, a recess from business; all which have two limitations on them, and no more; namely, that they be

1. Referred to their proper seasons.

2. Used with moderation.

Both these might give me subject to write many letters upon; but I study brevity, and desire rather to hint than dwell upon things which are serious and grave, because I would not tire you.

II. Duties of religion: these may be called necessities too in their kind, and that of the sublimest nature; and they ought not to be thrust at all out of their place, and yet they ought to be kept in their place too.

III. Duties of life, that is to say, business, or employment, or calling, which are divided into three kinds:

1. Labour, or servitude.

2. Employment.

3. Trade.

By labour, I mean the poor manualist, whom we properly call the labouring man, who works for himself indeed in one respect, but sometimes serves and works for wages, as a servant, or workman.

By employment, I mean men in business, which yet is not properly called trade, such as lawyers, physicians, surgeons, scriveners, clerks, secretaries, and such like: and

By trade I mean merchants and inland-traders, such as are already described in the introduction to this work.

To speak of time, it is divided among these; even in them all there is a just equality of circumstances to be preserved, and as diligence is required in one, and necessity to be obeyed in another, so duty is to be observed in the third; and yet all these with such a due regard to one another, as that one duty may not jostle out another; and every thing going on with an equality and just regard to the nature of the thing, the tradesman may go on with a glad heart and a quiet conscience.

This article is very nice, as I intend to speak to it; and it is a dangerous thing indeed to speak to, lest young tradesmen, treading on the brink of duty on one side, and duty on the other side, should pretend to neglect their duty to heaven, on pretence that I say they must not neglect their shops. But let them do me justice, and they will do themselves no injury; nor do I fear that my arguing on this point should give them any just cause to go wrong; if they will go wrong, and plead my argument for their excuse, it must be by their abusing my directions, and taking them in pieces, misplacing the words, and disjointing the sense, and by the same method they may make blasphemy of the Scripture.

The duties of life, I say, must not interfere with one another, must not jostle one another out of the place, or so break in as to be prejudicial to one another. It is certainly the duty of every Christian to worship God, to pay his homage morning and evening to his Maker, and at all other proper seasons to behave as becomes a sincere worshipper of God; nor must any avocation, either of business or nature, however necessary, interfere with this duty, either in public or in private. This is plainly asserting the necessity of the duty, so no man can pretend to evade that.

But the duties of nature and religion also have such particular seasons, and those seasons so proper to themselves, and so stated, as not to break in or trench upon one another, that we are really without excuse, if we let any one be pleaded for the neglect of the other. Food, sleep, rest, and the necessities of nature, are either reserved for the night, which is appointed for man to rest, or take up so little room in the day, that they can never be pleaded in bar of either religion or employment.

He, indeed, who will sleep when he should work, and perhaps drink when he should sleep, turns nature bottom upwards, inverts the appointment of providence, and must account to himself, and afterwards to a higher judge, for the neglect.

The devil—if it be the devil that tempts, for I would not wrong Satan himself—plays our duties often one against another; and to bring us, if possible, into confusion in our conduct, subtly throws religion out of its place, to put it in our way, and to urge us to a breach of what we ought to do: besides this subtle tempter—for, as above, I won't charge it all upon the devil—we have a great hand in it ourselves; but let it be who it will, I say, this subtle tempter hurries the well-meaning tradesman to act in all manner of irregularity, that he may confound religion and business, and in the end may destroy both.

When the tradesman well inclined rises early in the morning, and is moved, as in duty to his Maker he ought, to pay his morning vows to him either in his closet, or at the church, where he hears the six o'clock bell ring to call his neighbours to the same duty—then the secret hint comes across his happy intention, that he must go to such or such a place, that he may be back time enough for such other business as has been appointed over-night, and both perhaps may be both lawful and necessary; so his diligence oppresses his religion, and away he runs to transact his business, and neglects his morning sacrifice to his Maker.

On the other hand, and at another time, being in his shop, or his counting-house, or warehouse, a vast throng of business upon his hands, and the world in his head, when it is highly his duty to attend it, and shall be to his prejudice to absent himself—then the same deceiver presses him earnestly to go to his closet, or to the church to prayers, during which time his customer goes to another place, the neighbours miss him in his shop, his business is lost, his reputation suffers; and by this turned into a practice, the man may say his prayers so long and so unseasonably till he is undone, and not a creditor he has (I may give it him from experience) will use him the better, or show him the more favour, when a commission of bankrupt comes out against him.

Thus, I knew once a zealous, pious, religious tradesman, who would almost shut up his shop every day about nine or ten o'clock to call all his family together to prayers; and yet he was no presbyterian, I assure you; I say, he would almost shut up his shop, for he would suffer none of his servants to be absent from his family worship.

This man had certainly been right, had he made all his family get up by six o'clock in the morning, and called them to prayers before he had opened his shop; but instead of that, he first suffered sleep to interfere with religion, and lying a-bed to postpone and jostle out his prayers—and then, to make God Almighty amends upon himself, wounds his family by making his prayers interfere with his trade, and shuts his customers out of his shop; the end of which was, the poor good man deceived himself, and lost his business.

Another tradesman, whom I knew personally well, was raised in the morning very early, by the outcries of his wife, to go and fetch a midwife. It was necessary, in his way, to go by a church, where there was always, on that day of the week, a morning sermon early, for the supplying the devotion of such early Christians as he; so the honest man, seeing the door open, steps in, and seeing the minister just gone up into the pulpit, sits down, joins in the prayers, hears the sermon, and goes very gravely home again; in short, his earnestness in the worship, and attention to what he had heard, quite put the errand he was sent about out of his head; and the poor woman in travail, after having waited long for the return of her husband with the midwife, was obliged (having run an extreme hazard by depending on his expedition) to dispatch other messengers, who fetched the midwife, and she was come, and the work over, long before the sermon was done, or that any body heard of the husband: at last, he was met coming gravely home from the church, when being upbraided with his negligence, in a dreadful surprise he struck his hands together, and cried out, 'How is my wife? I profess I forgot it!'

What shall we say now to this ill-timed devotion, and who must tempt the poor man to this neglect? Certainly, had he gone for the midwife, it had been much more his duty, than to go to hear a sermon at that time.

I knew also another tradesman, who was such a sermon-hunter, and, as there are lectures and sermons preached in London, either in the churches or meeting-houses, almost every day in the week, used so assiduously to hunt out these occasions, that whether it was in a church or meeting-house, or both, he was always abroad to hear a sermon, at least once every day, and sometimes more; and the consequence was, that the man lost his trade, his shop was entirely neglected, the time which was proper for him to apply to his business was misapplied, his trade fell off, and the man broke.

Now it is true, and I ought to take notice of it also, that, though these things happen, and may wrong a tradesman, yet it is oftener, ten times for once, that tradesmen neglect their shop and business to follow the track of their vices and extravagence—some by taverns, others to the gaming-houses, others to balls and masquerades, plays, harlequins, and operas, very few by too much religion.

But my inference is still sound, and the more effectually so as to that part; for if our business and trades are not to be neglected, no, not for the extraordinary excursions of religion, and religious duties, much less are they to be neglected for vices and extravagances.

This is an age of gallantry and gaiety, and never was the city transposed to the court as it is now; the play-houses and balls are now filled with citizens and young tradesmen, instead of gentlemen and families of distinction; the shopkeepers wear a differing garb now, and are seen with their long wigs and swords, rather than with aprons on, as was formerly the figure they made.

But what is the difference in the consequences? You did not see in those days acts of grace for the relief of insolvent debtors almost every session of parliament, and yet the jails filled with insolvents before the next year, though ten or twelve thousand have been released at a time by those acts.

Nor did you hear of so many commissions of bankrupt every week in the Gazette, as is now the case; in a word, whether you take the lower sort of tradesman, or the higher, where there were twenty that failed in those days, I believe I speak within compass if I say that five hundred turn insolvent now; it is, as I said above, an age of pleasure, and as the wise man said long ago, 'He that loves pleasure shall be a poor man'— so it is now; it is an age of drunkenness and extravagance, and thousands ruin themselves by that; it is an age of luxurious and expensive living, and thousands more undo themselves by that; but, among all our vices, nothing ruins a tradesman so effectually as the neglect of his business: it is true, all those things prompt men to neglect their business, but the more seasonable is the advice; either enter upon no trade, undertake no business, or, having undertaken it, pursue it diligently: drive your trade, that the world may not drive you out of trade, and ruin and undo you. Without diligence a man can never thoroughly understand his business and how should a man thrive, when he does not perfectly know what he is doing, or how to do it? Application to his trade teaches him how to carry it on, as much as his going apprentice taught him how to set it up. Certainly, that man shall never improve in his trading knowledge, that does not know his business, or how to carry it on: the diligent tradesman is always the knowing and complete tradesman.

Now, in order to have a man apply heartily, and pursue earnestly, the business he is engaged in, there is yet another thing necessary, namely, that he should delight in it: to follow a trade, and not to love and delight in it, is a slavery, a bondage, not a business: the shop is a bridewell, and the warehouse a house of correction to the tradesman, if he does not delight in his trade. While he is bound, as we say, to keep his shop, he is like the galley-slave chained down to the oar; he tugs and labours indeed, and exerts the utmost of his strength, for fear of the strapado, and because he is obliged to do it; but when he is on shore, and is out from the bank, he abhors the labour, and hates to come to it again.

To delight in business is making business pleasant and agreeable; and such a tradesman cannot but be diligent in it, which, according to

Solomon, makes him certainly rich, and in time raises him above the world and able to instruct and encourage those who come after him.

CHAPTER VI
OVER-TRADING

It is an observation, indeed, of my own, but I believe it will hold true almost in all the chief trading towns in England, that there are more tradesmen undone by having too much trade, than for want of trade. Over-trading is among tradesmen as over-lifting is among strong men: such people, vain of the strengh, and their pride prompting them to put it to the utmost trial, at last lift at something too heavy for them, over-strain their sinews, break some of nature's bands, and are cripples ever after.

I take over-trading to be to a shopkeeper as ambition is to a prince. The late king of France, the great king Louis, ambition led him to invade the dominions of his neighbours; and while upon the empire here, or the states-general there, or the Spanish Netherlands on another quarter, he was an over-match for every one, and, in their single capacity, he gained from them all; but at last pride made him think himself a match for them all together, and he entered into a declared war against the emperor and the empire, the kings of Spain and Great Britain, and the states of Holland, all at once. And what was the consequence? They reduced him to the utmost distress, he lost all his conquests, was obliged, by a dishonourable peace, to quit what he had got by encroachment, to demolish his invincible towns, such as Pignerol, Dunkirk, &c., the two strongest fortresses in Europe; and, in a word, like a bankrupt monarch, he may, in many cases, be said to have died a beggar.

Thus the strong man in the fable, who by main strength used to rive a tree, undertook one at last which was too strong for him, and it closed upon his fingers, and held him till the wild beasts came and devoured him. Though the story is a fable, the moral is good to my present purpose, and is not at all above my subject; I mean that of a tradesman, who should be warned against over-trading, as earnestly, and with as much passion, as I would warn a dealer in gunpowder to be wary of fire, or a distiller or rectifier of spirits to moderate his furnace, lest the heads of his stills fly off, and he should be scalded to death.

For a young tradesman to over-trade himself, is like a young swimmer going out of his depth, when, if help does not come immediately, it is a thousand to one but he sinks, and is drowned. All rash adventures are condemned by the prudent part of mankind; but it is as hard to restrain youth in trade, as it is in any other thing, where the advantage stands in view, and the danger out of sight; the profits of trade are baits to the avaricious shopkeeper, and he is forward to reckon them up to himself, but does not perhaps cast up the difficulty which there may be to compass it, or the unhappy consequences of a miscarriage.

For want of this consideration, the tradesman oftentimes drowns, as I may call it, even within his depth—that is, he sinks when he has really the substance at bottom to keep him up—and this is all owing to an adventurous bold spirit in trade, joined with too great a gust of gain. Avarice is the ruin of many people besides tradesmen; and I might give the late South Sea calamity for an example in which the longest heads were most overreached, not so much by the wit or cunning of those they had to deal with as by the secret promptings of their own avarice; wherein they abundantly verified an old proverbial speech or saying, namely, 'All covet, all lose;' so it was there indeed, and the cunningest, wisest, sharpest, men lost the most money.

There are two things which may be properly called over-trading, in a young beginner; and by both which tradesmen are often overthrown.

I. Trading beyond their stock.

2. Giving too large credit.

A tradesman ought to consider and measure well the extent of his own strengh; his stock of money, and credit, is properly his beginning; for credit is a stock as well as money. He that takes too much credit is really in as much danger as he that gives too much credit; and the danger lies particularly in this, if the tradesman over-buys himself, that is, buys faster than he can sell, buying upon credit, the payments perhaps become due too soon for him; the goods not being sold, he must answer the bills upon the strength of his proper stock—that is, pay for them out of his own cash; if that should not hold out, he is obliged to put off his bills after they are due, or suffer the impertinence of being dunned by the creditor, and perhaps by servants and apprentices, and that with the usual indecencies of such kind of people.

This impairs his credit, and if he comes to deal with the same merchant, or clothier, or other tradesman again, he is treated like one that is but an indifferent paymaster; and though they may give him credit as before, yet depending that if he bargains for six months, he will take eight or nine in the payment, they consider it in the price, and use him accordingly; and this impairs his gain, so that loss of credit is indeed loss of money, and this weakens him both ways.

A tradesman, therefore, especially at his beginning, ought to be very wary of taking too much credit; he had much better slip the occasion of buying now and then a bargain to his advantage, for that is usually the temptation, than buying a greater quantity of goods than he can pay for, run into debt, and be insulted, and at last ruined. Merchants, and wholesale dealers, to put off their goods, are very apt to prompt young shopkeepers and young tradesmen to buy great quantities of goods, and take large credit at first; but it is a snare that many a young beginner has fallen into, and been ruined in the very bud; for if the young beginner does not find a vent for the quantity, he is undone; for at the time of payment the merchant expects his money, whether the goods are sold or not; and if he cannot pay, he is gone at once.

The tradesman that buys warily, always pays surely, and every young beginner ought to buy cautiously; if he has money to pay, he need never fear goods to be had; the merchants' warehouses are always open, and he may supply himself upon all occasions, as he wants, and as his customers call.

It may pass for a kind of an objection here, that there are some goods which a tradesman may deal in, which are to be bought at such and such markets only, and at such and such fairs only, that is to say, are chiefly bought there; as the cheesemongers buy their stocks of cheese and of butter, the cheese at several fairs in Warwickshire, as at Atherston fair in particular, or at fair in Gloucestershire, and at Sturbridge fair, near Cambridge; and their butter at Ipswich fair, in Suffolk; and so of many other things; but the answer is plain: those things which are generally bought thus, are ready money goods, and the tradesman has a sure rule for buying, namely, his cash. But as I am speaking of taking credit, so I must be necessarily supposed to speak of such goods as are bought upon credit, as the linen-draper buys of the Hamburgh and Dutch merchants, the woollen-draper of the Blackwell-hall men, the haberdasher of the thread merchants, the mercer of the weavers and Italian merchants, the silk-man of the Turkey merchants, and the like; here they are under no necessity of running deep into debt, but may buy sparingly, and recruit again as they sell off.

I know some tradesmen are very fond of seeing their shops well-stocked, and their warehouses full of goods, and this is a snare to them, and brings them to buy in more goods than they want; but this is a great error, either in their judgment or their vanity; for, except in retailers' shops, and that in some trades where they must have a great choice of goods, or else may want a trade, otherwise a well-experienced tradesman had rather see his warehouse too empty than too full: if it be too empty, he can fill it when he pleases, if his credit be good, or his cash strong; but a thronged warehouse is a sign of a want of customers, and of a bad market; whereas, an empty warehouse is a sign of a nimble demand.[14]

Let no young tradesman value himself upon having a very great throng of goods in hand, having just a necessary supply to produce a choice of new and fashionable goods—nay, though he be a mercer, for they are the most under the necessity of a large stock of goods; but I say, supposing even the mercer to have a tolerable show and choice of fashionable goods, that gives his shop a reputation, he derives no credit at all from a throng of old shopkeepers, as they call them, namely, out-of-fashion things: but in other trades it is much more a needful caution; a few goods, and a quick sale, is the beauty of a tradesman's warehouse, or shop either; and it is his wisdom to keep himself in that posture that his payments may come in on his front as fast as they go out in his rear; that he may be able to answer the demands of his merchants or dealers, and, if possible, let no man come twice for his money.

The reason of this is plain, and leads me back to where I began; credit is stock, and, if well supported, is as good as a stock, and will be as durable. A tradesman whose credit is good, untouched, unspotted, and who, as above, has maintained it with care, shall in many cases buy his goods as cheap at three or four months' time of payment, as another man shall with ready money—I say in some cases, and in goods which are ordinarily sold for time, as all our manufactures, the bay trade excepted, generally are.

---

[14] The keeping of a half empty shop will not suit the necessities of trade in modern times. Instead of following the advice of Defoe, therefore, the young tradesman is recommended to keep a sufficient stock of every kind of goods in which he professes to deal. A shopkeeper can hardly commit a greater blunder than allow himself to *be out* of any article of his trade. One of his chief duties ought to consist in keeping up a *fresh stock* of every article which there is a chance of being sought for, and, while avoiding the imprudence of keeping too large a stock of goods—which comes nearest to Defoe's meaning—it is certain that, by having on hand an abundant choice, the shop gains a name, and has the best chance of securing a concourse of customers.

He, then, that keeps his credit unshaken, has a double stock—I mean, it is an addition to his real stock, and often superior to it: nay, I have known several considerable tradesmen in this city who have traded with great success, and to a very considerable degree, and yet have not had at bottom one shilling real stock; but by the strength of their reputation, being sober and diligent, and having with care preserved the character of honest men, and the credit of their business, by cautious dealing and punctual payments, they have gone on till the gain of their trade has effectually established them, and they have raised estates out of nothing.

But to return to the dark side, namely, over-trading; the second danger is the giving too much credit. He that takes credit may give credit, but he must be exceedingly watchful; for it is the most dangerous state of life that a tradesman can live in, for he is in as much jeopardy as a seaman upon a lee-shore.

If the people he trusts fail, or fail but of a punctual compliance with him, he can never support his own credit, unless by the caution I am now giving; that is, to be very sure not to give so much credit as he takes.

By the word *so much*, I must be understood thus—either he must sell for shorter time than he takes, or in less quantity; the last is the safest, namely, that he should be sure not to trust out so much as he is trusted with. If he has a real stock, indeed, besides the credit he takes, that, indeed, makes the case differ; and a man that can pay his own debts, whether other people pay him or no, that man is out of the question—he is past danger, and cannot be hurt; but if he trusts beyond the extent of his stock and credit, even *he* may be overthrown too.

There were many sad examples of this in the time of the late war,[15] and in the days when the public credit was in a more precarious condition that it has been since—I say, sad examples, namely, when tradesmen in flourishing circumstances, and who had indeed good estates at bottom, and were in full credit themselves, trusted the public with too great sums; which, not coming in at the time expected, either by the deficiency of the funds given by parliament, and the parliament themselves not soon making good those deficiencies, or by other disasters of those times; I say, their money not coming in to answer their demands, they were ruined, at least their credit wounded, and

---

[15] The war of the Spanish succession, concluded by the treaty of Utrecht, 1713.

some quite undone, who yet, had they been paid, could have paid all their own debts, and had good sums of money left.

Others, who had ability to afford it, were obliged to sell their tallies and orders at forty or fifty per cent. loss; from whence proceeded that black trade of buying and selling navy and victualling bills and transport debts, by which the brokers and usurers got estates, and many thousands of tradesmen were brought to nothing; even those that stood it, lost great sums of money by selling their tallies: but credit cannot be bought too dear; and the throwing away one half to save the other, was much better than sinking under the burden; like sailors in a storm, who, to lighten the ship wallowing in the trough of the sea, will throw the choicest goods overboard, even to half the cargo, in order to keep the ship above water, and save their lives.

These were terrible examples of over-trading indeed; the men were tempted by the high price which the government gave for their goods, and which they were obliged to give, because of the badness of the public credit at that time; but this was not sufficient to make good the loss sustained in the sale of the tallies, so that even they that sold and were able to stand without ruin, were yet great sufferers, and had enough to do to keep up their credit.

This was the effect of giving over-much credit; for though it was the government itself which they trusted, yet neither could the government itself keep up the sinking credit of those whom it was indebted to; and, indeed, how should it, when it was not able to support its own credit? But that by the way. I return to the young tradesman, whom we are now speaking about.

It is his greatest prudence, therefore, after he has considered his own fund, and the stock he has to rest upon—I say, his next business is to take care of his credit, and, next to limiting his buying-liberty, let him be sure to limit his selling. Could the tradesman buy all upon credit, and sell all for ready money, he might turn usurer, and put his own stock out to interest, or buy land with it, for he would have no occasion for one shilling of it; but since that is not expected, nor can be done, it is his business to act with prudence in both parts—I mean of taking and giving credit—and the best rule to be given him for it is, never to give so much credit as he takes, by at least one-third part.

By giving credit, I do not mean, that even all the goods which he buys upon credit, may not be sold upon credit; perhaps they are goods which are usually sold so, and no otherwise; but the alternative is before him thus—either he must not give so much credit in quantity of goods, or not so long credit in relation to time—for example:

Suppose the young tradesman buys ten thousand pounds' value of goods on credit, and this ten thousand pounds are sold for eleven thousand pounds likewise on credit; if the time given be the same, the man is in a state of apparent destruction, and it is a hundred to one but he is blown up: perhaps he owes the ten thousand pounds to twenty men, perhaps the eleven thousand pounds is owing to him by two hundred men—it is scarce possible that these two hundred petty customers of his, should all so punctually comply with their payments as to enable him to comply with his; and if two or three thousand pounds fall short, the poor tradesman, unless he has a fund to support the deficiency, must be undone.

But if the man had bought ten thousand pounds at six or eight months' credit, and had sold them all again as above to his two hundred customers, at three months' and four months' credit, then it might be supposed all, or the greatest part of them, would have paid time enough to make his payments good; if not, all would be lost still.

But, on the other hand, suppose he had sold but three thousand pounds' worth of the ten for ready money, and had sold the rest for six months' credit, it might be supposed that the three thousand pounds in cash, and what else the two hundred debtors might pay in time, might stop the months of the tradesman's creditors till the difference might be made good.

So easy a thing is it for a tradesman to lose his credit in trade, and so hard is it, once upon such a blow, to retrieve it again. What need, then, is there for the tradesman to guard himself against running too far into debt, or letting other people run too far into debt to him: for if they do not pay him, he cannot pay others, and the next thing is a commission of bankrupt, and so the tradesman may be undone, though he has eleven thousand pounds to pay ten with?

It is true, it is not possible in a country where there is such an infinite extent of trade as we see managed in this kingdom, that either on one hand or another it can be carried on, without a reciprocal credit both taken and given; but it is so nice an article, that I am of opinion as many tradesmen break with giving too much credit, as break with taking it. The danger, indeed, is mutual, and very great. Whatever, then, the young tradesman omits, let him guard against both his giving and taking too much credit.

But there are divers ways of over-trading, besides this of taking and giving too much credit; and one of these is the running out into projects and heavy undertakings, either out of the common road which the tradesman is already engaged in, or grasping at too many undertakings at once, and having, as it is vulgarly expressed, too many irons in the fire at a time; in both which cases the tradesman is often wounded, and that deeply, sometimes too deep to recover.

The consequences of those adventures are generally such as these: first, that they stock-starve the tradesman, and impoverish him in his ordinary business, which is the main support of his family; they lessen his strength, and while his trade is not lessened, yet his stock is lessened; and as they very rarely add to his credit, so, if they lessen the man's stock, they weaken him in the main, and he must at last faint under it.

Secondly, as they lessen his stock, so they draw from it in the most sensible part—they wound him in the tenderest and most nervous part, for they always draw away his ready money; and what follows? The money, which was before the sinews of his business, the life of his trade, maintained his shop, and kept up his credit in the full extent of it, being drawn off, like the blood let out of the veins, his trade languishes, his credit, by degrees, flags and goes off, and the tradesman falls under the weight.

Thus I have seen many a flourishing tradesman sensibly decay; his credit has first a little suffered, then for want of that credit trade has declined—that is to say, he has been obliged to trade for less and less, till at last he is wasted and reduced: if he has been wise enough and wary enough to draw out betimes, and avoid breaking, he has yet come out of trade, like an old invalid soldier out of the wars, maimed, bruised, sick, reduced, and fitter for an hospital than a shop—such miserable havoc has launching out into projects and remote undertakings made among tradesmen.

But the safe tradesman is he, that avoiding all such remote excursions, keeps close within the verge of his own affairs, minds his shop or warehouse, and confining himself to what belongs to him there, goes on in the road of his business without launching into unknown oceans; and content with the gain of his own trade, is neither led by ambition or avarice, and neither covets to be greater nor richer by such uncertain and hazardous attempts.

CHAPTER VII
OF THE TRADESMAN IN DISTRESS, AND BECOMING BANKRUPT

In former times it was a dismal and calamitous thing for a tradesman to break. Where it befell a family, it put all into confusion and distraction; the man, in the utmost terror, fright, and distress, ran away with what goods he could get off, as if the house were on fire, to get into the Friars[16] or the Mint; the family fled, one one way, and one another, like people in desperation; the wife to her father and mother, if she had any, and the children, some to one relation, some to another. A statute (so they vulgarly call a commission of bankrupt) came and swept away all, and oftentimes consumed it too, and left little or nothing, either to pay the creditors or relieve the bankrupt. This made the bankrupt desperate, and made him fly to those places of shelter with his goods, where, hardened by the cruelty of the creditors, he chose to spend all the effects which should have paid the creditors, and at last perished in misery.

But now the case is altered; men make so little of breaking, that many times the family scarce removes for it. A commission of bankrupt is so familiar a thing, that the debtor oftentimes causes it to be taken out in his favour, that he may sooner be effectually delivered from all his creditors at once, the law obliging him only to give a full account of himself upon oath to the commissioners, who, when they see his integrity, may effectually deliver him from all further molestation, give him a part even of the creditors' estate; and so he may push into the world again, and try whether he cannot retrieve his fortunes by a better management, or with better success for the future.

Some have said, this law is too favourable to the bankrupt; that it makes tradesmen careless; that they value not breaking at all, but run on at all hazards, venturing without forecast and without consideration, knowing they may come off again so cheap and so easy, if they miscarry. But though I cannot enter here into a long debate upon that subject, yet I may have room to say, that I differ from those people very much; for, though the terror of the commission is in some measure abated, as indeed it ought to be, because it was before exorbitant and

---

[16] Whitefriars, in the neighbourhood of the Temple, London. This and the Mint were sanctuaries for debtors.

unreasonable, yet the terror of ruining a man's family, sinking his fortunes, blasting his credit, and throwing him out of business, and into the worst of disgrace that a tradesman can fall into, this is not taken away, or abated at all; and this, to an honest trading man, is as bad as all the rest ever was or could be.

Nor can a man be supposed, in the rupture of his affairs, to receive any comfort, or to see through his disasters into the little relief which he may, and at the same time cannot be sure he shall, receive, at the end of his troubles, from the mercy of the commission.

These are poor things, and very trifling for a tradesman to entertain thoughts of a breach from, especially with any prospect of satisfaction; nor can any tradesman with the least shadow of principle entertain any thought of breaking, but with the utmost aversion, and even abhorrence; for the circumstances of it are attended with so many mortifications, and so many shocking things, contrary to all the views and expectations that a tradesman can begin the world with, that he cannot think of it, but as we do of the grave, with a chillness upon the blood, and a tremor in the spirits. Breaking is the death of a tradesman; he is mortally stabbed, or, as we may say, shot through the head, in his trading capacity; his shop is shut up, as it is when a man is buried; his credit, the life and blood of his trade, is stagnated; and his attendance, which was the pulse of his business, is stopped, and beats no more; in a word, his fame, and even name, as to trade is buried, and the commissioners, that act upon him, and all their proceedings, are but like the executors of the defunct, dividing the ruins of his fortune, and at last, his certificate is a kind of performing the obsequies for the dead, and praying him out of purgatory.

Did ever tradesman set up on purpose to break? Did ever a man build himself a house on purpose to have it burnt down? I can by no means grant that any tradesman, at least in his senses, can entertain the least satisfaction in his trading, or abate any thing of his diligence in trade, from the easiness of breaking, or the abated severities of the bankrupt act.

I could argue it from the nature of the act itself, which, indeed, was made, and is effectual, chiefly for the relief of creditors, not debtors; to secure the bankrupt's effects for the use of those to whom it of right belongs, and to prevent the extravagant expenses of the commission, which before were such as often devoured all, ruining both the bankrupt and his creditors too. This the present law has providently put a stop to; and the creditors now are secure in this point, that what is to be had, what the poor tradesman has left, they are sure to have preserved for, and divided among them, which, indeed, before they were not. The case is so well known, and so recent in every tradesman's memory, that I need not take up any more of your time about it.

As to the encouragements in the act for the bankrupt, they are only these—namely, that, upon his honest and faithful surrender of his affairs, he shall be set at liberty; and if they see cause, they, the creditors, may give him back a small gratification for his discovering his effects, and assisting to the recovery of them; and all this, which amounts to very little, is upon his being, as I have said, entirely honest, and having run through all possible examinations and purgations, and that it is at the peril of his life if he prevaricates.

Are these encouragements to tradesmen to be negligent and careless of the event of things? Will any man in his wits fail in his trade, break his credit, and shut up his shop, for these prospects? Or will he comfort himself in case he is forced to fail—I say, will he comfort himself with these little benefits, and make the matter easy to himself on that account? He must have a very mean spirit that can do this, and must act upon very mean principles in life, who can fall with satisfaction, on purpose to rise no higher than this; it is like a man going to bed on purpose to rise naked, pleasing himself with the thoughts that, though he shall have no clothes to put on, yet he shall have the liberty to get out of bed and shift for himself.

On these accounts, and some others, too long to mention here, I think it is out of doubt, that the easiness of the proceedings on commissions of bankrupt can be no encouragement to any tradesman to break, or so much as to entertain the thoughts of it, with less horror and aversion than he would have done before this law was made.

But I must come now to speak of the tradesman in his real state of mortification, and under the inevitable necessity of a blow upon his affairs. He has had losses in his business, such as are too heavy for his stock to support; he has, perhaps, launched out in trade beyond his reach: either he has so many bad debts, that he cannot find by his books he has enough left to pay his creditors, or his debts lie out of his reach, and he cannot get them in, which in one respect is as bad; he has more bills running against him than he knows how to pay, and creditors dunning him, whom it is hard for him to comply with; and this, by degrees, sinks his credit.

Now, could the poor unhappy tradesman take good advice, now would be his time to prevent his utter ruin, and let his case be better or worse, his way is clear.

If it be only that he has overshot himself in trade, taken too much credit, and is loaded with goods; or given too much credit, and cannot get his debts in; but that, upon casting up his books, he finds his circumstances good at bottom, though his credit has suffered by his effects being out of his hands; let him endeavour to retrench, let him check his career in trade—immediately take some extraordinary measures to get in his debts, or some extraordinary measures, if he can, to raise money in the meantime, till those debts come in, that he may stop the crowd of present demands. If this will not do, let him treat with some of his principal creditors, showing them a true and faithful state of his affairs, and giving them the best assurances he can of payment, that they may be easy with him till he can get in his debts; and then, with the utmost care, draw in his trade within the due compass of his stock, and be sure never to run out again farther than he is able to answer, let the prospect of advantage be what it will; and by this method he may perhaps recover his credit again, at least he may prevent his ruin. But this is always supposing the man has a firm bottom, that he is sound in the main, and that his stock is at least sufficient to pay all his debts.

But the difficulty which I am proposing to speak of, is when the poor tradesman, distressed as above in point of credit, looking into his affairs, finds that his stock is diminished, or perhaps entirely sunk—that, in short, he has such losses and such disappointments in his business, that he is not sound at bottom; that he has run too far, and that his own stock being wasted or sunk, he has not really sufficient to pay his debts; what is this man's business?—and what course shall he take?

I know the ordinary course with such tradesmen is this:—'It is true,' says the poor man, 'I am running down, and I have lost so much in such a place, and so much by such a chapman that broke, and, in short, so much, that I am worse than nothing; but come, I have such a thing before me, or I have undertaken such a project, or I have such an adventure abroad, if it suceeds, I may recover again; I'll try my utmost; I'll never drown while I can swim; I'll never fall while I can stand; who knows but I may get over it?' In a word, the poor man is loth to come to the fatal day; loth to have his name in the Gazette, and see his wife and family turned out of doors, and the like; who can blame him? or who is not, in the like case, apt to take the like measures?—for it is natural to us all to put the evil day far from us, at least to put it as far off as we can. Though the criminal believes he shall be executed at last, yet he accepts of every reprieve, as it puts him within the possibility of an escape, and that as long as there is life there is hope; but at last the dead warrant comes down, then he sees death unavoidable, and gives himself up to despair.

Indeed, the malefactor was in the right to accept, as I say, of every reprieve, but it is quite otherwise in the tradesman's case; and if I may give him a rule, safe, and in its end comfortable, in proportion to his circumstances, but, to be sure, out of question, just, honest, and prudent, it is this:—

When he perceives his case as above, and knows that if his new adventures or projects should fail, he cannot by any means stand or support himself, I not only give it as my advice to all tradesmen, as their interest, but insist upon it, as they are honest men, they should break, that is, stop in time: fear not to do that which necessity obliges you to do; but, above all, fear not to do that early, which, if omitted, necessity will oblige you to do late.

First, let me argue upon the honesty of it, and next upon the prudence of it. Certainly, honesty obliges every man, when he sees that his stock is gone, that he is below the level, and eating into the estate of other men, to put a stop to it, and to do it in time, while something is left. It has been a fault, without doubt, to break in upon other men's estates at all; but perhaps a plea may be made that it was ignorantly done, and they did not think they were run so far as to be worse than nothing; or some sudden disaster may have occasioned it, which they did not expect, and, it may be, could not foresee: both which may indeed happen to a tradesman, though the former can hardly happen without his fault, because he ought to be always acquainting himself with his books, stating his expenses and his profits, and casting things up frequently, at least in his head, so as always to know whether he goes backward or forward. The latter, namely, sudden disaster, may happen so to any tradesman as that he may be undone, and it may not be his fault; for ruin sometimes falls as suddenly as unavoidably upon a tradesman, though there are but very few incidents of that kind which may not be accounted for in such a manner as to charge it upon his prudence.

Some cases may indeed happen, some disasters may befall a tradesman, which it was not possible he should foresee, as fire, floods of water, thieves, and many such—and in those cases the disaster is visible, the plea is open, every body allows it, the man can have no blame. A prodigious tide from the sea, joined with a great fresh or flood in the river Dee, destroyed the new wharf below the Roodee at West Chester, and tore down the merchants' warehouses there, and drove away not only all the goods, but even the buildings and altogether, into the sea. Now, if a poor shopkeeper in Chester had a large parcel of goods lying there, perhaps newly landed in order to be brought up to the city, but were all swept away, if, I say, the poor tradesman were ruined by the loss of those goods on that occasion, the creditors would see reason in it that they should every one take a share in the loss; the tradesman was not to blame.

Likewise in the distress of the late fire which began in Thames Street, near Bear Quay, a grocer might have had a quantity of goods in a warehouse thereabouts, or his shop might be there, and the goods perhaps might be sugars, or currants, or tobacco, or any other goods in his way, which could not be easily removed; this fire was a surprise, it was a blast of powder, it was at noonday, when no person coud foresee it. The man may have been undone and be in no fault himself, one way or other; no man can reasonably say to him, why did you keep so many goods upon your hands, or in such a place? for it was his proper business both to have a stock of goods, and to have them in such a place; every thing was in the right position, and in the order which the nature of his trade required.

On the other hand, if it was the breaking of a particular chapman, or an adventure by sea, the creditors would perhaps reflect on his prudence; why should any man trust a single chapman so much, or adventure so much in one single bottom, and uninsured, as that the loss of it would be his undoing?

But there are other cases, however, which may happen to a tradesman, and by which he may be at once reduced below his proper stock, and have nothing left to trade on but his credit, that is to say, the estates of his creditors. In such a case, I question whether it can be honest for any man to continue trading; for, first, it is making his creditors run an unjust hazard, without their consent; indeed, if he discovers his condition to one or two of them, who are men of capital stocks, and will support him, they giving him leave to pay others off, and go on at their risks, that alters the case; or if he has a ready money trade, that will apparently raise him again, and he runs no more hazards, but is sure he shall at least run out no farther; in these two cases, and I do not know another, he may with honesty continue.

On the contrary, when he sees himself evidently running out, and declining, and has only a shift here and a shift there, to lay hold on, as sinking men generally do; and knows, that unless something extraordinary happen, which, perhaps, also is not probable, he must fall, for such a man to go on, and trade in the ordinary way, notwithstanding losses, and hazards—in such a case, I affirm, he cannot act the honest man, he cannot go on with justice to his creditors, or his family; he ought to call his creditors together, lay his circumstances honestly before them, and pay as far as it will go. If his creditors will do any thing generously for him, to enable him to go on again, well and good, but he cannot honestly oblige them to run the risk of his unfortunate progress, and to venture their estates on his bottom, after his bottom is really nothing at all but their money.

But I pass from the honesty to the prudence of it—from what regards his creditors, to what regards himself—and I affirm, nothing can be more imprudent and impolite, as it regards himself and his family, than to go on after he sees his circumstances irrecoverable. If he has any consideration for himself, or his future happiness, he will stop in time, and not be afraid of meeting the mischief which he sees follows too fast for him to escape; be not so afraid of breaking, as not to break till necessity forces you, and that you have nothing left. In a word, I speak it to every declining tradesman, if you love yourself, your family, or your reputation, and would ever hope to look the world in the face again, *break* in time.

By breaking in time you will first obtain the character of an honest, though unfortunate man; it is owing to the contrary course, which is indeed the ordinary practice of tradesmen, namely, not to break till they run the bottom quite out, and have little or nothing left to pay; I say, it is owing to this, that some people think all men that break are knaves. The censure, it is true, is unjust, but the cause is owing to the indiscretion, to call it no worse, of the poor tradesmen, who putting the mischief as far from them as they can, trade on to the last gasp, till a throng of creditors coming on them together, or being arrested, and not able to get bail, or by some such public blow to their credit, they are brought to a stop or breach of course, like a man fighting to the last gasp who is knocked down, and laid on the ground, and then his resistance is at an end; for indeed a tradesman pushing on under irresistable misfortunes is but fighting with the world to the last drop, and with such unequal odds, that like the soldier surrounded with enemies, he must be killed; so the debtor must sink, it cannot be prevented.

It is true, also, the man that thus struggles to the last, brings upon him an universal reproach, and a censure, that is not only unavoidable, but just, which is worse; but when a man breaks in time, he may hold up his face to his creditors, and tell them, that he could have gone on a considerable while longer, but that he should have had less left to pay them with, and that he has chosen to stop while he may be able to give them so considerable a sum as may convince them of his integrity.

We have a great clamour among us of the cruelty of creditors, and it is a popular clamour, that goes a great way with some people; but let them tell us when ever creditors were cruel, when the debtor came thus to them with fifteen shillings in the pound in his offer. Perhaps when the debtor has run to the utmost, and there appears to be little or nothing left, he has been used roughly; and it is enough to provoke a creditor, indeed, to be offered a shilling or half-a-crown in the pound for a large debt, when, had the debtor been honest, and broke in time, he might have received perhaps two-thirds of his debt, and the debtor been in better condition too.

Break then in time, young tradesman, if you see you are going down, and that the hazard of going on is doubtful; you will certainly be received by your creditors with compassion, and with a generous treatment; and, whatever happens, you will be able to begin the world again with the title of an honest man—even the same creditors will embark with you again, and be more forward to give you credit than before.

It is true, most tradesmen that break merit the name of knave or dishonest man, but it is not so with all; the reason of the difference lies chiefly in the manner of their breaking—namely, whether sooner or later. It is possible, he may be an honest man who cannot, but he can never be honest that can, and will not pay his debts. Now he, that, being able to pay fifteen shillings in the pound, will struggle on till he sees he shall not be able to pay half-a-crown in the pound, this man was able to pay, but would not, and, therefore, as above, cannot be an honest man.

In the next place, what shall we say to the peace and satisfaction of mind in breaking, which the tradesman will always have when he acts the honest part, and breaks betimes, compared to that guilt and chagrin of the mind, occasioned by a running on, as I said, to the last gasp, when they have little to pay? Then, indeed, the tradesman can expect no quarter from his creditors, and will have no quiet in himself.

I might instance here the miserable, anxious, perplexed life, which the poor tradesman lives under; the distresses and extremities of his declining state; how harassed and tormented for money; what shifts he is driven to for supporting himself; how many little, mean, and even wicked things, will even the religious tradesman stoop to in his distress, to deliver himself—even such things as his very soul would abhor at another time, and for which he goes perhaps with a wounded conscience all his life after!

By giving up early, all this, which is the most dreadful part of all the rest, would be prevented. I have heard many an honest unfortunate man confess this, and repent, even with tears, that they had not learned to despair in trade some years sooner than they did, by which they had avoided falling into many foul and foolish actions, which they afterwards had been driven to by the extremity of their affairs.

CHAPTER VIII
THE ORDINARY OCCASIONS OF THE RUIN OF TRADESMEN

Since I have given advice to tradesmen, when they fell into difficulties, and find they are run behind-hand, to break in time, before they run on too far, and thereby prevent the consequences of a fatal running on to extremity, it is but just I should give them some needful directions, to avoid, if possible, breaking at all.

In order to this, I will briefly inquire what are the ordinary originals of a tradesman's ruin in business. To say it is negligence, when I have already pressed to a close application and diligence; that it is launching into, and grasping at, more business than their stock, or, perhaps, their understandings, are able to manage, when I have already spoken of the fatal consequences of over-trading; to say it is trusting carelessly people unable to pay, and running too rashly into debt, when I have already spoken of taking and giving too much credit—this would all be but saying the same thing over again—and I am too full of particulars, in this important case, to have any need of tautologies and repetitions; but there are a great many ways by which tradesmen precipitate themselves into ruin besides those, and some that need explaining and enlarging upon.

I. Some, especially retailers, ruin themselves by fixing their shops in such places as are improper for their business. In most towns, but particularly in the city of London, there are places as it were appropriated to particular trades, and where the trades which are placed there succeed very well, but would do very ill any where else, or any other trades in the same places; as the orange-merchants and wet-salters about Billingsgate, and in Thames Street; the coster-mongers at the Three Cranes; the wholesale cheesemongers in Thames Street; the mercers and drapers in the high streets, such as Cheapside, Ludgate Street, Cornhill, Round Court, and Grace-church Street, &c.

Pray what would a bookseller make of his business at Billingsgate, or a mercer in Tower Street, or near the Custom-house, or a draper in Thames Street, or about Queen-hithe? Many trades have their peculiar streets, and proper places for the sale of their goods, where people expect to find such shops, and consequently, when they want such goods, they go thither for them; as the booksellers in St Paul's churchyard, about the Exchange, Temple, and the Strand, &c., the mercers on both sides Ludgate, in Round Court, and Grace-church and Lombard Streets; the shoemakers in St Martins le Grand, and Shoemaker Row; the coach-makers in Long-acre, Queen Street, and Bishopsgate; butchers in Eastcheap; and such like.

For a tradesman to open his shop in a place unresorted to, or in a place where his trade is not agreeable, and where it is not expected, it is no wonder if he has no trade. What retail trade would a milliner have among the fishmongers' shops on Fishstreet-hill, or a toyman about Queen-hithe? When a shop is ill chosen, the tradesman starves; he is out of the way, and business will not follow him that runs away from it: suppose a ship-chandler should set up in Holborn, or a block-maker in Whitecross Street, an anchor-smith at Moorgate, or a coachmaker in Redriff, and the like!

It is true, we have seen a kind of fate attend the very streets and rows where such trades have been gathered together; and a street, famous some years ago, shall, in a few years after, be quite forsaken; as Paternoster Row for mercers, St Paul's Churchyard for woollen-drapers; both the Eastcheaps for butchers; and now you see hardly any of those trades left in those places.

I mention it for this reason, and this makes it to my purpose in an extraordinary manner, that whenever the principal shopkeepers remove from such a street, or settled place, where the principal trade used to be, the rest soon follow—knowing, that if the fame of the trade is not there, the customers will not resort thither: and that a tradesman's business is to follow wherever the trade leads. For a mercer to set up now in Paternoster Row, or a woollen-draper in St Paul's Churchyard, the one among the sempstresses, and the other among the chair-makers, would be the same thing as for a country shopkeeper not to set up in or near the market-place.[17]

The place, therefore, is to be prudently chosen by the retailer, when he first begins his business, that he may put himself in the way of business; and then, with God's blessing, and his own care, he may expect his share of trade with his neighbours.

---

[17] Paternoster Row has long been the chief seat of the bookselling and publishing trade in London; and there are now some splendid shops of mercers or haberdashers in St Paul's Churchyard, also in Ludgate hill adjoining.

2. He must take an especial care to have his shop not so much crowded with a large bulk of goods, as with a well-sorted and well-chosen quantity proper for his business, and to give credit to his beginning. In order to this, his buying part requires not only a good judgment in the wares he is to deal in, but a perfect government of his judgment by his understanding to suit and sort his quantities and proportions, as well to his shop as to the particular place where his shop is situated; for example, a particular trade is not only proper for such or such a part of the town, but a particular assortment of goods, even in the same way, suits one part of the town, or one town and not another; as he that sets up in the Strand, or near the Exchange, is likely to sell more rich silks, more fine Hollands, more fine broad-cloths, more fine toys and trinkets, than one of the same trade setting up in the skirts of the town, or at Ratcliff, or Wapping, or Redriff; and he that sets up in the capital city of a county, than he that is placed in a private market-town, in the same county; and he that is placed in a market-town, than he that is placed in a country village. A tradesman in a seaport town sorts himself different from one of the same trade in an inland town, though larger and more populous; and this the tradesman must weigh very maturely before he lays out his stock.

Sometimes it happens a tradesman serves his apprenticeship in one town, and sets up in another; and sometimes circumstances altering, he removes from one town to another; the change is very important to him, for the goods, which he is to sell in the town he removes to, are sometimes so different from the sorts of goods which he sold in the place he removed from, though in the same way of trade, that he is at a great loss both in changing his hand, and in the judgment of buying. This made me insist, in a former chapter, that a tradesman should take all occasions to extend his knowledge in every kind of goods, that which way soever he may turn his hand, he may have judgment in every thing.

In thus changing his circumstances of trade, he must learn, as well as he can, how to furnish his shop suitable to the place he is to trade in, and to sort his goods to the demand which he is like to have there; otherwise he will not only lose the customers for want of proper goods, but will very much lose by the goods which he lays in for sale, there being no demand for them where he is going.

When merchants send adventures to our British colonies, it is usual with them to make up to each factor what they call a *sortable cargo*; that is to say, they want something of every thing that may furnish the tradesmen there with parcels fit to fill their shops, and invite their customers; and if they fail, and do not thus sort their cargoes, the factors there not only complain, as being ill sorted, but the cargo lies by unsold, because there is not a sufficient quantity of sorts to answer the demand, and make them all marketable together.

It is the same thing here: if the tradesman's shop is not well sorted, it is not suitably furnished, or fitted to supply his customers; and nothing dishonours him more than to have people come to buy things usual to be had in such shops, and go away without them. The next thing they say to one another is, 'I went to that shop, but I could not be furnished; they are not stocked there for a trade; one seldom finds any thing there that is new or fashionable:' and so they go away to another shop; and not only go away themselves, but carry others away with them—for it is observable, that the buyers or retail customers, especially the ladies, follow one another as sheep follow the flock; and if one buys a beautiful silk, or a cheap piece of Holland, or a new-fashioned thing of any kind, the next inquiry is, where it was bought; and the shop is presently recommended for a shop well sorted, and for a place where things are to be had not only cheap and good, but of the newest fashion, and where they have always great choice to please the curious, and to supply whatever is called for. And thus the trade runs away insensibly to the shops which are best sorted.

3. The retail tradesman in especial, but even every tradesman in his station, must furnish himself with a competent stock of patience; I mean, that patience which is needful to bear with all sorts of impertinence, and the most provoking curiosity, that it is possible to imagine the buyers, even the worst of them, are or can be guilty of. A tradesman behind his counter must have no flesh and blood about him, no passions, no resentment. He must never be angry; no, not so much as seem to be so. If a customer tumbles him five hundred pounds' worth of goods, and scarce bids money for any thing—nay, though they really come to his shop with no intent to buy, as many do, only to see what is to be sold, and if they cannot be better pleased than they are at some other shop where they intend to buy, it is all one, the tradesman must take it, and place it to the account of his calling, that it is his business to be ill used, and resent nothing; and so must answer as obligingly to those that give him an hour or two's trouble and buy nothing, as he does to those who in half the time lay out ten or twenty pounds. The case is plain: it is his business to get money, to sell and please; and if

some do give him trouble and do not buy, others make him amends, and do buy; and as for the trouble, it is the business of his shop.

I have heard that some ladies, and those, too, persons of good note, have taken their coaches and spent a whole afternoon in Ludgate Street or Covent Garden, only to divert themselves in going from one mercer's shop to another, to look upon their fine silks, and to rattle and banter the journeymen and shopkeepers, and have not so much as the least occasion, much less intention, to buy any thing; nay, not so much as carrying any money out with them to buy anything if they fancied it: yet this the mercers who understand themselves know their business too well to resent; nor if they really knew it, would they take the least notice of it, but perhaps tell the ladies they were welcome to look upon their goods; that it was their business to show them; and that if they did not come to buy now, they might perhaps see they were furnished to please them when they might have occasion.

On the other hand, I have been told that sometimes those sorts of ladies have been caught in their own snare; that is to say, have been so engaged by the good usage of the shopkeeper, and so unexpectedly surprised with some fine thing or other that has been shown them, that they have been drawn in by their fancy against their design, to lay out money, whether they had it or no; that is to say, to buy, and send home for money to pay for it.

But let it be how and which way it will, whether mercer or draper, or what trade you please, the man that stands behind the counter must be all courtesy, civility, and good manners; he must not be affronted, or any way moved, by any manner of usage, whether owing to casualty or design; if he sees himself ill used, he must wink, and not see it—he must at least not appear to see it, nor any way show dislike or distaste; if he does, he reproaches not only himself but his shop, and puts an ill name upon the general usuage of customers in it; and it is not to be imagined how, in this gossiping, tea-drinking age, the scandal will run, even among people who have had no knowledge of the person first complaining. 'Such a shop!' says a certain lady to a citizen's wife in conversation, as they were going to buy clothes; 'I am resolved I won't go to it; the fellow that keeps it is saucy and rude: if I lay out my money, I expect to be well used; if I don't lay it out, I expect to be well treated.'

'Why, Madam,' says the citizen, 'did the man of the shop use your ladyship ill?'

Lady.—No, I can't say he used me ill, for I never was in his shop.

Cit.—How does your ladyship know he does so then?

Lady.—Why, I know he used another lady saucily, because she gave him a great deal of trouble, as he called it, and did not buy.

Cit.—Was it the lady that told you so herself, Madam?

Lady.—I don't know, really, I have forgot who it was; but I have such a notion in my head, and I don't care to try, for I hate the sauciness of shopkeepers when they don't understand themselves.

Cit.—Well; but, Madam, perhaps it may be a mistake—and the lady that told you was not the person neither?

Lady.—Oh, Madam, I remember now who told me; it was my Lady Tattle, when I was at Mrs Whymsy's on a visiting day; it was the talk of the whole circle, and all the ladies took notice of it, and said they would take care to shun that shop.

Cit.—Sure, Madam, the lady was strangely used; did she tell any of the particulars?

Lady.—No; I did not understand that she told the particulars, for it seems it was not to her, but to some other lady, a friend of hers; but it was all one; the company took as much notice of it as if it had been to her, and resented it as much, I assure you.

Cit.—Yet, and without examining the truth of the fact.

Lady.—We did not doubt the story.

Cit.—But had no other proof of it, Madam, than her relation?

Lady.—Why, that's true; nobody asked for a proof; it was enough to tell the story.

Cit.—What! though perhaps the lady did not know the person, or whether it was true or no, and perhaps had it from a third or fourth hand—your ladyship knows any body's credit may be blasted at that rate.

Lady.—We don't inquire so nicely, you know, into the truth of stories at a tea-table.

Cit.—No, Madam, that's true; but when reputation is at stake, we should be a little careful too.

Lady.—Why, that's true too. But why are you so concerned about it, Madam? do you know the man that keeps the shop?

Cit.—No otherwise, Madam, than that I have often bought there, and I always found them the most civil, obliging people in the world.

Lady.—It may be they know you, Madam.

Cit.—I am persuaded they don't, for I seldom went but I saw new faces, for they have a great many servants and journeymen in the shop.

Lady.—It may be you are easy to be pleased; you are good-humoured yourself, and cannot put their patience to any trial.

Cit.—Indeed, Madam, just the contrary; I believe I made them tumble two or three hundred pounds' worth of goods one day, and bought nothing; and yet it was all one; they used me as well as if I had laid out twenty pounds.

Lady.—Why, so they ought.

Cit.—Yes, Madam, but then it is a token they do as they ought, and understand themselves.

Lady.—Well, I don't know much of it indeed, but thus I was told.

Cit.—Well, but if your ladyship would know the truth of it, you would do a piece of justice to go and try them.

Lady.—Not I; besides, I have a mercer of my acquaintance.

Cit.—Well, Madam, I'll wait on your ladyship to your own mercer, and if you can't find any thing to your liking, will you go and try the other shop?

Lady.—Oh! I am sure I shall deal if I go to my mercer.

Cit.—Well, but if you should, let us go for a frolic, and give the other as much trouble as we can for nothing, and see how he'll behave, for I want to be satisfied; if I find them as your ladyship has been told, I'll never go there any more.

Lady.—Upon that condition I agree—I will go with you; but I will go and lay out my money at my own mercer's first, because I wont be tempted.

Cit.—Well, Madam, I'll wait on your ladyship till you have laid out your money.

After this discourse they drove away to the mercer's shop where the lady used to buy; and when they came there, the lady was surprised—the shop was shut up, and nobody to be seen. The next door was a laceman's, and the journeyman being at the door, the lady sent her servant to desire him to speak a word or two to her; and when he came, says the lady to him,

Pray, how long has Mr—'s shop been shut up?

Laceman.—About a month, madam.

Lady.—What! is Mr—dead?

Laceman.—No, madam, he is not dead.

Lady.—What then, pray?

Laceman.—Something worse, madam; he has had some misfortunes.

Lady.—I am very sorry to hear it, indeed. So her ladyship made her bow, and her coachman drove away.

The short of the story was, her mercer was broke; upon which the city lady prevailed upon her ladyship to go to the other shop, which she did, but declared beforehand she would buy nothing, but give the mercer all the trouble she could; and so said the other. And to make the thing more sure, she would have them go into the shop single, because she fancied the mercer knew the city lady, and therefore would behave more civilly to them both on that account, the other having laid out her money there several times. Well, they went in, and the lady asked for such and such rich things, and had them shown her, to a variety that she was surprised at; but not the best or richest things they could show her gave her any satisfaction—either she did not like the pattern, or the colours did not suit her fancy, or they were too dear; and so she prepares to leave the shop, her coach standing at a distance, which she ordered, that they might not guess at her quality.

But she was quite deceived in her expectation; for the mercer, far from treating her in the manner as she had heard, used her with the utmost civility and good manners. She treated him, on the contrary, as she said herself, even with a forced rudeness; she gave him all the impertinent trouble she was able, as above; and, pretending to like nothing he showed, turned away with an air of contempt, intimating that his shop was ill furnished, and that she should be easily served, she doubted not, at another.

He told her he was very unhappy in not having any thing that suited her fancy—that, if she knew what particular things would please her, he would have them in two hours' time for her, if all the French and Italian merchants' warehouses in London, or all the weavers' looms in Spitalfields, could furnish them. But when that would not do, she comes forward from his back shop, where she had plagued him about an hour and a half; and makes him the slight compliment of (in a kind of a scornful tone too), 'I am sorry I have given you so much trouble.'

'The trouble, madam, is nothing; it is my misfortune not to please you; but, as to trouble, my business is to oblige the ladies, my customers; if I show my goods, I may sell them; if I do not show them, I cannot; if it is not a trouble to you, I'll show you every piece of goods in my shop; if you do not buy now, you may perhaps buy another time.' And thus, in short, he pursued her with all the good words in the world, and waited on her towards the door.

As she comes forward, there she spied the city lady, who had just used the partner as the lady had used the chief master; and there, as if it had been by mere chance, she salutes her with, 'Your servant, cousin; pray, what brought you here?' The cousin answers, 'Madam, I am mighty glad to see your ladyship here; I have been haggling here a good while, but this gentleman and I cannot bargain, and I was just going away.'

'Why, then,' says the lady, 'you have been just such another customer as I, for I have troubled the gentleman mercer this two hours, and I cannot meet with any thing to my mind.' So away they go together to the door; and the lady gets the mercer to send one of his servants to bid her coachman drive to the door, showing him where the fellow stood.

While the boy was gone, she takes the city lady aside, and talking softly, the mercer and his partner, seeing them talk together, withdrew, but waited at a distance to be ready to hand them to the coach. So they began a new discourse, as follows:—

Lady.—Well, I am satisfied this man has been ill used in the world.

Cit.—Why, Madam, how does your ladyship find him?

Lady.—Only the most obliging, most gentleman-like man of a tradesman that ever I met with in my life.

Cit.—But did your ladyship try him as you said you would?

Lady.—Try him! I believe he has tumbled three thousand pounds' worth of goods for me.

Cit.—Did you oblige him to do so?

Lady.—I forced him to it, indeed, for I liked nothing.

Cit.—Is he well stocked with goods?

Lady.—I told him his shop was ill furnished.

Cit.—What did he say to that?

Lady.—Say! why he carried me into another inner shop, or warehouse, where he had goods to a surprising quantity and value, I confess.

Cit.—And what could you say, then?

Lady.—Say! in truth I was ashamed to say any more, but still was resolved not to be pleased, and so came away, as you see.

Cit.—And he has not disobliged you at all, has he?

Lady.—Just the contrary, indeed. (Here she repeated the words the mercer had said to her, and the modesty and civility he had treated her with.)

Cit.—Well, Madam, I assure you I have been faithful to my promise, for you cannot have used him so ill as I have used his partner—for I have perfectly abused him for having nothing to please me—I did as good as tell him I believed he was going to break, and that he had no choice.

Lady.—And how did he treat you?

Cit.—Just in the same manner as his partner did your ladyship, all mild and mannerly, smiling, and in perfect temper; for my part, if I was a young wench again, I should be in love with such a man.

Lady.—Well, but what shall we do now?

Cit.—Why, be gone. I think we have teazed them enough; it would be cruel to bear-bait them any more.

Lady.—No, I am not for teazing them any more; but shall we really go away, and buy nothing?

Cit.—Nay, that shall be just as your ladyship pleases—you know I promised you I would not buy; that is to say, unless you discharge me of that obligation.

Lady.—I cannot, for shame, go out of this shop, and lay out nothing.

Cit.—Did your ladyship see any thing that pleased you?

Lady.—I only saw some of the finest things in England—I don't think all the city of Paris can outdo him.

Cit.—Well, madam, if you resolve to buy, let us go and look again.

Lady.—'Come, then.' And upon that the lady, turning to the mercer—'Come, sir,' says she, 'I think I will look upon that piece of brocade again; I cannot find in my heart to give you all this trouble for nothing.'

'Madam,' says the mercer, 'I shall be very glad if I can be so happy as to please you; but, I beseech your ladyship, don't speak of the trouble, for that is the duty of our trade; we must never think our business a trouble.'

Upon this the ladies went back with him into his inner shop, and laid out between sixty and seventy pounds, for they both bought rich suits of clothes, and used his shop for many years after.

The short inference from this long discourse is this: That here you see, and I could give many examples very like this, how, and in what manner, a shopkeeper is to behave himself in the way of his business— what impertinences, what taunts, flouts, and ridiculous things, he must bear in his business, and must not show the least return, or the least signal of disgust—he must have no passions, no fire in his temper—he must be all soft and smooth: nay, if his real temper be naturally fiery and hot, he must show none of it in his shop—he must be a perfect complete hypocrite, if he will be a complete tradesman.[18]

---

[18] The necessity here insisted on seems a hard one, and scarcely consistent with a just morality. Yet, if the tradesman takes a right view of his situation, he will scarcely doubt the propriety of Defoe's advice. He must consider, that, in his shop, he is, as it were, acting a part. He performs a certain character in the drama of our social arrangements, one which requires all the civility and forbearance above insisted on. He is not called upon, in such circumstances, to feel, speak, and act, as he would find himself in honour required to do in his private or absolutely personal capacity—in his own house, for instance, or in any public place where he mingled on a footing of equality with his fellow-citizens. Accordingly, there is such a general sense of the justifiableness of his conducting himself in this submissive spirit, that no one would think of imputing it to him as a fault; but he would be more apt to be censured or ridiculed if he had so little sense as to take offence, in his capacity of tradesman, at any thing which it would only concern him to resent if it were offered to him in his capacity as a private citizen.

An incident, somewhat like that so dramatically related by Defoe, occurred a few years ago in the northern capital. A lady had, through whim, pestered a mercer in the manner related in the text, turning over all his goods, and only treating him with rudeness in return. When she finally turned to leave the shop, to inquire, as she said, for better and cheaper goods elsewhere, she found that a shower was falling, against which she had no protection. The tradesman, who had politely shown her to the door, observing her hesitate on the threshold at sight of the rain, requested her to wait a moment, and, stepping backwards for his umbrella, instantly returned, and, in the kindest accents, requested her to accept the loan of it. She took it, and went away, but in a few minutes returned it, in a totally different frame of spirit, and not only purchased extensively on this occasion, but became a constant customer for the future.

Another tradesman in the same city was so remarkable for his imperturbable civility, that it became the subject of a bet—an individual undertaking to irritate him, or, if he failed, to forfeit a certain sum. He went to the shop, and caused an immense quantity of the finest silks to be turned over, after which he coolly asked for a pennyworth of a certain splendid piece of satin. 'By all means,' said the discreet trader; 'allow me, Sir, to have your penny.' The coin

It is true, natural tempers are not to be always counterfeited—the man cannot easily be a lamb in his shop, and a lion in himself; but let it be easy or hard, it must be done, and it is done. There are men who have, by custom and usage, brought themselves to it, that nothing could be meeker and milder than they, when behind the counter, and yet nothing be more furious and raging in every other part of life—nay, the provocations they have met with in their shops have so irritated their rage, that they would go upstairs from their shop, and fall into phrensies, and a kind of madness, and beat their heads against the wall, and mischief themselves, if not prevented, till the violence of it had gotten vent, and the passions abate and cool. Nay, I heard once of a shopkeeper that behaved himself thus to such an extreme, that, when he was provoked by the impertinence of the customers, beyond what his temper could bear, he would go upstairs and beat his wife, kick his children about like dogs, and be as furious for two or three minutes as a man chained down in Bedlam, and when the heat was over, would sit down and cry faster then the children he had abused; and after the fit was over he would go down into his shop again, and be as humble, as courteous, and as calm as any man whatever—so absolute a government of his passions had he in the shop, and so little out of it; in the shop a soul-less animal that can resent nothing, and in the family a madman; in the shop meek like the lamb, but in the family outrageous like a Lybian lion.

The sum of the matter is this: it is necessary for a tradesman to subject himself, by all the ways possible, to his business; his customers are to be his idols: so far as he may worship idols by allowance, he is to bow down to them and worship them;[19] at least, he is not any way to

---

was handed to him, and, taking up the piece of satin, and placing the penny on the end of it, he cut round with his scissors, thus detaching a little bit of exactly the size and shape of the piece of money which was to purchase it. This, with the most polite air imaginable, he handed to his customer, whose confusion may be imagined.

[19] It appears to the editor that the case is here somewhat over-stated. While imperterbable good temper and civility are indispensible in the shopkeeper, it is not impossible that he may also err in displaying a *too great obsequiousness* of *manner*. This, by disgusting the common sense and good taste of customers, may do as much harm as want of civility. A too *pressing* manner, likewise, does harm, by causing the customer to feel as if he were *obliged* to purchase. The medium of an easy, obliging, and good-humoured manner, is perhaps what

displease them, or show any disgust or distaste at any thing they say or do. The bottom of it all is, that he is intending to get money by them; and it is not for him that gets money by them to offer the least inconvenience to them by whom he gets it; but he is to consider, that, as Solomon says, 'The borrower is servant to the lender,' so the seller is servant to the buyer.

When a tradesman has thus conquered all his passions, and can stand before the storm of impertinence, he is said to be fitted up for the main article, namely, the inside of the counter.

On the other hand, we see that the contrary temper, nay, but the very suggestion of it, hurries people on to ruin their trade, to disoblige the customers, to quarrel with them, and drive them away. We see by the lady above, after having seen the ways she had taken to put this man out of temper—I say, we see it conquered her temper, and brought her to lay out her money cheerfully, and be his customer ever after.

A sour, morose, dogmatic temper would have sent these ladies both away with their money in their pockets; but the man's patience and temper drove the lady back to lay out her money, and engaged her entirely.

---

suits best. But here, as in many other things, it is not easy to lay down any general rule. Much must be left to the goos sense and *tact* of the trader.

CHAPTER IX
OF OTHER REASONS FOR THE TRADESMAN'S DISASTERS: AND, FIRST, OF INNOCENT DIVERSIONS

A few directions seasonably given, and wisely received, will be sufficient to guide a tradesman in a right management of his business, so as that, if he observes them, he may secure his prosperity and success: but it requires a long and serious caveat to warn him of the dangers he meets with in his way. Trade is a straight and direct way, if they will but keep in it with a steady foot, and not wander, and launch out here and there, as a loose head and giddy fancy will prompt them to do.

The road, I say, is straight and direct; but there are many turnings and openings in it, both to the right hand and to the left, in which, if a tradesman but once ventures to step awry, it is ten thousand to one but he loses himself, and very rarely finds his way back again; at least if he does, it is like a man that has been lost in a wood; he comes out with a scratched face, and torn clothes, tired and spent, and does not recover himself in a long while after.

In a word, one steady motion carries him up, but many things assist to pull him down; there are many ways open to his ruin, but few to his rising: and though employment is said to be the best fence against temptations, and he that is busy heartily in his business, temptations to idleness and negligence will not be so busy about him, yet tradesmen are as often drawn from their business as other men; and when they are so, it is more fatal to them a great deal, than it is to gentlemen and persons whose employments do not call for their personal attendance so much as a shop does.

Among the many turnings and bye-lanes, which, as I say, are to be met with in the straight road of trade, there are two as dangerous and fatal to their prosperity as the worst, though they both carry an appearance of good, and promise contrary to what they perform; these are—

I. Pleasures and diversions, especially such as they will have us call innocent diversions.

II. Projects and adventures, and especially such as promise mountains of profit *in nubibus* [in the clouds], and are therefore the more likely to ensnare the poor eager avaricious tradesman.

I. I am now to speak of the first, namely, pleasures and diversions. I cannot allow any pleasures to be innocent, when they turn away either the body or the mind of a tradesman from the one needful thing which his calling makes necessary, and that necessity makes his duty—I mean, the application both of his hands and head to his business. Those pleasures and diversions may be innocent in themselves, which are not so to him: there are very few things in the world that are simply evil, but things are made circumstantially evil when they are not so in themselves: killing a man is not simply sinful; on the contrary, it is not lawful only, but a duty, when justice and the laws of God or man require it; but when done maliciously, from any corrupt principle, or to any corrupted end, is murder, and the worst of crimes.

Pleasures and diversions are thus made criminal, when a man is engaged in duty to a full attendance upon such business as those pleasures and diversions necessarily interfere with and interrupt; those pleasures, though innocent in themselves, become a fault in him, because his legal avocations demand his attendance in another place. Thus those pleasures may be lawful to another man, which are not so to him, because another man has not the same obligation to a calling, the same necessity to apply to it, the same cry of a family, whose bread may depend upon his diligence, as a tradesman has.

Solomon, the royal patron of industry, tells us, 'He that is a lover of pleasure, shall be a poor man.' I must not doubt but Solomon is to be understood of tradesmen and working men, such as I am writing of, whose time and application is due to their business, and who, in pursuit of their pleasures, are sure to neglect their shops, or employments, and I therefore render the words thus, to the present purpose—'The tradesman that is a lover of pleasure, shall be a poor man.' I hope I do not wrest the Scripture in my interpretation of it; I am sure it agrees with the whole tenor of the wise man's other discourses.

When I see young shopkeepers keep horses, ride a-hunting, learn dog-language, and keep the sportsmen's brogue upon their tongues, I will not say I read their destiny, for I am no fortuneteller, but I do say, I am always afraid for them; especially when I know that either their fortunes and beginnings are below it, or that their trades are such as in a particular manner to require their constant attendance. As to see a barber abroad on a Saturday, a corn-factor abroad on a Wednesday and Friday, or a Blackwell-hall man on a Thursday, you may as well say a country shopkeeper should go a-hunting on a market-day, or go a-feasting at the fair day of the town where he lives; and yet riding and hunting are otherwise lawful diversions, and in their kind very good for exercise and health.

I am not for making a galley-slave of a shopkeeper, and have him chained down to the oar; but if he be a wise, a prudent, and a diligent tradesman, he will allow himself as few excursions as possible.

Business neglected is business lost; it is true, there are some businesses which require less attendance than others, and give a man less occasion of application; but, in general, that tradesman who can satisfy himself to be absent from his business, must not expect success; if he is above the character of a diligent tradesman, he must then be above the business too, and should leave it to somebody, that, having more need of it, will think it worth his while to mind it better.

Nor, indeed, is it possible a tradesman should be master of any of the qualifications which I have set down to denominate him complete, if he neglects his shop and his time, following his pleasures and diversions.

I will allow that the man is not vicious and wicked, that he is not addicted to drunkenness, to women, to gaming, or any such things as those, for those are not woundings, but murder, downright killing. A man may wound and hurt himself sometimes, in the rage of an ungoverned passion, or in a phrensy or fever, and intend no more; but if he shoots himself through the head, or hangs himself, we are sure then he intended to kill and destroy himself, and he dies inevitably.

For a tradesman to follow his pleasures, which indeed is generally attended with a slighting of his business, leaving his shop to servants or others, it is evident to me that he is indifferent whether it thrives or no; and, above all, it is evident that his heart is not in his business; that he does not delight in it, or look on it with pleasure. To a complete tradesman there is no pleasure equal to that of being in his business, no delight equal to that of seeing himself thrive, to see trade flow in upon him, and to be satisfied that he goes on prosperously. He will never thrive, that cares not whether he thrives or no. As trade is the chief employment of his life, and is therefore called, by way of eminence, *his business*, so it should be made the chief delight of his life. The tradesman that does not love his business, will never give it due attendance.

Pleasure is a bait to the mind, and the mind will attract the body: where the heart is, the object shall always have the body's company. The great objection I meet with from young tradesmen against this argument is, they follow no unlawful pleasures; they do not spend their time in taverns, and drinking to excess; they do not spend their money in gaming, and so stock-starve their business, and rob the shop to supply the extravagant losses of play; or they do not spend their hours in ill company and debaucheries; all they do, is a little innocent diversion in riding abroad now and then for the air, and for their health, and to ease their thoughts of the throng of other affairs which are heavy upon them, &c.

These, I say, are the excuses of young tradesmen; and, indeed, they are young excuses, and, I may say truly, have nothing in them. It is perhaps true, or I may grant it so for the present purpose, that the pleasure the tradesman takes is, as he says, not unlawful, and that he follows only a little innocent diversion; but let me tell him, the words are ill put together, and the diversion is rather recommended from the word *little*, than from the word *innocent*: if it be, indeed, but little, it may be innocent; but the case is quite altered by the extent of the thing; and the innocence lies here, not in the nature of the thing, not in the diversion or pleasure that is taken, but in the time it takes; for if the man spends the time in it which should be spent in his shop or warehouse, and his business suffers by his absence, as it must do, if the absence is long at a time, or often practised—the diversion so taken becomes criminal to him, though the same diversion might be innocent in another.

Thus I have heard a young tradesman, who loved his bottle, excuse himself, and say, 'It is true, I have been at the tavern, but I was treated, it cost me nothing.' And this, he thinks, clears him of all blame; not considering that when he spends no money, yet he spends five times the value of the money in time. Another says, 'Why, indeed, I was at the tavern yesterday all the afternoon, but I could not help it, and I spent but sixpence.' But at the same time perhaps it might be said he spent five pounds' worth of time, his business being neglected, his shop unattended, his books not posted, his letters not written, and the like—for all those things are works necessary to a tradesman, as well as the attendance on his shop, and infinitely above the pleasure of being treated at the expense of his time. All manner of pleasures should buckle and be subservient to business: he that makes his pleasure be his business, will never make his business be a pleasure. Innocent pleasures become sinful, when they are used to excess, and so it is here; the most innocent diversion becomes criminal, when it breaks in upon that which is the due and just employment of the man's life. Pleasures rob the tradesman, and how, then, can he call them innocent diversions? They are downright thieves; they rob his shop of his attendance, and of the time which he ought to bestow there; they rob his family of their due support, by the man's neglecting that business by which they are to be supported and maintained; and they oftentimes rob the creditors of their just debts, the tradesman sinking by the inordinate use of those innocent diversions, as he calls them, as well by the expense attending them, as the loss of his time, and neglect of his business, by which he is at last reduced to the necessity of shutting up shop in earnest, which was indeed as good as shut before. A shop without a master is like the same shop on a middling holiday, half shut up, and he that keeps it long so, need not doubt but he may in a little time more shut it quite up.

In short, pleasure is a thief to business; how any man can call it innocent, let him answer that does so; it robs him every way, as I have said above: and if the tradesman be a Christian, and has any regard to religion and his duty, I must tell him, that when upon his disasters he shall reflect, and see that he has ruined himself and his family, by following too much those diversions and pleasures which he thought innocent, and which perhaps in themselves were really so, he will find great cause to repent of that which he insisted on as innocent; he will find himself lost, by doing lawful things, and that he made those innocent things sinful, and those lawful things unlawful to him. Thus, as they robbed his family and creditors before of their just debts—for maintenance is a tradesman's just debt to his family, and a wife and children are as much a tradesman's real creditors as those who trusted him with their goods—I say, as his innocent pleasures robbed his family and creditors before, they will rob him now of his peace, and of all that calm of soul which an honest, industrious, though unfortunate, tradesman meets with under his disasters.

I am asked here, perhaps, how much pleasure an honest-meaning tradesman may be allowed to take? for it cannot be supposed I should insist that all pleasure is forbidden him, that he must have no diversion, no spare hours, no intervals from hurry and fatigue; that would be to pin him down to the very floor of his shop, as John Sheppard was locked down to the floor of his prison.

The answer to this question every prudent tradesman may make for himself: if his pleasure is in his shop, and in his business, there is no danger of him; but if he has an itch after exotic diversions—I mean such as are foreign to his shop, and to his business, and which I therefore call *exotic*—let him honestly and fairly state the case between his shop and his diversions, and judge impartially for himself. So much pleasure, and no more, may be innocently taken, as does not interfere with, or do the least damage to his business, by taking him away from it.

Every moment that his trade wants him in his shop or warehouse, it is his duty to be there; it is not enough to say, I believe I shall not be wanted; or I believe I shall suffer no loss by my absence. He must come to a point and not deceive himself; if he does, the cheat is all his own. If he will not judge sincerely at first, he will reproach himself sincerely at last; for there is no fraud against his own reflections: a man is very rarely a hypocrite to himself.

The rule may be, in a few words, thus: those pleasures or diversions, and those only, can be innocent, which the man may or does use, or allow himself to use, without hindrance of, or injury to, his business and reputation.

Let the diversions or pleasures in question be what they will, and how innocent soever they are in themselves, they are not so to him, because they interrupt or interfere with his business, which is his immediate duty. I have mentioned the circumstance which touches this part too, namely, that there may be a time when even the needful duties of religion may become faults, and unseasonable, when another more needful attendance calls for us to apply to it; much more, then, those things which are only barely lawful. There is a visible difference between the things which we may do, and the things which we must do. Pleasures at certain seasons are allowed, and we may give ourselves some loose to them; but business, I mean to the man of business, is that needful thing, of which it is not to be said it *may*, but it *must* be done.

Again, those pleasures which may not only be lawful in themselves, but which may be lawful to other men, yet are criminal and unlawful to him. To gentlemen of fortunes and estates, who being born to large possessions, and have no avocations of this kind, it is certainly lawful to spend their spare hours on horseback, with their hounds or hawks, pursuing their game; or, on foot, with their gun and their net, and their dogs to kill the hares or birds, &c.—all which we call sport. These are the men that can, with a particular satisfaction, when they come home, say they have only taken an innocent diversion; and yet even in these, there are not wanting some excesses which take away the innocence of them, and consequently the satisfaction in their reflection, and therefore it was I said it was lawful to them to spend their spare hours—by which I am to be understood, those hours which are not due to more solemn and weighty occasions, such as the duties of religion in particular. But as this is not my present subject, I proceed; for I am not talking to gentlemen now, but to tradesmen.

The prudent tradesman will, in time, consider what he ought or ought not to do, in his own particular case, as to his pleasures—not what another man may or may not do. In short, nothing of pleasure or diversion can be innocent to him, whatever it may be to another, if it injures his business, if it takes either his time, or his mind, or his delight, or his attendance, from his business; nor can all the little excuses, of its being for his health, and for the needful unbending the bow of the mind, from the constant application of business, for all these must stoop to the great article of his shop and business; though I might add, that the bare taking the air for health, and for a recess to the mind, is not the thing I am talking of—it is the taking an immoderate liberty, and spending an immoderate length of time, and that at unseasonable and improper hours, so as to make his pleasures and diversions be prejudicial to his business—this is the evil I object to, and this is too much the ruin of the tradesmen of this age; and thus any man who calmly reads these papers will see I ought to be understood.

Nor do I confine this discourse to the innocent diversions of a horse, and riding abroad to take the air; things which, as above, are made hurtful and unlawful to him, only as they are hindrances to his business, and are more or less so, as they rob his shop or warehouse, or business, or his attendance and time, and cause him to draw his affections off from his calling.

But we see other and new pleasures daily crowding in upon the tradesman, and some which no age before this have been in danger of— I mean, not to such an excess as is now the case, and consequently there were fewer tradesmen drawn into the practice.

The present age is a time of gallantry and gaiety; nothing of the present pride and vanity was known, or but very little of it, in former times: the baits which are every where laid for the corruption of youth, and for the ruin of their fortunes, were never so many and so mischievous as they are now.

We scarce now see a tradesman's apprentice come to his fifth year, but he gets a long wig and a sword, and a set of companions suitable; and this wig and sword, being left at proper and convenient places, are put on at night after the shop is shut, or when they can slip out to go a-raking in, and when they never fail of company ready to lead them into all manner of wickedness and debauchery; and from this cause it is principally that so many apprentices are ruined, and run away from their masters before they come out of their times—more, I am persuaded, now, than ever were to be found before.

Nor, as I said before, will I charge the devil with having any hand in the ruin of these young fellows—indeed, he needs not trouble himself about them, they are his own by early choice—they anticipate temptation, and are as forward as the devil can desire them to be. These may be truly said to be drawn aside of their own lusts, and enticed—they need no tempter.

But of these I may also say, they seldom trouble the tradesmen's class; they get ruined early, and finish the tradesman before they begin, so my discourse is not at present directed much to them; indeed, they are past advice before they come in my way.

Indeed, I knew one of these sort of gentlemen-apprentices make an attempt to begin, and set up his trade—he was a dealer in what they call Crooked-lane wares: he got about £300 from his father, an honest plain countryman, to set him up, and his said honest father exerted himself to the utmost to send him up so much money.

When he had gotten the money, he took a shop near the place where he had served his time, and entering upon the shop, he had it painted, and fitted up, and some goods he bought in order to furnish it; but before that, he was obliged to pay about £70 of the money to little debts, which he had contracted in his apprenticeship, at two or three ale-houses, for drink and eatables, treats, and junketings; and at the barber's for long perukes, at the sempstress's for fine Holland-shirts, turn-overs, white gloves, &c, to make a beau of him, and at several other places.

When he came to dip into this, and found that it wanted still £30 or £40 to equip him for the company which he had learned to keep, he took care to do this first; and being delighted with his new dress, and how like a gentleman he looked, he was resolved, before he opened a shop, to take his swing a little in the town; so away he went, with two of his neighbour's apprentices, to the play-house, thence to the tavern, not far from his dwelling, and there they fell to cards, and sat up all night—and thus they spent about a fortnight; the rest just creeping into their masters' houses, by the connivance of their fellow-servants, and he getting a bed in the tavern, where what he spent, to be sure, made them willing enough to oblige him—that is to say, to encourage him to ruin himself.

They then changed their course, indeed, and went to the ball, and that necessarily kept them out the most part of the night, always having their supper dressed at the tavern at their return; and thus, in a few words, he went on till he made way through all the remaining money he had left, and was obliged to call his creditors together, and break before he so much as opened his shop—I say, his creditors, for great part of the goods which he had furnished his shop with were unpaid for; perhaps some few might be bought with ready money.

This man, indeed, is the only tradesman that ever I met with, that set up and broke before his shop was open; others I have indeed known make very quick work of it.

But this part rather belongs to another head. I am at present not talking of madmen, as I hope, indeed, I am not writing to madmen, but I am talking of tradesmen undone by lawful things, by what they call innocent and harmless things—such as riding abroad, or walking abroad to take the air, and to divert themselves, dogs, gun, country-sport, and city-recreation. These things are certainly lawful, and in themselves very innocent; nay, they may be needful for health, and to give some relaxation to the mind, hurried with too much business; but the needfulness of them is so much made an excuse, and the excess of them is so injurious to the tradesman's business and to his time, which should be set apart for his shop and his trade, that there are not a few tradesmen thus lawfully ruined, as I may call it—in a word, lawful or unlawful, their shop is neglected, their business goes behind-hand, and it is all one to the subject of breaking, and to the creditor, whether the man was undone by being a knave, or by being a fool; it is all one whether he lost his trade by scandalous immoral negligence, or by sober or religious negligence.

In a word, business languishes, while the tradesman is absent, and neglects it, be it for his health or for his pleasure, be it in good company or in bad, be it from a good or an ill design; and if the business languishes, the tradesman will not be long before he languishes too; for nothing can support the tradesman but his supporting his trade by a due attendance and application.[20]

---

[20] In the above admirable series of plain-spoken advices, the author has omitted one weighty reason why young tradesmen should not spend their evenings in frivolous, or otherwise improper company. The actual loss of time and of money incurred by such courses of conduct, is generally of less consequence than the losses arising from habitual distraction of mind, and the acquisition of an acquaintanceship with a set of idle or silly companions. It is of the utmost importance that young tradesmen should spend their leisure hours in a way

calculated to soothe the feelings, and enlarge the mind; and in the present day, from the prevalance of literature, and other rational means for amusement, they have ample opportunities of doing so.

CHAPTER X

OF EXTRAVAGANT AND EXPENSIVE LIVING; ANOTHER STEP TO A TRADESMAN'S DISASTER

Hitherto I have written of tradesmen ruined by lawful and innocent diversions; and, indeed, these are some of the most dangerous pits for a tradesman to fall into, because men are so apt to be insensible of the danger: a ship may as well be lost in a calm smooth sea, and an easy fair gale of wind, as in a storm, if they have no pilot, or the pilot be ignorant or unwary; and disasters of that nature happen as frequently as any others, and are as fatal. When rocks are apparent, and the pilot, bold and wilful, runs directly upon them, without fear or wit, we know the fate of the ship—it must perish, and all that are in it will inevitably be lost; but in a smooth sea, a bold shore, an easy gale, the unseen rocks or shoals are the only dangers, and nothing can hazard them but the skilfulness of the pilot: and thus it is in trade. Open debaucheries and extravagances, and a profusion of expense, as well as a general contempt of business, these are open and current roads to a tradesman's destruction; but a silent going on, in pursuit of innocent pleasures, a smooth and calm, but sure neglect of his shop, and time, and business, will as effectually and as surely ruin the tradesman as the other; and though the means are not so scandalous, the effect is as certain. But I proceed to the other.

Next to immoderate pleasures, the tradesman ought to be warned against immoderate expense. This is a terrible article, and more particularly so to the tradesman, as custom has now, as it were on purpose for their undoing, introduced a general habit of, and as it were a general inclination among all sorts of people to, an expensive way of living; to which might be added a kind of necessity of it; for that even with the greatest prudence and frugality a man cannot now support a family with the ordinary expense, which the same family might have been maintained with some few years ago: there is now (I) a weight of taxes upon almost all the necessaries of life, bread and flesh excepted, as coals, salt, malt, candles, soap, leather, hops, wine, fruit, and all foreign consumptions; (2) a load of pride upon the temper of the nation, which, in spite of taxes and the unusual dearness of every thing, yet prompts people to a profusion in their expenses.

This is not so properly called a *tax* upon the tradesmen; I think rather, it may be called *a plague* upon them: for there is, first, the dearness of every necessary thing to make living expensive; and secondly, an unconquerable aversion to any restraint; so that the poor will be like the rich, and the rich like the great, and the great like the greatest—and thus the world runs on to a kind of distraction at this time: where it will end, time must discover.

Now, the tradesman I speak of, if he will thrive, he must resolve to begin as he can go on; and if he does so, in a word, he must resolve to live more under restraint than ever tradesmen of his class used to do; for every necessary thing being, as I have said, grown dearer than before, he must entirely omit all the enjoyment of the unnecessaries which he might have allowed himself before, or perhaps be obliged to an expense beyond the income of his trade: and in either of these cases he has a great hardship upon him.

When I talk of immoderate expenses, I must be understood not yet to mean the extravagances of wickedness and debaucheries; there are so many sober extravagances, and so many grave sedate ways for a tradesman's ruin, and they are so much more dangerous than those hair-brained desperate ways of gaming and debauchery, that I think it is the best service I can do the tradesmen to lay before them those sunk rocks (as the seamen call them), those secret dangers in the first place, that they may know how to avoid them; and as for the other common ways, common discretion will supply them with caution for those, and their senses will be their protection.

The dangers to the tradesmen whom I am directing myself to, are from lawful things, and such as before are called innocent; for I am speaking to the sober part of tradesmen, who yet are often ruined and overthrown in trade; and perhaps as many such miscarry, as of the mad and extravagant, particularly because their number far exceeds them. Expensive living is a kind of slow fever; it is not so open, so threatening and dangerous, as the ordinary distemper which goes by that name, but it preys upon the spirits, and, when its degrees are increased to a height, is as fatal and as sure to kill as the other: it is a secret enemy, that feeds upon the vitals; and when it has gone its full length, and the languishing tradesman is weakened in his solid part, I mean his stock, then it overwhelms him at once.

Expensive living feeds upon the life and blood of the tradesman, for it eats into the two most essential branches of his trade, namely, his credit and his cash; the first is its triumph, and the last is its food: nothing goes out to cherish the exorbitance, but the immediate money;

expenses seldom go on trust, they are generally supplied and supported with ready money, whatever are not.

This expensive way of living consists in several things, which are all indeed in their degree ruinous to the tradesman; such as

1. Expensive house-keeping, or family extravagance.

2. Expensive dressing, or the extravagance of fine clothes.

3. Expensive company, or keeping company above himself.

4. Expensive equipages, making a show and ostentation of figure in the world.

I might take them all in bulk, and say, what has a young tradesman to do with these? and yet where is there a tradesman now to be found, who is not more or less guilty? It is, as I have said, the general vice of the times; the whole nation are more or less in the crime; what with necessity and inclination, where is the man or the family that lives as such families used to live?

In short, good husbandry and frugality is quite out of fashion, and he that goes about to set up for the practice of it, must mortify every thing about him that has the least tincture of frugality; it is the mode to live high, to spend more than we get, to neglect trade, contemn care and concern, and go on without forecast, or without consideration; and, in consequence, it is the mode to go on to extremity, to break, become bankrupt and beggars, and so going off the trading stage, leave it open for others to come after us, and do the same.[21]

To begin with house-keeping. I have already hinted, that every thing belonging to the family subsistence bears a higher price than usual, I may say, than ever; at the same time I can neither undertake to prove that there is more got by selling, or more ways to get it, I mean to a tradesman, than there was formerly; the consequence then must be, that the tradesmen do not grow rich faster than formerly; at least we may venture to say this of tradesmen and their families, comparing them

---

[21] Now, as in Defoe's time, a common observer is apt to be impressed with the idea, that expenses, with a large part of the community, exceed gains. Certainly, this is true at all times with a certain portion of society, but probably at no time with a large portion. There is a tendency to great self-deception in all such speculations; and no one ever thinks of bringing them to the only true test— statistical facts. The reader ought, therefore, to pay little attention to the complaints in the text, as to an increased extravagance in the expenses of tradesmen, and only regard the general recommendation, and the reasons by which that recommendation is enforced, to live within income.

with former times, namely, that there is not more got, and I am satisfied there is less laid up, than was then; or, if you will have it, that tradesmen get less and spend more than they ever did. How they should be richer than they were in those times, is very hard to say.

That all things are dearer than formerly to a house-keeper, needs little demonstration; the taxes necessarily infer it from the weight of them, and the many things charged; for, besides the things enumerated above, we find all articles of foreign importation are increased by the high duties laid on them; such as linen, especially fine linen; silk, especially foreign wrought silk: every thing eatable, drinkable, and wearable, are made heavy to us by high and exorbitant customs and excises, as brandies, tobacco, sugar; deals and timber for building; oil, wine, spice, raw silks, calico, chocolate, coffee, tea; on some of these the duties are more than doubled: and yet that which is most observable is, that such is the expensive humour of the times, that not a family, no, hardly of the meanest tradesman, but treat their friends with wine, or punch, or fine ale; and have their parlours set off with the tea-table and the chocolate-pot—treats and liquors all exotic, foreign and new among tradesmen, and terrible articles in their modern expenses; which have nothing to be said for them, either as to the expense of them, or the helps to health which they boast of: on the contrary, they procure us rheumatic bodies and consumptive purses, and can no way pass with me for necessaries; but being needless, they add to the expense, by sending us to the doctors and apothecaries to cure the breaches which they make in our health, and are themselves the very worst sort of superfluities.

But I come back to necessaries; and even in them, family-expenses are extremely risen, provisions are higher rated—no provisions that I know of, except only bread, mutton, and fish, but are made dearer than ever—house-rent, in almost all the cities and towns of note in England, is excessively and extremely dearer, and that in spite of such innumerable buildings as we see almost everywhere raised up, as well in the country as in London, and the parts adjacent.

Add to the rents of houses, the wages of servants. A tradesman, be he ever so much inclined to good husbandry, cannot always do his kitchen-work himself, suppose him a bachelor, or can his wife, suppose him married, and suppose her to have brought him any portion, be his bedfellow and his cook too. These maid-servants, then, are to be considered, and are an exceeding tax upon house-keepers; those who were formerly hired at three pounds to four pounds a-year wages, now demand five, six and eight pounds a-year; nor do they double anything upon us but their wages and their pride; for, instead of doing more work for their advance of wages, they do less: and the ordinary work of families cannot now be performed by the same number of maids, which, in short, is a tax upon the upper sort of tradesmen, and contributes very often to their disasters, by the extravagant keeping three or four maid-servants in a house, nay, sometimes five, where two formerly were thought sufficient. This very extravagance is such, that talking lately with a man very well experienced in this matter, he told me he had been making his calculations on that very particular, and he found by computation, that the number of servants kept by all sorts of people, tradesmen as well as others, was so much increased, that there are in London, and the towns within ten miles of it, take it every way, above a hundred thousand more maid-servants and footmen, at this time in place, than used to be in the same compass of ground thirty years ago;[22] and that their wages amounted to above forty shillings a-head per annum, more than the wages of the like number of servants did amount to at the same length of time past; the advance to the whole body amounting to no less than two hundred thousand pounds a-year.

Indeed, it is not easy to guess what the expense of wages to servants amounts to in a year, in this nation; and consequently we cannot easily determine what the increase of that expense amounts to in England, but certainly it must rise to many hundred thousand pounds a-year in the whole.

The tradesmen bear their share of this expense, and indeed too great a share, very ordinary tradesmen in London keeping at least two maids, and some more, and some a footman or two besides; for it is an ordinary thing to see the tradesmen and shopkeepers of London keep footmen, as well as the gentlemen: witness the infinite number of blue liveries, which are so common now that they are called the tradesmen's liveries; and few gentlemen care to give blue to their servants for that very reason.

In proportion to their servants, the tradesmen now keep their tables, which are also advanced in their proportion of expense to other things: indeed, the citizen's and tradesmen's tables are now the emblems, not of plenty, but of luxury, not of good house-keeping, but of profusion, and that of the highest kind of extravagance; insomuch,

---

[22] There can be little doubt, that the calculation of this experienced gentleman is grossly inconsistent with the truth. Nevertheless, this part of Defoe's work contains some curious traits of manners, which are probably not exaggerated

that it was the opinion of a gentleman who had been not a traveller only, but a nice observer of such things abroad, that there is at this time more waste of provisions in England than in any other nation in the world, of equal extent of ground; and that England consumes for their whole subsistence more flesh than half Europe besides; that the beggars of London, and within ten miles round it, eat more white bread than the whole kingdom of Scotland,[23] and the like.

But this is an observation only, though I believe it is very just; I am bringing it in here only as an example of the dreadful profusion of this age, and how an extravagant way of expensive living, perfectly negligent of all degrees of frugality or good husbandry, is the reigning vice of the people. I could enlarge upon it, and very much to the purpose here, but I shall have occasion to speak of it again.

The tradesman, whom I am speaking to by way of direction, will not, I hope, think this the way for him to thrive, or find it for his convenience to fall in with this common height of living presently, in his beginning; if he comes gradually into it after he has gotten something considerable to lay by, I say, if he does it then, it is early enough, and he may be said to be insensibly drawn into it by the necessity of the times; because, forsooth, it is a received notion, 'We must be like other folks:' I say, if he does fall into it then, when he will pretend he cannot help it, it is better than worse, and if he can afford it, well and good; but to begin thus, to set up at this rate, when he first looks into the world, I can only say this, he that begins in such a manner, it will not be difficult to guess where he will end; for a tradesman's pride certainly precedes his destruction, and an expensive living goes before his fall.

We are speaking now to a tradesman, who, it is supposed, must live by his business, a young man who sets up a shop, or warehouse, and expects to get money; one that would be a rich tradesman, rather than a poor, fine, gay man; a grave citizen, not a peacock's feather; for he that sets up for a Sir Fopling Flutter, instead of a complete tradesman, is not to be thought capable of relishing this discourse; neither does this discourse relish him; for such men seem to be among the incurables, and are rather fit for an hospital of fools (so the French call our Bedlam) than to undertake trade, and enter upon business.

---

[23] Defoe, from his having been employed for several years in Scotland at the time of the Union, must have well known how rare was then the use of white or wheaten bread in that country.

Trade is not a ball, where people appear in masque, and act a part to make sport; where they strive to seem what they really are not, and to think themselves best dressed when they are least known: but it is a plain visible scene of honest life, shown best in its native appearance, without disguise; supported by prudence and frugality; and like strong, stiff, clay land, grows fruitful only by good husbandry, culture, and manuring.

A tradesman dressed up fine, with his long wig and sword, may go to the ball when he pleases, for he is already dressed up in the habit; like a piece of counterfeit money, he is brass washed over with silver, and no tradesman will take him for current; with money in his hand, indeed, he may go to the merchant's warehouse and buy any thing, but no body will deal with him without it: he may write upon his edged hat, as a certain tradesman, after having been once broke and set up again, 'I neither give nor take credit:' and as others set up in their shops, 'No trust by retail,' so he may say, 'No trust by wholesale.' In short, thus equipped, he is truly a tradesman in masquerade, and must pass for such wherever he is known. How long it may be before his dress and he may suit, it not hard to guess.

Some will have it that this expensive way of living began among the tradesmen first, that is to say, among the citizens of London; and that their eager resolved pursuit of that empty and meanest kind of pride, called imitation, namely, to look like the gentry, and appear above themselves, drew them into it. It has indeed been a fatal custom, but it has been too long a city vanity. If men of quality lived like themselves, men of no quality would strive to live not like themselves: if those had plenty, these would have profusion; if those had enough, these would have excess; if those had what was good, these would have what was rare and exotic; I mean as to season, and consequently dear. And this is one of the ways that have worn out so many tradesmen before their time.

This extravagance, wherever it began, had its first rise among those sorts of tradesmen, who, scorning the society of their shops and customers, applied themselves to rambling to courts and plays; kept company above themselves, and spent their hours in such company as lives always above them; this could not but bring great expense along with it, and that expense would not be confined to the bare keeping such company abroad, but soon showed itself in a living like them at home, whether the tradesmen could support it or no.

Keeping high company abroad certainly brings on visitings and high treatings at home; and these are attended with costly furniture, rich clothes, and dainty tables. How these things agree with a tradesman's income, it is easy to suggest; and that, in short, these measures have sent so many tradesmen to the Mint and to the Fleet, where I am witness to it that they have still carried on their expensive living till they have come at last to starving and misery; but have been so used to it, they could not abate it, or at least not quite leave it off, though they wanted the money to pay for it.

Nor is the expensive dressing a little tax upon tradesmen, as it is now come up to an excess not formerly known to tradesmen; and though it is true that this particularly respects the ladies (for the tradesmen's wives now claim that title, as they do by their dress claim the appearance), yet to do justice to them, and not to load the women with the reproach, as if it were wholly theirs, it must be acknowledged the men have their share in dress, as the times go now, though, it is true, not so antic and gay as in former days; but do we not see fine wigs, fine Holland shirts of six to seven shillings an ell, and perhaps laced also, all lately brought down to the level of the apron, and become the common wear of tradesmen—nay, I may say, of tradesmen's apprentices—and that in such a manner as was never known in England before?

If the tradesman is thriving, and can support this and his credit too, that makes the case differ, though even then it cannot be said to be suitable; but for a tradesman to begin thus, is very imprudent, because the expense of this, as I said before, drains the very life-blood of his trade, taking away his ready money only, and making no return, but the worst of return, poverty and reproach; and, in case of miscarriage, infinite scandal and offence.

I am loth to make any part of my writing a satire upon the women; nor, indeed, does the extravagance either of dress or house-keeping, lie all, or always, at the door of the tradesmen's wives—the husband is often the prompter of it; at least he does not let his wife into the detail of his circumstances, he does not make her mistress of her own condition, but either flatters her with notions of his wealth, his profits, and his flourishing circumstances, and so the innocent woman spends high and lives great, believing that she is in a condition to afford it, and that her husband approves of it; at least, he does not offer to retrench or restrain her, but lets her go on, and indeed goes on with her, to the ruin of both.

I cannot but mention one thing here (though I purpose to give you one discourse on that subject by itself), namely, the great and indispensable obligation there is upon a tradesman always to acquaint his wife with the truth of his circumstances, and not to let her run on in ignorance, till she falls with him down the precipice of an unavoidable ruin—a thing no prudent woman would do, and therefore will never take amiss a husband's plainness in that particular case. But I reserve this to another place, because I am rather directing my discourse at this time to the tradesman at his beginning, and, as it may be supposed, unmarried.

Next to the expensive dressing, I place the expensive keeping company, as one thing fatal to a tradesman, and which, if he would be a complete tradesman, he should avoid with the utmost diligence. It is an agreeable thing to be seen in good company; for a man to see himself courted and valued, and his company desired by men of fashion and distinction, is very pleasing to any young tradesman, and it is really a snare which a young tradesman, if he be a man of sense, can very hardly resist. There is in itself indeed nothing that can be objected against, or is not very agreeable to the nature of man, and that not to his vicious part merely, but even to his best faculties; for who would not value himself upon being, as above, rendered acceptable to men both in station and figure above themselves? and it is really a piece of excellent advice which a learned man gave to his son, always to keep company with men above himself, not with men below himself.

But take me now to be talking, as I really am, not to the man merely, but to his circumstances, if he were a man of fortune, and had the view of great things before him, it would hold good; but if he is a young tradesman, such as I am now speaking of, who is newly entered into business, and must depend upon his said business for his subsistence and support, and hopes to raise himself by it—I say, if I am talking to such a one, I must say to him, that keeping company as above, with men superior to himself in knowledge, in figure, and estate, is not his business; for, first, as such conversation must necessarily take up a great deal of his time, so it ordinarily must occasion a great expense of money, and both destructive of his prosperity; nay, sometimes the first may be as fatal to him as the last, and it is oftentimes true in that sense of trade, that while by keeping company he is drawn out of his business, his absence from his shop or warehouse is the most fatal to him; and while he spends one crown in the tavern, he spends forty crowns' worth of his time; and with this difference, too, which renders it the worse to the tradesman, namely, that the money may be recovered, and gotten up again, but the time cannot. For example—

1. Perhaps in that very juncture a person comes to his warehouse. Suppose the tradesman to be a warehouse-keeper, who trades by commission, and this person, being a clothier in the country, comes to offer him his business, the commission of which might have been worth to him thirty to forty or fifty pounds per annum; but finding him abroad, or rather, not finding him at home and in his business, goes to another, and fixes with him at once. I once knew a dealer lose such an occasion as this, for an afternoon's pleasure, he being gone a-fishing into Hackney-marsh. This loss can never be restored, this expense of time was a fatal expense of money; and no tradesman will deny but they find many such things as this happen in the course of trade, either to themselves or others.

2. Another tradesman is invited to dinner by his great friend; for I am now speaking chiefly upon the subject of keeping high company, and what the tradesman sometimes suffers by it; it is true, that there he finds a most noble entertainment, the person of quality, and that professes a friendship for him, treats him with infinite respect, is fond of him, makes him welcome as a prince—for I am speaking of the acquaintance as really valuable and good in itself—but then, see it in its consequences. The tradesman on this occasion misses his 'Change, that is, omits going to the Exchange for that one day only, and not being found there, a merchant with whom he was in treaty for a large parcel of foreign goods, which would have been to his advantage to have bought, sells them to another more diligent man in the same way; and when he comes home, he finds, to his great mortification, that he has lost a bargain that would have been worth a hundred pounds buying; and now being in want of the goods, he is forced to entreat his neighbour who bought them to part with some of them at a considerable advance of price, and esteem it a favour too. Who now paid dearest for the visit to a person of figure?—the gentleman, who perhaps spent twenty shillings extraordinary to give him a handsome dinner, or the tradesman who lost a bargain worth a hundred pounds buying to go to eat it?

3. Another tradesman goes to 'Change in the ordinary course of his business, intending to speak with some of the merchants, his customers, as is usual, and get orders for goods, or perhaps an appointment to come to his warehouse to buy; but a snare of the like

kind falls in his way, and a couple of friends, who perhaps have little or no business, at least with him, lay hold of him, and they agree to go off Change to the tavern together. By complying with this invitation, he omits speaking to some of those merchants, as above, who, though he knew nothing of their minds, yet it had been his business to have shown himself to them, and have put himself in the way of their call; but omitting this, he goes and drinks a bottle of wine, as above, and though he stays but an hour, or, as we say, but a little while, yet unluckily, in that interim, the merchant, not seeing him on the Exchange, calls at his warehouse as he goes from the Exchange, but not finding him there either, he goes to another warehouse, and gives his orders to the value of £300 or £400, to a more diligent neighbour of the same business; by which he (the warehouse-keeper) not only loses the profit of selling that parcel, or serving that order, but the merchant is shown the way to his neighbour's warehouse, who, being more diligent than himself, fails not to cultivate his interest, obliges him with selling low, even to little or no gain, for the first parcel; and so the unhappy tradesman loses not his selling that parcel only, but loses the very customer, which was, as it were, his peculiar property before.

All these things, and many more such, are the consequences of a tradesman's absence from his business; and I therefore say, the expense of time on such light occasions as these, is one of the worst sorts of extravagance, and the most fatal to the tradesman, because really he knows not what he loses.

Above all things, the tradesman should take care not to be absent in the season of business, as I have mentioned above; for the warehouse-keeper to be absent from 'Change, which is his market, or from his warehouse, at the times when the merchants generally go about to buy, he had better be absent all the rest of the day.

I know nothing is more frequent, than for the tradesman, when company invites, or an excursion from business presses, to say, 'Well, come, I have nothing to do; there is no business to hinder, there is nothing neglected, I have no letters to write;' and the like; and away he goes to take the air for the afternoon, or to sit and enjoy himself with a friend—all of them things innocent and lawful in themselves; but here is the crisis of a tradesman's prosperity. In that very moment business presents, a valuable customer comes to buy, an unexpected bargain offers to be sold; another calls to pay money; and the like: nay, I would almost say, but that I am loth to concern the devil in more evils than he is guilty of—that the devil frequently draws a man out of his business when something extraordinary is just at hand for his advantage.

But not, as I have said, to charge the devil with what he is not guilty of, the tradesman is generally his own tempter; his head runs off from his business by a secret indolence; company, and the pleasure of being well received among gentlemen, is a cursed snare to a young tradesman, and carries him away from his business, for the mere vanity of being caressed and complimented by men who mean no ill, and perhaps know not the mischief they do to the man they show respect to; and this the young tradesman cannot resist, and that is in time his undoing.

The tradesman's pleasure should be in his business, his companions should be his books; and if he has a family, he makes his excursions up stairs, and no farther; when he is there, a bell or a call brings him down; and while he is in his parlour, his shop or his warehouse never misses him; his customers never go away unserved, his letters never come in and are unanswered. None of my cautions aim at restraining a tradesman from diverting himself, as we call it, with his fireside, or keeping company with his wife and children: there are so few tradesmen ruin themselves that way, and so few ill consequences happen upon an uxorious temper, that I will not so much as rank it with the rest; nor can it be justly called one of the occasions of a tradesman's disasters; on the contrary, it is too often that the want of a due complacency there, the want of taking delight there, estranges the man from not his parlour only, but his warehouse and shop, and every part of business that ought to engross both his mind and his time. That tradesman who does not delight in his family, will never long delight in his business; for, as one great end of an honest tradesman's diligence is the support of his family, and the providing for the comfortable subsistence of his wife and children, so the very sight of, and above all, his tender and affectionate care for his wife and children, is the spur of his diligence; that is, it puts an edge upon his mind, and makes him hunt the world for business, as hounds hunt the woods for their game. When he is dispirited, or discouraged by crosses and disappointments, and ready to lie down and despair, the very sight of his family rouses him again, and he flies to his business with a new vigour; 'I must follow my business,' says he, 'or we must all starve, my poor children must perish;' in a word, he that is not animated to diligence by the very sight and thought of his wife and children being brought to misery and distress, is a kind of a deaf adder that no music will charm, or a Turkish mute that no pity can move: in a word, he is a creature not to be called human, a wretch hardened against all the passions and affections that nature has furnished to other animals; and as there is no rhetoric of use to such a kind of man as that, so I am not talking to such a one, he must go among the incurables; for, where nature cannot work, what can argument assist?

CHAPTER XI
OF THE TRADESMAN'S MARRYING TOO SOON

It was a prudent provision which our ancestors made in the indenture of tradesmen's apprentices, that they should not contract matrimony during their apprenticeship; and they bound it with a penalty that was then thought sufficient. However, custom has taken off the edge of it since; namely, that they who did thus contract matrimony should forfeit their indentures, that is to say, should lose the benefit of their whole service, and not be made free.

Doubtless our forefathers were better acquainted with the advantages of frugality than we are, and saw farther into the desperate consequences of expensive living in the beginning of a tradesman's setting out into the world than we do; at least, it is evident they studied more and practised more of the prudential part in those cases, than we do.

Hence we find them very careful to bind their youth under the strongest obligations they could, to temperance, modesty, and good husbandry, as the grand foundations of their prosperity in trade, and to prescribe to them such rules and methods of frugality and good husbandry, as they thought would best conduce to their prosperity.

Among these rules this was one of the chief—namely, 'that they should not wed before they had sped?' It is an old homely rule, and coarsely expressed, but the meaning is evident, that a young beginner should never marry too soon. While he was a servant, he was bound from it as above; and when he had his liberty, he was persuaded against it by all the arguments which indeed ought to prevail with a considering man—namely, the expenses that a family necessarily would bring with it, and the care he ought to take to be able to support the expense before he brought it upon himself.

On this account it is, I say, our ancestors took more of their youth than we now do; at least, I think, they studied well the best methods of thriving, and were better acquainted with the steps by which a young tradesman ought to be introduced into the world than we are, and of the difficulties which those people would necessarily involve themselves in, who, despising those rules and methods of frugality, involved themselves in the expense of a family before they were in a way of gaining sufficient to support it.

A married apprentice will always make a repenting tradesman; and those stolen matches, a very few excepted, are generally attended with infinite broils and troubles, difficulties, and cross events, to carry them on at first by way of intrigue, to conceal them afterwards under fear of superiors, to manage after that to keep off scandal, and preserve the character as well of the wife as of the husband; and all this necessarily attended with a heavy expense, even before the young man is out of his time; before he has set a foot forward, or gotten a shilling in the world; so that all this expense is out of his original stock, even before he gets it, and is a sad drawback upon him when it comes.

Nay, this unhappy and dirty part is often attended with worse consequences still; for this expense coming upon him while he is but a servant, and while his portion, or whatever it is to be called, is not yet come into his hand, he is driven to terrible exigencies to supply this expense. If his circumstances are mean, and his trade mean, he is frequently driven to wrong his master, and rob his shop or his till for money, if he can come at it: and this, as it begins in madness, generally ends in destruction; for often he is discovered, exposed, and perhaps punished, and so the man is undone before he begins. If his circumstances are good, and he has friends that are able, and expectations that are considerable, then his expense is still the greater, and ways and means are found out, or at least looked for, to supply the expense, and conceal the fact, that his friends may not know it, till he has gotten the blessing he expects into his hands, and is put in a way to stand upon his own legs; and then it comes out, with a great many grieving aggravations to a parent to find himself tricked and defeated in the expectations of his son's marrying handsomely, and to his advantage; instead of which, he is obliged to receive a dish-clout for a daughter-in-law, and see his family propagated by a race of beggars, and yet perhaps as haughty, as insolent, and as expensive, as if she had blessed the family with a lady of fortune, and brought a fund with her to have supported the charge of her posterity.

When this happens, the poor young man's case is really deplorable. Before he is out of his time, he is obliged to borrow of friends, if he has any, on pretence his father does not make him a sufficient allowance, or he trenches upon his master's cash, which perhaps, he being the eldest apprentice, is in his hands; and this he does, depending, that when he is out of his time, and his father gives him wherewith to set up, he will make good the deficiency; and all this happens accordingly so that his reputation as to his master is preserved, and he comes off clear as to dishonesty in his trust.

But what a sad chasm does it make in his fortune! I knew a certain young tradesman, whose father, knowing nothing of his son's measures, gave him £2000 to set up with, straining himself to the utmost for the well introducing his son into the world; but who, when he came to set up, having near a year before married the servant-maid of the house where he lodged, and kept her privately at a great expense, had above £600 of his stock already wasted and sunk, before he began for himself; the consequence of which was, that going in partner with another young man, who had likewise £2000 to begin with, he was, instead of half of the profits, obliged to make a private article to accept of a third of the trade; and the beggar-wife proving more expensive, by far, than the partner's wife (who married afterwards, and doubled his fortune), the first young man was obliged to quit the trade, and with his remaining stock set up by himself; in which case his expenses continuing, and his stock being insufficient, he sank gradually, and then broke, and died poor. In a word, he broke the heart of his father, wasted what he had, and could never recover it, and at last it broke his own heart too.

But I shall bring it a little farther. Suppose the youth not to act so grossly neither; not to marry in his apprenticeship, not to be forced to keep a wife privately, and eat the bread he never got; but suppose him to be entered upon the world, that he has set up, opened shop, or fitted up his warehouse, and is ready to trade, the next thing, in the ordinary course of the world, at this time is *a wife*; nay, I have met with some parents, who have been indiscreet enough themselves to prompt their sons to marry as soon as they are set up; and the reason they give for it is, the wickedness of the age, that youth are drawn in a hundred ways to ruinous matches or debaucheries, and are so easily ruined by the mere looseness of their circumstances, that it is needful to marry them to keep them at home, and to preserve them diligent, and bind them close to their business.

This, be it just or not, is a bad cure of an ill disease; it is ruining the young man to make him sober, and making him a slave for life to make him diligent. Be it that the wife he shall marry is a sober, frugal, housewifely woman, and that nothing is to be laid to her charge but the mere necessary addition of a family expense, and that with the utmost moderation, yet, at the best, he cripples his fortune, stock-starves his business, and brings a great expense upon himself at first, before, by his success in trade, he had laid up stock enough to support the charge.

First, it is reasonable to suppose, that at his beginning in the world he cannot expect to get so good a portion with a wife, as he might after he had been set up a few years, and by his diligence and frugality, joined to a small expense in house-keeping, had increased both his stock in trade and the trade itself; then he would be able to look forward boldly, and would have some pretence for insisting on a fortune, when he could make out his improvements in trade, and show that he was both able to maintain a wife, and able to live without her. When a young tradesman in Holland or Germany goes a-courting, I am told the first question the young woman asks of him, or perhaps her friends for her, is, 'Are you able to pay the charges?' that is to say, in English, 'Are you able to keep a wife when you have got her?' The question is a little Gothic indeed, and would be but a kind of gross way of receiving a lover here, according to our English good breeding; but there is a great deal of reason in the inquiry, that must be confessed; and he that is not able to *pay the charges*, should never begin the journey; for, be the wife what she will, the very state of life that naturally attends the marrying a woman, brings with it an expense so very considerable, that a tradesman ought to consider very well of it before he engages.

But it is to be observed, too, that abundance of young tradesmen, especially in England, not only marry early, but by the so marrying they are obliged to take up with much less fortunes in their haste, than when they allow themselves longer time of consideration. As it stands now, generally speaking, the wife and the shop make their first show together; but how few of these early marriages succeed—how hard such a tradesman finds it to stand, and support the weight that attends it—I appeal to the experience of those, who having taken this wrong step, and being with difficulty got over it, are yet good judges of that particular circumstance in others that come after them.[24]

---

[24] Defoe's views on the subject of the too early marrying of young tradesmen, are in every particular sound. Though there are instances of premature marriages followed by no evil result, but rather the contrary, there can be no doubt, that the only prudent course is to wait till a settlement in life, and a regular income, have been secured. A young man, anxious for other reasons to marry, is sometimes heard to express his conviction that he might live more cheaply married than single. There could be no assertion more inconsistent with all common experience. Even if no positively ruinous consequences arise from an over-early marriage, it almost always occasions much hardship. It saddens a period of life which nature has designed to be peculiarly cheerful. The whole life of such a man becomes like a year in which there has been no

I know it is a common cry that is raised against the woman, when her husband fails in business, namely, that it is the wife has ruined him; it is true, in some particular cases it may be so, but in general it is wrong placed—they may say marrying has ruined the man, when they cannot say his wife has done it, for the woman was not in fault, but her husband.

When a tradesman marries, there are necessary consequences, I mean of expenses, which the wife ought not be charged with, and cannot be made accountable for—such as, first, furnishing the house; and let this be done with the utmost plainness, so as to be decent; yet it must be done, and this calls for ready money, and that ready money by so much diminishes his stock in trade; nor is the wife at all to be charged in this case, unless she either put him to more charge than was needful, or showed herself dissatisfied with things needful, and required extravagant gaiety and expense. Secondly, servants, if the man was frugal before, it may be he shifted with a shop, and a servant in it, an apprentice, or journeyman, or perhaps without one at first, and a lodging for himself, where he kept no other servant, and so his expenses went on small and easy; or if he was obliged to take a house because of his business and the situation of his shop, he then either let part of the house out to lodgers, keeping himself a chamber in it, or at the worst left it unfurnished, and without any one but a maid-servant to dress his victuals, and keep the house clean; and thus he goes on when a bachelor, with a middling expense at most.

But when he brings home a wife, besides the furnishing his house, he must have a formal house-keeping, even at the very first; and as children come on, more servants, that is, maids, or nurses, that are as necessary as the bread he eats—especially if he multiplies apace, as he ought to suppose he may—in this case let the wife be frugal and managing, let her be unexceptionable in her expense, yet the man finds his charge mount high, and perhaps too high for his gettings, notwithstanding the additional stock obtained by her portion. And what is the end of this but inevitable decay, and at last poverty and ruin?

Nay, the more the woman is blameless, the more certain is his overthrow, for if it was an expense that was extravagant and unnecessary, and that his wife ran him out by her high living and gaiety,

---

May or June. The grave cares of matrimony do not appear to be naturally suitable to the human character, till the man has approached his thirtieth, and the woman her twenty-fourth year.

he might find ways to retrench, to take up in time, and prevent the mischief that is in view. A woman may, with kindness and just reasoning, be easily convinced, that her husband cannot maintain such an expense as she now lives at; and let tradesmen say what they will, and endeavour to excuse themselves as much as they will, by loading their wives with the blame of their miscarriage, as I have known some do, and as old father Adam, though in another case, did before them, I must say so much in the woman's behalf at a venture. It will be very hard to make me believe that any woman, that was not fit for Bedlam, if her husband truly and timely represented his case to her, and how far he was or was not able to maintain the expense of their way of living, would not comply with her husband's circumstances, and retrench her expenses, rather than go on for a while, and come to poverty and misery. Let, then, the tradesman lay it early and seriously before his wife, and with kindness and plainness tell her his circumstances, or never let him pretend to charge her with being the cause of his ruin. Let him tell her how great his annual expense is; for a woman who receives what she wants as she wants it, that only takes it with one hand, and lays it out with another, does not, and perhaps cannot, always keep an account, or cast up how much it comes to by the year. Let her husband, therefore, I say, tell her honestly how much his expense for her and himself amounts to yearly; and tell her as honestly, that it is too much for him, that his income in trade will not answer it; that he goes backward, and the last year his family expenses amounted to so much, say £400—for that is but an ordinary sum now for a tradesman to spend, whatever it has been esteemed formerly—and that his whole trade, though he made no bad debts, and had no losses, brought him in but £320 the whole year, so that he was £80 that year a worse man than he was before, that this coming year he had met with a heavy loss already, having had a shopkeeper in the country broke in his debt £200, and that he offered but eight shillings in the pound, so that he should lose £120 by him, and that this, added to the £80 run out last year, came to £200, and that if they went on thus, they should be soon reduced.

What could the woman say to so reasonable a discourse, if she was a woman of any sense, but to reply, she would do any thing that lay in her to assist him, and if her way of living was too great for him to support, she would lessen it as he should direct, or as much as he thought was reasonable?—and thus, going hand in hand, she and he together abating what reason required, they might bring their expenses within the compass of their gettings, and be able to go on again comfortably.

But now, when the man, finding his expenses greater than his income, and yet, when he looks into those expenses, finds that his wife is frugal too, and industrious, and applies diligently to the managing her family, and bringing up her children, spends nothing idly, saves every thing that can be saved; that instead of keeping too many servants, is a servant to every body herself; and that, in short, when he makes the strictest examination, finds she lays out nothing but what is absolutely necessary, what now must this man do? He is ruined inevitably—for all his expense is necessary; there is no retrenching, no abating any thing.

This, I say, is the worst case of the two indeed; and this man, though he may say he is undone by marrying, yet cannot blame the woman, and say he is undone by his wife. This is the very case I am speaking of; the man should not have married so soon; he should have staid till he had, by pushing on his trade, and living close in his expense, increased his stock, and been what we call beforehand in the world; and had he done thus, he had not been undone by marrying.

It is a little hard to say it, but in this respect it is very true, there is many a young tradesman ruined by marrying a good wife—in which, pray take notice that I observe my own just distinction: I do not say they are ruined or undone by a good wife, or by their wives being good, but by their marrying—their unseasonable, early, and hasty marrying— before they had cast up the cost of one, or the income of the other— before they had inquired into the necessary charge of a wife and a family, or seen the profits of their business, whether it would maintain them or no; and whether, as above, they could pay the charges, the increasing necessary charge, of a large and growing family. How to persuade young men to consider this in time, and beware and avoid the mischief of it, that is a question by itself.

Let no man, then, when he is brought to distress by this early rashness, turn short upon his wife, and reproach her with being the cause of his ruin, unless, at the same time, he can charge her with extravagant living, needless expense, squandering away his money, spending it in trifles and toys, and running him out till the shop could not maintain the kitchen, much less the parlour; nor even then, unless he had given her timely notice of it, and warned her that he was not able to maintain so large a family, or so great an expense, and that, therefore, she would do well to consider of it, and manage with a straiter hand, and the like. If, indeed, he had done so, and she had not complied with him, then she had been guilty, and without excuse too; but as the woman cannot judge of his affairs, and he sees and bears a share in the riotous way of their living, and does not either show his dislike of it, or let her know, by some means or other, that he cannot support it, the woman cannot be charged with being his ruin—no, though her way of extravagant expensive living were really the cause of it. I met with a short dialogue, the other day, between a tradesman and his wife, upon such a subject as this, some part of which may be instructing in the case before us.

The tradesman was very melancholy for two or three days, and had appeared all that time to be pensive and sad, and his wife, with all her arts, entreaties, anger, and tears, could not get it out of him; only now and then she heard him fetch a deep sigh, and at another time say, he wished he was dead, and the like expressions. At last, she began the discourse with him in a respectful, obliging manner, but with the utmost importunity to get it out of him, thus:—

Wife.—My dear, what is the matter with you?

Husb.—Nothing.

Wife.—Nay, don't put me off with an answer that signifies nothing; tell me what is the matter, for I am sure something extraordinary is the case—tell me, I say, do tell me. [*Then she kisses him.*]

Husb.—Prithee, don't trouble me.

Wife.—I will know what is the matter

Husb.—I tell you nothing is the matter—what should be the matter?

Wife.—Come, my dear, I must not be put off so; I am sure, if it be any thing ill, I must have my share of it; and why should I not be worthy to know it, whatever it is, before it comes upon me.

Husb.—Poor woman! [*He kisses her.*]

Wife.—Well, but let me know what it is; come, don't distract yourself alone; let me bear a share of your grief, as well as I have shared in your joy.

Husb.—My dear, let me alone, you trouble me now, indeed.

[*Still he keeps her off.*]

Wife.—Then you will not trust your wife with knowing what touches you so sensibly?

Husb.—I tell you, it is nothing, it is a trifle, it is not worth talking of.

Wife.—Don't put me off with such stuff as that; I tell you, it is not for nothing that you have been so concerned, and that so long too; I have seen it plain enough; why, you have drooped upon it for this fortnight past, and above.

Husb.—Ay, this twelvemonth, and more.

Wife.—Very well, and yet it is nothing.

Husb.—It is nothing that you can help me in.

Wife.—Well, but how do you know that? Let me see, and judge whether I can, or no.

Husb.—I tell you, you cannot.

Wife.—Sure it is some terrible thing then. Why must not I know it? What! are you going to break? Come, tell me the worst of it.

Husb.—Break! no, no, I hope not—Break! no, I'll never break.

Wife.—As good as you have broke; don't presume; no man in trade can say he won't break.

Husb.—Yes, yes; I can say I won't break.

Wife.—I am glad to hear it; I hope you have a knack, then, beyond other tradesmen.

Husb.—No, I have not neither; any man may say so as well as I; and no man need break, if he will act the part of an honest man.

Wife.—How is that, pray?

Husb.—Why, give up all faithfully to his creditors, as soon as he finds there is a deficiency in his stock, and yet that there is enough left to pay them.

Wife.—Well, I don't understand those things, but I desire you would tell me what it is troubles you now; and if it be any thing of that kind, yet I think you should let me know it.

Husb.—Why should I trouble you with it?

Wife.—It would be very unkind to let me know nothing till it comes and swallows you up and me too, all on a sudden; I must know it, then; pray tell it me now.

Husb.—Why, then, I will tell you; indeed, I am not going to break, and I hope I am in no danger of it, at least not yet.

Wife.—I thank you, my dear, for that; but still, though it is some satisfaction to me to be assured of so much, yet I find there is something in it; and your way of speaking is ambiguous and doubtful. I entreat you, be plain and free with me. What is at the bottom of it?— why won't you tell me?—what have I done, that I am not to be trusted with a thing that so nearly concerns me?

Husb.—I have told you, my dear; pray be easy; I am not going to break, I tell you.

Wife.—Well, but let us talk a little more seriously of it; you are not going to break, that is, not just now, not yet, you said; but, my dear, if it is then not just at hand, but may happen, or is in view at some distance, may not some steps be taken to prevent it for the present, and to save us from it at last too.

Husb.—What steps could you think of, if that were the case?

Wife.—Indeed it is not much that is in a wife's power, but I am ready to do what lies in me, and what becomes me; and first, pray let us live lower. Do you think I would live as I do, if I thought your income would not bear it? No, indeed.

Husb.—You have touched me in the most sensible part, my dear; you have found out what has been my grief; you need make no further inquiries.

Wife.—Was that your grief?—and would you never be so kind to your wife as to let her know it?

Husb.—How could I mention so unkind a thing to you?

Wife.—Would it not have been more unkind to have let things run on to destruction, and left your wife to the reproach of the world, as having ruined you by her expensive living?

Husb.—That's true, my dear; and it may be I might have spoke to you at last, but I could not do it now; it looks so cruel and so hard to lower your figure, and make you look little in the eyes of the world, for you know they judge all by outsides, that I could not bear it.

Wife.—It would be a great deal more cruel to let me run on, and be really an instrument to ruin, my husband, when, God knows, I thought I was within the compass of your gettings, and that a great way; and you know you always prompted me to go fine, to treat handsomely, to keep more servants, and every thing of that kind. Could I doubt but that you could afford it very well?

Husb.—That's true, but I see it is otherwise now; and though I cannot help it, I could not mention it to you, nor, for ought I know, should I ever have done it.

Wife.—Why! you said just now you should have done it.

Husb.—Ay, at last, perhaps, I might, when things had been past recovery.

Wife.—That is to say, when you were ruined and undone, and could not show your head, I should know it; or when a statute of bankrupt had come out, and the creditors had come and turned us out of doors, then I should have known it—that would have been a barbarous sort of kindness.

Husb.—What could I do? I could not help it.

Wife.—Just so our old acquaintance G—W—did; his poor wife knew not one word of it, nor so much as suspected it, but thought him in as flourishing circumstances as ever; till on a sudden he was arrested in an action for a great sum, so great that he could not find bail, and the next day an execution on another action was served in the house, and swept away the very bed from under her; and the poor lady, that brought him £3000 portion, was turned into the street with five small children to take care of.

Husb.—Her case was very sad, indeed.

Wife.—But was not he a barbarous wretch to her, to let her know nothing of her circumstances? She was at the ball but the day before, in her velvet suit, and with her jewels on, and they reproach her with it every day.

Husb.—She did go too fine, indeed.

Wife.—Do you think she would have done so, if she had known any thing of his circumstances?

Husb.—It may be not.

Wife.—No, no; she is a lady of too much sense, to allow us to suggest it.

Husb.—And why did he not let her have some notice of it?

Wife.—Why, he makes the same dull excuse you speak of; he could not bear to speak to her of it, and it looked so unkind to do any thing to straiten her, he could not do it, it would break his heart, and the like; and now he has broke her heart.

Husb.—I know it is hard to break in upon one's wife in such a manner, where there is any true kindness and affection; but—

Wife.—But! but what? Were there really a true kindness and affection, as is the pretence, it would be quite otherwise; he would not break his own heart, forsooth, but chose rather to break his wife's heart! he could not be so cruel to tell her of it, and therefore left her to be cruelly and villanously insulted, as she was, by the bailiffs and creditors. Was that his kindness to her?

Husb.—Well, my dear, I have not brought you to that, I hope.

Wife.—No, my dear, and I hope you will not; however, you shall not say I will not do every thing I can to prevent it; and, if it lies on my side, you are safe.

Husb.—What will you do to prevent it? Come, let's see, what can you do?

Wife.—Why, first, I keep five maids, you see, and a footman; I shall immediately give three of my maids warning, and the fellow also, and save you that part of the expense.

Husb.—How can you do that?—you can't do your business.

Wife.—Yes, yes, there's nobody knows what they can do till they are tried; two maids may do all my house-business, and I'll look after my children myself; and if I live to see them grown a little bigger, I'll make them help one another, and keep but one maid; I hope that will be one step towards helping it.

Husb.—And what will all your friends and acquaintance, and the world, say to it?

Wife.—Not half so much as they would to see you break, and the world believe it be by my high living, keeping a house full of servants, and do nothing myself.

Husb.—They will say I am going to break upon your doing thus, and that's the way to make it so.

Wife.—I had rather a hundred should say you were going to break, than one could say you were really broke already.

Husb.—But it is dangerous to have it talked of, I say.

Wife.—No, no; they will say we are taking effectual ways to prevent breaking.

Husb.—But it will put a slur upon yourself too. I cannot bear any mortifications upon you, any more than I can upon myself.

Wife.—Don't tell me of mortifications; it would be a worse mortification, a thousand times over, to have you ruined, and have your creditors insult me with being the occasion of it.

Husb.—It is very kind in you, my dear, and I must always acknowledge it; but, however, I would not have you straiten yourself too much neither.

Wife.—Nay, this will not be so much a mortification as the natural consequence of other things; for, in order to abate the expense of our living, I resolve to keep less company. I assure you I will lay down all the state of living, as well as the expense of it; and, first, I will keep no visiting days; secondly, I'll drop the greatest part of the acquaintance I have; thirdly, I will lay down our treats and entertainments, and the like needless occasions of expense, and then I shall have no occasion for so many maids.

Husb.—But this, my dear, I say, will make as much noise almost, as if I were actually broke.

Wife.—No, no; leave that part to me.

Husb.—But you may tell me how you will manage it then.

Wife.—Why, I'll go into the country.

Husb.—That will but bring them after you, as it used to do.

Wife.—But I'll put off our usual lodgings at Hampstead, and give out that I am gone to spend the summer in Bedfordshire, at my aunt's, where every body knows I used to go sometimes; they can't come after me thither.

Husb.—But when you return, they will all visit you.

Wife.—Yes, and I will make no return to all those I have a mind to drop, and there's an end of all their acquaintance at once.

Husb.—And what must I do?

Wife.—Nay, my dear, it is not for me to direct that part; you know how to cure the evil which you sensibly feel the mischief of. If I do my part, I don't doubt you know how to do yours.

Husb.—Yes, I know, but it is hard, very hard.

Wife.—Nay, I hope it is no harder for you than it is for your wife.

Husb.—That is true, indeed, but I'll see.

Wife.—The question to me is not whether it is hard, but whether it is necessary.

Husb.—Nay, it is necessary, that is certain.

Wife.—Then I hope it is as necessary to you as to your wife.

Husb.—I know not where to begin.

Wife.—Why, you keep two horses and a groom, you keep rich high company, and you sit long at the Fleece every evening. I need say no more; you know where to begin well enough.

Husb.—It is very hard; I have not your spirit, my dear.

Wife.—I hope you are not more ashamed to retrench, than you would be to have your name in the Gazette.

Husb.—It is sad work to come down hill thus.

Wife.—It would be worse to fall down at one blow from the top; better slide gently and voluntarily down the smooth part, than to be pushed down the precipice, and be dashed all in pieces.

There was more of this dialogue, but I give the part which I think most to the present purpose; and as I strive to shorten the doctrine, so I will abridge the application also; the substance of the case lies in a few particulars, thus:—

I. The man was melancholy, and oppressed with the thoughts of his declining circumstances, and yet had not any thought of letting his wife know it, whose way of living was high and expensive, and more than he could support; but though it must have ended in ruin, he would rather let it have gone on till she was surprised in it, than to tell her the danger that was before her.

His wife very well argues the injustice and unkindness of such usage, and how hard it was to a wife, who, being of necessity to suffer in the fall, ought certainly to have the most early notice of it—that, if possible, she might prevent it, or, at least, that she might not be overwhelmed with the suddenness and the terror of it.

II. Upon discovering it to his wife, or rather her drawing the discovery from him by her importunity, she immediately, and most readily and cheerfully, enters into measures to retrench her expenses, and, as far as she was able, to prevent the blow, which was otherwise apparent and unavoidable.

Hence it is apparent, that the expensive living of most tradesmen in their families, is for want of a serious acquainting their wives with their circumstances, and acquainting them also in time; for there are very few ladies so unreasonable, who, if their husbands seriously informed them how things stood with them, and that they could not support their way of living, would not willingly come into measures to prevent their own destruction.

III. That it is in vain, as well as unequal, for a tradesman to preach frugality to his wife, and to bring his wife to a retrenching of her expenses, and not at the same time to retrench his own; seeing that keeping horses and high company is every way as great and expensive, and as necessary to be abated, as any of the family extravagances, let them be which they will.

All this relates to the duty of a tradesman in preventing his family expenses being ruinous to his business; but the true method to prevent all this, and never to let it come so far, is still, as I said before, not to marry too soon; not to marry, till by a frugal industrious management of his trade in the beginning, he has laid a foundation for maintaining a wife, and bringing up a family, and has made an essay by which he knows what he can and cannot do, and also before he has laid up and increased his stock, that he may not cripple his fortune at first, and be ruined before he has begun to thrive.

CHAPTER XII
OF THE TRADESMAN'S LEAVING HIS BUSINESS TO SERVANTS

It is the ordinary excuse of the gentlemen tradesmen of our times, that they have good servants, and that therefore they take more liberty to be out of their business, than they would otherwise do. 'Oh!' says the shopkeeper, 'I have an apprentice—it is an estate to have such a servant. I am as safe in him as if I had my eye upon the business from morning till night; let me be where I will, I am always satisfied he is at home; if I am at the tavern, I am sure he is in the counting-house, or behind the counter; he is never out of his post.

'And then for my other servants, the younger apprentices,' says he, 'it is all one as if I were there myself—they would be idle it may be, but he won't let them, I assure you; they must stick close to it, or he will make them do it; he tells them, boys do not come apprentices to play, but to work; not to sit idle, and be doing nothing, but to mind their master's business, that they may learn how to do their own.'

'Very well; and you think, Sir, this young man being so much in the shop, and so diligent and faithful, is an estate to you, and so indeed it is; but are your customers as well pleased with this man, too, as you are? or are they as well pleased with him, as they would be, if you were there yourself?'

'Yes, they are,' says the shopkeeper; 'nay, abundance of the customers take him for the master of the shop, and don't know any other; and he is so very obliging, and pleases so well, giving content to every body, that, if I am at any other part of the shop, and see him serving a customer, I never interrupt them, unless sometimes (he is so modest) he will call me, and turning to the ladies say, "There's my master, Madam; if you think he will abate you any thing, I'll call him;" and sometimes they will look a little surprised, and say, "Is that your master? indeed, we thought you had been the master of the shop yourself."'

'Well,' said I, 'and you think yourself very happy in all this, don't you? Pray, how long has this young gentleman to serve? how long is it before his time will be out?' 'Oh, he has almost a year and a half to serve,' says the shopkeeper. 'I hope, then,' said I, 'you will take care to have him knocked on the head, as soon as his time is out.' 'God forbid,' says the honest man; 'what do you mean by that?' 'Mean!' said I, 'why, if you don't, he will certainly knock your trade on the head, as soon as the year and a half comes to be up. Either you must dispose of him, as I say, or take care that he does not set up near you, no, not in the same street; if you do, your customers will all run thither. When they miss him in the shop, they will presently inquire for him; and as, you say, they generally take him for the master, they will ask whether the gentleman is removed that kept the shop before.'

All my shopkeeper could say, was, that he had got a salve for that sore, and that was, that when Timothy was out of his time, he resolved to take him in partner.

'A very good thing, indeed! so you must take Timothy into half the trade when he is out of his time, for fear he should run away with three-quarters of it, when he sets up for himself. But had not the master much better have been Timothy himself?—then he had been sure never to have the customers take Timothy for the master; and when he went away, and set up perhaps at next door, leave the shop, and run after him.'

It is certain, a good servant, a faithful, industrious, obliging servant, is a blessing to a tradesman, and, as he said, is an estate to his master; but the master, by laying the stress of his business upon him, divests himself of all the advantages of such a servant, and turns the blessing into a blast; for by giving up the shop as it were to him, and indulging himself in being abroad, and absent from his business, the apprentice gets the mastery of the business, the fame of the shop depends upon him, and when he sets up, certainly follows him. Such a servant would, with the master's attendance too, be very helpful, and yet not be dangerous; such a servant is well, when he is visibly an assistant to the master, but is ruinous when he is taken for the master. There is a great deal of difference between a servant's being the stay of his master, and his being the stay of his trade: when he is the first, the master is served by him; and when he is gone, he breeds up another to follow his steps; but when he is the last, he carries the trade with him, and does his master infinitely more hurt than good.

A good tradesman has a great deal of trouble with a bad servant, but must take heed that he is not wounded by a good one—the extravagant idle vagrant servant hurts himself, but the diligent servant endangers his master. The greater reputation the servant gets in his business, the more care the master has upon him, lest he gets within him, and worms him out of his business.

The only way to prevent this, and yet not injure a diligent servant, is that the master be as diligent as the servant; that the master be as much at the shop as the man. He that will keep in his business, need never fear keeping his business, let his servant be as diligent as he will. It is a hard thing that a tradesman should have the blessing of a good servant, and make it a curse to him, by his appearing less capable than his man.

Let your apprentice be in the business, but let the master be at the head of the business at all times. There is a great deal of difference between being diligent in the business *in* the shop, and leading the whole business *of* the shop. An apprentice who is diligent may be master of his business, but should never be master of the shop; the one is to be useful to his master, the other is to be master of his master; and, indeed, this shows the absolute necessity of diligence and application in a tradesman, and how, for want of it, that very thing which is the blessing of another tradesman's business is the ruin of his.

Servants, especially apprentices, ought to be considered, as they really are, in their moveable station, that they are here with you but seven years, and that then they act or move in a sphere or station of their own: their diligence is now for you, but ever after it is for themselves; that the better servants they have been while they were with you, the more dangerous they will be to you when you part; that, therefore, though you are bound in justice to them to let them into your business in every branch of it, yet you are not bound to give your business away to them; the diligence, therefore, of a good servant in the master's business, should be a spur to the master's diligence to take care of himself.

There is a great deal of difference also between trusting a servant in your business, and trusting him with your business: the first is leaving your business with him, the other is leaving your business to him. He that trusts a servant in his business, leaves his shop only to him; but he that leaves his business to his servant, leaves his wife and children at his disposal—in a word, such a trusting, or leaving the business to the servant, is no less than a giving up all to him, abandoning the care of his shop and all his affairs to him; and when such a servant is out of his time, the master runs a terrible risk, such as, indeed, it is not fit any tradesman should run—namely, of losing the best of his business.

What I have been now saying, is of the tradesman leaving his business to his apprentices and servants, when they prove good, when they are honest and diligent, faithful, and industrious; and if there are dangers even in trusting good servants, and such as do their duty perfectly well, what, then, must it be when the business is left to idle, negligent, and extravagant servants, who both neglect their masters' business and their own, who neither learn their trade for themselves, nor regard it for the interest of their masters? If the first are a blessing to their masters, and may only be made dangerous by their carrying away the trade with them when they go, these are made curses to their masters early, for they lose the trade for themselves and their masters too. The first carry the customers away with them, the last drive the customers away before they go. 'What signifies going to such a shop?' say the ladies, either speaking of a mercer or a draper, or any other trade; 'there is nothing to be met with there but a crew of saucy boys, that are always at play when you come in, and can hardly refrain it when you are there: one hardly ever sees a master in the shop, and the young rude boys hardly mind you when you are looking on their goods; they talk to you as if they cared not whether you laid out your money or no, and as if they had rather you were gone, that they might go to play again. I will go there no more, not I.'

If this be not the case, then you are in danger of worse still, and that is, that they are often thieves—idle ones are seldom honest ones—nay, they cannot indeed be honest, in a strict sense, if they are idle: but by dishonest, I mean downright thieves; and what is more dangerous than for an apprentice, to whom the whole business, the cash, the books, and all is committed, to be a thief?

For a tradesman, therefore, to commit his business thus into the hand of a false, a negligent, and a thievish servant, is like a man that travels a journey, and takes a highwayman into the coach with him: such a man is sure to be robbed, and to be fully and effectually plundered, because he discovers where he hides his treasure. Thus the tradesman places his confidence in the thief, and how should he avoid being robbed?

It is answered, that, generally tradesmen, who have any considerable trust to put into the hands of an apprentice, take security of them for their honesty by their friends, when their indentures are signed; and it is their fault then, if they are not secure. True, it is often so; but in a retail business, if the servant be unfaithful, there are so many ways to defraud a master, besides that of merely not balancing the cash, that it is impossible to detect them; till the tradesman, declining insensibly by the weight of the loss, is ruined and undone.

What need, then, has the tradesman to give a close attendance, and preserve himself from plunder, by acquainting himself in and with his business and servants, by which he makes it very difficult for them to deceive him, and much easier to him to discover it if he suspects them. But if the tradesman lives abroad, keeps at his country-house or lodgings, and leaves his business thus in the hands of his servants, committing his affairs to them, as is often the case; if they prove thieves, negligent, careless, and idle, what is the consequence?—he is insensibly wronged, his substance wasted, his business neglected; and how shall a tradesman thrive under such circumstances? Nay, how is it possible he should avoid ruin and destruction?—I mean, as to his business; for, in short, every such servant has his hand in his master's pocket, and may use him as he pleases.

Again, if they are not thieves, yet if they are idle and negligent, it is, in some cases, the same thing; and I wish it were well recommended to all such servants as call themselves honest, that it is as criminal to neglect their master's business as to rob him; and he is as really a thief who robs him of his time, as he that robs him of his money.

I know, as servants are now, this is a principle they will not allow, neither does one servant in fifty act by it; but if the master be absent, the servant is at his heels—that is to say, is as soon out of doors as his master, and having none but his conscience to answer to, he makes shift to compound with himself, like a bankrupt with his creditor, to pay half the debt—that is to say, half the time to his master, and half to himself, and think it good pay too.

The point of conscience, indeed, seems to be out of the question now, between master and servant; and as few masters concern themselves with the souls, nay, scarce with the morals of their servants, either to instruct them, or inform them of their duty either to God or man, much less to restrain them by force, or correct them, as was anciently practised, so, few servants concern themselves in a conscientious discharge of their duty to their masters—so that the great law of subordination is destroyed, and the relative duties on both sides are neglected; all which, as I take it, is owing to the exorbitant sums of money which are now given with servants to the masters, as the present or condition of their apprenticeship, which, as it is extravagant in itself, so it gives the servant a kind of a different figure in the family, places him above the ordinary class of servants hired for wages, and exempts him from all the laws of family government, so that a master seems now to have nothing to do with his apprentice, any other than in what relates to his business.

And as the servant knows this, so he fails not to take the advantage of it, and to pay no more service than he thinks is due; and the hours of his shop business being run out, he claims all the rest for himself, without the above restraint. Nor will the servants, in these times, bear any examinations with respect to the disposing of their waste time, or with respect to the company they keep, or the houses or places they go to.

The use I make of it is this, and herein it is justly applicable to the case in hand; by how much the apprentices and servants in this age are loose, wild, and ungovernable, by so much the more should a master think himself obliged not to depend upon them, much less to leave his business to them, and dispense with his own attendance in it. If he does, he must have much better luck then his neighbours, if he does not find himself very much wronged and abused, seeing, as I said above, the servants and apprentices of this age do very rarely act from a principle of conscience in serving their master's interest, which, however, I do not see they can be good Christians without.

I knew one very considerable tradesman in this city, and who had always five or six servants in his business, apprentices and journeymen, who lodged in his house; and having a little more the spirit of government in him than most masters I now meet with, he took this method with them. When he took apprentices, he told them beforehand the orders of his family, and which he should oblige them to; particularly, that they should none be absent from his business without leave, nor out of the house after nine o'clock at night; and that he would not have it thought hard, if he exacted three things of them:—

1. That, if they had been out, he should ask them where they had been, and in what company? and that they should give him a true and direct answer.

2. That, if he found reason to forbid them keeping company with any particular person, or in any particular house or family, they should be obliged to refrain from such company.

3. That, in breach of any of those two, after being positively charged with it, he would, on their promising to amend it, forgive them, only acquainting their friends of it; but the second time, he would dismiss them his service, and not be obliged to return any of the money he had with them. And to these he made their parents consent when

they were bound; and yet he had large sums of money with them too, not less than £200 each, and sometimes more.

As to his journeymen, he conditioned with them as follows:—

1. They should never dine from home without leave asked and obtained, and telling where, if required.

2. After the shutting in of the shop, they were at liberty to go where they pleased, only not to be out of the house after nine o'clock at night.

3. Never to be in drink, or to swear, on pain of being immediately dismissed without the courtesy usual with such servants, namely, of a month's warning.

These were excellent household laws; but the question is, how shall a master see them punctually obeyed, for the life of all laws depends upon their being well executed; and we are famous in England for being remiss in that very point; and that we have the best laws the worst executed of any nation in the world.

But my friend was a man who knew as well how to make his laws be well executed, as he did how to make the laws themselves. His case was thus: he kept a country-house about two miles from London, in the summer-time, for the air of his wife and children, and there he maintained them very comfortably: but it was a rule with him, that he who expects his servants to obey his orders, must be always upon the spot with them to see it done: to this purpose he confined himself to lie always at home, though his family was in the country; and every afternoon he walked out to see them, and to give himself the air too; but always so ordered his diversions, that he was sure to be at home before nine at night, that he might call over his family, and see that they observed orders, that is, that they were all at home at their time, and all sober.

As this was, indeed, the only way to have good servants, and an orderly family, so he had both; but it was owing much, if not all, to the exactness of his government; and would all masters take the same method, I doubt not they would have the like success; but what servants can a man expect when he leaves them to their own government, not regarding whether they serve God or the devil?

Now, though this man had a very regular family, and very good servants, yet he had this particular qualification, too, for a good tradesman, namely, that he never left his business entirely to them, nor could any of them boast that they were trusted to more than another.

This is certainly the way to have regular servants and to have business thrive; but this is not practised by one master to a thousand at this time—if it were, we should soon see a change in the families of tradesmen, and that very much for the better: nor, indeed, would this family government be good for the tradesman only, but it would be the servant's advantage too; and such a practice, we may say, would in time reform all the next age, and make them ashamed of us that went before them.

If, then, the morals of servants are thus loose and debauched, and that it is a general and epidemic evil, how much less ought tradesmen of this age to trust them, and still less to venture their all upon them, leave their great design, the event of all their business with them, and go into the country in pursuit of their pleasure.

The case of tradesmen differs extremely in this age from those in the last, with respect to their apprentices and servants; and the difference is all to the disadvantage of the present age, namely, in the last age, that is to say, fifty or sixty years ago, for it is not less, servants were infinitely more under subjection than they are now, and the subordination of mankind extended effectually to them; they were content to submit to family government; and the just regulations which masters made in their houses were not scorned and contemned, as they are now; family religion also had some sway upon them; and if their masters did keep good orders, and preserve the worship of God in their houses, the apprentices thought themselves obliged to attend at the usual hours for such services; nay, it has been known, where such orders have been observed, that if the master of the family has been sick, or indisposed, or out of town, the eldest apprentice has read prayers to the family in his place.

How ridiculous, to speak in the language of the present times, would it be for any master to expect this of a servant in our days! and where is the servant that would comply with it? Nay, it is but very rarely now that masters themselves do it; it is rather thought now to be a low step, and beneath the character of a man in business, as if worshipping God were a disgrace, and not an honour, to a family, or to the master of a family; and I doubt not but in a little while more, either the worship of God will be quite banished out of families, or the better sort of tradesmen, and such as have any regard to it, will keep chaplains, as other persons of quality do. It is confessed, the first is most probable, though the last, as I am informed, is already begun in the city, in some houses, where the reader of the parish is allowed a small additional salary to come once a-day, namely, every evening, to read prayers in the house.

But I am not talking on this subject; I am not directing myself to citizens or townsmen, as masters of families, but as heads of trade, and masters in their business; the other part would indeed require a whole book by itself, and would insensibly run me into a long satirical discourse upon the loss of all family government among us; in which, indeed, the practice of house-keepers and heads of families is grown not remiss only in all serious things, but even scandalous in their own morals, and in the personal examples they show to their servants, and all about them.

But to come back to my subject, namely, that the case of tradesmen differs extremely from what it was formerly: the second head of difference is this; that whereas, in former times, the servants were better and humbler than they are now, submitted more to family government, and to the regulations made by their masters, and masters were more moral, set better examples, and kept better order in their houses, and, by consequence of it, all servants were soberer, and fitter to be trusted, than they are now; yet, on the other hand, notwithstanding all their sobriety, masters did not then so much depend upon them, leave business to them, and commit the management of their affairs so entirely to their servants, as they do now.

All that I meet with, which masters have to say to this, is contained in two heads, and these, in my opinion, amount to very little.

I. That they have security for their servants' honesty, which in former times they had not.

II. That they receive greater premiums, or present-money, now with their apprentices, than they did formerly.

The first of these is of no moment; for, first, it does not appear that apprentices in those former days gave no security to their masters for their integrity, which, though perhaps not so generally as now, yet I have good reason to know was then practised among tradesmen of note, and is not now among inferior tradesmen: but, secondly, this security extends to nothing, but to make the master satisfaction for any misapplications or embezzlements which are discovered, and can be proved, but extend to no secret concealed mischiefs: neither, thirdly, do those securities reach to the negligence, idleness, or debaucheries of servants; but, which is still more than all the rest, they do not reach to the worst of robbery between the servant and his master, I mean the loss of his time; so that still there is as much reason for the master's inspection, both into his servants and their business, as ever.

But least of all does this security reach to make the master any satisfaction for the loss of his business, the ill management of his shop, the disreputation brought upon it by being committed to servants, and those servants behaving ill, slighting, neglecting, or disobliging customers; this does not relate to securities given or taken, nor can the master make himself any amends upon his servant, or upon his securities, for this irrecoverable damage. He, therefore, that will keep up the reputation of his shop, or of his business, and preserve his trade to his own advantage, must resolve to attend it himself, and not leave it to servants, whether good or bad; if he leaves it to good servants, they improve it for themselves, and carry the trade away with them when they go; if to bad servants, they drive his customers away, bring a scandal upon his shop, and destroy both their master and themselves.

Secondly, As to the receiving great premiums with their apprentices, which, indeed, is grown up to a strange height in this age, beyond whatever it was before, it is an unaccountable excess, which is the ruin of more servants at this time than all the other excesses they are subject to, nay, in some respect it is the cause of it all; and, on the contrary, is far from being an equivalent to their masters for the defect of their service, but is an unanswerable reason why the master should not leave his business to their management.

This premium was originally not a condition of indenture, but was a kind of usual or customary present to the tradesman's wife to engage her to be kind to the youth, and take a motherly care of him, being supposed to be young when first put out.

By length of time this compliment or present became so customary as to be made a debt, and to be conditioned for as a demand, but still was kept within bounds, and thirty or forty pounds was sufficient to a very good merchant, which now is run up to five hundred, nay, to a thousand pounds with an apprentice; a thing which formerly would have been thought monstrous, and not to be named.

The ill consequences of giving these large premiums are such and so many, that it is not to be entered upon in such a small tract as this; nor is it the design of this work: but it is thus far to the purpose here—namely, as it shows that this sets up servants into a class of gentlemen above their masters, and above their business; and they neither have a sufficient regard to one or other, and consequently are the less fit to be trusted by the master in the essential parts of his business; and this brings it down to the case in hand.

Upon the whole, the present state of things between masters and servants is such, that now more than ever the caution is needful and just, that he that leaves his business to the management of his servants, it is ten to one but he ruins his business and his servants too.

Ruining his business is, indeed, my present subject; but ruining his servants also is a consideration that an honest, conscientious master ought to think is of weight with him, and will concern himself about. Servants out of government are like soldiers without an officer, fit for nothing but to rob and plunder; without order, and without orders, they neither know what to do, or are directed how to do it.

Besides, it is letting loose his apprentices to levity and liberty in that particular critical time of life, when they have the most need of government and restraint. When should laws and limits be useful to mankind but in their youth, when unlimited liberty is most fatal to them, and when they are least capable of governing themselves? To have youth left without government, is leaving fire in a magazine of powder, which will certainly blow it all up at last, and ruin all the houses that are near it.

If there is any duty on the side of a master to his servant, any obligation on him as a Christian, and as a trustee for his parents, it lies here—to limit and restrain them, if possible, in the liberty of doing evil; and this is certainly a debt due to the trust reposed in masters by the parents of the youth committed to them. If he is let loose here, he is undone, of course, and it may be said, indeed, he was ruined by his master; and if the master is afterwards ruined by such a servant, what can be said for it but this? He could expect no other.

To leave a youth without government is indeed unworthy of any honest master; he cannot discharge himself as a master; for instead of taking care of him he indeed casts him off, abandons him, and, to put it into Scripture words, he leads him into temptation: nay, he goes farther, to use another Scripture expression: he delivers him over to Satan.

It is confessed—and it is fatal both to masters and servants at this time—that not only servants are made haughty, and above the government of their masters, and think it below them to submit to any family government, or any restraints of their masters, as to their morals and religion; but masters also seem to have given up all family government, and all care or concern for the morals and manners, as well as for the religion of their servants, thinking themselves under no obligation to meddle with those things, or to think any thing about them, so that their business be but done, and their shop or warehouse duly looked after.

But to bring it all home to the point in hand, if it is so with the master and servant, there is the less room still for the master of such servants to leave any considerable trust in the hands of such apprentices, or to expect much from them, to leave the weight of their affairs with them, and, living at their country lodgings, and taking their own diversions, depend upon such servants for the success of their business. This is indeed abandoning their business, throwing it away, and committing themselves, families, and fortunes, to the conduct of those, who, they have all the reason in the world to believe, have no concern upon them for their good, or care one farthing what becomes of them.

CHAPTER XIII
OF TRADESMEN MAKING COMPOSITION WITH DEBTORS, OR WITH CREDITORS

There is an alternative in the subject of this chapter, which places the discourse in the two extremes of a tradesman's fortunes.

I. The *fortunate tradesman*, called upon by his poor unfortunate neighbour, who is his debtor, and is become insolvent, to have compassion on him, and to compound with him for part of his debt, and accept his offer in discharge of the whole.

II. The *unfortunate tradesman* become insolvent and bankrupt himself, and applying himself to his creditor to accept of a composition, in discharge of his debt.

I must confess, a tradesman, let his circumstances be what they will, has the most reason to consider the disasters of the unfortunate, and be compassionate to them under their pressures and disasters, of any other men; because they know not—no, not the most prosperous of them—what may be their own fate in the world. There is a Scripture proverb, if I may call it so, very necessary to a tradesman in this case, 'Let him that thinketh he standeth, take heed lest he fall.'

N.B. It is not said, let him that standeth take heed, but him *that thinketh* he standeth. Men in trade can but think they stand; and there are so many incidents in a tradesman's circumstances, that sometimes when he thinks himself most secure of standing, he is in most danger of falling.

If, then, the contingent nature of trade renders every man liable to disaster that is engaged in it, it seems strange that tradesmen should be outrageous and unmerciful to one another when they fall; and yet so it is, that no creditor is so furious upon an unhappy insolvent tradesman, as a brother-tradesman of his own class, and who is at least liable to the same disaster, in the common event of his business.

Nay, I have lived to see—such is the uncertainty of human affairs, and especially in trade—the furious and outrageous creditor become bankrupt himself in a few years, or perhaps months after, and begging the same mercy of others, which he but just before denied to his not more unfortunate fellow-tradesman, and making the same exclamations at the cruelty and hard-heartedness of his creditors in refusing to comply with him, when, at the same time, his own heart must reproach him with his former conduct; how inexorable he was to all the entreaties and tears of his miserable neighbour and his distressed family, who begged his compassion with the lowest submission, who employed friends to solicit and entreat for them, laying forth their misery in the most lively expressions, and using all the arguments which the most moving distress could dictate, but in vain.

The tradesman is certainly wrong in this, as compassion to the miserable is a debt of charity due from all mankind to their fellow-creatures; and though the purse-proud tradesman may be able to say he is above the fear of being in the like circumstances, as some may be, yet, even then, he might reflect that perhaps there was a time when he was not so, and he ought to pay that debt of charity, in acknowledgement of the mercy that has set him above the danger.

And yet, speaking in the ordinary language of men who are subject to vicissitudes of fortune, where is the man that is sure he shall meet with no shock? And how have we seen men, who have to-day been immensely rich, be to-morrow, as it were, reduced to nothing! What examples were made in this city of such precipitations within the memory of some living, when the Exchequer shutting up ruined the great bankers of Lombard Street.[25] To what fell Sir Robert Viner—the great Alderman Backwell—the three brothers of the name of Forth, of whom King Charles II. made that severe pun, that ' *Three-fourths* of the city were broke?'

To what have we seen men of prodigious bulk in trade reduced—as Sir Thomas Cook, Sir Basil Firebrass, Sheppard, Coggs, and innumerable bankers, money-scriveners, and merchants, who thought themselves as secure against the shocks of trade, as any men in the world could be? Not to instance our late South Sea directors, and others, reduced by the terrible fate of bubbles, whose names I omit because they yet live, though sinking still under the oppression of their fortunes, and whose weight I would be far from endeavouring to make heavier.

Why, then, should any tradesman, presuming on his own security, and of his being out of the reach of disaster, harden his heart against the miseries and distresses of a fellow-tradesman, who sinks, as it were, by his side, and refuse to accept his offer of composition; at least, if he cannot object against the integrity of his representations, and cannot charge him with fraud and deceit, breaking with a wicked design to

---

[25] This event took place in 1671, Charles II. finding it necessary to suspend the national payments for a year.

cheat and delude his creditors, and to get money by a pretended breach? I say, why should any tradesman harden his heart in such a case, and not, with a generous pity, comply with a reasonable and fair proposal, while it is to be had?

I do acknowledge, if there is an evident fraud, if he can detect the bankrupt in any wicked design, if he can prove he has effects sufficient to pay his debts, and that he only breaks with a purpose to cheat his creditors, and he conceals a part of his estate, when he seems to offer a sincere surrender; if this be the case, and it can be made appear to be so—for in such a case, too, we ought to be very sure of the fact—then, indeed, no favour is due, and really none ought to be shown.

And, therefore, it was a very righteous clause which was inflicted on the fraudulent bankrupt, in a late act of Parliament, namely, that in case he concealed his effects, and that it appeared he had, though upon his oath, not given in a full account of his estate, but willingly and knowingly concealed it, or any part of it, with design to defraud his creditors, he should be put to death as a felon: the reason and justice of which clause was this, and it was given as the reason of it when the act was passed in the House of Commons, namely, that the act was made for the relief of the debtor, as well as of the creditor, and to procure for him a deliverance on a surrender of his effects; but then it was made also for the relief of the creditor, too, that he might have as much of his debt secured to him as possible, and that he should not discharge the debtor with his estate in his pocket, suffering him to run away with his (the creditor's) money before his face.

Also it was objected, that the act, without a penalty, would be only an act to encourage perjury, and would deliver the hard-mouthed knave that could swear what he pleased, and ruin and reject the modest conscientious tradesman, that was willing and ready to give up the utmost farthing to his creditors. On this account the clause was accepted, and the act passed, which otherwise had been thrown out.

Now, when the poor insolvent has thus surrendered his all, stript himself entirely upon oath, and that oath taken on the penalty of death if it be false, there seems to be a kind of justice due to the bankrupt. He has satisfied the law, and ought to have his liberty given him *as a prey*, as the text calls it, Jer. xxxix. 18., that he may try the world once again, and see, if possible, to recover his disasters, and get his bread; and it is to be spoken in honour of the justice as well as humanity of that law for delivering bankrupts, that there are more tradesmen recover themselves in this age upon their second endeavours, and by setting up again after they have thus failed and been delivered, than ever were known to do so in ten times the number of years before.

To break, or turn bankrupt, before this, was like a man being taken by the Turks; he seldom recovered liberty to try his fortune again, but frequently languished under the tyranny of the commissioners of bankrupt, or in the Mint, or Friars, or rules of the Fleet, till he wasted the whole estate, and at length his life, and so his debts were all paid at once.

Nor was the case of the creditor much better—I mean as far as respected his debt, for it was very seldom that any considerable dividend was made; on the other hand, large contributions were called for before people knew whether it was likely any thing would be made of the debtor's effects or no, and oftentimes the creditor lost his whole debt, contribution-money and all; so that while the debtor was kept on the rack, as above, being held in suspense by the creditors, or by the commissioners, or both, he spent the creditor's effects, and subsisted at their expense, till, the estate being wasted, the loss fell heavy on every side, and generally most on those who were least able to bear it.

By the present state of things, this evil is indeed altered, and the ruin of the creditor's effects is better prevented; the bankrupt can no more skulk behind the door of the Mint and Rules, and prevent the commissioners' inspection; he must come forth, be examined, give in an account, and surrender himself and effects too, or fly his country, and be seen here no more; and if he does come in, he must give a full account upon oath, on the penalty of his neck.

When the effects are thus surrendered, the commissioners' proceedings are short and summary. The assignees are obliged to make dividends, and not detain the estate in their own hands, as was the case in former days, till sometimes they became bankrupts themselves, so that the creditors are sure now what is put into the hands of the assignees, shall in due time, and without the usual delay, be fairly divided. On the other hand, the poor debtor having honestly discharged his part, and no objection lying against the sincerity of the discovery, has a certificate granted him, which being allowed by the Lord Chancellor, he is a clear man, and may begin the world again, as I have said above.

The creditor, being thus satisfied that the debtor has been faithful, does not answer the end of the act of Parliament, if he declines to assent to the debtor's certificate; nor can any creditor decline it, but on principles which no man cares to own—namely, that of malice, and the highest resentment, which are things a Christian tradesman will not easily act upon.

But I come now to the other part of the case; and this is supposing a debtor fails, and the creditors do not think fit to take out a commission of bankrupt against him, as sometimes is the case, at least, where they see the offers of the debtor are any thing reasonable: my advice in such case is (and I speak it from long experience in such things), that they should always accept the first reasonable proposal of the debtor; and I am not in this talking on the foot of charity and mercy to the debtor, but of the real and undoubted interest of the creditor; nor could I urge it, by such arguments as I shall bring, upon any other foundation; for, if I speak in behalf of the debtor, I must argue commiseration to the miserable, compassion and pity of his family, and a reflection upon the sad changes which human life exposes us all to, and so persuade the creditor to have pity upon not him only, but upon all families in distress.

But, I say, I argue now upon a different foundation, and insist that it is the creditor's true interest, as I hinted before, that if he finds the debtor inclined to be honest, and he sees reason to believe he makes the best offer he can, he should accept the first offer, as being generally the best the debtor can make;[26] and, indeed, if the debtor be wise as well as honest, he will make it so, and generally it is found to be so. And there are, indeed, many reasons why the first offers of the debtor are generally the best, and why no commission of bankrupt ordinarily raises so much, notwithstanding all its severities, as the bankrupt offers before it is sued out—not reckoning the time and expense which, notwithstanding all the new methods, attend such things, and are inevitable. For example—

When the debtor, first looking into his affairs, sees the necessity coming upon him of making a stop in trade, and calling his creditors together, the first thought which by the consequence of the thing comes to be considered, is, what offers he can make to them to avoid the having a commission sued out against him, and to which end common prudence, as well as honest principles, move him to make the best offers he can. If he be a man of sense, and, according to what I mentioned in another chapter, has prudently come to a stop in time, before things are run to extremities, and while he has something left to make an offer of that may be considerable, he will seldom meet with creditors so weak or

---

[26] The truth of this continues to be matter of daily observation in our own times.

so blind to their own interest not to be willing to end it amicably, rather than to proceed to a commission. And as this is certainly best both for the debtor and the creditor, so, as I argued with the debtor, that he should be wise enough, as well as honest enough, to break betimes, and that it was infinitely best for his own interest, so I must add, on the other hand, to the creditor, that it is always his interest to accept the first offer; and I never knew a commission make more of an estate, where the debtor has been honest, than he (the debtor) proposed to give them without it.

It is true, there are cases where the issuing out a commission may be absolutely necessary. For example—

1. Where the debtor is evidently knavish, and discovers himself to be so, by endeavours to carry off his effects, or alter the property of the estate, confessing judgments, or any the usual ways of fraud, which in such cases are ordinarily practised. Or—

2. Where some creditors, by such judgments, or by attachments of debts, goods delivered, effects made over, or any other way, have gotten some of the estate into their hands, or securities belonging to it, whereby they are in a better state, as to payment, than the rest. Or—

3. Where some people are brought in as creditors, whose debts there is reason to believe are not real, but who place themselves in the room of creditors, in order to receive a dividend for the use of the bankrupt, or some of his family.

In these, and such like cases, a commission is inevitable, and must be taken out; nor does the man merit to be regarded upon the foot of what I call compassion and commiseration at all, but ought to be treated like a *rapparee*,[27] or plunderer, who breaks with a design to make himself whole by the composition: and as many did formerly, who were beggars when they broke, be made rich by the breach. It was to provide against such harpies as these that the act of Parliament was made; and the only remedy against them is a commission, in which the best thing they can do for their creditors is to come in and be examined, give in a false account upon oath, be discovered, convicted of it, and sent to the gallows, as they deserve.

But I am speaking of honest men, the reverse of such thieves as these, who being brought into distress by the ordinary calamities of trade, are willing to do the utmost to satisfy their creditors. When such

---

[27] A name applied, in the seventeenth century, to a certain class of robbers in Ireland.

as these break in the tradesman's debt, let him consider seriously my advice, and he shall find—I might say, he shall *always* find, but I do affirm, he shall *generally* find—the first offer the best, and that he will never lose by accepting it. To refuse it is but pushing the debtor to extremities, and running out some of the effects to secure the rest.

First, as to collecting in the debts. Supposing the man is honest, and they can trust him, it is evident no man can make so much of them as the bankrupt. (1.) He knows the circumstances of the debtors, and how best to manage them; he knows who he may best push at, and who best forbear. (2.) He can do it with the least charge; the commissioners or assignees must employ other people, such as attorneys, solicitors, &c., and they are paid dear. The bankrupt sits at home, and by letters into the country, or by visiting them, if in town, can make up every account, answer every objection, judge of every scruple, and, in a word, with ease, compared to what others must do, brings them to comply.

Next, as to selling off a stock of goods. The bankrupt keeps open the shop, disperses or disposes of the goods with advantage; whereas the commission brings all to a sale, or an outcry, or an appraisement, and all sinks the value of the stock; so that the bankrupt can certainly make more of the stock than any other person (always provided he is honest, as I said before), and much more than the creditors can do.

For these reasons, and many others, the bankrupt is able to make a better offer upon his estate than the creditors can expect to raise any other way; and therefore it is their interest always to take the first offer, if they are satisfied there is no fraud in it, and that the man has offered any thing near the extent of what he has left in the world to offer from.

If, then, it be the tradesman's interest to accept of the offer made, there needs no stronger argument to be used with him for the doing it; and nothing is more surprising to me than to see tradesmen, the hardest to come into such compositions, and to push on severities against other tradesmen, as if they were out of the reach of the shocks of fortune themselves, or that it was impossible for them ever to stand in need of the same mercy—the contrary to which I have often seen.

To what purpose should tradesmen push things to extremities against tradesmen, if nothing is to be gotten by it, and if the insolvent tradesman will take proper measures to convince the creditor that his intentions are honest? The law was made for offenders; there needs no law for innocent men: commissions are granted to manage knaves, and hamper and entangle cunning and designing rogues, who seek to raise fortunes out of their creditors' estates, and exalt themselves by their own downfall; they are not designed against honest men, neither, indeed, is there any need of them for such.

Let no man mistake this part, therefore, and think that I am moving tradesmen to be easy and compassionate to rogues and cheats: I am far from it, and have given sufficient testimony of the contrary; having, I assure you, been the only person who actually formed, drew up, and first proposed that very cause to the House of Commons, which made it felony to the bankrupt to give in a false account. It cannot, therefore, be suggested, without manifest injustice, that I would with one breath prompt creditors to be easy to rogues, and to cheating fraudulent bankrupts, and with another make a proposal to have them hanged.

But I move the creditor, on account of his own interest, always to take the first offer, if he sees no palpable fraud in it, or sees no reason to suspect such fraud; and my reason is good, namely, because I believe, as I said before, it is generally the best.

I know there is a new method of putting an end to a tradesman's troubles, by that which was formerly thought the greatest of all troubles; I mean a fraudulent method, or what they call taking out friendly statutes; that is, when tradesmen get statutes taken out against themselves, moved first by some person in kindness to them, and done at the request of the bankrupt himself. This is generally done when the circumstances of the debtor are very low, and he has little or nothing to surrender; and the end is, that the creditors may be obliged to take what there is, and the man may get a full discharge.

This is, indeed, a vile corruption of a good law, and turning the edge of the act against the creditor, not against the debtor; and as he has nothing to surrender, they get little or nothing, and the man is as effectually discharged as if he had paid twenty shillings in the pound; and so he is in a condition to set up again, take fresh credit, break again, and have another commission against him; and so round, as often as he thinks fit. This, indeed, is a fraud upon the act, and shows that all human wisdom is imperfect, that the law wants some repairs, and that it will in time come into consideration again, to be made capable of disappointing the people that intend to make such use of it.

I think there is also wanting a law against twice breaking, and that all second commissions should have some penalty upon the bankrupt, and a third a farther penalty, and if the fourth brought the man to the gallows, it could not be thought hard; for he that has set up and broke, and set up again, and broke again, and the like, a third time, I think merits to be hanged, if he pretends to venture any more.

Most of those crimes against which any laws are published in particular, and which are not capital, have generally an addition of punishment upon a repetition of the crime, and so on—a further punishment to a further repetition. I do not see why it should not be so here; and I doubt not but it would have a good effect upon tradesmen, to make them cautious, and to warn them to avoid such scandalous doings as we see daily practised, breaking three or four, or five times over; and we see instances of some such while I am writing this very chapter.

To such, therefore, I am so far from moving for any favour, either from the law, or from their creditors, that I think the only deficiency of the law at this time is, that it does not reach to inflict a corporal punishment in such a case, but leaves such insolvents to fare well, in common with those whose disasters are greater, and who, being honest and conscientious, merit more favour, but do not often find it.

CHAPTER XIV
OF THE UNFORTUNATE TRADESMAN
COMPOUNDING WITH HIS CREDITORS

This is what in the last chapter I called an alternative to that of the fortunate tradesman yielding to accept the composition of his insolvent debtor.

The poor unhappy tradesman, having long laboured in the fire, and finding it is in vain to struggle, but that whether he strives or not strives, he must break; that he does but go backward more and more, and that the longer he holds out, he shall have the less to offer, and be the harder thought of, as well as the harder dealt with—resolves to call his creditors together in time, while there is something considerable to offer them, and while he may have some just account to give of himself, and of his conduct, and that he may not be reproached with having lived on the spoil, and consumed their estates; and thus, being satisfied that the longer he puts the evil day from him, the heavier it will fall when it comes; I say, he resolves to go no farther, and so gets a friend to discourse with and prepare them, and then draws up a state of his case to lay before them.

First, He assures them that he has not wasted his estate, either by vice and immorality, or by expensive and riotous living, luxury, extravagance, and the like.

Secondly, He makes it appear that he has met with great losses, such as he could not avoid; and yet such and so many, that he has not been able to support the weight of them.

Thirdly, That he could have stood it out longer, but that he was sensible if he did, he should but diminish the stock, which, considering his debts, was properly not his own; and that he was resolved not to spend one part of their debts, as he had lost the other.

Fourthly, That he is willing to show them his books, and give up every farthing into their hands, that they might see he acted the part of an honest man to them. And,

Fifthly, That upon his doing so, they will find, that there is in goods and good debts sufficient to pay them fifteen shillings in the pound; after which, and when he has made appear that they have a faithful and just account of every thing laid before them, he hopes they will give him his liberty, that he may try to get his bread, and to maintain his family in the best manner he can; and, if possible, to pay the remainder of the debt.

You see I go all the way upon the suggestion of the poor unfortunate tradesman being critically honest, and showing himself so to the full satisfaction of his creditors; that he shows them distinctly a true state of his case, and offers his books and vouchers to confirm every part of his account.

Upon the suggestion of his being thus sincerely honest, and allowing that the state of his account comes out so well as to pay fifteen shillings in the pound, what and who but a parcel of outrageous hot-headed men would reject such a man? What would they be called, nay, what would they say of themselves, if they should reject such a composition, and should go and take out a commission of bankrupt against such a man? I never knew but one of the like circumstances, that was refused by his creditors; and that one held them out, till they were all glad to accept of half what they said should be first paid them: so may all those be served, who reject such wholesome advice, and the season for accepting a good offer, when it was made them. But I return to the debtor.

When he looks into his books, he finds himself declined, his own fortune lost, and his creditors' stock in his hands wasted in part, and still wasting, his trade being for want of stock much fallen off, and his family expense and house-rent great; so he draws up the general articles thus:—

STOCK DEBTOR

To cash of my father (being my stock) to begin with in trade
£800 0 0
To cash of my father-in-law, being my wife's portion
600 0 0
To household-goods, plate, &c. of both
100 0 0
To profits in trade for ten years, as by the yearly balance
in the journal appears
2469 10 0
To debts abroad esteemed good, as by the ledger appears
1357 8 0
To goods in the warehouse at the prime cost
672 12 0
Plate and some small jewels of my wife's left, and old
household-goods altogether
103 0 0

£6102 10 0

Estate deficient to balance	1006	2	0

£7108 12

STOCK CREDITOR

By losses by bad debts in trade, in the year 1715	£ 50	0	0
By do. 1716	66	10	0
By do. 1717	234	15	0
By do. 1718	43	0	0
By do. 1719	25	0	0
By do. by the South Sea stock, 1720	1280	0	0
By do. in trade, 1721	42	0	0
By do. 1722	106	0	0
By do. 1723	302	0	0
By do. 1724	86	15	0
By house-keeping and expenses, taxes included, as by the cash-book appears, for ten years	1836	12	
By house-rents at £50 per annum	500	0	0
By credits now owing to sundry persons, as by the ledger appears	2536	0	

£7108 12

This account is drawn out to satisfy himself how his condition stands, and what it is he ought to do: upon the stating which account he sees to his affliction that he has sunk all his own fortune and his wife's, and is a thousand pounds worse than nothing in the world; and that, being obliged to live in the same house for the sake of his business and warehouse, though the rent is too great for him, his trade being declined, his credit sunk, and his family being large, he sees evidently he cannot go on, and that it will only be bringing things from bad to worse; and, above all the rest, being greatly perplexed in his mind that he is spending other people's estates, and that the bread he eats is not his own, he resolves to call his creditors all together, lay before them the true state of his case, and lie at their mercy for the rest.

The account of his present and past fortune standing as it did, and as appears above, the result is as follows, namely, that he has not sufficient to pay all his creditors, though his debts should prove to be all good, and the goods in his warehouse should be fully worth the price they cost, which, being liable to daily contingencies, add to the reasons which pressed him before to make an offer of surrender to his creditors both of his goods and debts, and to give up all into their hands.

The state of his case, as to his debts and credits, stands as follows:—

His debts esteemed good, as by the ledger, are	£1357 8 0
His goods in the warehouse	672 12 0

	£2030 0 0

His creditors demands, as by the same ledger appears, are	£3036 0 0

This amounts to fifteen shillings in the pound upon all his debts, which, if the creditors please to appoint an assignee or trustee to sell the goods, and collect the debts, he is willing to surrender wholly into their hands, hoping they will, as a favour, give him his household goods, as in the account, for his family use, and his liberty, that he may seek out for some employment to get his bread.

The account being thus clear, the books exactly agreeing, and the man appearing to have acted openly and fairly, the creditors meet, and, after a few consultations, agree to accept his proposals, and the man is a free man immediately, gets fresh credit, opens his shop again, and, doubling his vigilance and application in business, he recovers in a few years, grows rich; then, like an honest man still, he calls all his creditors together again, tells them he does not call them now to a second composition, but to tell them, that having, with God's blessing and his own industry, gotten enough to enable him, he was resolved to pay them the remainder of his old debt; and accordingly does so, to the great joy of his creditors, to his own very great honour, and to the encouragement of all honest men to take the same measures. It is true, this does not often happen, but there have been instances of it, and I could name several within my own knowledge.

But here comes an objection in the way, as follows: It is true this man did very honestly, and his creditors had a great deal of reason to be satisfied with his just dealing with them; but is every man bound thus to strip himself naked? Perhaps this man at the same time had a family to maintain, and had he no debt of justice to them, but to beg his household goods back of them for his poor family, and that as an alms?-and would he not have fared as well, if he had offered his creditors ten shillings in the pound, and took all the rest upon himself, and then he had reserved to himself sufficient to have supported himself in any new undertaking?

The answer to this is short and plain, and no debtor can be at a loss to know his way in it, for otherwise people may make difficulties where there are none; the observing the strict rules of justice and honesty will chalk out his way for him.

The man being deficient in stock, and his estate run out to a thousand pounds worse than nothing by his losses, &c, it is evident all he has left is the proper estate of his creditors, and he has no right to one shilling of it; he owes it them, it is a just debt to them, and he ought to discharge it fairly, by giving up all into their hands, or at least to offer to do so.

But to put the case upon a new foot; as he is obliged to make an offer, as above, to put all his effects, books, and goods into their power, so he may add an alternative to them thus, namely—that if, on the other hand, they do not think proper to take the trouble, or run the risk, of collecting the debts, and selling the goods, which may be difficult, if they will leave it to him to do it, he will undertake to pay them—shillings in the pound, and stand to the hazard both of debts and goods.

Having thus offered the creditors their choice, if they accept the proposal of a certain sum, as sometimes I know they have chosen to do, rather than to have the trouble of making assignees, and run the hazard of the debts, when put into lawyers' hands to collect, and of the goods, to sell them by appraisement; if, I say, they choose this, and offer to discharge the debtor upon payment, suppose it be of ten or twelve shillings in the pound in money, within a certain time, or on giving security for the payment; then, indeed, the debtor is discharged in conscience, and may lawfully and honestly take the remainder as a gift given him by his creditors for undertaking their business, or securing the remainder of their debt to them—I say, the debtor may do this with the utmost satisfaction to his conscience.

But without thus putting it into the creditors' choice, it is a force upon them to offer them any thing less than the utmost farthing that he is able to pay; and particularly to pretend to make an offer as if it were his utmost, and, as is usual, make protestations that it is the most he is able to pay (indeed, every offer of a composition is a kind of protestation that the debtor is not able to pay any more)—I say, to offer thus, and declare he offers as much as possible, and as much as the effects he has left will produce, if his effects are able to produce more, he is then a cheat; for he acts then like one that stands at bay with his creditors, make an offer, and if the creditors do not think fit to accept of it, they must take what methods they think they can take to get more; that is to say, he bids open defiance to their statutes and commissions of bankrupt, and any other proceedings: like a town besieged, which offers to capitulate and to yield upon such and such articles; which implies, that if those articles are not accepted, the garrison will defend themselves to the last extremity, and do all the mischief to the assailants that they can.

Now, this in a garrison-town, I say, may be lawful and fair, but in a debtor to his creditor it is quite another thing: for, as I have said above, the debtor has no property in the effects which he has in his hands; they are the goods and the estate of the creditor; and to hold out against the creditor, keep his estate by violence, and make him accept of a small part of it, when the debtor has a larger part in his power, and is able to give it—this is not fair, much less is it honest and conscientious; but it is still worse to do this, and at the same time to declare that it is the utmost the debtor can do; this, I say, is still more dishonest, because it is not true, and is adding falsehood to the other injustice.

Thus, I think, I have stated the case clearly, for the conduct of the debtor; and, indeed, this way of laying all before the creditors, and putting it into their choice, seems a very happy method for the comfort of the debtor, cast down and dejected with the weight of his circumstances; and, it may be, with the reproaches of his own conscience too, that he has not done honestly in running out the effects of his creditors, and making other families suffer by him, and perhaps poor families too—I say, this way of giving up all with an honest and single desire to make all the satisfaction he is able to his creditors, greatly heals the breach in his peace, which his circumstances had made before; for, by now doing all that is in his power, he makes all possible amends for what is past, I mean as to men; and they are induced, by this open, frank usage, to give him the reward of his honesty, and freely forgive him the rest of the debt.

There is a manifest difference to the debtor, in point of conscience, between surrendering his whole effects, or estate, to his creditors for satisfaction of their debts, and offering them a composition, unless, as I have said, the composition is offered, as above, to the choice of the creditor. By surrendering the whole estate, the debtor acknowledges the creditors' right to all he has in his possession, and gives it up to them as their own, putting it in their full power to dispose of it as they please.

But, by a composition, the debtor, as I have said above, stands at bay with the creditors, and, keeping their estates in his hands, capitulates with them, as it were, sword in hand, telling them he can give them no more, when perhaps, and too often it is the case, it is apparent that he is in condition to offer more. Now, let the creditors consent to these proposals, be what it will; and, however voluntary it may be pretended to be, it is evident that a force is the occasion of it, and the creditor complies, and accepts the proposal, upon the supposition that no better conditions can be had. It is the plain language of the thing, for no man accepts of less than he thinks he can get: if he believed he could have more, he would certainly get it if he could.

And if the debtor is able to pay one shilling more than he offers, it is a cheat, a palpable fraud, and of so much he actually robs his creditor. But in a surrender the case is altered in all its parts; the debtor says to his creditors, 'Gentlemen, there is a full and faithful account of all I have left; it is your own, and there it is; I am ready to put it into your hands, or into the hands of whomsoever you shall appoint to receive it, and to lie at your mercy.' This is all the man is able to do, and therefore is so far honest; whether the methods that reduced him were honest or no, that is a question by itself. If on this surrender he finds the creditors desirous rather to have it digested into a composition, and that they will voluntarily come into such a proposal, then, as above, they being judges of the equity of the composition, and of what ability the debtor is to perform it, and, above all, of what he may or may not gain by it, if they accept of such a composition, instead of the surrender of his effects, then the case alters entirely, and the debtor is acquitted in conscience, because the creditor had a fair choice, and the composition is rather their proposal to the debtor, than the debtor's proposal to them.

Thus, I think, I have stated the case of justice and conscience on the debtor's behalf, and cleared up his way, in case of a necessity, to stop trading, that he may break without wounding his conscience, as well as his fortunes; and he that thinks fit to act thus, will come off with the reputation of an honest man, and will have the favour of his creditors to begin again, with whatever he may have as to stock; and sometimes that favour is better to him than a stock, and has been the raising of many a broken tradesman, so that his latter end has been better than his beginning.

CHAPTER XV
OF TRADESMEN RUINING ONE ANOTHER BY RUMOUR AND CLAMOUR, BY SCANDAL AND REPROACH

I have dwelt long upon the tradesman's management of himself, in order to his due preserving both his business and his reputation: let me bestow one chapter upon the tradesman for his conduct among his neighbours and fellow-tradesmen.

Credit is so much a tradesman's blessing that it is the choicest ware he deals in, and he cannot be too chary of it when he has it, or buy it too dear when he wants it; it is a stock to his warehouse, it is current money in his cash-chest, it accepts all his bills, for it is on the fund of his credit that he has any bills to accept; demands would else be made upon the spot, and he must pay for his goods before he has them— therefore, I say, it accepts all his bills, and oftentimes pays them too; in a word, it is the life and soul of his trade, and it requires his utmost vigilance to preserve it.

If, then, his own credit should be of so much value to him, and he should be so nice in his concern about it, he ought in some degree to have the same care of his neighbour's. Religion teaches us not to slander and defame our neighbour, that is to say, not to raise or promote any slander or scandal upon his good name. As a good name is to another man, and which the wise man says, 'is better than life,' the same is credit to a tradesman—it is the life of his trade; and he that wounds a tradesman's credit without cause, is as much a murderer in trade, as he that kills a man in the dark is a murderer in matters of blood.

Besides, there is a particular nicety in the credit of a tradesman, which does not reach in other cases: a man is slandered in his character, or reputation, and it is injurious; and if it comes in the way of a marriage, or of a preferment, or post, it may disappoint and ruin him; but if this happens to a tradesman, he is immediately and unavoidably blasted and undone; a tradesman has but two sorts of enemies to encounter with, namely, thieves breaking open his shop, and ill neighbours blackening and blasting his reputation; and the latter are the worst thieves of the two, by a great deal; and, therefore, people should indeed be more chary of their discourse of tradesmen, than of other men, and that as they would not be guilty of murder. I knew an author of a book, who was drawn in unwarily, and without design, to publish a scandalous story of a tradesman in London. He (the author) was imposed upon by a set of men, who did it maliciously, and he was utterly ignorant of the wicked design; nor did he know the person, but rashly published the thing, being himself too fond of a piece of news, which he thought would be grateful to his readers; nor yet did he publish the person's name, so cautious he was, though that was not enough, as it proved, for the person was presently published by those who had maliciously done it.

The scandal spread; the tradesman, a flourishing man, and a considerable dealer, was run upon by it with a torrent of malice; a match which he was about with a considerable fortune was blasted and prevented, and that indeed was the malicious end of the people that did it; nor did it stop there—it brought his creditors upon him, it ruined him, it brought out a commission of bankrupt against him, it broke his heart, and killed him; and after his death, his debts and effects coming in, there appeared to be seven shillings in the pound estate, clear and good over and above all demands, all his debts discharged, and all the expenses of the statute paid.

It was to no purpose that the man purged himself of the crime laid to his charge—that the author, who had ignorantly and rashly published the scandal, declared himself ignorant; the man was run down by a torrent of reproach; scandal oppressed him; he was buried alive in the noise and dust raised both against his morals and his credit, and yet his character was proved good, and his bottom in trade was so too, as I have said above.

It is not the least reason of my publishing this to add, that even the person who was ignorantly made the instrument of publishing the scandal, was not able to retrieve it, or to prevent the man's ruin by all the public reparation he could make in print, and by all the acknowledgement he could make of his having been ignorantly drawn in to do it. And this I mention for the honest tradesman's caution, and to put him in mind, that when he has unwarily let slip anything to the wounding the reputation of his neighbour tradesman, whether in his trading credit, or the credit of his morals, it may not be in his power to unsay it again, that is, so as to prevent the ruin of the person; and though it may grieve him as long as he lives, as the like did the author I mention, yet it is not in his power to recall it, or to heal the wound he has given; and that he should consider very well of beforehand.

A tradesman's credit and a virgin's virtue ought to be equally sacred from the tongues of men; and it is a very unhappy truth, that as times now go, they are neither of them regarded among us as they ought to be.

The tea-table among the ladies, and the coffee-house among the men, seem to be places of new invention for a depravation of our manners and morals, places devoted to scandal, and where the characters of all kinds of persons and professions are handled in the most merciless manner, where reproach triumphs, and we seem to give ourselves a loose to fall upon one another in the most unchristian and unfriendly manner in the world.

It seems a little hard that the reputation of a young lady, or of a new-married couple, or of people in the most critical season of establishing the characters of their persons and families, should lie at the mercy of the tea-table; nor is it less hard, that the credit of a tradesman, which is the same thing in its nature as the virtue of a lady, should be tossed about, shuttle-cock-like, from one table to another, in the coffee-house, till they shall talk all his creditors about his ears, and bring him to the very misfortune which they reported him to be near, when at the same time he owed them nothing who raised the clamour, and owed nothing to all the world, but what he was able to pay.

And yet how many tradesmen have been thus undone, and how many more have been put to the full trial of their strength in trade, and have stood by the mere force of their good circumstances; whereas, had they been unfurnished with cash to have answered their whole debts, they must have fallen with the rest.

We need go no farther than Lombard Street for an exemplification of this truth. There was a time when Lombard Street was the only bank, and the goldsmiths there were all called bankers. The credit of their business was such, that the like has not been seen in England since, in private hands: some of those bankers, as I have had from their own mouths, have had near two millions of paper credit upon them at a time; that is to say, have had bills under their hands running abroad for so much at a time.

On a sudden, like a clap of thunder, King Charles II. shut up the Exchequer, which was the common centre of the overplus cash these great bankers had in their hands. What was the consequence? Not only the bankers who had the bulk of their cash there, but all Lombard Street, stood still. The very report of having money in the Exchequer brought a run upon the goldsmiths that had no money there, as well as upon those that had, and not only Sir Robert Viner, Alderman Backwell, Farringdon, Forth, and others, broke and failed, but several were ruined who had not a penny of money in the Exchequer, and only sunk by the rumour of it; that rumour bringing a run upon the whole street, and giving a check to the paper credit that was run up to such an exorbitant height.

I remember a shopkeeper who one time took the liberty (foolish liberty!) with himself, in public company in a coffee-house, to say that he was broke. 'I assure you,' says he, 'that I am broke, and to-morrow I resolve to shut up my shop, and call my creditors together.' His meaning was, that he had a brother just dead in his house, and the next day was to be buried, when, in civility to the deceased, he kept his shop shut; and several people whom he dealt with, and owed money to, were the next day invited to the funeral, so that he did actually shut up his shop, and call some of his creditors together.

But he sorely repented the jest which he put upon himself. 'Are you broke?' says one of his friends to him, that was in the coffee-house; 'then I wish I had the little money you owe me' (which however, it seems, was not much). Says the other, still carrying on his jest, 'I shall pay nobody, till, as I told you, I have called my people together.' The other did not reach his jest, which at best was but a dull one, but he reached that part of it that concerned himself, and seeing him continue carelessly sitting in the shop, slipped out, and, fetching a couple of sergeants, arrested him. The other was a little surprised; but however, the debt being no great sum, he paid it, and when he found his mistake, told his friends what he meant by his being broke.

But it did not end there; for other people of his neighbours, who were then in the coffee-house, and heard his discourse, and had thought nothing more of it, yet in the morning seeing his shop shut, concluded the thing was so indeed, and immediately it went over the whole street that such a one was broke; from thence it went to the Exchange, and from thence into the country, among all his dealers, who came up in a throng and a fright to look after him. In a word, he had as much to do to prevent his breaking as any man need to desire, and if he had not had very good friends as well as a very good bottom, he had inevitably been ruined and undone.

So small a rumour will overset a tradesman, if he is not very careful of himself; and if a word in jest from himself, which though indeed no man that had considered things, or thought before he spoke, would have said (and, on the other hand, no man who had been wise and thinking would have taken as it was taken)—I say, if a word taken from the tradesman's own mouth could be so fatal, and run such a dangerous length, what may not words spoken slyly, and secretly, and maliciously, be made to do?

A tradesman's reputation is of the nicest nature imaginable; like a blight upon a fine flower, if it is but touched, the beauty of it, or the flavour of it, or the seed of it, is lost, though the noxious breath which touched it might not reach to blast the leaf, or hurt the root; the credit of a tradesman, at least in his beginning, is too much at the mercy of every enemy he has, till it has taken root, and is established on a solid foundation of good conduct and success. It is a sad truth, that every idle tongue can blast a young shopkeeper; and therefore, though I would not discourage any young beginner, yet it is highly beneficial to alarm them, and to let them know that they must expect a storm of scandal and reproach upon the least slip they make: if they but stumble, fame will throw them down; it is true, if they recover, she will set them up as fast; but malice generally runs before, and bears down all with it; and there are ten tradesmen who fall under the weight of slander and an ill tongue, to one that is lifted up again by the common hurry of report.

To say I am broke, or in danger of breaking, is to break me: and though sometimes the malicious occasion is discovered, and the author detected and exposed, yet how seldom is it so; and how much oftener are ill reports raised to ruin and run down a tradesman, and the credit of a shop; and like an arrow that flies in the dark, it wounds unseen. The authors, no nor the occasion of these reports, are never discovered perhaps, or so much as rightly guessed at; and the poor tradesman feels the wound, receives the deadly blow, and is perhaps mortally stabbed in the vitals of his trade, I mean his trading credit, and never knows who hurt him.

I must say, in the tradesman's behalf, that he is in such a case to be esteemed a sacrifice to the worst and most hellish of all secret crimes, I mean envy; which is made up of every hateful vice, a complication of crimes which nothing but the worst of God's reasonable world can be guilty of; and he will indeed merit and call for every honest man's pity and concern. But what relief is this to him? for, in the meantime, though the devil himself were the raiser of the scandal, yet it shall go about; the blow shall take, and every man, though at the same time expressing their horror and aversion at the thing, shall yet not be able, no not themselves, to say they receive no impression from it.

Though I know the clamour or rumour was raised maliciously, and from a secret envy at the prosperity of the man, yet if I deal with him, it will in spite of all my abhorrence of the thing, in spite of all my willingness to do justice, I say it will have some little impression upon me, it will be some shock to my confidence in the man; and though I know the devil is a liar, a slanderer, a calumniator, and that his name *devil* is derived from it; and that I knew, if that, as I said, were possible, that the devil in his proper person raised and began, and carried on, this scandal upon the tradesman, yet there is a secret lurking doubt (about him), which hangs about me concerning him; the devil is a liar, but he may happen to speak truth just then, he may chance to be right, and I know not what there may be in it, and whether there may be any thing or no, but I will have a little care, &c.

Thus, insensibly and involuntarily, nay, in spite of friendship, good wishes, and even resolution to the contrary, it is almost impossible to prevent our being shocked by rumour, and we receive an impression whether we will or not, and that from the worst enemy; there is such a powerful sympathy between our thoughts and our interest, that the first being but touched, and that in the lightest manner imaginable, we cannot help it, caution steps on in behalf of the last, and the man is jealous and afraid, in spite of all the kindest and best intentions in the world.

Nor is it only dangerous in case of false accusations and false charges, for those indeed are to be expected fatal; but even just and true things may be as fatal as false, for the truth is not always necessary to be said of a tradesman: many things a tradesman may perhaps allow himself to do, and may be lawfully done, but if they should be known to be part of his character, it would sink deep into his trading fame, his credit would suffer by it, and in the end it might be his ruin; so that he that would not set his hand to his neighbour's ruin, should as carefully avoid speaking some truths, as raising some forgeries upon him.

Of what fatal consequence, then, is the raising rumours and suspicions upon the credit and characters of young tradesmen! and how little do those who are forward to raise such suspicions, and spread such rumours, consult conscience, or principle, or honour, in what they do! How little do they consider that they are committing a trading murder, and that, in respect to the justice of it, they may with much more equity break open the tradesman's house, and rob his cash-chest, or his shop; and what they can carry away thence will not do him half the injury that robbing his character of what is due to it from an upright and diligent conduct, would do. The loss of his money or goods is easily made up, and may be sometimes repaired with advantage, but the loss of credit is never repaired; the one is breaking open his house, but the other is burning it down; the one carries away some goods, but the other shuts goods out from coming in; one is hurting the tradesman, but the other is undoing him.

Credit is the tradesman's life; it is, as the wise man says, 'marrow to his bones;' it is by this that all his affairs go on prosperously and pleasantly; if this be hurt, wounded, or weakened, the tradesman is sick, hangs his head, is dejected and discouraged; and if he does go on, it is heavily and with difficulty, as well as with disadvantage; he is beholding to his fund of cash, not his friends; and he may be truly said to stand upon his own legs, for nothing else can do it.

And therefore, on the other hand, if such a man is any way beholding to his credit, if he stood before upon the foundation of his credit, if he owes any thing considerable, it is a thousand to one but he sinks under the oppression of it; that is to say, it brings every body upon him—I mean, every one that has any demand upon him—for in pushing for their own, especially in such cases, men have so little mercy, and are so universally persuaded that he that comes first is first served, that I did not at all wonder, that in the story of the tradesman who so foolishly exposed himself in the coffee-house, as above, his friend whom he said the words to, began with him that very night, and before he went out of the coffee-house; it was rather a wonder to me he did not go out and bring in half-a-dozen more upon him the same evening.

It is very rarely that men are wanting to their own interest; and the jealousy of its being but in danger, is enough to make men forget, not friendship only, and generosity, but good manners, civility, and even justice itself, and fall upon the best friends they have in the world, if they think they are in the least danger of suffering by them.

On these accounts it is, and many more, that a tradesman walks in continual jeopardy, from the looseness and inadvertency of men's tongues, ay, and women's too; for though I am all along very tender of the ladies, and would do justice to the sex, by telling you, they were not the dangerous people whom I had in view in my first writing upon this subject, yet I must be allowed to say, that they are sometimes fully even with the men, for ill usage, when they please to fall upon them in this nice article, in revenge for any slight, or but pretended slight, put upon them.

It was a terrible revenge a certain lady, who was affronted by a tradesman in London, in a matter of love, took upon him in this very article. It seems a tradesman had courted her some time, and it was become public, as a thing in a manner concluded, when the tradesman left the lady a little abruptly, without giving a good reason for it, and, indeed, she afterwards discovered, that he had left her for the offer of another with a little more money, and that, when he had done so, he reported that it was for another reason, which reflected a little on the person of the lady; and in this the tradesman did very unworthily indeed, and deserved her resentment: but, as I said, it was a terrible revenge she took, and what she ought not to have done.

First, she found out who it was that her former pretended lover had been recommended to, and she found means to have it insinuated to her by a woman-friend, that he was not only rakish and wicked, but, in short, that he had a particular illness, and went so far as to produce letters from him to a quack-doctor, for directions to him how to take his medicines, and afterwards a receipt for money for the cure; though both the letters and receipt also, as afterwards appeared, were forged, in which she went a dismal length in her revenge, as you may see.

Then she set two or three female instruments to discourse her case in all their gossips' companies, and at the tea-tables wherever they came, and to magnify the lady's prudence in refusing such a man, and what an escape she had had in being clear of him.

'Why,' says a lady to one of these emissaries, 'what was the matter? I thought she was like to be very well married.'

'Oh no, Madam! by no means,' says the emissary.

'Why, Madam,' says another lady, 'we all know Mr H———; he is a very pretty sort of a man.'

'Ay, Madam,' says the emissary again, 'but you know a pretty man is not all that is required.'

'Nay,' says the lady again, 'I don't mean so; he is no beauty, no rarity that way; but I mean a clever good sort of a man in his business, such as we call a pretty tradesman.'

'Ay,' says the lady employed, 'but that is not all neither.'

'Why,' says the other lady, 'he has a very good trade too, and lives in good credit.'

'Yes,' says malice, 'he has some of the first, but not too much of the last, I suppose.'

'No!' says the lady; 'I thought his credit had been very good.'

'If it had, I suppose,' says the first, 'the match had not been broke off.'

'Why,' says the lady, 'I understood it was broken off on his side.'

'And so did I,' says another.

'And so did I, indeed,' says a third.

'Oh, Madam!' says the tool, 'nothing like it, I assure you.'

'Indeed,' says another, I understood he had quitted Mrs———, because she had not fortune enough for him, and that he courted another certain lady, whom we all know.'

Then the ladies fell to talking of the circumstances of his leaving her, and how he had broken from her abruptly and unmannerly, and had been too free with her character; at which the first lady, that is to say, the emissary, or tool, as I call her, took it up a little warmly, thus:—

I. *Lady.*—Well, you see, ladies, how easily a lady's reputation may be injured; I hope you will not go away with it so.

2. *Lady.*—Nay, we have all of us a respect for Mrs———, and some of us visit there sometimes; I believe none of us would be willing to injure her.

I. *Lady.*—But indeed, ladies, she is very much injured in that story.

2. *Lady.*—Indeed, it is generally understood so, and every body believes it.

I. *Lady.*—I can assure you it is quite otherwise in fact.

2. *Lady.*—I believe he reports it so himself, and that with some very odd things about the lady too.

I. *Lady.*—The more base unworthy fellow he.

2. *Lady.*—Especially if he knows it to be otherwise.

I. *Lady.*—Especially if he knows the contrary to be true, Madam.

2. *Lady.*—Is that possible? Did he not refuse her, then?

I. *Lady.*—Nothing like it, Madam; but just the contrary.

2. *Lady.*—You surprise me!

3. *Lady.*—I am very glad to hear it, for her sake.

I. *Lady.*—I can assure you, Madam, she had refused him, and that he knows well enough, which has been one of the reasons that has made him abuse her as he has done.

2. *Lady.*—Indeed, she has been used very ill by him, or somebody for him.

I. *Lady.*—Yes, he has reported strange things, but they are all lies.

2. *Lady.*—Well; but pray, Madam, what was the reason, if we may be so free, that she turned him off after she had entertained him so long?

I. *Lady.*—Oh, Madam! reason enough; I wonder he should pretend, when he knew his own circumstances too, to court a lady of her fortune.

2. *Lady.*—Why, are not his circumstances good, then?

I. *Lady.*—No, Madam. Good! alas, he has no bottom.

2. *Lady.*—No bottom! Why, you surprise me; we always looked upon him to be a man of substance, and that he was very well in the world.

I. *Lady.*—It is all a cheat, Madam; there's nothing in it; when it came to be made out, nothing at all in it.

2. *Lady.*—That cannot be, Madam; Mr —— has lived always in good reputation and good credit in his business.

I. *Lady.*—It is all sunk again then, if it was so; I don't know.

2. *Lady.*—Why did she entertain him so long, then?

I. *Lady.*—Alas! Madam, how could she know, poor lady, till her friends inquired into things? But when they came to look a little narrowly into it, they soon found reason to give her a caution, that he was not the man she took him for.

2. *Lady.*—Well, it is very strange; I am sure he passed for another man among us.

I. *Lady.*—It must be formerly, then, for they tell me his credit has been sunk these three or four years; he had need enough indeed to try for a greater fortune, he wants it enough.

2. *Lady.*—It is a sad thing when men look out for fortunes to heal their trade-breaches with, and make the poor wife patch up their old bankrupt credit.

I. *Lady.*—Especially, Madam, when they know themselves to be gone so far, that even with the addition they can stand but a little while, and must inevitably bring the lady to destruction with them.

2. *Lady.*—Well, I could never have thought Mr —— was in such circumstances.

3. *Lady.*—Nor I; we always took him for a ten thousand pound man.

I. *Lady.*—They say he was deep in the bubbles, Madam.

2. *Lady.*—Nay, if he was gotten into the South Sea, that might hurt him indeed, as it has done many a gentleman of better estates than he.

I. *Lady.*—I don't know whether it was the South Sea, or some other bubbles, but he was very near making a bubble of her, and £3000 into the bargain.

2. *Lady.*—I am glad she has escaped him, if it be so; it is a sign her friends took a great deal of care of her.

1. *Lady.*—He won't hold it long; he will have his desert, I hope; I don't doubt but we shall see him in the Gazette quickly for a bankrupt.

2. *Lady.*—If he does not draw in some innocent young thing that has her fortune in her own hands to patch him up.

1. *Lady.*—I hope not, Madam; I hear he is blown where he went since, and there, they say, they have made another discovery of him, in a worse circumstance than the other.

2. *Lady.*—How, pray?

1. *Lady.*—Nothing, Madam, but a particular kind of illness, &c. I need say no more.

2. *Lady.*—You astonish me! Why, I always thought him a very civil, honest, sober man.

1. *Lady.*—This is a sad world, Madam; men are seldom known now, till it is too late; but sometimes murder comes out seasonably, and so I understand it is here; for the lady had not gone so far with him, but that she could go off again.

2. *Lady.*—Nay, it was time to go off again, if it were so.

1. *Lady.*—Nay, Madam, I do not tell this part of my own knowledge; I only heard so, but I am afraid there is too much in it.

Thus ended this piece of hellish wildfire, upon the character and credit of a tradesman, the truth of all which was no more than this—that the tradesman, disliking his first lady, left her, and soon after, though not presently, courted another of a superior fortune indeed, though not for that reason; and the first lady, provoked at being cast off, and, as she called it, slighted, raised all this clamour upon him, and persecuted him with it, wherever she was able.

Such a discourse as this at a tea-table, it could not be expected would be long a secret; it ran from one tittle-tattle society to another; and in every company, snow-ball like, it was far from lessening, and it went on, till at length it began to meet with some contradiction, and the tradesman found himself obliged to trace it as far and as well as he could.

But it was to no purpose to confront it; when one was asked, and another was asked, they only answered they heard so, and they heard it in company in such a place, and in such a place, and some could remember where they had it, and some could not; and the poor tradesman, though he was really a man of substance, sank under it prodigiously: his new mistress, whom he courted, refused him, and would never hear any thing in his favour, or trouble herself to examine whether it were true or no—it was enough, she said, to her, that he was laden with such a report; and, if it was unjust, she was sorry for it, but the misfortune must be his, and he must place it to the account of his having made some enemies, which she could not help.

As to his credit, the slander of the first lady's raising was spread industriously, and with the utmost malice and bitterness, and did him an inexpressible prejudice; every man he dealt with was shy of him; every man he owed any thing to came for it, and, as he said, he was sure he should see the last penny demanded; it was his happiness that he had wherewith to pay, for had his circumstances been in the least perplexed, the man had been undone; nay, as I have observed in another case, as his affairs might have lain, he might have been able to have paid forty shillings in the pound, and yet have been undone, and been obliged to break, and shut up his shop.

It is true, he worked through it, and he carried it so far as to fix the malice of all the reports pretty much upon the first lady, and particularly so far as to discover that she was the great reason of his being so positively rejected by the other; but he could never fix it so upon her as to recover any damages of her, only to expose her a little, and that she did not value, having, as she said wickedly, had her full revenge of him, and so indeed she had.

The sum of the matter is, and it is for this reason I tell you the story, that the reputation of a tradesman is too much at the mercy of men's tongues or women's either; and a story raised upon a tradesman, however malicious, however false, and however frivolous the occasion, is not easily suppressed, but, if it touches his credit, as a flash of fire it spreads over the whole air like a sheet; there is no stopping it.

My inference from all this shall be very brief; if the tongues of every ill-disposed envious gossip, whether man-gossip or woman-gossip, for there are of both sorts, may be thus mischievous to the tradesman, and he is so much at the mercy of the tattling slandering part of the world, how much more should tradesmen be cautious and wary how they touch or wound the credit and character of one another. There are but a very few tradesmen who can say they are out of the reach of slander, and that the malice of enemies cannot hurt them with the tongue. Here and there one, and those ancient and well established, may be able to defy the world; but there are so many others, that I think I may warn all tradesmen against making havoc of one another's reputation, as they would be tenderly used in the same case.

And yet I cannot but say it is too much a tradesman's crime, I mean to speak slightly and contemptibly of other tradesman, their neighbours, or perhaps rivals in trade, and to run them down in the characters they give of them, when inquiry may be made of them, as often is the case. The reputation of tradesmen is too often put into the hands of their fellow-tradesmen, when ignorant people think to inform themselves of their circumstances, by going to those whose interest it is to defame and run them down.

I know no case in the world in which there is more occasion for the golden rule, Do as you would be done unto; and though you may be established, as you may think, and be above the reach of the tongues of others, yet the obligation of the rule is the same, for you are to do as you would be done unto, supposing that you were in the same condition, or on a level with the person.

It is confessed that tradesmen do not study this rule in the particular case I am now speaking of. No men are apter to speak slightly and coldly of a fellow-tradesman than his fellow-tradesmen, and to speak unjustly so too; the reasons for which cannot be good, unless it can be pleaded for upon the foundation of a just and impartial concern in the interest of the inquirer; and even then nothing must be said but what is consistent with strict justice and truth: all that is more than that, is mere slander and envy, and has nothing of the Christian in it, much less of the neighbour or friend. It is true that friendship may be due to the inquirer, but still so much justice is due to the person inquired of, that it is very hard to speak in such cases, and not be guilty of raising dust, as they call it, upon your neighbour, and at least hurting, if not injuring him.

It is, indeed, so difficult a thing, that I scarce know what stated rule to lay down for the conduct of a tradesman in this case:—A tradesman at a distance is going to deal with another tradesman, my neighbour; and before he comes to bargain, or before he cares to trust him, he goes, weakly enough perhaps, to inquire of him, and of his circumstances, among his neighbours and fellow-tradesmen, perhaps of the same profession or employment, and who, among other things, it may be, are concerned by their interest, that this tradesman's credit should not rise too fast. What must be done in this case?

If I am the person inquired of, what must I do? If I would have this man sink in his reputation, or be discredited, and if it is for my interest to have him cried down in the world, it is a sore temptation to me to put in a few words to his disadvantage; and yet, if I do it in gratification of my private views or interest, or upon the foot of resentment of any kind whatever, and let it be from what occasion it will, nay, however just and reasonable the resentment is, or may be, it is utterly unjust and unlawful, and is not only unfair as a man, but unchristian, and is neither less nor more than a secret revenge, which is forbidden by the laws of God and man.

If, on the other hand, I give a good character of the man, or of his reputation, I mean, of his credit in business, in order to have the inquirer trust him, and at the same time know or believe that he is not a sound and good man (that is, as to trade, for it is his character in trade that I am speaking of), what am I doing then? It is plain I lay a snare for the inquirer, and am at least instrumental to his loss, without having really any design to hurt him; for it is to be supposed, before he came to me to inquire, I had no view of acting any thing to his prejudice.

Again, there is no medium, for to refuse or decline giving a character of the man, is downright giving him the worst character I can—it is, in short, shooting him through the head in his trade. A man comes to me for a character of my neighbouring tradesman; I answer him with a repulse to his inquiry thus—

A.—Good sir, do not ask me the character of my neighbours—I resolve to meddle with nobody's character; pray, do not inquire of me.

B.—Well, but, sir, you know the gentleman; you live next door to him; you can tell me, if you please, all that I desire to know, whether he is a man in credit, and fit to be trusted, or no, in the way of his business.

A.—I tell you, sir, I meddle with no man's business; I will not give characters of my neighbours—it is an ill office—a man gets no thanks for it, and perhaps deserves none.

B.—But, sir, you would be willing to be informed and advised, if it were your own case.

A.—It may be so, but I cannot oblige people to inform me.

B.—But you would entreat it as a favour, and so I come to you.

A.—But you may go to any body else.

B.—But you are a man of integrity; I can depend upon what you say; I know you will not deceive me; and, therefore, I beg of you to satisfy me.

A.—But I desire you to excuse me, for it is what I never do—I cannot do it.

B.—But, sir, I am in a great strait; I am just selling him a great parcel of goods, and I am willing to sell them too, and yet I am willing to be safe, as you would yourself, if you were in my case.

A.—I tell you, sir, I have always resolved to forbear meddling with the characters of my neighbours—it is an ill office. Besides, I mind my own business; I do not enter into the inquiries after other people's affairs.

B.—Well, sir, I understand you, then; I know what I have to do.

A.—What do you mean by that?

B.—Nothing, sir, but what I suppose you would have me understand by it.

A.—I would have you understand what I say—namely, that I will meddle with nobody's business but my own.

B.—And I say I understand you; I know you are a good man, and a man of charity, and loth to do your neighbours any prejudice, and that you will speak the best of every man as near as you can.

A.—I tell you, I speak neither the best nor the worst—I speak nothing.

B.—Well, sir, that is to say, that as charity directs you to speak well of every man, so, when you cannot speak well, you refrain, and will say nothing; and you do very well, to be sure; you are a very kind neighbour.

A.—But that is a base construction of my words; for I tell you, I do the like by every body.

B.—Yes, sir, I believe you do, and I think you are in the right of it—am fully satisfied.

A.—You act more unjustly by me than by my neighbour; for you take my silence, or declining to give a character, to be giving an ill character.

B.—No, sir, not for an ill character.

A.—But I find you take it for a ground of suspicion.

B.—I take it, indeed, for a due caution to me, sir; but the man may be a good man for all that, only—

A.—Only what? I understand you—only you won't trust him with your goods.

B.—But another man may, sir, for all that, so that you have been kind to your neighbours and to me too, sir—and you are very just. I wish all men would act so one by another; I should feel the benefit of it myself among others, for I have suffered deeply by ill tongues, I am sure.

A.—Well, however unjust you are to me, and to my neighbour too, I will not undeceive you at present; I think you do not deserve it.

He used a great many more words with him to convince him that he did not mean any discredit to his neighbour tradesman; but it was all one; he would have it be, that his declining to give his said neighbour a good character was giving him an ill character, which the other told him was a wrong inference. However, he found that the man stood by his own notion of it, and declined trusting the tradesman with the goods, though he was satisfied he (the tradesman) was a sufficient man.

Upon this, he was a little uneasy, imagining that he had been the cause of it, as indeed he had, next to the positive humour of the inquirer, though it was not really his fault; neither was the construction the other made of it just to his intention, for he aimed at freeing himself from all inquiries of that nature, but found there was no prevailing with him to understand it any other way than he did; so, to requite the man a little in his own way, he contrived the following method: he met with him two or three days after, and asked him if he had sold his goods to the person his neighbour?

'No,' says he; 'you know I would not.'

'Nay,' says the other, 'I only knew you said so; I did not think you would have acted so from what I said, nor do I think I gave you any reason.'

'Why,' says he, 'I knew you would have given him a good character if you could, and I knew you were too honest to do it, if you were not sure it was just.'

'The last part I hope is true, but you might have believed me honest too, in what I did say, that I had resolved to give no characters of any body.'

'As to that, I took it, as any body would, to be the best and modestest way of covering what you would not have be disclosed, namely, that you could not speak as you would; and I also judged that you therefore chose to say nothing.'

'Well, I can say no more but this; you are not just to me in it, and I think you are not just to yourself neither.'

They parted again upon this, and the next day the first tradesman, who had been so pressed to give a character of his neighbour, sent a man to buy the parcel of goods of the other tradesman, and offering him ready money, bought them considerably cheaper than the neighbour-tradesman was to have given for them, besides reckoning a reasonable discount for the time, which was four months, that the first tradesman was to have given to his neighbour.

As soon as he had done, he went and told the neighbour-tradesman what he had done, and the reason of it, and sold the whole parcel to him again, giving the same four months' credit for them as the first man was to have given, and taking the discount for time only to himself, gave him all the advantage of the buying, and gave the first man the mortification of knowing it all, and that the goods were not only for the same man, but that the very tradesman, whom he would not believe when he declined giving a character of any man in general, had trusted him with them.

He pretended to be very angry, and to take it very ill; but the other told him, that when he came to him for a character of the man, and he told him honestly, that he would give no characters at all, that it was not for any ill to his neighbour that he declined it, he ought to have believed him; and that he hoped, when he wanted a character of any of his neighbours again, he would not come to him for it.

This story is to my purpose in this particular, which is indeed very significant; that it is the most difficult thing of its kind in the world to avoid giving characters of our neighbouring tradesmen; and that, let your reasons for it be what they will, to refuse giving a character is giving a bad character, and is generally so taken, whatever caution or arguments you use to the contrary.

In the next place, it is hard indeed, if an honest neighbour be in danger of selling a large parcel of goods to a fellow, who I may know it is not likely should be able to pay for them, though his credit may in the common appearance be pretty good at that time; and what must I do? If I discover the man's circumstances, which perhaps I am let into by some accident, I say, if I discover them, the man is undone; and if I do not, the tradesman, who is in danger of trusting him, is undone.

I confess the way is clear, if I am obliged to speak at all in the case: the man unsound is already a bankrupt at bottom, and must fail, but the other man is sound and firm, if this disaster does not befall him: the first has no wound given him, but negatively; he stands where he stood before; whereas the other is drawn in perhaps to his own ruin. In the next place, the first is a knave, or rather thief, for he offers to buy, and knows he cannot pay; in a word, he offers to cheat his neighbour; and if I know it, I am so far confederate with him in the cheat.

In this case I think I am obliged to give the honest man a due caution for his safety, if he desires my advice; I cannot say I am obliged officiously to go out of my way to do it, unless I am any way interested in the person—for that would be to dip into other men's affairs, which is not my proper work; and if I should any way be misinformed of the circumstances of the tradesman I am to speak of, and wrong him, I may be instrumental to bring ruin causelessly upon him.

In a word, it is a very nice and critical case, and a tradesman ought to be very sure of what he says or does in such a case, the good or evil fate of his neighbour lying much at stake, and depending too much on the breath of his mouth. Every part of this discourse shows how much a tradesman's welfare depends upon the justice and courtesy of his neighbours, and how nice and critical a thing his reputation is.

This, well considered, would always keep a tradesman humble, and show him what need he has to behave courteously and obligingly among his neighbours; for one malicious word from a man much meaner than himself, may overthrow him in such a manner, as all the friends he has may not be able to recover him; a tradesman, if possible, should never make himself any enemies.

But if it is so fatal a thing to tradesmen to give characters of one another, and that a tradesman should be so backward in it for fear of hurting his neighbour, and that, notwithstanding the character given should be just, and the particular reported of him should be true, with how much greater caution should we act in like cases where what is suggested is really false in fact, and the tradesman is innocent, as was the case in the tradesman mentioned before about courting the lady. If a tradesman may be ruined and undone by a true report, much more may he be so by a false report, by a malicious, slandering, defaming tongue. There is an artful way of talking of other people's reputation, which really, however some people salve the matter, is equal, if not superior, in malice to the worst thing they can say; this is, by rendering them suspected, talking doubtfully of their characters, and of their conduct, and rendering them first doubtful, and then strongly suspected. I don't know what to say to such a man. A gentleman came to me the other day, but I knew not what to say; I dare not say he is a good man, or that I would trust him with five hundred pounds myself; if I should say so, I should belie my own opinion. I do not know, indeed, he may be a good man at bottom, but I cannot say he minds his business; if I should, I must lie; I think he keeps a great deal of company, and the like.

Another, he is asked of the currency of his payments, and he answers suspiciously on that side too; I know not what to say, he may pay them at last, but he does not pay them the most currently of any man in the street, and I have heard saucy boys huff him at his door for bills, on his endeavouring to put them off; indeed, I must needs say I had a bill on him a few weeks ago for a hundred pounds, and he paid me very currently, and without any dunning, or often calling upon, but it was I believe because I offered him a bargain at that time, and I supposed he was resolved to put a good face upon his credit.

A tradesman, that would do as he would be done by, should carefully avoid these people who come always about, inquiring after other tradesman's characters. There are men who make it their business to do thus; and as they are thereby as ready to ruin and blow up good fair-dealing tradesmen as others, so they do actually surprise many, and come at their characters earlier and nearer than they expect they would.

Tradesmen, I say, that will thus behave to one another, cannot be supposed to be men of much principle, but will be apt to lay hold of any other advantage, how unjust soever, and, indeed, will wait for an occasion of such advantages; and where is there a tradesman, but who, if he be never so circumspect, may some time or other give his neighbour, who watches for his halting, advantage enough against him. When such a malicious tradesman appears in any place, all the honest tradesmen about him ought to join to expose him, whether they are afraid of him or no: they should blow him among the neighbourhood, as a public nuisance, as a common *barrettor*, or raiser of scandal; by such a general aversion to him they would depreciate him, and bring him into so just a contempt, that no body would keep him company, much less credit any thing he said; and then his tongue would be no slander, and his breath would be no blast, and nobody would either tell him any thing, or hear any thing from him: and this kind of usage, I think, is the only way to put a stop to a defamer; for when he has no credit of his own left, he would be unable to hurt any of his neighbour's.

CHAPTER XVI
OF THE TRADESMAN'S ENTERING INTO PARTNERSHIP IN TRADE, AND THE MANY DANGERS ATTENDING IT

There are some businesses which are more particularly accustomed to partnerships than others, and some that are very seldom managed without two, three, or four partners, and others that cannot be at all carried on without partnership; and there are those again, in which they seldom join partners together.

Mercers, linen-drapers, banking goldsmiths, and such considerable trades, are often, and indeed generally, carried on in partnership; but other meaner trades, and of less business, are carried on, generally speaking, single-handed.

Some merchants, who carry on great business in foreign ports, have what they call houses in those ports, where they plant and breed up their sons and apprentices; and these are such as I hinted could not carry on their business without partnership.

The trading in partnership is not only liable to more hazards and difficulties, but it exposes the tradesman to more snares and disadvantages by a great deal, than the trading with a single hand does; and some of those snares are these:—

I. If the partner is a stirring, diligent, capable man, there is danger of his slipping into the whole trade, and, getting in between you and home, by his application, thrusting you at last quite out; so that you bring in a snake into your chimney corner, which, when it is warmed and grown vigorous, turns about at you, and hisses you out of the house. It is with the tradesman, in the case of a diligent and active partner, as I have already observed it was in the case of a trusty and diligent apprentice, namely, that if the master does not appear constantly at the head of the business, and make himself be known by his own application and diligence to be what he is, he shall soon look to be what he is not, that is to say, one not concerned in the business.

He will never fail to be esteemed the principal person concerned in the shop, and in the trade, who is principally and most constantly found there, acting at the head of every business; and be it a servant or a partner, the master or chief loses himself extremely by the advances the other makes of that kind; for, whenever they part again, either the apprentice by being out of his time, or the partner by the expiration of the articles of partnership, or by any other determination of their agreement, the customers most certainly desire to deal with the man whom they have so often been obliged by; and if they miss him, inquire after and follow him.

It is true, the apprentice is the more dangerous of the two, because his separation is supposed to be more certain, and generally sooner than the partner; the apprentice is not known, and cannot have made his interest among the buyers, but for perhaps a year, or a year and a half, before his time expired: sooner than that he could not put himself in the way of being known and observed; and then, when his time is out, he certainly removes, unless he is taken into the shop as a partner, and that, indeed, prolongs the time, and places the injury at a greater distance, but still it makes it the more influencing when it comes; and unless he is brought some how or other into the family, and becomes one of the house, perhaps by marriage, or some other settled union with the master, he never goes off without making a great chasm in the master's affairs, and the more, by how much he has been more diligent and useful in the trade, the wounds of which the master seldom if ever recovers.

If the partner were not an apprentice, but that they either came out of their times together, or near it, or had a shop and business before, but quitted it to come in, it may then be said that he brought part of the trade with him, and so increased the trade when he joined with the other in proportion to what he may be said to carry away when he went off; this is the best thing that can be said of a partnership; and then I have this to add, first, that the tradesman who took the partner in has a fair field, indeed, to act in with his partner, and must take care, by his constant attendance, due acquaintance with the customers, and appearing in every part of the business, to maintain not his interest only, but the appearance of his interest, in the shop or warehouse, that he may, on every occasion, and to every customer, not only be, but be known to be, the master and head of the business; and that the other is at best but a partner, and not a chief partner, as, in case of his absence and negligence, will presently be suggested; for he that chiefly appears will be always chief partner in the eye of the customers, whatever he is in the substance of the thing.

This, indeed, is much the same case with what is said before of a diligent servant, and a negligent master, and therefore I forbear to enlarge upon it; but it is so important in both cases, that indeed it cannot well be mentioned too often: the master's full application, in his own person, is the only answer to both. He that takes a partner only to ease him of the toil of his business, that he may take his pleasure, and leave the drudgery, as they call it, to the partner, should take care not to do it till about seven years before he resolves to leave off trade, that, at the end of the partnership, he may be satisfied to give up the trade to his partner, or see him run away with it, and not trouble himself about it.

But if he takes a partner at his beginning, with an intent, by their joint enlarged stock, to enlarge their business, and so carry on a capital trade, which perhaps neither of them were able to do by themselves, and which is the only justifiable reason for taking a partner at all, he must resolve then to join with his partner, not only in stock, but in mutual diligence and application, that the trade may flourish by their joint assistance and constant labour, as two oxen yoked together in the same draught, by their joint assistance, draw much more than double what they could either of them draw by their single strength; and this, indeed, is the only safe circumstance of a partnership: then, indeed, they are properly partners when they are assistants to one another, whereas otherwise they are like two gamesters striving to worm one another out, and to get the mastery in the play they are engaged in.

The very word *partner* imports the substance of the thing, and they are, as such, engaged to a mutual application, or they are no more partners, but rather one is the trading gentleman, and the other is the trading drudge; but even then, let them depend, the drudge will carry away the trade, and the profit too, at last. And this is the way how one partner may honestly ruin another, and for ought I know it is the only one: for it cannot be said but that the diligent partner acts honestly in acting diligently, and if the other did the same, they would both thrive alike; but if one is negligent and the other diligent, one extravagant and expensive, the other frugal and prudent, it cannot be said to be his fault that one is rich and the other poor—that one increases in the stock, and the other is lessened, and at last worked quite out of it.

As a partner, then, is taken in only for ease, to abate the first tradesman's diligence, and take off the edge of his application, so far a partner, let him be as honest and diligent as he will, is dangerous to the tradesman—nay, the more honest and the more diligent he is, the more dangerous he is, and the more a snare to the tradesman that takes him in; and a tradesman ought to be very cautious in the adventure, for, indeed, it is an adventure—that he be not brought in time to relax his diligence, by having a partner, even contrary to his first intention; for laziness is a subtle insinuating thing, and it is a sore temptation to a man of ease and indolence to see his work done for him, and less need of him in the business than used to be, and yet the business to go on well too; and this danger is dormant, and lies unseen, till after several years it rises, as it were, out of its ambuscade, and surprises the tradesman, letting him see by his loss what his neglect has cost him.

2. But there are other dangers in partnership, and those not a few; for you may not only be remiss and negligent, remitting the weight of the business upon him, and depending upon him for its being carried on, by which he makes himself master, and brings you to be forgot in the business; but he may be crafty too, and designing in all this, and when he has thus brought you to be as it were *nobody*, he shall make himself be all *somebody* in the trade, and in that particular he by degrees gets the capital interest, as well as stock in the trade, while the true original of the shop, who laid the foundation of the whole business, brought a trade to the shop, or brought commissions to the house, and whose the business more particularly is, is secretly supplanted, and with the concurrence of his own negligence—for without that it cannot be—is, as it were, laid aside, and at last quite thrust out.

Thus, whether honest or dishonest, the tradesman is circumvented, and the partnership is made fatal to him; for it was all owing to the partnership the tradesman was diligent before, understood his business, and kept close to it, gave up his time to it, and by employing himself, prevented the indolence which he finds breaking insensibly upon him afterwards, by being made easy, as they call it, in the assistance of a partner.

3. But there are abundance of other cases which make a partnership dangerous; for if it be so where the partner is honest and diligent, and where he works into the heart of the business by his industry and application, or by his craft and insinuation, what may it not be if he proves idle and extravagant; and if, instead of working him out, he may be said to play him out of the business, that is to say, prove wild, expensive, and run himself and his partner out by his extravagance?

There are but too many examples of this kind; and here the honest tradesman has the labouring oar indeed; for instead of being assisted by a diligent industrious partner, whom on that account he took into the trade, he proves a loose, extravagant, wild fellow, runs abroad into company, and leaves him (for whose relief he was taken in) to bear the burden of the whole trade, which, perhaps, was too heavy for him before, and if it had not been so, he had not been prevailed with to have taken in a partner at all.

This is, indeed, a terrible disappointment, and is very discouraging, and the more so, because it cannot be recalled; for a partnership is like matrimony, it is almost engaged in for better or for worse, till the years expire; there is no breaking it off, at least, not easily nor fairly, but all the inconveniences which are to be feared will follow and stare in your face: as, first, the partner in the first place draws out all his stock; and this sometimes is a blow fatal enough, for perhaps the partner cannot take the whole trade upon himself, and cannot carry on the trade upon his own stock: if he could, he would not have taken in a partner at all. This withdrawing the stock has sometimes been very dangerous to a partner; nay, has many times been the overthrow and undoing of him and of the family that is left.

He that takes a partner into his trade on this account—namely, for the support of his stock, to enjoy the assistance of so much cash to carry on the trade, ought seriously to consider what he shall be able to do when the partner, breaking off the partnership, shall carry all his stock, and the improvement of it too, with him: perhaps the tradesman's stock is not much increased, perhaps not at all; nay, perhaps the stock is lessened, instead of being increased, and they have rather gone backward than forward. What shall the tradesman do in such a case? And how shall he bear the breach in his stock which that separation would make?

Thus he is either tied down to the partner, or the partner is pinned down to him, for he cannot separate without a breach. It is a sad truth to many a partner, that when the partnership comes to be finished and expired, the man would let his partner go, but the other cannot go without tearing him all to pieces whom he leaves behind him; and yet the partner being loose, idle, and extravagant, in a word, will ruin both if he stays.

This is the danger of partnership in some of the best circumstances of it; but how hazardous and how fatal is it in other cases! And how many an honest and industrious tradesman has been prevailed with to take in a partner to ease himself in the weight of the business, or on several other accounts, some perhaps reasonable and prudent enough, but has found himself immediately involved in a sea of trouble, is brought into innumerable difficulties, concealed debts, and unknown incumbrances, such as he could no ways extricate himself out of, and so both have been unavoidably ruined together!

These cases are so various and so uncertain, that it is not easy to enumerate them: but we may include the particulars in a general or two.

1. One partner may contract debts, even in the partnership itself, so far unknown to the other, as that the other may be involved in the danger of them, though he was not at all concerned in, or acquainted with, them at the same time they were contracted.

2. One partner may discharge debts for both partners; and so, having a design to be knavish, may go and receive money, and give receipts for it, and not bringing it to account, or not bringing the money into cash, may wrong the stock to so considerable a sum as may be to the ruin of the other partner.

3. One partner may confess judgment, or give bonds, or current notes in the name, and as for the account of the company, and yet convert the effects to his own private use, leaving the stock to be answerable for the value.

4. One partner may sell and give credit, and deliver parcels of goods to what sum, or what quantity, he thinks fit, and to whom, and so, by his indiscretion, or perhaps by connivance and knavery, lose to the stock what parcel of goods he pleases, to the ruin of the other partner, and bring themselves to be both bankrupt together.

5. Nay, to sum up all, one partner may commit acts of bankruptcy without the knowledge of the other, and thereby subject the united stock, and both or all the partners, to the danger of a commission, when they may themselves know nothing of it till the blow is given, and given so as to be too late to be retrieved.

All these, and many more, being the ill consequences and dangers of partnership in trade, I cannot but seriously warn the honest industrious tradesman, if possible, to stand upon his own legs, and go on upon his own bottom; to pursue his business diligently, but cautiously, and what we call fair and softly; not eagerly pushing to drive a vast trade, and enjoy but half of it, rather carry on a middling business, and let it be his own.

There may be cases, indeed, which may have their exceptions to this general head of advice; partnerships may sometimes prove successful, and in some particular business they are more necessary than in others, and in some they tell us that they are absolutely necessary, though the last I can by no means grant; but be that as it will, there are so many cases more in number, and of great consequence too, which miscarry by the several perplexed circumstances, differing tempers, and open knavery of partners, that I cannot but give it as a friendly advice to all tradesmen—if possible, to avoid partnerships of all kinds.

But if the circumstances of trade require partnerships, and the risk must be run, I would recommend to the tradesman not to enter into partnerships, but under the following circumstances:—

I. Not to take in any partner who should be allowed to carry on any separate business, in which the partnership is not concerned. Depend upon it, whatever other business your partner carries on, you run the risk of it as much as you do of your own; and you run the risk with this particular circumstance too, that you have the hazard without the profit or success: that is, without a share in the profit or success, which is very unequal and unfair. I know cunning men will tell you, that there may be provision made so effectually in the articles of partnership, that the stock in partnership should be concerned in no other interest or engagements but its own; but let such cunning gentlemen tell me, if the partner meets with a disappointment in his other undertakings, which wounds him so deep as to break him, will it not affect the partnership thus far? I. That it may cause his stock to be drawn hastily out, and perhaps violently too. 2. That it touches and taints the credit of the partner to be concerned with such a man; and though a man's bottom may support him, if it be very good, yet it is a blow to him, touches his credit, and makes the world stand a little at a stay about him, if it be no more, for a while, till they see that he shows himself upon the Exchange, or at his shop-door again, in spite of all the apprehensions and doubts that have been handed about concerning him. Either of these are so essential to the tradesman, whose partner thus sinks by his own private breaches, in which the parnership is not concerned, that it is worth while to caution the tradesman against venturing. And I must add, too, that many a tradesman has fallen under the disaster by the partner's affairs thus affecting him, though the immediate losses which the partner had suffered have not been charged upon him; and yet I believe it is not so easy to avoid being fallen upon for those debts also.

It is certain, as I formerly noted, rumour will break a tradesman almost at any time. It matters not, at first, whether the rumour be true or false. What rumour can sit closer to a man in business—his own personal misfortunes excepted—than such as this-*that his partner is broke?* That his partner has met with a loss, suppose an insurance, suppose a fall of stocks, suppose a bubble or a cheat, or we know not what, the partner is sunk, no man knows whether the partnership be concerned in it or no; and while it is not known, every man will suppose it, for mankind always think the worst of every thing.

What can be a closer stroke at the poor tradesman? He knows not what his partner has done; he has reason to fear the worst; he even knows not himself, for a while, whether he can steer clear of the rocks or no; but soon recovers, knows his own circumstances, and struggles hard with the world, pays out his partner's stock, and gets happily over it. And it is well he does so, for that he is at the brink of ruin must be granted; and where one stands and keeps up his reputation and his business, there are twenty would be undone in the same circumstance.

Who, then, would run the venture of a partner, if it were possible to avoid it? And who, if they must have a partner, would have one that was concerned in separate business, in which the partnership was not engaged?

2. If you must have a partner, always choose to have the partner rather under than over you; by this I mean, take him in for a fifth, a fourth, or at most a third, never for a half. There are many reasons to be given for this, besides that of having the greater share of profits, for that I do not give as a reason here at all; but the principal reasons are these:—First, in case of any disaster in any of the particular supposed accidents which I have mentioned, and that you should be obliged to pay out your partner's stock, it will not be so heavy, or be so much a blow to you: and, secondly, you preserve to yourself the governing influence in your own business; you cannot be overruled, overawed, or dogmatically told, it shall, or shall not, be thus, or thus. He that takes in a partner for a third, has a partner servant; he that takes him in for a half, has a partner master—that is to say, a director, or preceptor: let your partner have always a lesser interest in the business than yourself, and be rather less acquainted with the business than yourself, at least not better. You should rather have a partner to be instructed, than a partner to instruct you; for he that teaches you, will always taunt you.

3. If you must have a partner, let him always be your junior, rather than your senior; by this I mean, your junior in business, whether he is so in years or not. There are many reasons why the tradesman should choose this, and particularly the same as the other of taking him in for a junior or inferior part of the trade—that is to say, to maintain the superiority of the business in his own hands; and this I mention, not at all upon account of the pride or vanity of the superiority, for that is a trifle compared to the rest; but that he may have the more authority to inspect the conduct of his partner, in which he is so much and so

essentially concerned; and to inquire whether he is doing any thing, or taking any measures, dangerous or prejudicial to the stock, or to the credit of the partnership, that so if he finds any thing, he may restrain him, and prevent in time the mischief which would otherwise be inevitable to them both.

There are many other advantages to a tradesman who is obliged to take a partner, by keeping in his own hands the major part of the trade, which are too long to repeat here; such as his being always able to put a check to any rash adventure, any launching out into bubbles and projects, and things dangerous to the business: and this is a very needful thing in a partnership, that one partner should be able to correct the rash resolves of another in hazardous cases.

By this correcting of rash measures, I mean over-ruling them with moderation and temper, for the good of the whole, and for their mutual advantage. The Romans frequently had two generals, or consuls, to command their armies in the field: one of which was to be a young man, that by his vigour and sprightly forwardness he might keep up the spirits and courage of the soldiers, encourage them to fight, and lead them on by his example; the other an old soldier, that by his experience in the military affairs, age, and counsels, he might a little abate the fire of his colleague, and might not only know how to fight, but know when to fight, that is to say, when to avoid fighting; and the want of this lost them many a victory, and the great battle of Cannae in particular, in which 80,000 Romans were killed in one day.

To compare small things with great, I may say it is just so in the affair of trade. You should always join a sober grave head, weighed to business, and acquainted with trade, to the young trader, who having been young in the work will the easier give up his judgment to the other, and who is governed with the solid experience of the other; and so you join their ways together, the rash and the sedate, the grave and the giddy.

Again, if you must go into partnership, be sure, if possible, you take nobody into partnership but such as whose circumstances in trade you are fully acquainted with. Such there are frequently to be had among relations and neighbours, and such, if possible, should be the man that is taken into partnership, that the hazard of unsound circumstances may be avoided. A man may else be taken into partnership who may be really bankrupt even before you take him; and such things have been done, to the ruin of many an honest tradesman.

If possible, let your partner be a beginner, that his stock may be reasonably supposed to be free and unentangled; and let him be one that you know personally, and his circumstances, and did know even before you had any thoughts of engaging together.

All these cautions are with a supposition that the partner must be had; but I must still give it as my opinion, in the case of such tradesmen as I have all along directed myself to, that if possible they should go on single-handed in trade; and I close it with this brief note, respecting the qualifications of a partner, as above, that, next to no partner, such a partner is best.

CHAPTER XVII
OF HONESTY IN DEALING, AND LYING

There is some difference between an honest man and an honest tradesman; and though the distinction is very nice, yet, I must say, it is to be supported. Trade cannot make a knave of an honest man, for there is a specific difference between honesty and knavery which can never be altered by trade or any other thing; nor can that integrity of mind which describes and is peculiar to a man of honesty be ever abated to a tradesman; the rectitude of his soul must be the same, and he must not only intend or mean honestly and justly, but he must do so; he must act honestly and justly, and that in all his dealings; he must neither cheat nor defraud, over-reach nor circumvent his neighbour, nor indeed anybody he deals with; nor must he design to do so, or lay any plots or snares to that purpose in his dealing, as is frequent in the general conduct of too many, who yet call themselves honest tradesmen, and would take it very ill to have any one tax their integrity.

But after all this is premised, there are some latitudes, like poetical licences in other cases, which a tradesman is and must be allowed, and which by the custom and usage of trade he may give himself a liberty in, which cannot be allowed in other cases to any man, no, nor to the tradesman himself out of his business—I say, he may take some liberties, but within bounds; and whatever some pretenders to strict living may say, yet that tradesman shall pass with me for a very honest man, notwithstanding the liberty which he gives himself of this kind, if he does not take those liberties in an exorbitant manner; and those liberties are such as these.

I. The liberty of asking more than he will take. I know some people have condemned this practice as dishonest, and the Quakers for a time stood to their point in the contrary practice, resolving to ask no more than they would take, upon any occasion whatsoever, and choosing rather to lose the selling of their goods, though they could afford sometimes to take what was offered, rather than abate a farthing of the price they had asked; but time and the necessities of trade made them wiser, and brought them off of that severity, and they by degrees came to ask, and abate, and abate again, just as other business tradesmen do, though not perhaps as some do, who give themselves a fuller liberty that way.

Indeed, it is the buyers that make this custom necessary; for they, especially those who buy for immediate use, will first pretend positively to tie themselves up to a limited price, and bid them a little and a little more, till they come so near the sellers' price, that they, the sellers, cannot find in their hearts to refuse it, and then they are tempted to take it, notwithstanding their first words to the contrary. It is common, indeed, for the tradesman to say, 'I cannot abate anything,' when yet they do and can afford it; but the tradesman should indeed not be understood strictly and literally to his words, but as he means it, namely, that he cannot reasonably abate, and that he cannot afford to abate: and there he may be in earnest, namely, that he cannot make a reasonable profit of his goods, if he is obliged to abate, and so the meaning is honest, that he cannot abate; and yet rather than not take your money, he may at last resolve to do it, in hopes of getting a better price for the remainder, or being willing to abate his ordinary gain, rather than disoblige the customer; or being perhaps afraid he should not sell off the quantity; and many such reasons may be given why he submits to sell at a lower price than he really intended, or can afford to do; and yet he cannot be said to be dishonest, or to lie, in saying at first he cannot, or could not, abate.

A man in trade is properly to be said not to be able to do what he cannot do to his profit and advantage. The English cannot trade to Hungary, and into Slavonia—that is to say, they cannot do it to advantage; but it is better for them to trade to Venice with their goods, and let the Venetians carry on a trade into Hungary through Dalmatia, Croatia, &c, and the like in other places.

To bring it down to particular cases: one certain merchant cannot deal in one sort of goods which another merchant is eminent for; the other merchant is as free to the trade as he, but he cannot do it to profit; for he is unacquainted with the trade, and it is out of his way, and therefore he cannot do it.

Thus, to the case in hand. The tradesman says he cannot sell his goods under such a price, which in the sense of his business is true; that is to say, he cannot do it to carry on his trade with the usual and reasonable advantage which he ought to expect, and which others make in the same way of business.

Or, he cannot, without underselling the market, and undervaluing the goods, and seeming to undersell his neighbour-shopkeepers, to whom there is a justice due in trade, which respects the price of sale; and to undersell is looked upon as an unfair kind of trading.

All these, and many more, are the reasons why a tradesman may be said not to lie, though he should say he *cannot* abate, or *cannot* sell his goods under such a price, and yet may after think fit to sell you his goods something lower than he so intended, or can afford to do, rather than lose your custom, or rather than lose the selling of his goods, and taking your ready money, which at that time he may have occasion for.

In these cases, I cannot say a shopkeeper should be tied down to the literal meaning of his words in the price he asks, or that he is guilty of lying in not adhering stiffly to the letter of his first demand; though, at the same time, I would have every tradesman take as little liberty that way as may be: and if the buyer would expect the tradesman should keep strictly to his demand, he should not stand and haggle, and screw the shopkeeper down, bidding from one penny to another, to a trifle within his price, so, as it were, to push him to the extremity, either to turn away his customer for a sixpence, or some such trifle, or to break his word: as if he would say, I will force you to speak falsely, or turn me away for a trifle.

In such cases, if, indeed, there is a breach, the sin is the buyer's: at least, he puts himself in the devil's stead, and makes himself both tempter and accuser; nor can I say that the seller is in that case so much to blame as the buyer. However, it were to be wished that on both sides buying and selling might be carried on without it; for the buyer as often says, 'I won't give a farthing more,' and yet advances, as the seller says, 'I can't abate a farthing,' and yet complies. These are, as I call them, *trading lies*; and it were to be wished they could be avoided on both sides; and the honest tradesman does avoid them as much as possible, but yet must not, I say, in all cases, be tied up to the strict, literal sense of that expression, *I cannot abate*, as above.[28]

2. Another trading licence is that of appointing, and promising payments of money, which men in business are oftentimes forced to make, and forced to break, without any scrupple; nay, and without any reproach upon their integrity. Let us state this case as clearly as we can, and see how it stands as to the morality of it, for that is the point in debate.

The credit usually given by one tradesman to another, as particularly by the merchant to the wholesale-man, and by the wholesale-man to the retailer, is such, that, without tying the buyer up

---

[28] The practice of haggling about prices is now very properly abandoned by all respectable dealers in goods, greatly to the comfort of both sellers and buyers.

to a particular day of payment, they go on buying and selling, and the buyer pays money upon account, as his convenience admits, and as the seller is content to take it. This occasions the merchant, or the wholesale-man, to go about, as they call it, *a-dunning* among their dealers, and which is generally the work of every Saturday. When the merchant comes to his customer the wholesale-man, or warehouse-keeper, for money, he tells him, 'I have no money, Sir; I cannot pay you now; if you call next week, I will pay you.' Next week comes, and the merchant calls again; but it is the same thing, only the warehouseman adds, 'Well, I will pay you next week, *without fail.'* When the week comes, he tells him he has met with great disappointments, and he knows not what to do, but desires his patience another week: and when the other week comes, perhaps he pays him, and so they go on.

Now, what is to be said for this? In the first place, let us look back to the occasion. This warehouse-keeper, or wholesale-man, sells the goods which he buys of the merchant—I say, he sells them to the retailers, and it is for that reason I place it first there. Now, as they buy in smaller quantities than he did of the merchant, so he deals with more of them in number, and he goes about among them the same Saturday, to get in money that he may pay his merchant, and he receives his bag full of promises, too, every where instead of money, and is put off from week to week, perhaps by fifty shopkeepers in a day; and their serving him thus obliges him to do the same to the merchant.

Again, come to the merchant. Except some, whose circumstances are above it, they are by this very usage obliged to put off the Blackwell-hall factor, or the packer, or the clothier, or whoever they deal with, in proportion; and thus promises go round for payment, and those promises are kept or broken as money comes in, or as disappointments happen; and all this while there is no breach of honesty, or parole; no lying, or supposition of it, among the tradesmen, either on one side or other.

But let us come, I say, to the morality of it. To break a solemn promise is a kind of prevarication; that is certain, there is no coming off of it; and I might enlarge here upon the first fault, namely, of making the promise, which, say the strict objectors, they should not do. But the tradesman's answer is this: all those promises ought to be taken as they are made—namely, with a contingent dependence upon the circumstances of trade, such as promises made them by others who owe them money, or the supposition of a week's trade bringing in money by retail, as usual, both of which are liable to fail, or at least to fall short;

and this the person who calls for the money knows, and takes the promise with those attending casualties; which if they fail, he knows the shopkeeper, or whoever he is, must fail him too.

The case is plain, if the man had the money in cash, he need not make a promise or appointment for a farther day; for that promise is no more or less than a capitulation for a favour, a desire or condition of a week's forbearance, on his assurance, that if possible he will not fail to pay him at the time. It is objected, that the words *if possible* should then be mentioned, which would solve the morality of the case: to this I must answer, that I own I think it needless, unless the man to whom the promise was made could be supposed to believe the promise was to be performed, whether it were possible or no; which no reasonable man can be supposed to do.

There is a parallel case to this in the ordinary appointment of people to meet either at place or time, upon occasions of business. Two friends make an appointment to meet the next day at such a house, suppose a tavern at or near the Exchange: one says to the other, 'Do not fail me at that time, for I will certainly be there;' the other answers, 'I will not fail.' Some people, who think themselves more religious than others, or at least would be thought so, object against these positive appointments, and tell us we ought to say, 'I will, if it pleases God.' or I will, life and health permitting;[29] and they quote the text for it, where our Saviour expressly commands to use such a caution, and which I shall say nothing to lessen the force of.

But to say a word to our present custom. Since Christianity is the public profession of the country, and we are to suppose we not only are Christians ourselves, but that all those we are talking to, or of, are also Christians, we must add that Christianity supposes we acknowledge that life, and all the contingencies of life, are subjected to the dominion of

---

[29] It was a fashion of trade in Defoe's time, and down to a somewhat later period, to thrust the phrase 'God willing' into almost every promise or announcement, the purport of which might possibly be thwarted by death or any other accident. The phrase, in particular, appeared at the beginning of all letters in which a merchant announced his design of visiting retail dealers in the provinces; as, 'God willing, I shall have the honour of waiting on you on the 15th proximo:' hence English *riders*, or commercial travellers, came to be known in Scotland by the nickname of God-willings.' This pious phraseology seems now to be banished from all mercantile affairs, except the shipping of goods.

Providence, and liable to all those accidents which God permits to befall us in the ordinary course of our living in the world, therefore we expect to be taken in that sense in all such appointments; and it is but justice to us as Christians, in the common acceptation of our words, that when I say, *I will certainly* meet my friend at such a place, and at such a time, he should understand me to mean, if it pleases God to give me life and health, or that his Providence permits me to come, or, as the text says, 'If the Lord will;' for we all know that unless the Lord will, I cannot meet, or so much as live.

Not to understand me thus, is as much as to say, you do not understand me to be a Christian, or to act like a Christian in any thing; and on the other hand, they that understand it otherwise, I ought not to understand them to be Christians. Nor should I be supposed to put any neglect or dishonour upon the government of Providence in the world, or to suggest that I did not think myself subjected to it, because I omitted the words in my appointment.

In like manner, when a man comes to me for money, I put him off: that, in the first place, supposes I have not the money by me, or cannot spare it to pay him at that time; if it were otherwise, it may be supposed I would pay him just then. He is then perhaps impatient, and asks me when I will pay him, and I tell him at such a time. This naturally supposes, that by that time I expect to be supplied, so as to be able to pay; I have current bills, or promises of money, to be paid me, or I expect the ordinary takings in my shop or warehouse will supply me to make good my promise: thus my promise is honest in its foundation, because I have reason to expect money to come in to make me in a condition to perform it; but so it falls out, contrary to my expectation, and contrary to the reason of things, I am disappointed, and cannot do it; I am then, indeed, a trespasser upon my creditor, whom I ought to have paid, and I am under affliction enough on that account, and I suffer in my reputation for it also; but I cannot be said to be a liar, an immoral man, a man that has no regard to my promise, and the like; for at the same time I have perhaps used my utmost endeavour to do it, but am prevented by many several men breaking promise with me, and I am no way able to help myself.

It is objected to this, that then I should not make my promises absolute, but conditional. To this I say, that the promises, as is above observed, are really not absolute, but conditional in the very nature of them, and are understood so when they are made, or else they that hear them do not understand them, as all human appointments ought to be understood; I do confess, it would be better not to make an absolute promise at all, but to express the condition or reserve with the promise, and say, 'I will if I can,' or, 'I will if people are just to me, and perform their promises to me.'

But to this I answer, the importunity of the person who demands the payment will not permit it—nothing short of a positive promise will satisfy—they never believe the person intends to perform if he makes the least reserve or condition in his promise, though, at the same time, they know that even the nature of the promise and the reason of the promise strongly implies the condition—I say, the importunity of the creditor occasions the breach, which he reproaches the debtor with the immorality of.[30]

Custom, indeed, has driven us beyond the limits of our morals in many things, which trade makes necessary, and which we cannot now avoid; so that if we must pretend to go back to the literal sense of the command; if our yea must be yea, and our nay nay; if no man must go beyond, or defraud his neighbour; if our conversation must be without covetousness, and the like—why, then, it is impossible for tradesmen to be Christians, and we must unhinge all business, act upon new principles in trade, and go on by new rules—in short, we must shut up shop, and leave off trade, and so in many things we must leave off living; for as conversation is called life, we must leave off to converse: all the ordinary communication of life is now full of lying; and what with table-lies, salutation-lies, and trading-lies, there is no such thing as every man speaking truth with his neighbour.

But this is a subject would launch me out beyond the bounds of a chapter, and make a book by itself. I return to the case particularly in hand—promises of payment of money. Men in trade, I say, are under this unhappy necessity, they are forced to make them, and they are forced to break them; the violent pressing and dunning, and perhaps threatening too, of the creditor, when the poor shopkeeper cannot

---

[30] Notwithstanding all this ingenious reasoning, we cannot help thinking that it would be better if conditional promises were made in conditional language. It is not necessarily to be understood in all cases that a direct unreserved promise means something conditional, so that there is a liability to being much deceived and grievously disappointed by all such promises. A sound morality certainly demands that the tradesman should use the practices described in the text as rarely, and with as much reluctance, as possible, and that, like other men, he should make his words, as nearly as may be, the echo of his thoughts.

comply with his demand, forces him to promise; in short, the importunate creditor will not be otherwise put off, and the poor shopkeeper, almost worried, and perhaps a little terrified too, and afraid of him, is glad to do and say any thing to pacify him, and this extorts a promise, which, when the time comes, he is no more able to perform than he was before, and this multiplies promises, and consequently breaches, so much of which are to be placed to the accounts of force, that I must acknowledge, though the debtor is to blame, the creditor is too far concerned in the crime of it to be excused, and it were to be wished some other method could be found out to prevent the evil, and that tradesmen would resolve with more courage to resist the importunities of the creditor, be the consequence what it would, rather than break in upon their morals, and load their consciences with the reproaches of it for all their lives after.

I remember I knew a tradesman, who, labouring long under the ordinary difficulties of men embarrassed in trade, and past the possibility of getting out, and being at last obliged to stop and call his people together, told me, that after he was broke, though it was a terrible thing to him at first too, as it is to most tradesmen, yet he thought himself in a new world, when he was at a full stop, and had no more the terror upon him of bills coming for payment, and creditors knocking at his door to dun him, and he without money to pay. He was no more obliged to stand in his shop, and be bullied and ruffled by his creditors, nay, by their apprentices and boys, and sometimes by porters and footmen, to whom he was forced to give good words, and sometimes strain his patience to the utmost limits: he was now no more obliged to make promises, which he knew he could not perform, and break promises as fast as he made them, and so lie continually both to God and man; and, he added, the ease of his mind which he felt upon that occasion was so great, that it balanced all the grief he was in at the general disaster of his affairs; and, farther, that even in the lowest of his circumstances which followed, he would not go back to live as he had done, in the exquisite torture of want of money to pay his bills and his duns.

Nor was it any satisfaction to him to say, that it was owing to the like breach of promise in the shopkeepers, and gentlemen, and people whom he dealt with, who owed him money, and who made no conscience of promising and disappointing him, and thereby drove him to the necessity of breaking his own promises; for this did not satisfy his mind in the breaches of his word, though they really drove him to the necessity of it: but that which lay heaviest upon him was the violence and clamour of creditors, who would not be satisfied without such promises, even when he knew, or at least believed, he should not be able to perform.

Nay, such was the importunity of one of his merchants, that when he came for money, and he was obliged to put him off, and to set him another day, the merchant would not be satisfied, unless he would swear that he would pay him on that day without fail. 'And what said you to him?' said I. 'Say to him!' said he, 'I looked him full in the face, and sat me down without speaking a word, being filled with rage and indignation at him; but after a little while he insisted again, and asked me what answer I would make him, at which I smiled, and asked him, if he were in earnest? He grew angry then, and asked me if I laughed at him, and if I thought to laugh him out of his money? I then asked him, if he really did expect I should swear that I would pay him the next week, as I proposed to promise? He told me, yes, he did, and I should swear it, or pay him before he went out of my warehouse.

I wondered, indeed, at the discourse, and at the folly of the merchant, who, I understood afterwards, was a foreigner; and though I thought he had been in jest at first, when he assured me he was not, I was curious to hear the issue, which at first he was loth to go on with, because he knew it would bring about all the rest; but I pressed him to know—so he told me that the merchant carried it to such a height as put him into a furious passion, and, knowing he must break some time or other, he was resolved to put an end to his being insulted in that manner; so at last he rose up in a rage, told the merchant, that as no honest man could take such an oath, unless he had the money by him to pay it, so no honest man could ask such a thing of him; and that, since he must have an answer, his answer was, he would not swear such an oath for him, nor any man living, and if he would not be satisfied without it, he might do his worst—and so turned from him; and knowing the man was a considerable creditor, and might do him a mischief, he resolved to shut up that very night, and did so, carrying all his valuable goods with him into the Mint, and the next day he heard that his angry creditor waylaid him the same afternoon to arrest him, but he was too quick for him; and, as he said, though it almost broke his heart to shut up his shop, yet that being delivered from the insulting temper of his creditor, and the perpetual perplexities of want of money to pay people when they dunned him, and, above all, from the necessity of making solemn promises for trifling sums, and then breaking them again, was to him like a load taken off his back when he was weary, and could stand under it no longer; it was a terror to him, he said, to be continually lying, breaking faith with all mankind, and making promises which he could not perform.

This necessarily brings me to observe here, and it is a little for the ease of the tradesman's mind in such severe cases, that there is a distinction to be made in this case between wilful premeditated lying, and the necessity men may be driven to by their disappointments, and other accidents of their circumstances, to break such promises, as they had made with an honest intention of performing them.

He that breaks a promise, however solemnly made, may be an honest man, but he that makes a promise with a design to break it, or with no resolution of performing it, cannot be so: nay, to carry it farther, he that makes a promise, and does not do his endeavour to perform it, or to put himself into a condition to perform it, cannot be an honest man. A promise once made supposes the person willing to perform it, if it were in his power, and has a binding influence upon the person who made it, so far as his power extends, or that he can within the reach of any reasonable ability perform the conditions; but if it is not in his power to perform it, as in this affair of payment of money is often the case, the man cannot be condemned as dishonest, unless it can be made appear, either

1. That when he made the promise, he knew he should not be able to perform it; or,

2. That he resolved when he made the promise not to perform it, though he should be in a condition to do it. And in both these cases the morality of promising cannot be justified, any more than the immorality of not performing it.

But, on the other hand, the person promising, honestly intending when he made the appointment to perform it if possible, and endeavouring faithfully to be able, but being rendered unable by the disappointment of those on whose promises he depended for the performance of his own; I cannot say that such a tradesman can be charged with lying, or with any immorality in promising, for the breach was not properly his own, but the people's on whom he depended; and this is justified from what I said before, namely, that every promise of that kind supposes the possibility of such a disappointment, even in the very nature of its making; for, if the man were not under a moral incapacity of payment, he would not promise at all, but pay at the time he promised. His promising, then, implies that he has only something future to depend upon, to capacitate him for the payment; that is to say, the appointments of payment by other tradesmen, who owe him (that promises) the money, or the daily supply from the ordinary course of his trade, suppose him a retailer in a shop, and the like; all which circumstances are subject to contingencies and disappointments, and are known to be so by the person to whom the promise is made; and it is with all those contingencies and possibilities of disappointment, that he takes or accepts the tradesman's promise, and forbears him, in hopes that he will be able to perform, knowing, that unless he receives money as above, he cannot.

I must, however, acknowledge, that it is a very mortifying thing to a tradesman, whether we suppose him to be one that values his credit in trade, or his principle as to honest dealing, to be obliged to break his word; and therefore, where men are not too much under the hatches to the creditor, and they can possibly avoid it, a tradesman should not make his promises of payment so positive, but rather conditional, and thereby avoid both the immorality and the discredit of breaking his word; nor will any tradesman, I hope, harden himself in a careless forwardness to promise, without endeavouring or intending to perform, from any thing said in this chapter; for be the excuse for it as good as it will, as to the point of strict honesty, he can have but small regard to his own peace of mind, or to his own credit in trade, who will not avoid it as much as possible.

CHAPTER XVIII
OF THE CUSTOMARY FRAUDS OF TRADE, WHICH HONEST MEN ALLOW THEMSELVES TO PRACTISE, AND PRETEND TO JUSTIFY

As there are trading lies which honest men tell, so there are frauds in trade, which tradesmen daily practise, and which, notwithstanding, they think are consistent with their being honest men.

It is certainly true, that few things in nature are simply unlawful and dishonest, but that all crime is made so by the addition and concurrence of circumstances; and of these I am now to speak: and the first I take notice of, is that of taking and repassing, or putting off, counterfeit or false money.

It must be confessed, that calling in the old money in the time of the late King William was an act particularly glorious to that reign, and in nothing more than this, that it delivered trade from a terrible load, and tradesmen from a vast accumulated weight of daily crime. There was scarce a shopkeeper that had not a considerable quantity or bag full of false and unpassable money; not an apprentice that kept his master's cash, but had an annual loss, which they sometimes were unable to support, and sometimes their parents and friends were called upon for the deficiency.

The consequence was, that every raw youth or unskilful body, that was sent to receive money, was put upon by the cunning tradesmen, and all the bad money they had was tendered in payment among the good, that by ignorance or oversight some might possibly be made to pass; and as these took it, so they were not wanting again in all the artifice and sleight of hand they were masters of, to put it off again; so that, in short, people were made bites and cheats to one another in all their business; and if you went but to buy a pair of gloves, or stockings, or any trifle, at a shop, you went with bad money in one hand, and good money in the other, proffering first the bad coin, to get it off, if possible, and then the good, to make up the deficiency, if the other was rejected.

Thus, people were daily upon the catch to cheat and surprise one another, if they could; and, in short, paid no good money for anything, if they could help it. And how did we triumph, if meeting with some poor raw servant, or ignorant woman, behind a counter, we got off a counterfeit half-crown, or a brass shilling, and brought away their goods

636

(which were worth the said half-crown or shilling, if it had been good) for a half-crown that was perhaps not worth sixpence, or for a shilling not worth a penny: as if this were not all one with picking the shopkeeper's pocket, or robbing his house!

The excuse ordinarily given for this practice was this—namely, that it came to us for good; we took it, and it only went as it came; we did not make it, and the like; as if, because we had been basely cheated by A, we were to be allowed to cheat B; or that because C had robbed our house, that therefore we might go and rob D.

And yet this was constantly practised at that time over the whole nation, and by some of the honestest tradesmen among us, if not by all of them.

When the old money was, as I have said, called in, this cheating trade was put to an end, and the morals of the nation in some measure restored—for, in short, before that, it was almost impossible for a tradesman to be an honest man; but now we begin to fall into it again, and we see the current coin of the kingdom strangely crowded with counterfeit money again, both gold and silver; and especially we have found a great deal of counterfeit foreign money, as particularly Portugal and Spanish gold, such as moydores and Spanish pistoles, which, when we have the misfortune to be put upon with them, the fraud runs high, and dips deep into our pockets, the first being twenty-seven shillings, and the latter seventeen shillings. It is true, the latter being payable only by weight, we are not often troubled with them; but the former going all by tale, great quantities of them have been put off among us. I find, also, there is a great increase of late of counterfeit money of our own coin, especially of shillings, and the quantity increasing, so that, in a few years more, if the wicked artists are not detected, the grievance may be in proportion as great as it was formerly, and perhaps harder to be redressed, because the coin is not likely to be any more called in, as the old smooth money was.

What, then, must be done? And how must we prevent the mischief to conscience and principle which lay so heavy upon the whole nation before? The question is short, and the answer would be as short, and to the purpose, if people would but submit to the little loss that would fall upon them at first, by which they would lessen the weight of it as they go on, as it would never increase to such a formidable height as it was at before, nor would it fall so much upon the poor as it did then.

First, I must lay it down as a stated rule or maxim, in the moral part of the question—that to put off counterfeit base money for good money, knowing it to be counterfeit, is dishonest and knavish.

Nor will it take off from the crime of it, or lessen the dishonesty, to say, 'I took it for good and current money, and it goes as it comes;' for, as before, my having been cheated does not authorise me to cheat any other person, so neither was it a just or honest thing in that person who put the bad money upon me, if they knew it to be bad; and if it were not honest in them, how can it be so in me? If, then, it came by knavery, it should not go by knavery—that would be, indeed, to say, it goes as it comes, in a literal sense; that is to say, it came by injustice, and I shall make it go so: but that will not do in matters of right and wrong.

The laws of our country, also, are directly against the practice; the law condemns the coin as illegal—that is to say, it is not current money, or, as the lawyers style it, it is not lawful money of England. Now, every bargain or agreement in trade, is in the common and just acceptation, and the language of trade, made for such a price or rate, in the current money of England; and though you may not express it in words at length, it is so understood, as much as if it were set down in writing. If I cheapen any thing at a shop, suppose it the least toy or trifle, I ask them, 'What must you have for it?' The shopkeeper answers—so much; suppose it were a shilling, what is the English but this—one shilling of lawful money of England? And I agree to give that shilling; but instead of it give them a counterfeit piece of lead or tin, washed over, to make it look like a shilling. Do I pay them what I bargained for? Do I give them one shilling of lawful money of England? Do I not put a cheat upon them, and act against justice and mutual agreement?

To say I took this for the lawful money of England, will not add at all, except it be to the fraud; for my being deceived does not at all make it be lawful money: so that, in a word, there can be nothing in that part but increasing the criminal part, and adding one knave more to the number of knaves which the nation was encumbered with before.

The case to me is very clear, namely, that neither by law, justice, nor conscience, can the tradesman put off his bad money after he has taken it, if he once knows it to be false and counterfeit money. That it is against the law is evident, because it is not good and lawful money of England; it cannot be honest, because you do not pay in the coin you agreed for, or perform the bargain you made, or pay in the coin expected of you; and it is not just, because you do not give a valuable consideration for the goods you buy, but really take a tradesman's goods away, and return dross and dirt to him in the room of it.

The medium I have to propose in the room of this, is, that every man who takes a counterfeit piece of money, and knows it to be such, should immediately destroy it—that is to say, destroy it as money, cut it in pieces; or, as I have seen some honest tradesmen do, nail it up against a post, so that it should go no farther. It is true, this is sinking so much upon himself, and supporting the credit of the current coin at his own expense, and he loses the whole piece, and this tradesmen are loth to do: but my answer is very clear, that thus they ought to do, and that sundry public reasons, and several public benefits, would follow to the public, in some of which he might have his share of benefit hereafter, and if he had not, yet he ought to do it.

First, by doing thus, he puts a stop to the fraud—that piece of money is no more made the instrument to deceive others, which otherwise it might do; and though it is true that the loss is only to the last man, that is to say, in the ordinary currency of the money, yet the breach upon conscience and principle is to every owner through whose hands that piece of money has fraudulently passed, that is to say, who have passed it away for good, knowing it to be counterfeit; so that it is a piece of good service to the public to take away the occasion and instrument of so much knavery and deceit.

Secondly, he prevents a worse fraud, which is, the buying and selling such counterfeit money. This was a very wicked, but open trade, in former days, and may in time come to be so again: fellows went about the streets, crying '*Brass money, broken or whole;*' that is to say, they would give good money for bad. It was at first pretended that they were obliged to cut it in pieces, and if you insisted upon it, they would cut it in pieces before your face; but they as often got it without that ceremony, and so made what wicked shifts they could to get it off again, and many times did put it off for current money, after they had bought it for a trifle.

Thirdly, by this fraud, perhaps, the same piece of money might, several years after, come into your hands again, after you had sold it for a trifle, and so you might lose by the same shilling two or three times over, and the like of other people; but if men were obliged to demolish all the counterfeit money they take, and let it go no farther, they they would be sure the fraud could go no farther, nor would the quantity be ever great at a time; for whatever quantity the false coiners should at any time make, it would gradually lessen and sink away, and not a mass of false and counterfeit coin appear together, as was formerly the case, and which lost the nation a vast sum of money to call in.

It has been the opinion of some, that a penalty should be inflicted upon those who offered any counterfeit money in payment; but besides that, there is already a statute against uttering false money, knowing it to be such. If any other or farther law should be made, either to enforce the statute, or to have new penalties added, they would still fall into the same difficulties as in the act.

1. That innocent men would suffer, seeing many tradesmen may take a piece of counterfeit money in tale with other money, and really and *bona fide* not know it, and so may offer it again as innocently as they at first took it ignorantly; and to bring such into trouble for every false shilling which they might offer to pay away without knowing it, would be to make the law be merely vexatious and tormenting to those against whom it was not intended, and at the same time not to meddle with the subtle crafty offender whom it was intended to punish, and who is really guilty.

2. Such an act would be difficultly executed, because it would still be difficult to know who did knowingly utter false money, and who did not; which is the difficulty, indeed, in the present law—so that, upon the whole, such a law would no way answer the end, nor effectually discover the offender, much less suppress the practice. But I am not upon projects and schemes—it is not the business of this undertaking.

But a general act, obliging all tradesmen to suppress counterfeit money, by refusing to put it off again, after they knew it to be counterfeit, and a general consent of tradesmen to do so; this would be the best way to put a stop to the practice, the morality of which is so justly called in question, and the ill consequences of which to trade are so very well known; nor will any thing but a universal consent of tradesmen, in the honest suppressing of counterfeit money, ever bring it to pass. In the meantime, as to the dishonesty of the practice, however popular it is grown at this time, I think it is out of question; it can have nothing but custom to plead for it, which is so far from an argument, that I think the plea is criminal in itself, and really adds to its being a grievance, and calls loudly for a speedy redress.

Another trading fraud, which, among many others of the like nature, I think worth speaking of, is the various arts made use of by tradesmen to set off their goods to the eye of the ignorant buyer.

I bring this in here, because I really think it is something of kin to putting off counterfeit money; every false gloss put upon our woollen manufactures, by hot-pressing, folding, dressing, tucking, packing, bleaching, &c, what are they but washing over a brass shilling to make it pass for sterling? Every false light, every artificial side-window, sky-light, and trunk-light we see made to show the fine Hollands, lawns, cambrics, &c. to advantage, and to deceive the buyer—what is it but a counterfeit coin to cheat the tradesman's customers?—an *ignis fatuus* to impose upon fools and ignorant people, and make their goods look finer than they are?

But where in trade is there any business entirely free from these frauds? and how shall we speak of them, when we see them so universally made use of? Either they are honest, or they are not. If they are not, why do we, I say, universally make use of them?—if they are honest, why so much art and so much application to manage them, and to make goods appear fairer and finer to the eye than they really are?—which, in its own nature, is evidently a design to cheat, and that in itself is criminal, and can be no other.

And yet there is much to be said for setting goods out to the best advantage too; for in some goods, if they are not well dressed, well pressed, and packed, the goods are not really shown in a true light; many of our woollen manufactures, if brought to market rough and undressed, like a piece of cloth not carried to the fulling or thicking mill, it does not show itself to a just advantage, nay, it does not show what it really is; and therefore such works as may be proper for so far setting it forth to the eye may be necessary. For example:

The cloths, stuffs, serges, druggets, &c, which are brought to market in the west and northern parts of England, and in Norfolk, as they are bought without the dressing and making up, it may be said of them that they are brought to market unfinished, and they are bought there again by the wholesale dealers, or cloth-workers, tuckers, and merchants, and they carry them to their warehouses and workhouses, and there they go through divers operations again, and are finished for the market; nor, indeed, are they fit to be shown till they are so; the stuffs are in the grease, the cloth is in the oil, they are rough and foul, and are not dressed, and consequently not finished; and as our buyers do not understand them till they are so dressed, it is no proper finishing the goods to bring them to market before—they are not, indeed, properly said to be made till that part is done.

Therefore I cannot call all those setting-out of goods to be knavish and false; but when the goods, like a false shilling, are to be set out with fraud and false colours, and made smooth and shining to delude the eye, there, where they are so, it is really a fraud; and though in some cases it extremely differs, yet that does not excuse the rest by any means.

The packers and hot-pressers, tuckers, and cloth-workers, are very necessary people in their trades, and their business is to set goods off to the best advantage; but it may be said, too, that their true and proper business is to make the goods show what really they are, and nothing else. It is true, as above, that in the original dress, as a piece of cloth or drugget, or stuff, comes out of the hand of the maker, it does not show itself as it really is, nor what it should and ought to show: thus far these people are properly called finishers of the manufactures, and their work is not lawful only, but it is a doing justice to the manufacture.

But if, by the exuberances of their art, they set the goods in a false light, give them a false gloss, a finer and smoother surface than really they have: this is like a painted jade, who puts on a false colour upon her tawny skin to deceive and delude her customers, and make her seem the beauty which she has no just claim to the name of.

So far as art is thus used to show these goods to be what they really are not, and deceive the buyer, so far it is a trading fraud, which is an unjustifiable practice in business, and which, like coining of counterfeit money, is making goods to pass for what they really are not; and is done for the advantage of the person who puts them off, and to the loss of the buyer, who is cheated and deceived by the fraud.

The making false lights, sky-lights, trunks, and other contrivances, to make goods look to be what they are not, and to deceive the eye of the buyer, these are all so many brass shillings washed over, in order to deceive the person who is to take them, and cheat him of his money; and so far these false lights are really criminal, they are cheats in trade, and made to deceive the world; to make deformity look like beauty, and to varnish over deficiencies; to make goods which are ordinary in themselves appear fine; to make things which are ill made look well; in a word, they are cheats in themselves, but being legitimated by custom, are become a general practice; the honestest tradesmen have them, and make use of them; the buyer knows of it, and suffers himself to be so imposed upon; and, in a word, if it be a cheat, as no doubt it is, they tell us that yet it is a universal cheat, and nobody trades without it; so custom and usage make it lawful, and there is little to be said but this, *Si populus vult decepi, decipiatur*—if the people will be cheated, let them be cheated, or they shall be cheated.

I come next to the setting out their goods to the buyer by the help of their tongue; and here I must confess our *shop rhetoric* is a strange kind of speech; it is to be understood in a manner by itself; it is to be taken, not in a latitude only, but in such a latitude as indeed requires as many flourishes to excuse it, as it contains flourishes in itself.

The end of it, indeed, is corrupt, and it is also made up of a corrupt composition; it is composed of a mass of rattling flattery to the buyer, and that filled with hypocrisy, compliment, self-praises, falsehood, and, in short, a complication of wickedness; it is a corrupt means to a vicious end: and I cannot see any thing in it but what a wise man laughs at, a good man abhors, and any man of honesty avoids as much as possible.

The shopkeeper ought, indeed, to have a good tongue, but he should not make a common prostitute of his tongue, and employ it to the wicked purpose of abusing and imposing upon all that come to deal with him. There is a modest liberty, which trading licence, like the poetic licence, allows to all the tradesmen of every kind: but tradesmen ought no more to lie behind the counter, than the parsons ought to talk treason in the pulpit.

Let them confine themselves to truth, and say what they will. But it cannot be done; a talking rattling mercer, or draper, or milliner, behind his counter, would be worth nothing if he should confine himself to that mean silly thing called *truth*—they must lie; it is in support of their business, and some think they cannot live without it; but I deny that part, and recommend it, I mean to the tradesmen I am speaking of, to consider what a scandal it is upon trade, to pretend to say that a tradesman cannot live without lying, the contrary to which may be made appear in almost every article.

On the other hand, I must do justice to the tradesmen, and must say, that much of it is owing to the buyers—they begin the work, and give the occasion. It was the saying of a very good shopman once upon this occasion, 'That their customers would not be pleased without lying; and why,' said he, 'did Solomon reprove the buyer?—he said nothing to the shopkeeper—"It is naught, it is naught," says the buyer; "but when he goes away, then he boasteth" (Prov. xx. 14.) The buyer telling us,' adds he, 'that every thing is worse than it is, forces us, in justifying its true value, to tell them it is better than it is.'

It must be confessed, this verbose way of trading is most ridiculous, as well as offensive, both in buyer and seller; and as it adds nothing to the goodness or value of the goods, so, I am sure, it adds nothing to the honesty or good morals of the tradesman, on one side or other, but multiplies trading-lies on every side, and brings a just reproach on the integrity of the dealer, whether he be the buyer or seller.

It was a kind of a step to the cure of this vice in trade, for such it is, that there was an old office erected in the city of London, for searching and viewing all the goods which were sold in bulk, and could not be searched into by the buyer—this was called *garbling*; and the garbler having viewed the goods, and caused all damaged or unsound goods to be taken out, set his seal upon the case or bags which held the rest, and then they were vouched to be marketable, so that when the merchant and the shopkeeper met to deal, there was no room for any words about the goodness of the wares; there was the garbler's seal to vouch that they were marketable and good, and if they were otherwise, the garbler was answerable.

This respected some particular sorts of goods only, and chiefly spices and drugs, and dye-stuffs, and the like. It were well if some other method than that of a rattling tongue could be found out, to ascertain the goodness and value of goods between the shopkeeper and the retail buyer, that such a flux of falsehoods and untruths might be avoided, as we see every day made use of to run up and run down every thing that is bought or sold, and that without any effect too; for, take it one time with another, all the shopkeeper's lying does not make the buyer like the goods at all the better, nor does the buyer's lying make the shopkeeper sell the cheaper.

It would be worth while to consider a little the language that passes between the tradesman and his customer over the counter, and put it into plain homespun English, as the meaning of it really imports. We would not take that usage if it were put into plain words—it would set all the shopkeepers and their customers together by the ears, and we should have fighting and quarrelling, instead of bowing and curtseying, in every shop. Let us hark a little, and hear how it would sound between them. A lady comes into a mercer's shop to buy some silks, or to the laceman's to buy silver laces, or the like; and when she pitches upon a piece which she likes, she begins thus:

Lady.—I like that colour and that figure well enough, but I don't like the silk—there is no substance in it.

Mer.—Indeed, Madam, your ladyship lies—it is a very substantial silk.

644

Lady.—No, no! you lie indeed, Sir; it is good for nothing; it will do no service.

Mer.—Pray, Madam, feel how heavy it is; you will find it is a lie; the very weight of it may satisfy you that you lie, indeed, Madam.

Lady.—Come, come, show me a better piece; I am sure you have better.

Mer.—Indeed, Madam, your ladyship lies; I may show you more pieces, but I cannot show you a better; there is not a better piece of silk of that sort in London, Madam.

Lady.—Let me see that piece of crimson there.

Mer.—Here it is, Madam.

Lady.—No, that won't do neither; it is not a good colour.

Mer.—Indeed, Madam, you lie; it is as fine a colour as can be dyed.

Lady.—Oh fy! you lie, indeed, Sir; why, it is not in grain.

Mer.—Your ladyship lies, upon my word, Madam; it is in grain, indeed, and as fine as can be dyed.

I might make this dialogue much longer, but here is enough to set the mercer and the lady both in a flame, and to set the shop in an uproar, if it were but spoken out in plain language, as above; and yet what is all the shop-dialect less or more than this? The meaning is plain—it is nothing but *you lie*, and *you lie*—downright Billingsgate, wrapped up in silk and satin, and delivered dressed finely up in better clothes than perhaps it might come dressed in between a carman and a porter.

How ridiculous is all the tongue-padding flutter between Miss Tawdry, the sempstress, and Tattle, my lady's woman, at the change-shop, when the latter comes to buy any trifle! and how many lies, indeed, creep into every part of trade, especially of retail trade, from the meanest to the uppermost part of business!—till, in short, it is grown so scandalous, that I much wonder the shopkeepers themselves do not leave it off, for the mere shame of its simplicity and uselessness.

But habits once got into use are very rarely abated, however ridiculous they are; and the age is come to such a degree of obstinate folly, that nothing is too ridiculous for them, if they please but to make a custom of it.

I am not for making my discourse a satire upon the shopkeepers, or upon their customers: if I were, I could give a long detail of the arts and tricks made use of behind the counter to wheedle and persuade the buyer, and manage the selling part among shopkeepers, and how easily and dexterously they draw in their customers; but this is rather work for a ballad and a song: my business is to tell the complete tradesman how to act a wiser part, to talk to his customers like a man of sense and business, and not like a mountebank and his merry-andrew; to let him see that there is a way of managing behind a counter, that, let the customer be what or how it will, man or woman, impertinent or not impertinent—for sometimes, I must say, the men customers are every jot as impertinent as the women; but, I say, let them be what they will, and how they will, let them make as many words as they will, and urge the shopkeeper how they will, he may behave himself so as to avoid all those impertinences, falsehoods, follish and wicked excursions which I complain of, if he pleases.

It by no means follows, that because the buyer is foolish, the seller must be so too; that because the buyer has a never-ceasing tongue, the seller must rattle as fast as she; that because she tells a hundred lies to run down his goods, he must tell another hundred to run them up; and that because she belies the goods one way, he must do the same the other way.

There is a happy medium in these things. The shopkeeper, far from being rude to his customers on one hand, or sullen and silent on the other, may speak handsomely and modestly, of his goods; what they deserve, and no other; may with truth, and good manners too, set forth his goods as they ought to be set forth; and neither be wanting to the commodity he sells, nor run out into a ridiculous extravagance of words, which have neither truth of fact nor honesty of design in them.

Nor is this middle way of management at all less likely to succeed, if the customers have any share of sense in them, or the goods he shows any merit to recommend them; and I must say, I believe this grave middle way of discoursing to a customer, is generally more effectual, and more to the purpose, and more to the reputation of the shopkeeper, than a storm of words, and a mouthful of common, shop-language, which makes a noise, but has little in it to plead, except to here and there a fool that can no otherwise be prevailed with.

It would be a terrible satire upon the ladies, to say that they will not be pleased or engaged either with good wares or good pennyworths, with reasonable good language, or good manners, but they must have the addition of long harangues, simple, fawning, and flattering language, and a flux of false and foolish words, to set off the goods, and wheedle them in to lay out their money; and that without these they are not to be pleased.

But let the tradesman try the honest part, and stand by that, keeping a stock of fashionable and valuable goods in his shop to show, and I dare say he will run no venture, nor need he fear customers; if any thing calls for the help of noise, and rattling words, it must be mean and sorry, unfashionable, and ordinary goods, together with weak and silly buyers; and let the buyers that chance to read this remember, that whenever they find the shopkeeper begins his noise, and makes his fine speeches, they ought to suppose he (the shopkeeper) has trash to bring out, and believes he has fools to show it to.

CHAPTER XIX
OF FINE SHOPS, AND FINE SHOWS

It is a modern custom, and wholly unknown to our ancestors, who yet understood trade, in proportion to the trade they carried on, as well as we do, to have tradesmen lay out two-thirds of their fortune in fitting up their shops.

By fitting up, I do not mean furnishing their shops with wares and goods to sell—for in that they came up to us in every particular, and perhaps went beyond us too—but in painting and gilding, fine shelves, shutters, boxes, glass-doors, sashes, and the like, in which, they tell us now, it is a small matter to lay out two or three hundred pounds, nay, five hundred pounds, to fit up a pastry-cook's, or a toy-shop.

The first inference to be drawn from this must necessarily be, that this age must have more fools than the last: for certainly fools only are most taken with shows and outsides.

It is true, that a fine show of goods will bring customers; and it is not a new custom, but a very old one, that a new shop, very well furnished, goes a great way to bringing a trade; for the proverb was, and still is, very true, that every body has a penny for a new shop; but that a fine show of shelves and glass-windows should bring customers, that was never made a rule in trade till now.

And yet, even now, I should not except so much against it, if it were not carried on to such an excess, as is too much for a middling tradesman to bear the expense of. In this, therefore, it is made not a grievance only, but really scandalous to trade; for now, a young beginner has such a tax upon him before he begins, that he must sink perhaps a third part, nay, a half part, of his stock, in painting and gilding, wainscoting and glazing, before he begins to trade, nay, before he can open his shop. As they say of building a watermill, two-thirds of the expense lies under the water; and when the poor tradesman comes to furnish his shop, and lay in his stock of goods, he finds a great hole made in his cash to the workmen, and his show of goods, on which the life of his trade depends, is fain to be lessened to make up his show of boards, and glass to lay them in.

Nor is this heavy article to be abated upon any account; for if he does not make a good show, he comes abroad like a mean ordinary fellow, and nobody of fashion comes to his shop; the customers are drawn away by the pictures and painted shelves, though, when they come there, they are not half so well filled as in other places, with goods fit for a trade; and how, indeed, should it be otherwise? the joiners and painters, glaziers and carvers, must have all ready money; the weavers and merchants may give credit; their goods are of so much less moment to the shopkeeper, that they must trust; but the more important show must be finished first, and paid first; and when that has made a deep hole in the tradesman's stock, then the remainder may be spared to furnish the shop with goods, and the merchant must trust for the rest.

It will hardly be believed in ages to come, when our posterity shall be grown wiser by our loss, and, as I may truly say, at our expense, that a pastry-cook's shop, which twenty pounds would effectually furnish at a time, with all needful things for sale, nay, except on an extraordinary show, as on twelfth-day at night for cakes, or upon some great feast, twenty pounds can hardly be laid out at one time in goods for sale, yet that fitting up one of these shops should cost upwards of £300 in the year 1710—let the year be recorded—the fitting up to consist of the following particulars:—

1. Sash windows, all of looking-glass plates, 12 inches by 16 inches in measure.

2. All the walls of the shop lined up with galley-tiles, and the back shop with galley-tiles in panels, finely painted in forest-work and figures.

3. Two large pier looking-glasses and one chimney glass in the shop, and one very large pier-glass seven feet high in the back shop.

4. Two large branches of candlesticks, one in the shop, and one in the back room.

5. Three great glass lanterns in the shop, and eight small ones.

6. Twenty-five sconces against the wall, with a large pair of silver standing candlesticks in the back room, value £25.

7. Six fine large silver salvers to serve sweetmeats.

8. Twelve large high stands of rings, whereof three silver, to place small dishes for tarts, jellies, &c., at a feast.

9. Painting the ceiling, and gilding the lanterns, the sashes, and the carved work, £55.

These, with some odd things to set forth the shop, and make a show, besides small plate, and besides china basins and cups, amounted to, as I am well informed, above £300.

Add to this the more necessary part, which was:—

1. Building two ovens, about £25.

2. Twenty pounds in stock for pies, cheese-cakes, &c.

So that, in short, here was a trade which might be carried on for about £30 or £40 stock, required £300 expenses to fit up the shop, and make a show to invite customers.

I might give something of a like example of extravagance in fitting up a cutler's shop, *Anglicé* a toyman, which are now come up to such a ridiculous expense, as is hardly to be thought of without the utmost contempt: let any one stop at the Temple, or at Paul's corner, or in many other places.

As to the shops of the more considerable trades, they all bear a proportion of the humour of the times, but do not call for so loud a remark. Leaving, therefore, the just reflection which such things call for, let me bring it home to the young tradesman, to whom I am directing this discourse, and to whom I am desirous to give solid and useful hints for his instruction, I would recommend it to him to avoid all such needless expenses, and rather endeavour to furnish his shop with goods, than to paint and gild it over, to make it fine and gay; let it invite customers rather by the well-filled presses and shelves, and the great choice of rich and fashionable goods, that one customer being well-served may bring another; and let him study to bring his shop into reputation for good choice of wares, and good attendance on his customers; and this shall bring a throng to him much better, and of much better people, than those that go in merely for a gay shop.

Let the shop be decent and handsome, spacious as the place will allow, and let something like the face of a master be always to be seen in it; and, if possible, be always busy, and doing something in it, that may look like being employed: this takes as much with the wiser observers of such things, as any other appearance can do.

I have heard of a young apothecary, who setting up in a part of the town, where he had not much acquaintance, and fearing much whether he should get into business, hired a man acquainted with such business, and made him be every morning between five and six, and often late in the evenings, working very hard at the great mortar; pounding and beating, though he had nothing to do with it, but beating some very needless thing, that all his neighbours might hear it, and find that he was in full employ, being at work early and late, and that consequently he must be a man of vast business, and have a great practice: and the thing was well laid, and took accordingly; for the neighbours, believing he had business, brought business to him; and the reputation of having a trade, made a trade for him.

The observation is just: a show may bring some people to a shop, but it is the fame of business that brings business; and nothing raises the fame of a shop like its being a shop of good trade already; then people go to it, because they think other people go to it, and because they think there is good choice of goods; their gilding and painting may go a little way, but it is the having a shop well filled with goods,[31] having good choice to sell, and selling reasonable—these are the things that bring a trade, and a trade thus brought will stand by you and last; for fame of trade brings trade anywhere.

It is a sign of the barrenness of the people's fancy, when they are so easily taken with shows and outsides of things. Never was such painting and gilding, such sashings and looking-glasses among the shopkeepers, as there is now; and yet trade flourished more in former times by a gread deal that it does now, if we may believe the report of very honest and understanding men. The reason, I think, cannot be to the credit of the present age, nor it it to the discredit of the former; for they carried on their trade with less gaiety, and with less expense, than we do now.[32]

---

[31] In another place, the author recommends a light stock, as showing a nimble trade. There can be little doubt that he is more reasonable here. A considerable abundance of goods is certainly an attraction to a shop. No doubt, a tradesman with little capital would only be incurring certain ruin having a larger stock than he could readily pay for. He must needs keep a small stock, if he would have a chance at all of doing well in the world. But this does not make it the less an advantage to a tradesman of good capital to keep an abundant and various stock of goods.

[32] It is really curious to find in this chapter the same contrast drawn between the *old* and the *new* style of fitting up shops, and carrying on business, as would be drawn at the present day by nine out of every ten common observers. The notion that the shops of the past age were plain, while those of the present are gaudy, and that the tradesmen of a past age carried on all their business in a quiet way and with little expense, is as strongly impressed on the minds of the present generation, as it is here seen to have been on those of Defoe's contemporaries, a hundred and twenty years ago, although it is quite impossible that the notion can be just in both cases. The truth probably is, that in Defoe's time, and at all former times, there were conspicuous, but not very numerous, examples of finely decorated shops, which seemed, and really were, very much of a novelty, as well as a rather striking exception from the style in which such places in general were then, and had for many years been furnished. So far, however, from these proving, as Defoe anticipates, a warning to future generations, the general appearance of shops has experienced a vast

My advice to a young tradesman is to keep the safe middle between these extremes; something the times must be humoured in, because fashion and custom must be followed; but let him consider the depth of his stock, and not lay out half his estate upon fitting up his shop, and then leave but the other half to furnish it; it is much better to have a full shop, than a fine shop; and a hundred pounds in goods will make a much better show than a hundred pounds' worth of painting and carved work; it is good to make a show, but not to be *all show.*

It is true, that painting and adorning a shop seems to intimate, that the tradesman has a large stock to begin with, or else they suggest he would not make such a show; hence the young shopkeepers are willing to make a great show, and beautify, and paint, and gild, and carve, because they would be thought to have a great stock to begin with; but let me tell you, the reputation of having a great stock is ill purchased, when half your stock is laid out to make the world believe it; that is, in short, reducing yourself to a small stock to have the world believe you have a great one; in which you do no less than barter the real stock for the imaginary, and give away your stock to keep the name of it only.

I take this indeed to be a French humour, or a spice of it turned English; and, indeed, we are famous for this, that when we do mimic the French, we generally do it to our hurt, and over-do the French themselves.

The French nation are eminent for making a fine outside, when perhaps within they want necessaries; and, indeed, a gay shop and a mean stock is something like the Frenchman with his laced ruffles, without a shirt. I cannot but think a well-furnished shop with a moderate outside is much better to a tradesman, than a fine shop and few goods; I am sure it will be much more to his satisfaction, when he casts up his year's account, for his fine shop will weigh but sorrily in his account of profit and loss; it is all a dead article; it is sunk out of his

---

improvement since those days; and the third-rate class are now probably as fine as the first-rate were at no distant period. At the same time, as in the reign of the first George, we have now also a few shops fitted up in a style of extraordinary and startling elegance, and thus forming that contrast with the general appearance of shops for the last forty years, which makes old people, and many others, talk of all the past as homely and moderate, and all the present as showy and expensive.

first money, before he makes a shilling profit, and may be some years a-recovering, as trade may go with him.

It is true that all these notions of mine in trade are founded upon the principle of frugality and good husbandry; and this is a principle so disagreeable to the times, and so contrary to the general practice, that we shall find very few people to whom it is agreeable. But let me tell my young tradesmen, that if they must banish frugality and good husbandry, they must at the same time banish all expectation of growing rich by their trade. It is a maxim in commerce, that money gets money, and they that will not frugally lay up their gain, in order to increase their gain, must not expect to gain as they might otherwise do; frugality may be out of fashion among the gentry, but if it comes to be so among tradesmen, we shall soon see that wealthy tradesmen will be hard to find; for they who will not save as well as gain, must expect to go out of trade as lean as they began.

Some people tell us indeed in many cases, especially in trade, that putting a good face upon things goes as far as the real merit of the things themselves; and that a fine, painted, gilded shop, among the rest, has a great influence upon the people, draws customers, and brings trade; and they run a great length in this discourse by satirising on the blindness and folly of mankind, and how the world are to be taken in their own way; and seeing they are to be deluded and imposed upon in such an innocent way, they ought to be so far deluded and imposed upon, alluding to the old proverbial saying, '*Si populus vult decipi, decipiatur;*' that it is no fraud, no crime, and can neither be against conscience, nor prudence; for if they are pleased with a show, why should they not have it? and the like.

This way of talking is indeed plausible; and were the fact true, there might be more in it than I think there is. But I do not grant that the world is thus to be deluded; and that the people do follow this rule in general—I mean, go always to a fine shop to lay out their money. Perhaps, in some cases, it may be so, where the women, and the weakest of the sex too, are chiefly concerned; or where the fops and fools of the age resort; and as to those few, they that are willing to be so imposed upon, let them have it.

But I do not see, that even this extends any farther than to a few toy-shops, and pastry-cooks; and the customers of both these are not of credit sufficient, I think, to weigh in this case: we may as well argue for the fine habits at a puppet-show and a rope-dancing, because they draw the mob about them; but I cannot think, after you go but one degree above these, the thing is of any weight, much less does it bring credit to the tradesman, whatever it may do to the shop.

The credit of a tradesman respects two sorts of people, first, the merchants, or wholesale men, or makers, who sell him his goods, or the customers, who come to his shop to buy.

The first of these are so far from valuing him upon the gay appearance of his shop, that they are often the first that take an offence at it, and suspect his credit upon that account: their opinion upon a tradesman, and his credit with them, is raised quite another way, namely, by his current pay, diligent attendance, and honest figure; the gay shop does not help him at all there, but rather the contrary.

As to the latter, though some customers may at first be drawn by the gay appearance and fine gilding and painting of a shop, yet it is the well sorting a shop with goods, and the selling good pennyworths, that will bring trade, especially after the shop has been open some time: this, and this only, establishes the man and the credit of the shop.

To conclude: the credit raised by the fine show of things is also of a different kind from the substantial reputation of a tradesman; it is rather the credit of the shop, than of the man; and, in a word, it is no more or less than a net spread to catch fools; it is a bait to allure and deceive, and the tradesman generally intends it so. He intends that the customers shall pay for the gilding and painting his shop, and it is the use he really makes of it, namely, that his shop looking like something eminent, he may sell dearer than his neighbours: who, and what kind of fools can so be drawn in, it is easy to describe, but satire is none of our business here.

On the contrary, the customers, who are the substantial dependence of a tradesman's shop, are such as are gained and preserved by good usage, good pennyworths, good wares, and good choice; and a shop that has the reputation of these four, like good wine that needs no bush, needs no painting and gilding, no carved works and ornaments;[33] it requires only a diligent master and a faithful servant, and it will never want a trade.

---

[33] The author seems here to carry his objections to decoration to an extreme. Good usage, good pennyworths, good wares, and good choice, are doubtless the four cardinal points of business; but a handsome shop also goes a considerable way in attracting customers, and is a principle which no prudent tradesman will despise.

CHAPTER XX
OF THE TRADESMAN'S KEEPING HIS BOOKS, AND CASTING UP HIS SHOP

It was an ancient and laudable custom with tradesmen in England always to balance their accounts of stock, and of profit and loss, at least once every year; and generally it was done at Christmas, or New-year's tide, when they could always tell whether they went backward or forward, and how their affairs stood in the world; and though this good custom is very much lost among tradesmen at this time, yet there are a great many that do so still, and they generally call it *casting up shop.* To speak the truth, the great occasion of omitting it has been from the many tradesmen, who do not care to look into things, and who, fearing their affairs are not right, care not to know how they go at all, good or bad; and when I see a tradesman that does not cast up once a-year, I conclude that tradesman to be in very bad circumstances, that at least he fears he is so, and by consequence cares not to inquire.

As casting up the shop is the way to know every year whether he goes backward or forward, and is the tradesman's particular satisfaction, so he must cast up his books too, or else it will be very ominous to the tradesman's credit.

Now, in order to doing this effectually once a-year, it is needful the tradesman should keep his books always in order; his day-book duly posted, his cash duly balanced, and all people's accounts always fit for a view. He that delights in his trade will delight in his books; and, as I said that he that will thrive must diligently attend his shop or warehouse, and take up his delight there, so, I say now, he must also diligently keep his books, or else he will never know whether he thrives or no.

Exact keeping his books is one essential part of a tradesman's prosperity. The books are the register of his estate, the index of his stock. All the tradesman has in the world must be found in these three articles, or some of them:—

Goods in the shop; Money in cash; Debts abroad.

The shop will at any time show the first of these upon a small stop to cast it up; the cash-chest and bill-box will show the second at demand; and the ledger when posted will show the last; so that a tradesman can at any time, at a week's notice, cast up all these three; and then, examining his accounts, to take the balance, which is a real trying what he is worth in the world.

It cannot be satisfactory to any tradesman to let his books go unsettled, and uncast up, for then he knows nothing of himself, or of his circumstances in the world; the books can tell him at any time what his condition is, and will satisfy him what is the condition of his debts abroad.

In order to his regular keeping his books, several things might be said very useful for the tradesman to consider:

I. Every thing done in the whole circumference of his trade must be set down in a book, except the retail trade; and this is clear, if the goods are not in bulk, then the money is in cash, and so the substance will be always found either there, or somewhere else; for if it is neither in the shop, nor in the cash, nor in the books, it must be stolen and lost.

II. As every thing done must be set down in the books, so it should be done at the very time of it; all goods sold must be entered in the books before they are sent out of the house; goods sent away and not entered, are goods lost; and he that does not keep an exact account of what goes out and comes in, can never swear to his books, or prove his debts, if occasion calls for it.

I am not going to set down rules here for book-keeping, or to teach the tradesman how to do it, but I am showing the necessity and usefulness of doing it at all. That tradesman who keeps no books, may depend upon it he will ere long keep no trade, unless he resolves also to give no credit. He that gives no trust, and takes no trust, either by wholesale or by retail, and keeps his cash all himself, may indeed go on without keeping any books at all; and has nothing to do, when he would know his estate, but to cast up his shop and his cash, and see how much they amount to, and that is his whole and neat estate; for as he owes nothing, so nobody is in debt to him, and all his estate is in his shop; but I suppose the tradesman that trades wholly thus, is not yet born, or if there ever were any such, they are all dead.

A tradesman's books, like a Christian's conscience, should always be kept clean and clear; and he that is not careful of both will give but a sad account of himself either to God or man. It is true, that a great many tradesmen, and especially shopkeepers, understand but little of book-keeping; but it is as true that they all understand something of it, or else they will make but poor work of shopkeeping.

I knew a tradesman that could not write, and yet he supplied the defect with so many ingenious knacks of his own, to secure the account of what people owed him, and was so exact doing it, and then took such care to have but very short accounts with any body, that he brought up his method to be every way an equivalent to writing; and, as I often told him, with half the study and application that those things cost him, he might have learned to write, and keep books too. He made notches upon sticks for all the middling sums, and scored with chalk for lesser things. He had drawers for every particular customer's name, which his memory supplied, for he knew every particular drawer, though he had a great many, as well as if their faces had been painted upon them; he had innumerable figures to signify what he would have written, if he could; and his shelves and boxes always put me in mind of the Egyptian hieroglyphics, and nobody understood them, or any thing of them, but himself.

It was an odd thing to see him, when a country-chap, came up to settle accounts with him; he would go to a drawer directly, among such a number as was amazing: in that drawer was nothing but little pieces of split sticks, like laths, with chalk-marks on them, all as unintelligible as the signs of the zodiac are to an old school-mistress that teaches the horn-book and primer, or as Arabic or Greek is to a ploughman. Every stick had notches on one side for single pounds, on the other side for tens of pounds, and so higher; and the length and breadth also had its signification, and the colour too; for they were painted in some places with one colour, and in some places with anther; by which he knew what goods had been delivered for the money: and his way of casting up was very remarkable, for he knew nothing of figures; but he kept six spoons in a place on purpose, near his counter, which he took out when he had occasion to cast up any sum, and, laying the spoons in a row before him, he counted upon them thus:

One, two, three, and another, one odd spoon, and t'other

By this he told up to six; if he had any occasion to tell any farther, he began again, as we do after the number ten in our ordinary numeration; and by this method, and running them up very quick, he would count any number under thirty-six, which was six spoons of six spoons, and then, by the strength of his head, he could number as many more as he pleased, multiplying them always by sixes, but never higher.

I give this instance to show how far the application of a man's head might go to supply the defect, but principally to show (and it does abundantly show it) what an absolute necessity there is for a tradesman to be very diligent and exact in keeping his books, and what pains those who understand their business will always take to do it.

This tradesman was indeed a country shopkeeper; but he was so considerable a dealer, that he became mayor of the city which he lived in (for it was a city, and that a considerable city too), and his posterity have been very considerable traders in the same city ever since, and they show their great-grandfather's six counting spoons and his hieroglyphics to this day.

After some time, the old tradesman bred up two of his sons to his business, and the young men having learned to write, brought books into the counting-house, things their father had never used before; but the old man kept to his old method for all that, and would cast up a sum, and make up an account with his spoons and his drawers, as soon as they could with their pen and ink, if it were not too full of small articles, and that he had always avoided in his business.

However, as I have said above, this evidently shows the necessity of book-keeping to a tradesman, and the very nature of the thing evidences also that it must be done with the greatest exactness. He that does not keep his books exactly, and so as that he may depend upon them for charging his debtors, had better keep no books at all, but, like my shopkeeper, score and notch every thing; for as books well kept make business regular, easy, and certain, so books neglected turn all into confusion, and leave the tradesman in a wood, which he can never get out of without damage and loss. If ever his dealers know that his books are ill kept, they play upon him, and impose horrid forgeries and falsities upon him: whatever he omits they catch at, and leave it out; whatever they put upon him, he is bound to yield to; so that, in short, as books well kept are the security of the tradesman's estate, and the ascertaining of his debts, so books ill kept will assist every knavish customer or chapman to cheat and deceive him.

Some men keep a due and exact entry or journal of all they sell, or perhaps of all they buy or sell, but are utterly remiss in posting it forward to a ledger; that is to say, to another book, where every parcel is carried to the debtor's particular account. Likewise they keep another book, where they enter all the money they receive, but, as above, never keeping any account for the man; there it stands in the cash-book, and both these books must be ransacked over for the particulars, as well of goods sold, as of the money received, when this customer comes to have his account made up; and as the goods are certainly entered when sold or sent away, and the money is certainly entered when it is received, this they think is sufficient, and all the rest superfluous.

I doubt not such tradesmen often suffer as much by their slothfulness and neglect of book-keeping, as might, especially if their business is considerable, pay for a book-keeper; for what is such a man's case, when his customer, suppose a country dealer, comes to town, which perhaps he does once a-year (as in the custom of other tradesmen), and desires to have his account made up? The London tradesman goes to his books, and first he rummages his day-book back for the whole year, and takes out the foot[34] of all the parcels sent to his chapman, and they make the debtor side of the account; then he takes his cash-book, if it deserves that name, and there he takes out all the sums of money which the chapman has sent up, or bills which he has received, and these make the creditor side of the account; and so the balance is drawn out, and this man thinks himself a mighty good accountant, that he keeps his books exactly; and so perhaps he does, as far as he keeps them at all; that is to say, he never sends a parcel away to his customer, but he enters it down, and never receives a bill from him, but he sets it down when the money is paid; but now take this man and his chap, together, as they are making up this account. The chapman, a sharp clever tradesman, though a countryman, has his pocket-book with him, and in it a copy of his posting-book, so the countrymen call a ledger, where the London tradesman's accounts are copied out; and when the city tradesman has drawn out his account, he takes it to his inn and examines it by his little book, and what is the consequence?

If the city tradesman has omitted any of the bills which the country tradesman has sent him up, he finds it out, and is sure to put him in mind of it. 'Sir,' says he, 'you had a bill from me upon Mr A.G. at such a time, for thirty pounds, and I have your letter that you received the money; but you have omitted it in the account, so that I am not so much in your debt by thirty pounds, as you thought I was.'

'Say you so!' says the city tradesman; 'I cannot think but you must be mistaken.'

'No, no!' says the other, 'I am sure I can't be mistaken, for I have it in my book; besides, I can go to Mr A.G., whom the bill was drawn upon, and there is, to be sure, your own endorsement upon it, and a receipt for the money.'

'Well,' says the citizen, 'I keep my books as exact as any body—I'll look again, and if it be there I shall find it, for I am sure if I had it, it is in my cash-book.'

---

[34] The sum at the bottom, or *foot*, of the account.

'Pray do, then,' says the countryman, 'for I am sure I sent it you, and I am sure I can produce the bill, if there be occasion.'

Away goes the tradesman to his books, which he pretends he keeps so exact, and examining them over again, he finds the bill for thirty pounds entered fairly, but in his running the whole year over together, as well he might, he had overlooked it, whereas, if his cash-book had been duly posted every week, as it ought to have been, this bill had been regularly placed to account.

But now, observe the difference: the bill for thirty pounds being omitted, was no damage to the country tradesman, because he has an account of it in his book of memorandums, and had it regularly posted in his books at home, whatever the other had, and also was able to bring sufficient proof of the payment; so the London tradesman's omission was no hurt to him.

But the case differs materially in the debtor side of the account; for here the tradesman, who with all his boasts of keeping his books exactly, has yet no ledger, which being, as I have said, duly posted, should show every man's account at one view; and being done every week, left it scarce possible to omit any parcel that was once entered in the day-book or journal—I say, the tradesman keeping no ledger, he looks over his day-book for the whole year past, to draw up the debtor side of his customer's account, and there being a great many parcels, truly he overlooks one or two of them, or suppose but one of them, and gives the chapman the account, in which he sums up his debtor side so much, suppose £136, 10s.: the chapman examining this by his book, as he did the cash, finds two parcels, one £7, 15s., and the other £9, 13s., omitted; so that by his own book his debtor side was £153, 18s.; but being a cunning sharp tradesman, and withal not exceeding honest, 'Well, well,' says he to himself, 'if Mr G. says it is no more than £136, 10s. what have I to do to contradict him? it is none of my business to keep his books for him; it is time enough for me to reckon for it when he charges me.' So he goes back to him the next day, and settles accounts with him, pays him the balance in good bills which he brought up with him for that purpose, takes a receipt in full of all accounts and demands to such a day of the month, and the next day comes and looks out another parcel of goods, and so begins an account for the next year, like a current chapman, and has the credit of an extraordinary customer that pays well, and clears his accounts every year; which he had not done had he not seen the advantage, and so strained himself to pay, that he might get a receipt in full of all accounts.

It happens some years after that this city tradesman dies, and his executors finding his accounts difficult to make up, there being no books to be found but a day-book and a cash-book, they get some skilful book-keeper to look into them, who immediately sees that the only way to bring the accounts to a head, is to form a ledger out of the other two, and post every body's account into it from the beginning; for though it were a long way back, there is no other remedy.

In doing this, they come to this mistake, among a great many others of the like kind in other chapmen's accounts; upon this they write to the chapman, and tell him they find him debtor to the estate of the deceased in such a sum of money, and desire him to make payment.

The country shopkeeper huffs them, tells them he always made up accounts with Mr. G., the deceased, once a-year, as he did with all his other chapmen, and that he took his receipt in full of all accounts and demands, upon paying the balance to him at such a time; which receipt he has to show; and that he owes him nothing, or but such a sum, being the account of goods bought since.

The executors finding the mistake, and how it happened, endeavour to convince him of it; but it is all one—he wants no convincing, for he knows at bottom how it is; but being a little of a knave himself, or if you please, not a little, he tells them he cannot enter into the accounts so far back—Mr G. always told him he kept his books very exactly, and he trusted to him; and as he has his receipt in full, and it is so long ago, he can say nothing to it.

From hence they come to quarrel, and the executors threaten him with going to law; but he bids them defiance, and insists upon his receipt in full; and besides that, it is perhaps six years ago, and so he tells them he will plead the statute of limitations upon them; and then adds, that he does not do it avoid a just debt, but to avoid being imposed upon, he not understanding books so well as Mr G. pretended to do; and having balanced accounts so long ago with him, he stands by the balance, and has nothing to say to their mistakes, not he. So that, in short, not finding any remedy, they are forced to sit down by the loss; and perhaps in the course of twenty years' trade, Mr G. might lose a great many such parcels in the whole; and had much better have kept a ledger; or if he did not know how to keep a ledger himself, had better have hired a book-keeper to have come once a-week, or once a-month, to have posted his day-book for him.

The like misfortune attends the not balancing his cash, a thing which such book-keepers as Mr G. do not think worth their trouble;

nor do they understand the benefit of it. The particulars, indeed, of this article are tedious, and would be too long for a chapter; but certainly they that know any thing of the use of keeping an exact cash-book, know that, without it, a tradesman can never be thoroughly satisfied either of his own not committing mistakes, or of any people cheating him, I mean servants, or sons, or whoever is the first about him.

What I call balancing his cash-book, is, first, the casting up daily, or weekly, or monthly, his receipts and payments, and then seeing what money is left in hand, or, as the usual expression of the tradesman is, what money is in cash; secondly, the examining his money, telling it over, and seeing how much he has in his chest or bags, and then seeing if it agrees with the balance of his book, that what is, and what should be, correspond.

And here let me give tradesmen a caution or two.

I. Never sit down satisfied with an error in the cash; that is to say, with a difference between the money really in the cash, and the balance in the book; for if they do not agree, there must be a mistake somewhere, and while there is a mistake in the cash, the tradesman cannot, at least he ought not to be, easy. He that can be easy with a mistake in his cash, may be easy with a gang of thieves in his house; for if his money does not come right, he must have paid something that is not set down, and that is to be supposed as bad as if it were lost; or he must have somebody about him that can find the way to his money besides himself, that is to say, somebody that should not come to it; and if so, what is the difference between that and having a gang of thieves about him?—for every one that takes money out of his cash without his leave, and without letting him know it, is so far a thief to him: and he can never pretend to balance his cash, nor, indeed, know any thing of his affairs, that does not know which way his money goes.

2. A tradesman endeavouring to balance his cash, should no more be satisfied if he finds a mistake in his cash one way, than another— that is to say, if he finds more in cash than by the balance of his cash-book ought to be there, than if he finds less, or wanting in cash. I know many, who, when they find it thus, sit down satisfied, and say, 'Well, there is an error, and I don't know where it lies; but come, it is an error on the right hand; I have more cash in hand than I should have, that is all, so I am well enough; let it go; I shall find it some time or other.' But the tradesman ought to consider that he is quite in the dark; and as he does not really know where it lies, so, for ought he knows, the error may really be to his loss very considerably—and the case is very plain,

that it is as dangerous to be over, as it would be to be under; he should, therefore, never give it over till he has found it out, and brought it to rights. For example:

If there appears to be more money in the cash than there is by the balance in the cash-book, this must follow—namely, that some parcel of money must have been received, which is not entered in the book; now, till the tradesman knows what sum of money this is, that is thus not entered, how can he tell but the mistake may be quite the other way, and the cash be really wrong to his loss? Thus,

My cash-book being cast up for the last month, I find, by the foot of the leaf, there is cash remaining in hand to balance £176, 10s. 6d.

To see if all things are right, I go and tell my money over, and there, to my surprise, I find £194, 10s. 6d. in cash, so that I have £18 there more than I should have. Now, far from being pleased that I have more money by me than I should have, my inquiry is plain, 'How comes this to pass?'

Perhaps I puzzle my head a great while about it, but not being able to find out, I sit down easy and satisfied, and say, 'Well, I don't much concern myself about it; it is better to be so than £18 missing; I cannot tell where it lies, but let it lie where it will, here is the money to make up the mistake when it appears.'

But how foolish is this! how ill-grounded the satisfaction! and how weak am I to argue thus, and please myself with the delusion! For some months after, it appears, perhaps, that whereas there was £38 entered, received of Mr B.K., the figure 3 was mistaken, and set down for a figure of 5, for the sum received was £58; so that, instead of having £18 more in cash than there ought to be, I have 40s. wanting in my cash, which my son or my apprentice stole from me when they put in the money, and made the mistake of the figures to puzzle the book, that it might be some time before it should be discovered.

Upon the whole, take it as a rule, the tradesman ought to be as unsatisfied when he finds a mistake to his gain in his cash, as when he finds it to his loss; and it is every whit as dangerous, nay, it is the more suspicious, because it seems to be laid as a bait for him to stop his mouth, and to prevent further inquiries; and it is on that account that I leave this caution upon record, that the tradesman may be duly alarmed.

The keeping a cash-book is one of the nicest parts of a tradesman's business, because there is always the bag and the book to be brought together, and if they do not exactly speak the same language, even to a farthing, there must be some omission; and how big or how little that omission may be, who knows, or how shall it be known, but by casting and recasting up, telling, and telling over and over again, the money?

If there is but twenty shillings over in the money, the question is, 'How came it there?' It must be received somewhere, and of somebody, more than is entered; and how can the cash-keeper, be he master or servant, know but more was received with it, which is not, and should have been, entered, and so the loss may be the other way? It is true, in telling money there may have been a mistake, and he that received a sum of money may have received twenty shillings too much, or five pounds too much—and such a mistake I have known to be made in the paying and receiving of money—and a man's cash has been more perplexed, and his mind more distracted about it, than the five pounds have been worth, because he could not find it out, till some accident has discovered it;[35] and the reason is, because not knowing which way it could come there, he could not know but some omission might be made to his loss another way, as in the case above mentioned.

I knew, indeed, a strong waterman, who drove a very considerable trade, but, being an illiterate tradesman, never balanced his cash-book for many years, nor scarce posted his other books, and, indeed, hardly understood how to do it; but knowing his trade was exceedingly profitable, and keeping his money all himself, he was easy, and grew rich apace, in spite of the most unjustifiable, and, indeed, the most intolerable, negligence; but lest this should be pleaded as an exception to my general rule, and to invalidate the argument, give me leave to add, that, though this man grew rich in spite of indolence, and a neglect of his book, yet, when he died, two things appeared, which no tradesman in his wits would desire should be said of him.

---

[35] This reminds the editor of an amusing anecdote he has heard, illustrative of the diseased accuracy, as it may be called, of a certain existing London merchant. On reckoning up his household book one year, he found that he had expended one penny more than was accounted for, and there was accordingly an error to that extent in his reckoning. The very idea of an error, however trifling the amount, gave him great uneasiness, and he set himself with the greatest anxiety to discover, if possible, the occasion. He employed the by-hours of weeks in the vain attempt; but at length, having one day to cross Waterloo Bridge, where there is a pontage of a penny for foot passengers, he all at once, to his inconceivable joy, recollected having there disbursed the coin in question about a twelvemonth before.

I. The servants falling out, and maliciously accusing one another, had, as it appeared by the affidavits of several of them, wronged him of several considerable sums of money, which they received, and never brought into the books; and others, of sums which they brought into the books, but never brought into the cash; and others, of sums which they took ready money in the shop, and never set down, either the goods in the day-book, or the money into the cash-book; and it was thought, though he was so rich as not to feel it, that is, not to his hurt, yet that he lost three or four hundred pounds a-year in that manner, for the two or three last years of his life; but his widow and son, who came after him, having the discovery made to them, took better measures afterwards.

II. He never did, or could know, what he was worth, for the accounts in his books were never made up; nor when he came to die, could his executors make up any man's account, so as to be able to prove the particulars, and make a just demand of their debt, but found a prodigious number of small sums of money paid by the debtors, as by receipts in their books and on their files, some by himself, and some by his man, which were never brought to account, or brought into cash; and his man's answer being still, that he gave all to the master, they could not tell how to charge him by the master's account, because several sums, which the master himself received, were omitted being entered in the same manner, so that all was confusion and neglect; and though the man died rich, it was in spite of that management that would have made any but himself have died poor.

Exact book-keeping is to me the effect of a man whose heart is in his business, and who intends to thrive. He that cares not whether his books are kept well or no, is in my opinion one that does not much care whether he thrives or no; or else, being in desperate circumstances, knows it, and that he cannot, or does not thrive, and so matters not which way it goes.

It is true, the neglect of the books is private and secret, and is seldom known to any body but the tradesman himself, at least till he comes to break, and be a bankrupt, and then you frequently hear them exclaim against him, upon that very account. 'Break!' says one of the assignees; 'how should he but break?—why, he kept no books; you never saw books kept in such a scandalous manner in your life; why, he has not posted his cash-book, for I know not how many months; nor posted his day-book and journal at all, except here and there an account that he perhaps wanted to know the balance of; and as for balancing his cash, I don't see any thing of that done, I know not how long. Why, this fellow could never tell how he went on, or how things stood with him: I wonder he did not break a long time ago.'

Now, the man's case was this: he knew how to keep his books well enough, perhaps, and could write well enough; and if you look into his five or six first years of trade, you find all his accounts well kept, the journal duly posted, the cash monthly balanced; but the poor man found after that, that things went wrong, that he went backwards, and that all went down-hill, and he hated to look into his books. As a profligate never looks into his conscience, because he can see nothing there but what terrifies and affrights him, makes him uneasy and melancholy, so a sinking tradesman cares not to look into his books, because the prospect there is dark and melancholy. 'What signify the accounts to me?' says he; 'I can see nothing in the books but debts that I cannot pay, and debtors that will never pay; I can see nothing there but how I have trusted my estate away like a fool, and how I am to be ruined for my easiness, and being a sot:' and this makes him throw them away, and hardly post things enough to make up when folks call to pay; or if he does post such accounts as he has money to receive from, that's all, and the rest lie at random, till, as I say, the assignees come to reproach him with his negligence.

Whereas, in truth, the man understood his books well enough, but had no heart to look in them, no courage to balance them, because of the afflicting prospect of them.

But let me here advise tradesmen to keep a perfect acquaintance with their books, though things are bad and discouraging; it keeps them in full knowledge of what they are doing, and how they really stand; and it brings them sometimes to the just reflections on their circumstances which they ought to make; so to stop in time, as I hinted before, and not let things run too far before they are surprised and torn to pieces by violence.

And, at the worst, even a declining tradesman should not let his books be neglected; if his creditors find them punctually kept to the last, it will be a credit to him, and they would see he was a man fit for business; and I have known when that very thing has recommended a tradesman so much to his creditors, that after the ruin of his fortunes, some or other of them have taken him into business, as into partnership, or into employment, only because they knew him to be qualified for business, and for keeping books in particular.

But if we should admonish the tradesman to an exact and regular care of his books, even in his declining fortunes, much more should it be his care in his beginning, and before any disaster has befallen him. I doubt not, that many a tradesman has miscarried by the mistakes and neglect of his books; for the losses that men suffer on that account are not easily set down; but I recommend it to a tradesman to take exact care of his books, as I would to every man to take care of his diet and temperate living, in order to their health; for though, according to some, we cannot, by all our care and caution, lengthen out life, but that every one must and shall live their appointed time,[36] yet, by temperance and regular conduct, we may make that life more comfortable, more agreeable, and pleasant, by its being more healthy and hearty; so, though the exactest book-keeping cannot be said to make a tradesman thrive, or that he shall stand the longer in his business, because his profit and loss do not depend upon his books, or the goodness of his debts depend upon the debtor's accounts being well posted, yet this must be said, that the well keeping of his books may be the occasion of his trade being carried on with the more ease and pleasure, and the more satisfaction, by having numberless quarrels, and contentions, and law-suits, which are the plagues of a tradesman's life, prevented and avoided; which, on the contrary, often torment a tradesman, and make his whole business be uneasy to him for want of being able to make a regular proof of things by his books.

A tradesman without his books, in case of a law-suit for a debt, is like a married woman without her certificate. How many times has a woman been cast, and her cause not only lost, but her reputation and character exposed, for want of being able to prove her marriage, though she has been really and honestly married, and has merited a good

---

[36] The correct doctrine is, we *may* not, by our utmost care and diligence, avoid the causes of an early and premature death; but he who acts according to the rules which promote health, and avoids all things which tend to endanger it, has a much better chance of living to the natural period appointed for human life than he who acts otherwise—besides, as stated in the text, making his life more agreeable. The author's illustration would be more properly drawn if we were to say, 'The tradesman, by keeping exact accounts, may not succeed in contending against certain unfavourable circumstances, no more than the man who lives according to the just rules of nature may thereby succeed in eviting other evils that tend to cut short life; but as the temperate man is most likely to be healthy, so is the tradesman, who keeps exact accounts, most likely to thrive in business.'

character all her days? And so in trade, many a debt has been lost, many an account been perplexed by the debtor, many a sum of money been recovered, and actually paid over again, especially after the tradesman has been dead, for want of hits keeping his books carefully and exactly when he was alive; by which negligence, if he has not been ruined when he was living, his widow and children have been ruined after his decease; though, had justice been done, he had left them in good circumstances, and with sufficient to support them.

And this brings me to another principal reason why a tradesman should not only keep books, but be very regular and exact in keeping them in order, that is to say, duly posted, and all his affairs exactly and duly entered in his books; and this is, that if he should be surprised by sudden or unexpected sickness, or death, as many are, and as all may be, his accounts may not be left intricate and unsettled, and his affairs thereby be perplexed.

Next to being prepared for death, with respect to Heaven and his soul, a tradesman should be always in a state of preparation for death, with respect to his books; it is in vain that he calls for a scrivener or lawyer, and makes a will, when he finds a sudden summons sent him for the grave, and calls his friends about him to divide and settle his estate; if his business is in confusion below stairs, his books out of order, and his accounts unsettled, to what purpose does he give his estate among his relations, when nobody knows where to find it?

As, then, the minister exhorts us to take care of our souls, and make our peace with Heaven, while we are in a state of health, and while life has no threatening enemies about it, no diseases, no fevers attending; so let me second that advice to the tradesman always to keep his books in such a posture, that if he should be snatched away by death, his distressed widow and fatherless family may know what is left for them, and may know where to look for it. He may depend upon it, that what he owes to any one they will come fast enough for, and his widow and executrix will be pulled to pieces for it, if she cannot and does not speedily pay it. Why, then, should he not put her in a condition to have justice done her and her children, and to know how and of whom to seek for his just debts, that she may be able to pay others, and secure the remainder for herself and her children? I must confess, a tradesman not to leave his books in order when he dies, argues him to be either.

1. A very bad Christian, who had few or no thoughts of death upon him, or that considered nothing of its frequent coming unexpected and sudden without warning; or,

2. A very unnatural relation, without the affections of a father, or a husband, or even of a friend, that should rather leave what he had to be swallowed up by strangers, than leave his family and friends in a condition to find, and to recover it.

Again, it is the same case as in matters religious, with respect to the doing this in time, and while health and strength remain. For, as we say very well, and with great reason, that the work of eternity should not be left to the last moments; that a death-bed is no place, and a sick languishing body no condition, and the last breath no time, for repentance; so I may add, neither are these the place, the condition, nor the time, to make up our accounts. There is no posting the books on a death-bed, or balancing the cash-book in a high fever. Can the tradesman tell you where his effects lie, and to whom he has lent or trusted sums of money, or large quantities of goods, when he is delirious and light-headed? All these things must be done in time, and the tradesman should take care that his books should always do this for him, and then he has nothing to do but make his will, and dispose of what he has; and for the rest he refers them to his books, to know where every thing is to be had.

CHAPTER XXI
OF THE TRADESMAN LETTING HIS WIFE BE ACQUAINTED WITH HIS BUSINESS

It must be acknowledged, that as this chapter seems to be written in favour of the women, it also seems to be an officious, thankless benefaction to the wives; for that, as the tradesman's ladies now manage, they are above the favour, and put no value upon it. On the contrary, the women, generally speaking, trouble not their heads about it, scorn to be seen in the counting house, much less behind the counter; despise the knowledge of their husbands' business, and act as if they were ashamed of being tradesmen's wives, and never intended to be tradesmen's widows.

If this chosen ignorance of theirs comes some time or other to be their loss, and they find the disadvantage of it too late, they may read their fault in their punishment, and wish too late they had acted the humbler part, and not thought it below them to inform themselves of what it is so much their interest to know. This pride is, indeed, the great misfortune of tradesmen's wives; for, as they lived as if they were above being owned for the tradesman's wife, so, when he dies, they live to be the shame of the tradesman's widow. They knew nothing how he got his estate when he was alive, and they know nothing where to find it when he is dead. This drives them into the hands of lawyers, attorneys, and solicitors, to get in their effects; who, when they have got it, often run away with it, and leave the poor widow in a more disconsolate and perplexed condition than she was in before.

It is true, indeed, that this is the women's fault in one respect, and too often it is so in many, since the common spirit is, as I observed, so much above the tradesman's condition; but since it is not so with every body, let me state the case a little for the use of those who still have ther senses about them; and whose pride is not got so much above their reason, as to let them choose to be tradesman's beggars, rather than tradesmen's widows.

When the tradesman dies, it is to be expected that what estate or effects he leaves, is, generally speaking, dispersed about in many hands; his widow, if she is left executrix, has the trouble of getting things together as well as she can; if she is not left executrix, she has not the trouble indeed, but then it is looked upon that she is dishonoured in not having the trust; when she comes to look into her affairs, she is more or less perplexed and embarrassed, as she has not or has acquainted herself, or been made acquainted, with her husband's affairs in his lifetime.

If she has been one of those gay delicate ladies, that valuing herself upon her being a gentlewoman, and that thought it a step below herself, when she married this mechanic thing called a tradesman, and consequently scorned to come near his shop, or warehouse, and by consequence acquainting herself with any of his affairs,[37] or so much as where his effects lay, which are to be her fortune for the future—I say, if this has been her case, her folly calls for pity now, as her pride did for contempt before; for as she was foolish in the first, she may be miserable in the last part of it; for now she falls into a sea of trouble, she has the satisfaction of knowing that her husband has died, as the tradesmen call it, well to pass, and that she is left well enough; but she has at the same time the mortification of knowing nothing how to get it in, or in what hands it lies. The only relief she has is her husband's books, and she is happy in that, but just in proportion to the care he took in keeping them; even when she finds the names of debtors, she knows not who they are, or where they dwell, who are good, and who are bad; the only remedy she has here, if her husband had ever a servant, or apprentice, who was so near out of his time as to be acquainted with the customers, and with the books, then she is forced to be beholden to him to settle the accounts for her, and endeavour to get in the debts; in return for which she is forced to give him his time and freedom, and let him into the trade, make him master of all the business in the world, and it may be at last, with all her pride, has to take him for a husband; and when her friends upbraid her with it, that she should marry her apprentice boy, when it may be she was old enough to be his mother, her answer is, 'Why, what could I do? I see I must have been ruined else; I had nothing but what lay abroad in debts, scattered about the world,

---

[37] Most of the wives of tradesmen above a certain rather humble condition would now smile at the idea of their being expected to attend their husbands' shops, in order to form an intimate acquaintance with their affairs. Doubtless, however, in the days of Defoe, when the capitals of tradesmen were less, when provision for widows by insurance upon lives was not practised, and when the comparative simplicity of the modes of conducting business admitted it, a female in that situation would only be exercising a prudent caution, and doing nothing in the least inconsistent with the delicacy of her sex, in obeying the rules laid down in the text.

and nobody but he knew how to get them in. What could I do? If I had not done it, I must have been a beggar.' And so, it may be, *she is* at last too, if the boy of a husband proves a brute to her, as many do, and as in such unequal matches indeed most such people do. Thus, that pride which once set her above a kind, diligent, tender husband, and made her scorn to stoop to acquaint herself with his affairs, by which, had she done it, she had been tolerably qualified to get in her debts, dispose of her shop-goods, and bring her estate together—the same pride sinks her into the necessity of cringing to a scoundrel, and taking her servant to be her master.

This I mention for the caution of those ladies who stoop to marry men of business, and yet despise the business they are maintained by; that marry the tradesman, but scorn the trade. If madam thinks fit to stoop to the man, she ought never to think herself above owning his employment; and as she may upon occasion of his death be left to value herself upon it, and to have at least her fortune and her children's to gather up out of it, she ought not to profess herself so unacquainted with it as not to be able to look into it when necessity obliges her.

It is a terrible disaster to any woman to be so far above her own circumstances, that she should not qualify herself to make the best of things that are left her, or to preserve herself from being cheated, and being imposed upon. In former times, tradesmen's widows valued themselves upon the shop and trade, or the warehouse and trade, that were left them; and at least, if they did not carry on the trade in their own names, they would keep it up till they put it off to advantage; and often I have known a widow get from £300 to £500 for the good-will, as it is called, of the shop and trade, if she did not think fit to carry on the trade; if she did, the case turned the other way, namely, that if the widow did not put off the shop, the shop would put off the widow; and I may venture to say, that where there is one widow that keeps on the trade now, after a husband's decease, there were ten, if not twenty, that did it then.

But now the ladies are above it, and disdain it so much, that they choose rather to go without the prospect of a second marriage, in virtue of the trade, than to stoop to the mechanic low step of carrying on a trade; and they have their reward, for they do go without it; and whereas they might in former times match infinitely to their advantage by that method, now they throw themselves away, and the trade too.[38]

But this is not the case which I particularly aim at in this chapter. If the women will act weakly and foolishly, and throw away the advantages that he puts into their hands, be that to them, and it is their business to take care of that; but I would have them have the opportunity put into their hands, and that they may make the best of it if they please; if they will not, the fault is their own. But to this end, I say, I would have every tradesman make his wife so much acquainted with his trade, and so much mistress of the managing part of it, that she might be able to carry it on if she pleased, in case of his death; if she does not please, that is another case; or if she will not acquaint herself with it, that also is another case, and she must let it alone; but he should put it into her power, or give her the offer of it.

First, he should do it for her own sake, namely, as before, that she may make her advantage of it, either for disposing herself and the shop together, as is said above, or for the more readily disposing the goods, and getting in the debts, without dishonouring herself, as I have observed, and marrying her 'prentice boy, in order to take care of the effects—that is to say, ruining herself to prevent her being ruined.

Secondly, he should do it for his children's sake, if he has any, that if the wife have any knowledge of the business, and has a son to breed up to it, though he be not yet of age to take it up, she may keep the trade for him, and introduce him into it, that so he may take the trouble off her hands, and she may have the satisfaction of preserving the father's trade for the benefit of his son, though left too young to enter upon it at first.

Thus I have known many a widow that would have thought it otherwise below her, has engaged herself in her husbands's business, and

---

[38] The number of widows, or at least females, carrying on trade in England, is still very considerable. In Scotland, it is a comparatively rare case. A native of the northern part of the island is apt to be strongly impressed with this fact, when, in the large manufacturing towns of England, he sees female names in so many cases inscribed upon the waggons used in the transport of goods. The complaint in the text, that females have, to such an extent, ceased to carry on the business of their deceased husbands, is probably, like many other complaints of the same kind already pointed out, merely a piece of querulousness on the part of our author, or the result of a very common mental deception.

carried it on, purely to bring her eldest son up to it, and has preserved it for him, and which has been an estate to him, whereas otherwise it must have been lost, and he would have had the world to seek for a new business.

This is a thing which every honest affectionate mother would, or at least should, be so willing to do for a son, that she, I think, who would not, ought not to marry a tradesman at all; but if she would think herself above so important a trust for her own children, she should likewise think herself above having children by a tradesman, and marry somebody whose children she would act the mother for.

But every widow is not so unnatural, and I am willing to suppose the tradesman I am writing to shall be better married, and, therefore, I give over speaking to the woman's side, and I will suppose the tradesman's wife not to be above her quality, and willing to be made acquainted with her husband's affairs, as well as to be helpful to him, if she can, as to be in a condition to be helpful to herself and her family, if she comes to have occasion. But, then, the difficulty often lies on the other side the question, and the tradesman cares not to lay open his business to, or acquaint his wife with it; and many circumstances of the tradesman draw him into this snare; for I must call it a snare both to him and to her.

I. The tradesman is foolishly vain of making his wife a gentlewoman, and, forsooth, he will have her sit above in the parlour, and receive visits, and drink tea, and entertain her neighbours, or take a coach and go abroad; but as to the business, she shall not stoop to touch it; he has apprentices and journeymen, and there is no need of it.

II. Some trades, indeed, are not proper for the women to meddle in, or custom has made it so, that it would be ridiculous for the women to appear in their shops; that is, such as linen and woollen drapers, mercers, booksellers, goldsmiths, and all sorts of dealers by commission, and the like—custom, I say, has made these trades so effectually shut out the women, that, what with custom, and the women's generally thinking it below them, we never, or rarely, see any women in those shops or warehouses.

III. Or if the trade is proper, and the wife willing, the husband declines it, and shuts her out—and this is the thing I complain of as an unjustice upon the woman. But our tradesmen, forsooth, think it an undervaluing to them and to their business to have their wives seen in their shops—that is to say, that, because other trades do not admit them, therefore they will not have their trades or shops thought less

674

masculine or less considerable than others, and they will not have their wives be seen in their shops.

IV. But there are two sorts of husbands more who decline acquainting their wives with their business; and those are, (I.) Those who are unkind, haughty, and imperious, who will not trust their wives, because they will not make them useful, that they may not value themselves upon it, and make themselves, as it were, equal to their husbands. A weak, foolish, and absurd suggestion! as if the wife were at all exalted by it, which, indeed, is just the contrary, for the woman is rather humbled and made a servant by it: or, (2.) The other sort are those who are afraid their wives should be let into the grand secret of all—namely, to know that they are bankrupt, and undone, and worth nothing.

All these considerations are foolish or fraudulent, and in every one of them the husband is in the wrong—nay, they all argue very strongly for the wife's being, in a due degree, let into the knowledge of their business; but the last, indeed, especially that she may be put into a posture to save him from ruin, if it be possible, or to carry on some business without him, if he is forced to fail, and fly; as many have been, when the creditors have encouraged the wife to carry on a trade for the support of her family and children, when he perhaps may never show his head again.

But let the man's case be what it will, I think he can never call it a hard shift to let his wife into an acquaintance with his business, if she desires it, and is fit for it; and especially in case of mortality, that she may not be left helpless and friendless with her children when her husband is gone, and when, perhaps, her circumstances may require it.

I am not for a man setting his wife at the head of his business, and placing himself under her like a journeyman, like a certain china-seller, not far from the East India House, who, if any customers came into the shop that made a mean, sorry figure, would leave them to her husband to manage and attend them; but if they looked like quality, and people of fashion, would come up to her husband, when he was showing them his goods, putting him by with a 'Hold your tongue, Tom, and let me talk.' I say, it is not this kind, or part, that I would have the tradesman's wife let into, but such, and so much, of the trade only as may be proper for her, not ridiculous, in the eye of the world, and may make her assisting and helpful, not governing to him, and, which is the main thing I am at, such as should qualify her to keep up the business for herself and children, if her husband should be taken away, and she be left destitute in the world, as many are.

Thus much, I think, it is hard a wife should not know, and no honest tradesman ought to refuse it; and above all, it is a great pity the wives of tradesmen, who so often are reduced to great inconvenience for want of it, should so far withstand their own felicity, as to refuse to be thus made acquainted with their business, by which weak and foolish pride they expose themselves, as I have observed, to the misfortune of throwing the business away, when they may come to want it, and when the keeping it up might be the restoring of their family, and providing for their children.

For, not to compliment tradesmen too much, their wives are not all ladies, nor are their children all born to be gentlemen. Trade, on the contrary, is subject to contingencies; some begin poor, and end rich; others, and those very many, begin rich, and end poor: and there are innumerable circumstances which may attend a tradesman's family, which may make it absolutely necessary to preserve the trade for his children, if possible; the doing which may keep them from misery, and raise them all in the world, and the want of it, on the other hand, sinks and suppresses them. For example:—

A tradesman has begun the world about six or seven years; he has, by his industry and good understanding in business, just got into a flourishing trade, by which he clears five or six hundred pounds a-year; and if it should please God to spare his life for twenty years or more, he would certainly be a rich man, and get a good estate; but on a sudden, and in the middle of all his prosperity, he is snatched away by a sudden fit of sickness, and his widow is left in a desolate despairing condition, having five children, and big with another; but the eldest of these is not above six years old, and, though he is a boy, yet he is utterly incapable to be concerned in the business; so the trade which (had his father lived to bring him up in his shop or warehouse) would have been an estate to him, is like to be lost, and perhaps go all away to the eldest apprentice, who, however, wants two years of his time. Now, what is to be done for this unhappy family?

'Done!' says the widow; 'why, I will never let the trade fall so, that should be the making of my son, and in the meantime be the maintenance of all my children.'

'Why, what can you do, child?' says her father, or other friends; 'you know nothing of it. Mr —— did not acquaint you with his business.'

'That is true,' says the widow; 'he did not, because I was a fool, and did not care to look much into it, and that was my fault. Mr —— did not press me to it, because he was afraid I might think he intended to put me upon it; but he often used to say, that if he should drop off before his boys were fit to come into the shop, it would be a sad loss to them—that the trade would make gentlemen of a couple of them, and it would be great pity it should go away from them.'

'But what does that signify now, child?' adds the father; 'you see it is so; and how can it be helped?'

'Why,' says the widow, 'I used to ask him if he thought I could carry it on for them, if such a thing should happen?'

'And what answer did he make?' says the father.

'He shook his head,' replied the widow, 'and answered, "Yes, I might, if I had good servants, and if I would look a little into it beforehand."'

'Why,' says the father, 'he talked as if he had foreseen his end.'

'I think he did foresee it,' says she, 'for he was often talking thus.'

'And why did you not take the hint then,' says her father, 'and acquaint yourself a little with things, that you might have been prepared for such an unhappy circumstance, whatever might happen?'

'Why, so I did,' says the widow, 'and have done for above two years past; he used to show me his letters, and his books, and I know where he bought every thing; and I know a little of goods too, when they are good, and when bad, and the prices; also I know all the country-people he dealt with, and have seen most of them, and talked with them. Mr—— used to bring them up to dinner sometimes, and he would prompt my being acquainted with them, and would sometimes talk of his business with them at table, on purpose that I might hear it; and I know a little how to sell, too, for I have stood by him sometimes, and seen the customers and him chaffer with one another.'

'And did your husband like that you did so?' says the father.

'Yes,' says she, 'he loved to see me do it, and often told me he did so; and told me, that if he were dead, he believed I might carry on the trade as well as he.'

'But he did not believe so, I doubt,' says the father.

'I do not know as to that, but I sold goods several times to some customers, when he has been out of the way.'

'And was he pleased with it when he came home? Did you do it to his mind?'

'Nay, I have served a customer sometimes when he has been in the warehouse, and he would go away to his counting-house on purpose, and say, "I'll leave you and my wife to make the bargain," and I have pleased the customer and him too.'

'Well,' says the father, 'do you think you could carry on the trade?'

'I believe I could, if I had but an honest fellow of a journeyman for a year or two to write in the books, and go abroad among customers.'

'Well, you have two apprentices; one of them begins to understand things very much, and seems to be a diligent lad.'

'He comes forward, indeed, and will be very useful, if he does not grow too forward, upon a supposition that I shall want him too much: but it will be necessary to have a man to be above him for a while.'

'Well,' says the father, 'we will see to get you such a one.'

In short, they got her a man to assist to keep the books, go to Exchange, and do the business abroad, and the widow carried on the business with great application and success, till her eldest son grew up, and was first taken into the shop as an apprentice to his mother; the eldest apprentice served her faithfully, and was her journeyman four years after his time was out; then she took him in partner to one-fourth of the trade, and when her son came of age, she gave the apprentice one of her daughters, and enlarged his share to a third, gave her own son another third, and kept a third for herself to support the family.

Thus the whole trade was preserved, and the son and son-in-law grew rich in it, and the widow, who grew as skilful in the business as her husband was before her, advanced the fortunes of all the rest of her children very considerably.

This was an example of the husband's making the wife (but a little) acquainted with his business; and if this had not been the case, the trade had been lost, and the family left just to divide what the father left; which, as they were seven of them, mother and all, would not have been considerable enough to have raised them above just the degree of having bread to eat, and none to spare.

I hardly need give any examples where tradesmen die, leaving nourishing businesses, and good trades, but leaving their wives ignorant and destitute, neither understanding their business, nor knowing how to learn, having been too proud to stoop to it when they had husbands, and not courage or heart to do it when they have none. The town is so full of such as these, that this book can scarce fall into the hands of any readers but who will be able to name them among their own acquaintance.

These indolent, lofty ladies have generally the mortification to see their husbands' trades catched up by apprentices or journeymen in the shop, or by other shopkeepers in the neighbourhood, and of the same business, that might have enriched them, and descended to their children; to see their bread carried away by strangers, and other families flourishing on the spoils of their fortunes.

And this brings me to speak of those ladies, who, though they do, perhaps, for want of better offers, stoop to wed a trade, as we call it, and take up with a mechanic; yet all the while they are the tradesmen's wives, they endeavour to preserve the distinction of their fancied character; carry themselves as if they thought they were still above their station, and that, though they were unhappily yoked with a tradesman, they would still keep up the dignity of their birth, and be called gentlewomen; and in order to this, would behave like such all the way, whatever rank they were levelled with by the misfortune of their circumstances.

This is a very unhappy, and, indeed, a most unseasonable kind of pride; and if I might presume to add a word here by way of caution to such ladies, it should be to consider, before they marry tradesmen, the great disadvantages they lay themselves under, in submitting to be a tradesman's wife, but not putting themselves in a condition to take the benefit, as well as the inconvenience of it; for while they are above the circumstances of the tradesman's wife, they are deprived of all the remedy against the miseries of a tradesman's widow; and if the man dies, and leaves them little or nothing but the trade to carry on and maintain them, they, being unacquainted with that, are undone.

A lady that stoops to marry a tradesman, should consider the usage of England among the gentry and persons of distinction, where the case is thus: if a lady, who has a title of honour, suppose it be a countess, or if she were a duchess, it is all one—if, I say, she stoop to marry a private gentleman, she ceases to rank for the future as a countess, or duchess, but must be content to be, for the time to come, what her husband can entitle her to, and no other; and, excepting the courtesy of the people calling her my Lady Duchess, or the Countess, she is no more than plain Mrs such a one, meaning the name of her husband, and no other.

Thus, if a baronet's widow marry a tradesman in London, she is no more my lady, but plain Mrs——, the draper's wife, &c. The application of the thing is thus: if the lady think fit to marry a mechanic, say a glover, or a cutler, or whatever it is, she should remember she is a glover's wife from that time, and no more; and to keep up her dignity, when fortune has levelled her circumstances, is but a piece of unseasonable pageantry, and will do her no service at all. The thing she is to inquire is, what she must do if Mr——, the glover, or cutler, should die? whether she can carry on the trade afterwards, or whether she can live without it? If she find she cannot live without it, it is her prudence to consider in time, and so to acquaint herself with the trade, that she may be able to do it when she comes to it.

I do confess, there is nothing more ridiculous than the double pride of the ladies of this age, with respect to marrying what they call below their birth. Some ladies of good families, though but of mean fortune, are so stiff upon the point of honour, that they refuse to marry tradesmen, nay, even merchants, though vastly above them in wealth and fortune, only because they are tradesmen, or, as they are pleased to call them, though improperly, mechanics; and though perhaps they have not above £500 or £1000 to their portion, scorn the man for his rank, who does but turn round, and has his choice of wives, perhaps, with two, or three, or four thousand pounds, before their faces.

The gentlemen of quality, we see, act upon quite another foot, and, I may say, with much more judgment, seeing nothing is more frequent than when any noble family are loaded with titles and honour rather than fortune, they come down into the city, and choose wives among the merchants' and tradesmen's daughters to raise their families; and I am mistaken, if at this time we have not several duchesses, countesses, and ladies of rank, who are the daughters of citizens and tradesmen, as the Duchess of Bedford, of A——e, of Wharton, and others; the Countess of Exeter, of Onslow, and many more, too many to name, where it is thought no dishonour at all for those persons to have matched into rich families, though not ennobled; and we have seen many trading families lay the foundation of nobility by their wealth and opulence—as Mr Child, for example, afterwards Sir Josiah Child, whose posterity by his two daughters are now Dukes of Beaufort and of Bedford, and his grandson Lord Viscount Castlemain, and yet he himself began a tradesman, and in circumstances very mean.

But this stiffness of the ladies, in refusing to marry tradesmen, though it is weak in itself, is not near so weak as the folly of those who first do stoop to marry thus, and yet think to maintain the dignity of their birth in spite of the meanness of their fortune, and so, carrying themselves above that station in which Providence has placed them, disable themselves from receiving the benefit which their condition offers them, upon any subsequent changes of their life.

This extraordinary stiffness, I have known, has brought many a well-bred gentlewoman to misery and the utmost distress, whereas, had they been able to have stooped to the subsequent circumstances of life, which Providence also thought fit to make their lot, they might have lived comfortably and plentifully all their days.

It is certainly every lady's prudence to bring her spirit down to her condition; and if she thinks fit, or it is any how her lot to marry a tradesman, which many ladies of good families have found it for their advantage to do—I say, if it be her lot, she should take care she does not make that a curse to her, which would be her blessing, by despising her own condition, and putting herself into a posture not to enjoy it.

In all this, I am to be understood to mean that unhappy temper, which I find so much among the tradesman's wives at this time, of being above taking any notice of their husband's affairs, as if nothing were before them but a constant settled state of prosperity, and it were impossible for them to taste any other fortune; whereas, that very hour they embark with a tradesman, they ought to remember that they are entering a state of life full of accidents and hazards, and that innumerable families, in as good circumstances as theirs, fall every day into disasters and misfortunes, and that a tradesman's condition is liable to more casualties than any other life whatever.

How many widows of tradesmen, nay, and wives of broken and ruined tradesmen, do we daily see recover themselves and their shattered families, when the man has been either snatched away by death, or demolished by misfortunes, and has been forced to fly to the East or West Indies, and forsake his family in search of bread?

Women, when once they give themselves leave to stoop to their own circumstances, and think fit to rouse up themselves to their own relief, are not so helpless and shiftless creatures as some would make them appear in the world; and we see whole families in trade frequently recovered by their industry: but, then, they are such women as can stoop to it, and can lay aside the particular pride of their first years; and who, without looking back to what they have been, can be content to look into what Providence has brought them to be, and what they must infallibly be, if they do not vigorously apply to the affairs which offer, and fall into the business which their husbands leave them the introduction to, and do not level their minds to their condition. It may, indeed, be hard to do this at first, but necessity is a spur to industry, and will make things easy where they seem difficult; and this necessity will humble the minds of those whom nothing else could make to stoop; and where it does not, it is a defect of the understanding, as well as of prudence, and must reflect upon the senses as well as the morals of the person.

CHAPTER XXII
OF THE DIGNITY OF TRADE IN ENGLAND MORE THAN IN OTHER COUNTRIES

It is said of England, by way of distinction, and we all value ourselves upon it, that it is a trading country; and King Charles II., who was perhaps that prince of all the kings that ever reigned in England, that best understood the country and the people that he governed, used to say, 'That the tradesmen were the only gentry in England.' His majesty spoke it merrily, but it had a happy signification in it, such as was peculiar to the bright genius of that prince, who, though he was not the best governor, was the best acquainted with the world of all the princes of his age, if not of all the men in it; and, though it be a digression, give me leave, after having quoted the king, to add three short observations of my own, in favour of England, and of the people and trade of it, and yet without the least partiality to our own country.

I. We are not only a trading country, but the greatest trading country in the world.

II. Our climate is the most agreeable climate in the world to live in.

III. Our Englishmen are the stoutest and best men (I mean what we call men of their hands) in the world.

These are great things to advance in our own favour, and yet to pretend not to be partial too; and, therefore, I shall give my reasons, which I think support my opinion, and they shall be as short as the heads themselves, that I may not go too much off from my subject.

I. We are the greatest trading country in the world, because we have the greatest exportation of the growth and product of our land, and of the manufacture and labour of our people; and the greatest importation and consumption of the growth, product, and manufactures of other countries from abroad, of any nation in the world.[39]

---

[39] We have here a pleasing trait of the superior sagacity of Defoe, in as far as it was a prevalent notion down to his time, and even later (nor is it, perhaps, altogether extinguished yet), that the prosperity of a country was marked by its excess of exports over imports. Defoe justly ranks the amount of importation on a level with that of exportation, as indicative of the well-being of the country.

2. Our climate is the best and most agreeable, because a man can be more out of doors in England than in other countries. This was King Charles II.'s reason for it, and I cannot name it, without doing justice to his majesty in it.

3. Our men are the stoutest and best, because, strip them naked from the waist upwards, and give them no weapons at all but their hands and heels, and turn them into a room, or stage, and lock them in with the like number of other men of any nation, man for man, and they shall beat the best men you shall find in the world.

From this digression, which I hope will not be disagreeable, as it is not very tedious, I come back to my first observation, that England is a trading country, and two things I offer from that head.

First, our tradesmen are not, as in other countries, the meanest of our people.

Secondly, some of the greatest and best, and most flourishing families, among not the gentry only, but even the nobility, have been raised from trade, owe their beginning, their wealth, and their estates, to trade; and, I may add,

Thirdly, those families are not at all ashamed of their original, and, indeed, have no occasion to be ashamed of it.

It is true, that in England we have a numerous and an illustrious nobility and gentry; and it is true, also, that not so many of those families have raised themselves by the sword as in other nations, though we have not been without men of fame in the field too.

But trade and learning have been the two chief steps by which our gentlemen have raised their relations, and have built their fortunes; and from which they have ascended up to the prodigious height, both in wealth and number, which we see them now risen to.

As so many of our noble and wealthy families are raised by, and derive from trade, so it is true, and, indeed, it cannot well be otherwise, that many of the younger branches of our gentry, and even of the nobility itself, have descended again into the spring from whence they flowed, and have become tradesmen; and thence it is, that, as I said above, our tradesmen in England are not, as it generally is in other countries, always of the meanest of our people.

Indeed, I might have added here, that trade itself in England is not, as it generally is in other countries, the meanest thing the men can turn their hand to; but, on the contrary, trade is the readiest way for men to raise their fortunes and families; and, therefore, it is a field for men of figure and of good families to enter upon.

N.B. By trade we must be understood to include navigation, and foreign discoveries, because they are, generally speaking, all promoted and carried on by trade, and even by tradesmen, as well as merchants; and the tradesmen are at this time as much concerned in shipping (as owners) as the merchants; only the latter may be said to be the chief employers of the shipping.

Having thus done a particular piece of justice to ourselves, in the value we put upon trade and tradesmen in England, it reflects very much upon the understanding of those refined heads, who pretend to depreciate that part of the nation, which is so infinitely superior in number and in wealth to the families who call themselves gentry, or quality, and so infinitely more numerous.

As to the wealth of the nation, that undoubtedly lies chiefly among the trading part of the people; and though there are a great many families raised within few years, in the late war, by great employments, and by great actions abroad, to the honour of the English gentry; yet how many more families among the tradesmen have been raised to immense estates, even during the same time, by the attending circumstances of the war, such as the clothing, the paying, the victualling and furnishing, &c, both army and navy! And by whom have the prodigious taxes been paid, the loans supplied, and money advanced upon all occasions? By whom are the banks and companies carried on?—and on whom are the customs and excises levied? Have not the trade and tradesmen born the burden of the war?—and do they not still pay four millions a-year interest for the public debts? On whom are the funds levied, and by whom the public credit supported? Is not trade the inexhausted fund of all funds, and upon which all the rest depend?

As is the trade, so in proportion are the tradesmen; and how wealthy are tradesmen in almost all the several parts of England, as well as in London! How ordinary is it to see a tradesman go off the stage, even but from mere shopkeeping, with from ten to forty thousand pounds' estate, to divide among his family!—when, on the contrary, take the gentry in England from one end to the other, except a few here and there, what with excessive high living, which is of late grown so much into a disease, and the other ordinary circumstances of families, we find few families of the lower gentry, that is to say, from six or seven hundred a-year downwards, but they are in debt and in necessitous circumstances, and a great many of greater estates also.

On the other hand, let any one who is acquainted with England, look but abroad into the several counties, especially near London, or within fifty miles of it. How are the ancient families worn out by time and family misfortunes, and the estates possessed by a new race of tradesmen, grown up into families of gentry, and established by the immense wealth, gained, as I may say, behind the counter, that is, in the shop, the warehouse, and the counting-house! How are the sons of tradesmen ranked among the prime of the gentry! How are the daughters of tradesmen at this time adorned with the ducal coronets, and seen riding in the coaches of the best of our nobility! Nay, many of our trading gentlemen at this time refuse to be ennobled, scorn being knighted, and content themselves with being known to be rated among the richest commoners in the nation. And it must be acknowledged, that, whatever they be as to court-breeding and to manners, they, generally speaking, come behind none of the gentry in knowledge of the world.

At this very day we see the son of Sir Thomas Scawen matched into the ducal family of Bedford, and the son of Sir James Bateman into the princely house of Marlborough, both whose ancestors, within the memory of the writer of these sheets, were tradesmen in London; the first Sir William Scawen's apprentice, and the latter's grandfather a porter upon or near London Bridge.

How many noble seats, superior to the palaces of sovereign princes (in some countries) do we see erected within few miles of this city by tradesmen, or the sons of tradesmen, while the seats and castles of the ancient gentry, like their families, look worn out, and fallen into decay. Witness the noble house of Sir John Eyles, himself a merchant, at Giddy-hall near Rumford; Sir Gregory Page on Blackheath, the son of a brewer; Sir Nathaniel Mead near Wealgreen, his father a linen-draper, with many others too long to repeat; and, to crown all, the Lord Castlemains at Wanstead, his father Sir Josiah Child, originally a tradesman.

It was a smart, but just repartee, of a London tradesman, when a gentleman, who had a good estate too, rudely reproached him in company, and bade him hold his tongue, for he was no gentleman. 'No, Sir,' says he, 'but I can buy a gentleman, and therefore I claim a liberty to speak among gentlemen.'

Again, in how superior a port or figure (as we now call it) do our tradesmen live, to what the middling gentry either do or can support! An ordinary tradesman now, not in the city only, but in the country, shall spend more money by the year, than a gentleman of four or five hundred pounds a-year can do, and shall increase and lay up every year too, whereas the gentleman shall at the best stand stock still, just where he began, nay, perhaps decline; and as for the lower gentry, from a hundred pounds a-year to three hundred, or thereabouts, though they are often as proud and high in their appearance as the other—as to them, I say, a shoemaker in London shall keep a better house, spend more money, clothe his family better, and yet grow rich too. It is evident where the difference lies; *an estate's a pond, but a trade's a spring*: the first, if it keeps full, and the water wholesome, by the ordinary supplies and drains from the neighbouring grounds, it is well, and it is all that is expected; but the other is an inexhausted current, which not only fills the pond, and keeps it full, but is continually running over, and fills all the lower ponds and places about it.

This being the case in England, and our trade being so vastly great, it is no wonder that the tradesmen in England fill the lists of our nobility and gentry; no wonder that the gentlemen of the best families marry tradesmen's daughters, and put their younger sons apprentices to tradesmen; and how often do these younger sons come to buy the elder son's estates, and restore the family, when the elder, and head of the house, proving rakish and extravagant, has wasted his patrimony, and is obliged to make out the blessing of Israel's family, where the younger son bought the birthright, and the elder was doomed to serve him.

Trade is so far here from being inconsistent with a gentleman, that, in short, trade in England makes gentlemen, and has peopled this nation with gentlemen; for after a generation or two the tradesmen's children, or at least their grand-children, come to be as good gentlemen, statesmen, parliament-men, privy-counsellors, judges, bishops, and noblemen, as those of the highest birth and the most ancient families, and nothing too high for them. Thus the late Earl of Haversham was originally a merchant; the late Secretary Craggs was the son of a barber; the present Lord Castlemain's father was a tradesman; the great-grandfather of the present Duke of Bedford the same; and so of several others. Nor do we find any defect either in the genius or capacities of the posterity of tradesmen, arising from any remains of mechanic blood, which it is pretended should influence them, but all the gallantry of spirit, greatness of soul, and all the generous principles, that can be found in any of the ancient families, whose blood is the most untainted, as they call it, with the low mixtures of a mechanic race, are found in these; and, as is said before, they generally go beyond them in knowledge of the world, which is the best education.

We see the tradesmen of England, as they grow wealthy, coming every day to the Herald's Office, to search for the coats-of-arms of their ancestors, in order to paint them upon their coaches, and engrave them upon their plate, embroider them upon their furniture, or carve them upon the pediments of their new houses; and how often do we see them trace the registers of their families up to the prime nobility, or the most ancient gentry of the kingdom!

In this search we find them often qualified to raise new families, if they do not descend from old; as was said of a certain tradesman of London that if he could not find the ancient race of gentlemen from which he came, he would begin a new race, who should be as good gentlemen as any that went before them. They tell us a story of the old Lord Craven, who was afterwards created Earl of Craven by King Charles II., that, being upbraided with his being of an upstart nobility, by the famous Aubery, Earl of Oxford, who was himself of the very ancient family of the Veres, Earls of Oxford, the Lord Craven told him, he (Craven) would cap pedigrees with him (Oxford) for a wager. The Earl of Oxford laughed at the challenge, and began reckoning up his famous ancestors, who had been Earls of Oxford for a hundred years past, and knights for some hundreds of years more; but when my Lord Craven began, he read over his family thus:—'I am William Lord Craven; my father was Lord Mayor of London, and my grandfather was the Lord knows who; wherefore I think my pedigree as good as yours, my lord.' The story was merry enough, but is to my purpose exactly; for let the grandfather be who he would, his father, Sir William Craven, who was Lord Mayor of London, was a wholesale grocer, and raised the family by trade, and yet nobody doubts but that the family of Craven is at this day as truly noble, in all the beauties which adorn noble birth and blood, as can be desired of any family, however ancient, or anciently noble.

In Italy, and especially at Venice, we see every day the sons of merchants, and other trades, who grow in wealth and estates, and can advance for the service of their country a considerable sum of money, namely, 60,000 to 100,000 dollars, are accepted to honour by the senate, and translated into the list of the nobility, without any regard to the antiquities of their families, or the nobility of blood; and in all ages the best kings and sovereign princes have thought fit to reward the extraordinary merit of their subjects with titles of honour, and to rank men among their nobility, who have deserved it by good and great actions, whether their birth and the antiquity of their families entitled them to it or not.

Thus in the late wars between England and France, how was our army full of excellent officers, who went from the shop, and from behind the counter, into the camp, and who distinguished themselves there by their merit and gallant behaviour. And several such came to command regiments, and even to be general officers, and to gain as much reputation in the service as any; as Colonel Pierce, Wood, Richards, and several others that might be named.

All this confirms what I have said before, namely, that trade in England neither is nor ought to be levelled with what it is in other countries; nor the tradesmen depreciated as they are abroad, and as some of our gentry would pretend to do in England; but that, as many of our best families rose from trade, so many branches of the best families in England, under the nobility, have stooped so low as to be put apprentices to tradesmen in London, and to set up and follow those trades when they have come out of their times, and have thought it no dishonour to their blood.

To bring this once more home to the ladies, who are so scandalised at that mean step, which they call it, of marrying a tradesman—it may be told them for their humiliation, that, however they think fit to act, sometimes those tradesmen come of better families than their own; and oftentimes, when they have refused them to their loss, those very tradesmen have married ladies of superior fortune to them, and have raised families of their own, who in one generation have been superior to those nice ladies both in dignity and estate, and have, to their great mortification, been ranked above them upon all public occasions.

The word tradesman in England does not sound so harsh as it does in other countries; and to say *a gentleman-tradesman*, is not so much nonsense as some people would persuade us to reckon it: and, indeed, as trade is now flourishing in England, and increasing, and the wealth of our tradesmen is already so great, it is very probable a few years will show us still a greater race of trade-bred gentlemen, than ever England yet had.

The very name of an English tradesman will, and does already obtain in the world; and as our soldiers by the late war gained the reputation of being some of the best troops in the world, and our seamen are at this day, and very justly too, esteemed the best sailors in the world, so the English tradesmen may in a few years be allowed to rank with the best gentlemen in Europe; and as the prophet Isaiah said of the merchants of Tyre, that 'her traffickers were the honourable of the earth,' (Isaiah, xxiii. 8.)

In the meantime, it is evident their wealth at this time out-does that of the like rank of any nation in Europe; and as their number is prodigious, so is their commerce; for the inland commerce of England—and it is of those tradesmen, or traffickers, that I am now speaking in particular—is certainly the greatest of its kind of any in the world; nor is it possible there should ever be any like it, the consumption of all sorts of goods, both of our own manufacture, and of foreign growth, being so exceeding great.

If the English nation were to be nearly inquired into, and its present opulence and greatness duly weighed, it would appear, that, as the figure it now makes in Europe is greater than it ever made before—take it either in King Edward III.'s reign, or in Queen Elizabeth's, which were the two chief points of time when the English fame was in its highest extent—I say, if its present greatness were to be duly weighed, there is no comparison in its wealth, the number of its people, the value of its lands, the greatness of the estates of its private inhabitants; and, in consequence of all this, its real strength is infinitely beyond whatever it was before, and if it were needful, I could fill up this work with a very agreeable and useful inquiry into the particulars.

But I content myself with turning it to the case in hand, for the truth of fact is not to be disputed—I say, I turn it to the case in hand thus: whence comes it to be so?—how is it produced? War has not done it; no, nor so much as helped or assisted to it; it is not by any martial exploits; we have made no conquests abroad, added no new kingdoms to the British empire, reduced no neighbouring nations, or extended the possession of our monarchs into the properties of others; we have grained nothing by war and encroachment; we are butted and bounded just where we were in Queen Elizabeth's time; the Dutch, the Flemings, the French, are in view of us just as they were then. We have subjected no new provinces or people to our government; and, with few or no exceptions, we are almost for dominion where King Edward I. left us; nay, we have lost all the dominions which our ancient kings for some hundreds of years held in France—such as the rich and powerful provinces of Normandy, Poictou, Gascoigne, Bretagne, and Acquitaine; and instead of being enriched by war and victory, on the contrary we have been torn in pieces by civil wars and rebellions, as well in Ireland as in England, and that several times, to the ruin of our richest families, and the slaughter of our nobility and gentry, nay, to the destruction even of monarchy itself, and this many years at a time, as in the long bloody wars between the houses of Lancaster and York, the many rebellions of the Irish, as well in Queen Elizabeth's time, as in King Charles I.'s time, and the fatal massacre, and almost extirpation of the English name in that kingdom; and at last, the late rebellion in England, in which the monarch fell a sacrifice to the fury of the people, and monarchy itself gave way to tyranny and usurpation, for almost twenty years.

These things prove abundantly that the rising greatness of the British nation is not owing to war and conquests, to enlarging its dominion by the sword, or subjecting the people of other countries to our power; but it is all owing to trade, to the increase of our commerce at home, and the extending it abroad.

It is owing to trade, that new discoveries have been made in lands unknown, and new settlements and plantations made, new colonies placed, and new governments formed in the uninhabited islands, and the uncultivated continent of America; and those plantings and settlements have again enlarged and increased the trade, and thereby the wealth and power of the nation by whom they were discovered and planted. We have not increased our power, or the number of our subjects, by subduing the nations which possessed those countries, and incorporating them into our own, but have entirely planted our colonies, and peopled the countries with our own subjects, natives of this island; and, excepting the negroes, which we transport from Africa to America, as slaves to work in the sugar and tobacco plantations, all our colonies, as well in the islands as on the continent of America, are entirely peopled from Great Britain and Ireland, and chiefly the former; the natives having either removed farther up into the country, or by their own folly and treachery raising war against us, been destroyed and cut off.

As trade alone has peopled those countries, so trading with them has raised them also to a prodigy of wealth and opulence; and we see now the ordinary planters at Jamaica and Barbadoes rise to immense estates, riding in their coaches and six, especially at Jamaica, with twenty or thirty negroes on foot running before them whenever they please to appear in public.

As trade has thus extended our colonies abroad, so it has, except those colonies, kept our people at home, where they are multiplied to that prodigious degree, and do still continue to multiply in such a manner, that if it goes on so, time may come that all the lands in England will do little more than serve for gardens for them, and to feed their cows; and their corn and cattle be supplied from Scotland and Ireland.

What is the reason that we see numbers of French, and of Scots, and of Germans, in all the foreign nations in Europe, and especially filling up their armies and courts, and that you see few or no English there?

What is the reason, that when we want to raise armies, or to man navies in England, we are obliged to press the seamen, and to make laws and empower the justices of the peace, and magistrates of towns, to force men to go for soldiers, and enter into the service, or allure them by giving bounty-money, as an encouragement to men to list themselves?—whereas the people of other nations, and even the Scots and Irish, travel abroad, and run into all the neighbour nations, to seek service, and to be admitted into their pay.

What is it but trade?—the increase of business at home, and the employment of the poor in the business and manufactures of this kingdom, by which the poor get so good wages, and live so well, that they will not list for soldiers; and have so good pay in the merchants' service, that they will not serve on board the ships of war, unless they are forced to do it?

What is the reason, that, in order to supply our colonies and plantations with people, besides the encouragement given in those colonies to all people that will come there to plant and to settle, we are obliged to send away thither all our petty offenders, and all the criminals that we think fit to spare from the gallows, besides what we formerly called the kidnapping trade?—that is to say, the arts made use of to wheedle and draw away young vagrant and indigent people, and people of desperate fortunes, to sell themselves—that is, bind themselves for servants, the numbers of which are very great.

It is poverty fills armies, mans navies, and peoples colonies. In vain the drums beat for soldiers, and the king's captains invite seamen to serve in the armies for fivepence a-day, and in the royal navy for twenty-three shillings per month, in a country where the ordinary labourer can have nine shillings a-week for his labour, and the manufacturers earn from twelve to sixteen shillings a-week for their work, and while trade gives thirty shillings per month wages to the seamen on board merchant ships. Men will always stay or go, as the pay gives them encouragement; and this is the reason why it has been so much more difficult to raise and recruit armies in England, than it has been in Scotland and Ireland, France and Germany.

The same trade that keeps our people at home, is the cause of the well living of the people here; for as frugality is not the national virtue of England, so the people that get much spend much; and as they work hard, so they live well, eat and drink well, clothe warm, and lodge soft—in a word, the working manufacturing people of England eat the fat, and drink the sweet, live better, and fare better, than the working poor of any other nation in Europe; they make better wages of their work, and spend more of the money upon their backs and bellies, than in any other country. This expense of the poor, as it causes a prodigious consumption both of the provisions, and of the manufactures of our country at home, so two things are undeniably the consequence of that part.

1. The consumption of provisions increases the rent and value of the lands, and this raises the gentlemen's estates, and that again increases the employment of people, and consequently the numbers of them, as well those who are employed in the husbandry of land, breeding and feeding of cattle, &c, as of servants in the gentlemen's families, who, as their estates increase in value, so they increase their families and equipages.

2. As the people get greater wages, so they, I mean the same poorer part of the people, clothe better, and furnish better, and this increases the consumption of the very manufactures they make; then that consumption increases the quantity made, and this creates what we call inland trade, by which innumerable families are employed, and the increase of the people maintained, and by which increase of trade and people the present growing prosperity of this nation is produced.

The whole glory and greatness of England, then, being thus raised by trade, it must be unaccountable folly and ignorance in us to lessen that one article in our own esteem, which is the only fountain from whence we all, take us as a nation, are raised, and by which we are enriched and maintained. The Scripture says, speaking of the riches and glory of the city of Tyre—which was, indeed, at that time, the great port or emporium of the world for foreign commerce, from whence all the silks and fine manufactures of Persia and India were exported all over the western world—'That her merchants were princes;' and, in another place, 'By thy traffic thou hast increased thy riches.' (Ezek. xxviii. 5.) Certain it is, that our traffic has increased our riches; and it is also certain, that the flourishing of our manufactures is the foundation of all our traffic, as well our merchandise as our inland trade.

The inland trade of England is a thing not easily described; it would, in a word, take up a whole book by itself; it is the foundation of all our wealth and greatness; it is the support of all our foreign trade, and of our manufacturing, and, as I have hitherto written, of the tradesmen who carry it on. I shall proceed with a brief discourse of the trade itself.

CHAPTER XXIII

OF THE INLAND TRADE OF ENGLAND, ITS MAGNITUDE, AND THE GREAT ADVANTAGE IT IS TO THE NATION IN GENERAL

I have, in a few words, described what I mean by the inland trade of England, in the introduction to this work. It is the circulation of commerce among ourselves.

I. For the carrying on our manufactures of several kinds in the several counties where they are made, and the employing the several sorts of people and trades needful for the said manufactures.

II. For the raising and vending provisions of all kinds for the supply of the vast numbers of people who are employed every where by the said manufactures.

III. For the importing and bringing in from abroad all kinds of foreign growth and manufactures which we want.

IV. For the carrying about and dispersing, as well our own growth and manufactures as the foreign imported growth and manufactures of other nations, to the retailer, and by them to the last consumer, which is the utmost end of all trade; and this, in every part, to the utmost corner of the island of Great Britain and Ireland.

This I call inland trade, and these circulators of goods, and retailers of them to the last consumer, are those whom we are to understand by the word tradesmen, in all the parts of this work; for (as I observed in the beginning) the ploughmen and farmers who labour at home, and the merchant who imports our merchandise from abroad, are not at all meant or included, and whatever I have been saying, except where they have been mentioned in particular, and at length.

This inland trade is in itself at this time the wonder of all the world of trade, nor is there any thing like it now in the world, much less that exceeds it, or perhaps ever will be, except only what itself may grow up to in the ages to come; for, as I have said on all occasions, it is still growing and increasing.

By this prodigy of a trade, all the vast importation from our own colonies is circulated and dispersed to the remotest corner of the island, whereby the consumption is become so great, and by which those colonies are so increased, and are become so populous and so wealthy as I have already observed of them. This importation consists chiefly of sugars and tobacco, of which the consumption in Great Britain is scarcely to be conceived of, besides the consumption of cotton, indigo, rice, ginger, pimento or Jamaica pepper, cocoa or chocolate, rum and molasses, train-oil, salt-fish, whale-fin, all sorts of furs, abundance of valuable drugs, pitch, tar, turpentine, deals, masts, and timber, and many other things of smaller value; all which, besides the employing a very great number of ships and English seamen, occasion again a very great exportation of our own manufactures of all sorts to those colonies; which being circulated again for consumption there, that circulation is to be accounted a branch of home or inland trade, as those colonies are on all such occasions esteemed as a branch of part of ourselves, and of the British government in the world.

This trade to our West Indies and American colonies, is very considerable, as it employs so many ships and sailors, and so much of the growth of those colonies is again exported by us to other parts of the world, over and above what is consumed among us at home; and, also, as all those goods, and a great deal of money in specie, is returned hither for and in balance of our own manufactures and merchandises exported thither—on these accounts some have insisted that more real wealth is brought into Great Britain every year from those colonies, than is brought from the Spanish West Indies to old Spain, notwithstanding the extent of their dominion is above twenty times as much, and notwithstanding the vast quantity of gold and silver which they bring from the mines of Mexico, and the mountains of Potosi.[40]

Whether these people say true or no, is not my business to inquire here; though, if I may give my opinion, I must acknowledge that I believe they do; but be it so or not, it is certain that it is an infinitely extended trade, and daily increasing; and much of it, if not all, is and ought to be esteemed as an inland trade, because, as above, it is a circulation among ourselves.

As the manufactures of England, particularly those of wool (cotton wool included), and of silk, are the greatest, and amount to the greatest value of any single manufacture in Europe,[41] so they not only employ more people, but those people gain the most money, that is to

---

[40] The amount of trade produced by the British colonies is still great; but it has been ascertained that it is not profitable to the nation at large, as much more is paid from the public purse for the military protection required by the colonies, than returns to individuals through the medium of business.

[41] The cotton manufacture has now the prominence which, in Defoe's time, was due to those of wool and silk.

say, have the best wages for their work of any people in the world; and yet, which is peculiar to England, the English manufactures are, allowing for their goodness, the cheapest at market of any in the world, too. Even France itself, after all the pains they are at to get our wool, and all the expense they have been at to imitate our manufactures, by getting over our workmen, and giving them even greater wages than they had here, have yet made so little proficiency in it, and are so far from outselling us in foreign markets, that they still, in spite of the strictest prohibitions, send hither, and to Holland and Germany, for English broad-cloths, druggets, duroys, flannels, serges, and several other sorts of our goods, to supply their own. Nor can they clothe themselves to their satisfaction with their own goods; but if any French gentleman of quality comes over hither from France, he is sure to bring no more coats with him than backs, but immediately to make him new clothes as soon as he arrives, and to carry as many new suits home with him at his return, as he can get leave to bring ashore when he comes there—a demonstration that our manufacture exceeds theirs, after all their boasts of it, both in goodness and in cheapness, even by their own confession. But I am not now to enter upon the particular manufactures, but the general trade in the manufacture; this particular being a trade of such a magnitude, it is to be observed for our purpose, that the greatness of it consists of two parts:—

1. The consumption of it at home, including our own plantations and factories.

2. The exportation of it to foreign parts, exclusive of the said plantations and factories.

It is the first of these which is the subject of my present discourse, because the tradesmen to whom, and for whose instruction these chapters are designed, are the people principally concerned in the making all these manufactures, and wholly and solely concerned in dispersing and circulating them for the home consumption; and this, with some additions, as explained above, I call *inland trade*.

The home-consumption of our own goods, as it is very great, so it has one particular circumstance attending it, which exceedingly increases it as a trade, and that is, that besides the numbers of people which it employs in the raising the materials, and making the goods themselves as a manufacture—I say, besides all this, there are multitudes of people employed, cattle maintained, with waggons and carts for the service on shore, barges and boats for carriage in the rivers, and ships and barks for carrying by sea, and all for the circulating these manufactures from one place to another, for the consumption of them among the people.

So that, in short, the circulation of the goods is a business not equal, indeed, but bearing a very great proportion to the trade itself.

This is owing to another particular circumstance of our manufacture, and perhaps is not so remarkably the case of any other manufacture or country in Europe, namely, that though all our manufactures are used and called for by almost all the people, and that in every part of the whole British dominion, yet they are made and wrought in their several distinct and respective countries in Britain, and some of them at the remotest distance from one another, hardly any two manufactures being made in one place. For example:

The broad-cloth and druggets in Wilts, Gloucester, and Worcestershire; serges in Devon and Somersetshire; narrow-cloths in Yorkshire and Staffordshire; kerseys, cottons, half-thicks, duffields, plains, and coarser things, in Lancashire and Westmoreland; shalloons in the counties of Northampton, Berks, Oxford, Southampton, and York; women's-stuffs in Norfolk; linsey-woolseys, &c, at Kidderminster; dimmeties and cotton-wares at Manchester; flannels at Salisbury, and in Wales; tammeys at Coventry; and the like. It is the same, in some respects, with our provisions, especially for the supply of the city of London, and also of several other parts: for example, when I speak of provisions, I mean such as are not made use of in the county where they are made and produced. For example:

Butter, in firkins, in Suffolk and Yorkshire; cheese from Cheshire, Wiltshire, Warwickshire, and Gloucestershire; herrings, cured red, from Yarmouth in Norfolk; coals, for fuel, from Northumberland and Durham; malt from the counties of Hertford, Essex, Kent, Bucks, Oxford, Berks, &c.

And thus of many other things which are the proper produce of one part of the country only, but are from thence dispersed for the ordinary use of the people into many, or perhaps into all the other counties of England, to the infinite advantage of our inland commerce, and employing a vast number of people and cattle; and consequently those people and cattle increasing the consumption of provisions and forage, and the improvement of lands; so true it is, and so visible, that trade increases people, and people increase trade.

This carriage of goods in England from those places is chiefly managed by horses and waggons; the number of which is not to be guessed at, nor is there any rule or art that can be thought of, by which any just calculation can be made of it, and therefore I shall not enter upon any particular of it at this time; it is sufficient to say, what I believe to be true, namely, that it is equal to the whole trade of some nations, and the rather because of the great improvement of land, which proceeds from the employing so many thousands of horses as are furnished for this part of business.

In other countries, and indeed, in most countries in Europe, all their inland trade, such as it is, is carried on by the convenience of navigation, either by coastings on the sea, or by river-navigation. It is true, our coasting trade is exceedingly great, and employs a prodigious number of ships, as well from all the shores of England to London, as from one port to another.

But as to our river-navigation, it is not equal to it, though in some places it is very great too; but we have but a very few navigable rivers in England, compared with those of other countries; nor are many of those rivers we have navigable to any considerable length from the sea. The most considerable rivers in England for navigation are as follows:—The Thames, the Trent, the Severn, the Wye, the Ouse, the Humber, the Air, and the Calder. These are navigable a considerable way, and receive several other navigable rivers into them; but except these there are very few rivers in England which are navigable much above the first town of note within their mouth.

Most of our other greatest and most navigable rivers are navigable but a very little way in; as the northern Ouse but to York, the Orwell but to Ipswich, the Yare but to Norwich; the Tyne itself but a very little above Newcastle, not in all above twelve miles; the Tweed not at all above Berwick; the great Avon but to Bristol; the Exe but to Exeter; and the Dee but to Chester; in a word, our river-navigation is not to be named for carriage, with the vast bulk of carriage by pack-horses and by waggons; nor must the carriage by pedlars on their backs be omitted[42]

This carriage is the medium of our inland trade, and, as I said, is a branch of the trade itself. This great carriage is occasioned by the situation of our produce and manufactures. For example—the Taunton and Exeter serges, perpetuanas, and duroys, come chiefly by land; the clothing, such as the broad-cloth and druggets from Wilts, Gloucester, Worcester, and Shropshire, comes all by land-carriage to London, and

---

[42] It is scarcely necessary to remind the reader, that the canal navigation of England has come into existence since the date of this work—the railway communication is but of yesterday.

goes down again by land-carriages to all parts of England; the Yorkshire clothing trade, the Manchester and Coventry trades, all by land, not to London only, but to all parts of England, by horse-packs—the Manchester men being, saving their wealth, a kind of pedlars, who carry their goods themselves to the country shopkeepers every where, as do now the Yorkshire and Coventry manufacturers also.

Now, in all these manufactures, however remote from one another, every town in England uses something, not only of one or other, but of all the rest. Every sort of goods is wanted every where; and where they make one sort of goods, and sell them all over England, they at the same time want other goods from almost every other part. For example:

Norwich makes chiefly woollen stuffs and camblets, and these are sold all over England; but then Norwich buys broad-cloth from Wilts and Worcestershire, serges and sagathies from Devon and Somersetshire, narrow cloth from Yorkshire, flannel from Wales, coal from Newcastle, and the like; and so it is, *mutatis mutandis*, of most of the other parts.

The circulating of these goods in this manner, is the life of our inland trade, and increases the numbers of our people, by keeping them employed at home; and, indeed, of late they are prodigiously multiplied; and they again increase our trade, as shall be mentioned in its place.

As the demand for all sorts of English goods is thus great, and they are thus extended in every part of the island, so the tradesmen are dispersed and spread over every part also; that is to say, in every town, great or little, we find shopkeepers, wholesale or retail, who are concerned in this circulation, and hand forward the goods to the last consumer. From London, the goods go chiefly to the great towns, and from those again to the smaller markets, and from those to the meanest villages; so that all the manufactures of England, and most of them also of foreign countries, are to be found in the meanest village, and in the remotest corner of the whole island of Britain, and are to be bought, as it were, at every body's door.

This shows not the extent of our manufactures only, but the usefulness of them, and how they are so necessary to mankind that our own people cannot be without them, and every sort of them, and cannot make one thing serve for another; but as they sell their own, so they buy from others, and every body here trades with every body: this it is that gives the whole manufacture so universal a circulation, and makes it so immensely great in England. What it is abroad, is not so much to our present purpose.

Again, the magnitude of the city of London adds very considerably to the greatness of the inland trade; for as this city is the centre of our trade, so all the manufactures are brought hither, and from hence circulated again to all the country, as they are particularly called for. But that is not all; the magnitude of the city influences the whole nation also in the article of provisions, and something is raised in every county in England, however remote, for the supply of London; nay, all the best of every produce is brought hither; so that all the people, and all the lands in England, seem to be at work for, or employed by, or on the account of, this overgrown city.

This makes the trade increase prodigiously, even as the city itself increases; and we all know the city is very greatly increased within few years past. Again, as the whole nation is employed to feed and clothe this city, so here is the money, by which all the people in the whole nation seem to be supported and maintained.

I have endeavoured to make some calculation of the number of shopkeepers in this kingdom, but I find it is not to be done—we may as well count the stars; not that they are equal in number neither, but it is as impossible, unless any one person corresponded so as to have them numbered in every town or parish throughout the kingdom. I doubt not they are some hundreds of thousands, but there is no making an estimate—the number is in a manner infinite. It is as impossible likewise to make any guess at the bulk of their trade, and how much they return yearly; nor, if we could, would it give any foundation for any just calculation of the value of goods in general, because all our goods circulate so much, and go so often through so many hands before they come to the consumer. This so often passing every sort of goods through so many hands, before it comes into the hands of the last consumer, is that which makes our trade be so immensely great. For example, if there is made in England for our home-consumption the value of £100,000 worth of any particular goods, say, for example, that it be so many pieces of serge or cloth, and if this goes through ten tradesmen's hands, before it comes to the last consumer, then there is £1,000,000 returned in trade for that £100,000 worth of goods; and so of all the sorts of goods we trade in.

Again, as I said above, all our manufactures are so useful to, and depend on, one another so much in trade, that the sale of one necessarily causes the demand of the other in all parts. For example, suppose the poorest countryman wants to be clothed, or suppose it be a gentleman wants to clothe one of his servants, whether a footman in a livery, or suppose it be any servant in ordinary apparel, yet he shall in some part employ almost every one of the manufacturing counties of England, for making up one ordinary suit of clothes. For example:

If his coat be of woollen-cloth, he has that from Yorkshire; the lining is shalloon from Berkshire; the waistcoat is of callamanco from Norwich; the breeches of a strong drugget from Devizes, Wiltshire; the stockings being of yarn from Westmoreland; the hat is a felt from Leicester; the gloves of leather from Somersetshire; the shoes from Northampton; the buttons from Macclesfield in Cheshire, or, if they are of metal, they come from Birmingham, or Warwickshire; his garters from Manchester; his shirt of home-made linen of Lancashire, or Scotland.

If it be thus of every poor man's clothing, or of a servant, what must it be of the master, and of the rest of the family? And in this particular the case is the same, let the family live where they will; so that all these manufactures must be found in all the remotest towns and counties in England, be it where you will.

Again, take the furnishing of our houses, it is the same in proportion, and according to the figure and quality of the person. Suppose, then, it be a middling tradesman that is going to live in some market-town, and to open his shop there; suppose him not to deal in the manufacture, but in groceries, and such sort of wares as the country grocers sell.

This man, however, must clothe himself and his wife, and must furnish his house: let us see, then, to how many counties and towns, among our manufactures, must he send for his needful supply. Nor is the quantity concerned in it; let him furnish himself as frugally as he pleases, yet he must have something of every necessary thing; and we will suppose for the present purpose the man lived in Sussex, where very few, if any, manufactures are carried on; suppose he lived at Horsham, which is a market-town in or near the middle of the county.

For his clothing of himself—for we must allow him to have a new suit of clothes when he begins the world—take them to be just as above; for as to the quality or quantity, it is much the same; only, that instead of buying the cloth from Yorkshire, perhaps he has it a little finer than the poor man above, and so his comes out of Wiltshire, and his stockings are, it may be, of worsted, not of yarn, and so they come from Nottingham, not Westmoreland; but this does not at all alter the case.

Come we next to his wife; and she being a good honest townsman's daughter, is not dressed over fine, yet she must have something decent, being newly married too, especially as times go, when the burghers' wives of Horsham, or any other town, go as fine as they do in other places: allow her, then, to have a silk gown, with all the necessaries belonging to a middling tolerable appearance, yet you shall find all the nation more or less concerned in clothing this country grocer's wife, and furnishing his house, and yet nothing at all extravagant. For example:

Her gown, a plain English mantua-silk, manufactured in Spitalfields; her petticoat the same; her binding, a piece of chequered-stuff, made at Bristol and Norwich; her under-petticoat, a piece of black callamanco, made at Norwith—quilted at home, if she be a good housewife, but the quilting of cotton from Manchester, or cotton-wool from abroad; her inner-petticoats, flannel and swanskin, from Salisbury and Wales; her stockings from Tewksbury, if ordinary, from Leicester, if woven; her lace and edgings from Stony Stratford the first, and Great Marlow the last; her muslin from foreign trade, as likewise her linen, being something finer than the man's, may perhaps be a guilick-Holland; her wrapper, or morning-gown, a piece of Irish linen, printed at London; her black hood, a thin English lustring; her gloves, lamb's-skin, from Berwick and Northumberland, or Scotland; her ribands, being but very few, from Coventry, or London; her riding-hood, of English worsted-camblet, made at Norwich.

Come next to the furniture of their house. It is scarce credible, to how many counties of England, and how remote, the furniture of but a mean house must send them, and how many people are every where employed about it; nay, and the meaner the furniture, the more people and places employed. For example:

The hangings, suppose them to be ordinary linsey-woolsey, are made at Kidderminster, dyed in the country, and painted, or watered, at London; the chairs, if of cane, are made at London; the ordinary matted chairs, perhaps in the place where they live; tables, chests of drawers, &c., made at London; as also looking-glass; bedding, &c., the curtains, suppose of serge from Taunton and Exeter, or of camblets, from Norwich, or the same with the hangings, as above; the ticking comes from the west country, Somerset and Dorsetshire; the feathers also from the same country; the blankets from Whitney in Oxfordshire; the rugs from Westmoreland and Yorkshire; the sheets, of good linen, from Ireland; kitchen utensils and chimney-furniture, almost all the brass and iron from Birmingham and Sheffield; earthen-ware from Stafford, Nottingham, and Kent; glass ware from Sturbridge in Worcestershire, and London.

I give this list to explain what I said before, namely, that there is no particular place in England, where all the manufactures are made, but every county or place has its peculiar sort, or particular manufacture, in which the people are wholly employed; and for all the rest that is wanted, they fetch them from other parts.[43]

But, then, as what is thus wanted by every particular person, or family, is but in small quantities, and they would not be able to send for it to the country or town where it is to be bought, there are shopkeepers in every village, or at least in every considerable market-town, where the particulars are to be bought, and who find it worth their while to furnish themselves with quantities of all the particular goods, be they made where and as far off as they will; and at these shops the people who want them are easily supplied.

Nor do even these shopkeepers go or send to all the several counties where those goods are made—that is to say, to this part for the cloth, or to that for the lining; to another for the buttons, and to another for the thread; but they again correspond with the wholesale dealers in London, where there are particular shops or warehouses for all these; and they not only furnish the country shopkeepers, but give them large credit, and sell them great quantities of goods, by which they again are enabled to trust the tailors who make the clothes, or even their neighbours who wear them; and the manufacturers in the several counties do the like by those wholesale dealers who supply the country shops.

Through so many hands do all the necessary things pass for the clothing a poor plain countryman, though he lived as far as Berwick-upon-Tweed; and this occasions, as I have said, a general circulation of

---

[43] Since Defoe's time, little alteration has taken place in the locality of a number of manufactures in England; but, in the interval, an entire change has been effected in Scotland, which now possesses various manufactures of importance in the commercial economy of the nation. We need only allude to the cambrics, gauzes, and silks of Paisley; the cottons and other goods of Glasgow; the plaidings of Stirlingshire; the stockings of Hawick; the printing-paper of Mid-Lothian; the carpets and bonnets of Kilmarnock; the iron of Muirkirk and Carron; the linens of Fife and Dundee; and the shawls of Edinburgh.

trade, both to and from London, from and to all the parts of England, so that every manufacture is sold and removed five or six times, and perhaps more, before it comes at the last consumer.

This method of trade brings another article in, which also is the great foundation of the increase of commerce, and the prodigious magnitude of our inland trade is much owing to it; and that is giving credit, by which every tradesman is enabled to trade for a great deal more than he otherwise could do. By this method a shopkeeper is able to stock his shop, or warehouses, with two or three times as much goods in value, as he has stock of his own to begin the world with, and by that means is able to trust out his goods to others, and give them time, and so under one another—nay, I may say, many a tradesman begins the world with borrowed stocks, or with no stock at all, but that of credit, and yet carries on a trade for several hundreds, nay, for several thousands, of pounds a-year.

By this means the trade in general is infinitely increased—nay, the stock of the kingdom in trade is doubled, or trebled, or more, and there is infinitely more business carried on, than the real stock could be able to manage, if no credit were to be given; for credit in this particular is a stock, and that not an imaginary, but a real stock; for the tradesman, that perhaps begins but with five hundred, or one thousand pounds' stock, shall be able to furnish or stock his shop with four times the sum in the value of goods; and as he gives credit again, and trusts other tradesmen under him, so he launches out into a trade of great magnitude; and yet, if he is a prudent manager of his business, he finds himself able to answer his payments, and so continually supply himself with goods, keeping up the reputation of his dealings, and the credit of his shop, though his stock be not a fifth, nay, sometimes not a tenth part, in proportion to the returns that he makes by the year: so that credit is the foundation on which the trade of England is made so considerable.

Nor is it enough to say, that people must and will have goods, and that the consumption is the same; it is evident that consumption is not the same; and in those nations where they give no credit, or not so much as here, the trade is small in proportion, as I shall show in its place.

CHAPTER XXIV
OF CREDIT IN TRADE, AND HOW A TRADESMAN OUGHT
TO VALUE AND IMPROVE IT: HOW EASILY LOST, AND
HOW HARD IT IS TO BE RECOVERED

Credit is, or ought to be, the tradesman's *mistress*; but I must tell him too, he must not think of ever casting her off, for if once he loses her, she hardly ever returns; and yet she has one quality, in which she differs from most of the ladies who go by that name—if you court her, she is gone; if you manage so wisely as to make her believe you really do not want her, she follows and courts you. But, by the way, no tradesman can be in so good circumstances as to say he does not want, that is, does not stand in need of credit.

Credit, next to real stock, is the foundation, the life and soul, of business in a private tradesman; it is his prosperity; it is his support in the substance of his whole trade; even in public matters, it is the strengh and fund of a nation. We felt, in the late wars, the consequence of both the extremes—namely, of wanting and of enjoying a complete fund of credit.

Credit makes war, and makes peace; raises armies, fits out navies, fights battles, besieges towns; and, in a word, it is more justly called the sinews of war than the money itself,[44] because it can do all these things without money—nay, it will bring in money to be subservient, though it be independent.

Credit makes the soldier fight without pay, the armies march without provisions, and it makes tradesmen keep open shop without stock. The force of credit is not to be described by words; it is an impregnable fortification, either for a nation, or for a single man in business; and he that has credit is invulnerable, whether he has money or no; nay, it will make money, and, which is yet more, it will make money without an intrinsic, without the *materia medica* (as the doctors have it); it adds a value, and supports whatever value it adds, to the meanest substance; it makes paper pass for money, and fills the Exchequer and the banks with as many millions as it pleases, upon demand. As I said in last chapter, it increases commerce; so, I may add,

---

[44] How strikingly was this proved in the last war, when the British government obtained credit for no less than six hundred millions to conduct warlike operations, and by these means was ultimately victorious.

it makes trade, and makes the whole kingdom trade for many millions more than the national specie can amount to.

It may be true, as some allege, that we cannot drive a trade for more goods than we have to trade with, but then it is as true, that it is by the help of credit that we can increase the quantity, and that more goods are made to trade with than would otherwise be; more goods are brought to market than they could otherwise sell; and even in the last consumption, how many thousands of families wear out their clothes before they pay for them, and eat their dinner upon tick with the butcher! Nay, how many thousands who could not buy any clothes, if they were to pay for them in ready money, yet buy them at a venture upon their credit, and pay for them as they can!

Trade is anticipated by credit, and it grows by the anticipation; for men often buy clothes before they pay for them, because they want clothes before they can spare the money; and these are so many in number, that really they add a great stroke to the bulk of our inland trade. How many families have we in England that live upon credit, even to the tune of two or three years' rent of their revenue, before it comes in!—so that they must be said to *eat the calf in the cow's belly*. This encroachment they make upon the stock in trade; and even this very article may state the case: I doubt not but at this time the land owes to the trade some millions sterling; that is to say, the gentlemen owe to the tradesmen so much money, which, at long run, the rents of their lands must pay.

The tradesmen having, then, trusted the landed men with so much, where must they have it but by giving credit also to one another? Trusting their goods and money into trade, one launching out into the hands of another, and forbearing payment till the lands make it good out of their produce, that is to say, out of their rents.

The trade is not limited; the produce of lands may be and is restrained. Trade cannot exceed the bounds of the goods it can sell; but while trade can increase its stock of cash by credit, it can increase its stock of goods for sale, and then it has nothing to do but to find a market to sell at; and this we have done in all parts of the world, still by the force of our stocks being so increased.

Thus, credit raising stock at home, that stock enables us to give credit abroad; and thus the quantity of goods which we make, and which is infinitely increased at home, enables us to find or force a vent abroad. This is apparent, our home trade having so far increased our manufacture, that England may be said to be able almost to clothe the whole world; and in our carrying on the foreign trade wholly upon the English stocks, giving credit to almost all the nations of the world; for it is evident, our stocks lie at this time upon credit in the warehouses of the merchants in Spain and Portugal, Holland and Germany, Italy and Turkey; nay, in New Spain and Brazil.

The exceeding quantity of goods thus raised in England cannot be supposed to be the mere product of the solid wealth and stocks of the English people; we do not pretend to it; the joining those stocks to the value of goods, always appearing in England in the hands of the manufacturers, tradesmen, and merchants, and to the wealth which appears in shipping, in stock upon land, and in the current coin of the nation, would amount to such a prodigy of stock, as not all Europe could pretend to.

But all this is owing to the prodigious thing called credit, the extent of which in the British trade is as hard to be valued, as the benefit of it to England is really not to be described. It must be likewise said, to the honour of our English tradesman, that they understand how to manage the credit they both give and take, better than any other tradesmen in the world; indeed, they have a greater opportunity to improve it, and make use of it, and therefore may be supposed to be more ready in making the best of their credit, than any other nations are.

Hence it is that we frequently find tradesmen carrying on a prodigious trade with but a middling stock of their own, the rest being all managed by the force of their credit; for example, I have known a man in a private warehouse in London trade for forty thousand pounds a-year sterling, and carry on such a return for many years together, and not have one thousand pounds' stock of his own, or not more—all the rest has been carried on upon credit, being the stocks of other men running continually through his hands; and this is not practised now and then, as a great rarity, but is very frequent in trade, and may be seen every day, as what in its degree runs through the whole body of the tradesmen in England.[45]

---

[45] The author's praises of credit must be received with caution. If his descriptions of the credit system of his own day are true, an improvement has since taken place, as business neither is nor can be now carried on to such an extent upon credit—a circumstance that redounds to the advantage of all parties.

Every tradesman both gives and takes credit, and the new mode of setting it up over their shop and warehouse doors, in capital letters, *No trust by retail*, is a presumption in trade; and though it may have been attempted in some trades, was never yet brought to any perfection; and most of those trades, who were the forwardest to set it up, have been obliged to take it down again, or act contrary to it in their business, or see some very good customers go away from them to other shops, who, though they have not brought money with them, have yet good foundations to make any tradesmen trust them, and who do at proper times make payments punctual enough.

On the contrary, instead of giving no trust by retail, we see very considerable families who buy nothing but on trust; even bread, beer, butter, cheese, beef, and mutton, wine, groceries, &c, being the things which even with the meanest families are generally sold for ready money. Thus I have known a family, whose revenue has been some thousands a-year, pay their butcher, and baker, and grocer, and cheesemonger, by a hundred pounds at a time, and be generally a hundred more in each of their debts, and yet the tradesmen have thought it well worth while to trust them, and their pay has in the end been very honest and good.

This is what I say brings land so much in debt to trade, and obliges the tradesman to take credit of one another; and yet they do not lose by it neither, for the tradesmen find it in the price, and they take care to make such families pay warmly for the credit, in the rate of their goods; nor can it be expected it should be otherwise, for unless the profit answered it, the tradesman could not afford to be so long without his money.

This credit takes its beginning in our manufactures, even at the very first of the operation, for the master manufacturer himself begins it. Take a country clothier, or bay-maker, or what other maker of goods you please, provided he be one that puts out the goods to the making; it is true that the poor spinners and weavers cannot trust; the first spin for their bread, and the last not only weave for their bread, but they have several workmen and boys under them, who are very poor, and if they should want their pay on Saturday night, must want their dinner on Sunday; and perhaps would be in danger of starving with their families, by the next Saturday.

But though the clothier cannot have credit for spinning and weaving, he buys his wool at the stapler's or fellmonger's, and he gets two or three months' credit for that; he buys his oil and soap of the country shopkeeper, or has it sent down from his factor at London, and he gets longer credit for that, and the like of all other things; so that a clothier of any considerable business, when he comes to die, shall appear to be £4000 or £5000 in debt.

But, then, look into his books, and you shall find his factor at Blackwell Hall, who sells his cloths, or the warehouse-keeper who sells his duroys and druggets, or both together, have £2000 worth of goods in hand left unsold, and has trusted out to drapers, and mercers, and merchants, to the value of £4000 more; and look into his workhouse at home, namely, his wool-lofts, his combing-shop, his yarn-chamber, and the like, and there you will find it—in wool unspun, and in yarn spun, and in wool at the spinners', and in yarn at and in the looms at the weavers'; in rape-oil, gallipoli oil, and perhaps soap, &c, in his warehouses, and in cloths at the fulling-mill, and in his rowing-shops, finished and unfinished, £4000 worth of goods more; so that, though this clothier owed £5000 at his death, he has nevertheless died in good circumstances, and has £5000 estate clear to go among his children, all his debts paid and discharged. However, it is evident, that at the very beginning of this manufacturer's trade, his £5000 stock is made £10,000, by the help of his credit, and he trades for three times as much in the year; so that £5000 stock makes £10,000 stock and credit, and that together makes £30,000 a-year returned in trade.

When you come from him to the warehouse-keeper in London, there you double and treble upon it, to an unknown degree; for the London wholesale man shall at his death appear to have credit among the country clothiers for £10,000 or £15,000, nay, to £20,000, and yet have kept up an unspotted credit all his days.

When he is dead, and his executors or widow come to look into things, they are frightened with the very appearance of such a weight of debts, and begin to doubt how his estate will come out at the end of it. But when they come to cast up his books and his warehouse, they find,

In debts abroad, perhaps £30,000 In goods in his warehouse £12,000

So that, in a word, the man has died immensely rich; that is to say, worth between £20,000 and £30,000, only that, having been a long standard in trade, and having a large stock, he drove a very great business, perhaps to the tune of £60,000 or £70,000 a-year; so that, of all the £30,000 owing, there may be very little of it delivered above four to six months, and the debtors being many of them considerable merchants, and good paymasters, there is no difficulty in getting in money enough to clear all his own debts; and the widow and children being left well, are not in such haste for the rest but that it comes in time enough to make them easy; and at length it all comes in, or with but a little loss.

As it is thus in great things, it is the same in proportion with small; so that in all the trade of England, you may reckon two-thirds of it carried on upon credit; in which reckoning I suppose I speak much within compass, for in some trades there is four parts of five carried on so, and in some more.

All these things serve to show the infinite value of which credit is to the tradesman, as well as to trade itself; and it is for this reason I have closed my instructions with this part of the discourse. Credit is the choicest jewel the tradesman is trusted with; it is better than money many ways; if a man has £10,000 in money, he may certainly trade for £10,000, and if he has no credit, he cannot trade for a shilling more.

But how often have we seen men, by the mere strength of their credit, trade for ten thousand pounds a-year, and have not one groat of real stock of their own left in the world! Nay, I can say it of my own knowledge, that I have known a tradesman trade for ten thousand pounds a-year, and carry it on with full credit to the last gasp, then die, and break both at once; that is to say, die unsuspected, and yet, when his estate has been cast up, appear to be five thousand pounds worse than nothing in the world: how he kept up his credit, and made good his payments so long, is indeed the mystery, and makes good what I said before, namely, that as none trade so much upon credit in the world, so none know so well how to improve and manage credit to their real advantage, as the English tradesmen do; and we have many examples of it, among our bankers especially, of which I have not room to enter at this time into the discourse, though it would afford a great many diverting particulars.[46]

I have mentioned on several occasions in this work, how nice and how dainty a dame this credit is, how soon she is affronted and disobliged, and how hard to be recovered, when once distasted and fled; particularly in the story of the tradesman who told his friends in a public coffee-house that he was broke, and should shut up his shop the next day. I have hinted how chary we ought to be of one another's

---

[46] Defoe speaks of such cases as if there were something laudable in them, whereas it is obviously for the interest of all honest traders, that no such men should be allowed to carry on business.

credit, and that we should take care as much of our neighbour tradesman's credit as we would of his life, or as we would of firing his house, and, consequently, the whole street.

Let me close all with a word to the tradesman himself, that if it be so valuable to him, and his friends should be all so chary of injuring his reputation, certainly he should be very chary of it himself. The tradesman that is not as tender of his credit as he is of his eyes, or of his wife and children, neither deserves credit, nor will long be master of it.

As credit is a coy mistress, and will not easily be courted, so she is a mighty nice touchy lady, and is soon affronted; if she is ill used, she flies at once, and it is a very doubtful thing whether ever you gain her favour again.

Some may ask me here, 'How comes it to pass, since she is so nice and touchy a lady, that so many clowns court and carry her, and so many fools keep her so long?' My answer is, that those clowns have yet good breeding enough to treat her civilly; he must be a fool indeed that will give way to have his credit injured, and sit still and be quiet-that will not bustle and use his utmost industry to vindicate his own reputation, and preserve his credit.

But the main question for a tradesman in this case, and which I have not spoken of yet, is, 'What is the man to do to preserve his credit? What are the methods that a young tradesman is to take, to gain a good share of credit in his beginning, and to preserve and maintain it when it is gained?'[47]

Every tradesman's credit is supposed to be good at first. He that begins without credit, is an unhappy wretch of a tradesman indeed, and may be said to be broke even before he sets up; for what can a man do, who by any misfortune in his conduct during his apprenticeship, or by some ill character upon him so early, begins with a blast upon his credit? My advice to such a young man would be, not to set up at all; or if he did, to stay for some time, till by some better behaviour, either as a journeyman, or as an assistant in some other man's shop or warehouse,

---

[47] Defoe almost appears in this place to lay capital out of the question, and to represent credit as all in all. Credit is a matter of great consequence; but we must not attempt to carry on business by its means alone. It should only be considered as an aid to capital. Those who, without capital, endeavour to set up in business by means of credit, or, when capital is exhausted, attempt to struggle on by means of credit alone, will, in general, only have a life of anxiety and dispeace for their pains.

he had recovered himself; or else to go and set up in some other place or town remote from that where he has been bred; for he must have a great assurance that can flatter himself to set up, and believe he shall recover a lost reputation.

But take a young tradesman as setting up with the ordinary stock, that is to say, a negative character, namely, that he has done nothing to hurt his character, nothing to prejudice his behaviour, and to give people a suspicion of him: what, then, is the first principle on which to build a tradesman's reputation? and what is it he is to do?

The answer is short. Two things raise credit in trade, and, I may say, they are the only things required; there are some necessary addenda, but these are the fundamentals.

1. Industry. 2. Honesty.

I have dwelt upon the first; the last I have but a few words to say to, but they will be very significant; indeed, that head requires no comment, no explanations or enlargements: nothing can support credit, be it public or private, but honesty; a punctual dealing, a general probity in every transaction. He that once breaks through his honesty, violates his credit—once denominate a man a knave, and you need not forbid any man to trust him.

Even in the public it appears to be the same thing. Let any man view the public credit in its present flourishing circumstances, and compare it with the latter end of the years of King Charles II. after the Exchequer had been shut up, parliamentary appropriations misapplied, and, in a word, the public faith broken; who would lend? Seven or eight per cent. was given for anticipations in King William's time, though no new fraud had been offered, only because the old debts were unpaid; and how hard was it to get any one to lend money at all!

But, after by a long series of just and punctual dealing, the Parliament making good all the deficient funds, and paying even those debts for which no provision was made, and the like, how is the credit restored, the public faith made sacred again, and how money flows into the Exchequer without calling for, and that at three or four per cent. interest, even from foreign countries as well as from our own people! They that have credit can never want money; and this credit is to be raised by no other method, whether by private tradesmen, or public bodies of men, by nations and governments, but by a general probity and an honest punctual dealing.

The reason of this case is as plain as the assertion; the cause is in itself; no man lends his money but with an expectation of receiving it again with the interest. If the borrower pays it punctually without hesitations and defalcations, without difficulties, and, above all, without compulsion, what is the consequence?—he is called an honest man, he has the reputation of a punctual fair dealer. And what then?—why, then, he may borrow again whenever he will, he may take up money and goods, or anything, upon his bare words, or note; when another man must give bondsmen, or *mainprize*, that is, a pawn or pledge for security, and hardly be trusted to neither. This is credit.

It is not the quality of the person would give credit to his dealing; not kings, princes, emperors, it is all one; nay, a private shopkeeper shall borrow money much easier than a prince, if the credit of the tradesman has the reputation of being an honest man. Not the crown itself can give credit to the head that wears it, if once he that wears it comes but to mortgage his honour in the matter of payment of money.

Who would have lent King Charles II. fifty pounds on the credit of his word or bond, after the shutting up the Exchequer? The royal word was made a jest of, and the character of the king was esteemed a fluttering trifle, which no man would venture upon, much less venture his money upon.

In King William's time the case was much the same at first; though the king had not broken his credit then with any man, yet how did they break their faith with the whole world, by the deficiency of the funds, the giving high and ruinous interest to men almost as greedy as vultures, the causing the government to pay great and extravagant rates for what they bought, and great premiums for what they borrowed— these were the injuries to the public for want of credit; nor was it in the power of the whole nation to remedy it; on the contrary, they made it still grow worse and worse, till, as above, the parliament recovered it. And how was it done? Not but by the same method a private person must do the same, namely, by doing justly, and fairly, and honestly, by every body.

Thus credit began to revive, and to enlarge itself again; and usury, which had, as it were, eaten up mankind in business, declined, and so things came to their right way again.

The case is the same with a tradesman; if he shuffles in payment, bargains at one time, and pays at another, breaks his word and his honour in the road of his business, he is gone; no man will take his bills, no man will trust him.

The conclusion is open and clear: the tradesman cannot be too careful of his credit, he cannot buy it too dear, or be too careful to preserve it: it is in vain to maintain it by false and loose doing business; by breaking faith, refusing to perform agreements, and such shuffling things as those; the greatest monarch in Europe could not so preserve his credit.

Nothing but probity will support credit; just, and fair, and honourable dealings give credit, and nothing but the same just, and fair, and honourable dealings will preserve it.

CHAPTER XXV
OF THE TRADESMAN'S PUNCTUAL PAYING HIS BILLS AND PROMISSORY NOTES UNDER HIS HAND, AND THE CREDIT HE GAINS BY IT

As I said that credit is maintained by just and honourable dealing, so that just dealing depends very much upon the tradesman's punctual payment of money in all the several demands that are upon him. The ordinary demands of money upon a tradesman are—

I. Promises of money for goods bought at time.

II. Bills drawn upon him; which, generally speaking, are from the country, that is to say, from some places remote from where he lives. Or,

III. Promissory notes under his hand, which are passed oftentimes upon buying goods: bought also at time, as in the first head.

IV. Bonds bearing interest, given chiefly for money borrowed at running interest.

I. Promises of money for goods bought at time. This indeed is the loosest article in a tradesman's payments; and it is true that a tradesman's credit is maintained upon the easiest terms in this case of any other that belongs to trade; for in this case not one man in twenty keeps to his time; and so easy are tradesmen to one another, that in general it is not much expected, but he that pays tolerably well, and without dunning, is a good man, and in credit; shall be trusted any where, and keeps up a character in his business: sometimes he pays sooner, sometimes later, and is accounted so good a customer, that though he owes a great deal, yet he shall be trusted any where, and is as lofty and touchy if his credit be called in question, as if he paid all ready money.

And, indeed, these men shall often buy their goods as cheap upon the credit of their ordinary pay, as another man shall that brings his money in his hand; and it is reasonable it should be so, for the ready-money man comes and buys a parcel here and a parcel there, and comes but seldom, but the other comes every day, that is to say, as often as he wants goods, buys considerably, perhaps deals for two or three thousand pounds a-year with you, and the like, and pays currently too. Such a customer ought indeed to be sold as cheap to, as the other chance customer for his ready money. In this manner of trade, I say, credit is maintained upon the easiest terms of any other, and yet here the tradesman must have a great care to keep it up too; for though it be the easiest article to keep up credit in, yet even in this article the tradesman may lose his credit, and then he is undone at once; and this is by growing (what in the language of trade is called) long-winded, putting off and putting off continually, till he will bear dunning; then his credit falls, his dealer that trusted him perhaps a thousand pounds previously, that esteemed him as good as ready money, now grows sick of him, declines him, cares not whether he deals with him or no, and at last refuses to trust him any longer. Then his credit is quite sunk and gone, and in a little after that his trade is ruined and the tradesman too; for he must be a very extraordinary tradesman that can open his shop after he has outlived his credit: let him look which way he will, all is lost, nobody cares to deal with him, and, which is still worse, nobody will trust him.

2. Bills drawn upon him from the country, that is to say, from some places remote from where he now dwells: it is but a little while ago since those bills were the loosest things in trade, for as they could not be protested, so they would not (in all their heats) always sue for them, but rather return them to the person from whom they received them.

In the meantime, let the occasion be what it will, the tradesman ought on all occasions to pay these notes without a public recalling and returning them, and without hesitation of any kind whatsoever. He that lets his bills lie long unpaid, must not expect to keep his credit much after them.

Besides, the late law for noting and protesting inland bills, alters the case very much. Bills now accepted, are protested in form, and, if not punctually paid, are either returned immediately, or the person on whom they are drawn is liable to be sued at law; either of which is at best a blow to the credit of the acceptor.

A tradesman may, without hurt to his reputation, refuse to accept a bill, for then, when the notary comes he gives his reasons, namely, that he refuses to accept the bill for want of advice, or for want of effects in his hands for account of the drawer, or that he has not given orders to draw upon him; in all which cases the non-acceptance touches the credit of the drawer; for in trade it is always esteemed a dishonourable thing to draw upon any man that has not effects in his hands to answer the bill; or to draw without order, or to draw and not give advice of it; because it looks like a forwardness to take the remitter's money without giving him a sufficient demand for it, where he expects and ought to have it.

A tradesman comes to me in London, and desires me to give him a bill payable at Bristol, for he is going to the fair there, and being to buy goods there, he wants money at Bristol to pay for them. If I give him a bill, he pays me down the money upon receipt of it, depending upon my credit for the acceptance of the bill. If I draw this bill where I have no reason to draw it, where I have no demand, or no effects to answer it, or if I give my correspondent no advice of it, I abuse the remitter, that is, the man whose money I take, and this reflects upon my credit that am the drawer, and the next time this tradesman wants money at Bristol fair, he will not come to me. 'No,' says he, 'his last bills were not accepted.' Or, if he does come to me, then he demands that he should not pay his money till he has advice that my bills are accepted.

But, on the other hand, if bills are right drawn, and advice duly given, and the person has effects in his hands, then, if he refuses the bill, he says to the notary he does not accept the bill, but gives no reason for it, only that he says absolutely, 'I will not accept it—you may take that for an answer;' or he adds, 'I refuse to accept it, for reasons best known to myself.' This is sometimes done, but this does not leave the person's credit who refuses, so clear as the other, though perhaps it may not so directly reflect upon him; but it leaves the case a little dubious and uncertain, and men will be apt to write back to the person who sent the bill to inquire what the drawer says to it, and what account he gives, or what character he has upon his tongue for the person drawn upon.

As the punctual paying of bills when accepted, is a main article in the credit of the acceptor, so a tradesman should be very cautious in permitting men to draw upon him where he has not effects, or does not give order; for though, as I said, it ought not to affect his reputation not to accept a bill where it ought not to be drawn, yet a tradesman that is nice of his own character does not love to be always or often refusing to accept bills, or to have bills drawn upon him where he has no reason to accept them, and therefore he will be very positive in forbidding such drawing; and if, notwithstanding that, the importunities of the country tradesman oblige him to draw, the person drawn upon will give smart and rough answers to such bills; as particularly, 'I refuse to accept this bill, because I have no effects of the drawer's to answer it.' Or thus, 'I refuse to accept this bill, because I not only gave no orders to draw, but gave positive orders not to draw.' Or thus, 'I neither will accept this bill, nor any other this man shall draw;' and the like. This thoroughly clears the credit of the acceptor, and reflects grossly on the drawer.

And yet, I say, even in this case a tradesman does not care to be drawn upon, and be obliged to see bills presented for acceptance, and for payment, where he has given orders not to draw, and where he has no effects to answer.

It is the great error of our country manufacturers, in many, if not in most, parts of England at this time, that as soon as they can finish their goods, they hurry them up to London to their factor, and as soon as the goods are gone, immediately follow them with their bills for the money, without waiting to hear whether the goods are come to a market, are sold, or in demand, and whether they are likely to sell quickly or not; thus they load the factor's warehouse with their goods before they are wanted, and load the factor with their bills, before it is possible that he can have gotten cash in his hand to pay them.

This is, first, a direct borrowing money of their factor; and it is borrowing, as it were, whether the factor will lend or no, and sometimes whether he can or no. The factor, if he be a man of money, and answers their bills, fails not to make them pay for advancing; or sells the goods to loss to answer the bills, which is making them pay dear for the loan; or refuses their bills, and so baulks both their business and their credit.

But if the factor, willing to oblige his employers, and knowing he shall otherwise lose their commission, accepts the bills on the credit of the goods, and then, not being able to sell the goods in time, is also made unable to pay the bills when due—this reflects upon his credit, though the fault is indeed in the drawer whose effects are not come in; and this has ruined many an honest factor.

First, it has hurt him by drawing large sums out of his cash, for the supply of the needy manufacturer, who is his employer, and has thereby made him unable to pay his other bills currently, even of such men's drafts who had perhaps good reason to draw.

Secondly, it keeps the factor always bare of money, and wounds his reputation, so that he pays those very bills with discredit, which in justice to himself he ought not to pay at all, and the borrower has the money, at the expense of the credit of the lender; whereas, indeed, the reproach ought to be to him that borrows, not to him that lends—to him that draws where there are no effects to warrant his draft, not to him that pays where he does not owe.

But the damage lies on the circumstances of accepting the bill, for the factor lends his employer the money the hour he accepts the bill, and the blow to his credit is for not paying when accepted. When the bill is accepted, the acceptor is debtor to the person to whom the bill is payable, or in his right to every indorser; for a bill of exchange is in this case different from a bond, namely, that the right of action is transferable by indorsement, and every indorser has a right to sue the acceptor in his own name, and can transfer that right to another; whereas in a bond, though it be given to me by assignment, I must sue in the name of the first person to whom the bond is payable, and he may at any time discharge the bond, notwithstanding my assignment.

Tradesmen, then, especially such as are factors,[48] are unaccountably to blame to accept bills for their employers before their goods are sold, and the money received, or within reach: if the employers cannot wait, the reproach should lie on them, not on the factor; and, indeed, the manufacturers all over England are greatly wrong in that part of their business; for, not considering the difference between a time of demand and a time of glut, a quick or a dead market, they go on in the same course of making, and, without slackening their hands as to quantity, crowd up their goods, as if it were enough to them that the factor had them, and that they were to be reckoned as sold when they were in his hands: but would the factor truly represent to them the state of the market—that there are great quantities of goods in hand unsold, and no present demand, desiring them to slack their hands a little in making; and at the same time back their directions in a plain and positive way, though with respect too, by telling them they could accept no more bills till the goods were sold. This would bring the trade into a better regulation, and the makers would stop their hands when the market stopped; and when the merchant ceased to buy, the manufacturers would cease to make, and, consequently, would not crowd or clog the market with goods, or wrong their factors with bills.

But this would require a large discourse, and the manufacturers' objections should be answered, namely, that they cannot stop, that they have their particular sets of workmen and spinners, whom they are obliged to keep employed, or, if they should dismiss them, they could not have them again when a demand for goods came, and the markets revived, and that, besides, the poor would starve.

These objections are easy to be answered, though that is not my present business; but thus far it is to my purpose—it is the factor's

---

[48] By factors, Defoe seems to mean the class of persons whom we now name commission-agents.

business to keep himself within compass: if the goods cannot be sold, the maker must stay till they can; if the poor must be employed, the manufacturer is right to keep them at work if he can; but if he cannot, without oppressing the factor, then he makes the factor employ them, not himself; and I do not see the factor has any obligation upon him to consider the spinners and weavers, especially not at the expense of his own credit, and his family's safety.

Upon the whole, all tradesmen that trade thus, whether by commission from the country, or upon their own accounts, should make it the standing order of their business not to suffer themselves to be overdrawn by their employers, so as to straiten themselves in their cash, and make them unable to pay their bills when accepted. It is also to be observed, that when a tradesman once comes to suffer himself to be thus overdrawn, and sinks his credit in kindness to his employer, he buys his employment so dear as all his employer can do for him can never repay the price.

And even while he is thus serving his employer, he more and more wounds himself; for suppose he does (with difficulty) raise money, and, after some dunning, does pay the bills, yet he loses in the very doing it, for he never pays them with credit, but suffers in reputation by every day's delay. In a word, a tradesman that buys upon credit, that is to say, in a course of credit, such as I have described before, may let the merchant or the warehouse-keeper call two or three times, and may put him off without much damage to his credit; and if he makes them stay one time, he makes it up again another, and recovers in one good payment what he lost in two or three bad ones.

But in bills of exchange or promissory notes, it is quite another thing, and he that values his reputation in trade should never let a bill come twice for payment, or a note under his hand stay a day after it is due, that is to say, after the three days *of grace,* as it is called. Those three days, indeed, are granted to all bills of exchange, not by law, but by the custom of trade: it is hard to tell how this custom prevailed, or when it began, but it is one of those many instances which may be given, where custom of trade is equal to an established law; and it is so much a law now in itself, that no bill is protested now, till those three days are expired; nor is a bill of exchange esteemed due till the third day; no man offers to demand it, nor will any goldsmith, or even the bank itself, pay a foreign bill sooner. But that by the way.

Bills of exchange being thus sacred in trade, and inland bills being (by the late law for protesting them, and giving interest and damage upon them) made, as near as can be, equally sacred, nothing can be of more moment to a tradesman than to pay them always punctually and honourably.

Let no critic cavil at the word *honourably*, as it relates to trade: punctual payment is the honour of trade, and there is a word always used among merchants which justifies my using it in this place; and that is, when a merchant draws a bill from abroad upon his friend at London, his correspondent in London answering his letter, and approving his drawing upon him, adds, that he shall be sure to *honour* his bill when it appears; that is to say, to accept it.

Likewise, when the drawer gives advice of his having drawn such a bill upon him, he gives an account of the sum drawn, the name of the person it is payable to, the time it is drawn at, that is, the time given for payment, and he adds thus—'I doubt not your giving my bill due honour;' that is, of accepting it, and paying it when it is due.

This term is also used in another case in foreign trade only, namely—a merchant abroad (say it be at Lisbon, or Bourdeaux) draws a bill of £300 sterling upon his correspondent at London: the correspondent happens to be dead, or is broke, or by some other accident the bill is not accepted; another merchant on the Exchange hearing of it, and knowing, and perhaps corresponding with, the merchant abroad who drew the bill, and loth his credit should suffer by the bill going back protested, accepts it, and pays it for him. This is called accepting it for the honour of the drawer; and he writes so upon the bill when he accepts it, which entitles him to re-draw the same with interest upon the drawer in Lisbon or Bourdeaux, as above.

This is, indeed, a case peculiar to foreign commerce, and is not often practised in home trade, and among shopkeepers, though sometimes I have known it practised here too: but I name it on two accounts, first—to legitimate the word honourable, which I had used, and which has its due propriety in matters of trade, though not in the same acceptation as it generally receives in common affairs; and, secondly, to let the tradesman see how deeply the honour, that is, the credit of trade, is concerned in the punctual payment of bills of exchange, and the like of promissory notes; for in point of credit there is no difference, though in matter of form there is.

There are a great many variations in the drawing bills from foreign countries, according as the customs and usages of merchants direct, and according as the coins and rates of exchange differ, and according as the same terms are differently understood in several places; as the word *usance*, and *two usance,* which is a term for the number of days given for payment, after the date of the bill; and though this is a thing particularly relating to merchants, and to foreign commerce, yet as the nature of bills of exchange is pretty general, and that sometimes an inland tradesman, especially in seaport towns, may be obliged to take foreign accepted bills in payment for their goods; or if they have money to spare (as sometimes it is an inland tradesman's good luck to have), may be asked to discount such bills—I say, on this account, and that they may know the value of a foreign bill when they see it, and how far it has to run, before it has to be demanded, I think it not foreign to the case before me, to give them the following account:—

I. As to the times of payment of foreign bills of exchange, and the terms of art ordinarily used by merchants in drawing, and expressed in the said bills: the times of payment are, as above, either—

(I.) At sight; which is to be understood, not the day it is presented, but three days (called days of grace) after the bill is accepted: (2.) usance: (3.) two usance.[49]

Usance between London and all the towns in the States Generals' dominions, and also in the provinces now called the Austrian Netherlands [Belgium], is one month. And two usance is two months; reckoning not from the acceptance of the bill, but from the date of it. Usance between London and Hamburgh is two months, Venice is three months; and double usance, or two usance, is double that time. Usance payable at Florence or Leghorn, is two months; but from thence payable at London, usance is three months. Usance from London to Rouen or Paris, is one month; but they generally draw at a certain number of days, usually twenty-one days' sight. Usance from London to Seville, is two months, as likewise between London and Lisbon, and Oporto, to or from. Usance from Genoa to Rome is payable at Rome ten days after sight. Usance between Antwerp and Genoa, Naples or Messina, is two months, whether to or from. Usance from Antwerp or Amsterdam, payable at Venice, is two months, payable in bank.

---

[49] All bills and promissory notes, inland or foreign, payable in this country, are allowed three days of grace beyond the actual period expressed upon them; thus, a bill drawn at thirty days after date, is payable only on the thirty-third day. If bills be not presented for payment on the last day of grace, they cannot be protested, and consitute only an evidence of the debt for legal recovery. If the last day of grace be a Sunday, the bill is presentible on the Saturday previous.

There are abundance of niceties in the accepting and paying of bills of exchange, especially foreign bills, which I think needless to enter upon here; but this I think I should not omit, namely—

That if a man pays a bill of exchange before it is due, though he had accepted it, if the man to whom it was payable proves a bankrupt after he has received the money, and yet before the bill becomes due, the person who voluntarily paid the money before it was due, shall be liable to pay it again to the remitter; for as the remitter delivered his money to the drawer, in order to have it paid again to such person as he should order, it is, and ought to be, in his power to divert the payment by altering the bill, and make it payable to any other person whom he thinks fit, during all the time between the acceptance and the day of payment.

This has been controverted, I know, in some cases, but I have always found, that by the most experienced merchants, and especially in places of the greatest business abroad, it was always given in favour of the remitter, namely, that the right of guiding the payment is in him, all the time the bill is running; and no bill can or ought to be paid before it is due, without the declared assent of the remitter, signified under his hand, and attested by a public notary. There are, I say, abundance of niceties in the matter of foreign exchanges, and in the manner of drawing, accepting, and protesting bills; but as I am now speaking with, and have confined my discourse in this work to, the inland tradesmen of England, I think it would be as unprofitable to them to meddle with this, as it would be difficult to them to understand it.[50]

---

[50] In consequence of the great extension of commerce since the time of Defoe, a short explanation of the principle and practice of drawing foreign bills of exchange now seems necessary. Foreign bills of exchange are used, in order to avoid the necessity of transmitting actual money from one country to another. A merchant, for instance, in Nova Scotia, is owing £100 to a manufacturer in Glasgow: he seeks out some one who is a creditor to that amount to some person in Britain; we shall say he finds a captain in the army who wishes to draw £100 from his agent in London. To this captain the Nova Scotia merchant pays £100, and gets his order or bill on the London agent, which bill he sends to the manufacturer in Glasgow, and the manufacturer transmits the bill to London for payment; any banker, indeed, will give him the money for it, deducting a small commission. Thus two debts are liquidated, without the transmission of a farthing in money. The demand for bills in foreign countries to send to Great Britain, has the effect of raising them to a premium, which is called the rate of exchange, and is a burden which falls on the purchaser of the

I return, therefore, to the subject in hand, as well as to the people to whom I have all along directed my discourse.

Though the inland tradesmen do not, and need not, acquaint themselves with the manner of foreign exchanges, yet there is a great deal of business done by exchange among ourselves, and at home, and in which our inland trade is chiefly concerned; and as this is the reason why I speak so much, and repeat it so often to the tradesman for whose instruction I am writing, that he should maintain the credit of his bills, so it may not be amiss to give the tradesman some directions concerning such bills.

He is to consider, that, in general, bills pass through a number of hands, by indorsation from one to another, and that if the bill comes to be protested afterwards and returned, it goes back again through all those hands with this mark of the tradesman's disgrace upon it, namely, that it has been accepted, but that the man who accepted it is not able to pay it, than which nothing can expose the tradesman more.

He is to consider that the grand characteristic of a tradesman, and by which his credit is rated, is this of paying his bills well or ill. If any man goes to the neighbours or dealers of a tradesman to inquire of his credit, or his fame in business, which is often done upon almost every extraordinary occasion, the first question is, 'How does he pay his bills?'

---

bill. Foreign bills of exchange drawn on parties in Great Britain, have expressed upon them the number of days after sight at which they are to be payable. Thus, a merchant on receiving a foreign bill drawn at 'thirty days after sight,' hastens to get it 'sighted,' or shown to the party on whom it is drawn, and that party accepts it, at the same time marking the date of doing so. The bill is then complete and negociable, and is presented for payment to the acceptor at the end of the time specified, allowing the usual three days of grace. Should the bill not be accepted on being 'sighted,' it is a dishonoured bill, and is returned with a legal protest to the foreign correspondent. To avert, as far as possible, the loss of foreign bills by shipwreck, a set of three bills is drawn for each transaction, called first, second, and third, of the same tenor. For example: 'Thirty days after sight pay this my first bill of exchange, for the sum of £100 sterling; second and third of the same tenor being unpaid.' This first bill is first sent, and by next conveyance the second is sent. Should the first arrive safely, the second, on making its appearance, is destroyed. The third is retained by the foreign correspondent till he hear whether the former two have arrived at their destination, and is sent only if they have been lost. On receiving whichever comes first, it is the duty of the receiver to communicate intelligence of the fact to the sender.

As when we go to a master or mistress to inquire the character of a maid-servant, one of the first questions generally is of her probity, 'Is she honest?' so here, if you would be able to judge of the man, your first question is, 'What for a paymaster is he? How does he pay his bills?'— strongly intimating, and, indeed, very reasonably, that if he has any credit, or any regard to his credit, he will be sure to pay his bills well; and if he does not pay his bills well, he cannot be sound at bottom, because he would never suffer a slur there, if it were possible for him to avoid it. On the other hand, if a tradesman pays his bills punctually, let whatever other slur be upon his reputation, his credit will hold good. I knew a man in the city, who upon all occasions of business issued promissory notes, or notes under his hand, at such or such time, and it was for an immense sum of money that he gave out such notes; so that they became frequent in trade, and at length people began to carry them about to discount, which lessened the gentleman so much, though he was really a man of substance, that his bills went at last at twenty per cent, discount or more; and yet this man maintained his credit by this, that though he would always take as much time as he could get in these notes, yet when they came due they were always punctually paid to a day; no man came twice for his money.

This was a trying case, for though upon the multitude of his notes that were out, and by reason of the large discount given upon them, his credit at first suffered exceedingly, and men began to talk very dubiously of him, yet upon the punctual discharge of them when due, it began presently to be taken notice of, and said openly how well he paid his notes; upon which presently the rate of his discount fell, and in a short time all his notes were at *par*; so that punctual payment, in spite of rumour, and of a rumour not so ill grounded as rumours generally are, prevailed and established the credit of the person, who was indeed rich at bottom, but might have found it hard enough to have stood it, if, as his bills had a high discount upon them, they had been ill paid too. All which confirms what I have hitherto alleged, namely, of how much concern it is for a tradesman to pay his bills and promissory notes very punctually.

I might argue here how much it is his interest to do so, and how it enables him to coin as many bills as he pleases—in short, a man whose notes are currently paid, and the credit of whose bills is established by their being punctually paid, has an infinite advantage in trade; he is a bank to himself; he can buy what bargains he pleases; no advantage in business offers but he can grasp at it, for his notes are current as another man's cash; if he buys at time in the country, he has nothing to do but to order them to draw for the money when it is due, and he gains all the time given in the bills into the bargain.

If he knows what he buys, and how to put it off, he buys a thousand pounds' worth of goods at once, sells them for less time than he buys at, and pays them with their own money. I might swell this discourse to a volume by itself, to set out the particular profit that such a man may make of his credit, and how he can raise what sums he will, by buying goods, and by ordering the people whom he is to pay in the country, to draw bills on him. Nor is it any loss to those he buys of, for as all the remitters of money know his bills, and they are currently paid, they never scruple delivering their money upon his bills, so that the countryman or manufacturer is effectually supplied, and the time given in the bill is the property of the current dealer on whom they are drawn.

But, then, let me add a caution here for the best of tradesmen not to neglect—namely, as the tradesman should take care to pay his bills and notes currently, so, that he may do it, he must be careful what notes he issues out, and how he suffers others to draw on him. He that is careful of his reputation in business, will also be cautious not to let any man he deals with over draw him, or draw upon him before the money drawn for his due. And as to notes promissory, or under his hand, he is careful not to give out such notes but on good occasions, and where he has the effects in his hand to answer them; this keeps his cash whole, and preserves his ability of performing and punctually paying when the notes become due; and the want of this caution has ruined the reputation of a tradesman many times, when he might otherwise have preserved himself in as good credit and condition as other men.

All these cautions are made thus needful on account of that one useful maxim, that the tradesman's *all* depends upon his punctual complying with the payment of his bills.

www.ingramcontent.com/pod-product-compliance
Lightning Source LLC
Chambersburg PA
CBHW070341030726
47504CB00001B/30